CLOUD COMPUTING LAW

Cloud Computing Law

Edited by
CHRISTOPHER MILLARD

OXFORD
UNIVERSITY PRESS

OXFORD
UNIVERSITY PRESS

Great Clarendon Street, Oxford, OX2 6DP,
United Kingdom

Oxford University Press is a department of the University of Oxford.
It furthers the University's objective of excellence in research, scholarship,
and education by publishing worldwide. Oxford is a registered trade mark of
Oxford University Press in the UK and in certain other countries

Published in the United States of America by Oxford University Press
198 Madison Avenue, New York, NY 10016, United States of America

British Library Cataloguing in Publication Data
Data available

Library of Congress Control Number: 2013940565

ISBN 978–0–19–967167–0 (hbk.)
ISBN 978–0–19–967168–7 (pbk.)

Printed in Great Britain by
CPI Group (UK) Ltd, Croydon, CR0 4YY

Preface

'What is distinctive about this new technological development and why does it merit special treatment by legislators, regulators, lawyers, and the business community?' This question, or a subset or variant of it, was often put to me in the early 1980s when I told people that I was a 'computer lawyer'. Three decades later, I often have a sense of déjà vu as I seek to explain why cloud computing gives rise to legal and regulatory challenges of sufficient importance, novelty, and complexity that 'cloud computing law' is worthy of attention as a specialist area of legal research, teaching, and practice. This should no longer surprise me, however, as along the way I encountered reactions ranging from bemusement to scepticism when I shifted my focus to encompass telecoms law (1984), Internet law (1994), and eCommerce law (1996). To be fair, when I moved on to cloud law in 2008, relatively few people had ever heard of 'the cloud', although many were already becoming reliant on cloud services unwittingly.

In one sense, the sceptics are of course right. Cloud computing, whereby computing resources are delivered as an online utility service, is in large part an evolution of existing technologies and business models, though there are some important differences as we will see in Part I of this book. Similarly, most of the law that has, or will have, an impact on cloud computing is not, and will not be, fundamentally new law. However, as Parts II–IV of the book should demonstrate, applying existing legal concepts and rules to cloud computing gives rise to various complex and challenging issues.[1] This is the case whether we are looking at contract law and intellectual property (Part II), privacy and data protection (Part III), or cloud regulation and governance in various contexts including competition law, consumer protection, and law enforcement access to data in clouds (Part IV). Moreover, as has been the case with regard to other aspects of computing, communications, the Internet, and eCommerce, legislators and regulators are already finding it difficult to resist the temptation to introduce sector-specific, and even technology-specific, rules to address particular aspects of cloud computing that they consider inadequately regulated.

This is not to say that the law should be static, nor that it is always inappropriate to introduce new rules in response to technological innovation or other developments. Finding the right balance can, however, be a significant challenge and this is a recurring theme in technology law discussions. As I wrote in the preface to a previous book (referencing Charles Dickens):

Even when it is not an ass, the law tends to be a rather slow moving animal. This intrinsic resistance to change is an ambivalent characteristic. In its favour, it must be said that the resultant continuity and certainty can be highly beneficial. Indeed, it is probably for these qualities more than any other that the law is invoked on a daily basis as a source of stability in social and economic relationships. Yet too much permanence in a highly impermanent world can be a recipe for friction and ultimately irrelevance.[2]

Questions of how best to find an appropriate balance between certainty and flexibility, and between continuity and innovation, will resurface in this book. As we will see, while such issues may be intriguing at a theoretical level (to lawyers at least) they are often also of considerable practical importance.

---

[1] Indeed, the disruptive potential of cloud computing extends to society more generally. As *The Economist* observed in a prescient report in 2008: 'The rise of the cloud is more than just another platform shift that gets geeks excited. It will undoubtedly transform the information technology industry, but it will also profoundly change the way people work and companies operate. It will allow digital technology to penetrate every nook and cranny of the economy and of society, creating some tricky political problems along the way.' 'Let it rise', *The Economist*, 23 October 2008, <http://www.economist.com/node/12411882>.

[2] Christopher Millard, *Legal Protection of Computer Programs and Data* (Toronto/London: Carswell/ Sweet & Maxwell, 1985).

A different, and potentially more important, objection to the subject matter of this book might be that laws have limited geographical reach and the laws of specific jurisdictions cannot apply to activities that take place in virtual contexts like 'clouds'. This too is merely a recasting of an old issue. The cyber-libertarian notion that the advent of the Internet rendered all governments impotent and that terrestrial laws had no application to online environments was quaint at the time it was first promulgated and with hindsight seems extremely naïve.[3] Rumours of the death of political geography and of the obsolescence of national laws turned out to be greatly exaggerated.[4] Having said that, it was true then, and remains the case now, that many laws do not work well in online environments and that it is much harder to make good rather than bad laws for cyberspace.[5] The central objectives of this book are to assess how various key legal constructs and rules apply to cloud computing, both in theory and in practice, and to facilitate a debate about how the governance of cloud computing might be improved.

A word about the origins of this book. In 2008, soon after I had started to speak and write on cloud-related issues, Microsoft asked me whether I would be interested in leading a research project to assess the legal and regulatory implications of cloud computing. Along with my academic colleagues Chris Reed and Ian Walden, I was delighted to agree and in 2009 the Cloud Legal Project was launched in the Centre for Commercial Law Studies at Queen Mary, University of London. I will say more about the Cloud Legal Project in the Acknowledgements but for now suffice to say that four years down the line we have certainly not run out of issues to tackle. This book represents a synthesis of our findings to date but the field is developing rapidly and we are now analysing the impact of cloud computing in various other legal and regulatory contexts. I hope that we will be able to incorporate at least some of those additional topics in a future edition of this book.

In terms of the conceptual scope of our current discussion of cloud computing, space will not permit a detailed exploration of the many ways in which cloud technologies and services may be used, and the legal consequences that can ensue. It is, however, worth noting that cloud computing is already a key enabler for a wide range of new business models and for a plethora of services delivered via apps on mobile and other devices. Big Data analytics also make extensive use of cloud technologies and services. These are important topics but our focus in this book will be on cloud computing itself. Where we do refer to cloud-based applications, ranging from social networking to the delivery of government services, this will be primarily for illustrative purposes.

Given the current pace of developments in relation to cloud computing technologies and services, and in many aspects of the legal and regulatory environment, it is inevitable that some details at least will have changed by the time you read this. As we go to press, significant areas of uncertainty include the ongoing EU data protection reform saga and the implications of reports of massive and systematic access to data in cloud environments by governments and law enforcement agencies. Procurement and contracting arrangements for cloud services are also evolving rapidly. In the light of such volatility, we have given examples of current technologies and market practices while endeavouring to explore the principles of cloud computing law in a way that will remain relevant for some time.

Christopher Millard
London, June 2013

---

[3] See John Perry Barlow, 'A Declaration of the Independence of Cyberspace' February 8, 1996, <https://projects.eff.org/~barlow/Declaration-Final.html>. For contemporaneous contrary views see Christopher Millard and Robert Carolina, 'Cyberspace and the "No Regulation" Fallacy', *Global Telecoms Business Yearbook 1995* and Christopher Millard and Robert Carolina, 'Commercial Transactions on the Global Information Infrastructure: A European Perspective' (1996) 14 *John Marshall J of Comp and Info Law*, 269–301.

[4] For multiple examples, and a thorough rebuttal of Barlow's cyber-libertarian thesis, see Jack Goldsmith and Tim Wu, *Who Controls the Internet?* (New York: Oxford University Press, 2006).

[5] See Chris Reed, *Making Laws for Cyberspace* (Oxford: Oxford University Press, 2012).

Acknowledgements

This book represents the combined, and very substantial, efforts over the past four years of the members of the Cloud Legal Project at the Centre for Commercial Law Studies (CCLS) at Queen Mary, University of London. I will say more about them in a moment. First, as I'm not sure when I will next have the opportunity to do so, I would like to acknowledge some other people to whom I am indebted.

Two of my final year teachers at The Manchester Grammar School had a particular impact. John Shoard not only made the study of history fascinating, but he instilled in me the importance of critical analysis of primary sources. Bryan Bass, sadly no longer with us, was a superb teacher of English language and literature who showed me how writing can work. At the University of Sheffield, Roger Brownsword (now at King's College, London) with whom I studied jurisprudence, and the late Ian Taylor who taught me criminology, together sparked my enduring interest in exploring the interface between law, society, and policy. Ian also urged me to apply for a scholarship to study in Canada where, in 1981–2, the faculty members of the University of Toronto's Centre for Criminology, especially Christopher Webster and the late Richard Ericson, opened my eyes to the richness of inter-disciplinary research. A year later, on the other side of the UofT campus at the Faculty of Law, Martin Friedland's incisive mind, good humour, eclectic knowledge of the law, and rigorous academic standards made him the perfect supervisor for the LLM thesis that became my first book on computer law.

I am very grateful to two pioneering scholars in the computer law field, Steve Saxby and Colin Tapper, for their encouragement when I was starting out in London. Colin also did me the great favour of introducing me to his then doctoral student Richard Susskind, with whom I have since had the pleasure of collaborating on many projects. Through Richard I met Ian Lloyd, another Scottish academic whose friendship has been much appreciated. Along the way, I have enjoyed the company of various kindred spirits who have pursued similar academic interests to me, mostly on top of their 'day jobs' advising clients, especially David Bender, Christopher Kuner, Ian Kyer, Michael Scott, Thomas Smedinghoff, and Graham Smith.

During the past three decades I have had the privilege of working with many innovative legal practitioners, including Robert Carolina, John Edwards, Joachim Fleury, Mark Ford, David Griffiths, Thomas Heymann, Liz Hiester, Deborah Ishihara, Richard Jones, Richard Kemp, Vanessa Marsland, Graham P. Smith, and Richard Thomas (all of whom were colleagues at Clifford Chance); Peter Church, Richard Cumbley, Julian Cunningham-Day, Javier Fernández-Samaniego, and Tanguy van Overstraeten at Linklaters; and the team at Bristows I have the good fortune to work with now, in particular Toby Crick, Hazel Grant, Mark Watts, and Philip Westmacott. It has also been a great pleasure to collaborate with hundreds of other technology lawyers and privacy specialists from around the world on client projects and in the work of various organizations including the International Bar Association, the Computer Law Association (now ITechLaw), and the International Association of Privacy Professionals. Many of them I now count as friends. Closer to home, the UK technology law market is characterized by collegiality and good-natured competition. This is evident, for example, in the educational work of the Society for Computers and Law and the Cambridge IT Law Summer School. It is epitomized in the London Computer Law Group which, since the mid-80s, has been the scene of countless lively debates and good dinners.

I have also been fortunate in having so many opportunities to work alongside clients on intriguing issues in technology law. Such assignments have demonstrated repeatedly that the law is of little or no use if it cannot be applied, and complied with, in practice. This is a frequent theme in this book. Although I didn't realize how important it was at the time, I am particularly grateful to Sir Bryan Carsberg, then Director General of the UK Office of Telecommunications, for the opportunity to work on the regulation of logically separate communications systems while I was on secondment to Oftel in 1989–90. This turned out to be highly relevant, both conceptually and technically, when I started looking at the implications of virtualization in cloud computing environments almost two decades later.

My association with CCLS began in 1986 when I started teaching computer law on the University of London inter-collegiate LLM programme. Adrian Sterling, as enthusiastic and inspiring then as he is to this day, had beaten me to it and was already pushing back the boundaries of IP and technology law. Soon after, Chris Reed arrived and took over, and greatly developed, the nascent LLM course in computer law. When Ian Walden joined in 1992 I was more than happy to hand over to him the LLM course in telecommunications law, which he also took to the next level and beyond. As time slipped by, Chris reminded me every so often that I had said I would try my hand at legal practice for 'just a few years' before moving to academia. Despite my extreme dilatoriness, in 2008 he very kindly organized a proper academic job for me. I am grateful to Spyros Maniatis, Director of CCLS, and all of the staff at the Centre for welcoming me into that vibrant community. I am also grateful to the members of the Oxford Internet Institute for the opportunity to collaborate with them as a Senior Research Fellow between 2008 and 2012 and since then as a Research Associate.

Working with the QMUL Cloud Legal Project team has been both intellectually stimulating and a lot of fun. In addition to their other work on the project, all members of the core team have contributed to this book, for which I am most grateful, namely Simon Bradshaw, Alan Cunningham, Kuan Hon, Julia Hörnle, Chris Reed, and Ian Walden. Thanks also to Laíse Da Corregio Luciano, who co-authored the competition law chapter, to Michaela Macdonald and Biddy Wyles who provided invaluable help in updating our comparative analysis of more than 30 cloud contracts, and to Leslie Lansman who provided rigorous and cheerful support in checking many of the citations and assisting with the copy editing.

As part of our research on negotiated cloud contracts (reported in Chapter 4) we conducted confidential interviews with individuals from more than 20 organizations comprising cloud providers, cloud users (both commercial and public sector), and other cloud market actors including law firms and insurance industry cyber risk specialists. As most did not wish to be named, none will be. We are, however, very grateful to all interviewees for giving their time and sharing their expertise and experiences.

The Cloud Legal Project, and this book which grew out of it, would not have happened at all without Microsoft Corporation's foresight and generous financial support by way of an academic research grant. Many at Microsoft have provided valuable insights and encouragement over the past four years, including Brad Smith and Ron Zink, who together had the original vision for the project, Stephen Bolinger, Stephen Collins, Steve Crown, Peter Cullen, Towney Feehan, John Frank, Sebastian Gerlach, Jean Gonié, Cornelia Kutterer, Mark Lange, Brendon Lynch, Craig Mundie, Steve Mutkoski, Rich Sauer, Nicolas Schifano, Lisa Tanzi, and Dervish Tayyip. We are very grateful to all of them, and others not listed, though the views expressed in this book are those of the authors alone.

The editorial and production teams at OUP did a great job and I would especially like to thank Ruth Anderson, Catherine Cotter, and Emma Hawes. It has also been a pleasure to work with Rhodri Jackson and his colleagues at OUP Law Journals on both the *International Journal of Law and Information Technology* and more recently on *International Data Privacy Law*.

As authors and editors often say, it takes a substantial commitment of time and energy to bring this kind of project to fruition. This has been no exception and I want especially to thank my wife Susan and our children Emily and Thomas for their love, patience, and encouragement, not only while I have been working on this book but more generally as I have shifted my primary focus from legal practice to academia.

Finally, I want to acknowledge my parents, John and Ruth Millard, who have been incredibly supportive and the most amazing role models. Sadly, my father died while this book was a work in progress. He is very greatly missed but his kindness, generosity, integrity, and hope will always inspire me.

Christopher Millard
London, June 2013

Contents

IV. CLOUD REGULATON AND GOVERNANCE

List of Contributors

The Editor

Christopher Millard is Professor of Privacy and Information Law at the Centre for Commercial Law Studies, Queen Mary, University of London and is Of Counsel to the law firm Bristows. He has over 30 years experience in technology law, both in academia and legal practice, and has led the QMUL Cloud Legal Project since it was established in 2009. He is a Fellow and former Chairman of the Society for Computers & Law and past-Chair of the Technology Law Committee of the International Bar Association. He has published widely in the computer law field and is a founding editor of the *International Journal of Law and IT* and of *International Data Privacy Law* (both Oxford University Press).

The Contributing Authors

Simon Bradshaw originally qualified in electronics and communications and served as an Engineering Officer in the Royal Air Force. His RAF experience included management of secure communications networks, technical analysis and IT project management. Having cross-qualified in Law he went on to undertake an LLM in Information Technology and Intellectual Property Law at Edinburgh, specializing in the IP implications of new technology. He subsequently trained as a barrister, was called to the Bar by Middle Temple and is now a member of Cornwall Street Chambers. From 2009–10 he was Project Co-ordinator and Research Assistant on the Queen Mary, University of London Cloud Legal Project and he is now a Visiting Fellow at the Centre for Commercial Law Studies at QMUL.

Alan Cunningham was the QMUL Cloud Legal Project Research Assistant for 2012–13. He completed his PhD (concerning the management of copyrights in a digital and online environment) at Queen Mary, University of London in 2007 and has taught Intellectual Property Law at Queen Mary and La Trobe University, Melbourne. He has published on law and technology issues in the *International Journal of Law and Information Technology*.

Laíse Da Correggio Luciano is Professor of EU Law at Fundação Getúlio Vargas—FGV—Rio de Janeiro, and Law Tutor at Queen Mary, University of London where she teaches ICT Competition Law on the Distance Learning LLM in Computer and Communications Law.

W Kuan Hon is an English solicitor and New York attorney (currently non-practising). She worked in the City of London focusing on finance-related English law (particularly banking, debt capital markets, and corporate insolvency) before obtaining an MSc in Computing Science with merit from Imperial College, London in 2009 and then an LLM in Computer and Communications Law with merit from Queen Mary, University of London in 2010. She also has an LLM from the University of Pennsylvania. From 2010–11 she was Project Co-Ordinator and Research Assistant on the QMUL Cloud Legal Project and has been a consultant to the project since 2011. She is currently a law and computer science PhD student at QMUL, researching cloud data protection law.

Julia Hörnle is Professor in Internet Law at the Centre for Commercial Law Studies, Queen Mary, University of London. She has also taught at universities in China, Germany, and Austria and has held a research position at Georgetown University, Washington DC. She is author of *Cross-border Internet Dispute Resolution* (Cambridge: Cambridge University Press, 2009) and *Cross-border Online Gambling Law & Policy* (Cheltenham: Elgar, 2010). Julia qualified as a solicitor in 1999 and practised with the law firm Eversheds in London and Brussels before joining QMUL in 2000. She is Managing Editor of the *International Journal of Law and Information Technology*. She has carried out research projects for the Chinese and UK governments and the European Commission.

Chris Reed is Professor of Electronic Commerce Law at the Centre for Commercial Law Studies, Queen Mary, University of London. He has published widely on many aspects of computer law and his books include *Making Laws for Cyberspace* (Oxford University Press, 2012), *Computer Law* (Editor and contributor, 7th edn, Oxford University Press, 2011) and *Internet Law* (2nd edn, Cambridge University Press, 2004). He consults to companies and law firms and is a past Chairman and Fellow of the Society for Computers and Law. Chris has acted as an Expert for the European Commission, represented the UK Government at the Hague Conference on Private International Law, and has been an invited speaker at OECD and G8 conferences.

Ian Walden is Professor of Information and Communications Law at the Centre for Commercial Law Studies, Queen Mary, University of London. His books include *Computer Crimes and Digital Investigations* (Oxford University Press, 2007), *Media Law and Practice* (Editor and contributor, Oxford University Press, 2009), *Telecommunications Law and Regulation* (Editor and contributor, 4th edn, Oxford University Press, 2012) and *Free and Open Source Software* (Editor and contributor, Oxford University Press, 2013). Ian has been involved in law reform projects for the World Bank, the European Commission, UNCTAD, UNECE, and the EBRD, as well as for a number of individual states. Ian is a solicitor, is Of Counsel to Baker & McKenzie, and is a member of the Press Complaints Commission. He was previously a Board Member and Trustee of the Internet Watch Foundation (2004–09).

List of Abbreviations

A29WP	Working Party established under Art 29 DPD
A&A	assurance and accreditation
AMI	Amazon Machine Image
ANSI	American National Standard Institute
API	Application Programming Interface
app	application
ASA	Advertising Standards Authority
AUP	Acceptable Use Policy
AWS	Amazon Web Services
BCAP	Broadcasting Committee of Advertising Practice
BCR	binding corporate rules
BIL	business impact level
CaaS	Communications/Content as a Service
CAP	Committee of Advertising Practice
CAS(T)	CESG Assured Service—Telecoms
CCLS	Centre for Commercial Law Studies, QMUL
CDN	content delivery network
CDPA	Copyright, Designs and Patents Act 1988
CEN	European Committee for Standardization
CENELEC	European Committee for Electrotechnical Standardization
CESG	Communications-Electronics Security Group (UK National Technical Authority for Information Assurance)
CIF	Cloud Industry Forum
CLAS	Communications-Electronics Security Group (CESG) Listed Advisers Scheme
CLP	Cloud Legal Project
CM	Certification Mark
CNIL	Commission nationale de l'informatique et des libertés
CPA	Consumer Protection Act 1987
CPDSR	Consumer Protection (Distance Selling) Regulations 2000
CRD	Consumer Rights Directive
CSA	Cloud Security Alliance
CSV	comma-separated values
DACAR	Data Capture and Auto Identification Reference Project
DES	Data Encryption Standard
DMTF	Distributed Management Task Force
DPA	Data Protection Act 1998
DPD	Data Protection Directive
DRM	digital rights management
EAL	Evaluation Assurance Level
EBS	Elastic Block Store
ECD	Electronic Commerce Directive
ECHR	European Convention on Human Rights
ECJ	European Court of Justice
ECPA	Electronic Communications Privacy Act
ECR	E-commerce Regulations
ECS	electronic communications services
ECtHR	European Court of Human Rights

EDRI	European Digital Rights
EEA	European Economic Area
EEW	European Evidence Warrant
EFF	Electronic Frontier Foundation
EIF	European Interoperability Framework
EIO	European Investigation Order
EIS	European Interoperability Strategy
EMEA	Europe, Middle East, and Africa
EPOF	European Privacy Officers Forum
ESO	European Standardization Organization
ETSI	European Telecommunications Standards Institute
EU	European Union
FIPS	Federal Information Processing Standards
FTC	Federal Trade Commission
GeM	Government eMarketplace
Gi	UK G-Cloud Framework v1
Gii	UK G-Cloud Framework v2
Giii	UK G-Cloud Framework v3
GPS	Government Procurement Service/the Authority
GSMA	GSM Association
GWS	Government Wide Services
IA	information assurance
IaaS	Infrastructure as a Service
IANA	Internet Assigned Numbers Authority
ICANN	Internet Council for Assigned Names and Numbers
ICC	International Chamber of Commerce
ICM	Independent Certification Mark
ICO	Information Commissioner's Office
ICT	Information and Communications Technology
IETF	Internet Engineering Task Force
IL	impact level
IL3	Impact Level 3
IP	Internet Protocol/intellectual property
IPR	Intellectual Property Right
ISO	International Organization for Standardization
ISS	information society services
IT	information technology
ITA	International Trade Administration
KPI	key performance indicator
LEA	law enforcement authority
LIBE	Committee on Civil Liberties, Justice and Home Affairs
MLA	mutual legal assistance
NIST	National Institute of Standards and Technology
NSA	National Security Agency
NSI	Network Solutions Inc.
OASIS	Organization for the Advancement of Structured Information Standards
OCC	Open Cloud Consortium
OCSI	Open Cloud Standards Incubator
OECD	Organization for Economic Cooperation and Development
OFT	Office of Fair Trading
OVF	Open Virtualization Format
PaaS	Platform as a Service

PbD	Privacy by Design
PCI	Payment Card Industry
PET	Privacy Enhancing Technology
PGA	pan-Government accreditation service
PIPEDA	Canadian Personal Information Protection and Electronic Documents Act 2000
PIUG	Patent Information User Group
PPN	Procurement Policy Note
PSN	Public Services Network
QMUL	Queen Mary, University of London
RAID	Redundant Array of Independent Disks
RAM	random-access memory
RIPA	Regulation of Investigatory Powers Act 2000
SaaS	Software as a Service
SAN	Storage Area Network
SGA	Sale of Goods Act 1979
SGSA	Supply of Goods and Services Act 1982
SLA	Service Level Agreement
SME	small to medium-sized enterprise
SNIA	Storage Networking Industry Association
SSAE	Statement on Standards for Attestation Engagements
SWIFT	Society for Worldwide Interbank Financial Telecommunication
TFEU	Treaty on the Functioning of the European Union
ToS	Terms of Service
TRIPS	(Agreement on) Trade-Related Aspects of Intellectual Property Rights
TV	television
UCE	User Controlled Encryption
UCTA	Unfair Contract Terms Act 1977
UK	United Kingdom
UKAS	United Kingdom Accreditation Service
US	United States (of America)
UTCCR	Unfair Terms in Consumer Contracts Regulations 1999
UTTC	(Directive on) Unfair Terms in Consumer Contracts
UV	UltraViolet
VAR	value-added reseller
VM	virtual machine
VMI	virtual machine image
VPN	virtual private network
WIPO	World Intellectual Property Organization

PART I

CLOUD COMPUTING ESSENTIALS

'Cloud computing' is often treated as one all-embracing concept. In fact, the term encompasses many different things. The purpose of this part of the book is to explain the key technical and commercial characteristics of cloud computing in sufficient detail to enable a non-technical reader to understand the concepts that will underpin the analysis of cloud legal and regulatory issues in the rest of the book. To analyse properly how laws apply to cloud computing, how contractual relationships work in clouds, and how the 'cloud ecosystem' is regulated, it is first necessary to differentiate between the main types of cloud computing services and consider how they work in structural and deployment terms. As will quickly become clear, layering of cloud services is common. Much depends on exactly how an individual service has been set up and implemented, including service layers that may not be obvious to users and may even be hidden deliberately.

In Chapter 1 we outline the main technical and commercial characteristics of cloud computing, including the central concept of 'X as a Service' and various other key elements. Common models for deployment of cloud resources are then described and are put in the broader context of the cloud supply chain.

The focus of Chapter 2 is on control, security, and risk in the cloud, including a description of how the so-called 'CIA Triad' (Confidentiality, Integrity, and Availability) works in cloud computing environments. The chapter also explains how cloud computing differs from traditional outsourcing arrangements and provides an overview of typical contractual structures for cloud services.

1

Cloud Technologies and Services

W Kuan Hon and Christopher Millard

1. What Is Cloud Computing?

At its simplest, cloud computing is a way of delivering computing resources as a utility service via a network, typically the Internet, scalable up and down according to user requirements. As such, the cloud may prove to be as disruptive an innovation as was the emergence of cheap electricity on demand a century or so ago.[1] Such computing resources may range from raw processing power and storage, such as servers or storage equipment, to full software applications. Users can 'rent' IT resources from third parties when needed, instead of purchasing their own, thus 'turning capex to opex' (capital expenditure into operating expenditure).

The scale, and scalability, of cloud computing make it ideally suited for environments where demand for IT resources may fluctuate widely and rapidly. Cloud may also prove to be a key enabling technology for releasing the latent power of 'Big Data', and for supporting the deployment of mobile devices and applications on a very large scale.[2] Market surveys and statistics abound but in terms of adoption to date, recent research indicates that more than half of US businesses already use cloud computing services.[3] In the EU, the cumulative economic impact of cloud computing has been predicted to be €940 billion and 3.8 million jobs for the period 2015–20.[4]

In slightly more technical terms, cloud computing is an arrangement whereby computing resources are provided on a flexible, location-independent basis that allows for rapid and seamless[5] allocation of resources on demand. Typically, cloud resources are provided to specific users from a pool shared with other customers with pricing, if any,[6] often proportional

---

[1] Nicholas Carr, *The Big Switch: Rewiring the World, from Edison to Google* (New York/London: WW Norton, 2009).

[2] For a discussion of the relationship between cloud, Big Data, and mobile, see David Linthicum, 'Understanding the Symbiosis of Cloud Computing, Big Data, and Mobile', <http://pro.gigaom.com/blog/understanding-the-symbiosis-of-cloud-computing-big-data-and-mobile/> (accessed 2 April 2013). For a brief introduction to Big Data, see Christopher Kuner, Fred Cate, Christopher Millard, and Dan Svantesson, 'The Challenge of "Big Data" for Data Protection' (2012) 2(2) *International Data Privacy Law* 47.

[3] Reuven Cohen, 'The Cloud Hits the Mainstream: More than Half of U.S. Businesses Now Use Cloud Computing' (*Forbes*, 16 April 2013), <http://www.forbes.com/sites/reuvencohen/2013/04/16/the-cloud-hits-the-mainstream-more-than-half-of-u-s-businesses-now-use-cloud-computing/> (accessed 1 June 2013).

[4] IDC, *Quantitative Estimates of the Demand for Cloud Computing in Europe and the Likely Barriers to Uptake*, 13 July 2012 Final Report for the European Commission, <http://ec.europa.eu/information_society/activities/cloudcomputing/docs/quantitative_estimates.pdf> (accessed 1 June 2013).

[5] 'Seamless' here means adding or removing capacity without specific action by the cloud user, or even awareness of such adjustment. Providers may offer users the option of requesting capacity manually when needed, or setting resources to vary automatically with demand.

[6] Many consumer services are funded by advertising. See Chapter 13 for a discussion of the status of such 'free' services.

to the resources used.[7] The delivery of cloud services often depends on complex, multilayered arrangements between various providers.[8]

Many permutations are possible, but cloud computing activities are often described as falling into one or more of the following three service categories:[9]

- Infrastructure as a Service ('IaaS'): raw computing resources, such as processing power ('compute') and storage.[10]
- Platform as a Service ('PaaS'): platforms for developing and deploying software applications.[11]
- Software as a Service ('SaaS'): end-user applications.[12]

Cloud users may run, typically via web browsers,[13] application software installed on remote servers which sends results to users over the Internet. This means that relatively simple devices, such as mobile phones or tablets, may be used to obtain access to vast computational resources.

The use of 'as a Service' emphasizes a change in focus, from obtaining products or licences, to renting the use of resources as services. These service models sit on a spectrum from IaaS to PaaS to SaaS, rather than being separate or discrete types of cloud computing. Generally, IaaS involves relatively low-level functionality for users, requiring greater user sophistication and expertise, including more hands-on, micromanagement of resources. However, it affords the user more flexibility and fine control. SaaS provides high-level functionality, and generally requires less user technical expertise, but offers less user control. PaaS sits in the middle. Users are spared the need to manage raw

---

[7] As outlined in Chapter 4, service charges may be calculated per user, per month. There are also other models. For example, PaaS provider AppFog charges according to the amount of RAM used. Alex Williams, 'AppFog Wants to Do for Developer Platforms What Google Did for Email' (*TechCrunch*, 25 July 2012), <http://techcrunch.com/2012/07/25/appfog-wants-to-do-for-developer-platforms-what-google-did-for-email> (accessed 1 March 2013).

[8] See Chapters 2, 3, and 4.

[9] Originally promulgated by the US National Institute of Standards and Technology: Peter Mell and Tim Grance, *The NIST Definition of Cloud Computing, Special Publication 800-145* (Gaithersberg, MD: US National Institute of Standards and Technology, 2011).

[10] The IT resources used over a network here essentially consist of computing hardware infrastructure (servers, storage, etc.) and tools to help users manage those resources. IaaS services include Rackspace, Amazon Web Services' EC2, and Google Compute Engine. Instead of investing in their own data centres or servers, users may install their operating systems and applications of choice on the provider's infrastructure. IaaS, as a data centre/computing hardware substitute, may be used, for example, by start-ups who avoid upfront capital expenditure on physical infrastructure by using IaaS to 'rent' use of a third party's computing and storage infrastructure.

[11] Accordingly, the IT resources used over a network in PaaS comprise platforms for programming, deploying, and hosting applications with application management tools. PaaS services include Google's App Engine, Microsoft's Windows Azure, and Heroku.

[12] With SaaS, the IT resource used over a network is application software, hence 'Software as a Service'. For example, instead of installing word-processing software to run on each user's local computer, Google Apps or Microsoft Office 365 SaaS may be used for online word processing. Other examples are webmail services such as Yahoo! Mail (instead of desktop email applications) and social networking services like Facebook. Salesforce's online customer relationship management service is an example of SaaS for enterprise cloud users. A subclass of SaaS is 'Storage as a Service', which provides the infrastructure and means for users to manage data storage, organization, and retrieval from any location over the Internet, for example Dropbox or Rackspace's Cloud Files.

[13] Although some services involve or allow installation of separate software on user devices to automate and synchronize storage of local files to the cloud, for example Dropbox, and other storage services, such as Google Drive, SugarSync, and SkyDrive. It is also very common for local applications ('apps') to be installed on mobile devices to facilitate access to specific cloud services.

processing/storage resources actively, and may focus on programming applications to be hosted via the service. Boundaries between them, particularly IaaS and PaaS, may blur; IaaS providers are increasingly offering higher-level functionality,[14] while PaaS providers may offer lower-level detailed control.[15]

SaaS is the most commonly used type of cloud service, particularly among consumers, which is unsurprising as it generally requires the least technical know-how on the part of users, and enables users to procure use of application software quickly without installing any specific software. According to a survey of 300 UK-based organizations in late 2011,[16] the SaaS applications most used were email, backup/disaster recovery, storage, and web hosting services.

Cloud deployment models can also be viewed in various ways, but a widely used classification is:

- Private cloud: where relevant infrastructure is owned by, or operated for, the benefit of a single large customer or a group of related entities.[17]

- Community cloud: where infrastructure is owned by, or operated for, and shared among a specific group of users with common interests, such as US government bodies,[18] UK local government, or the financial services industry.[19]

- Public cloud: where infrastructure is shared among multiple users using the same hardware and/or software.

- Hybrid cloud: involving a mixture of the above, for example, an organization with a private cloud may 'cloud burst' processing activities to a public cloud for 'load balancing' purposes during times of high demand.[20]

---

[14] For example, Amazon offers resources such as software development kits for Java, mobile (Android, iOS), PHP, Python, Ruby, and ASP.NET programmers. Amazon, 'Java Developer Center', available at <http://aws.amazon.com/java> (accessed 1 March 2013).

[15] For example, Azure PaaS allows use of VMs within cloud services. Windows Azure, 'How to Connect Virtual Machines in a Cloud Service', available at <http://www.windowsazure.com/en-us/manage/windows/how-to-guides/connect-to-a-cloud-service> (accessed 1 March 2013).

[16] Cloud Industry Forum, *Cloud UK: Paper Four Cloud Adoption and Trends for 2012* (2011).

[17] For example, the US state of Alaska. Cisco, 'State Government Deploys Private Cloud to Provide Services to Agencies' (2011), <http://www.cisco.com/en/US/solutions/collateral/ns340/ns517/ns224/state_of_alaska_cs.pdf> (accessed 1 March 2013).

[18] For example, Microsoft Office 365 SaaS as a 'multi-tenant service that stores US government data in a segregated community cloud'. Kirk Koenigsbauer, 'Announcing Office 365 for Government: A US Government Community Cloud' (30 May 2012), <http://blogs.office.com/b/microsoft_office_365_blog/archive/2012/05/30/announcing-office-365-for-government-a-us-government-community-cloud.aspx> (accessed 1 March 2013).

[19] For example, NYSE Euronext's Capital Markets Community cloud for financial services firms (launched in 2011 in partnership with storage provider EMC and virtualization firm VMware), offers applications and services to customers via its own 'app store', computing-on-demand services, and connections to NYSE Euronext's global trading network, including a market data feed. Tom Steinert-Threlkeld, 'Cloud Fundamental to NYSE IT Strategy' (*Information Management*, 28 August 2012), <http://www.information-management.com/news/cloud-fundamental-to-nyse-it-strategy-10023088-1.html?zkPrintable=true> (accessed 8 March 2013).
    A 'Trusted German Insurance Cloud' has also been launched, by the German Insurance Association: Federal Office for Information Security 'The BSI', available at <https://www.bsi.bund.de/ContentBSI/Presse/Pressemitteilungen/Presse2012/Trusted-German-Insurance-Cloud_08032012.html> (accessed 8 March 2013).

[20] For an explanation of how cloud bursting works, see Nati Shalom, 'What Is Cloud Bursting?' (*CloudCow.com*, 12 May 2012), <http://www.cloudcow.com/content/what-cloud-bursting> (accessed 1 March 2013).

Private/public should not be equated with on/off-premise. Infrastructure for cloud services may be located on users' premises, or at one or more external locations. Private clouds are not necessarily on-premise; the infrastructure/resources used could be managed, even owned, by a third party, but dedicated to the user concerned. Public clouds, however, are generally off-premise.

2. Cloud Computing Resources and Technologies

2.1 IaaS

Pooled computing resources in IaaS are used mainly for data processing ('compute' capability), storage, and networking or other connectivity services. These are outlined below because the application of certain laws relating to data location, data security, and handling of 'personal data' may be affected by the specific arrangements for processing, storing (including replicating and deleting), and transmitting data.[21]

2.1.1 Compute

For 'compute' a key enabler was the development of virtualization technologies. This facilitated the conceptual separation of different computing elements. Server hardware virtualization is the most common type of virtualization in cloud computing.

IaaS typically involves using 'virtual machines' (VMs). Via virtualization technology[22] a physical server may 'host' multiple VMs. Each VM operates as a virtual server, running independently with its own operating system[23] within which applications, or other software, may also be installed and run.[24]

Different users ('tenants', hence the term 'multi-tenancy') may thus independently create ('instantiate') and run their own VMs (and applications) within one physical server. They can terminate their VMs when no longer required, install their own firewalls, and manage their own virtual networks. Multiple users may share use of common physical infrastructure; this enables resource consolidation, economies of scale, and involves more efficient resource utilization than dedicating separate physical machines to different users (avoiding possible periods of non-use that may waste the machine's peak capacity).

VMs on one physical machine may share use of the same *physical* resources, including processors, hard disks, memory, and network interfaces. Users and their VMs are segregated or isolated from each other by virtualization software only, rather than through physical separation.[25] While shared use enables efficiencies, it also raises security

---

[21] See Chapters 8, 9, and 10.

[22] Virtualization software may be proprietary, such as Microsoft Hyper-V and VMWare Workstation, or open source, such as Xen, KVM, and Oracle VM VirtualBox. Amazon Web Services' set of (mainly IaaS) cloud computing services uses Amazon's modified version of Xen. Google Compute Engine IaaS is based on KVM.

[23] These may be proprietary (eg Windows), or open source (eg Linux).

[24] Assuming the operating system or other software's licence allows it to be installed and run in VMs instead of separate physical machines. See Chapter 4.

[25] As some users are concerned about this for compliance or security reasons, some providers (eg Amazon) offer services on separate, dedicated physical hardware. Amazon Web Services, 'Amazon EC2 Dedicated Instances', available at <http://aws.amazon.com/dedicated-instances> (accessed 1 March 2013).

concerns, including that the provider or another tenant may be able to access or interfere with the data or processing of another tenant using the same hardware.[26]

VMs are created and may be booted from stored files called virtual machine images ('VMIs') or virtual machine files.[27] Different virtualization technologies use or support different image formats.[28] VMIs allow quick deployment of multiple pre-configured VM instances from a single 'template' file.[29] For customers' convenience, some providers offer various pre-packaged template images with different operating systems pre-installed. Users may configure their own VMs with libraries or applications and so on, then capture or save 'snapshots' of their customized images,[30] and may even make images available publicly. VMs may also be cloned or 'live migrated' while running. If data operated on within a VM are not saved to persistent storage[31] before the VM's termination or failure, generally the data are lost. Depending on the service, even VM instances appearing to have attached storage may lose 'stored' data on 'taking down' the instance, unless actively saved to persistent storage first. The format, storage, and precise arrangements for using VMIs may have an impact on security, data location, and competition law.[32] Thus, several components may be involved in IaaS, from virtualization software and VMI files, to operating systems installed within VMs, and application or other software that users install and run on such operating systems.

Not all cloud computing requires the use of VMs, although it may still involve virtualization in the broad 'abstraction' sense. Some cloud computing involves the opposite: instead of one physical server running multiple VMs, multiple physical computers are harnessed to work together simultaneously, in parallel, on a single processing operation. Workloads are divided into sub-operations and distributed or 'mapped' among different physical servers, with the results of the distributed processing sub-operations being collected or 'reduced'.[33]

---

[26] Security is discussed further in Chapter 2. IEEEXplore Digital Library, 'Side-Channel Leaks in Web Applications: A Reality Today, a Challenge Tomorrow', available at <http://ieeexplore.ieee.org/xpl/login.jsp?tp=&arnumber=5504714&url=http%3A%2F%2Fieeexplore.ieee.org%2Fxpls%2Fabs_all.jsp%3Farnumber%3D5504714>; Thomas Ristenpart et al., 'Hey, You, Get off of My Cloud: Exploring Information Leakage in Third-party Compute Cloud' (*ACM Digital Library*, 2009), <http://dl.acm.org/citation.cfm?id=1653687>; and Yinqian Zhang et al., 'Cross-VM Side Channels and Their Use to Extract Private Keys' (*ACM Digital Library*, 2012), <http://dl.acm.org/citation.cfm?id=2382230> (all accessed 1 March 2013).

[27] Virtual disk files (virtual disk images), which may be stored on physical disks, are 'images' of virtual hard disks (ie the contents of a VM's virtual hard disk drive). VMs may use virtual disks as physical hard disks. Virtual disks may store operating systems, data, and applications that may be run from the disk within a VM.

[28] For example, VMWare, Workstation, Microsoft Hyper-V, and VirtualBox use different formats (but VirtualBox supports several formats).

[29] Amazon's VMIs use Amazon's own proprietary format and are called Amazon Machine Images ('AMIs'). Amazon Web Services, 'Amazon Machine Images (AMIs)', available at <https://aws.amazon.com/amis> (accessed 1 March 2013).

[30] 'Virtual appliances' are software applications ('software appliances') that run within VMs, usually one application per appliance. A virtual appliance *image* incorporates VMI plus 'pre-installed' software appliances. An open standard for packaging and distributing virtual appliances, Open Virtualization Format ('OVF'), has been accepted by standards organizations ANSI and ISO. OVF has seen some, but not universal, support (eg by IBM and VMWare). Distributed Management Task Force, 'Open Virtualization Format Specification' (12 January 2010), <http://dmtf.org/sites/default/files/standards/documents/DSP0243_1.1.0.pdf> (accessed 1 March 2013).

[31] Usually one or more hard disk drives or SSD flash storage.

[32] See Chapters 7, 8, and 12.

[33] A popular open-source framework for scalable distributed applications handling large quantities of unstructured data is the Apache Hadoop project. The project is based on Google's MapReduce framework for massive distributed processing using low-cost commodity systems. Hadoop uses 'clusters' of 'nodes' or servers fragmenting data across nodes automatically, and also replicating data automatically,

Other types of virtualization feature in cloud. Just as operating systems may be made independent of hardware through hardware virtualization, applications may be decoupled from operating systems through application virtualization. Virtualization methods vary, but the end result is the logical 'abstraction' of computing from physical resources, a broader concept which runs through cloud computing and enables users to focus on desired functions and actions at a higher, simpler, and more general level, rather than having to micromanage underlying resources.

2.1.2 *Storage*

Storage 'virtualization' makes it possible for a user to have access to what appears to be a single file or document while the relevant data are stored in a physically distributed fashion across different pieces of hardware (eg a Storage Area Network or SAN), with specialized software managing storage and retrieval. The intention is that users need not be concerned with the details of physical storage as this is handled automatically for them. RAID[34] is a storage virtualization technology resilient to individual physical drive failure. Multiple drives, a RAID array, behave as one logical drive. Data fragments are 'striped' across those drives automatically and, possibly, also replicated or 'mirrored' in different ways, depending on the RAID scheme or 'level' used. RAIDs may be combined into larger RAIDs.

Providers often offer persistent non-volatile data storage, enabling data retrieval, for example after a VM instance terminates.[35] Cloud service providers employ various, in some cases proprietary, systems to manage large-scale distributed data storage and retrieval across different hardware, including distributed file systems and distributed databases.[36] Database management systems, operating at a higher level than file

attempting to use different racks for fault-tolerance. Organizations such as eBay, Facebook, and Yahoo! use Hadoop heavily to provide cloud services to their external users, as well as for internal purposes, including private cloud computing to support public-facing services. Dhruba Borthakur, 'Facebook Has the World's Largest Hadoop Cluster!' (*HDFS*, 9 May 2010), <http://hadoopblog. blogspot.co.uk/2010/05/facebook-has-worlds-largest-hadoop.html>; Ashish Thusoo et al., 'Data Warehousing and Analytics Infrastructure at Facebook' (*ACM Digital Library*, 2010), <http://delivery .acm.org/10.1145/1810000/1807278/p1013-thusoo.pdf>; Yahoo, 'Hadoop at Yahoo!', available at <http://developer.yahoo.com/hadoop/>; and Anil Madan, 'Hadoop—The Power of the Elephant' (*Ebay Tech Blog*, 29 October 2010), <http://www.ebaytechblog.com/2010/10/29/hadoop-the-power-of -the-elephant> (all accessed 1 March 2013). Although Hadoop does not use VMs, there is increasing interest in running Hadoop on VMs. See also Chris Brenton, 'The Basics of Virtualization Security', <https://cloudsecurityalliance.org/wp-content/uploads/2011/11/virtualization-security.pdf> (accessed 1 March 2012).

[34] Originally an acronym for Redundant Array of Inexpensive Disks, RAID is now used to mean Redundant Array of Independent Disks.

[35] Storage systems include Amazon's S3, SimpleDB, or Elastic Block Storage, and Windows Azure's SQL Azure, blob, table storage, or XDrive.

[36] For example, Amazon's Dynamo for structured data storage underlies many services, including its S3 storage. Giuseppe Decandia et al., 'Dynamo: Amazon's Highly Available Key-value Store' (*ACM Digital Library*, 2007), <http://dl.acm.org/citation.cfm?id=1294281> (accessed 1 March 2012).

Google's proprietary software developed for fault-tolerant distributed storage and processing using cheap commodity hardware includes BigTable, for structured data, and Google File System, a distributed file system. Fay Chang et al., 'Bigtable: A Distributed Storage System for Structured Data' (*ACM Digital Library*, 2 June 2008), <http://dl.acm.org/citation.cfm?id=1365816> (accessed 1 March 2012).

Many cloud databases are 'NoSQL' databases, for example the open-source MongoDB used by Twitter and (on Amazon EC2) location-based social media service FourSquare, 'Show and Tell: MongoDB at Foursquare', available at <http://engineering.foursquare.com/2011/12/21/ show-and-tell-mongodb-at-foursquare>. Some consider that NoSQL databases handle huge quantities of distributed data better than traditional relational SQL databases. To prioritize high availability, cloud services usually tolerate weaker data consistency, hence the term 'eventual consistency': on updating data, replicas are updated to be consistent—but only eventually, not instantly. For example, Amazon

systems, are effectively applications enabling easier and more structured logical management of data than file systems (although ultimately database files are stored in file systems). However, the same database, or even database table, may hold more than one user's data, so it is not just physical storage, but logical storage that may be shared among different users, again, with software handling the segregation.[37] Thus, users rely on such software for security, to ensure one user cannot access another user's data deliberately or inadvertently.

Cloud computing uses the RAID concept at larger scale: one data set may be dispersed in fragments (chunks or 'shards' in database terms) among servers or other storage equipment,[38] to be reunited and delivered to a user logging in with the correct credentials. Sharding is based on the provider's sharding policies, which vary with space constraints and performance considerations.[39] Applications' requests for data are automatically sent to some or all servers hosting relevant fragments and results are coalesced by the application. Sharding assists availability, as smaller fragments are retrieved faster and response times improved. While 'sharding', or 'partitioning', most commonly refers to fragmenting databases,[40] data not within a structured database may also be fragmented for storage or operations.[41] Data fragmentation is relevant to data location and may give rise to questions as to whether data fragments are intelligible or constitute 'personal data'.[42]

In summary, multiple users' data may be stored on common physical equipment, with software handling the storage and retrieval of a particular user's data. IaaS users may choose among available data-storage mechanisms, which may include database and caching tools, and may even use their own applications to manage data storage. Therefore, different degrees of control over data storage and data location are possible.

SimpleDB and Google BigTable use eventual consistency. Werner Vogels, 'Eventually Consistent' (*Practice*, January 2009), <http://citeseerx.ist.psu.edu/viewdoc/download?doi=10.1.1.187.8545&rep =rep1&type=pdf>; and David Bermbach et al., 'Eventual Consistency: How Soon Is Eventual? An Evaluation of Amazon S3's Consistency Behavior' (*ACM Digital Library*, 2011), <http://dl.acm.org/ citation.cfm?id=2093186> (all accessed 1 March 2013).

[37] Ways to segregate users' data exist, even so: 'Technische und organisatorische Anforderungen an die Trennung con automatisierten Verfahren bei der Benutzung einer gemeinsamen IT—Infrastruktur' (10 November 2012), <http://www.lda.brandenburg.de/sixcms/media.php/4055/TOP08_20121011 _OH_Mandantenfaehigkeit_v10_b.pdf> (accessed 1 March 2013: regarding technical and organizational separation requirements for automated data processing on shared IT systems, by a working group on technical and organizational data-protection matters, part of the Conference of the German Data Protection Commissioners).

[38] While servers' physical hard drives can store data, storage arrays attached to servers may also handle persistent storage of data.

[39] For example, to equalize workload across different servers and/or data centres. LA Barroso and U Hölzle, 'The Datacenter as a Computer: An Introduction to the Design of Warehouse-scale Machines' in Mark D Hill (ed.), *Synthesis Lectures on Computer Architecture* (Morgan & Claypool, 2009) at 1.

[40] Users may partition or 'shard' cloud databases logically; we use 'sharding' to mean only automatic data fragmentation by providers' systems. Users have no say in such automated sharding, although some providers, for example Amazon and Microsoft (Azure), allow users to confine to broad geographically circumscribed regions, for example the EU or Europe, the storage (and presumably other processing) of the resulting shards. See Chapters 3 and 10.

[41] For example, Amazon's Elastic Block Store ('EBS') appears to users as physical hard drives, but data are stored as EBS snapshots on Amazon's S3 storage service, first broken into chunks whose size depends on Amazon's optimizations. Amazon, 'Amazon Elastic Block Store (EBS)' (2011), <http://aws .amazon.com/ebs> (accessed 1 March 2013).

[42] This is discussed further in Chapter 7.

Whatever the service type, providers may back up data to multiple locations to protect against data corruption or loss due to hardware or software weaknesses or failure,
and to preserve data and service availability. Some providers may, for business continuity reasons, replicate stored data to separate equipment within the *same* data centre.
Replication may even be 'synchronous', that is in real time or near real time. Providers
may or may not back up further, for instance to tapes (which may be stored in the
same or different physical locations). Some providers also automatically replicate data
to other, geographically separated, data centres.[43] If irrecoverable data loss occurs, for
example due to a natural disaster affecting one data centre, copies may be retrievable
from data centres holding replicas (disaster recovery). Similarly, upon any failure, users
may be switched over ('failover') to using another data centre, maintaining availability
and giving the illusion of instantaneous data 'migration' to another location.[44] However,
not all providers back up data, particularly across different data centres (rather than
just within the same one). Large providers may have sufficient infrastructure, whereas
smaller providers might not.

Providers are increasingly allowing users to choose a processing region, for instance
'Europe'. However, it is not always clear whether all stored data and replicas will also be
restricted to the chosen region, and it may be difficult as a technical matter for users, or
for example their auditors, to verify that their data and processing are indeed confined
to the specified physical location.

Finally, in terms of data location and security, data may also be stored, albeit often
only temporarily, on a hard disk or memory[45] during active processing, and deletion
methods of such temporary copies may vary. If a user runs processing operations on data
using cloud resources, generally the data exist only ephemerally unless, and until, saved
to persistent storage. During operations, data retrieved from and saved to persistent
storage may be temporarily cached automatically, perhaps in distributed fragments, to
speed up operations.[46] Data may also be cached in particular locations to speed up data
delivery to those geographical areas (content delivery networks or CDNs). Therefore,
data may also be located in any server operating on the data (usually in the same data
centre from which such data were retrieved, but technically it could differ), and any
temporary caches holding the data.

---

[43] Google and Microsoft maintain two replicas of each data set, typically in different data centres.
Rajen Sheth, 'Disaster Recovery by Google' (*Official Google Enterprise Blog*, 4 March 2010), <http://
googleenterprise.blogspot.com/2010/03/disaster-recovery-by-google.html> and Brad Calder et al.,
'Windows Azure Storage: A Highly Available Cloud Storage Service with Strong Consistency' (2011),
<http://sigops.org/sosp/sosp11/current/2011-Cascais/printable/11-calder.pdf> (both accessed 1
March 2013). Replication strategies vary. 'Facebook replicates data with all writes going through a
single master data center...Yahoo! mail partitions data across [data centres] based on user...Facebook
design has a single master coordinate replication—this speeds up lookups but concentrates load on the
master for update operations', Albert Greenberg et al., 'The Cost of a Cloud: Research Problems in Data
Center Networks', <http://research.microsoft.com/en-us/um/people/dmaltz/papers/dc-costs-ccr-editorial.pdf>.
Google claims 'live' synchronous (real-time) replication, for example for Google Apps SaaS: Sheth, ibid.

[44] This is the main circumstance when cloud data might be perceived to 'move' from one data
centre to another, but clearly does not involve deletion of data from one data centre and recreation
in another.

[45] Increasingly, to enhance performance, data may be stored simply in memory and backed up
to persistent storage: Amazon Web Services, 'SAP HANA One—Now Available for Production Use
on AWS', available at <http://aws.typepad.com/aws/2012/10/sap-hana-now-available-for-production-use
.html> (accessed 1 March 2013).

[46] Just as, when using application software on a desktop computer to operate on data, some data may
be cached temporarily.

2.1.3 Networking

With network virtualization, multiple—often distributed—networking hardware and software resources may be combined into a single logical unit, for instance, to increase network capacity or resilience; however, users perceive one virtual network.[47] Conversely, multiple virtualized networks, isolated from each other, may use shared physical infrastructure simultaneously. Thus, as above, software decouples virtual networks from hardware, and multiple resources may be pooled. As with physical networks, virtual networks may also involve virtual Internet Protocol (IP) addresses, virtual routers, virtual switches, virtual firewalls, and virtual links. Again, IaaS users may manage their own virtual networks, such as virtual private networks (VPNs) connecting VMs of their choice. Similar risks arise as above regarding the security of shared infrastructure, for example whether one user can ever 'see' another user's network traffic, and the adequacy of the software to enforce segregation between users.

2.1.4 Resource management

To share hardware among different users it is necessary to manage or orchestrate the automated use and release of processing, storage, and networking resources to distribute and balance different users' workloads across the available resource pool, scaling up or down as needed across different equipment. The aim is to provide the on-demand, seamlessly scalable, efficient use of resources characteristic of cloud. For example, if a physical server is 'full' to capacity, and hosting the maximum number of VMs it can hold, then, unless a VM running in the server has terminated making room in the server's memory to host another VM, any new VM that subsequently needs to be created must be instantiated on a different physical server. Similarly, different users' data may be stored not only on the same physical system (the same hardware), but also on the same logical system (the same database or even database table), again separated only by software. Storage and retrieval of users' data on a common infrastructure will also need to be managed.

Software 'cloud platforms',[48] 'cloud fabric', or 'cloud operating systems'[49] enable such automated resource management across pools of shared, distributed hardware and software infrastructure at scale.[50] They automate 'bringing up' (or 'spinning up', or 'provisioning') VM instances, spinning them down as needed in different physical machines, or related clusters of machines, according to available capacity and VM 'health', including

---

[47] Many organizations have long used virtual private networks (VPNs) to provide private networks over the Internet.

[48] Not to be confused with the specialized use of 'platform' in PaaS (an application development and hosting 'platform'), or for example Google's use of 'cloud platform'. Here, we consider 'platform' to be the software infrastructure of cloud computing.

[49] 'Cloud fabric' and 'cloud operating system' are not (yet) terms of art and no common definition has emerged to describe them.

[50] Such 'cloud platforms' may be proprietary, for example IBM SmartCloudEnterprise, VMware vSphere, and what underlies Amazon Web Services; or, they may be open source, such as the Eucalyptus cloud computing platform, OpenNebula, CloudStack (acquired by Citrix in 2011), and OpenStack (developed more recently by US agency NASA and Internet hosting organization Rackspace, and used in Citrix's Webex web conferencing service <http://www.openstack.org/user-stories/cisco-webex/>). Open Stack, 'A Collaborative Cloud', <http://www.openstack.org/user-stories/cisco-webex/a-collaborative -cloud> (accessed 1 March 2013). The Hadoop framework (see n. 33) may also be considered such a platform.

A user may install proprietary or open-source cloud platforms on its own infrastructure for private cloud computing, for example OpenStack. Turn-key enterprise Hadoop platforms for private cloud include Cloudera's, IBM's, and Nimbula/MapR.

monitoring, tracking, and migrating VMs as needed. They can manage networks and virtual networks, not just monitoring in-coming traffic and handling security, but also 'load balancing' to distribute in-coming traffic to suitable available instances,[51] typically through automated software with algorithms to optimize resource allocation and usage based on defined policies and parameters. They can also manage storage and retrieval of data (including structured data in databases) across different equipment. They include tools to enable users to manage their own quota of resources.

Cloud platform software may be hosted, for example, installed on a provider's infrastructure and offered as a service to users (including 'data centre as a service'), or may be installed on user-controlled infrastructure for use as private cloud.[52] Service providers can install applications on IaaS to offer PaaS or SaaS to their own users.[53] IaaS users may install applications for internal use. Installed software could be developed by whoever installs it, or a third party.[54] Thus, IaaS offers users considerable control and flexibility. IaaS may (subject to any technical or contractual restrictions imposed by providers)[55] be used for any purposes for which a user's own computing infrastructure may be used, whether for internal applications, PaaS platforms, or SaaS applications offered to the user's own customers, or even website hosting. This may be important in terms of liability for content (such as infringement of intellectual property rights), and responsibility for compliance (eg under data protection law).

2.2 PaaS

Whereas IaaS users must manage their own virtual computing resources, PaaS involves what technologists term a higher level of 'abstraction'. PaaS effectively provides an integrated computing infrastructure and programming/hosting platform, usually including database and web server services.

PaaS users need not manage VMs or other computing resources at a low level, but can focus on programming application code. After the code of the user's choice is deployed to the PaaS service as an application, the user's application may be run via the Internet, for example as SaaS. The provider's platform automatically handles management and load balancing of computing resources, virtualized or otherwise, to serve and scale the application as necessary, including data storage and replication.

Users have some choice over data-storage mechanisms, including how their application accesses stored data. However, while freed from detailed resource management, PaaS users are restricted to coding applications using only programming languages, frameworks, libraries, and so on supported by the PaaS provider, and user applications must meet any other provider limitations (imposed for scalability and security or other

---

[51] Amazon's Elastic Load Balancer redirects traffic among an 'Auto-Scaling' group of multiple VM instances. Amazon Web Services, 'New Features for Amazon EC2: Elastic Load Balancing, Auto Scaling and Amazon CloudWatch', <http://aws.typepad.com/aws/2009/05/new-aws-load-balancing -automatic-scaling-and-cloud-monitoring-services.html>; 'AWS Management Console Now Supports Elastic Load Balancing', <http://aws.typepad.com/aws/2009/12/aws-management-console-now -supports-elastic-load-balancing.html> (both accessed 1 March 2013).

[52] Amazon IaaS is only available as a hosted service; Eucalyptus may be installed on a user's own infrastructure.

[53] For example, Heroku's PaaS service is built on Amazon's IaaS service, as is Dropbox's SaaS storage service.

[54] Third-party software licences for installation on a user's own servers on-premise may not necessarily permit installation on VMs or external clouds, so licence terms may need checking and, if necessary, renegotiation. See Chapter 4.

[55] See Chapters 3 and 4.

reasons).[56] Compared with IaaS, users may also have less visibility into what resources are used to run their application, and how they are provided. PaaS platforms may even be built on other providers' IaaS platforms.[57] Accordingly, PaaS offers users less flexibility and control than IaaS. However, PaaS users do control the code they deploy, and therefore have control over the security of their application, which may affect responsibility and liability.

As with IaaS platforms, PaaS cloud platforms may be used as provider-hosted services, or installed on users' infrastructure for private cloud computing.[58] Also, PaaS applications may be for use by the user's employees only, or offered to the user's own customers as SaaS. For example, a software developer wishing to provide online applications to consumers as SaaS may program and host those applications using PaaS (or IaaS) instead of buying its own servers. Like IaaS, PaaS may be used for highly scalable web hosting.[59]

2.3 SaaS

SaaS sits at an even higher level of abstraction than PaaS. Users need not be concerned even with application code; they simply use the application(s) provided. How underlying resources are deployed to provide the service is managed by providers, and as mentioned above some SaaS providers base their services on other providers' IaaS or PaaS, although others may use their own physical or software infrastructure.

While users can set preferences for some SaaS applications, and control how their own quota is used (for instance, storage space), their ability to customize applications is usually limited, and they cannot control how providers manage underlying resources. Some SaaS services even use a single running application to serve multiple users. Again, different users' data may be stored in the same database, even database table, posing potential security risks. Users must rely on the SaaS software to enforce separation.

While SaaS applications often originate from the SaaS provider, third-party SaaS applications may be installed on a SaaS provider's infrastructure for offering as a service, or on a private cloud for internal use.[60]

3. Cloud Supply Chain: Key Concepts

The cloud supply chain is complex. One cloud service may combine hardware and/or software components from different suppliers or providers. Also, cloud services themselves may be combined or layered.

---

[56] For example, Google's App Engine supports applications coded using Python and Java, Heroku is for Ruby on Rails programs, VMWare's Cloud Foundry supports Java, Ruby, Node.js, and Scala, while RedHat's OpenShift Origin and Microsoft's Windows Azure support multiple languages.

[57] For example, Engine Yard PaaS uses Amazon Web Services IaaS.

[58] For example, Microsoft's proprietary Windows Azure, or VMWare's open-source Cloud Foundry. Some PaaS platforms are only available as a service; for example, Google's App Engine, hosted by Google, is not available for installation on a user's own infrastructure.

[59] For example, Accenture used Google App Engine to build the 2011 UK Royal Wedding website, available at <http://www.officialroyalwedding2011.org> (accessed 8 March 2013).

[60] For example, Microsoft Office 365 application software may be licensed for internal use in a private cloud, or for offering in a public cloud, such as by telecommunications provider Vodafone UK 'Microsoft Office 365 from Vodafone', available at <http://www.vodafone.com/content/index/about/what/business/productivity_services/office_365.html> (accessed 8 March 2013), or could be used as a full SaaS service on Microsoft-run infrastructure.

3.1 Combining components

Cloud services ultimately employ physical infrastructure: equipment housed in physical locations, typically data centres. The data centre ecosystem may involve different players providing physical space, equipment (whether servers, storage, or networking), software infrastructure and services (including, of course, cloud services), and related ancillary services. Cloud platforms used as software infrastructure for cloud services may be proprietary or open source, hosted-only or available as installable software, and may not necessarily involve virtualization. Cloud service providers need not use their own cloud platforms or application software. Therefore, the owner, operator, manager, and user of a physical or software component may be different entities.

As a concrete illustration, a person X may buy or lease a dedicated data centre, or rent space in a third party's data centre where others also rent space (colocation). X could buy or rent servers or storage devices from other third parties. Servers and other equipment could be dedicated to X, or shared with others. X might manage 'its' servers itself, with only its own employees having access to them, for example in a locked cage or room, perhaps with biometric controls for entry, and so on. Or, X might use a third-party service provider to help run and maintain its servers. On those servers, X could install a proprietary or open-source cloud platform.[61] Some suppliers even sell physical servers with open-source or proprietary cloud software infrastructure pre-installed. X could offer the use of its cloud infrastructure to others as IaaS.[62] Or, X could build its own PaaS platform on this infrastructure, to develop and host its own applications for private cloud, or to offer PaaS services to others. PaaS platforms, whether stand-alone or built on existing IaaS platforms, may also be installable on X's equipment, for X's own use or offering to others as hosted services. Physical and software infrastructure could be managed by X, or a third party on its behalf, such as a systems integrator. X might have a separate consultancy, or other services contract, with an integrator to help it set up, manage, or support its cloud. X could install, on its own or third-party cloud infrastructure, application software it developed internally, or licensed from third parties. It could use these applications internally, as private cloud, or offer them as a service to others, as a SaaS provider. These illustrate that many combinations are possible, and users may not necessarily know how a cloud service has been put together or who supplies, provides, or operates different components.

Users may also combine different cloud providers' services. Ancillary support for primary cloud services includes analytics, monitoring, and cloud-based billing systems. SaaS across different providers is increasingly integrated.[63] Providers may use third-party cloud security providers, and integrate applications with, or support, 'non-cloud' components.

Cloud use is becoming increasingly sophisticated. With traditional IT, organizations may install and operate different applications, while with cloud, customers increasingly integrate different cloud applications and support services, with each other and with legacy internal systems.

---

[61] For instance, Canonical's Ubuntu Enterprise Cloud, which itself leverages OpenStack. This illustrates that even cloud platform software is not a single concept; there may be different kinds at different levels, for example with more user functionality added, such as with Ubuntu Cloud.

[62] For example, European telecommunications and managed services provider Colt uses VMWare's vCloud platform to offer private and public cloud services as 'virtual data centres' in Colt's physical data centres, and Colt also provides connectivity for those services.

[63] Google Apps MarketPlace enables customers of this SaaS productivity suite to use third-party SaaS integrated with, managed, and accessed through, Google Apps. 'Google Apps Marketplace Now Launched' (*Google Apps*, 10 March 2010), <http://googleappsupdates.blogspot.com/2010/03/google-apps-marketplace-now-launched.html> (accessed 8 March 2013).

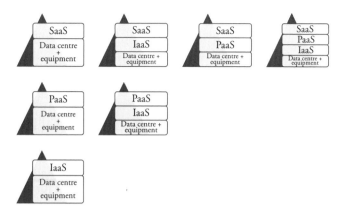

Figure 1.1 Cloud layers—different architectures

3.2 Layers or chains of cloud services

Cloud computing often involves a combination of 'layers'[64] of services and such layering may not be transparent to users. The classification of a service depends on exactly which layers and actors are under consideration. For example, customers of Dropbox may consider that they obtain a SaaS storage service from Dropbox. However, from the perspective of Dropbox, which built its SaaS service on Amazon's IaaS infrastructure, Amazon provides an IaaS service, which Dropbox uses to offer SaaS to its own customers.[65] Thus, Dropbox is both a cloud user (of Amazon IaaS) and cloud provider (of SaaS storage, to its customers).

Furthermore, as already mentioned, PaaS may be layered on IaaS, SaaS on PaaS or IaaS; triple layers are possible. Figure 1.1, albeit in a simplified way, illustrates the main alternatives.

Examples of the different alternatives are:

1. 'Unlayered'[66] IaaS, such as Amazon Web Services, RackSpace, GoGrid, or Google Compute Engine.

2. 'Unlayered' PaaS, such as Google App Engine, Microsoft Windows Azure, or Salesforce's Force.com.

3. PaaS on IaaS, such as dotCloud, Engine Yard, or Heroku (all built on Amazon IaaS).

4. 'Unlayered' SaaS, for example social networking or sharing services such as Facebook[67] and Flickr, webmail services such as Gmail and Outlook.com, and Salesforce's customer relationship management service.

---

[64] 'Layer' is not a defined term of art in this context.

[65] See Chapter 3 for a discussion of the contractual implications of this type of arrangement.

[66] Here, 'unlayered' refers to the cloud service. As mentioned in Section 3.1, physical infrastructure may be provided by parties other than the cloud service provider. Figure 1.1 shows 'data centre + equipment' as the implicit bottom, physical 'layer'.

[67] Facebook allows developers to create applications operating within Facebook, ie provides a 'platform' for developers to offer applications to Facebook users. However, strictly speaking Facebook does not provide PaaS, but only a way for applications to *interface* with its proprietary social networking platform. Facebook apps are, in fact, hosted elsewhere, such as on Amazon IaaS: Amazon Web Services, 'Facebook Application Hosting', available at <http://aws.amazon.com/facebook-application-hosting> (accessed 8 March 2013).

5. SaaS on IaaS, such as Dropbox, or Mozy (both on Amazon IaaS); indeed, any SaaS service built on Amazon, such as location-based consumer SaaS service Foursquare.

6. SaaS on PaaS, such as any SaaS service built on App Engine or Azure.[68]

7. SaaS on PaaS on IaaS: any SaaS service built on IaaS-based PaaS services, such as dotCloud or Heroku.[69]

This multiplicity of possible architectures for what appears, to the end user, to be a single cloud service, means that users may be dependent on several different providers and sub-providers,[70] including physical infrastructure providers. Different contractual arrangements for supply or provision of different components may also exist between different parties. Despite the potential importance for users of multiple dependencies, it is often difficult for users to know who is involved in 'hidden' service layers behind the direct provider, or to assess the risks of a hidden provider's service or equipment failing.

It is possible that a particular cloud user might be the only entity involved in a private cloud arrangement and might have direct control over every component of its cloud service 'stack'. In almost all cases, however, cloud computing arrangements are a new way of sourcing different IT resources from multiple providers and it is common for there to be complex relationships between users and providers and between providers and sub-providers.

It is tempting to regard cloud computing as just a new form of outsourcing. Many commercial, legal, and regulatory issues relevant to outsourcing do indeed apply to cloud computing. However, cloud computing has some fundamental characteristics that distinguish it from traditional outsourcing and which may affect the provider's or user's position in relation to risk management, contractual terms, and so on. In particular, there is considerable scope for confusion in dealing with layered services, particularly as regards assurances relating to security and sub-contractors.[71]

---

[68] Toyota's planned SaaS services for its car owners will run on Azure. Sharon Pian Chan, 'Microsoft and Toyota Bringing Cloud Computing to the Car' (*The Seattle Times*, 6 April 2011), <http://seattletimes .nwsource.com/html/microsoftpri0/2014698772_microsoftwillbuild.html> (accessed 8 March 2013).

[69] Many SaaS apps offered to users of Facebook or the Apple iPhone smartphone are developed and deployed using Heroku. For example, Heroku, 'Facebook Apps that Scale with Heroku', <http:// success.heroku.com/cardinal_blue>; and 'Heroku Fuels Social App Development with New Facebook Program' (*Heroku*, 9 November 2010), <http://news.heroku.com/news_releases/heroku-fuels-social -app-development-with-new-facebook-program> (both accessed 8 March 2013).

A concrete example: Chase Jarvis's Best Camera app for the iPhone smartphone was produced and deployed using Heroku. A user of that app may use an iPhone to photograph another person, then store and share that photo via the app, ultimately on Amazon's servers. Here, we have three providers: Chase Jarvis provides the iPhone app to the end user; Heroku (sub-provider) provides the platform used by Chase Jarvis to build and deliver the app; and Amazon (sub-sub-provider) provides the underlying computing infrastructure. The end user may not know, and may not necessarily be concerned to know, that Best Camera uses Heroku/Amazon. Best Camera App, available at <http://thebestcamera.com/ app.html> and Heroku, 'Launched Top iPhone App & Social Site with Heroku', <http://success.heroku .com/ubermind> (both accessed 8 March 2013).

[70] For example, when Amazon Web Services suffered an outage in its US East Region in April 2011, SaaS providers who relied on Engine Yard and Heroku were also affected: Derrick Harris, 'Cloud Platforms Heroku, DotCloud & Engine Yard Hit Hard by Amazon Outage' (*Gigaom*, 21 April 2011), <http://gigaom.com/cloud/more-than-100-sites-went-down-with-ec2-including-your-paas -provider> (accessed 8 March 2013).

[71] These issues are explored further in Chapter 2, Section 5. See also Chapter 4 and W Kuan Hon and Christopher Millard, 'Cloud Computing vs Traditional Outsourcing—Key Differences' (*Social Science Research Network*, 12 September 2012), <http://papers.ssrn.com/sol3/papers.cfm?abstract _id=2200592> (accessed 8 March 2012).

3.3 Cloud compared with grid and utility computing

Grid computing[72] also involves distributed computing harnessing multiple physical machines. However, a key difference lies in how resources are allocated, and perhaps also in cloud's greater 'on demand' capability.[73] With grid computing, large amounts of data are requested by a small number of users (few but large allocation requests are made), whereas cloud computing better suits environments with many users requesting small amounts of data (many but small allocation requests): ' "Grids are well suited for complex scientific work in virtual organizations," ... Clouds, on the other hand, are well suited for simple work such as many short-running jobs.'[74] Or, to look at it another way, 'In a computational grid, one large job is divided into many small portions and executed on multiple machines. This characteristic is fundamental to a grid; not so in a cloud'.[75]

Utility computing is used generally to refer to the commoditization of computing, whereby computing services are delivered like water, electricity, gas, and telecommunications utilities. Cloud computing is one way to deliver utility computing, including access on demand and paying only for what is used.[76]

4. Concluding Remarks

To summarize, many components may be involved in one cloud service, with different possible deployment models and layers, and cloud supply chains and contractual relationships may be complex. Chapter 2 explores what this means in terms of control, risk, and security in the cloud.

---

[72] For a detailed comparison of cloud computing and grid computing, by business model, architecture, resource management and programming, application and security models, see Ian Foster et al., 'Cloud Computing and Grid Computing 360-Degree Compared', available at <http://arxiv.org/ftp/arxiv/papers/0901/0901.0131.pdf> (accessed 8 March 2013).

[73] Judith Myerson, 'Cloud Computing versus Grid Computing' (*IBM*, 3 March 2009), <http://www.ibm.com/developerworks/web/library/wa-cloudgrid> (accessed 8 March 2013).

[74] Jennifer Schiff, 'Grid Computing and the Future of Cloud Computing' (*Enterprise Storage Forum*, 21 January 2010), <http://www.enterprisestorageforum.com/outsourcing/features/article.php/3859956/Grid-Computing-and-the-Future-of-Cloud-Computing.htm>; and Thorsten, 'Cloud Computing vs Grid Computing' (*RightScale Blog*, 7 July 2008), <http://blog.rightscale.com/2008/07/07/cloud-computing-vs-grid-computing> (both accessed 8 March 2013).

[75] Karishma Sundaram, 'Cloud Computing vs Grid Computing' (*Bright Hub*, 20 May 2011), <http://www.brighthub.com/environment/green-computing/articles/68785.aspx> (accessed 8 March 2013)—thus, Hadoop (n. 33) might be considered close to grid computing.

[76] Rajkumar Buyaa et al., 'Cloud Computing and Emerging IT Platforms: Vision, Hype and Reality for Delivering Computing as the 5th Utility' (*Science Direct*, June 2009), <http://www.sciencedirect.com/science/article/pii/S0167739X08001957> (accessed 8 March 2013); although as mentioned earlier in this chapter, some cloud services are free, and others are charged on, for example, a per-month per-user basis rather than on amount used.

2

Control, Security, and Risk in the Cloud

W Kuan Hon and Christopher Millard

1. Introduction

A major feature of cloud computing is that it enables abstraction, whereby user function-ality can be separated from resource management. But, reliance on abstracted resources that are controlled by third parties, and whose use is shared, carries risks.[1] Concerns are often raised about decreased user control and increased provider control of data in cloud, particularly data security (confidentiality, integrity, and availability), fuelled perhaps by the relative lack of information available to users regarding details of cloud providers' components, suppliers, and mechanics.[2]

Colocation risks may also exist: if hardware thought to contain a third party's target data is seized by authorities, data of other tenants sharing that hardware may be exposed also.[3] Similarly, data that happen to be stored on the same equipment or database as that of another user, who is targeted remotely, could also be at risk. Whether the targeting is local or remote, other users' data stored on the same hardware or database as targeted data would be more at risk than if they were stored on hardware or a database that is not targeted for attack or seizure. Where data are stored on a third party's infrastructure, there is also the risk of data no longer being available to a user if its provider is targeted, for example if its equipment is seized, made inaccessible, or its business closed down.[4]

However, cloud services differ in the degree of control and flexibility afforded to users (and accordingly in responsibility for security), and the extent to which providers or sub-providers can access user data. Much depends on a service's type and design.

---

[1] See generally, Wayne Jansen et al., 'Guidelines on Security and Privacy in Public Cloud Computing' (*National Institute of Standards and Technology*, December 2011), <http://csrc.nist.gov/publications/nist-pubs/800-144/SP800-144.pdf>; Thomas Haeberlen et al., 'Cloud Computing Benefits, Risks and Recom-mendations for Information Security' (*European Network and Information Security Agency*, December 2012), <https://resilience.enisa.europa.eu/cloud-security-and-resilience/cloud-computing-benefits-risks-and-recommendations-for-information-security/at_download/file>; Cloud Security Alliance, 'Security Guidance for Critical Areas of Focus in Cloud' (2011), available at <https://cloudsecurityalliance.org/guidance/csaguide.v3.0.pdf>; Federal Office for Information Security, 'Security Recommendations for Cloud Computing Providers' available at <https://www.bsi.bund.de/SharedDocs/Downloads/EN/BSI/Publications/Minimum_information/SecurityRecommendationsCloudComputingProviders.pdf?__blob=publicationFile> (all accessed 6 March 2013).

[2] For example, EU data protection regulators cite loss of control and lack of transparency as major risks of cloud. See Article 29 Data Protection Working Party, *Opinion 05/2012 on Cloud Computing*, WP196. Security information, issues, and audits are discussed in detail in Chapter 3, including con-tractual provisions regarding cloud security. Data protection issues are discussed in Part III of this book.

[3] FBI server seizures, although not cloud-specific, have affected innocent businesses whose data happened to be hosted on the target server. James Urquhart, 'FBI Seizures Highlight Law as Cloud Impediment' (*CNET*, 16 April 2009), <http://news.cnet.com/8301-19413_3-10220786-240.html> (accessed 6 March 2013).

[4] As when US authorities closed down cloud storage service Megaupload over copyright infringe-ment allegations, depriving all its users of access to their stored data (even if not copyright-infringing). Nick Perry, 'Popular File-sharing Website Megaupload Shut Down' (*USA Today*, 20 January 2012), <http://www.usatoday.com/tech/news/story/2012-01-19/megaupload-feds-shutdown/52678528/1> (accessed 6 March 2013).

2. Confidentiality

Confidentiality is at risk only if providers or others can access users' data in intelligible form.

2.1 Cryptography[5]

Unauthorized access can be prevented or minimized by users encrypting their data strongly before upload to the cloud. Cryptographic applications may transform an entire data set by applying an 'algorithm' to it, for instance, translating information into another language so only those knowing that language can understand the translation.[6] One-way cryptography ('hashing') applies one-way functions (cryptographic hash functions) to data, producing fixed-length 'hashes' or 'hash values'; it is intended to be irreversible.[7] Two-way cryptography ('encryption') is reversible, enabling reconstitution of the original data set ('decryption'), but only by certain persons, or in certain circumstances. Thus, cryptography may be used to protect data confidentiality.

Factors affecting encrypted data's security against unauthorized decryption include strength of encryption method (the algorithm's cryptographic strength),[8] encryption key length (longer keys are generally more secure against attacks), and key management, including decryption key storage, security, and key access control.[9] Some encryption methods have been 'broken' or 'cracked'.[10] We consider information 'strongly' encrypted

---

[5] On encryption generally, see Ross Anderson, *Security Engineering: A Guide to Building Dependable Distributed Systems* 2nd edn (Indianapolis: John Wiley & Sons, 2008), Ch. 5.

[6] Similarly, encrypted data are intended for use only by whoever holds and can use the decryption key, typically whoever knows the password or passphrase required to generate and to use the key, itself usually encrypted.

[7] Passwords are often one-way 'hashed', that is a one-way cryptographic 'hash function' applied to the password, and the resulting hash value stored. A password later entered is similarly hashed. If the two hash values are identical, the password is accepted. This avoids insecurely storing 'cleartext' passwords. Comparing hashes also enables integrity checking, that is detecting changes or corruption to original data. Hashes can be transmitted and/or stored with the original data. If integrity is compromised, the hashes will differ. Hashing can therefore be used to check if files are identical (even with encrypted files), for example to 'deduplicate' files stored by users, as has been publicized in relation to storage service Mega. Robert David Graham, 'Mega and Encrypted Cloud Deduplication' (*Errata Security*, 21 January 2013), <http://erratasec.blogspot. co.uk/2013/01/mega-and-encrypted-cloud-deduplication.html> (accessed 6 March 2013).

Deduplication may weaken security, depending on how it has been implemented. Dropbox, for example, received some negative publicity regarding its deduplication practices. Mathew J Schwartz, 'Dropbox Accused of Misleading Customers on Security' (*InformationWeekUK*, 16 May 2011), <http://www. informationweek.com/storage/security/dropbox-accused-of-misleading-customers/229500683> (accessed 6 March 2013).

[8] Even one-way cryptography may be broken, and original data reconstituted. Cloud computing, using Amazon's EC2 GPU cluster instances, was employed to reconstruct 14 passwords of 1–6 characters long from their SHA-1 hashes in under an hour, for about US$2. Jack Clark, 'Hacker Uses Cloud Computing to Crack Passwords' (*ZDNet*, 16 November 2010), <http://www.zdnet.com/ hacker-uses-cloud-computing-to-crack-passwords-4010021067/> (accessed 2 April 2013).

[9] Matt Blaze et al., *Minimal Key Lengths for Symmetric Ciphers to Provide Adequate Commercial Security* (US Defense Technical Information Center, 1996), <http://www.dtic.mil/cgi-bin/GetTRDoc? AD=ADA389646>. The publication of secret US embassy cables on the WikiLeaks website illustrates the importance of restricting key access. While data were stored securely, the overall measures were not conducive to security because it seems too many people had key access. Greg Miller, 'CIA to examine impact of files recently released by WikiLeaks', (*The Washington Post,* 22 December 2010), <http://www.washingtonpost. com/wp-dyn/content/article/2010/12/21/AR2010122105498.html> (accessed 6 March 2013).

[10] Encryption techniques found vulnerable have required replacement by more secure algorithms. Also, technological advances, including cloud, facilitate decryption via 'brute force' attacks, whereby numerous computers rapidly try different keys to find what 'fits'. For example, messages encrypted using Data Encryption Standard (DES) were decrypted by the US Electronic Frontier Foundation—see

if it is secure against decryption for most practical purposes most of the time in the real world;[11] in particular, if it is encrypted, and decryption keys are secured' to recognized industry standards and best practices.[12]

Cryptography may be applied to data within an electronic file, folder, database, or other collection of information. Users may apply cryptography to parts or, perhaps more commonly, to all of a data set or database before storing it in the cloud. For example, one-way or two-way cryptography may be applied only to names, but other data left readable as 'plaintext'. Alternatively, two-way cryptography may be applied to a whole data set before storage for future use. Cryptography may be applied within a user's computer prior to transmission, using its own software, or the provider's.[13] Even where users intend to process data unencrypted in the cloud, providers may encrypt all or part of data received, in order to store data more securely, or before using or selling anonymized or pseudonymized personal data (eg, applying cryptography to identifiers).[14]

Decrypting and re-encrypting data reduces performance: one disadvantage of cryptography. Furthermore, even with data that are strongly encrypted to military grade, in order to enable applications to process data actively, such as for sorting, analysis, indexing, for full-text searching, retention management, data format conversion, or other use, currently encrypted data must first be decrypted (even if re-encrypted thereafter).[15] Data that exist 'in the clear' in unencrypted form *at any point* in the cloud, may be vulnerable to access by providers or third parties. The only way to avoid this vulnerability is to download encrypted data to the user's own systems, then decrypt locally. Secure operations on data that remain encrypted, for example inside encrypted 'containers', are technically possible. Hopefully, such secure computation involving 'homomorphic encryption'[16] will become workable.[17] However, currently such operations would take an unfeasibly long time,[18] meaning encryption to secure cloud data confidentiality is

Electronic Frontier Foundation, 'Cracking DES' (July 1998), available at <http://w2.eff.org/Privacy/Crypto/Crypto_misc/DESCracker> (accessed 6 March 2013).

[11] When weaknesses are discovered in cryptographic systems, the system will not necessarily become suddenly insecure. However, practical attacks using techniques discovered will probably be possible someday. So, such discoveries impel migration to more secure techniques, rather than signifying that everything encrypted with that system is immediately insecure. Bruce Schneier, 'Cryptanalysis of SHA-1' (*Schneier on Security*, 18 February 2005), <http://www.schneier.com/blog/archives/2005/02/cryptanalysis_o.html> (accessed 6 March 2013).

[12] See US Code of Federal Regulations 45 CFR Part 170, Health Information Technology: Initial Set of Standards, Implementation Specifications, and Certification Criteria for Electronic Health Record Technology, US Department of Health and Human Services (Federal Register, 28 July 2010). §170.210 stipulates standards to which §170.302 generally requires electronic health information to be encrypted: 'Any encryption algorithm identified by the National Institute of Standards and Technology (NIST) as an approved security function in Annex A of the Federal Information Processing Standards (FIPS) Publication 140–2.'

[13] For example, Mozilla Weave, now Firefox Sync. Christopher Soghoian, 'Caught in the Cloud: Privacy, Encryption, and Government Back Doors in the Web 2.0 Era' (2010) *Journal on Telecommunications and High Technology Law*, 8(2) 359, which suggests why cloud security measures are relatively lacking, for instance in encryption, and offers possible solutions.

[14] Anonymized and pseudonymized personal data in the cloud are discussed in Chapter 7.

[15] Tim Mather, Subra Kumaraswamy, Shahed Latif, *Cloud Security and Privacy: An Enterprise Perspective on Risks and Compliance* (Sebastopol, CA: O'Reilly, 2009), 62 and Miranda Mowbray, 'The Fog over the Grimpen Mire: Cloud Computing and the Law' (2009) 6:1 *SCRIPTed* 129, 135–6.

[16] N Smart and F Vercauteren, 'Fully Homomorphic Encryption with Relatively Small Key and Ciphertext Sizes' in Phong Q Nguyen and David Pointcheval (eds), *Public Key Cryptography—PKC 2010*, 420 (Berlin/Heidelberg: Springer, 2010).

[17] R Chow et al., 'Controlling Data in the Cloud: Outsourcing Computation Without Outsourcing Control' in Radu Sion and Dawn Song (chairs), *Proceedings of the 2009 ACM Workshop on Cloud Computing Security*, 85–90 (Chicago, IL: ACM, 2009).

[18] Bruce Schneier, 'Homomorphic Encryption Breakthrough', *Schneier on Security* (9 July 2009), <http://www.schneier.com/blog/archives/2009/07/homomorphic_enc.html> (accessed 2 April 2013).

only practicable in certain situations, notably, pure passive storage of encrypted data that are decrypted only on the user's machine after download, and where the data do not need to be operated on in-cloud. In practice, the current potential benefits of operating on data actively using cheap, flexible cloud services can only be realized where data are unencrypted or decrypted beforehand. One compromise solution has been to process only obfuscated[19] or tokenized[20] data in the cloud, keeping sensitive confidential data on-premise.

While some services claim to encrypt data on users' computers before transfer to the cloud,[21] whether providers can access decryption keys, and therefore read intelligible user data, varies with the individual service: some services involve provider key access, whereas others do not.[22] Some users even give providers key access.[23] Many SaaS services involve providers, or their software, accessing intelligible user data. That may be required, for example, for indexing data for user search functionality, or for analysing data to display advertisements relevant to data content. However, with layered services, sub-providers may not necessarily have access. Consider SaaS built on PaaS or IaaS infrastructure. Even if the SaaS application gives the SaaS provider access to decryption keys for encrypted data stored by its application, the application is unlikely to give the PaaS or IaaS provider such access. And, as mentioned above, with SaaS involving mere storage, the SaaS provider may not have key access if users encrypt data strongly before transmission.

With unencrypted data, unauthorized access is possible if intruders can access data on the provider's systems; therefore, intrusion prevention and detection systems, such as firewalls, are important. Many systems are designed to give providers 'backdoors', a technical ability to access user data (at least if unencrypted), as providers may need access for maintenance or support purposes. In such cases, increased confidentiality would require access control restrictions: minimizing class(es) of employees with technical access and restricting

---

[19] Miranda Mowbray, Siani Pearson, and Yun Shen, 'Enhancing Privacy in Cloud Computing via Policy-based Obfuscation', *The Journal of Supercomputing* (online 31 March 2010), Vol. 61, Issue 2, August 2012, 267–91 and M Mowbray and S Pearson, 'A Client-based Privacy Manager for Cloud Computing', *Proceedings of Fourth Conference on Communication System Software and Middleware* (Dublin, 2009).

[20] See n. 27 and accompanying text.

[21] SpiderOak SaaS storage, Mozilla Firefox Sync for browser information storage/synchronization, LastPass password storage.

[22] Several cloud providers hold user keys: Chris Foresman, 'Apple Holds the Master Decryption Key When it Comes to iCloud Security, Privacy' (*ArsTechnica*, 3 April 2012), <http://arstechnica.com/apple/2012/04/apple-holds-the-master-key-when-it-comes-to-icloud-security-privacy>. SpiderOak SaaS storage states it cannot access users' keys. However, where providers' software is used to encrypt data, users without security expertise and access to relevant code must rely on providers' assurances that they have no such access. For example, storage service Dropbox had to clarify that it in fact held keys and could access users' encrypted data. Ryan Singel, 'Dropbox Lied to Users About Data Security, Complaint to FTC Alleges' (*Wired*, 13 May 2011), <http://www.wired.com/threatlevel/2011/05/dropbox-ftc> (both accessed 11 March 2013).

[23] A 2012 global survey of 4,000 managers on cloud encryption found nearly half of respondents stated their organization already transferred sensitive or confidential data to the cloud, although 39% admitted 'their security posture has been reduced as a result', clearly demonstrating that, for many organizations, economic benefits of cloud 'outweigh security concerns'. 82% of organizations had transferred or planned to transfer sensitive or confidential data to cloud, of whom 64% felt *providers* had primary responsibility for protecting data, 'even though a similar number have little or no knowledge about what measures their providers have put in place to protect data'. About half of them encrypted data *before* transfer to the cloud; the rest relied on providers. 36% considered *users* are primarily responsible for key management (22% providers). Nevertheless, even with organizations that encrypted data internally, over half gave providers control of their keys. Thales, 'New Global Study by Thales and Ponemon Institute First to Focus on Data Protection and Encryption in the Cloud' (*Thales e-Security*, 7 August 2012), <http://www.thales-esecurity.com/en/Press/Press%20Releases/2012/Ponemon%20Cloud%20report.aspx> (accessed 11 March 2013).

their access, use, or disclosure of accessed data (eg by contract, including imposing legally binding confidentiality obligations).[24] Users who control their own employees' access to their cloud data also must manage such access properly, to prevent employees from misusing or disclosing such data without authority. Strong authentication methods would also be desirable in both cases.[25]

Unauthorized access is possible if data are intercepted during transmission. With data in transmission ('data in flight' or 'data in motion'), the *connection* for transmitting unencrypted or encrypted data may be unencrypted or encrypted,[26] normally depending on the provider's systems. But, if users transmit unencrypted personal data, even via secure channels, providers will still receive unencrypted data as such. Conversely, encrypted channels may not be required for confidential transmission of already strongly encrypted data, as anyone monitoring transmissions would only obtain encrypted data.

Finally, ways to use encryption (short of homomorphic encryption) and other methods to protect data have been developed, and more seem likely to emerge. While not necessarily cloud-specific, many of these methods could be, and are being, used for cloud data. For example, particularly sensitive data, such as credit card numbers, could be replaced by non-sensitive 'tokens', whether for one-time or multiple use. Only tokenized data are processed. Tokens are not encrypted data and often are generated randomly, sometimes in a format similar to that of the original data. Tokens are mapped to, and used to reference, original data that are stored separately and securely, for example in a secure on-premise database or cache, and the map or 'look-up table' of tokens and corresponding 'real' values is similarly stored securely. Accordingly, tokens have no value to attackers and need no particular protection; the security of an individual token relies mainly on the near-impossibility of determining the original data from only the token's value. Tokenization systems are widely used for payment card data in transmission, storage, or to protect against unauthorized attempts to gain access to card data.[27]

So-called encryption, tokenization, or cloud protection 'gateways' are being offered to prospective cloud users to install on-premise, and in order to protect data at the application layer. Rather than encrypting all data, selected data known to be sensitive (not just payment data but webpage fields, such as email subject, body, and attachments) are encrypted or tokenized automatically at the gateway, so that only encrypted or tokenized data are processed in-cloud, and are decrypted or de-tokenized automatically on passing

---

[24] Provider employees with full administrative rights may abuse their privileges: Adrian Chen, 'GCreep: Google Engineer Stalked Teens, Spied on Chats' (*Gawker*, 14 September 2010), <http://gawker.com/5637234> (accessed 11 March 2013).

[25] For instance, verifying someone logging in to a system is who they purport to be, by using passwords or stronger, two factor authentication methods where codes generated by keyfobs, or sent to mobile phones, are needed to log in, in addition to passwords.

[26] The TLS/SSL protocol is used to secure transmission of, for example, credit card details between browsers and remote servers (https). Connections may also be secured using virtual private networks (VPNs): IaaS provider Amazon offers VPN connections between 'Virtual Private Clouds' on its infrastructure and users' own data centres.

[27] Scoping SIV, Tokenization Taskforce PCI Security Standards Council, 'PCI DSS Tokenization Guidelines' (August 2011), <https://www.pcisecuritystandards.org/documents/Tokenization_Guidelines_Info_Supplement.pdf>; Visa, 'Visa Best Practices for Tokenization Version 1.0' (14 July 2010), <http://usa.visa.com/download/merchants/tokenization_best_practices.pdf>. For comparisons of encryption and tokenization, see Stuart Lisk, 'Is Tokenization or Encryption Keeping You up at Night?' (*Cloud Security Alliance*, 20 April 2011), <https://blog.cloudsecurityalliance.org/2011/04/20/is-tokenization-or-encryption-keeping-you-up-at-night>; Ian Huynh, 'Encryption is Better Equipped Than Tokenization to Secure Data in the Cloud' (*SC Magazine*, 1 October 2010), <http://www.scmagazine.com/encryption-is-better-equipped-than-tokenization-to-secure-data-in-the-cloud/article/178963> (all accessed 11 March 2013).

back through the gateway. Encryption/decryption keys and token maps or vaults are stored locally in the user's gateway, which gateway providers claim they cannot access; only the user controls keys/mappings and locally stored sensitive data, and end users may use cloud services as normal, ostensibly with no latency or performance reduction. Thus, cloud providers cannot access anything beyond encrypted or tokenized data, should they attempt, or be required by law enforcement authorities, to view the user's cloud data. Even searching and sorting of data may be possible, as with 'plaintext' data in cloud applications. Gateway products now exist that are designed to be compatible with common cloud services such as Amazon Web Services, Gmail, Office 365 and Salesforce, or databases in-cloud, for example Windows Azure SQL Database. Such products can even be adapted by users for use with other cloud applications, and may provide automatic detailed logging of all usage for compliance and audit purposes.[28] Gateway providers argue that restrictions on data location may be met by processing only tokenized data in-cloud, as the 'real data' remain behind the user's firewall.

Encryption techniques have also been used to enable transmission of 'self-destructing' messages or files. Silent Circle, devised by PGP cryptography pioneer Phil Zimmerman, has received some attention. Initially for secure phone calls and SMS texts, it now enables secure transfers of encrypted files from smartphones or tablets using peer-to-peer encryption. Senders may set timers to delete the transmitted data automatically from both devices after, say, seven minutes. By design Silent Circle will not store metadata, for example times of transmissions, and IP addresses are deleted after seven days. In response to pressure from security experts, Silent Circle's code has begun to be released publicly so that its security may be verified.[29] A similar prototype precursor termed Vanish, which allowed self-destructing data, for example webmail, private messages on social networking services such as Facebook, or documents on Google Docs, was cracked not long after its release.[30] It remains to be seen whether use of self-destructing data will be adopted more broadly; currently, a service called Snapchat for self-destructing photos and messages seems to be popular, particularly among teenagers.[31] With all such services there remains the risk that the recipient could capture a screenshot of the received 'ephemeral' data before it self-destructs.

---

[28] Gateway providers include CipherCloud and Perspecsys. For examples of gateway use, including for defence and health data, see Ellen Messmer, 'How Joining Google Gmail with Encryption System Helps High-tech Firm Meet Government Security Rules' (*Network World*, 7 February 2013), <http://www.networkworld.com/news/2013/020713-novati-itar-266514.html>; Ellen Messmer, 'CipherCloud Widens Cloud-based Encryption Options' (*Network World*, 6 September 2012), <http://www.networkworld.com/news/2012/090612-ciphercloud-262151.html> (both accessed 11 March 2013).

[29] Ryan Gallagher, 'The Threat of Silence' (*Slate*, 4 February 2013), <http://www.slate.com/articles/technology/future_tense/2013/02/silent_circle_s_latest_app_democratizes_encryption_governments_won_t_be.html>; Jon Matonis, 'Pressure Increases on Silent Circle to Release Application Source Code' (*Forbes*, 6 February 2013), <http://www.forbes.com/sites/jonmatonis/2013/02/06/pressure-increases-on-silent-circle-to-release-application-source-code>, code available at Github, <https://github.com/SilentCircle> (all accessed 11 March 2013).

[30] Roxana Geambasu et al., 'Vanish: Increasing Data Privacy with Self-Destructing Data', available at <http://vanish.cs.washington.edu/pubs/usenixsec09-geambasu.pdf> (accessed 11 March 2013). Scott Wolchok et al., 'Defeating Vanish with Low-Cost Sybil Attacks Against Large DHTs', available at <http://z.cs.utexas.edu/users/osa/unvanish/papers/vanish-broken.pdf> (accessed 2 April 2013).

[31] Jenna Wortham, 'A Growing App Lets You See It, Then You Don't' (*The New York Times*, 8 February 2013), <http://www.nytimes.com/2013/02/09/technology/snapchat-a-growing-app-lets-you-see-it-then-you-dont.html?pagewanted=all> (accessed 11 March 2013). Facebook has followed suit with a similar application, Poke.

2.2 Data deletion

Different degrees of 'deletion' exist in cloud, as with local computers. If a user actively deletes data, data may move to a 'recycle bin' or 'trash', but not actually be 'deleted' for a period of time, for instance 30 days or until 'emptying' the bin.[32] When a contract terminates, user data may not be deleted immediately, but only after a certain period, which users may indeed prefer because it gives them time to retrieve their data.[33] Use of trash cans and delayed deletion after termination may therefore assist other aspects of security, namely integrity and availability, for example by protecting against inadvertent or accidental user deletion of data.

However, even on emptying bins and so on, often data are not actually deleted. Instead, 'pointers', which contain metadata-referencing locations of fragments comprising the data set, are deleted; the actual data are gradually overwritten over time by fresh data, saved by the same or different users.[34] Furthermore, where data are processed in, or moved between, different physical servers, fragments may remain on disks used, including temporary physical storage, until overwritten.

Data remanence, residual representations of nominally erased or removed data, may therefore be an issue. Remaining fragments of 'deleted' data may or may not be intelligible or re-unitable, depending on service type and design, particularly with VMs where 'deleted' fragments may be exposed to users sharing the physical infrastructure. Effective confidentiality, therefore, requires overwriting deleted data a minimum number of times,[35] the ultimate measure being demagnetizing or securely destroying physical storage media. With strongly encrypted data, however, actions such as overwriting may be irrelevant. Simply destroying keys may be sufficient, or unnecessary, if providers and other third parties can never access users' keys.[36] However, deleting data selectively from bulk backup tapes may be difficult. Also, providers may not record locations of particular users' data on a backup (tape or otherwise), or may not link data with backups so that deleting originals deletes all copies.

Accordingly, deleting data securely may require deletion from multiple locations and media, and different levels of deletion exist, up to destroying the physical hardware. The degree needed depends on the desired level of security: more sensitive data may require stronger security, and overwriting more times on deletion. With private cloud, users may have more control of physical infrastructure, and greater ability to require and verify deletion. However, more secure deletion is more expensive (particularly destroying

---

[32] There may be a user education issue; some users are unaware that 'deleting' may simply move data to 'trash' without deleting it.

[33] Discussed further in Chapter 3.

[34] Google Apps SaaS terms specify this, for example on termination: '10.3 (iii) after a commercially reasonable period of time, Google will delete Customer Data by removing pointers to it on Google's active and replication servers and overwriting it over time'. Google, 'Google Apps for Education Agreement', available at <http://www.google.com/apps/intl/en/terms/education_terms.html>; 'Google Apps (Free) Agreement', available at <http://www.google.com/apps/intl/en/terms/standard_terms.html>; see also Section 11.5 of 'Google Apps for Business (Online) Agreement', available at <http://www.google.com/apps/intl/en-GB/terms/premier_terms_ie.html> (all accessed 2 April 2013).

[35] Data protection regulators consider that personal data in the cloud must be overwritten multiple times for proper deletion. See Article 29 Data Protection Working Party, *Opinion 05/2012 on Cloud Computing*, WP196.

[36] A poll by security firm Trend Micro in mid-2012 found that, to address data destruction concerns, of 149 respondents 33% encrypted data; 31% left deletion to cloud providers; and 10% demagnetized disks (not possible without access to the physical disks). Christine Drake, 'Cloud Data Destruction: Is Your Old Data Still Accessible?' (*Cloud Security Blog*, 15 August 2012), <http://cloud.trendmicro.com/cloud-data-destruction> (accessed 11 March 2013).

rather than redeploying hardware). Accordingly, providers, particularly of public cloud services, may not employ more secure methods unless necessary, and may attempt to pass on costs to users. Deletion seems as much a financial as a technical issue.[37]

Furthermore, some SaaS storage services make a feature of not destroying data, but *keeping* all versions of files, enabling users to retrieve previous revisions.[38] Similarly, some database systems automatically keep 'deleted' versions. With databases it might be possible to check the code to see how deletion operations are implemented, but providers may not agree to this, and implementations may vary.

Deletion of cloud data, therefore, raises problematic issues for legal and regulatory compliance as well as for confidentiality.[39]

2.3 Application access

Cloud applications may access stored data. In IaaS and PaaS, users control the security of their application: for instance, if the user's application permits unauthorized or inadvertent disclosure of data through the user's coding errors, that is not within the control of the provider. PaaS providers control how user code is deployed, even though they cannot control the security of the code itself.

3. Integrity

Integrity, that is securing data against unauthorized destruction, loss, or modification, depends on access and systems. Preventing unauthorized access to preserve integrity involves the same issues as preventing access to preserve confidentiality; for example, application errors may cause data corruption or inadvertent deletion. Because some providers back up or replicate data to protect integrity and availability, cloud data may be located physically in multiple sets of equipment, possibly even different data centres. This is sometimes said to increase risks to confidentiality, as data may be accessible in multiple locations.[40] Whatever the service type, users often back up their cloud data, whether to internal servers or to other cloud services.[41]

4. Availability

4.1 Service disruptions

Some aspects of availability, that is securing against disruption of, and ensuring timely and reliable access and use to data, have been discussed above. Backups with failover are one way to help maintain availability. Availability may be compromised if providers do not protect their systems, for example against distributed denial of service attacks which 'flood' networks and reduce, or prevent, connectivity. However, users' own Internet connections may fail or be disrupted, even if providers' networks are operational, and causes of connectivity

---

[37] This issue is discussed further in Chapter 3.   [38] For example, Dropbox.

[39] Discussed in Chapter 3.

[40] However, that assumes whoever has access to a physical location, for example a data centre operator, may retrieve, in intelligible form, data stored there—which may be impossible with encrypted data, and, with unencrypted data, difficult or impossible without knowing both storage and representation formats used.

[41] See Chapter 4.

interruptions may not always be pinpointed easily. Users are thus also dependent on their own Internet access service. Some cloud terms of service include service level agreements (SLAs) that cover minimum requirements regarding availability levels and performance. SLAs can be contentious, particularly as standards for measuring service levels have not yet become established.[42]

4.2 Data portability, application portability, interoperability

Also relevant to availability is 'lock-in': a major concern for users is the risk of overdependence on one provider's, often proprietary, service. Lock-in is relevant not only as a practical issue, which users may consider in relation to their cloud contracts, but also in terms of intellectual property law, data protection law, and competition law. If the service is terminated for whatever reason, users will normally want to recover their data and metadata in formats that are easily accessible, readable, and importable into other applications, whether running internally or in another provider's cloud. This is commonly called 'data portability'.[43]

There are several aspects to data portability: data format, what assistance (if any) providers will give users, what if anything providers charge for such assistance, and the data retention period. Because cloud data may be stored in proprietary formats, to what extent will providers allow user data to be exported in a non-proprietary, or at least in a standard or common format, which enables re-use by users? If data are only available in the provider's proprietary format, which cannot be read except via its service, the data are not portable. How easily and quickly may users download or otherwise recover their data? Some providers may, for a fee, post or courier data to users on disk; this can be important for data in large quantities. A related issue is the length of the 'grace period' that providers allow for users to self-retrieve data after contract termination.

Data portability, while often mentioned in the cloud context, is sometimes used to encompass application portability and interoperability also. Strictly, these are separate concepts. Application portability is an equally, if not more, important aspect of dependence risk, particularly for IaaS and PaaS. Custom applications running on IaaS or PaaS services typically utilize and integrate with the provider's Application Programming Interfaces (APIs), usually proprietary. It may be difficult or impossible to migrate applications to run in-house, or on another provider's service, without rewriting the application's code substantially, unless APIs are the same.[44] Well-advised users may verify application and data portability using test data and applications before contracting for cloud services, rather than taking the risk of contractual assurances on portability proving untrue, and leaving the user with no practical ability to retrieve its data.

Finally, note that 'interoperability' is, like data portability, often used broadly to mean application portability. 'Interoperability' may also mean 'federation': not moving

---

[42] See Chapter 4.

[43] Lock-in and data portability issues are discussed further in Chapters 4, 6, and 12.

[44] For example, the Eucalyptus cloud platform supports Amazon EC2 and S3 APIs; OpenStack does not. Joe Brockmeier, 'Amazon Taps Eucalyptus as Private Cloud Partner' (*Readwrite*, 21 March 2012), <http://www.readwriteweb.com/cloud/2012/03/amazon-taps-eucalyptus-as-private-cloud-partner.php> (accessed 11 March 2013). Services are emerging like AppFog, based on Cloud Foundry PaaS, that enable applications to run on, or across, different IaaS/PaaS services (Amazon, Azure, HP OpenStack, and Rackspace), supporting multiple programming languages and offering application portability 'with single click, zero-code migrations' between different IaaS providers and indeed internal infrastructure supporting Cloud Foundry'. Appfog Feature Roadmap, available at <http://docs.appfog.com/roadmap#infras>; Lucas, 'If PaaS Is Expensive and Slow, Why Not Use a VPS?' (*Appfog*), <http://blog.appfog.com/if-paas-is-expensive-and-slow-why-not-use-a-vps> (both accessed 11 March 2013).

applications and/or data between clouds, but having different cloud systems, perhaps from different providers, working together, *interacting*, and exchanging data or instructions. 'Interoperability' and 'federation' are sometimes used interchangeably or together.[45] Standards for cloud interoperability are still developing.[46]

5. Control and Flexibility in Practice

In traditional outsourcing, users control their service providers through contract and instructions to processors. While it is often thought that cloud users lose all control, much depends on the service. Figure 2.1 illustrates that, with different service types, a user ('tenant') may have varying degrees of control, and therefore varying degrees of responsibility for different aspects of public[47] cloud computing. For some aspects, tenants have sole control; for others, providers. In other cases, both have some control. An individual system's design may affect what is controllable, and by whom.

Generally, users have more control and flexibility with IaaS than with PaaS or SaaS.[48] With IaaS, providers manage much of the basic infrastructure, notably hardware maintenance. However, although automation of VM management is increasing, users must handle 'back end' configuration and administration of their resources, operating systems, frameworks, and applications installed within VMs and so on, including managing load balancing and failover clusters, and security. This could include installing and updating firewalls, applying operating system and application security patches, and enforcing encrypted connections to their VMs. PaaS users also have control over their application's code. Users decide what applications they wish to install and host on IaaS/PaaS, and such applications may be user-developed, and therefore user-controlled. In contrast, SaaS users utilize standardized applications, provided by SaaS providers, and in environments that users cannot control, relying on providers to secure applications as well as environments. Thus, SaaS systems generally involve more provider control but still differ regarding provider access to intelligible user data.[49]

---

[45] European Commission Information Society and Media Expert Group Report, 'The Future of Cloud Computing', available at <http://cordis.europa.eu/fp7/ict/ssai/docs/cloud-report-final.pdf> (accessed 11 March 2013).

[46] See Cloud-standards.org, 'Welcome to the Cloud Standards Wiki', available at <http://cloud-standards.org/wiki/index.php?title=Main_Page>; OASIS, 'OASIS to Standardize Cloud Application Management for Platforms (CAMP)' (*OASIS*, 12 November 2012), <https://www.oasis-open.org/news/pr/camp-tc> (both accessed 11 March 2013). One of three key actions identified by the EU cloud strategy was identifying the necessary standards and developing EU-wide voluntary certification schemes: European Commission, 'Communication from the Commission to the European Parliament, The Council, the European Economic and Social Committee and the Committee of the Regions' (27 September 2012), <http://ec.europa.eu/information_society/activities/cloudcomputing/docs/com/com_cloud.pdf> (accessed 11 March 2013).

[47] With some uses of private cloud, users might control physical infrastructure themselves.

[48] Indeed, the introduction by Google and Microsoft of IaaS services in mid-2012 (to supplement their existing PaaS and SaaS products) may have been in response to demand for services affording more user control.

[49] One writer suggests that PaaS provides users with the best security compromise. Wh1t3Rabbit, 'Is PaaS the Optimal Cloud Service Model Option for Security? (Part 1 of 2)' (*HP*, 29 November 2012), <http://h30499.www3.hp.com/t5/Following-the-Wh1t3-Rabbit/Is-PaaS-the-optimal-cloud-service-model-option-for-security-Part/ba-p/5884443>; Wh1t3Rabbit, 'Why PaaS Is the Optimal Cloud Service Model Option for Security (Part 2 of 2)' (*HP*, 11 December 2012), <http://h30499.www3.hp.com/t5/Following-the-Wh1t3-Rabbit/Why-PaaS-is-the-optimal-cloud-service-model-option-for-security/ba-p/5895495> (both accessed 11 March 2013).

SERVICE OWNER	SaaS	PaaS	IaaS
Data	Joint	Tenant	Tenant
Application	Joint	Joint	Tenant
Compute	Provider	Joint	Tenant
Storage	Provider	Provider	Joint
Network	Provider	Provider	Joint
Physical	Provider	Provider	Provider

Figure 2.1 Who controls what in cloud computing—typical scenarios
Source: © Cloud Security Alliance, reproduced with permission.

Users do not necessarily lose all control in cloud, particularly regarding security measures. Often, users may encrypt or obfuscate data, and may back up data whatever the service type; IaaS users may install their own firewalls or anti-malware and so on. Users who wish to ensure the security of their data will need to use applications (whether IaaS, PaaS, or SaaS) responsibly; for example, they must not disclose their access credentials to unauthorized parties who would thereby be enabled to access the data or employ inappropriate access or sharing settings. As there are significant differences between services, a more nuanced approach is needed. Treating all cloud services alike as 'one size fits all', as if they were the same as traditional outsourcing, and as if all cloud services posed equal risks to privacy or security, is over-simplistic and unsatisfactory, and could lead to inappropriate regulation, which may stifle innovation and impede cloud development and use without necessarily protecting users' privacy or security.

A final point is that, in the real world, security involves trade-offs. Indeed, there may even be trade-offs between different aspects of security, for instance confidentiality and integrity as opposed to availability. Some maintain that cloud should not be used unless perfect security can be ensured, but the better question may be, is the particular service's security *worse than* the user's existing security arrangements? At least one survey has found that on-premise applications and data were, at the time of the survey, subject to more security incidents (third-party attacks) than in-cloud systems.[50] Moreover, there have been some high-profile expressions of confidence in cloud's potential to be at least as secure as on-premise, if not more secure.[51]

Initiatives are progressing to increase awareness regarding the nuances of cloud security and the respective responsibilities of user and provider, as well as to improve cloud security generally.[52]

5.1 Passive provision of resources

Many current laws[53] assume traditional outsourcing procedures. Classic outsourcing of data processing, for instance payroll processing, involves users giving instructions to agents who are provided with data and tasked with processing the data actively for users according to the user's mandate. Agents may themselves engage sub-processor(s) to assist with this processing. The cloud computing model is fundamentally different as cloud users do not hire others to process data for them. Rather, they process data themselves, in self-service fashion, using cloud providers' infrastructure and resources. To assess that argument, let us run through a series of situations.

If I sell you a computer, you control the data you process using that computer. I am clearly not your processor. You process data yourself, using the supplied computer. It cannot be said that I process any data *for you*. If the computer includes preloaded software, created by me or a third party, which you use to process data, I am still not your processor; I merely supplied you with hardware and software, even if we agree, probably for a fee, that whenever the software producer releases updates, I will come and upgrade the software for you.

Now say I rent you my computer, which you use on your premises to process data. Again, *I* do not process data, even if you use software I supplied, with the computer I leased you, and even if I undertake to maintain and keep upgraded both hardware and software. If my employees physically visit your premises occasionally for maintenance or to fix a problem, they may be able to access incidentally any data you stored on the computer during their visit. However, ability to access data incidentally in such situations should not make me your 'processor'. Similarly, if I repossess the computer on termination or breach, I may then be able to access any data you had left unencrypted on the computer, but again I am not your 'processor'.

Next, say my computer is kept on my own premises, but I let you come and use it for your data processing whenever you wish. It is still you processing data, albeit using

---

[50] Neil MacDonald, 'Cloud Computing Can Be More Secure' (*Gartner*, 31 March 2012), <http://blogs.gartner.com/neil_macdonald/2012/03/31/cloud-computing-can-be-more-secure> (accessed 11 March 2013).

[51] 'HMRC First for New IT Contract', <http://hmrc.presscentre.com/Press-Releases/HMRC-first-for-new-IT-contract-680b1.aspx>; Patrick Thibodeau, 'Cloud Security Fears Exaggerated, Says Federal CIO' (*Computerworld*, 28 July 2011), <http://www.computerworld.com/s/article/9218702/Cloud_security_fears_exaggerated_says_federal_CIO>; Rohan Pearce, ' "Absolute Garbage": Comm Bank CIO Dismisses Security, Data Sovereignty as Cloud Barriers' (*CIO*, 13 November 2012), <http://www.cio.com.au/article/441854/_absolute_garbage_comm_bank_cio_dismisses_security_data_sovereignty_cloud_barriers> (all accessed 11 March 2013).

[52] Notably by the Cloud Security Alliance: Cloud Controls Matrix, available at <https://cloudsecurityalliance.org/research/ccm>; Cloud Security Alliance, 'Cloud Security Alliance Recommends the Cloud Security Readiness Tool' (*CSA*, 17 January 2013), <https://cloudsecurityalliance.org/csa-news/csa-recommends-cloud-security-readiness-tool> (both accessed 11 March 2013). Standards that the EU cloud strategy (see n. 46) is to focus on include security standards.

[53] Notably data protection; see Part III of this book.

resources I provide to you. Now, I keep a battery, or a farm of computers in my building, and my customers may use available computers for their own processing; if customers want processing power meeting specified requirements, I check which free machine suits their needs, and point them to it. Customers can install whatever operating system and software they wish, and pay me based on how powerful and fast the machine they use is, and how long they use it for.

I now let customers 'save' particular machines, configured to their specifications, with an operating system and applications pre-installed, which I store for them. They can, thereafter, simply fetch their preconfigured machine to use whenever they wish. The service I provide is not a data-processing service; I am still only providing customers with hardware and software resources they use to process data as they wish even if I am also maintaining resources, keeping hardware in good order, replacing defective machines, perhaps updating operating systems, ensuring security software such as firewalls and antivirus software is installed, or even upgrading security software.

Now I have several buildings, with machines preconfigured for all my customers. Whenever needed, a customer may fetch out their preconfigured machine and use it on a spare table. They may bring a USB memory stick holding data they wish to process using my resources, to which they may save resulting data. For space and cost reasons, multiple customers may share a table, with vertical panels between. I thus benefit from economies of scale, and may pass some cost savings on to customers. However, the fact that different customers share use of my resources does not make me a 'processor', any more than it makes an Internet cafe a 'processor'.

I next use 'load balancer' software to automate analysis of which building has spare tables, and which tables have free space, in order to direct customers automatically to suitable spaces. Load balancers may consider customer preferences: some may only be interested in buildings in location X because others are too far away to get to quickly. This facilitates customers' use of resources I provide, but again does not make me a 'processor' of any data they operate on using my resources.

I may make available computers with only one kind of application software installed, for example email, customer-relationship management, or word processing, for customers who want only those applications, which I keep upgraded. I might let customers authorize their employees, or indeed their own customers, to visit my building to use resources allocated to that customer. I may even let customers 'sub-lease' my infrastructure to others, or assist them to use my resources, perhaps providing their own supporting resources. These may make my resources more useful to customers, but again do not render me a processor.

Essentially, my buildings, with tables and computers, are analogous to data centres, server farms, and the cloud service models. Making available computers with specific applications pre-installed is like SaaS. Providing computers where customers can install their operating systems and application software of choice, which some may authorize their own employees or customers to use, is like IaaS. Finally, providing computers that customers can use to develop their own application software, and to deploy such software for use by their own employees or customers, is like PaaS.

Cloud computing differs from these analogies mainly in how customers access resources (remotely, over the Internet), and use of virtualization. Cloud users, their customers, or employees access relevant services via the Internet, rather than by visiting buildings in person. Does that make the provider a 'processor'? Arguably not: it is still the user who processes data regardless of the means by which they access the resources made available to them by providers. What about virtualization? Instead of using a different physical computer for each customer, providers may use VMs, emulating physical machines (the computers

I keep at the back), operating within physical servers' random-access memory (RAM) (the tables where customers may use computers). Instead of customers preconfiguring physical machines, they save on my systems a snapshot, or 'virtual machine image', of their configured machine (which I make available in all my buildings). Then, to use my resources, they create an 'instance' of their VM on a physical server with room for another VM (bring out their preconfigured machine to use on a table with spare capacity). They terminate the instance (move it from the table back to the room) when no longer needed. This is more efficient than buying and dedicating different physical servers to customers, which may go unused whenever the customer is not processing data. It does mean that customers (tenants) may have to share physical servers and RAM (tables) with other customers' VMs, depending on where there is spare server capacity (table space). However, it is arguable that virtualization still doesn't make me a processor of my customers' data. The resources may be provided in a different way, but customers are still the ones using them.

Provider performance monitoring, and checking that software and hardware are up to date and operating properly, again may be characterized as maintaining resources provided to users, rather than 'processing' data. This should not make providers 'processors' either; nor should users' dependency on availability of providers' resources for access to their data. Users may depend on hardware or software they use not failing or crashing, whether sold, leased, or licensed to them, but that does not render sellers, lessors, or licensors 'processors' for users. Finally, if layers of cloud services are used, the above analysis is unaffected. Thus, many cloud services are merely passive providers of computing resources, utilized by users to perform their own processing.[54]

5.2 Key differences from traditional outsourcing

Many current laws are difficult to apply to cloud arrangements because they do not cater adequately for the distinctive characteristics of cloud computing, including those arising from individual services' designs or from service type, particularly with public shared-infrastructure IaaS and PaaS. Hence, analysing legal issues with cloud is not always straightforward.

The key differences between traditional outsourcing and cloud, which it is important to bear in mind when considering legal issues, are:[55]

1. **Active agency versus passive resources for self-service usage.** Unlike with traditional outsourcing, public cloud providers do not act as agents that process data actively for users, but at most they passively store data which users choose to store and otherwise process on the provider's infrastructure. Providers may be active in maintaining and supporting the infrastructure and environment within which users process their data, but data processing is generally performed, not by providers, but by users operating the provider's resources on a self-service basis.

2. **'Direction of travel' and sequence of events.** In classic outsourcing, successive contracts 'down the chain' of processors may be easily tailored, from both timing

---

[54] However, where users choose to store, on providers' infrastructure, data that includes 'personal data', the provider will be a 'processor' under data protection laws, because merely holding personal data is treated as 'processing' it. Also, a provider will become a 'controller' under such laws if it processes stored personal data for its own purposes, for example analysing such data using automated software to display advertisements to users based on data content, or disclosing data to third parties. See Chapter 8.
[55] For a more detailed analysis of this topic, see W Kuan Hon and Christopher Millard, 'Cloud Computing vs Traditional Outsourcing—Key Differences', <http://papers.ssrn.com/sol3/papers.cfm?abstract_id=2200592>.

and control perspectives. However, cloud involves the opposite sequence of events and 'direction of travel'. Many cloud services are pre-packaged, standardized, and commoditized services, which may be built on existing sub-provider services on sub-provider standard terms. The 'sub-service' in turn may be based on other services. A user chooses the provider and pre-built package that it thinks best meets its specific processing and other needs. It may, therefore, be difficult if not impossible to change, particularly in different ways for different customers, sub-contracts between the provider and its sub-providers, because it has pre-built its service using standardized sub-service(s), rather than being commissioned to provide a service to order.

3. **Standardized shared infrastructure and environments.** Public cloud providers offer standardized, shared infrastructure and environments, often using relatively cheap commodity hardware, rather than tailoring them to each customer. Customization of services is sometimes possible, but costs extra time and money. Although IaaS affords a great degree of user control over individual resources, it is still provided in a standardized environment using the provider's standardized system. Private cloud allows the most customization and control, especially if on a user's own infrastructure and managed by the user, and, if it is on third-party infrastructure and/or managed by a third party, it is closest to traditional outsourcing. Traditional outsourced processing may use standardized infrastructure, sometimes at large scale, but it is unlikely to be shared to such an extent as in cloud. With shared infrastructure where users' data are segregated, not through their being stored in separate physical equipment, but through their being separated 'logically' using software, users are reliant on the software separation being implemented properly and securely.

4. **Knowledge.** In traditional outsourcing, processors are entrusted with the processing of specific data or types of data. In cloud, depending on the service, some providers may not even know the nature of data (eg, personal data) processed using their services, or how users are processing data, unless and until the provider chooses actively to access such data, assuming no encryption. In this sense, some providers are mere hosts renting out resources, and ought not to be treated in the same way as providers who access and utilize user data for their own purposes. Thus, the 'cloud of unknowing' works both ways: users may not have much knowledge regarding the supply chain, but providers may not have much knowledge regarding data or processing either.[56]

5. **Degrees of control.** We cover below the different degrees of control that may exist in cloud.

6. Cloud Services and Commercial Arrangements, Contractual Structures, and the IT Channel

The cloud sector is expanding rapidly, with providers ranging from major technology companies to small start-ups. While some specialize in specific types of cloud service and/or market, others offer cloud products covering the spectrum of cloud activities.

Most cloud service arrangements, especially for consumers and small to medium-sized enterprises (SMEs), are established via non-negotiable, standard-form, 'click-through'

---

[56] Providers' knowledge (or lack thereof) is discussed in more detail, in relation to personal data, in Chapter 8.

contracts. Such terms of service tend to favour providers and often contain specific provisions, including in privacy policies, which are disadvantageous to customers and possibly unenforceable, or even illegal. Terms and conditions may be complex and obscure, and it is not uncommon for providers to claim rights to change them unilaterally without notice.[57] Transparency is generally regarded as a fundamental prerequisite for certain compliance purposes such as effective privacy protection; it is also important that affected individuals have an appropriate degree of control over how information about them is used. Providers, and the contractual terms on which they operate, vary significantly in how they address (or fail to address) issues such as privacy and data security.

A relatively small, but growing, number of cloud contracts is negotiated, typically where cloud customers insist on specific arrangements and providers consider that the financial or strategic value of a deal merits special treatment. Although such deals typically involve corporate or government customers, privacy and security provisions are among the most commonly negotiated terms, and can be deal-breakers.[58]

Of growing significance in cloud is the IT channel, termed by the Cloud Industry Forum (CIF) the 'Reseller, Service Provider, and Outsourcer', comprising IT consultancies,[59] managed services providers, systems integrators, specialist resellers, technical value-added resellers (VARs), IT outsourcers, distributors, volume resellers, and IT retailers. We use 'integrator' to mean 'reseller, service provider, or outsourcer'. Integrators are increasingly providing cloud consultancy and systems integration services, for example assisting users to convert legacy applications to run in-cloud. The importance of such intermediaries looks set to grow.

Integrators are potentially very large users of IaaS or PaaS, based upon which they provide services (particularly SaaS) to their end users. Integrators may also provide cloud services on infrastructure they control.[60] They also offer customized cloud services, particularly private or hybrid cloud. Integrators may play multiple roles, sometime on the same deal. They may offer mixed cloud and non-cloud services, particularly to large users. Thus, cloud computing may be just one service forming a part, perhaps only a small part, of a larger package of services, or 'whole business' deal, or traditional large outsourcing deal, including, for example, Internet connectivity services, consultancy, or other professional services. Integrators contract with both end users and providers, unless their end users contract directly with providers.[61] Therefore, in many ways, integrators are like providers who use other providers to offer services to their own end users.

Figure 2.2 illustrates some typical contractual structures. In Figure 2.2., 'provider' means provider of an IaaS, PaaS, or SaaS service (as opposed to components). Thus 'Direct' may cover providers who use their own infrastructure, and also those using an IaaS or a PaaS service (sub-provider) to provide their own service. Even a user who contracts directly with a provider (the 'Direct' example) may have been referred by a reseller or partner, who in turn may receive a commission.[62]

---

[57] See Chapter 3.   [58] See Chapter 4.

[59] Which may provide advice on migration to cloud, building cloud hardware or software (on clients' or third-party infrastructure), support, training, and so on.

[60] For example, IBM's Smart Enterprise Cloud.

[61] 43% of UK cloud services' resellers contracted directly with end-user customers, 12% required customers to contract with providers (typically on commission), and 28% offered a mix dependent on solutions required. 48% offered back-to-back terms between supplier and customer. Cloud Industry Forum (CIF), *Cloud UK: Paper Three Contracting Cloud Services: A Guide to Best Practices* (2011) 5.

[62] Google Apps for Business may be sold by resellers, for instance, but the contract for cloud services is between the user and Google.

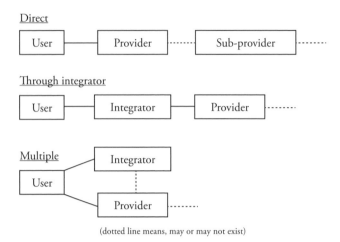

(dotted line means, may or may not exist)

Figure 2.2 Some typical cloud contract structures

Chains of contracts may therefore exist in relation to a single cloud service, not always back to back. Indeed, lack of mirroring of terms in sub-contracts may pose a risk for integrators. Contracts in relation to underlying components such as servers, storage equipment and data centre space may also exist, but are generally beyond the scope of this book. More generally, lack of awareness regarding how cloud arrangements work has resulted in some lawyers treating cloud contracts as though they were software licences, or technology product sales, rather than contracts for services. This problem tends to arise, in particular, where users seek to deploy their standard procurement terms in cloud negotiations.[63] Lack of negotiating power on the part of consumers and small businesses has also been a concern. One pillar of the EU's cloud strategy is the development of model cloud contract terms to cover key issues, such as data preservation after termination, data disclosure and integrity, data location and transfer, ownership of data, direct and indirect liability, change of service by cloud providers, and sub-contracting.[64]

7. Insurance as a Tool for Managing Cloud Risks

Prospective cloud users may manage their cloud risks not just through technological or contractual means, but also through insurance. Insurers may cover cloud users, treating cloud as outsourcing, as many policies covering outsourcing risks may already extend to cloud, or they may insure against specific cloud risks. They may also insure providers in relation to liability to users or others under errors and omissions policies.[65] Insurers may influence the promulgation of best practices among both cloud users and providers, for example by insisting on a security certification as a precondition for cover, or possibly for a pricing discount. The role of insurers in cloud seems set to grow, particularly if stricter legal requirements are imposed on cloud users in future.

---

[63] See Chapters 4 and 5.
[64] <http://ec.europa.eu/digital-agenda/en/european-cloud-computing-strategy>.
[65] Marsh Ltd, *The Cloud Risk Framework: Informing Decisions About Moving to the Cloud* (2012). See Chapter 4.

8. Concluding Remarks

To summarize, many components may be involved in a particular cloud service, with different possible deployment models and layers, as detailed in Chapter 1.

Cloud is not just one thing. Individual service type and system design matter. In particular, IaaS allows for far more user control, and therefore responsibility, than SaaS. In considering legal implications, it is important to pinpoint and analyse the exact service and component concerned. Is the potential cloud user procuring an end-user application? Does it need consultancy services to install and support cloud fabric on physical infrastructure it controls, for its private cloud? What software is involved: open source, proprietary, or perhaps acquired with hardware? If users wish to run third-party applications (not supplied by the provider as part of its service), what contracts or licences are needed? What are the wider legal and regulatory issues surrounding the particular intended cloud use?

Cloud is not 'all or nothing'. A 'mix and match' approach is possible, and indeed preferred by some users. Before using cloud services, well-advised users may undertake cost/benefit and risk/reward assessments, involving, as appropriate, their security, risk, legal, and compliance functions. Users may have differing risk tolerances for different functions or workloads: the question is whether the particular service suits the risk profile and operational requirements of a particular function or workload. Some workloads may not be suitable for cloud or at least for certain types of cloud arrangement. For example, highly confidential data might be kept on-premise, or only be moved to a private or community cloud with appropriate security safeguards.

Cloud need not be all at once. In practice, organizations are unlikely to adopt cloud computing fully in one move, except perhaps for start-ups without legacy hardware or software where benefits may outweigh costs and risks. For legacy applications, and/or data involving existing investments in expensive, possibly stand-alone hardware, and/or software, potential benefits may not justify the costs of migrating to cloud. Some legacy workloads may not be easily scalable; for example, database systems may need significant re-engineering to utilize cloud efficiencies. With cloud applications, developers also need to assume systems will fail, and build in resilience accordingly, instead of assuming systems will always be available and will not be allowed to fail.[66] Thus, migration to cloud does not always involve simply migrating data; applications may also need rewriting to work in cloud or integrate with cloud applications.[67] Organizations considering cloud may start small, with specific applications such as email, in order to test the waters and assess the potential for full roll-outs.

Clouds may coexist, with each other, as well as with internal systems and external non-cloud services. A user may employ different cloud services for different business processes or functions. For example, one global user stated to a researcher from the Queen Mary, University of London (QMUL) Cloud Legal Project that its approach was to try different cloud services, most of which it considered as 'tactical', contracting directly with providers; however, it was also beginning to use 'strategic' cloud services, initially via integrators. Organizations may also use in-house applications, or systems

---

[66] See Charles Babcock, 'Amazon's Vogels Challenges IT: Rethink App Dev' (*InformationWeek*, 30 November 2012), <http://www.informationweek.com/cloud-computing/infrastructure/amazons-vogels-challenges-it-rethink-app/240142928> (accessed 11 March 2013).

[67] However, it seems organizations are increasingly willing to migrate applications, even mission-critical applications, to the cloud: SailPoint, 'As Cloud Adoption Increases, Enterprises Are Increasingly at Risk' (*SailPoint*, 11 December 2012), <http://www.sailpoint.com/news/press/press-release.php?release=112> (accessed 11 March 2013).

in parallel with similar cloud applications or systems, such as for customer-relationship management.

Cloud may require complementary services. Users may need to consider support services, for example additional provisions for further support from providers, allowing for extra fees and perhaps under a separate agreement, particularly in the early stages of using IaaS/PaaS. For example, they may need assistance in creating or migrating applications to the provider's service, as well as general technical support. With large deals, which tend to have more in common with classic outsourcing, paid-for support services throughout the term are typical.

Closed clouds may be costly. Private clouds, with servers and storage dedicated to one user or a corporate group, are more expensive to develop and maintain, even with some shared components, and deal values may need to be large to justify investment in private infrastructure. Some users with existing data centres and hardware may consider using them for their own private clouds, perhaps with their own proprietary private cloud software infrastructure, to leverage existing investments in physical infrastructure, rather than using public cloud.

Cloud users may benefit from community. There is scope for highly regulated sectors, such as the pharmaceutical and financial services industries, to develop community clouds based on shared but segregated infrastructure. Such clouds could be designed to enable compliance with regulatory obligations, such as permitting independent audits to recognized industry standards by agreed qualified third-party auditors, and their results could be shared with regulators, with regular audits conducted of the whole infrastructure and system, rather than per user.

Cloud should not be treated in a 'one size fits all' manner. In particular, users do not necessarily lose control in cloud, and may be able to exercise self-help, for example by encrypting data. Regulation of cloud computing needs to take account of how particular cloud technologies operate, and differences between cloud and traditional outsourcing, as well as the realities of the Internet age.

PART II

CLOUD COMPUTING TRANSACTIONS

As we saw in Part I, cloud computing has many features that are attractive to users, including rapid deployment, high scalability, and flexible pricing. We also saw, however, that technical and commercial arrangements for delivering cloud services are often complex and opaque. In this part of the book, we explore the current state of the market for cloud transactions by analysing various types of cloud contracts and we consider whether current contracting models deal appropriately with the complexity and risk involved in procurement of cloud services. We also look at specific issues that arise in relation to ownership and use of information in cloud environments.

Chapter 3 focuses on non-negotiable, standard-form, contracts. A practical perspective is given based on surveys of cloud contracts conducted by the Cloud Legal Project at Queen Mary, University of London. The research comprised more than 30 sets of contractual terms offered to customers by a range of cloud providers for a variety of types of cloud service. An initial survey in 2010 of cloud Terms of Service (ToS), including terms and conditions, service level agreements, acceptable user policies, and privacy policies, identified 20 main categories into which provisions fell. The 20 categories of terms are discussed in this chapter in three broad categories: contractual form and applicable law; data handling; and liabilities and responsibilities. The chapter also reports the findings of a further survey in 2013 which identified changes in the ToS of individual providers and highlighted areas in which market practice is evolving.

Most cloud computing arrangements are based on standard ToS, and indeed that appears to be the only basis on which many providers will make their services available. Cloud procurement practices are, however, becoming more sophisticated, driven by users' attempts to negotiate providers' standard terms, as well as market developments on the provider side, particularly among cloud integrators. Chapter 4 draws on research, also undertaken by the Cloud Legal Project, into instances where users have requested changes to providers' standard terms, and the extent to which providers agreed to such changes. Particular attention is paid to the provisions that are most commonly negotiated and which, if not agreed, are likely to constitute 'deal-breakers'.

Special arrangements for procuring cloud services are also emerging in the public sector. Many governments and other public sector organizations are evaluating cloud computing services as part of a policy agenda that includes improving efficiency and reducing expenditure. Chapter 5 contains a detailed analysis of the cloud computing framework developed by the UK government between 2011 and 2013. This case study identifies some of the key challenges facing cloud providers when selling their services to public sector customers, and explores how obstacles to procurement are being tackled. Take-up of cloud services among public sector organizations has so far been limited but it is anticipated that agreed contracting frameworks, such as the UK's G-Cloud, will facilitate more widespread adoption.

A further potential obstacle to the development of the cloud market is uncertainty regarding ownership of information stored, created, processed, and distributed in cloud environments. Chapter 6 addresses these issues in the context of information flows between cloud providers, their customers, and various third parties. Distinctions are drawn between content that is stored and processed by users, as compared with information generated by cloud providers. The chapter also explores practical techniques for managing access to information in clouds and issues arising from the use of cloud models for the distribution of existing content. Finally, the uncertain proprietary status of Application Programming Interfaces (APIs) is considered in the context of the growing importance of APIs as a means of facilitating both interoperability between cloud environments, and portability of data between specific cloud services.

3

Standard Contracts for Cloud Services

*Simon Bradshaw, Christopher Millard, and Ian Walden**

1. Introduction

This chapter originated in a survey (undertaken as part of the Cloud Legal Project at Queen Mary, University of London) of various Terms of Service (ToS) under which cloud computing services are offered to customers. The ToS surveyed were available online or supplied to us by a range of cloud service providers. It should be noted that these are standard ToS as offered to customers. In the case of large commercial or government cloud contracts, such ToS will sometimes be negotiated and tailored to fit the specific requirements of the customer.[1] To date, the terms of such specific transactions have only been made public in a few cases. This chapter is focused on, and restricted to, a review of standard ToS. Furthermore, this review is carried out from the basis of a European (and specifically English) legal perspective, although the international nature of cloud services is noted where appropriate.

An initial overview survey in early 2010 identified 20 main categories into which ToS elements fell. Each set of ToS was then analysed against these categories. In some categories there was little variation between providers; all or most of them set out very similar terms. In others, a much wider range of approaches was seen. Furthermore, it became apparent that where there was significant variation from provider to provider; the terms offered were clearly related to the type of service in question, the target market it was aimed at, and the commercial legacy of the provider, such as outsourcing, retail, or software.[2]

A further survey was carried out in January 2013 with the aim of identifying changes in the ToS of individual providers. The objective was to analyse the evolution both of specific sets of ToS, and of the features of ToS seen across the range of services covered by the survey.

Given the speed of development of the market, it was unsurprising that in the 2013 review we could not find matches for all the providers and services covered in the 2010 survey. In the intervening period some providers had closed down or withdrawn services from the market, or had merged with or been bought by others. In other cases the provider's services had changed sufficiently that it was difficult to identify a directly comparable service. In such cases we sought in the 2013 survey to identify as close an equivalent product as possible, and in addition several services were added to the survey in place of those that had been discontinued.

* The authors are most grateful to Michaela MacDonald and Biddy Wyles for their assistance with the detailed analysis, reported in this chapter, of how standard cloud contracts evolved between 2010 and 2013.

[1] See Chapters 4 and 5.

[2] As will be seen, particularly in areas such as the extent to which a provider disclaims responsibility for failure of a cloud service, the approach of a provider may reflect the extent to which it has a corporate culture of building long-term trust relationships with its customers.

2. Classifying Cloud Services and Cloud Provider ToS Documents

For the purposes of this study a 'provider' is the business organization that offers a cloud service, while a 'service' is the particular cloud service in question. For some providers, such as ADrive, Dropbox, or Facebook, the core cloud service is the provider's only product of substance, and the two are essentially congruent. For other providers, the cloud service may be only one of a number of products, or even a number of cloud products, that the provider offers. Indeed, some of the providers covered by this survey offered cloud services that were sufficiently distinct that it was considered worthwhile to analyse the ToS of more than one of them. The initial survey in 2010 covered 31 cloud services offered by 27 discrete providers; the intent was to take as broad a sample as possible of providers offering cloud services targeted towards the US and European markets.

All the contract terms analysed in this survey were standard terms that were available on the provider's website for review by potential and current customers. Indeed, as will be noted below, many providers assert that rather than there being an obligation on the provider to notify customers regarding changes to the ToS for a service, customers are required to review the ToS as hosted on the provider's website on a regular basis to check whether there have in fact been any changes.[3] The ToS, as originally reviewed, were downloaded in the first week of January 2010, with a follow-up review of the ToS available in July 2010 for the same services. A comprehensive second survey was undertaken in January 2013; this included a number of additional providers and services, both to broaden the survey base and to address the withdrawal of a number of the services covered by the original survey.

Table 3.1 lists the cloud services covered by this survey together with a broad description of the type of service offered. Unless otherwise indicated, the service name was the same in 2013 as in 2010. References in footnotes are to the current or most recent version of the ToS.

Table 3.1 Cloud providers covered by survey

Provider	Service	Type of Service
37signals	Basecamp[4]	Collaborative project management tool
3tera (2010) CenturyLink (2013)	AppLogic (2010) Savvisdirect[5] (2013)	Virtualized application hosting via IaaS
ADrive	ADrive[6]	File hosting and backup via SaaS
Akamai	Hosting (2010) Terra[7] (2013)	Web acceleration via IaaS distributed caching

---

[3] As will be discussed later in this chapter, this may be an onerous task, especially if the provider does not flag up changes to the ToS documents or indicate the date of last change or review.

[4] Service description available at <http://basecamp.com>, and ToS at <http://basecamp.com/terms> (both accessed 25 March 2013).

[5] Service description available at <http://www.savvisdirect.com>, and ToS at <http://www.savvisdirect.com/terms-conditions> (both accessed 25 March 2013).

[6] Service description available at <http://www.adrive.com>, and ToS at <http://www.adrive.com/terms> (both accessed 25 March 2013).

[7] Service description available at <http://www.akamai.com/html/solutions/terra-solutions.html>, and ToS at <http://www.akamai.com/html/policies/index.html> (both accessed 25 March 2013).

Provider	Service	Type of Service
Amazon	Amazon Web Services[8]	Virtualized application hosting and data storage via IaaS
Apple	iWork.com (2010) iCloud[9] (2013)	Collaborative document review via SaaS
Apple	MobileMe (2010) iCloud (2013)	Email, file hosting, and personal information management via SaaS
Decho	MozyHome/Mozypro[10]	File hosting and backup via SaaS
Dropbox	Dropbox[11]	File hosting and backup via SaaS
ElasticHosts	ElasticHosts Cloud[12]	Application hosting via IaaS
Facebook	Facebook[13]	Social networking (including application sharing) via SaaS
Flexiant (formerly Xcalibre)	FlexiScale[14]	Application hosting via IaaS
G.ho.st	G.ho.st (closed)[15]	Former virtualized desktop via SaaS
GoGrid	GoGrid[16]	Virtualized application hosting and data storage via IaaS
Google	Google Apps Premier (2010) Google Apps for Business[17] (2013)	Application creation and hosting via PaaS
Google	Google Docs[18] (2010) Google Drive[19] (2013)	Document creation and sharing via SaaS

Continued

[8] Service description available at <http://aws.amazon.com>, and ToS at <http://aws.amazon.com/agreement> (both accessed 25 March 2013).

[9] Service description available at <https://www.icloud.com>, and ToS at <http://www.apple.com/legal/icloud/ww> (both accessed 25 March 2013).

[10] Service description available at <http://mozy.com/products>, and ToS at <http://mozy.com/terms> (both accessed 25 March 2013).

[11] Service description available at <https://www.dropbox.com/features>, and ToS at <https://www.dropbox.com/terms> (both accessed 25 March 2013).

[12] Service description available at <http://www.elastichosts.com>, and ToS at <http://www.elastichosts.com/cloud-hosting/terms-of-service> (both accessed 25 March 2013).

[13] Service description available at <http://www.facebook.com/help>, and ToS at <http://www.facebook.com/terms.php> and <http://www.facebook.com/policy.php> (all accessed 25 March 2013).

[14] Service description available at <http://www.flexiant.com>, and ToS at <http://www.flexiant.com/products/flexiscale/terms> (both accessed 25 March 2013).

[15] Service description (archived) at <http://web.archive.org/web/20080616200715/http://www.g.ho.st>, and ToS (archived) at <http://web.archive.org/web/20080511011825/www.g.ho.st/TermsOfService.html> (both accessed 25 March 2013).

[16] Service description available at <http://www.gogrid.com/cloud-hosting>, and ToS at <http://www.gogrid.com/legal/terms-service.php> (both accessed 25 March 2013).

[17] Service description available at <http://www.google.com/intl/en_uk/enterprise/apps/business>, and ToS at <http://www.google.com/apps/intl/en-GB/terms/premier_terms.html> (both accessed 25 March 2013).

[18] Service description at <http://www.google.com/google-d-s/intl/en/tour1.html>, and ToS at <http://www.google.com/google-d-s/intl/en/terms.html> (both accessed 25 March 2013).

[19] Service description available at <https://drive.google.com>, and ToS at <http://www.google.co.uk/intl/en/policies/terms/regional.html> (both accessed 25 March 2013).

Table 3.1 *Continued*

Provider	Service	Type of Service
IBM	Smart Business Cloud (2010) Smart Cloud Enterprise[20] (2013)	Virtualized application hosting and data storage via IaaS
Iron Mountain	LiveVault(No longer offered to new customers 2013)	Data archiving via SaaS
Joyent	Joyent Cloud[21]	Application hosting via IaaS
Microsoft	.Net[22]	Application development and hosting via PaaS/IaaS
Microsoft	Live Mesh (2010) Windows Live & Skydrive[23] (2013)	Data sharing and sync via SaaS
Microsoft	SQL Azure Database (2010) SQL Database[24] (2013)	Data storage and search via IaaS
Nirvanix	Storage Delivery Network[25] (2010) Cloud Storage Network (2013)	Data storage via IaaS
PayPal	PayPal Merchant Services[26] (2010) PayPal Services (2013)	Payment and accounts handling via SaaS
Rackspace UK	Rackspace Cloud (2010) Rackspace Cloud Servers[27] (2013)	Virtualized application hosting and data storage via IaaS
Salesforce	Salesforce CRM (2010) Sales Cloud[28] (2013)	HR and CRM services via SaaS
Symantec	Norton Online (2010) Norton Online Backup[29] (2013)	Backup via SaaS

[20] Service description available at <http://www-935.ibm.com/services/uk/en/cloud-enterprise>, and ToS at <http://www-935.ibm.com/services/us/en/cloud-enterprise/contracts/sc_agreement.html> (both accessed 25 March 2013).

[21] Service description available at <http://joyent.com/products>, and ToS at <http://joyent.com/company/policies/terms-of-service> (both accessed 25 March 2013).

[22] Service description available at <http://www.microsoft.com/net/overview.aspx>; ToS not available online.

[23] Service description available at <https://skydrive.live.com>, and ToS at <http://windows.microsoft.com/en-gb/windows-live/microsoft-services-agreement> (both accessed 25 March 2013).

[24] Service description available at <http://www.microsoft.com/windowsazure/sqlazure> (accessed 25 March 2013); ToS not available online.

[25] Service description available at <http://www.nirvanix.com/products-services/storage-delivery-network/index.aspx>, and ToS at <http://www.nirvanix.com/how-to-buy/terms.aspx> (both accessed 25 March 2013).

[26] Service description available at <https://www.paypal.com/uk/webapps/mpp/home-merchant>, and ToS at <https://cms.paypal.com/cms_content/GB/en_GB/files/ua/ua.pdf> (both accessed 25 March 2013).

[27] Service description available at <http://www.rackspace.co.uk/cloud-hosting>, and ToS at <http://www.rackspace.co.uk/rackspace-home/legal/general-terms> (both accessed 25 March 2013).

[28] Service description available at <https://www.salesforce.com/crm/products.jsp>, and ToS at <https://www.salesforce.com/company/legal/agreements.jsp> (both accessed 25 March 2013).

[29] Service description available at <http://uk.norton.com/online-backup>, and ToS at <http://www.symantec.com/content/en/us/about/media/NOBU_TOS_21_USE.pdf> (both accessed 25 March 2013).

Provider	Service	Type of Service
The Planet (2010) SoftLayer (2013)	The Planet (2010) SoftLayer[30] (2013)	Virtualized application hosting and data storage via IaaS
UKFast	CloudHosts[31]	Application hosting via IaaS
Zecter	ZumoDrive Closed 2012	File hosting and backup via SaaS
ZoHo	Zoho Services[32]	Document creation and sharing via SaaS
In addition, the following services were examined by the 2013 survey		
500px	500px[33]	Image hosting via SaaS
Box	Box Personal/Business[34]	Document creation and sharing via SaaS
Dell	Dell vCloud[35]	Data Hosting via IaaS
Linux	Linode[36]	Virtual Server Hosting via IaaS
Oracle	Exalogic Elastic Cloud[37]	Virtual Server Hosting via IaaS
Oracle	Optimized Solution for Enterprise Cloud Infrastructure[38]	Enterprise Cloud Management
Mega	Mega[39]	Storage via SaaS
Canonical	Ubuntu One[40]	Storage via SaaS

In this study we use ToS to refer to the document containing the terms governing the relationship between the customer and the cloud service provider. We also use ToS in a broader sense to include related documents that cover other aspects of this relationship. Such ToS come in a number of forms, from relatively short and simple,

[30] Service description available at <http://www.softlayer.com/services>, and ToS at <http://www.softlayer.com/about/legal/standard-msa> (both accessed 25 March 2013).

[31] Service description available at <http://www.ukfast.co.uk/cloud-hosting.html>, and ToS at <http://www.ukfast.co.uk/terms.html> (both accessed 25 March 2013).

[32] Service description available at <http://www.zoho.com/index.html>, and ToS at <http://www.zoho.com/terms.html> (both accessed 25 March 2013).

[33] Service description available at <http://500px.com>, and ToS at <http://500px.com/terms> (both accessed 25 March 2013).

[34] Service description available at <https://www.box.com>, and ToS at <https://www.box.com/static/html/terms.html> (both accessed 25 March 2013).

[35] Service description available at <http://www.dell.com/Learn/us/en/555/by-service-type-cloud-services-cloud-hosting?c=us&l=en&s=biz>, and ToS at <http://www.dell.com/Learn/us/en/19/solutions/cloud-solutions-agreement?c=us&l=en&s=dhs> (both accessed 25 March 2013).

[36] Service description available at <http://www.linode.com>, and ToS at <http://www.linode.com/tos.cfm> (both accessed 25 March 2013).

[37] Service description available at <http://www.oracle.com/uk/products/middleware/exalogic/overview/index.html>, and ToS at <http://www.oracle.com/us/legal/terms/index.html> (both accessed 25 March 2013).

[38] Service description available at <http://www.oracle.com/us/solutions/oos/enterprise-cloud-infrastructure/overview/index.html>, and ToS at <http://www.oracle.com/us/legal/terms/index.html> (both accessed 25 March 2013).

[39] Service description available at <https://mega.co.nz/#privacycompany>, and ToS at <https://mega.co.nz/#terms> (both accessed 25 March 2013).

[40] Service description available at <https://one.ubuntu.com>, and ToS at <https://one.ubuntu.com/terms> (both accessed 25 March 2013).

to lengthy, complex, and split over several sub-documents, but generally include the following:

- **Terms of Service** (ToS). This document details the overall relationship between the customer and the provider. It usually contains the commercial terms, if the service is paid for, and includes legal clauses such as choice of law and disclaimers. If there are other ToS documents it typically incorporates them by reference.

- **Service Level Agreement** (SLA). This document specifies the level of service the provider aims to deliver together with the process for compensating customers if the actual service falls short of that. Accordingly, SLAs are associated only with paid-for services.

- **Acceptable Use Policy** (AUP). This document details the permitted (or in practice, forbidden) uses of the service.

- **Privacy Policy**. This document describes the provider's approach to using and protecting the customer's personal information. Although usually termed a 'Privacy Policy', it often incorporates terms specifically relating to data protection.

Although some providers publish all four ToS documents separately, it is quite common to see the AUP folded into the ToS, while many services, even some paid ones, do not offer an SLA. However, a separate privacy policy is usually made available; this may be because the provider has a single privacy policy applying to all its online services rather than just cloud provision, and also reflects the fact that privacy policies tend to address compliance rather than contractual issues.[41] Where separate ToS documents are presented, one will typically incorporate the others by reference.

This analysis is based on the full range of ToS documents issued by the surveyed providers. We noted that even where there are separate documents comprising the ToS, specific terms are not always allocated as neatly as the above definitions might suggest. In particular, we noted several instances where terms relating to privacy were found in the ToS or AUP, as well as the Privacy Policy.

One important point to note is that several large providers have more than one set of ToS documents for a given service. Depending on location, a customer may be offered ToS tailored to the appropriate local laws. Such localization was seen in relation to services from major providers such as Microsoft and Google. Other providers, such as IBM, offered ToS that included a range of optional elements that applied depending upon the location of the customer.[42]

3. Categorizing and Analysing Terms

An initial review of the ToS documents covered in this survey indicated that although they vary considerably in content and length there are many features that commonly appear. We have identified, in particular, 20 types of term that are either common or, if rare, are of sufficient interest to our analysis to merit specific note when they are seen.

For the purposes of this analysis we have divided these terms into three categories: contractual form and applicable law; data handling; and liabilities and responsibilities.

---

[41] For a more detailed discussion of data protection issues, see Chapters 7–10.
[42] See Sections 3.1.2 (Applicable law) and 3.3.2 (Direct liability) for examples.

3.1 Contractual form and applicable law

3.1.1 Contract

The general basis on which providers and customers enter into a relationship falls into two broad categories, depending on whether the provider is offering a paid service or a free one. However, there is an element of overlap between the two. For instance, some 'free' services may impose non-monetary costs on the customer, such as contextual advertising, or the imposition of licence terms that allow the provider to re-use the customer's data for its own purposes.[43] Equally, paid services themselves fall into a spectrum between those entered into on the basis of the standard-form contract of the provider, and those where the contract terms are fully negotiated, depending on the relative bargaining power of provider and customer.[44] Furthermore, some services may offer a free trial period conditional on the customer giving payment details, which then converts into a paid contract; such a service is classed as 'paid' for the purposes of this analysis.

Nonetheless, one can observe a distinction between the ToS of cloud services that are offered as a paid utility service, and those provided on an at least notionally free or low-cost, flat-rate basis. The former typically include IaaS infrastructure provision, as exemplified by Amazon Web Services' EC2 and S3 products. The latter are typically directed at consumers and offer services such as email, file storage, or content hosting.

For paid services, ToS typically specify the initial duration of the contract, its renewal period and payment structure, and the steps to be taken by either party to terminate the contract. It is not unusual to see a provision that the contract will continue indefinitely until it is terminated. For example, Amazon Web Services' ToS provide that:

The Agreement will remain in effect until terminated by you or us in accordance with this Section 7.2.[45]

Contracts for paid services typically include clauses defining breaches by the customer that will result either in managed termination of the contract (eg, after one payment period in default) or immediate termination for cause. The most common justification specified for immediate termination is a serious breach by the customer of the provider's AUP (as discussed further below).

For free services there is no periodic payment structure, and thus no fixed contract term.[46] Nonetheless, the provider will generally specify the means by which it can bring the relationship to an end so as to avoid indefinite obligations to host customer data. One of these, as with paid contracts, will often be a breach of the AUP (eg 37Signals, ADrive, and Google Docs). Another will typically be an 'inactive account' clause by which a provider can excuse itself from supporting accounts that are not being paid for (being free) but which are not being used.

---

[43] For more detailed discussion of this point, see Section 3.2.6.

[44] As explained in the Introduction, this chapter concentrates on standard-form contracts for cloud computing services; negotiated contracts are addressed in Chapter 4.   [45] See n. 8.

[46] Indeed, under some models of contract formation it may be questionable whether an enforceable contract exists between the provider and customer. Under English law, for example, the customer may be held not to have provided any consideration; see, for example, *Spreadex Ltd v Colin Cochrane* [2012] EWHC 1290 (Comm). However, it could be held that the customer has acted to his or her detriment in some other manner (eg, permitting commercial use to be made of personal data, or agreeing to abide by terms such as exclusion clauses) that forms valid consideration. Even if the agreement between the provider and customer does not form a valid contract, it may well comprise a conditional licence by which the provider offers a free service in return for the customer abiding by the provider's terms. As such, for the purposes of this analysis it will be assumed that the ToS for the service are valid and enforceable to the extent local law permits, be it under contract or (for the provider) as the terms of a conditional licence.

This chapter does not seek to make a detailed analysis of the enforceability of specific terms, although it does make reference to relevant case law where such terms have been considered by the courts.[47]

Little change was observed between 2010 and 2013 in this area. However, it is notable that a number of the providers surveyed have terms entitling them to terminate services immediately without notice, particularly where the customer is alleged to have contravened the ToS.[48] In such cases, providers often stated that customers would have no right of access to data following termination.[49] A number of providers even asserted a right to terminate the service without cause.[50]

3.1.2 Applicable law

The majority of the ToS surveyed include terms that assert that the contract is covered by the laws of a specific jurisdiction. This is typically the jurisdiction in which the provider has its principal place of business, but in the case of some providers (typically with international operations) the ToS may specify that differing legal systems apply depending on the location of the customer. Out of the 31 ToS analysed in 2010, and the 36 reviewed or added to the survey in 2013, the breakdown of choice of law is as listed in Table 3.2.

Table 3.2 Breakdown of choice of law

Choice of law	2010 (out of 31)	2013 (out of 36)
The law of a particular US state.	15	17
English law, for providers based in England.	4	6
English law, for providers based outside England but in respect of their customers in Europe or EMEA.	4	2
The law of other EU jurisdictions for European customers.	2	3
Canadian law.	0	1
New Zealand law.	0	1
Scottish law.	1	0
The customer's local law.	2	4
No choice of law expressed or implied, or an ambiguous choice given (eg 'UK law').	3	2

It should be noted that for the purposes of this analysis the ToS obtained were those that would be offered to a prospective customer in England. Some of the larger providers offer ToS tailored to customers in England/the UK, Europe, or the Europe, Middle East, and Africa (EMEA) region. The survey showed that for the set of providers examined in

---

[47] See Chapter 13 for a more detailed consideration of consumer protection law as it applies to cloud contracts and services.
[48] For example, Rackspace Terms of Service, 'Termination' (see n. 27).
[49] Rackspace ToS, 'Access to Data'.
[50] For example, Google (for free services), Joyent, 500px.

2010 a customer in England was offered a contract governed by English law in ten out of 31 cases: in four because the provider operated under English law; in four because the provider selected English law as a regional choice; and in two because the provider adopted local law. For the other cases, the customer was offered a contract governed by Scottish law, other European law (Irish or Luxembourg law), or the law of one of five different US states. In some, the customer was not offered a valid choice of law at all.[51]

By 2013 a significant evolution was seen. Three providers (Apple, Decho Mozy, and IBM) that had previously specified the law of another jurisdiction for customers based in the UK now apply the law of the customer's usual place of residence or business address. Conversely, Google moved away from applying English law to customers in the EMEA region to mandating California state law. The one provider (Flexiant) that had stipulated Scottish law in its ToS now specifies English law instead; it is possible this reflects the establishment of its European HQ in London as distinct from its development and support centre in Edinburgh.

For those providers surveyed for the first time in 2013, all had chosen to apply the jurisdiction of their corporate base. It may, therefore, be that there is a pattern to choice-of-law terms: providers initially assert the law of their own jurisdiction for all customers, but as a wider market develops they begin to offer terms reflecting the law applicable to customers. However, this can lead to a provider offering a range of ToS to suit different legal systems, and it is interesting to note that Google appears to have taken a step the other way by applying its local law to all customers.

A somewhat more complicated approach was to specify one choice of law for some aspects of the contract and another for other aspects. For instance, Microsoft specifies for customers in the EMEA region that contract breaches will be resolved under the law of Luxembourg, whereas other disputes (eg consumer protection) will be dealt with under the law of the country to which services are directed. In 2010 this approach was seen for both Microsoft's SQL and Livemesh/Skydrive services, but by 2013 it was used for only the latter.

IBM's Smartcloud agreement adopts a particularly thorough approach; having set out default terms, it then lists variations to those terms applying to some 45 different states or groups of states. The resulting ToS are unusually long and complicated, but far more fine-grained as regards applicable local law than any other ToS surveyed.

It should be noted that choice-of-law terms may be more significant for corporate or SME customers, since, as noted above, individual consumers may, depending on the applicable law, be shielded by consumer protection laws from contract terms that purport to impose a foreign legal system. A large corporate customer would presumably seek to tailor a cloud contract to ensure that it was not subject to a legal system the customer felt inappropriate; while for government customers, or other public sector bodies, subjecting themselves to a foreign law will often be completely unacceptable.

3.1.3 Jurisdiction

The position with choice of forum for settling disputes between the provider and customer is very similar to that with choice of law. Not surprisingly (as it would be of questionable wisdom for a provider to seek to do otherwise) both the 2010 and 2013 surveys

---

[51] In such cases a European court would apply the 'Rome I' Regulations to determine the applicable law (Regulation (EC) 593/2008 on the law applicable to contractual obligations, OJ L177/6, 4.7.2008). For a consumer customer, Art. 6 of these Regulations would generally apply the law of the consumer's domicile.

found that providers generally specify a jurisdiction compatible with the specified legal system. In many cases, especially where the law of a particular US state is asserted, the provider will include a term stating that claims against it must be brought in the courts of a particular city within that state.

Where the 2013 review found that providers had changed the law asserted to govern the agreement, the specified jurisdiction was also changed accordingly. This has generally had the effect of ensuring that any claim would be dealt with in the customer's own jurisdiction; it may be that this reflects a recognition of the likely position for consumers under EU consumer protection law.[52]

Jurisdiction clauses are usually phrased as being exclusive in respect of claims brought by a customer against a provider, but a number of providers include terms giving themselves a choice of venue for claims against the customer. Such clauses may bear heavily on customers who take advantage of the international nature of cloud computing services, although they may of course not be enforceable against consumers, depending on local consumer protection law.[53]

In addition to asserting jurisdiction, several providers seek to impose relatively short limitation periods within which a customer must bring a claim in respect of the service. IBM and Rackspace require claims to be brought within two years, Apple within one year, and ADrive within six months.[54] Again, such terms may well not be enforceable, particularly against European consumers.[55]

3.1.4 Arbitration

A cloud computing service contract, in common with many other sorts of commercial contract, may give the option of commercial arbitration as an alternative to litigation or may even seek to require it. Although common in business-to-business contracts, such terms may be deemed to impose unfair constraints upon a consumer's ability to seek a remedy.[56]

Seven of the 31 ToS analysed in 2010 included some form of clause seeking to impose arbitration. Three providers (ADrive, Nirvanix, and Zoho) required customer disputes to be resolved through arbitration in all cases. 3Tera stipulated arbitration for claims valued at more than US$500; its successor, CenturyLink, required all disputes to be referred to arbitration. IBM, Iron Mountain, and Microsoft (for LiveMesh) all had

---

[52] See Chapter 13. It is worth noting here that there may be further practical obstacles to a customer bringing a claim, even where the provider's ToS stipulate local jurisdiction. For example, PayPal's ToS state that PayPal accepts the jurisdiction of the English courts. However, PayPal's European operations are undertaken through PayPal SarL and the only address given for legal correspondence is in Luxembourg. At first sight, therefore, a UK-based customer of PayPal seeking to issue proceedings might conclude that the only route to do so would be to issue out of the jurisdiction, with the attendant additional expense and legal complication. The authors of this chapter are aware of a such a dispute with PayPal in which the claimant obtained the address of a PayPal branch office in England and successfully effected service on the company there, but this example indicates that acceptance of jurisdiction may not give customers an immediate accessible route of remedy.

[53] Similar considerations as to enforceability, especially against individual consumer customers, apply as for choice of law.

[54] ADrive Terms of Service, B.24 (see n. 6).

[55] See sub-paragraph (q) of the Annex to Council Directive 93/13/EEC of 5 April 1993 on Unfair Terms in Consumer Contracts.

[56] For example, terms seeking to impose compulsory arbitration against consumer customers within the UK are highlighted as being potentially unfair under the UTCC Directive (see n. 55), while in the US, such clauses have been held to be valid, see *Hill v Gateway 2000 Inc.* 105 F 3d 1147 (7th Cir 1997).

terms that imposed arbitration on customers in some countries but not others. IBM, for its Smart Business cloud, mandated arbitration for disputes arising in the People's Republic of China, South-East Asian states, and states within Eastern Europe or the Former Soviet Union. Such terms are likely to reflect a lack of confidence in the effectiveness of the judicial systems in such countries. Where such clauses apply they generally stipulate a forum for arbitration and a recognized arbitration body.

Little had changed by the time of the 2013 review of ToS, although some refinements were noted. 3Tera's former customers now use Savvisdirect as provided by Century Link, whose ToS provide that it will pay the cost of a customer's arbitration filing fee if that exceeds the local court filing fee, and that it will pay the costs of arbitration.[57]

3.1.5 *Acceptable use*

Rules regarding the manner in which customers may use (and, more specifically, may not abuse) the service, often presented in a separate AUP, are present in some form in every one of the ToS analysed, and reflect concerns of providers to shield themselves from liability arising out of the conduct of their customers.[58] At first sight they vary in their extent and detail, from brief injunctions against illegal conduct to extremely broad-ranging and detailed lists of prohibited behaviour, but on careful examination they prove to be very similar in their scope and effect.

The vast majority of acceptable use terms prohibit a consistent set of activities that providers consider to be improper or outright illegal uses of their service. These include bulk unsolicited commercial email ('spam'), fraud, gambling, hacking into other systems, or the hosting of content that is obscene, defamatory, or such as to promote discrimination or incite hatred. In many cases, the difference between shorter and longer AUPs is the level of detail with which such activities are described. A good example of a short AUP is that imposed by ZoHoServices, which prohibits behaviour that is 'unlawful, defamatory, harassing, libellous, invasive of another's privacy, abusive, threatening, harmful, vulgar, pornographic, obscene, or is otherwise objectionable, offends religious sentiments, promotes racism, contains viruses, or that which infringes or may infringe intellectual property or other rights of another'.[59]

Although other providers' AUPs may be much more extensive and detailed than this, they tend to prohibit very much the same forms of behaviour and misuse.[60] A number of providers do go further than this in setting out examples of unacceptable activity.

---

[57] Savviisdirect Terms & Conditions, 23 'Governing Law, Disputes' (see n. 5).

[58] The English courts have held the extent to which hosts have sought to control the illicit behaviour of users to be very relevant in determining their liability for such misconduct. In *L'Oréal SA v eBay International AG* [2009] R.P.C. 21, eBay escaped joint liability for trademark infringements because of its proactive efforts to restrain such behaviour by users; by contrast, in *Twentieth Century Fox Film Corporation v Newzbin Ltd* [2010] E.C.C. 13, Newzbin was held liable for copyright infringement owing to its failure to prevent (and indeed its tacit encouragement of) illicit file-sharing by its users. (Massey, 'Case Comment: *Twentieth Century Fox Film Corporation v Newzbin Ltd*' C.T.L.R. 2010, 16(6), 164–166.) The question of host liability was again considered in *Tamiz v Google Inc.* [2013] EWCA Civ 68 in which the Court of Appeal took the view that Google was not deemed to be the publisher of comments posted to a blog it hosted before being notified of them, but that it could become a publisher, and thus attract liability, once it had been so notified, depending on the action it took. See Graham Smith, '*Tamiz v Google*: The Court of Appeal Verdict', <http://www.scl.org> (accessed 19 March 2013).

[59] Zoho Terms of Service, 'Spamming and Illegal Activities' (see n. 32).

[60] It should be noted though that this survey is of providers in the US and European markets, where there is likely to be a more or less a common 'Western' set of cultural and legal assumptions about what constitutes 'acceptable' behaviour.

Some, such as ElasticHosts, prohibit the use of their service for 'safety-critical' applications where the failure of the service may result in injury or loss of life. Others, such as Rackspace, have terms prohibiting some quite unusual activities, such as any use in connection with the design of weapons of mass destruction![61] In a similar vein, several US-based providers such as ADrive do not permit their services to be used by, or to host material for, nationals of a list of nations including Cuba, Iran, and North Korea.[62]

At the time of the initial survey in 2010 there was little in the way of evidence of such AUP terms actually being invoked. In late 2010, however, this topic attracted considerable media attention through the well-publicized decision of cloud providers such as Amazon to terminate their relationships with the WikiLeaks website.[63] Furthermore, the backlash against Amazon from WikiLeaks supporters, which manifested itself both in terms of calls for a boycott and through cyber-attacks on Amazon's services, indicates the possible risks to cloud customers arising from the conduct of cloud providers or fellow customers, although the apparent ineffectiveness of such attacks may itself illustrate the resilience of cloud services.[64]

The applicability of acceptable use terms for online services was recently considered by the English High Court in *Overy v PayPal (Europe) Ltd* [2012] EWHC 2659.[65] The dispute arose from the termination by PayPal of payment services provided to the claimant, Mr Overy, who was using them for the purposes of running a competition for which his house was offered as the prize. PayPal sought to rely upon its acceptable use policy's prohibition against use for lottery or gambling activities. His Honour Judge Hegarty QC, having earlier held that the prohibition was valid and enforceable against the claimant, considered the extent to which the claimant could rely upon either the Unfair Terms in Consumer Contracts Regulations 1999 (UTCCR 1999), or the Unfair Contract Terms Act 1977 (UCTA 1977) applied to this and other terms.

Although HH Judge Hegarty QC held that Mr Overy had represented himself to PayPal in such a way as to exclude operation of UTCCR 1999,[66] he nonetheless considered the application of the Regulations to PayPal's ToS. In doing so, he held that the terms upon which PayPal had relied were not intrinsically unfair, and in the case of the provisions regarding gambling were justified in terms of the regulatory risks to PayPal of allowing its services to be used for such activities.[67]

3.1.6 Variation of contract terms

Eight of the providers surveyed in 2010 made no mention of any process for varying their contract terms, but the remainder reserved the right to do this. However, even among those, the procedure for doing so varied considerably. Thirteen of the providers incorporated a term that stated that they may amend their ToS simply by posting an

---

[61] Rackspace General Terms and Conditions, 8 'Export Matters' (see n. 27).

[62] Countries subject to embargoes and economic sanctions imposed by US law and enforced by the US Office of Foreign Assets Control.

[63] P Thibodeau, 'With WikiLeaks, Amazon Shows Its Power over Customers' (*Computerworld*, 2 December 2010).

[64] J Vijayan, 'Amazon.com Appears to Repel Anonymous DDoS Attack' (*TechWorld*, 10 December 2010), <http://news.techworld.com/security/3252813/amazoncom-appears-to-repel-anonymous-ddos-attack> (accessed 27 March 2013).

[65] The cited report covers only the judge's principal conclusions at paragraphs 169–81 of the judgment. The full judgment is available as of February 2013 via BAILII (<www.bailii.org>) under neutral citation [2012] EWHC 2659 (QB).

[66] *Overy v PayPal*, [181].   [67] *Overy v PayPal*, [228], [252].

updated version on their website, and that continued use of the service by the customer was deemed as acceptance of the new ToS. Where the services were provided under a paid contract, such a term would typically include reference to a break clause by which a customer who does not wish to accept the amended ToS may withdraw from the agreement.

By the time of the review in 2013, only one provider (Akamai) did not have a term allowing ToS to be varied. Those that had introduced such a provision followed the pattern noted above, asserting the right to vary terms via unilateral notice. Such notices may well contravene consumer protection law; for instance, UTCCR 1999 specify such terms as among those which may be regarded as unfair in a consumer contract under English law.[68] Similar provisions apply throughout the EU as a result of the relevant Directive.[69]

Only three providers, Google Apps Premier, Iron Mountain (in 2010), and Salesforce CRM, state that changes to the ToS may only be in writing with the agreement of both parties. The extent to which providers undertook positively to notify customers of changes was variable, with some, for example Canonical, committing to notify changes via email, but the majority stating that the mere posting of an update would constitute sufficient notice. Salesforce links from its ToS page to an archive of all previous versions of its Master Subscription Agreement back to 1999.[70] The topic of notification of ToS changes is addressed further at Section 4.1.

3.2 Data handling

3.2.1 Data integrity

The majority of providers surveyed in 2010 expressly included terms in their ToS making it clear that ultimate responsibility for preserving the confidentiality and integrity of the customer's data lay with the customer. A number (eg Amazon, GoGrid, and Microsoft) asserted that they would make 'best efforts' to preserve such data, but nonetheless included such a disclaimer. A number of providers went so far as to recommend that the customer encrypt data stored in the provider's cloud (eg GoGrid, Microsoft), or specifically placed responsibility on the customer to make separate backup arrangements. Amazon's ToS for Amazon Web Services (AWS), for example, did this, and went on to note that: 'We will have no liability to you for any unauthorized access or use, corruption, deletion, destruction or loss of any of Your Content or Applications.'[71]

The review in 2013 found little change; providers continue to firmly place the onus for ensuring data integrity onto customers. All of the providers surveyed for the first time in 2013 incorporated such terms, although, perhaps to assuage possible customer concerns, especially among consumers, as well as regulatory obligations under data protection law—a number of providers made non-binding assurances about the measures they took to safeguard customer data. Linode, for instance, referred in its privacy policy to 'industry-standard technical safeguards' and 'other storage system access control mechanisms'.[72] However, without any specific details such generic assurances may be

---

[68] SI 1999/2083, Sch. 2, para. 1(k).

[69] Council Directive 93/13/EEC of 5 April 1993 on unfair terms in consumer contracts.

[70] Salesforce, 'Master Subscription Agreement Archive', available at <https://www.salesforce.com/company/legal/MSA-archive.jsp> (accessed 27 March 2013).

[71] AWS Customer Agreement, 7.2 (see n. 8).

[72] Linode.com, 'Security and Data Integrity', available at <http://www.linode.com/privacy.cfm> (accessed 27 March 2013).

of limited comfort to even the most technically sophisticated customer; indeed, such customers might find them especially concerning.

Significantly, such terms are imposed by storage providers such as ADrive and Apple for services that for many (especially individual) customers will be their 'separate backup arrangement'. In effect, a number of providers of consumer-oriented cloud services appear to disclaim the specific fitness of their services for the specific purpose(s) for which many customers will have signed up to use them.[73] Some providers (eg Rackspace) state that data integrity will only be guaranteed where the customer has paid for additional specific backup services.

A small number of the providers surveyed give more positive assurances. For example, Salesforce CRM's ToS state that appropriate measures will be taken to safeguard customer data. It was interesting to note in the 2010 survey that two providers that offered specific backup services, Symantec and Iron Mountain, made no mention of data integrity in their ToS. It may well be that both providers assumed it to be implicit from the nature of their service that they would assure such protection, and saw no need to provide for it expressly. However, as noted above, other providers offering storage and backup services specifically disclaim such representations. The distinction tends to be between those services that provide backup facilities for no fee, where there is no assurance, and those which charge for such facilities, where there is.

3.2.2 Data preservation

An important issue for many customers is what will happen to their data after the relationship with the provider comes to an end.[74] In fact, there are two issues here: whether there will be any opportunity for the customer to gain access to the data (eg, to retrieve it for use elsewhere) once the contract has ended, and whether there is assurance from the provider that data will effectively be deleted after this stage. The former point is likely to be significant for many customers because they are likely to want assurance that data put into the cloud may be recovered in a managed fashion. The significance of the latter point is likely to be that customers will be concerned as to whether data they entrust to a cloud service provider will ever be deleted comprehensively from the service.

Most of the providers surveyed fall into three broad camps in respect of the way in which they state that they will deal with customer information following the end of the relationship between them and the customer.

The first set of providers asserts that they will normally preserve customer data for a set period of time following the end of a service contract. Amazon, ElasticHosts, and Box all stipulate 30 days (or one month) as the grace period during which a former customer may access data. However, this grace period may not apply if the contract is terminated for cause, such as breach of the relevant AUP. Other providers offer shorter grace periods: Nirvanix grants 15 days, and Decho granted only three in its 2010 ToS and gives no such period at all in its current ones. IBM, in its 2013 ToS, states that data will not be deleted from an account closed by a customer until the customer has confirmed that data have been exported and backed up, or six months has elapsed.

The second set of providers asserts that customer data will be deleted immediately when the relationship between customer and provider ends. In this respect it is notable

---

[73] An alternative, and perhaps more charitable, interpretation is that such terms encourage customers not to rely on what may prove to be a single point of failure.

[74] See Commission Staff Working Document, SWD (2012) 271/2, [3.5].

that Apple took such an approach for its former MobileMe product, even though this was a paid service. A similar policy is in place for the replacement iCloud product; although the basic service is free, the ToS make no distinction in this respect between basic free storage and additional storage a user may have purchased.

Such terms raise the question of the provider's position should a court later decide that termination of the contract was ineffective. The provider could be in breach of contract, or of a potential duty in bailment[75] to preserve the customer's data. Indeed, it might even be liable to criminal prosecution for offences regarding the unauthorized deletion of data.[76]

The third set takes a hybrid approach, with providers stating that they will be under no obligation to preserve data after the end of the relationship, but not undertaking to delete data, or noting that a grace period may apply at their discretion. For example, Softlayer says that customer data access is not guaranteed, while Google, for its Google Docs service, states that it will make a reasonable effort to give a customer the opportunity to export data. For its paid Google Apps for Business service, Google provides for a 'commercially reasonable period' for data to be extracted, which offers users little reassurance and no certainty.[77]

Some 'free' providers, offering storage to private customers, may not have a specific contract period. As such they may state that they will delete data in apparently dormant accounts. An example is Zoho, which defines delinquency as 120 days without access.[78]

Other providers have more unusual terms owing to the nature of their service. Facebook has a facility for 'memorializing' the accounts of users who have died, preserving the content and allowing limited posting of comments. In the case of PayPal, customer data may include electronic cash, and so a very long grace period of three years is applied during which PayPal will attempt to return unused funds.

Specific assurances as to data deletion are less common. One of the few examples seen was originally provided by 3Tera in its 2010 ToS, which stated that '*All customer data remaining after the cancellation date will be destroyed for security and privacy reasons*'. Century Link has retained this term in its replacement service.

Data deletion is a concern for customers who may have reservations about the degree to which a provider can assure that potentially sensitive data is no longer present in any form once it has notionally been removed from storage, or indeed once the relationship between customer and provider has come to an end. It should perhaps also be a concern for providers, since they may assume responsibility for the security of any non-deleted personal data submitted by the user.[79] This mirrors on a larger scale existing concerns about the challenge of ensuring that sensitive data are purged from magnetic media.[80]

3.2.3 Data disclosure

In terms of the circumstances in which providers will, or may, disclose customer information (including customer data stored on the provider's cloud), we see a spectrum of

---

[75] The possibility that a duty in bailment might arise is explored in Chapter 6.

[76] For example, UK Computer Misuse Act 1990, s. 3.

[77] Google Apps Terms of Service, Section 11.2 'Effects of Termination' (see n. 17).

[78] Zoho Terms of Service, 'Inactive User Accounts Policy' (see n. 32).

[79] See discussion in Chapter 8 of the respective roles and responsibilities of data controllers and data processors.

[80] See, for example, Mary K Pratt, 'Have You Resold Your Data to Crooks?' (*Computerworld*, 16 February 2007), <http://www.computerworld.com/s/article/9011459/Have_you_resold_your_data_to_crooks> (accessed 27 March 2013).

approaches ranging from providers that have a very high threshold for justifying disclosure to others that have a much lower one.

All providers that mention this issue[81] state that they will disclose such data in response to a valid court order. Some purport to establish procedural safeguards. For example, the ToS for Salesforce CRM provide that the customer will be given advance notice of a requested disclosure, unless such notice is prohibited, and that Salesforce will assist the customer in opposing such orders.[82]

A number of providers have a slightly lower threshold for disclosure, accepting requests (as distinct from enforceable orders) from recognized law enforcement agencies, or where there is a clear and immediate need to disclose information in the public interest or to protect life. Facebook, for instance, will disclose customer contact information to authorities in such circumstances.[83] Others go further, with ADrive asserting that the decision to disclose is broadly at its discretion, and may be triggered by conduct perceived to expose ADrive to legal liability.[84] Some providers, such as Zoho and Dell, have terms by which they may disclose data if, in their 'reasonable' or 'good faith' belief, it is necessary to do so in order to protect the interests of the provider or a third party.

An unusual approach is that taken by IBM. IBM expressly states that it has no duty of confidentiality regarding customer data stored in its cloud, and places responsibility for keeping it confidential on the customer, for example via encryption.[85] However, where the data are stored under arrangements where IBM specifically has root (as in privileged) access to VMs, considerably tighter disclosure protection is specified. This appears to reflect the difference between customer data that IBM is not required to have access to for the provision of the service (eg straightforward data storage) and data where the nature of the service requires that IBM has unencrypted access to it (eg the hosting of VMs).

For some cloud services, however, disclosure may well form an inherent part of the service. As Edwards and Brown have noted, social networking sites are built upon the sharing of personal information, and are to a large extent crafted to encourage behaviour antithetical to conventional notions of privacy.[86] The boundary between social networking and hosting sites is increasingly blurred, with hosting sites such as Flickr offering 'family' and 'friend' contacts, special-interest groups, and blogging.[87] Such sites will have to address concerns arising from the conflicting expectations of customers who wish both to share data, and to understand and control whom it is shared with. The issues experienced by Facebook in particular have led to it making repeated changes to its ToS as it has sought to balance fine-grained privacy control with ease of use.[88] It is unlikely to

---

[81] In 2010, not all those surveyed did: one provider, Zecter, was silent on the issue of third-party disclosure. All providers surveyed or reviewed in 2013 had terms addressing this point.

[82] 8.3—Compelled Disclosure. 'The Receiving Party may disclose Confidential Information of the Disclosing Party if it is compelled by law to do so, provided the Receiving Party gives the Disclosing Party prior notice of such compelled disclosure (to the extent legally permitted) and reasonable assistance, at the Disclosing Party's cost, if the Disclosing Party wishes to contest the disclosure.' (See n. 28.)

[83] Facebook Privacy Policy, Section 6 'How We Share Information' (see n. 13).

[84] ADrive Privacy Policy, Section (q) 'No Warranties' (see n. 6).

[85] For further discussion of issues surrounding the duty of confidence a cloud computing provider may have in respect of data it hosts, see Chapter 6.

[86] Lilian Edwards and Ian Brown, 'Data Control and Social Networking: Irreconcilable Ideas?' in A. Matwyshyn (ed.) *Harboring Data: Information Security, Law, and the Corporation* (Palo Alto: Stanford University Press, 2009).

[87] <http://www.flickr.com/help/contacts>; <http://www.flickr.com/help/groups>; <http://www.flickr.com/help/blogging> (all accessed 27 March 2013).

[88] Hicks, 'Through the Privacy Wall' (2010) 98 *European Lawyer* 51. Before being revised in May 2010, Facebook's Privacy Policy was, at 5,830 words, noted as being longer than the US Constitution (BBC, 'Facebook Mulls U-turn on Privacy', 19 May 2010, <http://www.bbc.co.uk/news/10125260> (accessed 27 March 2013).

be the only networking/hosting cloud site to experience such challenges in drafting ToS appropriate to the complex and disparate needs of large user communities.

3.2.4 Data location/transfer

One of the oft-cited selling points of cloud computing is that data and processing capacity can be flexed between a provider's resources, potentially on a global scale. However, this has led to one of the most frequently raised legal concerns regarding cloud computing: that a customer's data may be stored or processed in a totally different, and potentially unknown, jurisdiction.[89] Some major cloud providers, such as Amazon, offer 'regional zones' in which a customer may be assured that data will remain. Furthermore, the EU Data Protection regime acts as a strong brake on unfettered transfer of personal data out of Europe;[90] while, conversely, US long-arm statutes may encourage attempts to avoid the jurisdictional reach of the US authorities.[91] As well as location, the international nature of the cloud raises questions about the extent to which data are protected in transit, be it between the customer and provider, or within the provider's own infrastructure.

Perhaps surprisingly, given the prominence often attached to these issues, few of the providers surveyed actually undertake to store data in a particular location or zone. Even Amazon does not describe its regional system in its ToS, although this feature is arguably incorporated by representation via its website FAQ and sign-up process.[92] Indeed, for the 31 sets of ToS reviewed in 2010, 15 made no mention of data location or transit protection whatsoever. Of those that did, seven asserted compliance with US Safe Harbor procedures,[93] while some of those that did not (eg Norton) stated that they would only transfer personal data to locations providing an equivalent or greater level of protection for personal data to that applicable where the data originated.[94] For one of its online services (.Net), Microsoft mentioned in its 2010 ToS that it was subject to US Safe Harbor obligations but stated that 'Personal information collected on Microsoft sites and services may be stored and processed in the United States or any other country in which Microsoft or its affiliates, subsidiaries or service providers maintain facilities'.

---

[89] Mowbray, 'The Fog over the Grimpen Mire: Cloud Computing and the Law' (2009) 6:1 *SCRIPTed* 129; Nauwelaerts and Le Bousse, 'Cloud Bursting' (2009) 20(4) *Computing & Law*.

[90] Directive 95/46/EC (OJ L 281/31, 23.11.1995), at Arts 25 and 26.

[91] See further Chapter 11. See also Sachevda, 'International Jurisdiction in Cyberspace: A Comparative Perspective' (2007) 13(8) *CTLR* 245; Maier, 'How Has the Law Attempted to Tackle the Borderless Nature of the Internet?' (2010) 18(2) *IJL&IT* 142; Raul, McNicholas, and Jillson, 'Reconciling European Data Privacy Concerns with US Discovery Rules: Conflict and Comity' (2009) 2(3) *Global Competition Litigation Review* 119; Kuner, 'Data Protection Law and International Jurisdiction on the Internet' (2010) 18(2) *IJL&IT* 176 (Part 1), 18(3) *IJL&IT* 227 (Part 2).

[92] During the sign-up phase for AWS S3 a customer is offered one of nine Regions: US (Standard), US West (Oregon), US (Northern California), EU (Ireland), Asia Pacific (Singapore), Asia Pacific (Tokyo), Asia Pacific (Sydney), South America (São Paulo), and GovCloud (US). Statements, such as the comment in the Amazon S3 service description, 'You can choose a Region to optimize for latency, minimize costs, or address regulatory requirements . . . Objects stored in a Region never leave the Region unless you transfer them out. For example, objects stored in the EU (Ireland) Region never leave the EU', would likely be taken under English law as representations inducing the customer to enter into a contract. Further details of Amazon's storage domain policy are available at <http://aws.amazon.com/s3/faqs/#Where_is_my_data_stored> (accessed 30 March 2013).

[93] The 'Safe Harbor' procedure was established by the US Department of Commerce, in consultation with the European Commission, to facilitate the transfer of personal data between the EU and the US. See Chapter 10, Section 5.1.

[94] By 2013, detailed provisions on transfers had been introduced. See clauses 5.1 and 12 of Symantec's 'Complete Privacy Statement', <http://www.symantec.com/en/uk/about/profile/policies/privacy.jsp>.

The same statement was repeated in its Online Privacy Statement as of 2013.[95] Similar terms are asserted by a number of providers (including PayPal, Dell, and Canonical) in the ToS surveyed or reviewed in 2013; it appears there is growing acknowledgement of the international nature of cloud storage.

As well as the question of where customer data are stored, a further concern is the security of data in transit. The international nature of cloud services means that customer data will usually be transferred between customer and provider over the Internet. Furthermore, if (as many larger cloud providers do) the provider has multiple data centres, then, unless the provider has built or leased its own secure network and facilities, transfers between data centres may well also be over Internet connections. Several providers (eg 37Signals and UKFast) caution in their ToS that customer data may be transferred unencrypted over inherently insecure networks in such a manner. By contrast, Dropbox specifically states, albeit on its website rather than in its ToS, that all data transfers are encrypted, and identifies Amazon S3 as the underlying storage service provider.[96]

3.2.5 Monitoring by provider

It is not just disclosure of content to third parties that customers may be concerned about. Customers may equally not wish their use of a cloud service to be monitored by the provider, be this because such monitoring might be the precursor to third-party disclosure, or because it may disclose the customer's confidential data to the provider. This latter point may still apply even if only traffic data (eg frequency and volume of data movement) is monitored; sustained analysis of such data can reveal a considerable amount of information about the use of even encrypted services.[97]

Providers appear to fall into three categories in relation to their policy on monitoring the use of their services by customers. One set (including Nirvanix, PayPal, and Zoho) is silent in their ToS on the subject. This does not, of course, mean that they do not undertake such monitoring, only that they do not declare a policy on doing so.

A second set (including Elastichosts and Flexiant) state that they monitor customer use, but only in terms of the nature and pattern of use (eg bandwidth consumption) and may well state that this is specifically for the purpose of ensuring a good quality of service provision.

The third set state that they may monitor the data the customer uploads to their cloud, typically for purposes of enforcing their AUP (eg Rackspace and GoGrid). It is not generally made clear in ToS whether such monitoring is proactive or in response to specific suspicions of disapproved activity; it may be that the providers do not wish to constrain themselves in this respect, or that they do not wish to assume responsibility for policing their content.[98]

---

[95] Microsoft, 'Microsoft Online Privacy Statement', <http://privacy.microsoft.com/en-us/fullnotice.mspx> (accessed 27 March 2013).

[96] Dropbox Security Overview, available at <https://www.dropbox.com/privacy#security>, 'Secure Storage' (accessed 30 March 2013).

[97] Shuo Chen et al., 'Side-Channel Leaks in Web Applications: A Reality Today, a Challenge Tomorrow' (2010), *Proc. IEEE Symposium on Security and Privacy* (Oakland), IEEE Computer Society, May 2010.

[98] The degree to which cloud providers were under a duty to actively monitor data uploaded by customers in respect of copyright infringement was the subject of a substantial claim brought by Viacom against Google regarding material uploaded to YouTube. This claim was dismissed in June 2010 but illustrates the potential for major disputes in this area. *Viacom International et al. v YouTube et al.* (SDNY, 23 June 2010).

Provider monitoring was one area where significant evolution of terms was seen between 2010 and 2013. A number of providers that in 2010 had not stated a policy on monitoring or had stated that it was only carried out for service provision purposes had amended their ToS by 2013 to state much more clearly that data were monitored for compliance with terms such as acceptable use policies. Two major providers in particular did this: Apple and Google. Apple's 2010 ToS for iWork and MobileMe both indicated that monitoring was for the purpose of providing the service. By 2013, the ToS for iCloud required the user to consent to monitoring of account data and location services, and asserted Apple's right to prescreen, move, refuse, modify, or remove data at any time.[99] Google, which in 2010 had been silent in its ToS on this point, asserted a right in 2013 to monitor use of the Google Apps for Business service to prevent abuse. Interestingly, it also imposed via its ToS a duty upon customers of this service to screen for and prevent abusive use of the email component of the service.

The extensive scope of such monitoring clauses may be indicative of growing concerns regarding the hosting of illegal or otherwise inappropriate content. Notwithstanding the challenges of filtering the vast amounts of content hosted by large providers grows,[100] such providers are supplementing existing 'notice and takedown' provisions with authorizations to adopt a more proactive approach.

3.2.6 *Rights over service/content*

The first version of this survey in 2010 found no evidence of any provider seeking to assert intellectual property (IP) rights over content and data uploaded to the cloud by customers. Indeed, the most common term relating to IP was one stating, at greater or lesser length, that both provider and customer retained the IP relating to their service and data respectively. In a few cases (eg Decho, Flexiant, and Joyent) this term referred only to the provider's IP, and no mention was made to that of the customer.

A typical example of a reciprocal term can be found in the ToS for Google Apps Premier (now Google Apps for Business). After noting that Google retains IP in elements of its service, the ToS go on to state that it does not own third-party content on the service, and that such material remains the property of the content owner.

What is seen from several providers, however, is a term asserting that the customer grants the provider a compulsory licence to republish some or all of the customer's data for the purpose of provision of the service. This is particularly so for consumer-focused services that encourage hosting as well as storage of customer content, for example, Apple and Google.

It may be argued that this merely formalizes what would be a licence implied by business efficacy or necessity, but that it does so in a way that allows the scope of the licence to be clearly established. The scope of the explicit licence may be significantly greater than would have been implied. Facebook, for example, requires customers to grant such a licence for the use of shared content that covers a very broad range of activities, including (as has been the subject of some controversy) advertising by Facebook.[101]

---

[99] iCloud Terms and Conditions, 'Removal of Content' (see n. 9).

[100] In the first instance judgment in *Tamiz v Google* (qv) Eady J observed that 'the blogs on Blogger. com contain, I am told, more than half a trillion words and 250,000 new words are added every minute. In these circumstances, it is virtually impossible for the corporation to exercise editorial control over content'. *Tamiz v Google* [2012] EWHC 449 (QB) [35].

[101] C Walters, 'Facebook's New Terms of Service: "We Can Do Anything We Want with Your Content. Forever"' (*Consumerist*, 15 February 2009), <http://consumerist.com/2009/02/facebooks-new-terms-of-service-we-can-do-anything-we-want-with-your-content-forever.html> (accessed 27 March

The review in 2013 found that the position was unchanged, with providers stating that IP in customer data remains with the customer. There continues to be widespread use of terms by which the provider asserts that it has a compulsory licence for the purposes of providing the service. The period since the 2010 review has seen a number of cases of poorly drafted or misinterpreted ToS appearing to allow, or being construed as allowing, the provider to claim IP rights over customer data. A widely publicized example involved the image-hosting provider Instagram which updated its ToS in December 2012 to include a provision that was viewed as giving it the right to sell its customers' photographs to third parties without notification or compensation.[102] This change led to widespread criticism and the contentious elements of the ToS were removed.[103]

3.2.7 Proprietary rights and duties

This topic relates specifically to terms that describe whether the contract for cloud services gives rise to any form of non-ownership right or relationship, such as a bailment or fiduciary duties.[104] Here, it is easy to classify providers: the vast majority make no reference whatsoever to such a concept. Those few that do refer to proprietary rights do so in terms that on examination appear not to relate to data in the provider's cloud. Amazon, for example, asserts that no right of bailment arises in respect of data sent to it for import into the S3 cloud, but on close reading it is apparent that this term applies to data in the form of physical media, and that Amazon is really asserting that if a customer sends it physical media it has no special duty of care to look after the media. Similarly, The Planet, in its 2010 ToS, appeared to define customer data as 'property' but immediately went on to assert ownership only over physical property left by the customer with it after the end of a contract. In short, the question of whether a bailment or similar such relationship exists in respect of customer data actually in the cloud is simply not addressed by any of the providers surveyed.

3.3 Liabilities and responsibilities

3.3.1 Warranty

Of the elements of cloud provider ToS analysed by this survey, perhaps the greatest area of commonality was in respect of terms regarding the warranty given by the provider to

---

2013); Graham and Anderson, 'Are Individuals Waking up to the Privacy Implications of Social Networking Sites?' (2010) 32(3) *EIPR* 99. Although Facebook subsequently withdrew some of the most contentious terms (such as the perpetual nature of the asserted licence) it still claims a very wide range of permissible uses. From Section 2 of the Statement of Rights and Responsibilities (see n. 13): 'For content that is covered by intellectual property rights, like photos and videos ("IP content"), you specifically give us the following permission, subject to your privacy and application settings: you grant us a non-exclusive, transferable, sub-licensable, royalty-free, worldwide license to use any IP content that you post on or in connection with Facebook ("IP License"). This IP License ends when you delete your IP content or your account unless your content has been shared with others, and they have not deleted it.'

[102] Julianne Pepitone, 'Instagram Can Now Sell Your Photos for Ads' (*CNNMoney*, 18 December 2012), <http://money.cnn.com/2012/12/18/technology/social/instagram-sell-photos/index.html> (accessed 30 March 2013).

[103] Declan McCullagh and Donna Tam, 'Instagram Apologizes to Users: We Won't Sell Your Photos' (*CNET*, 18 December 2012), <http://news.cnet.com/8301-1023_3-57559890-93/instagram-apologizes-to-users-we-wont-sell-your-photos> (accessed 20 March 2013).

[104] For a discussion regarding the ownership of data stored in or processed via cloud computing services, see Chapter 6.

the customer for performance of the service. Almost without exception, every provider went to considerable, and in some cases extraordinary, lengths to deny that any such warranty existed.

Where there was a difference visible it was in the approach taken by those providers which asserted the law and jurisdiction of US states and those which claimed to be governed by the laws of a European country. In a clear reflection of differing commercial practices, and of differing approaches to consumer protection, US-based providers were far more comprehensive in disclaiming any warranty. For an example of a very comprehensive disclaimer, see that given by GoGrid in respect of its cloud service:

GOGRID MAKES NO EXPRESS OR IMPLIED WARRANTIES, INCLUDING WITHOUT LIMITATION WARRANTIES OF TITLE, NONINFRINGEMENT, MERCHANTABILITY, OR FITNESS FOR A PARTICULAR PURPOSE. GoGrid does not warrant that the Service will be uninterrupted, error-free, or free from viruses or other harmful components. The Service is provided with no warranties regarding security, reliability, protection from attacks, data integrity, or data availability (including without limitation data integrity or availability related to cloud storage features of the Service). Except to the extent specifically provided in the SLA, THE SERVICE IS PROVIDED ON AN 'AS IS' AND 'AS AVAILABLE' BASIS. No communication between Customer and GoGrid will create a warranty or in any way alter or restrict any disclaimer of warranty or limitation of liability set forth in this Section 8 or elsewhere in this Agreement.[105]

This very full disclaimer is more detailed than most others seen, but not fundamentally different from them; many providers, including Facebook and Amazon, exclude express or implied warranties that the service provided will be fit for purpose or merchantable. Some of those providers that claim European jurisdiction either do not exclude any such warranties (eg UKFast) or accept statutory implied warranties where they apply (eg IBM, Google). However, at the time of the initial survey in 2010 a number of providers claiming European law and jurisdiction disclaimed any such warranties (eg Apple and G.ho.st), notwithstanding consumer protection law rules to the contrary. By 2013, a more nuanced approach was observed; Apple, for instance, notes in its ToS for iCloud that some jurisdictions do not permit the exclusion of certain warranties. Where providers that had previously asserted US law now specified that of a European state, the warranty provisions generally reflected the European approach to consumer law. Decho, for example, asserted Utah state law in its 2010 ToS and excluded all warranties for fitness for purpose or reliability. By contrast, its 2013 ToS specify English law for customers in the UK and contain a provision stating that nothing in them excludes, restricts, or affects the customer's statutory rights, a clause that is absent from the corresponding part of the ToS for US-based customers. It is evident that many providers not only accept the case for providing localized ToS but also understand the necessity of properly tailoring them to comply with local consumer protection law.

It is worth noting that, following discussions with the UK Office of Fair Trading, Apple agreed in late 2009 to revise the ToS for its iTunes music service, in particular for terms that sought to exclude liability for faulty services or which sought to allow it unilaterally to vary the terms of the contract.[106] Given that many cloud computing ToS (including Apple's) have such terms, it will be interesting to see if corresponding changes are requested in respect of them.

---

[105] See n. 16.
[106] Office of Fair Trading, 'Apple Agrees to Improve Terms and Conditions', 27 November 2009, <http://www.oft.gov.uk/news/press/2009/136-09> (accessed 27 March 2013).

3.3.2 Direct liability

The contrasting approaches to disclaiming warranties of service by US-based and Europe-based cloud providers are to a large extent mirrored in terms seeking to exclude direct liability for damage caused to the customer by the provider. In this context, 'direct liability' is taken to mean liability for losses to the customer relating to the loss or compromise of data hosted on the cloud service. All US-based providers surveyed seek to deny liability for direct damage as far as possible, be it in very general terms or phrased as relating to the consequences of inability to access data. Again, a particularly comprehensive example can be found in GoGrid's ToS, which exclude liability for losses arising from security breaches, data breach or loss, denial of service, performance failures, or the accuracy of the service. Indeed, GoGrid excludes such liability even where a customer has specifically contracted for security or backup features.[107]

Providers based in Europe tend to be less overt about seeking to exclude direct liability, presumably on the basis that in most European legal systems it is difficult to do so. Such exclusions as there are tend to be based on, for instance, *force majeure* (as with Flexiant or ElasticHosts). A noticeable evolution from 2010 to 2013 was that many providers took more care in seeking to specify what did or did not constitute a direct loss. For example, IBM has terms specific to Ireland and the UK that exclude liability for special, incidental, and exemplary damages, and for losses arising from wasted management time or lost profits, business, revenue, goodwill, or anticipated savings.[108]

3.3.3 Indirect liability

Disclaimers against indirect liability, such as for indirect, consequential, or economic losses arising from a breach by the provider, are even more common. This is no doubt due to the potentially very large scope of such damages. It may prove difficult to quantify the direct loss, if any, resulting from the deletion of customer data by a cloud provider. However, if such data are essential to, for instance, the operation of an online retail system, the resulting loss of business may be very large. As such, with the exception of Flexiant, which did not make a specific reference to such losses, every single provider surveyed specifically excluded them. Such variations as there were related to detail, for example, excluding indirect losses that were specifically within the contemplation of both parties.[109] To quote UKFast's ToS for CloudHosts, such losses are excluded 'even if the event was foreseeable by, or the possibility thereof is or has been brought to the attention of the Company'.[110] Some ToS purport to exclude 'incidental losses' that might actually be considered to be direct losses; UKFast, for example, seeks via its ToS to exclude liability for 'indirect, consequential or economic loss' said to include 'damage, costs or expenses'.[111]

Whether such terms will be effective is another matter, however. The question of remoteness and foreseeability of loss for the purposes of exclusions in IT contracts was addressed by the English High Court in *GB Gas Holdings v Accenture* [2009] EWHC

---

[107] GoGrid Terms of Service, Section 8(c) (see n. 16).

[108] IBM Terms of Service, Section 17.7.2 (see n. 20).

[109] In English law, *Hadley v Baxendale* 'Limb 2' losses, such as those potential losses associated with the particular contract in question and known to both parties in advance, as distinct from 'Limb 1' losses identified in *Hadley v Baxendale* (1854) 9 Ex Ch 341 as those common to such contracts.

[110] UKFast Terms of Service, 9.3 (see n. 31).

[111] UKFast Terms of Service, 9.3.

2966 (Comm).[112] The Court held that a number of the claimant's business losses arising from the defendant's delay in implementing the contract were in fact direct losses occasioned by the breach of contract. Cloud computing contracts that seek to define and exclude losses consequential on service failure as being indirect may therefore not, at least if brought before an English court, insulate the provider from wider liability for such losses.

This question was explored in the case (described in more detail earlier) of *Overy v PayPal*. HH Judge Hegarty considered whether PayPal's term excluding liability for loss of profits was reasonable within the meaning of UCTA 1977, as applied to the scenario (as will be the case for cloud services with standard ToS) where one party deals on the written standard terms of the other. HH Judge Hegarty held that, in the business circumstances PayPal operated under, it was not unreasonable to exclude such liability, or indeed more general liability for indirect loss.[113]

This analysis, however, was specifically on the facts of the dispute in question and, in particular, the potential liabilities faced by PayPal. In his judgment, HH Judge Hegarty referred to section 11(4) UCTA 1977, which deals with cases where by reference to a contract term or notice a party seeks to restrict liability to a specified sum of money, and which provides that the reasonableness of such a term should be assessed with regard to the resources available for meeting such a liability and the feasibility of insuring against it. It is by no means certain that cloud providers offering other sorts of service, for example data storage, would face the wide-ranging and extensive liabilities that HH Judge Hegarty QC held that PayPal did, and against which it was held reasonable for PayPal to exclude liability.

3.3.4 Limit of liability

Notwithstanding the denial of warranties and exclusions of liability commonly seen throughout the surveyed ToS, it is also common to find terms seeking to limit the extent of any damages that the provider may be liable for.

In 2010, the majority of providers surveyed (19 out of the 31 ToS analysed) took the approach of setting a maximum liability that was some multiple of the amount paid in service fees by the customer over a set period, often with an upper limit. For example, GoGrid and Salesforce CRM limited their liability to the total amount paid by the customer over the previous 12 months; Rackspace to 12 times the monthly fee; and UKFast and ElasticHosts to only one month's fees. Decho, which offers both paid and free services, limits its liability to the total amount paid by the customer, and specifically notes that for free services this equates to a total denial of liability.[114]

Seven of the providers surveyed did not specify a liability limit but denied all direct and indirect liability (see the discussion above); it has thus been assumed that in effect they simply denied liability without limit.

Such limits of liability were considered by HH Judge Hegarty QC in *Overy v PayPal*. Although, as noted above, he held that it was reasonable in the circumstances for PayPal to exclude indirect liability, he was less persuaded that PayPal could reasonably, as per its ToS, limit liability to the greater of either the value of the transaction in dispute or the fees paid by the other party to PayPal in the previous 12 months. HH Judge Hegarty QC

---

[112] The decision was upheld in the Court of Appeal, [2010] EWCA Civ 912.
[113] *Overy v PayPal*, para. 268. For source, see n. 65.
[114] Mozy Terms of Service, 'Limitation of Liability'. See n. 10.

could not see any justification for these limits, and held that PayPal would not be entitled to rely upon them against Mr Overy.

Where a flat liability is specified, be it as a general limit or as a cap to a pro rata liability, the amount varies significantly depending on the nature of the provider's service and the expected customers for it. ADrive, which offers a consumer storage service, has a liability limit of US$100, as do Dropbox and Facebook; UKFast, a host catering to SMEs, has a liability limit of £5,000. Some providers set higher limits; as of 2013 IBM sets a limit of $25,000, or €25,000 for customers in the UK or Republic of Ireland. It is notable though that this figure is itself a significant reduction on the €500,000 limit set in IBM's 2010 ToS. In light of HH Judge Hegarty QC's judgment in *Overy v PayPal* though, the effectiveness of such limits under English law must be considered doubtful.

Notwithstanding such judicial concerns, the 2013 survey found that this approach to capping liability remained common, although some providers had amended such terms to reflect a more nuanced approach. For instance, in 2010 Flexiant asserted a liability cap of twice the amount paid in fees in any service period. By 2013, this had been amended to the greater of the amount paid in fees in the previous three months, or £15,000.[115]

3.3.5 Indemnification

As well as seeking to deny or strictly limit liability, most cloud providers incorporate indemnification clauses into their ToS. For 24 out of the 31 ToS analysed in 2010, the customer was required to indemnify the provider against any claim against the provider arising from the customer's use of the service. From the consumer or SME perspective, it is worth noting that such terms are currently imposed not only by providers that charge for cloud services but also by the free-to-use service providers surveyed, such as Dropbox and Facebook. As of the time of drafting this chapter, for instance, some one billion Facebook users, none of whom pay for the service they use, have by signing up agreed to the following indemnification term:

If anyone brings a claim against us related to your actions, content or information on Facebook, you will indemnify and hold us harmless from and against all damages, losses, and expenses of any kind (including reasonable legal fees and costs) related to such claim.

Conversely, a number of providers undertake to indemnify the customer in certain circumstances. In 2010, four providers, 3Tera, Akamai, Google (for Google Apps Premier), and Salesforce (for Salesforce CRM), indemnified the customer against claims brought against them for IP infringement arising from use of the provider's service. Such a claim might be one brought for IP infringement in relation to the provider's technology or software that the cloud provider had licensed.[116] By 2013, 3Tera's successor CenturyLink no longer offered such an indemnity, but Dell (a provider newly surveyed in 2013) did. Such an indemnity may be stated to be conditional; for instance, Google Apps for Business' indemnification clause requires the customer to allow Google to control the conduct of litigation.

---

[115] Flexiant Terms of Service, Section 15.1. See n. 14.
[116] For example, the 2010 dispute between Microsoft and SalesForce.com over patents for cloud computing technology; Ina Fried, 'Microsoft, Salesforce Settle Patent Dispute' (*CNET*, 4 August 2010), <http://news.cnet.com/8301-13860_3-20012674-56.html> (accessed 27 March 2013).

3.3.6 Service availability

Where a provider offers service credits, it will specify a service performance target that it will aim to meet. This target may often appear quite optimistic (Flexiant, Joyent, and GoGrid all set 100 per cent service uptime targets) but, as noted in the discussion of service credits, the target will usually exclude a wide range of potential causes of loss of service. ElasticHosts, for example, states a 100 per cent availability target but excludes the following sources of potential downtime:

- Your payments not covering your use, including but not limited to when your subscriptions or prepaid balance run out.
- Acts or omissions of you or your users.
- Software running within your virtual servers.
- Scheduled maintenance which we have announced at least 24 hours in advance.
- Factors outside our control, including but not limited to any force majeure events; failures, acts or omissions of our upstream providers or failures of the internet.
- Actions of third parties, including but not limited to security compromises, denial of service attacks and viruses.
- Violations of our Acceptable Use Policy.
- Law enforcement activity.[117]

Conversely, many providers expressly disclaim any availability target. Fifteen out of the 31 ToS surveyed in 2010 incorporated terms by which the provider stated that the service was 'as-is' or 'best-efforts', or that it may be suspended or discontinued at any time. For the 2013 survey, 20 out of 36 providers featured such terms in their ToS. Furthermore, such terms were seen across the full range of cloud services covered by this survey, ranging from those aimed at consumers to those, such as Amazon Web Services, aimed at a market primarily of other cloud providers, and major corporate and government users.

3.3.7 Service credits

Although many providers seek to deny or limit liability, a number (particularly those offering commercial services) provide a mechanism for compensating customers for failure to deliver the service to set levels. Such compensation is invariably by service credit, allowing the customer a rebate against future billing; no exceptions were found to this in all the providers surveyed. Both ElasticHosts and GoGrid, for example, offer service credits of 100 times the cost of the lost service (eg a six-minute outage would attract a rebate of ten hours' service charges) capped at one month's service fees.[118] For both providers, this provision was present in their 2010 and 2013 ToS. When first surveyed in 2010, The Planet offered a more complex rebate mechanism, with customers receiving a 5 per cent monthly fee rebate for the first five minutes of lost service, and then a further 5 per cent for each additional 30 minutes; this presumably recognized that service failures that last more than a few minutes may be quite prolonged.[119] By the time its successor service from SoftLayer was reviewed in 2013, the rebate mechanism had changed significantly, providing only for 5 per cent monthly rebates for each 30 minutes of outage. Significantly, outages of less than 30 minutes are explicitly excluded from triggering a service credit; this might be viewed as an indication that short outages may be relatively frequent.

---

[117] ElasticHosts Terms of Service, SLA, and AUP, 'Service Level Agreement' (see n. 12).
[118] See nn. 12, 16.   [119] See n. 30.

Service credits are typically governed by a separate Service Level Agreement, which will usually exclude such causes of downtime as scheduled maintenance or any factors outside the provider's immediate control, such as routing or traffic issues affecting Internet links (see the discussion above of terms relating to 'service availability').

Service credits may also be offered under very restrictive conditions; for example, ElasticHosts specifies that it will be sole arbiter of eligibility for and the extent of credits, and that such credits are the sole remedy available to the customer for service deficiency.[120]

4. Practical Findings

4.1 Tracking changes in ToS

Six months after the 2010 survey, the ToS of the providers covered by it were revisited for the purpose of comparison. This allowed for further examination of an issue noted in Section 3.1.6: the extent to which a provider notifies customers of changes to ToS.

The ToS for all the providers covered by the initial survey were revisited, save for G.ho.st, which had ceased operation during this period. For each provider, all ToS documents were examined to see whether they had been changed since the initial sample and the extent, if at all, to which changes had been highlighted to users.

It will be apparent that there are four possible statuses for each document:

- *Changed and Notified*: This means that the document had changed since the January 2010 sample and that there is notice of this within the document, for example an issue date more recent than this. 18 documents were in this category, representing 11 providers. 15 of those documents were from 8 providers that either put the customer on notice to review terms or made no mention of policy for contract variation. As such, a diligent customer would note that there had been a change, although in no case was there a positive indication (eg by highlighting) of what the change had been.

- *Unchanged and Notified*: This means that the document contained an issue date that was before January 2010 and which, indeed, matched that of the previous sample copy of that document. 28 documents were in this category, representing 18 providers. 16 of those documents were from 10 providers that either put the customer on notice to review terms or made no mention of policy for contract variation. A customer seeking to confirm the status of his or her ToS could thus readily discern that these documents had not changed.

- *Unchanged and Not Notified*: This meant that there was no indication of the change status or last issue date of the document in question, but that comparison of the June 2010 version with the one archived in January 2010 revealed no changes. 19 documents from 12 providers were in this category. 14 of those documents were from 8 providers that either put the customer on notice to review terms, or made no mention of policy for contract variation. Customers of these providers are thus

---

[120] 'We will be the sole arbiter regarding the award of credit and our decision will be final and binding. The award of credit by us to you as described in this Service Level Agreement will be the sole and exclusive remedy for unavailability of stored data or virtual servers or loss of stored data. Credits will only be provided against future service and for the avoidance of doubt may not be exchanged for cash or other forms of payment.' (See n. 12.)

faced with a careful review of often lengthy ToS documents to reassure themselves that there has been no contract variation.[121]

- *Changed and Not Notified*: These documents also had no indication of change status or last issue date, but comparison between the January 2010 and June 2010 versions revealed changes. 4 documents from 3 providers were in this category. 3 of those documents were from 2 providers that either put the customer on notice to review terms or made no mention of policy for contract variation. As such, there were changes that a customer could only have discovered by regular diligent review of the published ToS. (The one document that was from a provider that said it would notify customers of changes had a minor change in terminology that the provider presumably did not consider worthy of notification.)

It is worth noting that many of the providers that lacked a positive notification policy did in fact make it clear when their published ToS had last changed, usually by including a review date. In some cases, as noted, the changes were very minor; nonetheless, it is useful for customers to see that the document has been at the very least reviewed recently. However, it is a matter of concern that such a policy is not universal. In particular, where a provider places the burden of monitoring its ToS for changes onto its customers, it would seem incumbent upon it to make it clear if such changes have actually taken place. Even those that did date their ToS did not, for instance, mark up revised passages or note specific changes. Were a provider to update its AUP without making it clear to its customers that it had done so, some customers could find that hitherto permitted activities were now proscribed.[122]

This exercise has not been repeated for the 2013 survey because at the time of drafting only a single sample of the newly surveyed ToS was available. However, it was noted in the course of the survey that several providers take steps to ensure that users are aware of, or can find, the history of changes to their ToS. As mentioned in Section 3.1.6, Salesforce provides an online archive of previous versions of its Master Service Agreement. PayPal provides a similar archive,[123] as well as a page summarizing ToS changes that have been announced but are yet to come into effect.[124]

4.2 Comparing and categorizing ToS

One of the overarching aims of this analysis was to identify and evaluate patterns in the ToS offered by the providers covered by the 2010 and 2013 surveys. Both common features and distinctive approaches were noted. The patterns that emerged fall into three main categories:

- Aspects of the ToS that are distinctly segmented among providers; in other words, some providers adopt one approach to such terms, while others take a clearly different one.

---

[121] In the case of some ToS documents we resorted to document version comparison software to ascertain whether changes had been made.

[122] Although if the AUP was amended to reflect legislative changes (eg to restrict behaviour newly made illegal) the provider could argue that the customers had not been disadvantaged in that such behaviour was now proscribed by law. Nonetheless, it would seem prudent to ensure that customers were advised of such changes.

[123] PayPal, *Past Policy Updates* (effective date 1 March 2013).

[124] PayPal, *Upcoming Policy Updates* (effective date 16 May 2013).

- Aspects of the ToS where the opposite is seen, with most or all providers adopting a common approach to a particular area of ToS.
- Areas of ToS where most or all providers take a common basic approach but some then develop this approach further. This is termed a 'spectrum' approach, in that providers are seen to lie on a spectrum of greater or lesser variation from a default position.

In respect of the first type of ToS term, the clearest segmentation among cloud providers is that between those for services that are paid for and those that are 'free', or at least not funded by direct subscription. Such a distinction is not surprising as the commercial obligations of a provider are likely to be in proportion to the consideration provided by a customer. This is seen most clearly in respect of data retention beyond the termination of the customer/provider relationship. Such retention requires the provider to commit resources such as storage and account management; indeed, even if access is provided only for the customer to withdraw data, this requires effort on the part of the provider, as non-standard access to the cloud is required.

Another clear distinction observed was between providers that asserted that their ToS were governed by the laws of US states, and those that claimed to be covered by the laws of European countries. Very extensive disclaimers of warranty or limitations of liability were much more common among the former than the latter. Again, this is not a surprising distinction. European legal systems tend to be less tolerant than those of US states regarding terms that limit the duty of one party, particularly if it is the more powerful one, to perform its obligations under a contract. This is most clearly enshrined in EU law in respect of consumer transactions, such as the Unfair Contract Terms Directive[125] and Distance Selling Directive.[126] As noted in Section 3.1.2, little change was seen between 2010 and 2013 in terms of the proportion of those providers surveyed that asserted the law of a US state and that of a European country, although slightly more providers now specify the local law of the customer.

A more general distinction observed is that between SaaS products and IaaS products. Put simply, the ToS of IaaS products tend to resemble one another more than those of SaaS products. This, again, is readily explicable; IaaS providers are selling the computing equivalent of raw commodities: processing power, storage capacity, and bandwidth. Although the exact details of a VM may vary between two providers, both are selling what in essence is the same product. By contrast, a SaaS provider offering an online document processing service is selling something very different from one offering cloud-based customer-management services. This distinction continued to be observed in 2013, with the ToS for IaaS products being less varied than those for SaaS products.

Other areas where providers fell into clear groups in respect of their ToS include monitoring of customer activity and variation of the ToS themselves. In respect of monitoring, providers adopt one of three approaches: they do not state that they do so,[127] they

---

[125] Directive 93/13/EEC of 5 April 1993 on unfair terms in consumer contracts (OJ L 95, 21.4.1993) 29.

[126] Directive 97/7/EC of 20 May 1997 on the protection of consumers in respect of distance contracts (OJ L 144, 4.6.1999) 19.

[127] In 2010, 37Signals, 3Tera, Akamai, Google, IBM, Nirvanix, PayPal, Salesforce, Zecter, and Zoho made no mention of monitoring, and UKFast stated that it would not proactively monitor customer compliance with the AUP. In 2013, 37Signals, Facebook, Nirvanix, PayPal, Salesforce, Zoho, Box, Dell, and Canonical made no mention of monitoring, while Centurylink, Akamai, Dropbox, Google, Norton, UKFast, and Linode either said that they did not monitor user data or did no more than reserve the right to do so. Mega explicitly states that it does not monitor user content.

note that they do so for the claimed purpose of maintaining service quality,[128] or they claim to do so explicitly so as to police their AUP.[129, 130] Although there is no clear segmentation in the market in terms of approach to monitoring, there is an apparent predominance of IaaS hosting providers in the third group. It may well be that this is because IaaS products provide the greatest scope for active abuse of services (eg by running 'spam' software) rather than just hosting of inappropriate content.

As for ToS variation, there is a division between those providers that state that they will provide written notice (in some cases even conditional on mutual acceptance), and those which require the customer to monitor published ToS for unilateral changes. Here, it was noticeable that the former group included providers such as Salesforce and Iron Mountain that provide SaaS products in areas such as CRM and archiving where long-term trusted customer relationships are important.

In respect of the second type of ToS term, that which varies little between providers, the clearest example is seen by comparing the AUP for cloud services. At first sight there seems to be significant variations between them; the AUP for 37Signals, for instance, simply reserves the right to delete content that is 'unlawful, offensive, threatening, libellous, defamatory, pornographic, obscene or otherwise objectionable',[131] whereas that for Rackspace is a lengthy separate document.[132] On closer inspection though, Rackspace's AUP prohibits fundamentally the same types of behaviour as 37Signals'; it is just that one AUP goes into much more detail in describing them than the other. This pattern is seen across the providers covered by this survey; without exception every provider incorporates some form of AUP in its ToS, and for the most part these consistently prohibit broadly the same set of activities that fall outside the generally accepted bounds of legitimate conduct in the European/US marketplace that was covered in this survey.

A further area of consistency is in the approach providers take to limiting their liability to customers. Where such liability is not denied altogether, it is typically subject either to a simple cap, or a ceiling described in terms of the total amount paid by the customer over a period ranging from the previous month to the previous year. It is also common to see terms that seek to exclude any express or implied warranty for fitness for purpose, or for indirect losses arising from use of the provider's service. Where the provider issues an SLA, this also usually excludes responsibility for service outages from such causes as scheduled maintenance or Internet connectivity problems. Such SLAs also invariably limit the remedy available to customers to a credit specifically against future use of the provider's service.

As for the third type of ToS term, the 'spectrum' of approaches, a good example is seen in the policy that providers say they will take towards requests for disclosure of customer data. Of the providers that address this point, all say that they will give such disclosure in response to an enforceable order of a court of competent jurisdiction. However, some go further and say that they will disclose customer data on mere request from government and law enforcement agencies, with a few going even further than that and stating

---

[128] In 2010, Apple, Decho, Dropbox, Facebook, Flexiant, and Microsoft mentioned monitoring for service quality or traffic-management purposes. By 2013, no provider cited this as a basis for monitoring.

[129] In 2010, ADrive, Amazon, Elastichosts, G.ho.st (now defunct), GoGrid, Joyent, Rackspace, Symantec, and The Planet asserted some level of monitoring for compliance with ToS. By 2013, ADrive, Amazon, Apple, Elastichosts, Flexiant, GoGrid, Google (for Google Apps), Joyent, Microsoft, and Rackspace had such terms.

[130] It is, of course, possible that providers that make no mention of a monitoring policy in their ToS nonetheless do so for either of the reasons quoted.

[131] See n. 4, 'General Conditions', paragraph 6.

[132] Rackspace, 'Legal information', <http://www.rackspace.co.uk/legal/aup> (accessed 27 March 2013).

that they will disclose customer data where they consider it is in their business interests to do so.

Another example of a 'spectrum' term is in relation to IP rights over customer data. Those providers that state a policy in this area state that the customer retains ownership of the IP in its data and content. However, some providers then go on to impose via the ToS a licence by which the customer authorizes the provider to copy and reuse such data for the purpose of providing the service. Again, at least one provider (Facebook) goes further in specifying a range of uses it may then put such data to.

4.3 ToS—what a prospective customer should expect

A prospective customer of cloud computing services may ask if this analysis sheds any light on the nature of the ToS that should or could be expected. As the discussion above notes, it is indeed possible to discern patterns in cloud ToS and at a minimum these may act as a guide to what the range of industry practice is in a particular area of a contract. For example, a customer seeking to enter into a paid contract for IaaS provision may well, on the basis of the ToS examined, expect to see a clause limiting liability to between one month's and one year's total customer payment; a total denial of liability would be less usual. Similarly, such a prospective customer should be aware that the SLA will almost certainly limit remedies for service outages to a rebate against future billing for the service in question.

The following points are noted as general guidance by way of a checklist of points to bear in mind when examining cloud ToS:[133]

- Cloud service providers will generally, but not invariably, use their principal place of business as the basis for the legal system and litigation forum governing their ToS. This means that many cloud services are offered under the laws of US states and subject to terms that purport to restrict legal disputes to the courts of those states. Some larger providers, however, have localized legal frameworks, a policy seen more in 2013 than during the original survey in 2010. Customers may be more comfortable with the prospect of signing contracts governed by legal systems for which they can more readily obtain advice and which provide expressly for more local resolution of disputes.

- Most cloud providers will seek to exclude, as far as possible under the legal system applying to the contract, any warranty of service or acceptance of liability. Such liability as cannot be disclaimed altogether will typically be strictly limited. Those providers asserting that their ToS are governed by the laws of US states will generally have more wide-ranging disclaimers of liability than those which claim to be governed by, for instance, English law or the law of another EU state.

- Customers should consider carefully terms by which the provider seeks to allow itself to vary the ToS unilaterally, or to impose termination conditions for the contract based on criteria for which it is the sole arbiter. As the WikiLeaks experience has demonstrated, this may be particularly important for terms regarding acceptable use.[134]

---

[133] They are emphatically not legal advice and do not, and should not, provide a substitute for careful examination of the ToS of a cloud service, and professional legal advice if appropriate.

[134] As noted, for example, by Hal Roberts, 'Amazon's Wikileaks Takedown' (*Berkman Center for Internet & Society*), <http://blogs.law.harvard.edu/hroberts/2010/12/03/amazons-wikileaks-takedown> (accessed 27 March 2013).

- Where a prospective customer has specific security concerns, the ToS should be consulted to assess the provider's approach to securing and protecting data. Those customers wishing to use a cloud-based solution for backup of important data should, in particular, take note of terms by which a provider advises or requires customers separately to back up data placed on their cloud service (in other words, where the proposed backup solution itself disclaims responsibility for being a reliable backup).

- Data protection and privacy issues need to be considered via careful scrutiny of ToS, not least because exclusions and disclaimers relating to them may well, on the evidence of these surveys, not be exclusively in the part of the ToS specifically labelled as relating to privacy. The threshold for disclosure, and policy regarding, monitoring of customer activities can both vary considerably from provider to provider. Furthermore, few providers are explicit as to the location or even general zone that data are stored in, or the identity of any underlying service providers; if such considerations are important to a customer (eg, where there is a risk that personal data may be exported from the EEA) then if the ToS are not clear on the point, further investigation would be advisable.

- Data retention post termination of the contract is an area where providers differ sharply in approach. 'Free' services may often not provide such retention; if coupled with termination clauses that allow the provider to terminate the relationship at its own discretion with little or no notice, this may result in the risk of the customer losing access to all data. Paid services generally allow a grace period, but customers should check to ensure how long this lasts and whether there might be, for instance, additional costs involved.

- Care should be taken in selecting a cloud service on the basis of features or policies that are not specifically mentioned in the ToS. Unless a particular feature is clearly referred to in the process of signing up to the service it may not comprise either a term of the agreement or a representation deemed to have induced it.

4.4 A more open approach?

A natural concern of any prospective customer of cloud services is whether the ToS on offer are clear and straightforward to understand. Consumers and SME customers are not likely to seek specialist legal advice on the interpretation of ToS, particularly where those terms are offered on a standard-form 'take it or leave it' basis with little or no scope for negotiation.[135]

A number of providers not considered in 2010 were included in the 2013 survey; in some cases these were new services the ToS for which would presumably have been freshly drafted. One set of ToS, in particular, showed evidence of a different drafting approach to that seen elsewhere: those offered by image hosting provider 500px for its service of the same name.

500px's ToS contained terms drafted in a manner reminiscent of those of other ToS seen in the survey. However, these terms were presented in the left-hand column of the ToS document, with each section having a corresponding sentence or short paragraph in the right-hand column presented in larger print that sought to summarize the terms

---

[135] Negotiated cloud contracts are considered in detail in Chapter 4.

in question in clear and simple language. For example, the section entitled 'Fair Usage Policy' set out terms as follows:

500px maintains a fair usage policy to ensure stable and fast service to all users.

Free accounts are limited to a maximum of 10 new photographs/images per week and 2,000 photographs/images in total (approximately 60Gb of storage) and 1Gb of data transfer from profile and portfolios per month. Any additional usage may result in restrictions on your account including limited access to your portfolio or a requirement to upgrade if the limit is exceeded for several months.

Premium accounts are limited to maximum of 1,000 new photographs/images per week 100,000 photographs/ images in total (approximately 3,000Gb of storage) and 10Gb of data transfer per month. Awesome accounts that exceed a limit for several months will be notified of their usage and restrictions may be imposed if usage is not corrected.

Presented next to these terms (in a significantly larger font) was:

Basically,

If you use more than your fair share, we may gradually limit your account.

500px's ToS attracted considerable attention when released in 2012. Although much comment was positive, focusing on the perceived 'user-friendliness' of the ToS,[136] concerns were also expressed that the short-version summaries might over-simplify the legal effect of the associated ToS clauses and in doing so may lead customers to assume that the legal consequences of such clauses were other than their actual effect might be.[137] This criticism would appear to have some force; as with the following term:

No agency, partnership, joint venture, or employment is created as a result of the Terms and you do not have any authority of any kind to bind 500px in any respect whatsoever. The failure of either party to exercise in any respect any right provided for herein shall not be deemed a waiver of any further rights hereunder. 500px shall not be liable for any failure to perform its obligations hereunder where such failure results from any cause beyond 500px's reasonable control, including, without limitation, mechanical, electronic or communications failure or degradation (including 'line-noise' interference). If any provision of the Terms is found to be unenforceable or invalid, that provision shall be limited or eliminated to the minimum extent necessary so that the Terms shall otherwise remain in full force and effect and enforceable. 500px may transfer, assign or delegate the Terms and its rights and obligations without consent. The Terms shall be governed by and construed in accordance with the laws of Ontario, as if made within Ontario between two residents thereof, and the parties submit to the exclusive jurisdiction of Ontario courts. Both parties agree that the Terms is the complete and exclusive statement of the mutual understanding of the parties and supersedes and cancels all previous written and oral agreements, communications and other understandings relating to the subject matter of the Terms, and that all modifications must be in a writing signed by both parties, except as otherwise provided herein.

The term was summarized in the adjacent column as follows:

Basically,

Things can happen—we are not responsible.

---

[136] Megan Garber, 'Behold, a Terms of Service Agreement That Is Actually User-Friendly', *The Atlantic*, 12 April 2012.

[137] Knowlton Thomas, 'Toronto Startup 500px Ignites Controversy over TOS: Is it Helping Users or Tricking Them?', (*Techvibes*), 12 April 2012, <http://www.techvibes.com/blog/toronto-startup-5 00px-ignites-controversy-over-tos-is-it-helping-users-or-tricking-them-2012-04-12> (accessed 30 March 2013).

It would seem very doubtful that 'things can happen—we are not responsible' could in any way be described as an adequate summary of a paragraph that includes terms relating to exclusion of liability, choice of law and jurisdiction, and interpretation. Moreover, this paragraph itself includes an 'entire agreement' clause ('Both parties agree that the Terms is the complete and exclusive statement of the mutual understanding of the parties') that is silent as to whether the informal summaries form part of the ToS. If they do, and they do not accurately reflect the corresponding 'formal' terms, then the ToS will contain inconsistent clauses. In such circumstances a court, particularly one applying English common law, may well refer to the well-established principle that a party which seeks to rely upon terms that may be construed in two ways is bound by that which is least beneficial to itself.[138]

5. Conclusions

Our examination of the ToS for a broad range of cloud services has revealed both common elements and contrasts. Many cloud providers include elements in their ToS asserting wide-ranging disclaimers of liability or of any warranty that the service will operate as described, or indeed at all. SLAs are often couched in such terms as to exclude the majority of causes of a cloud service outage, and provide remedies only in the form of credits against future service. Conversely, prospective customers may find that the threshold for disclosure to a third party, the extent to which data will be preserved following the end of a contract, and the legal system under which the contract is offered will vary greatly from provider to provider.

On the basis of our analysis some patterns can be discerned. Where a customer explicitly pays for a service, the provider is likely to provide more in the way of remedies for service outages (albeit usually subject to heavy caveats) and will often facilitate access to data post termination of a contract. Those providers based in Europe or which assert the law of a European state for customers in Europe will typically be less forceful in denying liability than those which are based in, and assert the legal governance of, a US state. And while the terms governing acceptable (or rather unacceptable) use of a service may seem to vary widely, in practical terms they usually proscribe a very similar list of activities.

How are cloud ToS likely to develop? We have already noted[139] that the complex and often conflicting expectations of users of social networking sites can force the rapid evolution of ToS, especially in customer-sensitive areas such as privacy. Where providers of hosting and utility services aimed at consumers seek to incorporate elements of social networking into their products they are likely to encounter similar pressures. We anticipate that producing ToS that are clear, comprehensive, and concise in respect of matters such as privacy will provide an ongoing challenge and further work should be undertaken to monitor and assess the evolution of such terms.

Another area likely to be of growing relevance to consumers, but also of importance to enterprise and government customers, is the approach providers take to resolution of disputes. Our research has found extensive use of terms seeking to impose arbitration or the provider's choice of law and forum for litigation. Although such terms may be ineffective against consumers they may still pose obstacles to customers with a grievance. It avails a customer little to be told that she can, notwithstanding a cloud provider's ToS, sue that provider in her local court if the chances of obtaining an enforceable judgment

---

[138] *Munn v Baker* (1817) 2 Stark 255.   [139] See Section 3.2.5 of this chapter.

against it are minimal because all its business and assets are in a remote jurisdiction. Such issues are, of course, not new but, as with so many of the legal concerns arising from cloud computing, the nature of cloud business makes it easier for ordinary users to encounter them. As the use of global cloud services grows it is likely that more customers will find themselves party to international disputes regarding services delivered to their desktop or mobile device; while the cloud may be location-independent, legal remedies are not.[140] Enterprise and government customers may be in an even more difficult position, as they will not be shielded by consumer protection laws.

It would not be surprising if consumers, accustomed to strong legal protection in disputes with suppliers, start to see cloud services as lacking an accessible and enforceable dispute resolution mechanism. Meanwhile, corporate customers may become wary of ToS that impose unfamiliar legal systems. The widespread exclusion of liability claimed in many ToS is likely to aggravate such concerns.

Providers may seek to reassure customers by tailoring ToS to conform more closely to local expectations. We have already seen such 'localization' in the ToS of some of the providers surveyed in this study.[141] Large providers may make a virtue of offering locally tailored ToS, while smaller, local providers may seek to emphasize their connection to the jurisdiction of their customers.

If a significant number of providers do adapt or localize their ToS to counter potential or actual customer concerns, we may see a 'virtuous circle' setting in through customer pressure. Once customers start to note that some providers offer ToS that offer more in the way of enforceable rights than others do, the presence or absence of such rights may well become a selling point. Alternatively, public or administrative law intervention or regulatory pressure may be brought to bear against providers to ensure that, for example, European consumers are offered ToS that are compliant with EU consumer protection law.

Another approach that has been seen in at least one instance in our survey (500px) is to draft ToS that are made 'user friendly' by, for instance, including brief summaries of clauses so as to make it clear to customers what their rights and obligations under the ToS agreement are. At first sight this is an attractive concept, in that it would seem to address one of the most common concerns about ToS for online services: that they are incomprehensible to the vast majority of users. However, unless care is taken both to summarize terms accurately and to make clear whether the summaries are themselves a legally effective part of the ToS, there is a risk to the provider that this may actually complicate the legal position.

As of 2013, there has been little litigation concerning ToS of online providers, although matters arising from such terms have come before the courts, as in *Overy v PayPal*. The relative disparity in bargaining power between cloud service providers and consumers or SMEs obviously mitigates against disputes being escalated to court unless the dispute is of unusually high value (as in *Overy*). Nonetheless, the legal issues that may arise from standard-form ToS are such that there is abundant scope for such litigation, especially as cloud services become more pervasive and reliance on such services continues to grow.

---

[140] Although a provider might assert that it was acting in the best interests of customers by imposing arbitration on the basis that a recognized arbitration procedure and forum is more likely to be accessible to a customer than the legal system and courts of a foreign cloud provider. Nonetheless, consumer protection law may view such imposed arbitration as unfair, as per n. 56.

[141] See Sections 3.1.2 and 3.3.1.

4

Negotiated Contracts for Cloud Services[1]

W Kuan Hon, Christopher Millard, and Ian Walden

1. Introduction

Following the Cloud Legal Project's (CLP) initial survey and analysis of standard terms,[2] the CLP conducted qualitative research into situations where users had requested changes to providers' standard terms, and the extent to which providers agreed them. From our research, we identify themes which we believe reasonably reflect key market concerns at this relatively immature stage of cloud adoption.

Based on our research, users consider that providers' standard contract terms do not sufficiently accommodate customer needs; the top six types of terms most negotiated were as follows, with the third and fourth issues ranking roughly equally in importance (depending on type of user/service):

1. exclusion or limitation of liability and remedies, particularly regarding data integrity and disaster recovery;

2. service levels, including availability;

3. security and privacy,[3] particularly Data Protection Directive (DPD) issues;[4]

4. lock-in and exit, including term, termination rights, and return of data on exit;

5. providers' ability to change service features unilaterally; and

6. Intellectual property rights (IPRs).

In this chapter, we first describe our research methodology and scope. We then outline providers' perspectives on cloud contract terms, users' perspectives on cloud contracts, and factors influencing why users request certain terms and why providers may agree them, including the role of integrators. Then, we discuss the key types of terms negotiated. Finally, we give views on how we consider cloud contracts are likely to develop as the market matures.

---

[1] A version of this chapter was previously published as: W Kuan Hon, Christopher Millard, and Ian Walden, 'Negotiating Cloud Contracts: Looking at Clouds from Both Sides Now' (2012) 16 *Stan Tech L Rev* 81.

[2] See Chapter 3. The initial survey was in 2010 and a follow-up survey, with comparative analysis, was undertaken in 2013 in preparation for this book.

[3] 62% of UK enterprise decision-makers polled in 2011 cited data security, and 55% data privacy, as their biggest concerns with cloud adoption: Cloud Industry Forum (CIF), *Cloud UK: Paper Four Cloud Adoption and Trends for 2012* (2012) (CIF4)—cf 64% and 62% respectively, in a previous CIF poll conducted a year previously: CIF, *Cloud UK: Paper One Adoption and Trends 2011* (2011) (CIF1).

In a more recent CIF survey, of existing UK cloud users, the two biggest concerns expressed during the internal decision-making process were data security (82%) and data privacy (69%): CIF, *Cloud UK: Paper Eight UK Cloud Adoption and Trends for 2013* (2013).

[4] See Part III of this book.

2. Methodology and Scope

2.1 Methodology

We offer a qualitative analysis, based on our sources, of cloud contract[5] negotiations over a particular time period. Our sources comprised reports of experiences at public conferences/seminars or in informal discussions with cloud actors, plus detailed confidential interviews[6] of at least an hour each, conducted between December 2010 and early 2012, with more than 20[7] organizations, comprising:[8]

- cloud providers: UK-based or global SaaS, PaaS, and IaaS providers, including integrators, and EU and non-EU telecommunications providers;
- cloud users: businesses serving consumers, financial services businesses, and UK public sector organizations, including educational institutions; and
- other cloud market actors: law firms and insurance industry firms.

Our sources discussed specific deals they had been involved with, and their experiences and personal views. Some providers and law firms provided generalized experiences regarding users and clients.

2.2 Scope

We analyse only contracts between cloud users and providers (including integrators[9]) of SaaS, PaaS, or IaaS *services* to users, but not end-user software licences regarding cloud infrastructure or applications running thereon. Cloud users' services may include rights to run software owned by providers (or licensed by providers from rights owners in order to provide services to third parties who, in using the provider's services, run such software in-cloud). However, cloud users procure primarily services, not licences.

Possible chains of services and providers (often unbeknown to users)[10] means users may rely on multiple parties, with multiple possible points of failure. Cloud users generally also depend on Internet connectivity.[11] We do not discuss contracts with telecommunications providers, contracts for consultancy or advisory services regarding users'

---

[5] We relied solely on our interviewees' information regarding their experiences negotiating cloud contracts. We could not verify terms were as stated, as contracts were confidential to the parties. Not all types of terms were discussed with all sources, as some users had not reached the stage of considering certain terms (eg ongoing audit rights).

[6] Most interviewees were UK-based lawyers. In some organizations, both legal and technical experts participated. We are very grateful to our sources for their participation and assistance. As most did not wish to be named, no names are given.

[7] For qualitative research 15–20 interviews are generally considered adequate to obtain a good range of views before reaching 'saturation', the point where no new information or themes are observed and the same information starts recurring. Greg Guest, Arwen Bunce, and Laura Johnson, 'How Many Interviews Are Enough? An Experiment with Data Saturation and Variability' (2006) 18(1) *Field Methods* 59. We did not attempt quantitative surveys, although we reference certain surveys conducted by others (eg CIF).

[8] More detailed breakdowns are omitted as they could identify interviewees or organizations who required anonymity. Mention of an organization's name in this chapter does not imply its participation in our interviews.

[9] See Chapter 2, Section 6.   [10] See Chapter 1, Section 3.

[11] Indeed, some sources felt the biggest issue for cloud, although little discussed, was responsibility for the underlying network, and who takes the risk of its failure (sometimes, integrators).

adoption of cloud computing (sometimes within a larger package), or contracts for supporting services for or working with the primary cloud service.

Also, while cloud users' own individual end users (eg employees or customers) may use services procured, we focus only on the user's relationship with its provider, not its own end users. The sole exception involves integrators, where we discuss wholesale contracts with their providers, where they are users, and their customers, where they are providers.

3. Cloud Providers' Perspectives

The starting point for cloud contracts is usually providers' standard terms. Generally these are provider-favourable and designed for high-volume, low-cost, standard commoditized services on shared multi-tenant infrastructure. However, as many providers' standard terms do not accommodate enterprise users' requirements, cloud users have sought to make terms more balanced and appropriate to their circumstances. There seems to have been some movement, particularly for large users. Nevertheless, our research indicates that some providers' negotiations are very process-driven, particularly at the lower price end, where providers seemed unable or unwilling to accommodate differences such as corporate structures entailing (for users) separate localized contracts for non-US affiliates.

4. Cloud Users' Perspectives

4.1 Introduction

Before discussing changes requested by users, we first discuss why they may want changes, and the factors that influence whether providers accede.

Drivers for users to seek changes to providers' standard terms may be internal or external. Internal reasons obviously include commercial issues, such as required high service levels for mission-critical services, and risk allocation between user and provider (particularly provider liability). External drivers are chiefly regulatory: the need to comply with laws and regulations, including regulatory action. However, other external drivers are possible. Insurers' role in cloud market evolution is likely to increase.[12] Insurers may influence terms by, for example, insisting on certain certifications before agreeing to insure services; although according to one specialist UK cloud insurer, more providers than users were insuring, mainly for liability/errors and omissions.

Factors affecting cloud contract terms' development will be both demand and supply led. Large users such as governments are demanding more customer-friendly terms. Integrators, smaller or niche/specialist providers, and market entrants are offering or agreeing to such terms, making contract terms a source of competitive advantage. Accordingly, we believe standard terms will improve for users as the market develops.

Our findings tie in with a CIF survey of 450 decision-makers in private and public sector organizations, which found that while 48 per cent of organizations polled were already using cloud, only 52 per cent of those (particularly larger organizations) had negotiated

---

[12] Currently, many insurers view cloud as outsourcing, which many policies already cover.

their contracts. 45 per cent had no opportunity to negotiate (click-through terms, discussed below). Therefore, about half of such users' cloud contracts were negotiated.[13]

4.2 Risk management, internal controls, governance, and awareness: the click-through 'trap'?

Many providers' roots lie in click-through web services offered to consumers or SMEs. Users are presented with providers' standard contract terms and 'click through' to accept, without any opportunity for negotiation. With many services, the only additional step is for users to enter credit card details, whereupon they may start using the service. This history seems reflected in cloud services' terms and sign-up procedures generally. These are often click-through, as cloud services' nature enables use of a click-through consumer-based distribution model. Some providers deliberately choose that model for cloud. Others maintain generic click-through terms for 'self-service' customer-managed services, targeting smaller or trial users, but (possibly regionalized) framework or master agreements for larger users, enabling online purchase of specific services.

For providers, click-through may eliminate negotiation costs and reduce legal liabilities and other risks.[14] Some users noted that some providers, even large ones, had insufficient in-house legal resources to deal with users' requests to change terms, which might be another reason why they refuse to negotiate. One IaaS provider stated that no customer had ever requested changes to its click-through terms. Another provider was considering moving to 'click-through only' specifically to avoid negotiation time/costs.

However, for users, click-through fosters a bypass, sometimes deliberate, of institutional procurement processes.[15] A 2010 survey found 50 per cent of IT and IT security specialists (44 per cent in Europe) were unaware of at least some cloud computing resources deployed in their organizations.[16] Of decision-makers accountable for cloud services, a 'surprisingly high' number responded 'don't know' to several key questions in a 2011 survey.[17]

While click-through may enable more efficient and flexible IT services provisioning, users' risk exposures may be affected. As certain data protection regulators have noted,[18] click-through's speed and ease means some customers may be tempted to accept providers' standard terms online, to obtain the desired service quickly, without considering fully those terms' nature or effect, or undergoing their organization's standard

---

[13] CIF, *Paper Three Contracting Cloud Services—A Guide to Best Practice* (2011) (CIF3).

[14] However, non-negotiated standard terms may be unenforceable in some circumstances, even against businesses (eg under the UK Unfair Contract Terms Act 1977). See Chapter 13.

[15] Possibly encouraged by some IT functions' perceived lack of responsiveness, and a desire to deploy quickly without the perceived delays of dealing with internal IT, security or legal functions—for example David Linthicum, '3 Reasons Cloud App Development Is Taking Off' (*InfoWorld*, 20 October 2011), <http://www.infoworld.com/d/cloud-computing/3-reasons-cloud-app-development-taking-176439> (accessed 5 March 2013): 'Employees frustrated with the wait for corporate IT to solve a business problem simply hire their own developers and use PaaS as a cheap way to get their applications built, tested, and deployed.' A survey found that many organizations allowed 'rogue cloud use' that bypassed IT functions, for costs-saving reasons. Symantec, 'Avoiding the Hidden Costs of Cloud' (*Symantec*, 2013).

Perhaps, also, users are habituated to 'clicking through' to agree terms automatically from websites' standard processes for online sales of consumer products or services. In this sense, click-through for cloud contracts reflects the influence of consumer distribution models.

[16] Ponemon Institute, *Security of Cloud Computing Users: A Study of US and Europe IT Practitioners* (2010).

[17] A poll of some 450 decision-makers on behalf of CIF—CIF3 (n. 13).

[18] Der ArbeitskreiseTechnik und Medien der Konferenz der Datenschutzbeauftragten des Bundes und der Länder, *Orientierungshilfe—Cloud Computing version 1.0* (2011).

procurement procedures (such as legal or data protection review, security evaluation, or other risk assessments).

Upon discovering their employees' subscriptions for cloud services on providers' standard terms, some users have attempted to negotiate more acceptable terms. One SaaS provider noted some users were unaware that other internal departments used its service; the user could consolidate its services only after its IT department discovered the position. Some cloud services have been used without any written contract, whether because they were free, and/or being trialled as a pilot or test.[19]

Some employees may bypass internal procurement procedures because services are free of charge, at least for basic services. However, 'free of charge' or 'low cost' does not mean 'free of risk' or 'low risk'. Legal, regulatory, or reputational risks may exist, particularly if data involved are not 'fake' test data but 'real', perhaps even confidential or personal data. Furthermore, organizations may be charged for essential supporting services or 'extras' beyond the 'free' component, for example Postini spam filtering for Google Apps SaaS.

Even with negotiated contracts, some users' lawyers commented that their involvement had not been sought early enough: 'Business or procurement people negotiate without lawyers in the room; eventually the contract gets to legal staff, but not soon enough!' It is difficult for lawyers to change contract terms when told that terms have already been agreed to, and that services are going live shortly, being asked to 'just do a quick review'.

Not involving lawyers from the outset may, in some organizations, be prevalent with other types of contracts too. But while attempts to circumvent legal scrutiny may expedite deals, they may also expose organizations to liability and other legal risks. Sometimes, users' lawyers were asked to draft or review cloud contracts without being told the service's nature or purpose. This also poses risks: IaaS differs from SaaS. SaaS storage services for managing customers' personal data should be approached differently from services that, for instance, only record meteorological readings.

Providers have greater control in cloud, particularly with SaaS, with correspondingly reduced user control, as witness publicity regarding limitations in Microsoft Office 365's 'P' Plan. Here, the number of emails users could receive in 24 hours was restricted.[20] This provider constraint, which would not be possible with email applications on internal servers, illustrates that users need to scrutinize contractual terms before sign-up. However, procedurally, sometimes providers make terms available only late in the sign-up process, which may make it harder for users to compare offerings at an early stage.

The above suggests that some organizations may need to consider and address governance and cultural issues in their overall risk-management strategy, both internally and in relations with providers. Without scrutiny of policies, procedures, and practices,

---

[19] For example, in response to a freedom of information request regarding Chelsea and Westminster Hospital's tests of cloud computing for health care involving Flexiant, the Data Capture and Auto Identification Reference Project (DACAR) based at Chelsea and Westminster Hospital, and Edinburgh Napier University, the hospital replied: 'There is no contractual agreement between Flexiant and Chelsea and Westminster Hospital Foundation Trust at this time.' Letter dated 3 August 2011 (on file with authors).

CIF, Paper eight UK Cloud adoption and trends for 2013 (2013) (CIF8) 12 confirmed that 59% of cloud users surveyed favour 'try-before-you-buy', conducting pilots/trials before contracting formally for a cloud service they had not used before.

[20] Ed Bott, 'Small Businesses, Beware the Office 365 Fine Print' (*ZDNet*, 21 October 2011), <http://www.zdnet.com/blog/bott/small-businesses-beware-the-office-365-fine-print/4151> (accessed 5 March 2013).

including training, some may find themselves committed[21] to contracts on terms unfavourable to them, exposing them to legal risk, including breach of legal or regulatory obligations with possible civil, or even criminal, liability.

Some users, such as News International, flag credit card charges by employees signing up for Amazon Web Services' IaaS and the like, partly to secure better block pricing.[22] However, flagging may be impossible with free services. Another user, which is also a provider, bans employees from clicking through on standard cloud contracts.

There may also be an educational issue for users' lawyers. Some providers' lawyers pointed out that users' lawyers sometimes raised points on providers' standard terms for the 'wrong reasons', such as 'going to town' to justify their fees! The main reason was such lawyers' lack of understanding about cloud and what the user was buying. Many approached cloud contracts as software licences or technology acquisitions, rather than contracts for services. Others treated them as classic IT outsourcing, without taking proper account of cloud's unique features. One SaaS provider found that the largest users negotiated least, whether because the deal was relatively small for them, or because they understood SaaS better, so did not seek terms inappropriate to cloud. However, it must be said that users' lawyers have also suggested that some providers' terms are too software licence-orientated and could be more cloud-appropriate. Indeed, our sources considered that, even in the IT industry, many intermediaries treated cloud computing as involving the supply of products or licences rather than provision of services. This all seems to indicate the market's immaturity.

While not the key focus of this chapter, precontractual due diligence should not be overlooked. This may include security,[23] disaster recovery, data return/retention/format on exit, and exit strategies[24] discussed below.

4.3 To negotiate, or not to negotiate?

Users may decide that small initial pilots or tests of moving specific workloads or processes to the cloud do not justify the time/costs of negotiating providers' standard terms. For example, the UK government online services prototype Alpha.gov.uk employed Amazon's IaaS on Amazon's standard click-through terms.[25] Similarly, Warwickshire County Council's pilot of Google Apps[26] commenced in late 2011 on Google's standard terms. Only when considering full migration of the relevant function, or processing of 'real' data, particularly personal data, might such users scrutinize contract terms.

However, can users negotiate? As with any commercial agreement, much depends on relative bargaining power. Large providers generally decline to change their standard

---

[21] Assuming relevant employees at least have ostensible authority to bind the organization, which seems likely.

[22] Paul Cheesbrough (CIO, News International), presentation (Amazon Summit 2011, London, 14 June 2011).

[23] For precontractual security checks (not limited to data protection), EU data protection authorities have suggested European Network and Information Security Agency, *Cloud Computing Information Assurance Framework* (2009).

[24] However, it seems only 45% of UK cloud users had a plan to migrate to another provider upon any service interruption or termination (with 12% responding 'don't know'). Similarly, only 45% of integrators had such a plan. CIF3 (n. 13) 9.

[25] Government Digital Service response to freedom of information request, 22 December 2011.

[26] Kathleen Hall, 'Warwickshire County Council Signs Google to Pilot G-Cloud E-mail Service' (*ComputerWeekly.com*, 19 September 2011), <http://www.computerweekly.com/news/2240105636/Warwickshire-County-Council-signs-Google-to-pilot-G-Cloud-e-mail-service> (accessed 5 March 2013).

terms, insisting on 'take it or leave it', even when requested by large users, for example integrators. Some users have had to 'take it', negotiating only commercial terms (price, payment frequency, or perhaps availability levels), because 'We needed them more than they needed us'. Others have walked away.

Some users have accepted providers' standard terms when faced with providers' refusal to negotiate.[27] Nevertheless, even large providers have departed from their standard terms to secure deals they perceive as sufficiently worthwhile, whether for financial, strategic, or reputational 'trophy' value. Examples are Google's deals to provide Google Apps SaaS to the City of Los Angeles[28] and the University of Cambridge.[29] Some smaller SaaS providers will consider larger customers' requests to change standard terms.

Generally, bigger users, particularly from regulated industries, try to negotiate more. Some even require contracts to be on *their* standard IT services or outsourcing terms, on a 'take it or leave it' basis. Such users, mainly government bodies and financial institutions, may have more purchasing power. Also, their internal procedures may make it difficult and time-consuming to contract on terms other than their own (eg, banks may require director sign-off for changes to their standard terms). To secure such users' business quickly, some providers may accept the user's terms, even though some terms may not be cloud-appropriate.[30]

Thus, both providers and large users want to contract on their own standard terms, although generally neither set of terms seems optimal for cloud arrangements.

4.4 Role of integrators

Our research suggests integrators are in a better position than end users to negotiate terms with providers.[31] Integrators may have ongoing relationships with providers, and perhaps stronger bargaining positions (with larger business volumes) if they use the same provider to service multiple customers. However, with large providers, even global integrators have had difficulty obtaining the changes that they, or their customers, needed for data protection or security purposes.

We found some end users contracted with integrators, rather than providers, because some integrators were prepared to give greater assurances than providers. For instance, some interviewees mentioned users contracting with integrators for Office 365, rather than using Office 365 on Microsoft's infrastructure, to obtain contractual assurances from integrators regarding liability/liability caps, service levels/credits, support, and backups that were not obtainable from Microsoft.

However, if the integrator's contract with the provider is not truly 'back to back', integrators bear the risks of any mismatch in obligations and liabilities. 'If we use a

---

[27] Text to n. 13.

[28] Although, reportedly, there have been problems: Jon Brodkin, 'Google Apps Hasn't Met LAPD's Security Requirements, City Demands Refund' (*ArsTechnica*, 20 October 2011), <http://arstechnica.com/business/news/2011/10/google-apps-hasnt-met-lapds-security-requirements-city-demands-refund.ars> (accessed 5 March 2013).

[29] Google, 'Google Apps Education Edition Agreement' (10 January 2010). Available at <http://www.ucs.cam.ac.uk/googleapps/google-apps-cambridge-contract.pdf> (accessed 5 March 2013).

[30] See Chapter 5.

[31] CIF findings were similar. For example, a (provider-favourable) right for providers to change contracts unilaterally was agreed in contracts with 33% of users, but only 19% of integrators—CIF, *Cloud UK Paper two: The Impact upon the IT Supply Chain* (2011) (CIF2). Available at <http://www.cloudindustryforum.org/white-papers/cloud-the-impact-upon-it-supply> (accessed 1 June 2013). Despite their seemingly better bargaining position, however, only 40% of integrators (cf 52% of end users) 'consciously negotiated' (ie presumably were aware their organization had negotiated) provider contracts. CIF2, 12.

cloud service, as a systems integrator we have to be very careful about what the customer requires, because we might not be able to get that from the cloud service provider', one stated. 'We're taking a big slice of the risk pie', another noted. It appears that at least some integrators make a calculated decision to take that risk, to gain or retain users' business by better meeting their needs. They consider that risks in some respects may be spread over end users, and take a pragmatic approach to aggregated risk. This position may also receive some encouragement from insurers.[32]

Nevertheless, integrators' greater willingness to assume risk is not unlimited. Integrators noted that where users insisted on a particular provider, if the integrator could not persuade the provider to amend its terms to meet customer requirements, it had to make that clear to the customer, sometimes leaving the customer to contract directly with the provider. Hence, while some integrators do not wish to invest in infrastructure, others already are, or are considering providing cloud services on infrastructure they control. This enables them to offer users such as banks the assurances needed while managing their own exposure.

Integrators may also offer mixed cloud/non-cloud services, particularly to large users, where the cloud service is part of a larger package of services or 'whole business' deal, including, for example, Internet connectivity or consultancy services. Similarly, customers may seek SaaS management or monitoring tools within more traditional large outsourcing deals. Contracts for such deals will obviously reflect the cloud component's relatively minor position.

4.5 Other relevant factors

The extent users need to negotiate contracts depends on how much control over users' applications and/or data the particular system's design affords users and providers, and how 'customer-friendly' a provider's standard terms are.

With paid-for services, providers are generally more willing to accept liability (or greater liability), and agree to other user-requested commitments or measures, than they would with free services.[33] The more providers are paid, the more they are willing to concede.

Market factors are also relevant. A global user noted that one large provider was more flexible than others because it was trying to 'catch up' in cloud, and indeed was more flexible with cloud than other contract types.

5. Cloud Contract Terms: Detailed Analysis

5.1 Liability: exclusion/limits and remedies for breach of warranties/indemnities

Providers' exclusion of liability, particularly for outages and data loss, was generally the biggest issue for users.[34] Providers try to exclude liability altogether,[35] or restrict liability

---

[32] Marsh Ltd, *The Cloud Risk Framework: Informing Decisions About Moving to the Cloud* (2012).
[33] See Chapter 3.
[34] In a CIF survey, providers excluded liability for data loss for 34% of UK cloud users, accepting capped liability for data loss and breach of contract for 54%. With integrators, providers accepted more liability: 20% of providers excluded liability; 31% agreed capped liability; and 27% accepted full liability. CIF3 (n. 13).
[35] See Chapter 3.

as much as possible,[36] because they provide commoditized services. Understandably, providers may not wish to be exposed to, for example, £100 million of liability for a deal worth £1 million; unlimited liability could put smaller providers out of business.

According to our research, providers usually state that liability is non-negotiable, and 'everyone else accepts it'. Even large users had difficulty getting providers to accept any monetary liability. One global user stated that generally it 'had to lump it'. Another stated, 'They won't move'. Refusal to accept any liability was cited as a 'deal-breaker' by several users. Although liability exclusion is more widespread and more acceptable under US jurisdictions, some US users still refused to deal with some providers who excluded liability.

However, some global users negotiated successfully for provider liability. This might be more common where cloud is part of a larger deal, such as telecommunications. If liability was agreed upon, it was almost invariably accepted only in limited circumstances, restricted to narrowly defined types of damage: typically, 'direct' losses only, with no liability for indirect or consequential losses. Where liability was accepted for 'direct losses', that term's definition might be much discussed.[37]

Some users, particularly those who could insist on their own standard terms, such as financial institutions or government, secured unlimited liability for defined types of breach or loss, notably breach of confidentiality, privacy or data protection laws, or breach of regulatory or security requirements, such as breaches giving rise to regulatory fines. One integrator commented, 'For privacy breaches there is no cap that people will agree that would be sufficient'.

However, more commonly, liability was capped, sometimes with different caps for different types of losses, often limited according to amounts paid in total or over a period, such as 100 per cent or 125 per cent of six months' fees.[38] Some providers agreed to a higher percentage or longer period of fees for certain deals, such as where fees were paid up front.[39] Users who could impose their own terms might cap liability at a higher proportion, for instance 150 per cent of charges paid over the last year.

Some telecommunications providers appeared more willing to accept some liability, perhaps because they control Internet connections to users and therefore have greater control regarding connectivity and service availability. Smaller providers also seemed more flexible: one enterprise-oriented SaaS provider accepted liability for outages as standard if caused by Internet connectivity failures at its data centres, whereas many large providers reject any monetary liability for outages, however caused. As previously mentioned, some integrators also seemed more willing to accept liability: for example, a global user contracted with an integrator who accepted liability for data loss when the provider would not accept liability.

Conversely, providers have argued that customers want to have their cake and eat it, seeking services that are cheap (because commoditized) while requesting greater assurances (no or reduced liability exclusions/limitations or higher service levels). More technologically sophisticated users stated that they arranged backups themselves, for

---

[36] For example, in the UK, liability cannot be excluded for negligence causing death or personal injury. Unfair Contract Terms Act 1977 (UCTA), s. 2(1).

[37] See Chapter 3 for a discussion of the scope of 'direct loss'.

[38] Interestingly, an integrator commented that some providers who indicated willingness to offer capped liability subsequently reverted to total liability exclusion. Also, one SaaS provider observed that its liability ceiling was not negotiated as often as one might think, although it was questioned more in higher-value deals.

[39] CIF recommends providers consider offering higher caps for higher fees—CIF3 (n. 13) 13.

example to their own servers, while a provider noted that users were beginning to understand that they could not expect much provider liability for low-cost services.[40]

Some SaaS providers emphasized that they provide services, not licences, and preferred not to include any contractual software licences in order to avoid associated risks. With open-source software, providers excluded liability for IPR infringement. Many users wanted warranties that IPRs regarding application software used in the cloud were the provider's, and that the service did not infringe any third-party rights, with appropriate indemnities. This might be impossible where providers licensed applications from third parties to offer SaaS services. To address third-party IPRs, for instance IPRs of the provider's own suppliers, some users requested copies of third-party indemnities to providers, seeking back-to-back indemnities from providers. The indemnity's scope might require scrutiny for suitability. For example, one global provider, whose SaaS service included supply of content, limited its liability to copyright infringement, excluding patent-related infringements. Generally, as with other kinds of liability, IPR indemnities were limited to direct losses and capped. One global user declined to deal with a SaaS provider who restricted IPR indemnities to certain countries' IPRs only, with limited amount and losses covered.

When considering provider liability, contractual provisions are not the only factor. Several sources noted that providers offering unlimited liability may not be creditworthy should losses arise; yet, users may find it easier to propose to their directors contracts where providers assume rather than exclude liability. Focusing on contractual terms rather than, for example, financial standing, may thus be too narrow for risk-management purposes.

5.2 Resilience, availability, performance, and service levels

5.2.1 Data integrity, resilience, and business continuity

A common theme was business continuity and disaster recovery: how to ensure integrity and availability of cloud data and applications. One user noted, 'Providers tend to say cloud is very redundant, fault-tolerant, there's no need for disaster recovery—but there is'.

In practice, many providers make backups. Some undertake to do so; however, most will not warrant data integrity, or accept liability for data loss. Where a SaaS service included supply of certain data, liability was limited to replacing any lost data.

Under confidentiality provisions, providers may be liable for data security breaches, because unauthorized accesses to user data may breach confidentiality; however, data loss or corruption might not constitute confidentiality breaches. Therefore, additional specific warranties (with liability) regarding data loss/corruption may be important. Some global users secured such warranties; for example, unlimited liability for data loss/corruption (for one financial institution), and even monetary compensation for data loss including recovery costs (for another global user).

One non-European telecommunications provider undertakes to back up data and guarantees their integrity, commenting that Amazon did not because its charges are low. Many providers, including Amazon, offer backup as a separate service: if users pay extra,

---

[40] Even short guides on cloud recommend user backups: Cloudtweaks, 'Cloud Computing Security—10 Tips for Keeping Your Cloud Data Safe', 5 October 2012, <http://www.cloudtweaks.com/2012/10/cloud-computing-security-10-tips-for-keeping-your-cloud-data-safe> (accessed 5 March 2013).

the provider undertakes to make backups and assumes liability for backup integrity and data loss.[41]

Providers such as Amazon stress that cloud involves shared responsibility. Both users and providers have responsibility for data integrity, backup and security, and allocation of responsibilities and risks that needs careful consideration.[42] Users generally have more control with IaaS/PaaS than with SaaS.[43] Our interviewees who were more technically aware, such as technology businesses or integrators, tended to recognize the need for their own backup strategy, rather than expecting providers' basic services to include backup. An integrator using cloud to provide SaaS services to its own users implemented its own disaster recovery procedures, backing up or 'failing over' to the same or separate data centres or another provider, depending on end users' risk tolerance.

5.2.2 *Service levels, service credits*

Approaches to service level agreements (SLAs), for instance commitments on availability levels and performance, varied. This was probably because availability levels are often quite high, and capacities/throughput, performance, and service levels are normally negotiable commercial issues varying with user requirements, rather than legal issues.[44]

Standards are still lacking, making comparison of different services difficult. In large deals, methods for measuring service levels are often debated, with users wanting numerous key performance indicators (KPIs). At the low end, providers stipulate the metrics, generally not exceeding 5 or 10 KPIs.

Providers state that, because they provide commoditized services, they cannot negotiate service levels. One enterprise-oriented SaaS provider did not even offer SLAs. Only about 0.2 per cent of its users had requested SLAs; fewer still wanted as high as 99.7 per cent uptime. Possibly, this was because its service was designed for very high uptime levels, and information on historic levels was published.

If availability, reliability, and performance are vital, as with mission-critical applications or real-time services, users may consider how load on providers' infrastructure from other users can affect the user's application performance; how well the service handles peak spikes; how sufficient robustness is ensured, and so on.[45] One issue which has seen little discussion is the risk of additional users adversely affecting the service, because cloud capacity is not in fact unlimited. This may result in SLA breaches, yet reportedly users generally did not try to restrict how quickly providers added new users, or how much capacity they could offer new users.

Users with mission-critical applications may accordingly seek higher availability levels, warranties regarding response times, undertakings not to terminate services without notification and consent, longer prior notification of proposed maintenance downtime, and perhaps notification of usage exceeding agreed limits (to allow user investigation and management) rather than immediately throttling usage and slowing performance

---

[41] One enterprise-oriented SaaS provider noted that *force majeure* was often raised regarding provider liability, depending on whether it was required to make backups, and whether the *force majeure* incident also affected the backup.

[42] See Amazon.com Inc., 'Amazon Web Services: Overview of Security Processes' (March 2013).

[43] See Chapter 2.

[44] For example, guaranteeing different levels at different prices. CIF recommends providers should document management systems, processes, and resources for consistent service delivery, and specify whether users may audit business continuity or disaster recovery processes, as well as publishing average availability times: CIF3 (n. 13) 12.

[45] See Chapter 3.

without consulting users. However, providers are unlikely to warrant latency (network and systems response time), unless perhaps they control the network. For example, some telecommunications providers or integrators will warrant low latencies, for a price. One provider considered that what users truly want, but providers did not offer, was guaranteed application performance, for example, X simultaneous users with maximum Y response time. It believed focus on application performance management/monitoring would increase if this were offered.

Users may also consider methods and time to restore data from backup if systems fail or data are lost. One integrator commented that providers' response time requirements were 'Nothing like what clients insist upon'.[46] Time lag varies with providers, from seconds for some business-oriented services (which accordingly charge more), to days.

SLAs are often referenced by linking to providers' published website details, which providers may amend. This puts the burdensome onus on users to monitor providers' sites for changes,[47] so some users have required prenotification of impending SLA changes.

For SLA breaches, remedies are normally excluded, except as specifically provided. Providers generally exclude remedies other than service credits, even for total service failures. However, some allow optional termination if SLAs fall below a certain percentage, even accepting liability for monetary compensation if (but only if) terminated. Standard terms generally limit circumstances when service credits are given; for example, only for failures arising from matters under the provider's control, or only if credits are claimed within a certain period, and so on. Although perhaps counter-intuitive, one global user, who uses cloud to provide real-time services to end users, did not insist on performance warranties or even service credits, as any outage would be highly detrimental reputationally, so monetary compensation would probably be inadequate, and credits were difficult to quantify. Therefore, it decided simply to accept standard SLAs.

Even where service levels are non-negotiable, service credits for SLA breaches may be. While preferring service credits, some providers offer benchmarked 'money back' rebates or monetary compensation.

5.2.3 Transparency

Our research indicated two main ways for users to obtain availability data. Users may monitor availability themselves, or providers may provide information: for example, specific webpages that are kept updated which users may check.

A global user stated that, for contracts incorporating SLAs, it further required statistics reporting. Similarly, a non-European telecom provider offered SLAs according to users' requests, and would commit to keeping users informed proactively within certain boundaries ('tell them before they tell us').

Where availability was critical, users might monitor services or applications themselves, such as for failure of VM instances, using provider tools or (as many providers disallow user access to their tools) public tools, or the user's own tools. However, excessive user monitoring may affect application performance and increase usage charges. After assessing the impact of monitoring, one large user was persuaded not to monitor. One global user also noted that providers' usage monitoring for billing purposes might

---

[46] CIF recommends providers should specify protocols and SLAs for restoring data from backups—CIF3 (n. 13) 11.

[47] See Chapter 3.

affect performance. Therefore, for services requiring near real-time responses, some users sought rights to require providers to pause or stop monitoring if materially detrimental to performance. One integrator stated that it usually monitored charges itself, depending on the service's set-up.

It seems providers generally could improve transparency regarding availability, service levels, and so on by providing data to users proactively. Illustrating that greater transparency is possible technically, trust.salesforce.com and Microsoft Dynamics CRM were cited as services enabling users to check, even in real time, data on service performance and availability. Such transparency may involve providers in technical changes and costs. Generally, it is providers with large enterprise customer bases who provide such data.

5.2.4 Users' liability?

Another issue is users' liability to providers, particularly where users employ cloud to deliver services to their end users. Unsurprisingly, users who could negotiate their contracts would not accept liability to providers. One global user declined to contract with a provider who required such liability.

Cloud users also declined to indemnify providers for actions of the users' customers as they cannot control such actions, even if they constituted breaches of providers' terms and caused loss to providers. A compromise was for providers to terminate or suspend the service, with sufficient prior notice for users to investigate and terminate the culprit's account if necessary. Such users also ensured their contracts with end users allowed termination for misconduct, with indemnities from end users.

5.3 Regulatory issues

Generally, the role of providers regarding their users' compliance obligations seems ill-defined, misunderstood, or poorly accommodated by providers. A common theme was that many providers, in standard terms or even negotiations, would not consider that users have regulatory or other legal obligations, and that they may need to demonstrate compliance to regulators. Some users expressed frustration at providers' lack of empathy with their compliance obligations, especially in Europe. Some users addressed this issue by using cloud only in less highly regulated jurisdictions, for example certain Asian countries. Integrators are 'caught in the middle', as the compliance responsibilities are generally not theirs but their end users'.

Some providers seemingly have not considered the impact of regulatory requirements on their terms; several users noted this.[48] One discovered, after protracted negotiations, that a global provider had never conducted a regulatory review of its own services or terms, let alone its contract with its own sub-provider. Reportedly, some users, to save costs, decided to use cloud despite inadequate contract terms, 'taking a view' on regulators discovering and enforcing any non-compliance. However, one integrator

---

[48] To some extent, this may reflect some users' lack of focus on regulatory or legal issues when procuring cloud services, as mentioned in Section 4.2 above. For example. see Edward F Moltzen, 'Analysis: Dropbox Carries Risks for SMBs' (*CRN*, 4 November 2011) <http://www.crn.com/news/cloud/231902380/analysis-dropbox-carries-risks-for-smbs.htm> (accessed 5 March 2013), noting that the then new Dropbox for Teams cloud storage service did not meet Payment Card Industry requirements, the US Health Insurance Portability and Accountability Act, or the Sarbanes-Oxley Act. Dropbox responded that customers who beta-tested the service before launch were concerned with collaboration and ease-of-sharing, not these requirements or laws.

commented that, although providers refused to negotiate privacy and security issues, some agreed changes upon users refusing to sign otherwise.

Regulatory issues varied with jurisdiction. More issues reportedly arose with, for example Germany or France, than with the UK. But with European users generally, and users outside government/financial sectors, data protection laws were the most commonly cited regulatory issue. This seems unsurprising: data protection laws are 'horizontal' not 'vertical', regulating all sectors, and data controllers remain responsible when processing data in the cloud. Financial sector regulation was another key regulatory issue.

For customers generally, data location and confidentiality were the top data protection law concerns, followed by data processor/transfer agreements and sub-providers' roles, while for financial institutions the biggest issues were security requirements and audit rights.

5.3.1 Data location and data export

Users were less concerned about colocation[49] within a third party's data centre than about data centre location. Many users were concerned about locations of data centre(s) employed by their providers, particularly if outside the European Economic Area (EEA). Conversely, other users specifically wanted data kept offshore, such as 'in the Channel Islands but never in the USA'.

The DPD prohibits transfers of 'personal data' outside the EEA except in specified circumstances.[50] This prohibition is significant. Global users have refused to contract with providers who declined to include terms to comply with such transfer requirements.

The CIF recommends providers offering EEA-only locations should inform users accordingly. Indeed, EEA users might consider this a selling point. It also recommends that providers disclose all data centre locations, including those used for backups, and whether data may be transferred outside the EEA.[51] However, some providers will not disclose such locations.

Users have sought, and sometimes obtained, warranties or undertakings that all data centres used for their data were in the EU/EEA, or that data were kept within the EU. One UK-based global user stated that, although it did not process personal data in the cloud, it still required its global provider to confine processing to EU data centres, and, should it nevertheless transfer data to the US, it must be certified under Safe Harbor and comply with its principles.

Some services allow users to choose locations of data centres used to process users' data, for example EU-only.[52] Providers are increasingly offering, albeit with exceptions, to restrict data to users' chosen locations as standard.[53]

Verifying that data are actually processed in the claimed locations is difficult technically. One provider noted that some providers were misleadingly labelling servers as 'EU', when data could be processed elsewhere. A public sector user felt warranties of UK-only data location could be untrue, citing a hosted services provider that stated data storage was UK-only, but whose IP address indicated a US location.[54]

---

[49] Sharing hardware or software with other customers in the same location: see Chapter 1.
[50] See Chapter 10.   [51] CIF3 (n. 13) 11.   [52] See Chapter 10.
[53] Amazon's terms (15 March 2012) Section 3.2 state: 'We will not move Your Content from your selected AWS regions without notifying you, unless required to comply with the law or requests of governmental entities.' Available at <http://aws.amazon.com/agreement> (accessed 5 March 2013). See also Chapter 10.
[54] However, an IP address may not always reflect geographical location. A multinational corporate may, for example, route all communications through its US HQ, thus identifying it externally as having US IP addresses, irrespective of local offices' locations.

Users may need location information for reasons other than the DPD transfer restriction. The DPD requires controllers to choose processors providing 'sufficient guarantees' regarding security measures for processing, and ensure compliance with those measures. This may be difficult without more transparency regarding providers' systems, data centre locations, and transmissions.

Although the DPD allows transfers *within* the EEA, many users, particularly public sector users, further require data centres to be within their own country. One provider stated that because it did not currently use any UK data centres, it could not offer its solution to UK central government departments such as the Cabinet Office, or the Department for Work and Pensions, which required use of UK data centres only.[55] Integrators also noted this position.

Our research is consistent with CIF surveys that found that most UK users considered it important for data to be stored in the EEA, with a significant proportion believing data must be confined to the UK.[56]

Providers' attempts to address these issues include using partners with data centres in the required countries, or using private clouds. While data location can be circumscribed by such commercial or technical means, this involves greater costs, because providers may be unable to use resources efficiently.

Salesforce was cited as allowing users to check their data's location in near real time with its trust.salesforce.com webpage. Possibly, this is because, historically, it serves business users, whereas many other cloud services' initial customer base mainly comprised individual consumers. Technically, providers may be able to engineer their systems to offer similar information. However, the expense involved may be passed on to customers, and, as mentioned above, verifying claimed locations is still difficult technically.

Data location is a problematic, even emotionally charged, issue. One global user said that if it could not confine its data to the EU, it would nevertheless avoid the US because of the USA PATRIOT Act and litigation issues; financial institutions particularly raised this legislation. EU providers and others have suggested that data would be safer in, for example, a German-only cloud.[57] However, the US is not the only nation that may access data to combat terrorism or crime, and this Act's high profile might reflect some marketing opportunism and political concerns regarding the US exercising powers extraterritorially, more than legal differences.[58] We discuss law enforcement access provisions below.

As data are often accessed remotely, data centre location is not the only factor affecting data location. Many sources noted that an EEA provider with EEA-only data centres may, to provide round-the-clock 'follow the sun' services, use non-EEA support staff, or sub-contractors who have (or are given) access to customer data or metadata. Remote access to user data by affiliates, support staff, or sub-contractors may involve 'transfer'. Even where such personnel cannot log in to user accounts, they may be able

---

[55] Although see Chapter 5. This seems similar to US regulation, such as the International Traffic in Arms Regulatory framework, requiring that certain cloud services for the federal government be housed in US-located IT infrastructure accessible only to vetted US citizens. For example, Amazon launched a cloud service to comply with these requirements. Werner Vogels (Amazon CTO), 'Expanding the Cloud—The AWS GovCloud (US) Region' (*All Things Distributed*, 16 August 2011), <http://www.allthingsdistributed.com/2011/08/aws_govcloud_region.html>, and 'AWS Security and Compliance Center', available at <http://aws.amazon.com/security/#features> (both accessed 5 March 2013).

[56] CIF3 (n. 13) 8; CIF8 (n. 19) 9.

[57] Cornelius Rahn, 'Deutsche Telekom Wants "German Cloud" to Shield Data from US' (*Bloomberg*, 13 September 2011).

[58] See Chapter 11.

to view metadata, such as email delivery times. To troubleshoot account issues, users may give login details, including passwords, to support staff, in which case user consent may be assumed. However, consent cannot necessarily be assumed where users have not been informed that non-EEA support staff have technical ability to access personal data remotely, even when not given login details by individuals seeking assistance. One user called potential access by support staff 'a huge hole', citing a provider who insisted its service involved no international data transfers because its data centre was in the EU, seemingly overlooking the fact that its support, maintenance, even code debugging might occur in India, and that therefore data could be transferred to staff in India. Some providers address this issue by using a recognized method of transfer to non-EEA staff or sub-contractors, such as establishing contracts based on model clauses.[59]

Irrespective of data protection, existing contracts may restrict data location. For example, one global user's service, provided to end users as a cloud service, includes provision to end users of licensed content subject to third-party IPRs. Certain content licences required this user to store the content on its own secured servers, and to know its location always. Obviously, such content cannot be stored in-cloud in circumstances involving possible distribution or transfer across different data centres. Even within one data centre, a user's stored data may migrate locations, depending on systems used. Thus, some IPR licensing schemes may hinder cloud adoption, and raising licensors' awareness of how cloud storage works may be important.

Other regulatory issues are possible. For example, locations of providers and data centres may be relevant under export control laws, mentioned as restricting transfer of certain information or software to particular countries, with remote access again raising issues.

5.3.2 *Data processor agreements, and sub-processors*

Users who are 'controllers' of 'personal data' under the DPD must meet certain requirements when engaging 'processors' to process personal data for them. The DPD's minimum requirements differ across the EEA, having been increased by some Member States.[60]

Many providers' standard terms are silent on status, or they state that the provider acts only as 'data processor'. This seems mainly for providers' protection, to try to ensure they are not regarded as 'controllers' (with greater obligations and liabilities), although contractual labels are not determinative.

The DPD requires the contract between user/controller and provider/processor to contain an agreement, often termed a 'data processor agreement', requiring the processor to process personal data only according to the controller's instructions and to take certain security measures. Some enterprise-oriented providers' standard terms may, to assist users' DPD compliance, specifically include a data processor agreement. Otherwise, users who are controllers of personal data may want it included. It is common, for example, in financial institutions' standard contracts.

However, some providers would not go beyond stating 'processor' status. The underlying reason may be that the DPD ill suits cloud. Even treating infrastructure providers as 'processors' may be inappropriate, as they provide IT resources and suitable (but standardized) environments for users to use those resources, rather than actively processing data for users. Providers have therefore considered it inappropriate to agree to 'process' data only on users' instructions, as it is for *users* to control their own processing.

---

[59] See Chapter 10.   [60] See Chapter 8.

With shared, standardized, multi-tenant infrastructure and environment, it would be difficult or impossible to comply should different customers issue conflicting instructions regarding the resources or environment.[61]

Nevertheless, some providers have accepted a data processor agreement. Conversely, where providers would only agree to general obligations to comply with data protection laws, one global user stated it had accepted these terms with large providers who it knew, from previous dealings, had implemented proper data protection processes.

Providers' terms generally entitle them to use sub-contractors, for example for support services. One fundamental issue is, are cloud sub-providers 'sub-processors' of personal data? Although the matter is arguable, this chapter assumes they are. EU data protection authorities consider that, for compliance, controllers must know all possible cloud sub-processors, perhaps even to data centre operator level.[62]

Whatever the data type, some users wanted contracts to restrict sub-contracting (including of support services), and to stipulate that providers' contractual obligations were unaffected by any sub-contracting. Users in large deals normally prohibited sub-contracting without their consent, except on certain mandatory terms to providers on preapproved lists. Users sometimes asked to see the sub-contract, or even contracted directly with sub-contractors for obligations including confidentiality. One global user required rights to vet and veto any sub-contractors who had access to any data it stored or processed in-cloud, or who provided services worth over a certain percentage of contract value, as with managed services. For smaller deals, it wanted notification of any such sub-contractors' identities, but not necessarily veto rights. With SaaS, it still inquired as to who the sub-providers were and their locations. Similarly, other global users indicated they would not allow sub-contracting or assignments without express prior consent. One SaaS provider confirmed that some users insisted on consent as a precondition for assignments. Therefore, at least some users who were able to negotiate contracts have required the safeguards and precontract information stipulated by data protection authorities.

In summary, current data protection law puts both users and providers in difficult positions, with one or the other having to 'take a view' on contract terms, accepting that, with personal data, a data processor agreement is necessary by law, but may be meaningless or impossible to comply with in-cloud. Compliance may also necessitate investigation of any sub-providers and data centres used.

5.3.3 Data subject rights

If data subjects request their personal data from users, one SaaS provider noted that, as users have access to and control over data (including personal data) they choose to process in-cloud, provider involvement is unnecessary: users can retrieve requested personal data directly themselves. Nevertheless, one global user secured from a global provider an obligation to cooperate with it as necessary to respond to subject access requests. Similar wording is standard in UK government contracts, including the G-Cloud v1 framework agreement.[63]

Again, these sorts of terms, suitable for processing agents who have sole control of outsourced data, do not recognize cloud's 'self-service', tools-based nature.

---

[61] A possible exception involves private clouds outsourced to integrators, where integrators could follow instructions regarding infrastructure dedicated to and customized for the user concerned.

[62] See Chapter 8 and Article 29 Data Protection Working Party, WP196, *Opinion 05/2012 on Cloud Computing* (WP196).

[63] See Chapter 5.

5.4 Confidentiality, and rights to monitor/access/disclose/use customer data

5.4.1 Confidentiality

Providers may receive or have access to two main kinds of confidential data: data disclosed by users during contract negotiations (such as information on the service's intended purpose and usage), and data processed using the service. Both kinds may include personal or commercially sensitive data. Users may accordingly want confidentiality and/or non-disclosure agreements from providers. Sometimes, users secured unlimited liability for the former; liability for the latter proved more difficult, and can be a 'show stopper'.

Many users persuaded providers to accept liability, usually capped, for breach of confidentiality. Generally, users sought higher caps here. Users preferred capped liability from integrators, over no, or restricted liability, under providers' standard terms. Providers had, although rarely, accepted uncapped liability for breach of confidentiality, data disclosure, or data protection breaches, at least where limited to direct losses excluding contingent liabilities or consequential damage. Enterprise-oriented providers seemed more flexible with highly regulated users, even giving indemnities for breach of data protection obligations. Conversely, one non-EU provider always rejected any liability for confidentiality breaches.

Definitions of confidentiality breach and the cap's amount obviously involved careful consideration for users and providers, as did definitions of direct, indirect, and consequential losses. Some providers also considered that data loss per se was not a confidentiality breach, particularly with SaaS, capping such liability accordingly.[64]

Users negotiated for confidentiality obligations to survive contract termination, typically for five to seven years, depending on the data's nature. Some users wanted such obligations to continue indefinitely.

5.4.2 Access to user data; disclosure

Users fear unauthorized access to their data. Many providers have 'back doors' to access users' data, and contractually reserve access rights[65] for maintenance, servicing, support, or even security purposes. Other providers stated they had no such access, although they could terminate users' access.

Even some providers, who professed inability to access user data without customer login details, reserved access rights for maintenance and so on, acknowledging that certain employees *could* access data in 'emergencies'. Also, users may volunteer login details to staff when seeking support, although the scope of resulting access depends on the user's access privileges.

While some users had not negotiated service usage monitoring, others stipulated that information obtained from such monitoring, or from support/maintenance activities, must be treated as subject to confidentiality provisions. Some users restricted purposes for which providers could monitor usage: for example, only for security (filtering email for spam or malware), to establish and substantiate charges payable (how many end users had used the service), or to verify compliance with terms (size/capacity/bandwidth

---

[64] On 'personal data' in cloud computing see Chapter 7 and on responsibility for personal data in cloud computing, Chapter 8.

[65] See Chapter 3.

limits). Some users wanted to prohibit the use of resulting data for other purposes, and prohibit monitoring for other purposes. However, some providers rejected any restrictions on their monitoring rights. Others stated they could not technically monitor users' processing, for example within users' VMs.

Standard terms usually authorize providers to disclose users' data on court order, or if *requested* by law enforcement authorities.[66] Some providers' standard terms require them to notify a user immediately upon law enforcement or other official authorities' requests for that user's data, although, where laws forbid such notification, the term is qualified accordingly. Otherwise, users have required providers to notify them promptly on receiving any third-party requests (unless prohibited by law), to pass them on to the user (with integrators sending them to end users/customers), and to allow the user to make representations against disclosure. Indeed, financial institutions' standard terms may prohibit disclosure without their consent, although they accept that disclosures may be required under laws or court orders which would prevent providers from notifying users. Sometimes, providers felt that users under specific lawful intercept obligations, notably telecommunications users, endeavoured to 'pass off' those obligations to providers.

One SaaS provider's users had specific requirements regarding data location and ability to access data. For example, never outside country X, must be duplicated in country Y and elsewhere, never in country Z. It addressed by using affiliates and partners operating data centres in different countries. If an entity in one country was required by that country's laws to access data in a data centre in another country, it could not, as only the affiliate or partner had control over the data.

5.5 Security requirements, audit rights, security breaches or incidents, and incident response

Security is often cited as an issue in cloud computing, partly because of general concerns regarding loss of user control, partly because data protection laws require controllers to take security measures protecting personal data. It may also be easier for users to obtain board approval for contracts specifying detailed security requirements and audit rights, demonstrating considered, structured decisions on security risks.

Accordingly, security often arose in precontract discussions, particularly as many providers were not forthcoming regarding their security arrangements. One global user noted, 'It is a challenge to find out what protection providers are providing'. Worryingly, a 2011 report on cloud providers' security found that most providers, including large ones, did not prioritize security.[67]

Several sources cited problems with audit rights. In particular, financial services users require extensive audit rights for themselves, their financial auditors, and regulators.[68]

---

[66] See Chapters 3 and 11. Nevertheless, 54% of UK users believed providers would give data to third parties only if required by court order; 93% of UK users expected providers to contact them before releasing data—CIF3 (n. 13).

[67] Ponemon Institute, *Security of Cloud Computing Providers Study* (2011) reporting a survey of 103 cloud service providers in the US, 24 in six European countries. A more recent survey of 300 senior European technology leaders found that, of respondents who ranked cloud as a 'top 3' potential growth area, security (data protection and centralization) was one feature stated to most drive their adoption of cloud (58%). DLA Piper, *The European Technology Index: Fostering Growth in a Challenging Market* (2012), <http://www.dlapiper.com/files/Uploads/Documents/DLA_Piper_European_Technology_Index.pdf>.

[68] See the UK Financial Services Authority's SYSC 8.1.8 on outsourcing.

Deals have foundered because providers would not compromise on audit rights. One integrator commented that users did not appreciate how strongly providers resisted audit rights. Audit rights and certifications have been contentious with shared services generally, not just cloud.

Education is important. Some users still lack knowledge about cloud components and services. For example, audit rights were requested of an integrator who only provided application software running on users' own infrastructure.

5.5.1 Providers' security measures—precontractual audits

What security measures should be taken? Who's best placed to take them? These vary with service nature and type. Generally, with IaaS and PaaS, users may have more control over security, while with SaaS, providers may.[69]

Regarding precontractual audits, for data protection and other reasons, users wanted information on providers' physical and digital security measures. They wanted to ensure providers had adequate security policies and underpinning systems, and that issues were addressed in practice, with appropriate approval processes for configuration and change management, and so on. Users' security questionnaires might include many detailed questions, for example fire extinguisher locations.

However, providers generally considered that, particularly with shared infrastructure, providing details of policies and practices to all prospective customers, or allowing data centre visits, would impair security and contravene their own security policies: excessive transparency about security can itself compromise security.

One global user requests all potential providers' security standards, which its security team reviews, and stated: 'Where we know we will be struggling with the provider because of their security standards, and they're not prepared to negotiate or change them, we'll go elsewhere.' Some providers provided documentation or other information showing they take security measures. Generally, providers would at most allow users (or users' security teams) to see a summary or high-level overview of security policies, measures, and standards. Providers rarely supplied more detailed information than they made available generally. However, for the right deal or customer, typically government or financial services, one enterprise-oriented provider had, subject to non-disclosure agreements, allowed prospective users' security-vetted personnel to make escorted visits to data centres, view specific documentation (eg its ISO27001[70] policies and procedures and other detailed information given to its certifier to support its certification), and discuss issues with teams providing or supporting services and application security and security monitoring, and so on. However, they could only view hard copies in closed rooms, without taking copies.

One global user commented that Salesforce emphasizes its willingness to allow users to visit its data centres; others are less receptive to audits of physical or logical storage and systems. Understandably, providers may be unwilling to allow numerous prospective small customers to visit data centres, although a SaaS provider, who disallows 'pen testing',[71] allowed physical site 'walk-rounds', and a global provider permitted site visits. The degree of provider control may affect the position. If it controls all relevant data centres, escorted 'tours' are less problematic, although still involving resources and costs for

---

[69] See Chapter 2.
[70] ISO27001 is an industry standard security framework for implementing information security management systems within an organization.
[71] Defined at Section 5.5.4 below.

providers (passed on to users). Some queried the value of physical visits. Data protection authorities have recognized that visits may be inappropriate with shared infrastructure, 'Since data from several players are stored in the same premises and access opportunities for all who store the data would result in security risks in itself',[72] and that 'Individual audits of data hosted in a multi-party, virtualised server environment may be impractical technically and can in some instances serve to increase risks to those physical and logical network security controls in place'.[73]

Sometimes, obtaining information about providers' security measures suffices for users. One global user might not negotiate detailed security terms if, having seen documentation and receiving access to the provider's systems, it was satisfied with its security.

5.5.2 *Whose security policy?*

Can users dictate security policies or practices? In a pre-cloud, single-user scenario, such as traditional outsourcing to managed services providers, providers might agree to follow users' security policies.

However, with standardized multi-tenanted infrastructure, it may be difficult or impossible for providers to comply with all users' security policies as requirements may differ, or even conflict. Nevertheless, users often wanted providers' undertakings to comply with minimum measures specified in users' security policies (which they considered appropriate to the data's sensitivity), typically scheduled or annexed. Providers generally refused ('take it or leave it'), at most undertaking to follow their *own* policies, perhaps stated to be based on industry best practices (eg ISO27001), and usually with rights to change policies unilaterally. One global user noted that, having reviewed a provider's policy, pragmatically this was acceptable, at least for relatively low-risk data. Even where providers' security policies already covered, for example, encrypting stored data, they might not commit to that contractually, although they might agree that, for instance, only qualified, vetted employees who needed access to user data would have access.

Depending on data sensitivity, users may want assurance of minimum-security levels beyond compliance with providers' own policies. Some users wanted encryption of all data at rest and all connections.[74] Most could not compel providers to undertake additional security measures. Some large users, such as banks, did. After much negotiation, some providers agreed to follow one global user's own security policies; others refused. For another user, some providers agreed minor changes; about half refused to meet higher standards. This may partly be due to reluctance to incur costs, sometimes significant, in obtaining and maintaining industry-standard certifications. A non-European telecommunications provider stated that in one large deal the user considered even ISO27001 inadequate; there, the provider considered specific requests and implementation costs. Again, deal value seems relevant. For the right price and users, such as financial institutions, some smaller providers accepted higher security requirements: one SaaS provider even agreed to a financial institution's full standard security schedule.

Our sources indicated many deals have collapsed, or 'not even got to first base', due to providers' unwillingness to follow users' security policies. One global provider felt that, if so, the user was simply not ready for cloud.

---

[72] Datainspektionen, *Tillsynenligtpersonuppgiftslagen (1998:204)—Salemskommunstyrelse* (2011) (Google translation).
[73] WP196. Discussed further in Chapter 8.
[74] Whether providers may access decryption keys is a different, important issue: see Chapter 8.

5.5.3 Certifications

Independent certifications to objective industry standards represent one possible compromise. Cloud security-specific standards and certifications are developing, with initiatives by organizations like the Cloud Security Alliance (CSA) and the Open Data Centre Alliance. The standards adopted must be cloud-appropriate. One provider commented that some customers, especially governments (US, EU including UK) or government contractors, required Evaluation Assurance Level (EAL) certification under Common Criteria security evaluation standards.[75] These specify particular hardware/software rigidly, so changing any such hardware/software invalidates certifications. Therefore, they ill suit cloud where hardware may be unknown and products evolve quickly. That provider stated, 'It is complex and expensive to get official certification for so little certainty'.

While all customers of one enterprise-oriented SaaS provider raised security issues, it stated that after conducting due diligence and noting the service's certifications for credit cards (PCI/DSS),[76] ISO27001, SAS70,[77] and so on, they were reassured; indeed, some considered its security exceeded their internal protections. Some providers undertook to obtain and maintain industry standard certifications such as ISO27001, providing users with copy certifications, and so on. One global provider underwent regular independent SAS70 type II audits, and shared reports with users.

Other software infrastructure certifications or security assurances are possible, such as on virtualization platforms' effectiveness for segregating users. In 2011, the CESG (UK National Technical Authority for Information Assurance) assured VMWare's VSphere 4.0 for hosting VMs for UK public sector information protectively marked Restricted (Business Impact Level 3 or IL3[78]) and below.[79]

5.5.4 Precontractual penetration testing

Users' precontractual due diligence measures may include security penetration testing ('pen testing'), to check security issues such as integrity or robustness of providers' security policy and IT systems, and how (and how well) users' data or VMs are separated from other users'.

Many users, particularly highly regulated users, sought precontractual pen testing. Most providers refused, because it might affect other users' services or data. One enterprise-oriented public SaaS provider often received such requests from large organizations, particularly financial institutions. It occasionally agreed, subject to the user's acceptance of unlimited liability for any damage caused, and testing constraints (timing,

---

[75] Common Criteria, *Common Criteria for Information Technology Security Evaluation* (2009).

[76] PCI Security Standards Council, *Payment Card Industry (PCI) Data Security Standard* (2010). A provider's PCI/DSS compliance does not ensure its users' compliance: that requires further action 'above the hypervisor', within users' control rather than providers'—Marcia Savage, 'PCI DSS Compliant Cloud Providers: No PCI Panacea' (*TechTarget*, 22 March 2011), <http://searchcloudsecurity.techtarget.com/news/2240033583/PCI-DSS-compliant-cloud-providers-No-PCI-panacea> (accessed 5 March 2013). Cloud-specific PCI-DSS guidance was issued in January 2013: Cloud Special Interest Group, 'PCI DSS Cloud Computing Guidelines' (February 2013).

[77] American Institute of Certified Public Accountants, *Statement on Auditing Standards (SAS) No 70, Service Organizations*—replaced in 2011 by *Statement on Standards for Attestation Engagements (SSAE) No. 16*.

[78] See CESG and Cabinet Office, *Extract from HMG IA Standard No.1 Business Impact Level Tables* (2009). See also Chapter 5.

[79] See CESG, 'CESG and VMware Deliver Trusted Platform for Hosting Multi-Level Environments' (14 September 2011), <http://www.cesg.gov.uk/Publications/Documents/cesg-vmware_joint-statement14-09-11.pdf> (accessed 5 March 2013).

from which IP address, etc.). Such testing was usually confined to a sandbox, or a special segregated area, to avoid damage to systems that could affect others. Numerous such pen tests were conducted annually. Some automated scanning of the application was permitted, at weekends only. However, that provider rejected unlimited pen testing.

Providers that disallow user testing may conduct their own tests (or use a third party), sharing results with current or prospective users. One SaaS provider organizes regular independent tests, including after application upgrades, showing users summarized results. Some users required sight of such results before contracting. Others still wanted their own or their chosen third-party pen tests. Another SaaS provider was obtaining SAS70 certification[80] to address users' desire to conduct pen testing.

Ongoing tests were unusual. One global user, after conducting precontractual pen testing on a global provider without physical site audits, was satisfied by that test together with undertakings to comply with security measures, and did not require rights to conduct future tests.

As a non-European telecommunications provider noted, users cannot be prevented from pen testing. Interestingly, although it had several large users, including banks, none had sought prior testing, although all requested security certifications.

5.5.5 Ongoing audit rights[81]

Many financial services users felt they needed rights to require post-contract audits, at least when the user's regulator (or end user's regulator) required it. However, most providers refused, for security and costs reasons; providers were more willing to allow audits if users met all costs. Even enterprise-oriented SaaS providers that allowed audits would not offer the unfettered rights financial institutions required, but generally restricted audits narrowly, for instance, once annually per user, only if required by the user's regulator, or only with the provider's consent. Or, they agreed only to 'commercially reasonable' cooperation, rather than full audit rights.

EU data protection authorities consider that users need technical and practical means to investigate suspected unauthorized accesses to personal data, whether within the user or provider, meaning contractual rights to logs or audits. Some providers offer users not just logs but tools, for example for real-time 24-hour monitoring, to check who has accessed which accounts, what they viewed, and what they did. One SaaS provider undertakes to log all accesses as standard. It commented that, once this undertaking was pointed out, most users who requested audit rights accepted logs instead. Provision of tools by more providers may help to increase user trust by both increasing transparency and assisting with legal compliance. EU data protection authorities consider that, to check providers' compliance with the required security measures, the contract 'should' provide for, not only logging, but also ongoing audit rights against all *sub*-providers too, IaaS, PaaS, perhaps even data centre operators.[82] Clarity from regulators is needed regarding how far down the 'stack' users must go.

A global integrator commented that providers' reluctance to allow audits might partly arise from their inability to pinpoint data locations.[83] Also, providers may lack sufficient control or rights to allow audits, particularly if using sub-providers. Consider

---

[80] Replaced by SSAE 16 from June 2011—n. 77.
[81] For a detailed survey and guide to ongoing security SLAs, see ENISA, *Survey and Analysis of Security Parameters in Cloud SLAs across the European Public Sector* (2011) and *Procure Secure: A Guide to Monitoring of Security Service Levels in Cloud Contracts* (2012).
[82] Datainspektionen (n. 72) and WP196. See also Chapter 8.   [83] See Chapter 10.

a SaaS provider using a PaaS service, which may itself use another's IaaS infrastructure or data centre. The SaaS provider may allow inspection of its application code to verify application security, but it might have no right to allow users to audit its PaaS/IaaS providers, visit data centres, or even to conduct its own audits of sub-providers. Therefore, rights to audit sub-providers may be problematic. Nevertheless, one financial institution obtained comprehensive audit rights from a US SaaS provider for itself, affiliates, and regulators, including of sub-providers and sub-contractors.

One compromise was for providers to agree to share audit reports with integrators, or at least allow the integrator to view reports and ideally (though many providers might disagree) allow results to be shared with the integrator's users and their regulators. Where audits are disallowed and no independent audits are conducted or shared with users, users must rely on any security undertakings from providers; verifying compliance is impossible. A global user noted, 'The only way to find out if they have actually complied is if they have a major breach or loss of confidential information!'

The general lack of audit rights causes difficulties, especially for integrators whose customers require such rights, possibly including the right to select auditors. This issue may become more prominent as audit rights increasingly come to the fore, described by one user as a 'headache', with users being dependent on (the not necessarily consistent) views and actions of individual national regulators. Ongoing third-party audits to industry standards are a possible solution, as are precontractual audits, but legislators and regulators need to consider these issues, particularly the extent to which users may rely on such audits for liability purposes.[84]

5.5.6 Security breach notification

Many providers' standard terms did not require reporting of security incidents and so on to users. This might be for operational reasons: many providers' systems and processes were not set up to enable easy and quick notification of incidents to users.

Users have requested notification of data losses or security breaches at the provider level in, say, 24 hours, sometimes even when only other users were affected. Some providers agreed to notify users promptly of breaches or losses, at least where affecting that user (but possibly not if only affecting other users). Others, while not committing contractually to notify users, would in practice attempt to notify users as soon as possible, although faster notification might be possible if users paid for higher support levels. Still other providers would not commit to notifying users, except perhaps for users such as telecommunications providers who by law need that capability, but were implementing systems and organizational measures to enable notifications.

For large users, if the matter went to a senior enough level, some providers accepted additional obligations to use commercially reasonable efforts to monitor for and detect breaches, and to notify breaches (at least where affecting that user), perhaps also with termination rights for the user. Notification periods may be short, for example within one business day after the provider becomes aware of an actual or potential threat, at least where it may adversely impact on the user's service (eg unauthorized access). As with

---

[84] Some data protection authorities (eg Sweden's—*Salems*, n. 72) consider that independent third-party audits would not absolve controllers from responsibility to ensure appropriate security measures were taken. However, WP196 (p. 22) recognized that 'third-party audits chosen by the controller and certification may also be acceptable providing full transparency is guaranteed (eg by providing for the possibility to obtain a copy of a third-party audit certificate or a copy of the audit report verifying certification)'.

other important notices, users may require written notification to a particular physical address, not just email notification.

What actions must providers take after security breaches? Agreed security standards usually addressed this issue, for instance by requiring isolation or quarantine of affected areas, and otherwise remedying the situation. On receiving notification, some users wanted rights for their security team to investigate and consider whether the required security standards had been met, and, if not, serve notice to remedy the breach if not already remedied, or even to terminate the agreement. However, unlike with traditional outsourcing, many providers refused any joint breach analysis with users, insisting on handling breaches themselves.

5.6 Lock-in and exit

Many cloud users cited lock-in as one of their top concerns. Lock-in involves several aspects. Exit strategy and end-of-contract transition were major user concerns, including data portability; retaining metadata as well as data was considered important. Users were wary of being 'locked in' for too long an initial contract term. This issue, covered later, is often pricing-related, and sometimes negotiable.

A major lock-in concern is risk of (over-)dependence on one provider's, often proprietary, service. As cloud use becomes more widespread and sophisticated, we believe contracts may extend beyond addressing data portability to cover application portability, VM portability, and perhaps even interoperability.[85]

5.6.1 Data retention/deletion and data portability

Two issues arise with data retention and deletion. First, will providers retain users' data when needed by users, enabling users to retrieve data in usable format? Secondly, will providers delete user data when required?

Users may wish providers to retain data in two main circumstances: retention for regulatory, litigation, or other legal reasons affecting users; and contract termination, where users want their data to be retained for long enough to allow their recovery.

Our sources indicated that retention for legally required purposes, for example e-discovery or evidence preservation upon law enforcement request, has not been negotiated much yet. A large enterprise-oriented SaaS provider stated no prospective user had raised the issue before early 2011. We think this will become increasingly important. One aspect is how much assistance, if any, providers must give users. An enterprise-oriented provider stated that users who needed to retain data for longer periods, such as for tax reasons, must arrange storage themselves. One global user was concerned about using a large provider because it did not know what, if any, processes were implemented for e-discovery, whereas another platform it used had such processes. Another global user secured a global provider's agreement to retain, segregate, and secure data if specifically requested, while a SaaS provider specializing in email continuity provides, as standard, e-discovery support tools, allowing users to choose retention periods (longer periods cost more).

These examples illustrate that data retention for compliance and so on is technically possible. However, cloud e-discovery tools have been lacking. One user commented that providers often had difficulty understanding that users would need help should they receive a

---

[85] See Chapter 2.

relevant request. Some users have defined contractually exactly what assistance they may need from providers here.[86]

Users' ability to have data returned upon contract termination has seen more negotiation. Process simplicity may be as important as data format. A UK public sector educational institution chose one provider's SaaS service over another's partly because it believed data retrieval from the former would be easier.

There are several aspects here: format, what assistance (if any) providers give users and at what price, and retention period.

Some, especially enterprise-oriented providers, routinely commit to returning data in standard format (typically comma-separated values (CSV)) on termination, at least upon the user so requesting. Several Salesforce SaaS users mentioned that one benefit was return of data in CSV format and, with certain services, possible weekly data downloads or emails. Some global users requested contractual commitments to return data in their required format after termination for whatever reason. Some providers agreed (at least for reasonable formats), although perhaps charging more for substantial data quantities.

Most providers offered no assistance, even contracted paid assistance. However, a SaaS provider provides data in another format for a set fee if users so request. A user noted that some providers/integrators will agree to provide assisted migration at contract end. A non-European telecommunications provider assists with migration-in ('onboarding'), and, while willing to assist migrations-out, found even smaller users did not need it, taking direct copies themselves.[87]

Another lock-in issue is, how long do users have after termination to recover data before deletion? Many providers deleted data immediately, or after a short period (often 30 days). Some users obtained longer grace periods, for instance two months, perhaps requiring notice to users before deletion. Some providers offered 90 days. For large deals, 18 months to two years might be agreed, with migration assistance offered, mimicking classic outsourcing deals. Six months might suffice if providers agreed to provide 'reasonable assistance'. How long users need to migrate applications and data may vary with their circumstances.[88]

Standard terms may require data deletion after termination only if upon user request, or are silent on deletion. Depending on type of service and intended usage,[89] users have sought contractual commitments to ensure deletion of data from the provider's systems (including duplicates or backups). This is relevant both when users delete data while using a cloud service, and after contract termination. Deletion after termination may be particularly important with personal data, including data held by any sub-processors.

Data may require deletion from different locations and media, with different levels of deletion, up to securely destroying hardware.[90] The degree of deletion needed depends on the level of security required for the data concerned. For example, if cloud data move

---

[86] Providers are increasingly implementing e-discovery tools, for example in early 2012 Google introduced 'Vault' archiving and e-discovery tools for Google Apps customers. Jack Halprin, 'Google Apps Vault Brings Information Governance to Google Apps' (*Google Enterprise Blog*, March 2012), <http://googleenterprise.blogspot.co.uk/2012/03/google-apps-vault-brings-information.html> (accessed 5 March 2013).

[87] The CIF recommends providers should assist with migration or at least allow users sufficient time to self-migrate. CIF3 (n. 13) 15.

[88] This paragraph was based on interviews. The CIF recommends that providers give at least 30 days' notice before deletion. CIF3 (n. 13).

[89] Data deletion is often an issue in-cloud, but may be considered unimportant for some services. For example, for a SaaS service involving temporary processing but no permanent data storage, a global user was not concerned about data deletion provisions, although personal data might be involved.

[90] See Chapter 2 and Chapter 5.

between different equipment automatically, data may remain in previous devices until overwritten.[91] One SaaS provider splits data into smaller portions randomly after contract termination, so it would be virtually impossible for users (although not the provider) to reconstruct data. It would not agree to requests to commit to stronger deletion, although it would certify it no longer held data after their return. A global provider would agree to delete all duplicates (although it was unclear to what standard), and to certify deletions.

More secure deletion is more expensive (particularly destroying rather than redeploying equipment). Accordingly, providers only employed more secure methods where necessary, and wanted to pass on costs to users. Deletion seems as much a financial as a technical issue. Costs may be partly why, as a global user noted, data deletion has not hitherto been a particular focus of cloud. A global integrator commented that, while willing to delete data, providers were reluctant to do so to ISO standards, as they wished to reuse hardware. Where secure deletion was vital, as with financial institutions or telecommunications providers, some providers were willing to guarantee it, usually only at greater cost.

Some global users persuaded providers to agree to delete data if requested, providing evidence of permanent deletion of all copies. Some users would not contract with providers who refused. A non-European telecommunications provider agreed terms requiring deletion, including specific provisions for overwriting data to recognized data deletion standards to make data unrecoverable, if larger users requested. One global user secured additional obligations to deliver all backups of stored data and applications within a short period after termination. However, the most another global user secured was acknowledgement of data confidentiality, with warranties that data would be deleted following termination.

Some users wanted rights to ensure data they deleted during the term were deleted permanently, including all duplicates, for example after receiving complaints about end-user IPR breach, or law enforcement deletion requests. To assure third parties regarding deletion of all offending content, one compromise involved agreeing that providers must use reasonable endeavours to delete data and erase relevant storage media upon specific user request. Providers might need capabilities to quarantine rather than delete data, for example with IPR disputes.

Education may be an issue: users and third parties may need more explanation regarding degrees of deletion, depending on the nature and sensitivity of content. If certain data are no longer accessible for most purposes that might suffice in some situations; more sensitive data, such as customer payment records, might require more secure deletion (and more stringent or frequent audits), if not absolute destruction. Similarly, secure deletion may be required where third-party contracts, like certain content licences, restrict where users may store data or applications. One provider noted another educational issue: users may need to make employees aware that, for instance, with SaaS services, 'deletion' often merely transfers data to a 'recycle bin', stored for say 90 or 180 days before deletion.

5.7 Term and termination

5.7.1 Minimum term, renewals, and notice periods

Our sources felt that, before contracting, users should consider carefully the minimum and maximum acceptable term, their exit strategy, and ensure practical requirements were addressed contractually if necessary. A long initial term may be one aspect of lock-in.

---

[91] Contracts did not generally address this issue, although it was noted, for example, in German data protection authorities' cloud guidance—n. 18. See also Chapter 2, Section 2.2.

One global user noted some 'cloud washing': certain services described as 'cloud' did not utilize typical cloud pricing models or cloud technologies; for instance, they required minimum revenue and term commitments (unlike the common 'pay as you go' cloud model), and new servers had to be procured if more capacity was needed, instead of instantly increasing capacity on demand and so on. However, even with acknowledged cloud services like Salesforce, a minimum term was often said to be required. A global user pointed out that larger users were better able to 'beat cloud providers down on price', and therefore deals might be less commercially viable for providers unless they were longer-term. Bigger deals, or deals involving more sophisticated or customized services, were more likely to involve an initial minimum term. There are indications that initial fixed terms are increasingly common. Initial minimum term is more of a commercial than legal issue; some providers may reduce unit or per-user prices for longer initial terms. Some providers wanted early termination fees (which might be 'huge') if users terminated fixed-term contracts earlier for convenience, as fixed set-up costs were intended to be recovered over the term.

Rather than rolling monthly contracts, providers preferred fixed-term contracts (or an initial fixed term, continuing thereafter unless terminated on giving, say, a month's notice). Standard terms typically stipulate a one- to three-year initial term, sometimes renewing automatically unless terminated. CIF research[92] indicated that 46 per cent of UK users' contracts renew automatically, particularly with smaller organizations, but only 38 per cent of integrators' contracts. The critical difference: 64 per cent of integrators' internal business practices incorporated early warning systems to manage renewals proactively.

Contracts often require non-renewal notices to be submitted within a set period before expiry. Users might miss the window. Many users successfully requested deletion of automatic renewal provisions, or increases in the period before term expiry within which users could give notice, say from 30 to 60 days. Because some users apparently did not understand the rollover mechanism, one SaaS provider even sent automated reminders at intervals in advance of that period. It seems users' contract terms and/or internal processes regarding renewals could be improved.

Length of initial term, and therefore period of lock-in, varied with type of service and deals. Some basic click-through SaaS services may use a rolling basis, say monthly or 90 days. Other SaaS services, particularly large deals, may have an initial fixed term and may involve master agreements. Terms sought by integrators depend on their customers' requirements. Some users, like financial institutions, might require even longer initial terms, with guaranteed renewals, because they needed price ceilings over a longer period and required significant transition periods. However, providers generally did not offer initial periods as long as five years, so such users had to agree to shorter terms than they wished, and devise advance plans for dealing with end-of-term issues.

Where terms permit termination for convenience by either party, notice period was another issue. To have enough time to migrate providers, users often needed longer notice from providers regarding service termination than for mere service changes, for example several months instead of one; particularly with mission-critical applications or IaaS/PaaS where users might need to modify their hosted application's code to run on another provider's cloud. Accordingly, many users stated they always requested longer than the typical 30 days. Thus, portability and migration of applications, not just data, can be important for users. Ideally, those aspects should be checked during due diligence (such as testing ability to export data to desired formats), rather than relying on the

---

[92] CIF3 (n. 13); CIF2 (n. 31) 12.

contract. Data and applications may require migration not only on contract termination, but also if providers become insolvent or close down.

Conversely, some users wanted rights to terminate for convenience on shorter notice. For example, one global user negotiated longer notice from its provider than it had to give itself, although identical notice periods for both are not uncommon.

Users also risk lock-in *in practice* if, for example, their developers mainly use one provider's IaaS/PaaS service. They can develop and leverage expertise in that service, but may also prefer to keep using it, given inevitable learning curves with other providers' services. Some users therefore encouraged employees to use several providers, to avoid over-reliance on one provider's service and its (possibly proprietary) APIs. If cloud services become standardized, the 'internal expertise' issue may become less important. The use of proprietary versus open-source cloud infrastructure looks set to become more significant.

5.7.2 *Termination events*

Insolvency and material breach are common events allowing termination. One global user did not want providers to terminate for anything except non-payment, as even an insolvent user may need continued use of cloud services while winding down. A financial institution using its own standard terms stipulated non-payment as the only event allowing provider termination. However, generally providers seemed unwilling to remove other termination events like material breach or insolvency. One provider considered its termination events 'set in stone' and rejected any changes, unless perhaps the deal was large enough, and the user would withdraw without that change.

Some users increased the notice period given by providers before termination for non-payment. For other breaches, integrators, and other users who use cloud to service their own end users, had problems with providers' rights to terminate immediately on material breach, breach of acceptable use policies (AUPs) (covered below), or on receiving complaints regarding breach of third-party IPRs and so on. Such users did not wish one end user/customer's actions to trigger rights to terminate the whole service.[93]

However, many services lack granularity. An IaaS provider may be unable to locate and terminate the offending VM instance, and therefore can only terminate the entire service. Providers, while acknowledging this deficiency, still refused to change terms, but stated they would take a commercial approach to discussions should issues arise. Nevertheless, some users managed, not without difficulty, to negotiate for provider notification of any third-party complaints regarding IPR infringement and so on, for no service termination or suspension without further notification, and for cooperation with the user's attempts to resolve the matter with the relevant end user or third party, perhaps by terminating just the offending end user's account. Users with multiple applications also sought to limit termination to a particular application, rather than all applications hosted with that provider.

Breach of providers' AUP may be a specific termination event, or a material breach entitling providers to terminate.[94] AUPs tend to be 'take it or leave it' and were rarely negotiated, possibly because such terms were generally accepted as reasonably standardized, and providers considered them 'hardcore'. For instance, continually exceeding agreed usage limits would be considered unacceptable. Nevertheless, one global user

---

[93] 46% of UK integrators had actively engaged with providers to define and determine termination events. CIF3 (n. 13) 9. Perhaps smaller integrators had not yet focused on this issue, and/or few integrators polled were providers themselves.

[94] CIF research showed 70% of UK users had checked AUPs to ensure they were comfortable with them. CIF3 (n. 13) 9.

negotiated successfully with a global provider for a less restrictive AUP, with fewer usages being stipulated as unacceptable.

For many users, AUPs were unimportant; although rights for providers to change AUPs unilaterally were not, as AUP breaches usually entitle providers to terminate. As mentioned, AUPs were problematic for integrators and others using cloud to serve end users, particularly consumers. One end user/customer breaching a provider's AUP may enable the provider to terminate services for the user/integrator and all other end users. Therefore, such users/integrators contractually obligated their end users to comply with providers' AUPs, making end-user accounts terminable for breach. Rejecting standard terms that enabled instant termination, they required notice from providers before termination for AUP breach (except perhaps for material breaches) of, say, 30 days to enable users to remedy breaches, obliging providers to consult before termination. One global integrator considered this a 'huge' issue, which did not get attention because of emphasis on liability and service levels. In its experience, most providers were willing to give some notice before termination, but not necessarily to afford users opportunities to remedy breaches which the provider considered vital.

Some users ('only the better lawyers', one SaaS provider noted) wanted rights to terminate for change in control of providers; for example, takeover by the user's competitor, with the usual issues regarding definitions and scope of 'change of control'. Providers generally refused, except perhaps for large deals in specific circumstances with clear definitions of 'competitor'. Users such as financial institutions wanted rights to terminate if required by regulators, law, or regulation. While material breach was a common basis for termination, some users secured specific termination rights for defined breaches, including breach of confidentiality, security policies, or IPR provisions.

5.7.3 Suspension

Providers' standard terms usually reserve rights to suspend services (eg for non-payment). Some providers had no suspension rights, preferring simply to terminate for breach.

Like termination, suspension for breach of AUPs, and so on, was particularly problematic for users with multiple end users, as all end users' services could be suspended for one end user's actions or omissions. Accordingly, one global user would not permit suspension except with prior notice and its agreement. An integrator would not allow suspension for anything except non-payment, unless prior notice was given with reasons for suspension, so that it could notify its end users and discuss it with them as appropriate. Another global user similarly required prior written notice of non-payment, with a final notice before suspension, and commitments to restore services within X days after payment. Other global users, including an integrator, agreed to suspension for breach, but again only after reasonable prior notice (quite long, in some cases) and good faith consultation, and so on. One financial institution did not permit suspension on any grounds, which the provider agreed to.

Suspension for reasons unrelated to users may be necessary, as in following security incidents or to address technical service problems. Users generally agreed to that kind of suspension.

5.8 Changing service description/features

Many standard terms allow providers to change certain or all contract terms unilaterally.[95] Interviewed users considered this unacceptable. Again, enterprise-oriented providers were

---

[95] See Chapter 3.

more likely to agree, or provide as standard, that that amendment was only permitted if agreed in writing by users, or at least that users would receive prior notification, whereupon they could terminate.[96] The latter was more common.

Providers' right to change unilaterally service features, functions, or even service description was much negotiated. One non-European telecommunications provider notified its (enterprise) users of feature changes, but would not contractually undertake to do so. A SaaS provider stated that it never discontinued features, but only introduced improvements, which customers could choose to enable. Its standard terms already stipulated that new features must not materially decrease users' functionality. The importance of this issue, and how much users negotiated it, varied with type and usage of service, extent of termination rights, and so on. For example, where users could terminate for convenience on giving notice; if a user disliked a feature change it might simply terminate.

With commoditized SaaS services, users might have to accept providers' rights to change features, although many users still wanted qualifications that changes must not adversely affect their service. For IaaS and PaaS, changes might be more significant. Changes could force users to rewrite application code created to integrate with proprietary provider APIs, which users wished to avoid. With large deals for mission-critical services, for instance, a global user's main platform for servicing end users, a provider's refusal to change this term could be a 'deal-breaker'. Therefore, users have insisted providers cannot change core services without consent, although minor changes to service features or support aspects might be permitted without notification. Service improvements were permitted, but if changes were materially detrimental to their service, some users negotiated rights to terminate (or even reject changes), at least upon the current contract period expiring, without liability, but possibly without any rebates.

Users generally wanted longer prior notification of key changes and their impact (at least 30 days). Certain providers who insisted on rights to change service features unilaterally still agreed to give notice of changes, although not necessarily longer or prior notice. Users wanted enough notice to assess changes, discuss them with their own customers where relevant and, for changes considered detrimental, perhaps negotiate with alternative providers. If providers guaranteed a longer lead-time, say a year, before introducing notified changes, users were more comfortable with being able to adapt in time.

5.9 IPRs

IPR issues frequently arise regarding cloud-processed data and/or applications, including cloud services themselves. Indeed, for one global SaaS provider, they were negotiated the most.

Providers' terms may specify that they own deliverables (eg documentation). Some users wanted clarification that users retained ownership of cloud-processed data and confidential information, and so on. Some providers' standard terms do so provide.[97]

Standard terms may not address rights to *applications* that users develop or deploy on IaaS/PaaS. Some users wanted clarification that users own such IPR. However, the line is sometimes unclear between user's application and provider's platform/integration tools. In one deal, involving customization, a global user secured only an exclusive-use period. Where integrators develop applications for their own customers, customers

---

[96] The CIF recommends providers should not be entitled to change terms without consent, or at least should give users notice and allow them to terminate. CIF3 (n. 13) 14.

[97] CIF research found nearly 75% of UK users (and 68% of integrators) were content that providers' contracts did not allow providers to take ownership of data/IPR. CIF3 (n. 13) 9. See Chapter 6.

might require ownership, or at least rights to use the software free after contract termination or transfer.

Another contentious issue concerned rights to service improvements arising from users' suggestions, bug fixes, and so on. Providers may require users to assign such rights. Yet, users may not want their suggested improvements made available to competitors. Such users sought to prohibit provision of those improvements to providers' other customers without the user's consent. This issue arose even in a deal involving open-source software where the user could not claim rights, let alone forbid using bug fixes and so on for competitors.

Where cloud services include application licences, some users wanted clarification that pricing covered such licences. However, other services include no application licences. To install user-sourced third-party applications on IaaS/PaaS, even some SaaS, users must 'bring their own' licences. Providers wanted express clarification that users were entitled to load/use such applications on providers' infrastructure, even if the provider could not run them itself.

Only some licensors let users 'port' on-premise licences to the cloud. Although not directly affecting contract terms, such licensing may be problematic for users. For instance, logging usage in a VM may be unworkable because VMs are continually instantiated or terminated, which may make it impossible to identify VM locations and which ones run licensed software. Rights to bring a set number of licences to the cloud, irrespective of VM location, would assist. One SaaS provider noted that, even when existing licences could be 'converted' to cloud, including the payment model, licensors' sales/marketing teams did not necessarily publicize that benefit, possibly because the commission structure was not so remunerative!

Licences were charged on different bases, for example annually in advance for on-premise or monthly rolling 'per user' for in-cloud.[98] Some licensing schemes were preferred by SaaS providers as better matching provider–user payment models, and better suiting public multi-tenanted cloud environments: Citrix, for example, allows monthly per-user payments, compared with Oracle which charges based on the number of processor cores (CPU sockets) in the system used.[99]

6. Concluding Remarks

With many early adopters of cloud computing being individual consumers or SMEs, cloud computing epitomizes IT's increasing consumerization as well as commoditization. The common use of providers' standard terms in cloud computing reflects the consumer distribution model. However, factors are combining to force more flexibility in providers' terms.

From the supply side, integrators, traditional IT services vendors, and telecommunications providers who are willing to accept more risk are increasingly entering the market. They see the opportunity to sell more robust, enterprise-grade services with

---

[98] The CIF predicts that organizations will still favour predictability of cost over 'pay-as-you-go' metering, from a pragmatic planning perspective. CIF8 (n. 19) 16.

[99] Bill Claybrook, 'Warning: Not All Cloud Licensing Models Are User-friendly' (*SearchCloud Computing*, August 2011), <http://searchcloudcomputing.techtarget.com/feature/Warning-Not-all-cloud-licensing-models-are-user-friendly> (accessed 5 March 2013). Oracle's charges equate each virtual core with a physical core (although one physical core could support several virtual cores), or vary with the number of virtual cores in Amazon EC2 instances used.

contract terms to match, rather than the 'as is, where is' services offered by the likes of Amazon and Google. Increasing availability of open-source components, for example OpenStack, may also facilitate market entry by new providers, which may increase competition.

The market, while becoming more sophisticated and transparent, may be fragmenting. There will still be bigger providers offering generalized 'one-size-fits-all' commodity services. However, niche providers and integrators are emerging, who are more willing to tailor contract terms or service features to user needs. Therefore, to remain competitive, providers may need better awareness of user concerns, more flexibility in negotiations, and more willingness to demonstrate their services' security and robustness.

Even large providers are realizing that, to gain or keep customers from certain sectors, they must adapt. Several global providers are offering different services with different pricings and terms, from consumer- to enterprise-orientated, with specific terms for certain market sectors or functionality (eg third-party-certified services).

Large users who could require contracts on their own standard terms are making their terms cloud-friendlier, with some financial institutions considering producing standard SaaS, possibly even IaaS, terms. Indeed, there may be scope for financial institutions to collaborate on producing suitably balanced standard terms for cloud contracts in consultation with providers, obviously subject to competition law restrictions.

In the middle- and low-value markets, choice and information are still limited, and many contract terms remain inadequate or inappropriate for users' needs; these users may lack bargaining power to compel changes. Negotiations by large users have helped to educate providers about users' issues such as privacy and security, so that providers take due account of users' compliance concerns. These will probably filter down to the middle market at least, because that market is large and, therefore, attractive to providers. That may result in standard terms offered for mid-sized deals becoming more user-appropriate over time.

For low-value deals, legislative or regulatory action regarding inadequate contract terms may be needed (eg by consumer protection or data protection authorities). However, legislators and regulators also need education regarding cloud technologies and business structures, to enable cloud to be used in a balanced way that enables its potential economic benefits to be realized. Some current difficulties arise, not because contract terms are poor, but because data protection and financial services laws make assumptions that do not hold in cloud. In particular, current laws assume one-to-one relationships not one-to-many, dedicated not shared infrastructure, and controllers' absolute control over processors who process data actively for controllers, instead of renting out self-service resources.[100]

With customized, managed private cloud services on dedicated infrastructure, providers may show more flexibility on contract terms. However, commoditized public cloud services on shared infrastructure are very different. They are cheap because of standardization. One provider felt that the biggest challenge was that users wanted the lowest price for the highest specifications or features, for example location monitoring or audit rights. Forcing providers to accept greater liability and to incur costs to upgrade infrastructure, while charging only low commodity prices, is likely to be unappealing to providers, and may itself undermine market development. If one provider's infrastructure is insufficiently secure for personal data, controllers may instead choose another who provides adequate security.

---

[100] See Chapter 2 and Chapter 8.

Rather than stipulating mandatory terms for commodity cloud, it may be better for policymakers to encourage a greater range of cloud services (with different sets of terms) which users can assess, choosing whichever best suits their needs. These could include cheap public clouds for data that are neither personal data nor commercially confidential, more expensive 'personal data' clouds, or even more costly high-security, auditable private, or community clouds, for example sector-specific clouds for financial services or health-care institutions.

Even mid-sized organizations wishing to process confidential or personal data in-cloud may lack expertise to assess providers' security measures. Therefore, to enable consumers and SMEs to consider and compare cloud services properly, work is also needed on industry standards and certifications on security, data portability, and interoperability, for sub-providers as well as providers. Suitable standards and certifications, with provision for both self-certification and independent third-party certifications, might then form the basis for laws that recognize appropriate certificates, trustmarks, or seals as adequate for various compliance purposes.

For legislators and regulators to accept standards and certifications, providers need to be more open and transparent. They need to provide clearer, more detailed explanations of how data location relates to data security; and how data may be secured against remote access by unauthorized persons, even if located inside the EEA, or moved between different equipment, including data fragmentation and data structures. They need to explain clearly how they can access users' data or monitor users' processing, if at all. They should perhaps also develop tools to, for example, enable users to verify accurately locations of data and VM instances.

Insurers' increasing involvement in cloud is also relevant. Insurers may be better able than smaller users to assess risks. However, users may also need to consider actively insuring against risks like provider's breaches, outages, and data loss, checking their coverage.[101] One provider noted that, almost irrespective of how much liability providers accept, it was critical for users to understand cloud 'layers'[102] and data location. Some smaller users have contracted without understanding virtualization, the vertical supply chain, or provider layering; some even had no idea who provided the service. Ignorance of cloud structures may result in risks not being properly addressed. It is clearly important to help users climb the cloud learning curve. Users may, for example, need to consider which, if any, functions should be migrated to cloud and how, for instance, starting with pilots only, conducting risk assessments, and implementing internal controls. They need to recognize that, apart from scrutinizing contract terms, other practical measures may be required: notably, precontractual due diligence and testing, encryption of data as appropriate, backing up internally or to another provider when using low-cost services without guaranteed backup, and post-contract monitoring.

In summary, while larger users have negotiated contract terms, the SME user market is unlikely to benefit in the short to medium term. While changes to providers' standard terms should filter down from large deals, and up from regulatory action regarding consumer and other deals, a multi-pronged approach may be best, involving all types of

---

[101] CIF3 (n. 13) 9–43% of users had insurance for business interruption due to the provider's disaster or data leak, but 37% did not know if they would be covered, although 65% of users expected their providers to cover these risks!

[102] As a consumer example illustrating risks of ignorance regarding layers, users of online backup service Backify, based on the Livedrive service, lost their data after a dispute between Backify and Livedrive. Brid-Aine Parnell, 'Punters Lose Backups in Cloud Storage Biz Spat' (*The Register*, 17 November 2011), <http://www.theregister.co.uk/2011/11/17/livedrive_backify_dispute> (accessed 5 March 2013).

players to encourage development of a full variety of cloud services and contract terms, priced at different levels, with standards and certifications to assist legal certainty regarding compliance.

It is encouraging that the three key actions under the European Commission's 2012 cloud strategy[103] included cutting through the standards 'jungle', and developing 'safe and fair contract terms'. Regarding the first, intended steps include promoting trusted and reliable cloud offerings by tasking the European Telecommunications Standards Institute to coordinate openly and transparently with stakeholders to identify by 2013 a detailed map of necessary standards (including for security, interoperability, data portability, and reversibility). These include enhancing trust in cloud services by recognizing at EU level technical specifications in information and communication technologies for protecting personal information in accordance with the new Regulation on European Standardization, working with ENISA and other relevant bodies to assist development of EU-wide voluntary certification schemes in cloud (including regarding data protection), and establishing a list of such schemes by 2014.

As regards contract terms, actions intended by the end of 2013 included developing with stakeholders model terms for cloud service level agreements for contracts between cloud providers and professional cloud users, taking into account developing EU *acquis*, proposing for consumers and small firms European model contract terms for issues falling within the proposed Common European Sales Law,[104] standardizing key contract terms, and providing best practice terms for cloud services on aspects relating to supply of 'digital content'. An expert group (including industry) was to identify before the end of 2013 safe and fair contract terms for consumers and small firms (with a similar optional instrument for cloud-related issues falling outside the Common European Sales Law's scope), to review standard contractual clauses for transfer of personal data to third countries to adapt them, as needed, to cloud services, and to work with industry to agree on a code of conduct for cloud providers[105] to support uniform application of data protection rules, which may be submitted to the Article 29 Working Party to ensure legal certainty and compliance with EU law.

---

[103] 'Unleashing the potential of cloud computing in Europe' COM(2012) 529 final, 27.9.2012.
[104] See also Chapter 13.
[105] For example, the CIF has developed a voluntary Code of Practice—see Chapter 14.

5

Public Sector Cloud Contracts

W Kuan Hon, Christopher Millard, and Ian Walden

1. Introduction

Governments are interested in cloud computing as part of a policy agenda that includes improving efficiency and reducing public expenditure.[1] With much initial cloud market growth occurring in the US, it is unsurprising that the US government led the way, with then US Federal CIO Vivek Kundra's 25-point implementation plan in December 2010 announcing a shift to a 'Cloud First' policy for US federal government. The UK government also moved to a 'Cloud First' policy in May 2013, as did Australia shortly afterwards.[2]

Furthermore, one of three key pillars of the EU cloud strategy[3] is 'Promoting Common Public Sector Leadership through a European Cloud Partnership' between industry experts and public sector users to produce common public sector procurement requirements for cloud, noting that the public sector, as the EU's largest buyer of IT services, can 'set stringent requirements for features, performance, security, interoperability and data portability and compliance with technical requirements. It can also lay down requirements for certification'.

This chapter describes and assesses the 2011–12 pilot cloud computing framework of the UK government ('Government'), G-Cloud v1 (termed 'Gi' by the G-Cloud programme), and Government's innovative approach to cloud procurement through using successive multiple G-Cloud frameworks. As at 1 June 2013 there have been two further G-Cloud procurements, 'Gii'[4] and 'Giii'[5], and responsibility for the once-specialist programme is being transitioned over to the more stably resourced 'business as usual' Government Digital Service.[6] We discuss some early lessons learned, particularly

---

[1] For example, HM Government, *Government Cloud Strategy* (2011).

[2] <https://cio.gov/documents25-point-implementation-plan-to-reform-federal-itpdf/>. For instance, the US Interior Department now uses Google Apps SaaS for 90,000 employees <http://www.nytimes.com/2012/12/26/technology/google-apps-moving-onto-microsofts-business-turf.html> and the US Navy has issued a cloud policy <http://www.doncio.navy.mil/ContentView.aspx?id=4695>, while the US Central Intelligence Agency has reportedly engaged Amazon to build a private cloud for it: <http://fcw.com/articles/2013/03/18/amazon-cia-cloud.aspx> although this decision has been challenged by IBM <http://online.wsj.com/article/SB10001424127887324904004578539722533 829106.html>. UK announcement <https://www.gov.uk/government/news/government-adopts-cloud-first-policy-for-public-sector-it>; Australia <http://www.dbcde.gov.au/__data/assets/pdf_file/0008/163844/2013-292_National_Cloud_Computing_Strategy_Accessible_FA.pdf>.

[3] European Commission, *Unleashing the Potential of Cloud Computing in Europe*, COM(2012) 529 final.

[4] Invitation to tender documents available at <https://online.contractsfinder.businesslink.gov.uk/Common/View%20Notice.aspx?site=1000&lang=en&noticeid=792275&fs=true>; final form of framework agreement and Gii suppliers at <https://online.contractsfinder.businesslink.gov.uk/Common/View%20Notice.aspx?site=1000&lang=en&noticeid=720055&fs=true>.

[5] Invitation to tender documents available at <https://online.contractsfinder.businesslink.gov.uk/Common/View%20Notice.aspx?site=1000&lang=en&noticeid=806731&fs=true>.

[6] Denise McDonagh, 'G-Cloud—Goodbye and Thank You' (*G-Cloud blog*, 4 June 2013), <http://gcloud.civilservice.gov.uk/2013/06/04/g-cloud-goodbye-and-thank-you/> (accessed 14 June 2013).

regarding contractual and other legal issues. Governments' contractual concerns are in some respects different, and in other respects similar, to those of other cloud users.[7] We compare and contrast these against our other findings,[8] and also highlight some key changes in Gii and Giii.

Then G-Cloud programme director, Denise McDonagh, reported 50–90 per cent 'total cost of ownership' savings through using cloud.[9] For example, the UK Department of Health reduced website hosting costs by 96 per cent to £25,000 (from some £800,000 in 2011–12), by switching from a large integrator to an SME procured through G-Cloud.[10]

Government wanted an electronic marketplace covering a range of cloud and supporting services that had undergone some prior vetting, and would be available on baseline contractual terms, enabling Government buyers[11] to procure desired services easily and quickly. Government's CloudStore[12] for public sector users went live in beta form on Sunday 19 February 2012, cataloguing more than 1,700 services from 257 suppliers,[13] with services then undergoing vetting in staged tranches. Nearly 300 suppliers tendered.[14] CloudStore, hosted on Microsoft's Windows Azure PaaS service on standard Azure terms including pay-as-you-go, was developed for the G-Cloud programme for free by UK supplier Solidsoft in just four weeks,[15] although it has since been replaced.[16] Within two weeks after CloudStore's opening, the first purchase, by the Maritime and Coastguard Agency, was concluded within 24 hours from initiation.[17]

Government's first invitation to tender for G-Cloud framework agreements, leading to CloudStore, was issued on 18 October 2011[18] and has been described as 'the fastest framework procurement in UK government'.[19] The Gi exercise highlighted some

---

[7] This chapter generally uses Government terminology: 'suppliers' for cloud providers, 'buyers' for Government organizations which may procure cloud services, and 'sub-contractors' for sub-providers.

[8] See Chapter 4.

[9] <http://www.computerweekly.com/news/2240179128/Cabinet-Office-hands-government-public-cloud-first-mandate>.

[10] <http://dxw.com/2013/03/the-department-of-health-moves-its-wordpress-sites-to-dxw/>.

[11] Potential buyers are listed in Section VI.3 of the contract notice (n. 18).

[12] At <http://www.gov.uk/cloudstore>.

[13] <http://gcloud.civilservice.gov.uk/2012/02/21/the-launch/> and Chris Chant, 'Response to Proact: Why We Declined to Bid for G-Cloud Work' (*G-Cloud blog*, 29 February 2012) <http://gcloud.civilservice.gov.uk/2012/02/29/response-to-proact-why-we-declined-to-bid-for-g-cloud-work/>.

[14] G-Cloud Programme (tweet, 20 December 2011), <https://twitter.com/#!/G_Cloud_UK/status/149058999000637440> (accessed 16 March 2012).

[15] Eleanor Stewart, 'CloudStore Open for Business' (*G-Cloud blog*, 19 February 2012), <http://gcloud.civilservice.gov.uk/2012/02/19/cloudstore-open-for-business/> (accessed 16 March 2012), and Cabinet Office email, 2 March 2012.

[16] N. 114.

[17] Jo Best, 'CloudStore Breaks Its Duck as MCA Makes First Buy from Cloud Catalogue' (*Government Computing*, 5 March 2012), <http://www.guardian.co.uk/government-computing-network/2012/mar/05/cloudstore-g-cloud-purchase-mca-training> (accessed 16 March 2012).

[18] Contract notice 332461-2011 was published on 22 October 2011 at <http://ted.europa.eu/udl?uri=TED:NOTICE:332461-2011:TEXT:EN:HTML>. For related documents (including invitation to tender, forms of draft framework agreement, and compliance certificates), see <http://www.contractsfinder.businesslink.gov.uk/Common/View%20Notice.aspx?site=1000&lang=en&noticeid=306906&fs=true> supplemented by <http://www.contractsfinder.businesslink.gov.uk/Common/View%20Ojeu%20Notice.aspx?site=1000&lang=en&NoticeId=303918> (accessed 16 March 2012).
The final form of framework agreement is available at <https://online.contractsfinder.businesslink.gov.uk/Common/View%20Notice.aspx?site=1000&lang=en&NoticeId=625234>, but appears different to the final form of framework agreement as received from the G-Cloud team, email to first author of 4 April 2012, for example it does not include all the added liability provisions discussed below.

[19] Chris Chant, 'The Launch' (*G-Cloud blog*, 21 February 2012), <http://gcloud.civilservice.gov.uk/2012/02/21/the-launch/>.

uncertainties regarding cloud as a service, including issues as basic as its definition.[20] It also demonstrated some difficulties arising from suppliers' possible use of 'layered' services, of which buyers may be unaware. Finally, it illustrated some key concerns buyers or providers may have regarding cloud contract terms.

One explicit objective was to involve small and medium-sized enterprises ('SMEs')[21] as potential suppliers to Government. About 50 per cent of suppliers accepted for CloudStore were corporate SMEs.[22] This also meant Government received numerous queries from potential suppliers, many of whom had never tendered for Government contracts, regarding tender procedures, requirements, and cloud. Gii's submission deadline was postponed twice due to the influx of queries, while Giii's deadline was also extended.[23]

Key legal points related to:

1. contractual structure used, including public procurement law issues and cloud providers' liability;

2. sub-providers' role and treatment—given cloud services' often complex, multilayered nature;

3. audit rights regarding suppliers and sub-providers;

4. data location and other data protection law issues; and

5. data deletion and extraction.

Gi brought out other issues, particularly uncertainties for potential SME providers, who would benefit from more structure and guidance. However, those issues generally will not be discussed in detail here.

2. Background

Gi did not involve choosing only 'best of breed' suppliers but rather selecting, for CloudStore listing, suppliers meeting set minimum criteria, leaving buyers to narrow down selection further themselves if appropriate.[24]

Strictly, CloudStore is not an 'app store', although previously described as such.[25] Buyers cannot find a CloudStore-listed service, click to pay, then immediately 'add' and

---

[20] Gi elicited questions from suppliers, consolidated in Government Procurement Service, *Tender Questions and Answers* (12 December 2011), plus further sets of questions/answers on the draft framework agreement, 'Document 1', 'Document 2', and 'Document 3'. All were linked to at <http://www.buyingsolutions.gov.uk/categories/ICT/G-Cloud> but are now unavailable there. Unless otherwise stated, numerical references in this chapter (eg 108) are to numbered questions/answers in *Tender Questions and Answers*, now available at <http://gcloud.civilservice.gov.uk/files/2012/01/Tender-Clarification-Questions-Final-Version-12th-Dec.pdf> accessed 1 June 2013. We refer to Documents 1–3 using the same names.

[21] Definition based on number of employees and either turnover or balance sheet total—European Commission Recommendation of 6 May 2003 concerning the definition of micro, small and medium-sized enterprises [2003] OJ L124/36, 20.5.2003.

[22] Chris Chant, 'Stand (Up) and Deliver—Can SMEs Handle It' (*G-Cloud blog*, 24 February 2012). G-Cloud was cited as a successful example of encouraging Government procurement from SMEs—Cabinet Office, *SME Case Studies—Celebrating SMEs Winning Government Business* (2012).

[23] <http://gcloud.civilservice.gov.uk/2012/07/11/gii-extension-deadline/>; <http://gcloud.civilservice.gov.uk/2012/08/16/g-cloud-ii-framework-extension/>; and <http://gcloud.civilservice.gov.uk/2013/02/26/giii-submission-date-change/>.

[24] For example, 233.   [25] For example, Cabinet Office, *CloudStore Open for Business* (2012).

use it, unlike with smartphone app stores. Instead, CloudStore is a catalogue enabling buyers to locate suitable services, discuss them with suppliers as appropriate, then procure the chosen service relatively quickly. Buyers must still enter into 'call-off' contracts with suppliers, although intended to be on predefined mandatory minimum terms, then perform any necessary set-up and deployment.

Gi was not meant to provide the ultimate UK G-Cloud solution. It was intended as a pilot, to establish likely supply and demand for cloud services to help inform future procurements.[26] That is why, unlike some other Government procurement frameworks, Gi had a lifetime of only six months, extendible by Government to nine months,[27] but terminable by it at any time.[28] Call-off contracts under Gi had a maximum term of one year,[29] so could outlive Gi, but again this term is shorter than under some other Government procurements.[30]

Short durations were also intended to avoid lock-in, and move away from a culture of long-term contracts with large suppliers. Several suppliers queried the relatively short-term nature of Gi and call-off contracts. One felt its investment was difficult to justify for short terms; another requested three to five years.[31] However, issues other than contract term may affect lock-in.[32]

Gi was not intended to be the *exclusive* way for Government bodies to procure cloud services.[33] It simply provided one means of procuring cloud services, which buyers could use if they wished, knowing that a framework agreement had already been entered into and certain minimum assurance and accreditation ('A&A') procedures undergone centrally, so that buyers need not spend further time or money 'reinventing the wheel', unless further assurances were needed for particular uses.

Government bodies may procure cloud services outside of G-Cloud. Indeed, independently of G-Cloud, some have invited tenders for cloud services, typically on a pilot or trial basis.[34] Similarly, pre-existing cloud contracts were unaffected. For instance, solutions provider Savvis's IaaS platform, termed Government Wide Services (GWS), previously used by the Home Office, was adopted by the Ministry of Justice in March 2011 as a secure platform to support enterprise resource planning shared services (designed by Steria, implemented by Accenture).[35]

Suppliers who missed Gi's December 2011 deadline could not participate in Gi. Even those who met the deadline could offer only the services included in their bids.[36] However, suppliers could tender in other Government cloud procurements and centralized frameworks such as Gii and Giii, the G-Cloud frameworks that followed Gi.

---

[26] 4.
[27] And extended in July 2012 to 13 November 2012, following 'the unprecedented level of feedback' from suppliers, much of which related to G-Cloud's basic philosophy and mechanics. See Denise McDonagh, 'Gi and Gii to be extended' (*G-Cloud blog*, 6 July 2012), <http://gcloud.civilservice.gov.uk/2012/07/06/gi-gii-extended/>.
[28] 245; Gi framework agreement (n. 18).   [29] For example, 18.
[30] 268. Termination of a supplier's framework agreement would not automatically terminate call-off contracts under that agreement, although 'then the grounds for that termination may have some bearing on that supplier's Call-off contracts'; 292.
[31] For example, 4, 56, 324.   [32] See Chapter 4, Section 5.6.   [33] 214.
[34] For example, the BBC's December 2011 invitation to tender for SaaS testing services.
[35] Savvis, *United Kingdom Ministry of Justice Selects Savvis for GBP 14m Infrastructure-as-a-Service Contract* (2011), <http://www.savvis.com/en-us/company/news/press/pages/unitedkingdomministryofjusticeselectssavvisforgbp14minfrastructure-as-a-servicecontract.aspx> (accessed 16 March 2012).
[36] For example, 6. But see Section 4.2 below on suppliers' ability to update terms, which technically could include new services.

3. Which Cloud Computing Services?

The invitation to tender for Gi (ITT) stated Government's intention to utilize public cloud by default, 'utilising private cloud only where essential criteria cannot be met by public cloud delivery model offerings'. For example, Government-accredited data centre services and infrastructure dedicated to Government use might be necessary for processing information with higher security requirements. However, Government expected that how its essential criteria were met would evolve as the cloud market innovated and matured, possibly reducing the need for private cloud.

Another interesting aspect was Government's view that, for G-Cloud, private and community cloud meant the same thing. The public sector should be treated as one organization for cloud services: 'this means that there will be only one private cloud ... that is able to be accessed by all public sector consumers'.[37] Its aspiration was that components of this 'single' private cloud would be delivered by multiple suppliers/organizations, in an interconnected and interoperable manner, available to all.[38] It seems too early for much to crystallize regarding cloud standards, interoperability, or federation, and Gi did not stipulate requirements in those areas, but some suppliers raised queries about them. Government did ask suppliers to identify all open standards supported by their service and to document technical and service interfaces/boundaries, stating that, as G-Cloud services matured, it might issue additional interface/interoperability specifications/standards in future.[39] Given the current lack of such cloud standards, an interconnected Government private cloud provided by different suppliers may be some way off, but, if driven through by Government, could influence development of the UK cloud market.

Gi sought tenders of cloud services classified into four 'lots', seeking at least three suppliers per lot,[40] totalling in aggregate £60 million:[41]

- IaaS;
- PaaS;
- SaaS;[42] and
- 'Specialist services', to comprise: 'Onboarding services, Design Authority, Project/Programme Management, Business Analysis, Design and Development, Project Specification and Selection, Service Integration, Deployment, Transition Management, Service Management and User Management'.

Gi adopted the 'cloud computing' definition promulgated by the US NIST.[43] The first three lots covered 'pure' cloud services within this definition; the fourth comprised supporting services, such as consultancy services to help deploy or migrate data and/or applications or users to the cloud.[44]

Gi was not aimed at procuring free ad-supported services, such as social media used by some Government bodies, but such suppliers were not barred from bidding.[45]

There was some uncertainty regarding resellers.[46] One reseller hoped lot-four suppliers could resell services of other suppliers which had been accredited in lots one to three.

---

[37]　However, there may be different private clouds for different security levels. ITT 12.4.
[38]　ITT 12.4.　　　[39]　For example, 76.　　　[40]　For example, 5, 169.
[41]　Contract notice (n. 18): £20 million for IaaS; £10 million for PaaS; £20 million for SaaS; and £10 million for 'specialist services'. This low value is due to Gi being a pilot.
[42]　For example, customer-relationship management. Others will be considered for the future—180.
[43]　See discussion in Chapter 1.　　　[44]　429.　　　[45]　54.
[46]　For example, 78, 100. See Chapter 2.

Government clarified that resellers could tender, even if the supplier whose service was to be resold was also tendering, and vice versa. But it was unclear whether a reseller's tender should answer questions regarding themselves or suppliers of the services resold.[47] For value-added resellers, the accreditation-scoping document asked which components reuse other already-accredited services.[48] However, that seems more appropriate to SaaS services built on IaaS/PaaS services, than to resellers who simply market others' services without providing any cloud services themselves.

4. Contractual Structure

4.1 Framework agreement and call-off contracts

Uncertainties arose regarding Gi's contractual structure, in particular the difference between framework agreements and call-off contracts, their different parties, the role of suppliers' own contract terms, and suppliers' ability to negotiate framework agreements and/or call-off contracts. Underlining this, many issues raised by suppliers on framework agreement terms were in fact more relevant to call-off contracts.[49]

A framework agreement is simply an umbrella agreement, setting up the overall contractual structure, terms and procedures, the framework, under which individual 'call-off contracts' for buying goods or services may, during the framework agreement's lifetime,[50] be entered into between buyers and relevant suppliers. Under Gi, approved suppliers entered into framework agreements with the Government Procurement Service[51] ('GPS' or 'the Authority'). A call-off contract would comprise an order form[52] (completed by the buyer), which would incorporate the supplier's own terms subject to certain mandatory call-off terms, discussed below.[53] Government bodies need not 'buy' anything from suppliers who had entered into framework agreements with the GPS. Similarly, suppliers were not required to accept orders from buyers, although two or more failures to accept orders would entitle the GPS to suspend the supplier from Gi. However, the framework agreement was intended to simplify and speed up any subsequent procurement of cloud services from the supplier by an individual Government body ('Contracting Body'), through the Contracting Body making a separate call-off

---

[47] 100—which asked, *in relation to whom* should answers be given, reseller or underlying supplier? Stating the bidder should answer tender questions makes no sense for questions regarding underlying services; perhaps the question was misunderstood.

[48] Government 'AccreditCamp' webinar on A&A for suppliers, 13 February 2012—audio recording and slides at <http://www.slideshare.net/G-Cloud/accredcamp-slides-audio>. The scoping document template is at <http://gcloud.civilservice.gov.uk/files/2012/02/G-Cloud-Service-Accreditation-Scope-Template-.doc>.

[49] For example, 122, 194, 195, 213.   [50] 179.

[51] An executive agency of Government's Cabinet Office, to provide procurement savings for Government generally, and specifically centralized procurement for central Government departments. <http://gps.cabinetoffice.gov.uk/about-government-procurement-service/about-us> (accessed 1 June 2013).

[52] Framework agreement Sch. 2 contained an example order form, incorporating by reference the supplier's own terms, plus overlay terms discussed below.

[53] The final form of framework agreement defined 'Call-Off Agreement' as 'a legally binding agreement (entered into pursuant to the provisions of this Framework Agreement) for the provision of G-Cloud Services made between a Contracting Body and the Supplier comprising of an Order Form and the Call-Off Terms as may be amended pursuant to Paragraph 3.1.2 of Framework Schedule 3

contract with the supplier under Gi, with its own expiry date and termination provisions. The GPS would not be party to call-off contracts.[54]

There was a further twist. Government indicated that a Gi supplier would supply services under its own terms, to be incorporated into its call-off contract with the Contracting Body. However, those terms would be subject to an 'overlay' of certain overriding call-off terms, specified in the framework agreement. To participate in Gi, a supplier must agree that such overlay terms take precedence over its own terms, should they conflict.[55] The intention was that a supplier and buyer could agree minor amendments to the supplier's own terms, for example different or additional terms, with the sample order form referring to 'special terms', but not so as to alter the overlay terms.[56]

Queries were raised regarding, for instance, service level agreements (SLAs),[57] found in some cloud contracts but not covered in the framework agreement. SLAs were intended to be addressed in the supplier's service description or elsewhere in its tender response, or its own 'subsequent' terms.[58] Similarly, Government expected suppliers' terms to cover their right to terminate, acceptable use policies, general customer obligations, invoicing for charges, payment terms, indemnities, right for parties to seek injunctive relief, intellectual property rights, and interest on late payments.[59]

Government specified that:

- Suppliers passing certain basic checks (covered below) would sign a framework agreement with the GPS for a six-month term, extendible by Government to nine months.

- An intending buyer (Government department, local authority, etc.) of cloud services from such a supplier would, during the lifetime of the supplier's framework agreement, enter into a separate call-off contract with the supplier, for a term not exceeding one year. Thus, some provisions of the framework agreement, between the Authority and supplier, were replicated in the standard terms to 'overlay' any call-off contract between the Contracting Body and supplier.[60]

- The buyer–supplier contract would be on the supplier's own terms, with certain mandatory terms, stipulated by the framework agreement, overriding the supplier's terms in case of conflict.

Figure 5.1 illustrates the contractual relationships: both Supplier A and Supplier B have made framework agreements with the GPS, Government Buyer 1 has made call-off contracts with Supplier A and Supplier B, but Government Buyer 2 has made a call-off contract only with Supplier A.

(Call-Off Ordering Procedure including Award Criteria)' [sic—Sch. 3 did not contain a para. 3.1.2 or another provision on amending contract terms].

'Call-Off Terms' were defined as 'terms and conditions (including the Supplier's terms and conditions) in Framework Schedule 2 (Order Form and Call-Off Terms)'. However, there seemed no express provision for mandatory terms to override *order form* terms inserted by a buyer as agreed with the supplier, in case of conflict. Gii added reference to the order form in the precedence clause.

[54] 245.   [55] Framework agreement (n. 18) Sch. 2, para. 2.
[56] For example, 122.
[57] Covering 'performance, availability and other operational factors of that service'—361. See text to n. 85.
[58] 211—'Service Levels are provided by the supplier in the Tender response and catalogue entry or on any subsequent Terms & Conditions provided by the supplier.' This suggested tender responses were part of the framework agreement, and that suppliers could provide terms subsequently (ie change them). Also, for example, 44, 66.
[59] For example, 451. This changed in Gii/Giii.   [60] For example, 191.

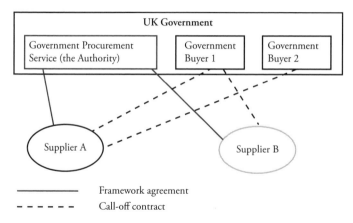

Figure 5.1 Contractual relationships between GPS, Government buyers, and suppliers

4.2 The overlay approach

Three potential issues arose with Gi's contractual approach: a risk exposure if any issues were not covered in any of the documents; the potential for disputes over whether terms conflicted; and whether the documents complied with public procurement rules.

An overlay approach carries legal risks for buyers and suppliers. For suppliers, the overlay terms override suppliers' own terms should they conflict, and in this regard it is interesting that enterprise SaaS provider Salesforce submitted specially tailored terms for Gii, rather than its usual standard terms.[61]

For Government, its overlay terms only take priority where there is a conflict, so one risk is that, if overlay terms do not cover a situation addressed in a supplier's terms, the latter would govern. This means the overlay terms must be carefully thought through, to ensure they cover *all* intended situations, without important gaps. For example, several suppliers were concerned that the draft overlay terms did not contain any limitation of their liability. In reality, this omission would have meant that the suppliers' own terms controlled the liability position, for example excluding or substantially restricting their liability.[62] So, that omission was more an issue for Government than suppliers. Ultimately, Government changed the draft framework agreement to limit expressly each party's liability for breach of framework agreement or any call-off contracts (and with 'direct' losses expressed to include losses from data loss or corruption, namely data integrity).[63] Without this change, suppliers' own terms would very likely have excluded or restricted their liability.

Second, it is not always straightforward to assess whether and to what extent a supplier's terms and overlay terms conflict, as they could be inconsistent only indirectly. This can result in disputes, with the parties disagreeing as to whether a conflict exists.

The third issue relates to public procurement contracts, not cloud contracts more generally. This chapter focuses on contractual terms, so procurement issues are not

---

[61] Search CloudStore for Salesforce. Direct links to specific CloudStore entries were not possible as at March 2013.

[62] See Chapter 3.

[63] Clause 24, and clause 9.1, Sch. 2, final form of framework agreement received April 2012 (see n. 18), although the final wording's meaning was unclear. The liability provisions in framework agreement and call-off terms differed, but were based on amounts paid under the relevant agreement. The December 2011 and April 2012 versions of the liability wording are reproduced at <http://cloudlegalproject.org/Research/71492.html>. Numerous suppliers queried their liability, for example 108.

discussed in detail. Nevertheless, we outline them because they may be relevant to other similar Government procurements.[64]

EU public procurement laws[65] aim to provide value for money for taxpayers while ensuring equal treatment, non-discrimination, and transparency. Several alternative procedures are possible for awarding Government contracts. Non-compliance can render a commercial agreement void.

Gi's purpose was clear: 'The buying process should be quick and easy (select from catalogue) and shouldn't need negotiation.'[66] Was that purpose achieved? For multiple suppliers to tender to supply Government with cloud services under framework agreements between each approved supplier and GPS, Gi employed what's termed the 'open' procedure.[67] To comply with public procurement law and allow buyers to obtain cloud services without having to reopen competition at call-off stage, the contractual structure and terms must satisfy certain requirements. Notably, the framework agreement must include 'all the terms of the proposed contract' (the call-off contract), to avoid reopening competition, and call-off contract terms cannot be 'substantially amended' from those in the signed framework agreement. Because the 'open procedure' was used, framework agreement terms as proposed by GPS could not be negotiated,[68] although amendments by suppliers and/or GPS to clarify terms or correct errors were permitted.[69] Also, when establishing a framework, the basis of call-offs must be made clear in advance, as it may inform suppliers' bid responses. Failing to do so, or amending the basis for making call-offs after concluding the framework agreement, would breach transparency requirements and, therefore, public procurement laws.

It may be queried whether Gi met those requirements, for several reasons. First, in December 2011, changes were made to the framework agreement, such as to include liability limitation, allow third-party audits and other provisions,[70] which seemed to go beyond mere clarification and error correction, and might therefore be inconsistent with the open procedure. It was changed again between December 2011 and February 2012 to expand the liability provisions from a paragraph to a page.[71]

Second, although suppliers had to submit their own terms with their tender,[72] it was unclear to what extent the framework agreement included the supplier's own terms (albeit with mandatory overlay), as those terms were not explicitly incorporated into or, it seems, attached to, the signed framework agreement. While the framework agreement included a sample order form, buyers were not obliged to use that form, and suppliers could reject orders if they considered customer service requirements or implementation requests, as specified at order stage, too onerous. Furthermore, the order form completed by the buyer could include terms not provided in, or different from, those in the framework agreement, such as the service requirements just mentioned, testing requirements and 'Special Terms such as Service Descriptions and Service Standards'. It was unclear to what extent such terms might constitute 'substantial' amendment.

---

[64] On public procurement law, we are grateful for input from Kevin Calder, partner, Mills & Reeve LLP.
[65] Implemented in the UK by the Public Contracts Regulations 2006 (SI 2006/5) and the Public Contracts (Scotland) Regulations 2006 (SI 2006/1), each as amended. Regulations 15 and 19 of the former contain requirements on the open procedure and framework agreements.
[66] Chant (n. 13).   [67] 436; ITT 7.8.   [68] For example, 123, 176.   [69] 123, 436.
[70] See n. 63 on liability limitation. Provisions on freedom of information, official secrets, and so on, initially omitted for brevity (110), were also added, as were typographical/cross-reference corrections.
[71] Framework agreement (final form) clause 24, and Sch. 2, 9.1—see n. 63.   [72] 55, 155.

Third, suppliers could update catalogue entries, including service description and contract terms, meaning a supplier's terms, as incorporated into a call-off contract, could differ from those at the date of the framework agreement. Although Government intended only that suppliers should be able to update service description and pricing, not contract terms,[73] the framework agreement specifically entitled suppliers to vary catalogue entries 'with all new prices and/or other terms being effective in respect of all orders placed thereafter'.[74]

Amending an existing public sector contract may sometimes constitute a 'new' contract award, which may be invalid if processes for new procurements were not followed. Amendments may constitute 'new' awards if 'materially different in character from the original contract', thereby demonstrating the parties' intention to renegotiate the contract's essential terms. 'Material' amendments include ones extending the contract's scope 'considerably to encompass services not initially covered', or changing the economic balance in favour of the contractor in a manner not provided by the initial contract.[75]

Where the original contract builds in express mechanisms envisaging and permitting specific types of changes, such as annual retail price index-based price increases, that may be permissible under procurement laws. Gi allowed suppliers to update 'all new prices and/or other terms', not mentioning specific terms other than prices. Allowing amendments to 'other terms', while expressly permitted by the framework agreement, is extremely broad, seemingly allowing amendments to suppliers' terms of any nature and scope, subject to the overlay. Similarly, 'all new prices' does not restrict how much or how prices may change. The effect of such broad provisions under procurement laws is difficult to assess. However, if updated 'other terms', or large price increases, were 'substantially' or 'materially' different from the original, questions must arise regarding whether any contract incorporating the updated terms would effectively be a fresh contract, requiring a new procurement, therefore possibly entailing case-by-case review by potential buyers of suppliers' terms against initially submitted terms.

It was unclear whether the call-off contract must attach the supplier's terms (incorporated by reference in the sample order form—but which version of those terms?), and whether the catalogue would flag changes to terms made by suppliers to alert buyers to check for differences between original and updated suppliers' terms. It was also unclear whether the catalogue would retain initial as well as latest uploaded terms, to enable checking for compliance with public procurement laws. Therefore, there must be some uncertainty regarding which version of a supplier's terms would be incorporated into a call-off contract, and whether suppliers' later terms made material or substantial amendments requiring a new procurement.

Although the 'Store' designation, and various statements on the official G-Cloud blog, suggested that Gi had established a simpler buying process, the issues mentioned above could have been problematic, and interestingly the framework agreement itself seemed to envisage some call-offs could involve further negotiations and possibly even competition.[76] In fact, no challenge to Gi on any of these bases was mounted. However, there are ways to ensure compliance with public procurement requirements while

---

[73] Telephone conversation with Authority representative, 29 February 2012.

[74] If Government intended to incorporate supplier's terms as at the date of the framework agreement, the contractual documentation did not make this explicit, and indeed the agreement's wording seemed to allow suppliers to change terms thereafter.

[75] Case C-454/06 *pressetext Nachrichtenagentur GmbH v Austria* [2008] ECR I-4401.

[76] Framework agreement Sch. 3 (Call-Off Ordering Procedure) and text to n. 117.

avoiding the need for buyers to engage in competitive tendering at call-off stage. While it may be difficult to strike the desired balance between protecting Government and facilitating supplier bids, many uncertainties could have been eliminated by, for example, including specific framework agreement provisions explicitly annexing and incorporating the supplier's terms into that agreement, requiring those incorporated terms (and no other versions) to be part of any call-off contracts, subject to mandatory call-off terms, and prohibiting G-Cloud suppliers from amending those incorporated terms in any call-off contracts, for example by the supplier updating its catalogue entry (although incorporated terms could expressly permit changes such as price increases, as mentioned above). Alternatively, which might involve less risk of breaching procurement rules, a form of framework agreement could be used covering all required issues comprehensively (including a full call-off contract, without incorporating any suppliers' terms).[77]

Another important issue, in assessing compliance with public procurement laws, is evaluating suppliers' terms. Where suppliers may amend framework agreement terms (including call-off terms), or submit their own terms superseding elements of those terms, Government would need to ensure there was a basis for evaluating the impact of suppliers' terms on whether the relevant bid was the most economically advantageous tender, given the 'value for money' objective of public procurement laws. Clearly, onerous supplier terms would have an overall impact on value. This point is relevant to an approach where some areas are not addressed in Government terms, but covered only by supplier terms, such as SLAs. If buyers' evaluations did not encompass supplier terms, arguably that would constitute unequal treatment, as different services might not be evaluated on an equivalent basis.

5. G-Cloud Security—A&A

The G-Cloud frameworks addressed assurance and accreditation separately. 'Assurance' involves verifying claimed functionality/service management aspects of the service, for example that service criteria in suppliers' catalogue entries and service definitions are stated clearly and unambiguously, and commercial assurance (financial viability, via credit checks). All G-Cloud suppliers underwent assurance.[78] 'Accreditation' involves information security assurance, defined as 'the formal assessment of the ICT system against its information assurance (IA) requirements, resulting in the acceptance of residual risks in the context of the business requirement. It is a prerequisite to approval to operate'.[79] To avoid duplication, accreditation for the G-Cloud frameworks is performed centrally by the pan-Government accreditation service ('PGA').[80] This section focuses on accreditation.

---

[77] And see 330.

[78] CloudStore, under the 'Further Documents' tab, 'Assurance Details URL'. Assurance results are currently cloud-hosted on Google Sites, and seem to include services not themselves directly on G-Cloud frameworks, such as Google Mail <https://sites.google.com/a/gcloud.cabinet-office.gov.uk/assurance-result-details/home/g033-004-google-mail>.

[79] Emma Gawen, 'Introducing Accreditation' (*G-Cloud blog*, 9 February 2012), <http://gcloud.civilservice.gov.uk/2012/02/09/introducing-accreditation/>. For fuller details, see ITT Appendix 3, 'Service Assurance/Accreditation' and Emma Gawen, 'Accreditation Myths and Confusion' (*G-Cloud blog*, 3 April 2012), <http://gcloud.civilservice.gov.uk/2012/04/03/accreditation-myths-and-confusion/> (each accessed 16 March 2012).

[80] Provided by Government's National Technical Authority for Information Assurance and Cabinet Office (formerly Communications–Electronics Security Group, still commonly called 'CESG').

UK central Government departments must assess what's called the 'business impact level' ('BIL' or 'IL') of information assets or IT systems, for risks to confidentiality, integrity, and availability. Some suppliers were unclear regarding this classification system, or its requirements.[81] IL0 means zero impact, while IL6 indicates maximum possible negative impact. For example, if certain information is assessed at 0-0-0 (or 000), this means its loss is considered to have zero impact on Government in terms of confidentiality, integrity, and availability, respectively. Impact may vary with business sector, and may increase with data aggregation.[82] Standard Government protective markings for confidentiality affect IL: information marked 'PROTECT', 'RESTRICTED', 'CONFIDENTIAL', 'SECRET', and 'TOP SECRET' would have ILs for confidentiality of 2, 3, 4, 5, and 6 respectively. However, the reverse does not hold: for example, an asset with IL5 for confidentiality would not necessarily be marked 'SECRET'. Government considers that impact levels should be assessed no differently when using cloud.[83]

With G-Cloud, to help meet one of Government's principles of driving commoditization, ILs were expressed as follows: IL0-0-X, IL1-1-X, IL2-2-X, IL3-3-X. Thus, 'IL1' was shorthand for IL1-1-X, 'IL2' for IL2-2-X, and so on. X was undefined.[84] This was because Government, not knowing what levels of availability suppliers might wish to propose, left it to suppliers to express their service's availability (including options) in service definitions in a way meaningful for service type and customers.[85] In short, Government, rather than stipulating minimum availability levels, wanted suppliers' tenders to include information about their own levels (the undefined X), perhaps with different levels priced differently, so that buyers could choose the level meeting their individual needs.

CloudStore was itself unavailable for several hours on 29 February 2012 due to an Azure outage.[86] While this might seem to underscore the risks of cloud, Chant explained that Government had chosen an Azure installation without 'multi-service deployment' because CloudStore was not considered a 'critical Government system' justifying higher costs for higher guaranteed uptime. Email was used to obtain information needed to continue working. This incident, therefore, might alternatively be taken to illustrate that higher availabilities are possible, at a price, and that buyers may, and do, evaluate cost/risk trade-offs. Here, for a catalogue service, Government chose not to pay the premium.[87]

G-Cloud accreditations rely on ISO27001[88] accreditation, obtained at suppliers' own expense, rather than IL accreditation. While lack of existing IL accreditation did not bar suppliers from G-Cloud, G-Cloud services at IL1 or above required ISO27001 accreditation, whose scope must be agreed with the PGA, performed by United Kingdom

[81] 364, 379.   [82] 53.
[83] CESG, *Extract from HMG IA Standard No. 1—Business Impact Level Tables* (2009). Simplifications are planned, partly because G-Cloud accreditations have proved more involved and time-consuming than desired. Derek du Perez, 'Government Plans to Halve Number of Security Levels to Simplify Accreditation' (*ComputerWorldUK*, 12 June 2012), <http://www.computerworlduk.com/news/public-sector/3363496/government-plans-to-halve-number-of-security-levels-to-simplify-accreditation/>.
[84] Cf the Public Services Network, a 'network of networks' for Government based on existing commercial networks, which requires IL4 for availability.
[85] 410.
[86] CloudStore later moved to ProcServe's GeM (n. 112)—a non-cloud service which also suffered access issues in 2012: <https://twitter.com/G_Cloud_UK/statuses/228134794838556672>.
[87] Chris Chant, 'CloudStore and the Microsoft Azure Outage' (*G-Cloud blog*, 1 March 2012), <http://gcloud.civilservice.gov.uk/2012/03/01/cloudstore-and-the-microsoft-azure-outage/> (accessed 16 March 2012).
[88] ISO/IEC, *ISO/IEC 27001:2005—Information Technology—Security Techniques—Information Security Management Systems—Requirements* (2005).

Accreditation Service (UKAS)-accredited third parties who would review evidence and conduct site visits as appropriate. As IL1 and IL2 accreditations are similar, Government decided to require IL2 accreditation for IL1 services. While wanting notification of any existing IL1/2 accreditations, Government favoured specific ISO27001 accreditation for G-Cloud IL2, with the PGA checking the existing accreditation's scope. Thus, suppliers with existing ISO27001 accreditation might not require much further action, at least for IL2, if the scope was considered acceptable. For example, for services hosted in an ISO27001 (IaaS/PaaS) facility, where the SaaS software had no ISO27001 accreditation, Government stated that, for IL1/2, suitably scoped ISO27001 accreditation would be required for the software and surrounding support/management process, but a componentized (or layered) approach would be taken to accreditation, placing reliance on the existing IaaS/PaaS accreditation. For IL3 ('RESTRICTED'), where security of network connections is also important, suppliers without existing accreditations were advised to consult Communications-Electronics Security Group (CESG) Listed Advisers Scheme (CLAS) consultants.[89]

Some suppliers were uncertain regarding A&A requirements and timing, partly because full correct details of procedures/requirements, needed by some to determine pricing and even whether to bid, were unavailable before December 2011.[90] A Security Accreditation Scope template[91] was provided in January 2012. Accreditation information was, and continues to be, published on the G-Cloud blog and webpages.[92] Detailed A&A guidance on G-Cloud was issued in May 2012.[93] This guidance is expected to be revised for lessons learned and to reflect planned changes in Government's protective marking scheme.[94]

Initially, it was unclear whether a service could be added to CloudStore or purchasable before passing full A&A, and indeed whether all CloudStore services must be ISO27001-accredited at least 'for the ILs at which ISO 27001 is [sic]'. However, CloudStore listed unaccredited services. Some services, particularly lot four, were considered not to require accreditation. CloudStore services could be procured for IL0 situations. However, for IL1 or higher, buyers could only use appropriately accredited services, for example for IL1/2 purposes, services accredited to IL2.[95]

The first accreditations were not completed until August 2012, involving nine services from supplier SCC, several at IL3.[96] A webpage lists accredited services;[97] at

---

[89] 3, 90; 304, 375; 408, 409; 393; 409; 411 (the answer seemed to suggest both SaaS and IaaS/PaaS require A&A, but any existing IaaS/PaaS accreditation may be relied on); Authority (n. 73); AccreditCamp (n. 48). CLAS consultants are members of the CLAS.

[90] 47, 70c, 118, 265 (although the agreed change is not in the final framework agreement), 412, 480. Insufficient prior information on A&A requirements may also cause procurement law problems—see paragraph after n. 69.

[91] N. 48.

[92] <http://gcloud.civilservice.gov.uk/supplier-zone/accreditation/>; <http://gcloud.civilservice.gov.uk/supplier-zone/accreditation-qa/>; and more generally <http://gcloud.civilservice.gov.uk/category/accreditation/>.

[93] HM Government, *G-Cloud Information Assurance Requirements and Guidance* (2012) <http://gcloud.civilservice.gov.uk/files/2012/05/G-Cloud-Services-IA-Requirements-and-Guidance-version-1-0-_for-publication_1-2.pdf>.

[94] The Cabinet Office's review of Government's protective marking system (n. 83) proposes three tiers of protective markings, with 'the lower tier' intended to manage risk to most Government and personal data, including BIL2 information as well as sensitive information that is BIL 3, subject to low (typical commercial) threat conditions. Controls for services at this lower tier will probably be based on principles in the G-Cloud guidance—n. 93, paras 60–1.

[95] 3, 471; 3; 373; 473; AccreditCamp (n. 48), Chant (n. 19).

[96] <http://gcloud.civilservice.gov.uk/2012/08/22/accreditation-go/>.

[97] <http://gcloud.civilservice.gov.uk/customer-zone/accreditation-status/>.

March 2013, only one other supplier, Skyscape,[98] had achieved IL3, but several services had achieved IL2 ('PROTECT'), including collaboration SaaS service Huddle and Microsoft's Office 365 SaaS.

Regarding the public cloud risks of shared systems,[99] bidders must provide 'proof of adequate separation between non-government users and government users of IL2 and IL3 services'.[100] This suggested buyers could use public cloud services freely for IL0/1, but subsequent guidance stated that 'Protections must be in place to ensure that different tenants within a multi-tenanted environment can only gain access to their own information within the service. For customers consuming the service at BIL 00x, 11x and 22x, the use of an appropriate assured product might provide this separation, or alternatively a penetration test which tests the strength of the separation in the design can be performed'.[101] For IL2-2-x, suppliers must explain how they achieve data separation and secure data transfer to/from the public cloud.[102]

Government wanted the accreditation process to be as similar as possible to that for the Public Services Network ('PSN'),[103] with similar governance regime and involvement of the PSN accreditation panel, and 2-2-x accreditation being akin to CESG Assured Service – Telecoms (CAS(T)) telecommunications services certification.[104] As not all services require accreditation, rather than accrediting all accepted suppliers procedures were developed for suppliers to apply for accreditation, with one 'window' each month. The G-Cloud programme provided advice and non-financial assistance to suppliers regarding A&A (which might include, eg, whether the supplier, in fact, needed its target accreditation level), rather than eliminating it immediately for non-compliance, in line with Government's SME agenda.[105]

Gi was very technology-led, with some reliance on A&A to iron out certain issues overlapping with law or regulation. For example, if 'personal data is within the scope of the service', suppliers seeking accreditation for IL 11x/22x services had to complete a Data Protection Act 1998 ('DPA') checklist, produced by the G-Cloud programme, regarding suppliers' management of personal data.[106]

Accredited services will be reviewed and reapproved 'at least every 12 months and/ or if there is a substantial change to the accredited service or a change in the perceived threat, whichever is soonest. Any significant change or shortfall in the configuration of G-Cloud relevant systems and services, or the physical, personnel or procedural security measures in place at the corresponding locations may invalidate accreditation and require the G-Cloud service to undergo re-accreditation. The PGA may at random select to inspect a G-Cloud relevant supplier and supporting service site/locations'.[107]

---

[98] Set up by QinetiQ, VMware, Cisco, EMC, and Ark Continuity, <http://www.skyscapecloud.com/skyscape-press/g-cloud-expert-skyscape-awarded-highest-level-of-pan-government-accreditation>.
[99] See Chapter 2.
[100] 45, 52.   [101] N. 93.   [102] AccreditCamp (n. 48).
[103] A 'network of networks' for the public sector, from existing commercial networks: <http://gps.cabinetoffice.gov.uk/contracts/rm860>.
[104] AccreditCamp (n. 48).   [105] N. 92.
[106] N. 93. CESG (n. 83) categorizes 'Loss of control of a citizen's personal data beyond those authorised by the citizen' as BIL1, 'Loss of control of many citizens' personal data beyond those authorised by each citizen' as BIL2, 'Loss of control of a citizen's sensitive data beyond those authorised by the citizen. A compromise to the identity or financial status of an individual citizen' as BIL3, and so on. It also covers BILs for 'Impact on the Identity of the Citizen'.
[107] Gii ApplyCamp <http://gcloud.civilservice.gov.uk/files/2012/06/ApplyCampJune-2012QA.docx>.

6. CloudStore

Gi's CloudStore catalogue entries were created from accepted suppliers' tender submission spreadsheets. CloudStore beta was the 'parking area', with entries for listed services marked 'WAITING TO BE ASSURED'. Certain aspects were searchable, such as supplier name, service, and IL. At CloudStore's launch, for most listed services 'Service description' contained no descriptions or links, and initially there were few links to pricing. However, many details are now publicly available on CloudStore, including suppliers' service definitions and terms.

Suppliers must pay the GPS a monthly management charge of 0.5 per cent of all (VAT-exclusive) 'Charges' payable by Contracting Bodies to the supplier for orders placed, and provide monthly 'Management Information' reports to the GPS, including information on orders received, and invoices raised during the month reported on, to enable invoicing by the GPS.[108] These reports are also the source of regularly published G-Cloud sales information, including buyer, supplier, and amount.[109] The catalogue is also published periodically in downloadable form.[110]

The GPS wanted to publish 'Catalogue Entries, Service Definitions, supplier prices, supplier terms and conditions, assurance and accreditation verification results, performance feedback from Customer Satisfaction monitoring and from Authority Management Information'—but not 'supplier designs or processes, supplier IPR or the details from accreditation supporting documentation', which would only be available to buyers because security control information is considered commercially sensitive.[111] Initially, the catalogue was to be hosted on the pre-existing Government eMarketplace (GeM) platform,[112] viewable only by registered buyers.[113] That may be partly why a specially created CloudStore was launched, publicly accessible without login. However, with the initial CloudStore, buyers could not see tender information withheld from the public catalogue. For reasons including buyers' desire to view such detailed information, the catalogue part of CloudStore moved to the GeM in May 2012,[114] remaining publicly accessible. The GeM may be replaced later in 2013.[115]

Under Gi, as mentioned above, suppliers could vary catalogue entries, including descriptions of services offered. Hence, a 'catalogue builder tool' was to be provided to suppliers for future changes of catalogue entries.[116] As previously discussed, despite Government's contrary intention, the Gi framework agreement permitted suppliers to change terms, including prices. It is unknown what mechanisms Government implemented for notifications whenever suppliers updated their catalogue entries using the tool, and how it checked what changes were made. However, Gii and Giii attempted to restrict updates, discussed below.

---

[108] Gi framework agreement clause 11, Sch. 4, para. 1.3.
[109] <http://gcloud.civilservice.gov.uk/about/sales-information/>.
[110] <http://data.gov.uk/dataset/cloudstore_catalogue_version>.
[111] 243 (cf 70c), framework agreement clause 33.4. On information to be redacted from the framework agreement, and presumably also the catalogue, see 485.
[112] ProcServe, *Government eMarketplace & Dynamic Marketplace*, <http://www.procserve.com/solutions/governmentemarketplace.html> (accessed 16 March 2012).
[113] For example, 220.
[114] Eleanor Stewart, 'CloudStore—the Next Iteration' (*G-Cloud blog*, 18 March 2012), <http://gcloud.civilservice.gov.uk/2012/05/18/cloudstore-the-next-iteration/> (accessed 15 August 2012).
[115] Webcast Q&A, <http://gcloud.civilservice.gov.uk/files/2012/11/CloudStore-for-Suppliers-QA-Final-External.xls>, 179, 125.
[116] For example, 43; clause 6.2, framework agreement. Indeed, suppliers *must* keep entries updated: clause 6.1.

Government intended that a buyer would use CloudStore as follows:

1. derive a longlist of services meeting its essential minimum requirements;

2. produce a shortlist of offerings providing a suitable service within its available budget;

3. award directly based on lowest price or, if unable to identify which service best met its needs, further evaluate shortlisted offerings using the same evaluation model based on criteria 'Whole life cost', 'Functional fit', 'Non-functional characteristics', and 'Service management', to which it could apply its own weightings. It could conduct tests and demonstrations or set service descriptions or standards as necessary to enable it to establish which shortlisted offering provided the most economically advantageous solution for it;[117]

4. suppliers would hear from a potential buyer only if it needed clarification on a catalogue entry, or if they had been shortlisted (including on how their offering performed in evaluation, if unsuccessful); and

5. if buyer and supplier were agreed, they would sign a call-off contract comprising an order form incorporating the supplier's standard terms, subject to overlay terms.[118]

7. Gi Contractual Documents

7.1 Layering of services

A cloud services supplier who contracts directly with a customer may 'layer' its service on other services obtained from sub-providers, who themselves may use other sub-providers.[119] Normally, the supplier would have a direct contract only with its immediate provider. One uncertainty therefore was, which if any of these other actors would be considered a G-Cloud supplier's 'Sub-Contractor', and what did G-Cloud require in relation to them?[120]

The first issue concerns A&A. It was unclear how far down the layers A&A would need to go. For instance, Government confirmed that a SaaS supplier finalizing contracts with an IaaS partner could tender, but its service would not 'be placed in the assured/accredited catalogue (from which customers can place call-off contracts) until such time as it has gone through assurance/accreditation'.[121] The question therefore was, exactly what 'it' must undergo A&A? Which services must pass A&A before a supplier's tender could be accepted for G-Cloud? Only its SaaS service, the PaaS service it used, the IaaS service on which the PaaS service was built, the ultimate data centre's service? Would it depend on a buyer's intended IL, for example down to the data centre layer for IL3 and above, but only the SaaS layer for IL0?

Government stated that use of sub-contractors and third parties would be covered 'as part of the scope of the ISO27001 certification or accreditation of the service'.[122]

---

[117] At least one buyer has published a further Request for Information from Gii suppliers—see <https://online.contractsfinder.businesslink.gov.uk/Common/View%20Notice.aspx?site=1000&lang=en&noticeid=819867&fs=true>.

[118] 37; framework agreement Sch. 2, Sch. 3; 33. Buyers must also ensure that A&A activities suit their risk profiles, and should consider the service in their internal accreditation process—406—so further security measures could be required at call-off stage.

[119] See Chapter 1. [120] See, for example, 307, although the question itself was unclear.

[121] 23.

[122] 303: the query was whether, for transfer of Authority personal data to sub-contractors as part of providing G-Cloud services (as per, for example, 444), blanket consent could be given for public cloud services at IL2 or below. The response did not address the consent issue as such. Presumably, if the PGA approved such sub-contractors, the Authority would consent—but this was not clarified.

However, how would they be 'covered'; how many layers down the cloud 'stack' would the A&A process go? It seems that, for SaaS hosted on IaaS/PaaS, accreditation of the IaaS/PaaS layer would be required, because Government had stated that any existing accreditation of that layer could be relied upon, although the SaaS software must still undergo appropriate ISO27001 accreditation.[123] However, Government did not clarify whether IaaS/PaaS layers *not* already accredited would require accreditation. Furthermore, this seems inconsistent with the answer to another query regarding whether, to offer a SaaS service, the platform hosting that implementation must itself be on CloudStore or be accredited. There, Government stated: 'No, the SaaS provision includes the necessary elements of platform and infrastructure.'[124] Also, for a consortium bid, it was considered acceptable for the main supplier to be ISO27001-certified, even if a partner was not.[125]

Government stated that, for services at IL2 ('RESTRICTED') and higher, the nature and extent of the supplier's dependence on lower layers (including third-party data centres) and their security would need careful consideration, implying that any PaaS/IaaS service relied on must be accredited to IL2 or IL3, as appropriate. Also, it stated that if data centres used had existing certifications, those could be relevant as evidence when accrediting the supplier's service.[126]

However, it remains unclear exactly what needs to be considered, and what kinds of accreditations for lower 'layers' will be acceptable. If a supplier partners with a sub-provider to offer its service,[127] the supplier may secure the sub-provider's active cooperation, and even agreement to subject the sub-provider's service to G-Cloud A&A, and it might be able to negotiate the terms of its sub-provider contract. However, another supplier may use standardized sub-services on the sub-provider's standard terms, often on a 'click-through' basis. If so, it might be unable to negotiate the sub-provider contract, or persuade the sub-provider to agree to undergo A&A or provide other assistance for the supplier's G-Cloud tender. Thus, suppliers may wish to know beforehand what checks, certifications, accreditations, or audits are required regarding sub-providers, sub-sub-providers, and so on, before deciding whether to bid, so they can assess whether the requirements could be met. Providing such advance information to suppliers would also avoid risks of procurement law breaches through giving insufficient information.

In future frameworks, advance provision of more information about precisely how use of lower layers would be covered for accreditation purposes would assist potential suppliers, particularly SMEs. Gii and Giii have clarified that suppliers need only disclose sub-contractors 'who directly contribute to the Potential Provider's ability to meet its obligations under the Framework Agreement (including under any Call-Off Contract). There is no need to specify those sub-contractors providing general services to the Potential Provider (such as window cleaners, lawyers, desktop software providers etc) that indirectly enable the Potential Provider to perform the Framework Agreement'. However, clarity regarding IaaS/PaaS services, data centre operators, and data centre equipment suppliers is still needed.

The next issue relates to compliance certificates. For Gi, bidding suppliers had to provide a certificate of compliance regarding offered services, information provided, acceptance of framework agreement and terms, and so on. Suppliers also had to give any named sub-contractors copies of G-Cloud documentation. Furthermore, suppliers' sub-contractors (or consortium members) must sign similar certificates regarding the accuracy of information in the supplier's tender regarding them or their services, which

---

[123] 411.   [124] 167.   [125] 383.   [126] AccreditCamp (n. 48).
[127] For example, 23—SaaS supplier partnering with IaaS provider.

presupposes they would see at least part of that tender. Government stated that certificates for known sub-contractors must be submitted with tenders.[128]

Again, this approach, based on traditional outsourcing, raises uncertainties for cloud services. Who is a 'sub-contractor' of the cloud supplier? With layered services, are certificates required not just for the SaaS supplier, but also its PaaS/IaaS sub-provider? One supplier even asked whether certificates were needed for its hardware and software suppliers, to which the answer was, perhaps not entirely helpfully, that certificates must be completed for 'all Subcontractors that will acting on your behalf, provide any goods and/or services in accordance with the framework agreement'.[129]

Uncertainties regarding 'Sub-Contractors' also arose from suggestions that only entities explicitly listed in a supplier's tender would be 'Sub-Contractors'. However, it was stated that sub-contractors need not, but 'can', be listed or referred to in the supplier's service definition 'if you consider them integral to your service offering'; otherwise, 'please register a list of your sub-contractors with GPS (Government Procurement Service) after the award of the framework'.[130]

In situations such as audits, it seems clear Government intended only to include sub-contractors with whom suppliers had direct contracts. However, sub-sub-providers' services and underlying physical infrastructure may well affect the security of G-Cloud suppliers' services. Therefore, for A&A, Government might well wish to vet lower-layer services. For example, storage equipment used could have 'backdoors'. Whether bidding suppliers may require sub-providers to undergo such vetting is a different matter. Perhaps intending suppliers of SaaS to Government will migrate to using only IaaS and PaaS providers who have themselves tendered and been approved for G-Cloud ('Accepted Infrastructure Providers'). Indeed, Government had stated that Accepted Infrastructure Providers providing services to other intending G-Cloud suppliers must commit to doing so on terms no less favourable than those applying to direct provision of IaaS/PaaS services to Government under Gi.[131] Such non-discrimination provisions will encourage resellers/integrators in the market and may also incentivize IaaS/PaaS providers to tender for G-Cloud and seek accreditation, so that Government may influence cloud market development. However, while CloudStore service definitions currently indicate whether the service is available to other G-Cloud suppliers, there seems no contractual requirement for services to be so made available *on no less favourable terms*, such as pricing.

7.2 Audit rights

A major issue from our research on negotiated cloud contracts involved audit rights, namely rights of customers and/or their regulators, auditors, and so on to audit cloud providers' services, particularly Government and financial services customers.[132] Gi highlighted potential suppliers' similar concerns regarding audit rights to verify compliance, particularly rights to inspect data centres used for relevant services. Several

---

[128] 416; and seemingly even known sub-contractors who the supplier may not use—434.

[129] 39, 416.

[130] 285. The 'Sub-Contractor' definition in the final framework agreement was amended to remove references to persons specifically listed by the supplier, suggesting that Government intended to include all sub-contractors.

[131] Gi invitation to tender, 12.13. However, the Gi framework agreement contained no such undertaking, and this requirement was not stated in the Giii invitation to tender documents.

[132] See Chapter 4.

suppliers pointed out that audit provisions failed to recognize that public cloud utilizes shared infrastructure. Many suppliers refuse customers access to inspect or audit data-processing activities or data centres because of disruption and privacy and security concerns regarding the data of suppliers and other customers on the same infrastructure, instead managing audits and verification through independent third-party auditors.[133]

For IL3xx or higher, Government declined to limit inspections to independent third parties, as the PGA (or agents) may need to conduct site visits. While PGA visits aimed to reduce the need for multiple visits, buyers were 'still accountable for the information risk and therefore must still have the right of inspection if they so wish'.[134]

However, for IL2 and lower, it amended the draft framework agreement so that inspection and audit certificates from 'an independent third party'[135] would be acceptable. It expected 'no site visits will be required at IL2[2x] as this will have been covered by the ISO 27001 audit', but the Accreditation Panel would require penetration testing reports, although any forensic seizures requirement has not yet been publicized.[136] For IL22x services, site visits might be required for ISO27001 certification, 'if the paper-based submission [for ISO27001 certification] generated the requirement for further information on implementation and execution of information assurance and security controls at all locations relevant to delivery of the service, including site visits and audit by the PGA or their agent'. However, at IL22x any site visits and audit by the PGA would only be 'when absolutely required'. It was 'intended that these will be very much the exception rather than the rule', but if required would be discussed with the supplier during the accreditation process.

Suppliers were also concerned about the breadth of audit rights, particularly possibly unlimited audits. Government stated that the purpose of audit rights was simply to enable it to obtain monthly management information accurately reflecting services sold and management charges payable to the GPS and, as Gi was relatively short-term, GPS expected to invoke this right only if there was 'cause for concern that a supplier may not be fulfilling its obligations under the Framework Agreement'. Buyers also had audit rights under call-off contracts, but presumably the same applied regarding their short-term nature.[137]

While allowing third-party audits for IL2 and below seemed a reasonable compromise, to make the framework more supplier-friendly future frameworks might spell out, for example, that audits would not be required for IL0 or even IL1, and that site visits for IL2 would only be required in exceptional circumstances (detailing them). Suppliers might well seek such provisions even for relatively short-term contracts.

Layering issues arise again. SaaS suppliers using PaaS/IaaS services may be concerned, not just about audit frequency, but also, more fundamentally, whether they can persuade PaaS/IaaS sub-providers to agree to allow the PGA to inspect or audit their services or data centres. This may drive business to larger IaaS/PaaS providers that can afford ISO27001 certifications and G-Cloud accreditations.

7.3 Data location and data protection issues

Gi's draft framework agreement contained standard Government data protection clauses, including on data location, for both framework agreement and call-off contracts. The

---

[133] For example, 249.   [134] For example, 199.
[135] Without stipulating the third party's required expertise or qualifications.   [136] 75.
[137] N. 126. 494 expressed concern about certain requirements to reimburse audit costs.

Accreditation Scope template required suppliers to specify locations where the offered service (including support locations) 'reside', including 'any elements of offshoring of any element of the service (defined as outside the UK)', with overseas locations required at least at country level, while, for accreditation of services to hold personal data, the DPA checklist similarly required information on geographical location and adequate protection of personal data to be held outside the European Economic Area ('EEA').

EU data protection laws, designed for stand-alone databases, ill suit cloud computing. An oft-cited feature of cloud computing is that data may automatically flow between different equipment, in the same or different data centres, even to different countries. Sometimes, even the supplier cannot precisely pinpoint certain data's location within a data centre. Therefore, unsurprisingly, numerous queries and requests (more than on liability) arose on Gi's standard clauses on data location and other data protection law matters.[138] Also unsurprisingly, given current laws, Government felt unable to accommodate most such requests.

In Gi, data location was relevant for two reasons. First, Government must comply with EU data protection laws implemented by the DPA, which prohibits transfer of 'personal data' outside the EEA except in limited circumstances.[139] Second, 'offshoring', namely transfer or storage of UK government data outside the UK (even within the EEA), may be restricted for security reasons, irrespective of data protection. Government data or services concerning or directly supporting national security that is marked 'RESTRICTED' or above (IL3 or higher), should not normally be offshored, whether or not constituting 'personal data'. Otherwise, in principle nothing prohibits offshoring of IL2 (and, presumably, lower-level) information, although DPA compliance and other issues require consideration, and assurance levels should be no lower offshore than onshore.[140]

Gi seems to have used 'Safe Harbor' as shorthand for several different circumstances where EU law permits transfer of personal data outside the EEA for reasons of adequate protection, of which Safe Harbor is just one.[141] Gi's framework agreement seemed to require both the GPS's and relevant buyer's prior written consent before transferring personal data outside the UK. Suppliers queried the acceptability of services, particularly public cloud services, involving transfers to data centres, sub-contractors, or affiliates outside the UK or EEA. They also requested blanket consent to such transfers (rather than per transfer) provided Safe Harbor or other recognized adequate protection was in place. Government acknowledged that Safe Harbor was not the only method to achieve adequacy, but also stressed that acceptance onto Gi did not signify its consent to such transfers, nor would it automatically agree transfers simply because a recognized method was used. Although, initially, Government stated that it would depend on the buyer's requirements, it amended its response to clarify that A&A would assess whether the supplier's implementation was satisfactory to allow such transfers and intra-EEA offshoring, including its method of achieving adequacy for data protection law purposes.[142] Thus, for personal data it seemed buyers must await A&A before procuring offshore services via CloudStore. Even for UK-only services, A&A would check that, for example,

[138] A G-Cloud blog post discussed data location issues. Emma Gawen, '#Accreditcamp, Accreditation and the Off-shoring of Data' (*G-Cloud blog*, 14 February 2012), <http://gcloud.civilservice.gov.uk/2012/02/14/accreditcamp-accreditation-and-the-off-shoring-of-data/> (accessed 16 March 2012).

[139] See Chapter 10.

[140] Cabinet Office, *Government ICT Offshoring (International Sourcing) Guidance* (2011).

[141] Use of model contract clauses or binding corporate rules (464) being some others. See Chapter 10.

[142] For example, Document 1, clause 30.3.3.

the data centres concerned were indeed in the UK.[143] It is noteworthy that, in May 2013, Salesforce and Oracle, both large providers now listed on CloudStore as suppliers, announced plans to open data centres physically located in the UK, with the avowed intention of servicing UK public sector customers via G-Cloud. Furthermore, Oracle's facility will be available to other providers wishing to offer cloud services to UK government bodies, although on what terms is unclear.[144]

One supplier asked how suppliers with data centres in the EU, but not the UK, could comply with Gi's prohibition on processing personal data outside the UK without the GPS's prior written consent. The GPS answered that this could be achieved by the supplier establishing a data storage facility in the UK, seeking prior consent before utilizing any offshore storage, or by specifying non-UK processing location(s) clearly in its service description and including customer consent to processing in such location(s) in the supplier's own terms.[145] This seems to contradict the position that consideration of data location is part of A&A. Perhaps the intention was that including consent in the supplier's terms would address the legal issue but that, until location was considered as part of PGA accreditation, buyers could not use the service concerned for anything above IL0. It would be helpful if Government clarified the position, for example by stating that, for G-Cloud services accredited for certain ILs, consent may be deemed when using them for those levels (but no higher), with the supplier undertaking not to transfer data outside the countries originally specified, without consent.

One supplier pointed out, consistently with cloud's 'self-service' nature, that data centre location may well be within the customer's control: if so, it was for buyers to choose processing location. If a service gave customers a choice of multiple data centre locations for storage, processing, transfer, or accessing of personal data, it should be solely the customer's responsibility to ensure it did not select locations outside the EEC [sic] to process personal data. However, Government declined to modify its standard data protection clauses in this regard, stating that suppliers' own terms could include such provision.[146]

The current widespread treatment of cloud providers, including G-Cloud suppliers, as 'processors' for data protection law purposes is also problematic.[147] If a customer stores data with a provider to hold passively until the customer retrieves or deletes the data, under current laws the provider/storer is technically a 'processor', even if it has no idea what type of data customers store with it. As one supplier put it, 'Suppliers of infrastructure services do not access customer data in the ordinary course of providing the infrastructure services'. Accordingly, some suppliers noted that it was within the customer's control, and should, therefore, be for buyers (rather than suppliers) to access or extract data, for example to deal with freedom of information requests or data subjects' requests for access to their personal data.[148] Again, this reflects the self-service nature of cloud.

---

[143] 127. However, if a supplier declares its service uses only specified data centres, clearly located in the UK, it may be impossible to verify that its processing occurs only in those locations. See Chapter 10.

[144] On Salesforce, see <http://www.zdnet.com/salesforce-com-readies-uk-datacentre-aims-for-government-contracts-7000014818/> and on Oracle, see <http://news.techworld.com/data-centre/3447070/oracle-opens-second-uk-data-centre-to-support-government-g-cloud/>, and see text containing n. 131.

[145] 175, 444.   [146] 481.   [147] See Chapter 8.

[148] 200 (freedom of information requests), Document 1, clause 30.2.9(e) (provision of personal data held). On the latter, Government agreed to limit this to circumstances 'where the Authority is not in possession of or have [sic] access to such data'. The final framework agreement did not so provide.

Some suppliers queried terms requiring them to comply with controllers' obligations or other data protection legislation, as 'suppliers do not collect data at source from the relevant data subjects'; at most they can only comply as 'processors', who have only incidental access to data in conjunction with providing the services, and have no knowledge of the data's nature or content, so they 'cannot be responsible for maintaining the Authority's obligations under the Data Protection Legislation'. Similarly, 'A Supplier of infrastructure services is not in a position to understand the Authority's obligations under the Data Protection Legislation and to act in a manner that will not result in the Authority's breach of those obligations. Will the Authority strike this provision or agree that it will not process or store any data subject to Data Protection Legislation when utilizing a Supplier's services?' Government responded, 'Where the supplier does have access to customer data this would apply (eg your billing systems). However, where a supplier has no access to customer this would not apply'.[149] It did not amend the framework agreement accordingly. The meaning of its statement was not entirely clear. It suggested that only personal data relating to the customer *as such*, for example for billing, would be treated as personal data for this purpose. However, if 'access' means 'technical ability to access', irrespective of actual access, then many suppliers will 'have access'. Interestingly, Government explicitly recognized that 'a cloud provider may not have access to data as a typical "data processor" would', although nevertheless declining to amend its terms.[150]

Related issues arose with Government's contractual requirement, reflecting current law, that suppliers must 'process' personal data 'only in accordance with instructions' from Government. In cloud, suppliers are not paid to process data actively for customers following customers' instructions, but instead provide standardized environments within which customers may process data using defined resources. Suppliers would have practical difficulties if they had to follow (possibly differing) instructions from myriad customers regarding that environment's set-up or maintenance.[151] Accordingly, some suppliers, emphasizing the standardized nature of their services, queried that term, or asked for change control provisions regarding instructions given. Declining to change the term, Government stated that 'the supplier must show how their service will allow the appropriate risk management of the information and compliance with legalisation [sic] and regulation'.[152] While demonstrating risk management and compliance (presumably as part of A&A) may be a practical solution, the legal requirement for 'instructions' remains an issue.[153] Perhaps, as with processing location choice, suppliers' terms could oblige customers not to give instructions inconsistent with the service's capabilities!

Data protection law also does not cater properly for layered cloud services, typically SaaS built on PaaS or IaaS. As mentioned above, the PaaS/IaaS provider would probably be considered a 'Sub-Contractor'. However, under standard Government provisions, 'transfer' of personal data to others, including sub-contractors, requires prior written consent.[154] Is the PaaS provider a sub-contractor? Will using this SaaS service involve 'transfer' to that provider because its infrastructure is used? If another layer lies behind the PaaS provider, is there a 'transfer' to the underlying provider too? Is there a 'transfer' to the data centre operator, if a third party? What if the data are encrypted at the SaaS

[149] For example, 200.   [150] Document 1, 30.2.9(d).   [151] See Chapter 8.
[152] Document 1, 30.2.1; 173; 302.
[153] Gi's wording refers to 'reasonable' instructions, with permitted offshoring.
[154] Framework agreement clause 30.2.5 (transfer to Sub-Contractor), call-off terms 3.1.2.5.

or customer level? Again, Government refused requests to agree to 'disclosure' only to provide the service, or to ensure sub-contractors process data according to the contract (rather than requiring consent), or for blanket consent to use sub-contractors for public cloud services or make transfers to US affiliates (instead of 'per transfer' consent). 'The use of sub-contractors and 3rd parties will be covered as part of the scope of the ISO27001 certification or accreditation.' Government also would not agree to allow disclosure to comply with any request of a governmental or regulatory body (including subpoenas or court orders), stating: 'Any request from regulators or the Courts in respect of Authority Personal Data must be referred to the Authority and not dealt with by the Supplier.' Also, it would not agree a request that the *supplier's* prior consent should be required before Government used its services for processing or storing personal data (which request underlines infrastructure suppliers' general ignorance regarding the nature of customer data).[155]

Difficulties with applying data protection laws to cloud were highlighted further by requirements on security measures. Reflecting data protection law requirements, Government's standard clause required suppliers to implement appropriate technical and organizational measures to protect [Authority/Customer] Personal Data against unauthorized or unlawful processing and against accidental loss, destruction, damage, alteration, or disclosure.[156] However, in cloud, particularly commoditized, standardized infrastructure services involving 'self-service' customer usage, it may be difficult to comply, again because such suppliers generally lack knowledge about the content, or even nature, of data customers choose to process using their services. One supplier queried:

How can the Authority expect a Supplier to be able to deliver security measures 'appropriate' to the Data when the Authority can migrate the data at will, add additional services through portal provisioning, and flex their cloud services. The Supplier cannot reasonably be expected to assess all the data that that the Authority may add/remove to the services. The only assurances the Supplier can provide will be that the measures will be appropriate to the Impact Level classification in the service description. It will then be the Authorities [sic] responsibility to assess whether that impact level is appropriate for the data the Authority puts onto the cloud.[157]

Government responded that forthcoming guidance[158] would cover the issue, again emphasizing the importance of A&A to G-Cloud. Under this guidance, suppliers applying for accreditation must state if they wish to be approved to hold personal data in their service and how they would meet DPA compliance in terms of geographical locations and access, completing a DPA checklist.

7.4 Data extraction and deletion

With outsourced data processing, customers wish to recover their data from the supplier on exit, that is after the contract ends. This is termed 'off-boarding', as opposed to the 'on-boarding' process of moving data and processing to the cloud.[159]

Gi's call-off terms provided that the parties must comply with 'the Exit and Service Transfer Arrangements as per the Supplier's terms and conditions'. 'Exit' and 'Service Transfer Arrangements' were undefined. However, the framework agreement, which would override the supplier's terms, required formats for transfer of customer data to be

---

[155] 174, Document 1, clause 30.2.5. This provision would cause difficulties for suppliers required by law to disclose information without notifying customers. See Chapter 11.
[156] Clause 30.2.3 framework agreement, 3.1.23 call-off terms.   [157] 242.
[158] N. 93.   [159] For example, 360, 455.

open or readily translated to other formats required by the customer, obliging suppliers to demonstrate 'data extraction capability' if requested. Inability to so demonstrate was grounds for termination. The call-off terms also required the 'return', within ten working days after termination, of 'any data (including (if any) Customer Data) and Customer Confidential Information in the Supplier's possession, power or control,[160] either in its then current format or in a format nominated by the Customer (in which event the Customer will reimburse the Supplier's pre-agreed and reasonable data conversion expenses)'. The term 'Customer Data' was defined broadly as 'data that is owned or managed by the Customer'.

Several suppliers pointed out that, with self-service commoditized cloud, many suppliers do not actively transfer or extract data themselves as 'professional services', but would make data available for extraction by the customer, such as via APIs, as was common in cloud; data extraction was the customer's responsibility. One supplier also suggested that any functional demonstration of data extraction should be done before ordering, as part of the buyer's selection process, and 'Any cancellation clause due to failure by customer to verify standard functionality is contrary to standard industry practice'. Taking the point, Government amended the draft Gi framework agreement to recognize that a supplier does not necessarily transfer data directly, removing the right to terminate for failure to demonstrate data extraction capability.[161] However, the Gi call-off terms, arguably more significant in practice, were not correspondingly adapted, still requiring suppliers to 'return' data after exit.

Similarly, one supplier queried its obligation to 'extract' customer data to comply with freedom of information requests; the customer should be able to extract its data itself, although the provider might have incidental access to data.[162]

The framework agreement did not deal explicitly with extraction of metadata, that is data generated by the cloud service about processing performed on data placed in the service by users, such as access frequency, context, and relational data. Metadata was mentioned in relation to SaaS eDiscovery tools,[163] but its extraction was not discussed. In many respects metadata is, increasingly, more useful and valuable than underlying data, so perhaps future agreements may specifically entitle buyers to copies of metadata.[164]

Another issue was deletion of data from suppliers' systems on exit. As Chapter 2 noted, there are degrees of deletion. The framework agreement stipulated that, subject to specific buyer requirements, 'whenever the Supplier extracts customer data it must use its best efforts, consistent with the sensitivity of the data, to ensure that any residual image of the data is deleted'. However, what degree of deletion would suffice? Government expected 'appropriate measures at IL2 in accordance with the ISO27001 certification. At IL3, there is no specific action beyond normal customer separation requirements'. It added that for IL3 there was a separate need for IS5 type destruction when the supplier wished to scrap equipment used, but this was not anticipated to be when the customer left the service. It stated that details would be covered during the A&A process for each

---

[160] See Chapter 11, Section 4.   [161] For example, 315, 335.

[162] 483. That question seemed to relate to 'extraction' of data for return to buyers after contract expiry. However, the response addressed freedom of information requests made directly to providers, stating that Government data held by cloud providers alone 'will not be subject to FOIA where it is held "on behalf of" a public authority, most typically where the contractor is processing information belonging to a public authority as part of its contract'. This answer, apparently referring to Cabinet Office guidance (n. 140) paras 26–9, assumes cloud involves active 'processing' by providers, which is not necessarily true (see Chapter 8).

[163] 25.

[164] 'Customer Data' is 'data that is owned or managed by the Customer'. However, much cloud metadata may be owned by the supplier. See Chapter 6.

service. Another supplier suggested that tools used to delete data should be agreed as part of the Service Description, to ensure all parties understood and agreed how data were to be removed at exit. The GPS agreed. However, regarding a separate aspect of deletion, it declined to modify its deletion clause when a supplier suggested that the wording would not work if multiple Government bodies share one user account.[165]

This illustrates that no fully satisfactory approach to deletion of buyers' data on exit has been settled, but reviewing the issue as part of A&A seems sensible, which hopefully will lead to more guidance for future procurements, which may also need to cover extraction of metadata specifically.

7.5 Other contractual issues

Possibly because of many providers' consumer-oriented origins, in cloud contracts providers often reserve the right to change their terms at any time, unilaterally binding customers to updated terms even for pre-existing services, thus placing the burden squarely on customers to keep checking terms (usually on the provider's website) for changes.[166]

The risk of Gi suppliers changing service descriptions or terms between signing of framework agreement and call-off contract could have been eliminated, properly reflecting Government's intention to disallow wider changes, through drafting changes as previously described.[167] Gii and Giii have since attempted to address this risk, discussed below.

As Government reserved rights to vary the Gi framework, some suppliers were concerned about whether any such variations would affect pre-existing orders. Normally, these are typical concerns of customers regarding *suppliers'* ability to vary their terms.[168]

There was some confusion regarding pricing, and uncertainty about how to price offerings, as pricing might depend on IL. Government intended that 'All services must include a price, the price on the catalogue is not fixed; suppliers are welcome to reduce at any time. Once ordered by a customer, the price quoted (from the catalogue pricing) would be the ceiling for the duration of that (up to) 12-month contract. Responses that do not include pricing information would not be compliant'. Suppliers also asked for index-linking to allow price increases, which Government was willing to consider for future frameworks provided this was clear in the supplier's terms/service definition/pricing.[169]

Some suppliers considered Government termination rights too broad or vague, such as for change of control, fraud, grave misconduct, and security concerns. However, Government would not amend those terms, but would consider termination for 'security concerns' in the next framework.[170]

8. After Gi

Gii and Giii were, respectively, announced in May 2012 (commencing November 2012, expiring November 2013) and January 2013 (overlapping with Gii).[171] Gii went live

---

[165] 75c; Document 2, clause 14.4; 51.   [166] See Chapter 3.   [167] Section 4.2.

[168] For example, 294. See Chapter 3.

[169] For example, 140, 206. Technically, the Gi framework agreement allowed suppliers to increase, not just reduce, prices, although the wording might be too broad for procurement law purposes.

[170] For example, 142. Gii duly deleted this termination option.

[171] Giii, originally to launch in December 2012, was delayed when all GPS ICT frameworks were paused in October 2012 pending Government review <https://www.gov.uk/government/news/

with some 450 suppliers (75 per cent SMEs) offering more than 3,000 services, nearly double the number of suppliers and services as Gi, with a broader range of services including hosting, storage, email, document-management systems, collaboration tools, and virtual desktops.[172] Giii, seeking an even wider range of services (including identity services), went live in May 2013, and Giv's launch is planned for summer 2013.[173]

For both Gii and Giii, the framework agreement term was increased to 12 months (over Gi's six months). Gii's term was extendible by six months, but Giii reverted to a three-month extension option. Both Gii and Giii allowed a longer maximum call-off contract period of 24 months. As at March 2013, some £7.3 million of reported purchases had been made through Gi over its nine-month lifetime and £1.2 million through Gii, the majority with SMEs.[174] This may seem small compared with the total permitted spend,[175] but, reflecting Government's commitment to G-Cloud, in both Gii and Giii the total amount of purchases permitted under the framework was increased, from £60 million under Gi to £100 million and £200 million under Gii and Giii respectively.

To cater for potential conflicts between the nature of fast-changing commodity services and procurement law, Government chose not to adopt a dynamic procurement system, but instead to emulate one, by embarking on a series of multiple, relatively short-duration, overlapping frameworks, currently once every three to six months. These continuous iterative procurements, in both process and documentation, aimed to take account of feedback from buyers, suppliers, and other interested parties, refreshing CloudStore by maintaining and expanding the range of services available to buyers and enabling new and different suppliers, services, and contract terms to be considered for G-Cloud frameworks on a regular basis. This approach was considered to address procurement law requirements, fixing suppliers' services and terms as at the time of their tenders, but enabling any later material updates needed, for example due to market changes, to be accommodated by allowing updated services or terms to be submitted for a subsequent framework.[176]

One aim was to enable existing G-Cloud framework suppliers to be fast-tracked onto successive frameworks, to 'rollover' their services to a new G-Cloud framework easily 'as long as there are no material changes from the original service description', but 'If you want to refresh or add new services under Giii, any rolled-over and new services will all need to be submitted as part of your tender response'. Some suppliers found the rollover into Gii inordinately complicated and time-consuming, resulting in a different application system being introduced for Giii to streamline the process further, for example prepopulating information on online submission forms for suppliers.[177]

---

review-to-assess-effectiveness-of-government-ict-framework-agreements>. It was green-lighted in December 2012: <http://gcloud.civilservice.gov.uk/2012/12/20/its-full-steam-ahead-for-g-cloud-iii-procurement/>.

[172] <http://gps.cabinetoffice.gov.uk/sites/default/files/contracts/Cloud%20II%20Suppliers%20Per%20Lot%20%282%29.pdf> and <http://gcloud.civilservice.gov.uk/2012/10/26/g-cloud-ii-now-open-for-business/>.

[173] <http://gcloud.civilservice.gov.uk/2013/03/18/an-update-on-giii/>.

[174] <http://gcloud.civilservice.gov.uk/files/2012/06/130222_G-Cloud-Total-Spend.csv>—increased as at 19 March 2013 to some £7.65 million (Gi) and nearly £4.3 million (Gii); <http://gcloud.civilservice.gov.uk/files/2012/06/G-Cloud-Total-Spend-19-03-13.csv>.

[175] The relatively low spend through G-Cloud has been noted—<http://www.computerworlduk.com/in-depth/public-sector/3420389/g-cloud-iii--is-the-framework-getting-any-better/>. However, small purchase values could represent far larger cost savings for Government—see text to n. 10 and <http://www.guardian.co.uk/public-leaders-network/2013/mar/13/vivek-kundra-leading-questions-government-data-cloud>.

[176] Numerous mentions in the G-Cloud webpages and blog, particularly <http://gcloud.civilservice.gov.uk/applying-to-g-cloud/>.

[177] <http://gcloud.civilservice.gov.uk/2013/01/11/g-cloud-iii-launch/>.

Despite Government's various attempts at process simplification and assistance and guidance for suppliers, queries from suppliers have continued unabated, presumably due in part to the drive to engage SME suppliers. In Gii, queries mainly related to contractual documentation and differences between Gi and Gii,[178] to the extent that Government further amended Gii's terms and produced detailed guidance for suppliers on the terms, as it was clear 'that certain areas were difficult to interpret and we recognise that this has been a barrier to application from some suppliers'. Guidance on how suppliers should complete their service definitions was also issued.[179]

Initially, most G-Cloud purchases were of 'Lot 4' ancillary/supporting services rather than of true cloud IT resources; even some purchases designated as 'Lot 1' IaaS in fact appeared to be for professional services. However, September 2012 saw the first major IaaS purchase, by the Government Digital Service from Skyscape (whose services had received IL2 or IL3 accreditation).[180] In November 2012, the Ministry of Defence procured hosting for its digital staff engagement/innovation system from Skyscape via G-Cloud.[181] In January 2013, the Care Quality Commission chose Gii supplier Ixis's unaccredited hosting and support service (using the open-source content-management system Drupal) after running a parallel traditional procurement process, making 'significant savings' partly by taking a commoditized approach to IT.[182]

As at March 2013, relatively few large cloud providers have been accepted in G-Cloud frameworks, apart from Microsoft (Gi; 17 purchases reported so far, including Office 365 SaaS and two Azure PaaS) and Salesforce (Gii; no purchases reported to date). Neither Amazon nor Google has been accepted as a direct G-Cloud provider yet, although they had submitted expressions of interest, which seems inconsistent with a report that for Gi 'Amazon had concerns over the stipulation that the UK government could audit US data centres', while others believe that they are not ready for Government's terms and other detailed requirements, particularly given their reliance on non-UK data centres.[183] It was suggested that Amazon might participate in Giii, but it did not.[184]

CloudStore does list some 'channel' resellers of Google Apps SaaS and Amazon Web Services IaaS, and suppliers of migration/support services for such cloud services. At March 2013, no purchases of Google services from such providers had been reported (or were shown as such in the spreadsheet made public by Government), but there was one 'AWS instance' purchase.[185] In such cases, presumably buyers would contract directly with the ultimate provider on Google or Amazon's standard terms, without

[178] <http://gcloud.civilservice.gov.uk/2012/07/06/gi-gii-extended/>.

[179] <http://gcloud.civilservice.gov.uk/2012/08/20/revised-g-cloud-ii-terms-conditions-guidance/>, linking to Guidance on G-Cloud ii framework agreement and schedules ('Gii Guidance'); <http://gcloud.civilservice.gov.uk/files/2012/08/120809-Guidance-on-G-Cloud-Framework-and-Call-Off-V0D03.doc>; and <http://gcloud.civilservice.gov.uk/2012/07/26/revised-framework-published/> linking to <http://gcloud.civilservice.gov.uk/files/2012/07/Guidance-on-Terms-and-Conditions-final.doc>.

[180] <http://gcloud.civilservice.gov.uk/2012/09/18/first-iaas-purchase-completed/> and <http://digital.cabinetoffice.gov.uk/2012/09/18/introducing-a-new-supplier-skyscape/>.

[181] <http://www.skyscapecloud.com/skyscape-press/ministry-of-defence-starts-to-adopt-the-cloud>.

[182] <http://www.computerworlduk.com/in-depth/public-sector/3426139/health-watchdog-g-cloud-was-our-plan-b-but-it-beat-plan/>.

[183] <http://www.techweekeurope.co.uk/news/amazon-google-g-cloud-security-government-100303>.

[184] <http://www.theregister.co.uk/2012/11/09/amazon_on_g_cloud_uk/>.

[185] By English Heritage, from Arcor.

Government's overlay terms applying to such contracts.[186] Might this undermine the purpose of having overriding terms to protect Government buyers? What procurement process applies to those direct contracts? It seems inconsistent that such resellers have been accepted (particularly given these issues), along with a myriad of supporting services that are not true 'cloud', yet the G-Cloud programme will not entertain suppliers of software suitable for installation on private clouds (which might allow buyers to procure SaaS software from one supplier for installation on IaaS or private cloud procured from another supplier), but rather requires all cloud services offered to be supplier-hosted.[187]

Gii and Giii maintained the overlay approach, with its attendant uncertainties. Here, it is noteworthy that, presumably to minimize such uncertainties, SaaS provider Salesforce submitted terms tailored to G-Cloud, rather than its standard terms.[188] Overall, there were some documentation improvements, for instance eliminating some provisions unnecessary in the framework agreement and, in Giii, making documentation more cloud-appropriate. However, legal uncertainties remained or were heightened in some cases. Drafting and usage, particularly of new or changed defined terms such as 'Confidential Information', 'Customer's Confidential Information', 'Customer's Data', and 'Customer Personal Data', and the relationships between them, could still be clearer and more consistent.[189]

As regards public procurement law issues, the initial draft framework agreement for Gii was also amended following supplier queries,[190] primarily to make the terms more cloud-appropriate, but again carrying the risk that some changes might be considered to exceed clarification or error correction, although again, as with Gi, Gii has not been challenged on this basis. For example, a 'best endeavours' obligation to prevent malware in systems, itself changed from 'all steps, in accordance with Good Industry Practice' in Gi, became 'reasonable endeavours' (a classic change during contract negotiations); requirements, carried over from Gi, to 'provide a written description of the technical and organisational methods employed' by the supplier for processing personal data were deleted; and an obligation to 'supply Customer Data' on request was changed to 'supply (or make available)', as better befits the self-service nature of cloud. A right for GPS to verify 'the costs of the Supplier (including Sub-Contractors)', in a schedule regarding GPS access rights to enable it to verify management charges, was deleted.[191] A new Gii obligation to comply with the customer's security policy in relation to systems holding

---

[186] 'Arcus AWS instance Amazon Web Services capacity can be purchased directly from Amazon through G-Cloud if available, or through Arcus.' <https://sites.google.com/a/arcusglobal.com/g-cloud/lot-4/amazon-deployment-integration-and-migration/full-definition>.

[187] <http://gcloud.civilservice.gov.uk/files/2012/08/20120816-Cloud-QA-v11-20-08-final.xlsx> ('Gii Q&A') 18.   [188] See text to n. 61.

[189] Space does not permit a full list, but for example, drafting changes in Gii and Giii have arguably made the crucial relationship between 'order form', 'call-off terms', and suppliers' terms less clear, particularly regarding incorporation of suppliers' terms, the overriding nature of the call-off terms, mandatory use of the order form (to avoid material changes through buyers using another form), and the order of precedence clause. Also, failure to consider all consequential changes following changes to definitions means that, for instance, prohibitions on processing personal data or disclosing confidential information without consent would not apply when required by 'Law' (introduced in Gii, in the latter case). Because 'Law' in Gi and Gii included 'directives or requirements of any Regulatory Body', and the definition of 'Regulatory Body' was changed in Gii to include bodies entitled to regulate 'the Supplier or its Parent Company', this could be interpreted so as to allow, for example, US suppliers to disclose customer data if required by a US regulatory body or indeed US law, which surely cannot have been intended. Some duplications and erroneous numbering and cross-references also persist in Giii.

[190] <http://gcloud.civilservice.gov.uk/2012/08/20/revised-g-cloud-ii-terms-conditions-guidance/> and <http://gcloud.civilservice.gov.uk/2012/07/26/revised-framework-published/>.

[191] See also n. 198.

'Customer Data'[192] was changed to 'Supplier security policy', following several suppliers' comments regarding its unworkability for multiple customers, with Government stating that the supplier's security policy would be reviewed for adequacy as part of accreditation if relevant.[193]

What of suppliers' ability to change their terms? The Gii framework agreement permitted suppliers to vary only prices and service definition, 'subject to the Authority's Approval (that shall not be unreasonably withheld or delayed)'. This was modified during the tender period. Giii improved on this further by specifically prohibiting material changes, although from a public procurement viewpoint it ought to make clear that material changes are barred absolutely, even if GPS wishes to approve them, and deleting a provision which could have allowed suppliers to change terms anytime before their very first CloudStore order, reinstating explicit reference to suppliers being able to reduce their prices. Gii also deleted a provision entitling Government to 'change the way the procurement vehicle operates including making reasonable consequential variations to the terms of this Framework Agreement'.

The Gii order form, largely unchanged in Giii, allowed buyers to require a parent company guarantee, already briefly noted in the Gi order form, but without specifying guarantee scope, terms, or form. It also permitted buyers to specify services required, and quality standards and technical standards (already in Gi). A section was introduced permitting an overall liability limit (although uncapped for certain areas, see below), to be inserted. Similarly, a termination notice period could be specified in the form. The scope for buyers and suppliers to modify services or terms through the order form, expanded in Gii, may increase the risk of 'material' changes. The order of precedence clause was also amended to refer expressly to the order form (as well as supplier's terms), suggesting that the order form might contain different terms from the framework agreement and call-off contract, which could 'change' them, perhaps even materially. The Gii Guidance[194] explained that elements that could be changed through the order form include, but were not limited to: the call-off liability cap; late payment terms; supplier terms on termination for convenience; 'Movement of personal data out of the EEA'; format of data to be made available/supplied on termination; and/or 'In exceptional circumstances Call-Off specific terms and conditions'.

However, in Giii, guidance notes were inserted in the body of the order form itself, attempting to minimize this risk and clarify that the order form was not an open-ended way to change terms but to 'fill in the blanks' in a more constrained way. For example, 'The Order Form cannot be used to alter existing terms or add any supplementary terms that materially change the G-Cloud Service offered by the Supplier and defined in the tender documents that include, but are not limited to, the Service Definition and Supplier terms. There are a small number of terms within the Call-Off contract that may be defined in the Order Form these are denoted in the contract with the use of square brackets', and 'where a given G-Cloud Services offers multiple standards one should indicate which one(s) are required e.g. if multiple file formats are offered and need to

---

[192] Whose definition, see Gii framework agreement p. 52, was *not* stated to include 'Customer Personal Data', itself defined as 'the personal data supplied by the Customer to the Supplier in the course of the use of the service' which (unlike 'Customer Data') arguably may not be enough to cover personal data processed by the customer *using* the supplier's services, although that was clearly the intention.

[193] Gii Q&A (n. 187), for example 122. Although obliging suppliers to comply only with their own security policies may not seem to give buyers much contractual comfort, there were, and continue to be in Giii, separate and slightly duplicative obligations regarding, for example, 'adequate security arrangements'.   [194] N. 179.

be stipulated at the time of order. This section cannot be used to stipulate Quality or Technical standards not already offered or defined in the G-Cloud Service as either a requirement or acceptance criteria'. Nonetheless, the form 'may', not 'must', be used by buyers, and this coupled with the ability to make certain changes via the form means procurement law risks were not eliminated, particularly as the Gii order form introduced a section 'Additional and/or Alternative Clauses' (deleted in Giii).

Very broadly speaking, it seems that Gii adopted terms more suited to traditional procurements, with supplier queries resulting in a few changes 'back' to more cloud-appropriate provisions, generally maintained by Giii, whose initial draft was much more cloud-appropriate. For example, Gii's order form in the onboarding section added provisions for delay payments from suppliers if milestones were not achieved, unless 'otherwise agreed', and provisions on payment timings and issue of invoices, which would normally be standardized in terms.

In Gii, and again in Giii, the liability and data protection provisions were revamped, and these areas may continue to be contentious. Seemingly relying on its bargaining power as a large user, in Gii Government required greater liability from suppliers, including unlimited liability in certain cases. As one supplier put it, pointing out key changes in the liability position from Gi:[195]

The most concerning is that relating to (i) Loss of or corruption of Customer Data (ii) Misuse of Personal Data (iii) the requirement for supplier systems to be 'secure' and (iv) Non Compliance with customer's security policy. The importance of these issues is appreciated, however, uncapped liability provisions for loss of data and for not having a 'secure' system is unworkable for G-Cloud. Smaller suppliers are reliant on cloud infrastructure providers, who will not guarantee secure systems, nor provide uncapped liability for loss of data. In addition, uncapped liability is not insurable. Furthermore, most services to be procured under this Framework are likely to be of small value and therefore would not merit taking significant risks that outweigh the service revenues. Please will the Authority reconsider these provisions.

Government declined, stating that 'Unlimited liability provisions in relation to: Bribery and Corruption, Fraud, Confidentiality, Protection of Customer Data and Personal Data are an essential part of public sector provisions. These are not onerous obligations and will remain as drafted'. The Gii Guidance[196] also explained the intention: 'There are a number of clauses in the contract that deal with liabilities in the case of loss of data. As with similar clauses these are not intended to overrides a supplier's contract in any ordinary course of events. Thus, if a supplier states certain availability criteria for a service and customer personal data on that service is unavailable, then the supplier SLA's (if any) would apply. However, it is possible that a supplier may act in a way that is outside of the services that in some way impacts these data – these situations would be covered by provisions in the DPA which the agreement would default to (see below).' However, the supplier's point would seem to have some validity. Public cloud is cheap partly because of limited or no liability on the part of providers, so requiring unlimited liability will inevitably affect pricing,[197] and it is interesting that Giii saw the deletion of these unlimited liability provisions and liability for data integrity (including notification of remedial action the supplier would take on suspecting loss or corruption), leaving the overall cap to apply in most cases.

Changes in Gii relevant to data protection included removal of certain provisions recognized as irrelevant between the GPS and suppliers, retaining them in call-off contract

---

[195] Gii Q&A (n. 187) 83. See also <http://gcloud.civilservice.gov.uk/2012/07/06/gi-gii-extended /#comment-1909>.
[196] N. 179.   [197] See Chapter 4.

provisions. Other changes included new definitions of 'Customer's Confidential Information' and 'Customer Personal Data'; prohibiting (except with consent) processing of personal data outside the EEA (not just the UK); deletion of certain GPS security compliance audit rights from the Schedule on records and audit access;[198] express supplier obligations to customers to maintain adequate security arrangements meeting requirements of 'Good Industry Practice', with obligations to notify and cooperate with the customer regarding any breach of security relating to 'Customer Confidential Information' (whose definition, clearly intended to encompass commercially confidential information also, includes 'Customer Personal Data', but did not mention 'Customer Data'); explicit liability for integrity of 'Customer Personal Data' (limited to reconstitution costs, and deleted in Giii); restrictions in call-off contracts on supplier use of 'Customer's Confidential Information'; specific rights to equitable relief regarding suppliers' obligations relating to 'Personal Data'; and unlimited liability, indeed indemnities, for breach of these and certain other provisions as mentioned above. Two pages in the Gii Guidance explained these provisions,[199] including the status of suppliers as controller or processor, and that, while approval for transfers of personal data outside the EEA was required, 'This prior permission can be granted at the time of order by simply including it as part of the supplier's order form'.[200]

Other key changes in Gii included new insurance requirements on suppliers, including professional indemnity insurance for 'Sub-Contractors'. The issue of who are considered to be 'Sub-Contractors' remains problematic, whether regarding insurance or audit rights.[201]Provisions regarding termination for change of control and insolvency were amended. Gii also removed the requirement for compliance certificates to be signed by sub-contractors, but suppliers must still warrant that they have supplied copies of procurement documentation to any sub-contractors and/or consortium members named in their tender.[202]

Gii's draft terms, following a public discussion,[203] were to represent 'a standardised set going forward, including improved wording in the Data Protection clauses to ensure that they more fully take into account the complexities of cloud computing'.[204] The terms have, indeed, moved closer to being cloud-appropriate, although arguably the relationship between order

---

[198] Gii deleted 'to review the Supplier's compliance with its security obligations'. However, this Schedule continued to entitle the GPS to inspect suppliers' 'records and accounts' for purposes including 'to review the integrity, confidentiality and security of the Authority Personal Data held or used by the Supplier' and 'to review the Supplier's compliance with the Data Protection Legislation in accordance with this Framework Agreement and any other Laws'. Both these purposes were finally deleted in Giii, presumably to reflect better that Schedule's objective, namely to check management charges payable to the GPS, not data protection compliance.

[199] N. 179.   [200] See also Gii Q&A (n. 187) 48, 268, 375, 376.

[201] Gii Q&A (n. 187) 54, 133, 145, 345, 372, 373, 404. For example, 286: 'Are the definitions of Sub-Contract and Sub-Contractor intended to capture any vendors or suppliers from which Supplier has purchased commercially available off-the-shelf items, and who are not involved in day-to-day management or support of the cloud computing services? Cloud computing providers purchase servers and other hardware from a broad range of potential vendors; however, since those vendors are not providing goods specific to the G-Cloud services or involved in the actual management/support of the services, it is unlikely that the provider would be able to negotiate (or that the vendors would agree to provide) the specific audit rights, insurance provisions, or other provisions in the Framework Agreement. Can either the definitions or the relevant agreement provisions be narrowed to apply only to those sub-contracts or sub-contractors that Supplier has specifically engaged to provide the actual services?' Answer: 'The definition of the Sub-Contractor clearly includes agreement between the Supplier and the Sub-Contractor to provide to the Supplier the G-Cloud Services or any part thereof. Sub-Contractor definition equally refers to any person engaged by the Supplier in connection with the provision of the G-Cloud Services. This includes both commodity and non-commodity services. However any terms relating to sub-contractors will take into account the nature of the sub-contract where relevant.'

[202] Gii invitation to tender 7.6 and compliance certificate—see n. 4.   [203] N. 213.

[204] <http://gcloud.civilservice.gov.uk/2013/01/11/g-cloud-iii-launch/>.

form, call-off terms, and suppliers' terms has become muddier, hopefully offset by process improvements. Giii expanded the data protection provisions further, for example adding an express requirement to 'provide the Customer with such information as the Customer may reasonably request to satisfy itself that the Supplier is complying with its obligations under the DPA', and an explicit requirement to notify security breaches regarding personal data to the customer.[205] Supplier obligations regarding personal data were, however, qualified with, 'To the extent that the Supplier is Processing the Order Personal Data',[206] which, while seemingly acknowledging that suppliers may in fact be controllers, or neither controllers nor processors,[207] may leave buyers exposed, because buyers are likely to need suppliers to be under contractual obligations regarding, for example, implementation of appropriate security measures, reliability of supplier staff, and provision of information regarding compliance with data protection obligations, regardless of the status of the supplier under data protection laws. Where the Customer consents to export of personal data, Giii required suppliers to incorporate standard and/or model clauses 'or warrant that the obligations set out in the Supplier Terms provide Adequate protection for Personal Data', with 'Adequate' defined by reference to the relevant contractual clauses providing sufficient safeguards under Article 26(2) DPD.[208]

As regards public sector buyers, there seems to have been some buyer confusion, for example believing they need to run, or wanting to run, further mini-competitions, or uncertainty about how much further customization was possible.[209] The G-Cloud programme's efforts to educate and assist potential buyers on the benefits of using G-Cloud frameworks have included several blog posts outlining the buying process, and guest posts from buyers who purchased through G-Cloud, to increase public sector 'buy in'.[210]

Government's insistence on CloudStore being publicly accessible, an 'open marketplace' to foster a transparent and competitive marketplace enabling service comparisons[211] (including of prices), may have produced one side benefit, presumably intended by Government: namely price reductions for Government from its traditional IT suppliers, notably integrators wishing to remain competitive with G-Cloud.[212]

Government has striven for increased transparency. G-Cloud procurements involved heavy use of social media for Government announcements or other communications with prospective providers, through the G-Cloud blog or Twitter rather than press releases, which have proved very open and interactive, and a YouTube channel. Gi and Gii document links were published on the G-Cloud blog, and Government even published draft Giii documentation for consultation,[213] although unlike with Gii any post-clarification changes to Giii documents have not as at March 2013 been published

---

[205] Although there was already a security breach notification requirement regarding 'Customer's Confidential Information', which includes 'Customer Personal Data', defined in Giii to include 'Order Personal Data' and/or 'Service Personal Data', adding levels of complexity which seem unnecessary. There is no definition of 'Customer Confidential Information', although a court would presumably equate that with 'Customer's Confidential Information'.

[206] Another new definition, see the previous footnote.   [207] See Chapter 8.

[208] See Chapter 10.

[209] For example, <http://gcloud.civilservice.gov.uk/customer-zone/buyers-faqa/#comment-2016>.

[210] For example, <http://gcloud.civilservice.gov.uk/2012/09/13/g-cloud-is-it-legal/>; <http://gcloud.civilservice.gov.uk/2012/09/05/university-hertfordshire-cms/>; <http://digital.cabinetoffice.gov.uk/2012/09/18/introducing-a-new-supplier-skyscape/>; <http://gcloud.civilservice.gov.uk/2012/11/30/a-tale-of-two-councils/>; and <http://www.computerworlduk.com/in-depth/public-sector/3426139/health-watchdog-g-cloud-was-our-plan-b-but-it-beat-plan/>.

[211] <http://gcloud.civilservice.gov.uk/2013/01/11/g-cloud-iii-launch/>.

[212] <http://www.sourcingfocus.com/site/newsitem/6995/>.

[213] <http://gcloud.civilservice.gov.uk/2012/11/19/so-what-do-you-think/>—very few comments were posted, perhaps because of the pre-Christmas timing and relatively short 11-day consultation period.

on the G-Cloud blog. The CloudStore catalogue is downloadable, and sales information regularly provided, although improvements are possible, for example further details of services purchased.

Outside the G-Cloud frameworks, Government cloud procurements have occurred, for example because contracts longer than the G-Cloud call-off maximum of two years were desired to justify migration costs,[214] or specialist needs existed. In January 2013, Informatics Merseyside entered into a five-year £30 million framework agreement with integrator SCC for the UK's first 'healthcare cloud', effectively a private or community cloud platform designed to deliver secure data centre services at 'significant savings' (15 per cent or £1.5 million envisaged), covering applications including patient administration services, email provision, SharePoint and Business Intelligence Systems. Any partner organization (participating NHS Trusts) could procure cloud and colocation services through this partnership 'on any scale'. Mersey Care NHS Trust was the first partner organization to sign a call-off contract under this framework; 15 TB of its data will be transferred from 90 in-house servers to the cloud platform, to provide 'greater flexibility and certainty around spending commitments, requiring payment only for what is used and removing the need to invest in, maintain or upgrade own on-site data centres'.[215] For sensitive data like health data, private clouds seem the more likely course.

9. Making Contracts Cloud-appropriate?

In many ways, cloud computing is simply one way to outsource IT resources.[216] Therefore, many outsourcing issues are also relevant to cloud, but not all of them are, and cloud has its own unique features.

There are indications that, perhaps due to time constraints, the legal documentation for Gi was not as complete or as suited to cloud or the intent behind Gi as it could have been.[217] It is likely that suppliers wishing to participate in Gi 'took a view' on the terms, although some declined to tender altogether.[218] The Gi and Gii framework agreements seem to have been based on standard IT outsourcing contracts, which, as seen from suppliers' queries discussed above, may not suit cloud entirely, and need to be adapted accordingly. We have highlighted specific areas where suppliers did not consider such terms suitable. Of particular concern is whether suppliers can undertake to provide security measures 'appropriate' to specific processing activities given the self-service nature of many cloud services, and many suppliers' lack of knowledge as to the nature or content of data processed.[219] However, Giii was more cloud-appropriate, no doubt taking account of supplier feedback. It seems clear that lessons learned from Gi, and particularly Gii, have overall resulted in incrementally better guidance and documentation, informing successive frameworks on legal as well as technological fronts.

---

[214] Chapter 4 Section 5.7.1 reported that some large users felt cloud contracts offered were not long-term enough for their needs.
[215] <http://www.imerseyside.nhs.uk/news_and_events/news/first_uk_healthcare_nhs_cloud.aspx> and <http://www.imerseyside.nhs.uk/news_and_events/news/cloud_computing.aspx>; see also <http://www.scc-cloud-computing.com/2012/11/scc-delivers-first-uk-healthcare-cloud/> and <http://cloud.governmentcomputing.com/news/nhs-trust-to-put-its-data-in-the-cloud>.
[216] See Chapter 2.
[217] For example, 18, and the liability issue. Call-off terms clause 2.1.3 referred erroneously to 'Framework Agreement'.
[218] Chant (n. 13)—inability to negotiate terms was one factor cited by that supplier.
[219] 242.

While successive G-Cloud frameworks have become more streamlined in some respects, some fluctuations in contract terms and systems/procedures suggest that the G-Cloud programme is still finding its feet, and it may be a while before G-Cloud frameworks are fully standardized, whether in terms of process or documentation. In all G-Cloud frameworks to date, deadlines for suppliers to submit tenders had to be extended due to the volume of queries from prospective providers—perhaps inevitable with SMEs. Pausing to take stock, which might appear desirable, has not seemed possible given the rapidity with which successive new G-Cloud frameworks have been and are to be launched. Nevertheless, there remains scope for future frameworks' contractual documentation to strike a better balance between making frameworks sufficiently cloud-friendly so as to draw in greater numbers of suppliers, particularly SMEs, and sufficiently protective of public sector buyers and the public purse, as well as better reflecting Government intentions.[220] Process improvements also seem possible.

To further Government policy of encouraging procurement from SME suppliers, even more guidance would be helpful, and it is being developed from the G-Cloud frameworks.[221] In particular, derived from suppliers' queries to date, clarification could be provided, for example in consolidated 'FAQs', regarding issues such as what service changes are possible before suppliers must apply under a new G-Cloud framework, the treatment of layered services and use of IaaS/PaaS providers already accepted for the CloudStore (which could help to incentivize large IaaS/PaaS providers such as Amazon to participate), who qualifies as 'Sub-Contractors', the requirements regarding resellers, and clearly separating out what issues relate to contractual/regulatory requirements, as opposed to accreditation purposes. As with other things cloud, it will be important to continue to educate both suppliers and buyers.

Notwithstanding some continuing legal and teething issues, G-Cloud has been hailed by Cabinet Office Minister Francis Maude as 'the model of an innovative, more cost-effective and open way for the government to buy and operate IT',[222] and, indeed, G-Cloud seems to have made a start on reducing the burden on the public purse[223] and enabling simpler, faster Government IT procurements, particularly from SMEs. In March 2013, Cabinet Office minister Francis Maude revealed proposals for Government to adopt a 'Public Cloud First' mandate, so that Government bodies should consider public cloud computing services ahead of other options to meet its IT needs.[224]

The G-Cloud programme has also illustrated that, while not unique to cloud, public procurement activities can impact on contractual terms and indeed the cloud market, and it is valuable to identify those areas where pressure may be felt. No doubt the G-Cloud experience will help to inform the work of the European Cloud Partnership.

---

[220] Drafting improvements could also be made: see n. 189 and text to that note.

[221] For example, some SMEs queried concepts such as ILs, Safe Harbor, and so on—for example 145. The G-Cloud team is providing continuing guidance on many areas via the blog, 'ApplyCamps', webinars for suppliers, and 'BuyCamps' for buyers.

[222] <https://www.gov.uk/government/news/g-cloud-celebrates-first-birthday-on-a-high>.

[223] Chant estimated that Government saved £90 million in the first year of G-Cloud: <https://twitter.com/cantwaitogo/status/314119029122031616> and <https://twitter.com/cantwaitogo/status/314316686843080704>.

[224] <https://www.gov.uk/government/news/government-adopts-cloud-first-policy-for-public-sector-it> and see Chapter 12, Section 4.1.

6

Ownership of Information in Clouds

Chris Reed and Alan Cunningham

1. Introduction

This chapter will explore a number of issues relating to how information is stored, created, processed, and/or distributed in the cloud environment, and any subsequent ownership claims or issues that arise. In addition to more normative ownership models, such as those established by intellectual property (IP), confidentiality actions, or contract, we explore how cloud computing has implications for open models of ownership as well. We also address the implications cloud computing has for the commercial distribution of content, such as that created and distributed by film companies. Finally, because of the connection with copyright and the implications for the development of the cloud industry as a whole, we also explore the question of the ownership of the application programming interfaces (APIs) that are essential for the interoperability of cloud services.

We first address content stored or processed by the user (or customer) of the cloud service and also, briefly, content or information stored or processed by the service provider itself. Such content, irrespective of whether it is controlled by the user or the service provider, will be generated either outside or inside the cloud.

2. User Content Stored and Processed in the Cloud

A conceptual map of the information flows in the cloud relationship between provider and customer might look something like Figure 6.1.

Although this map is apparently complex, it can be further simplified as follows.

Information generated outside the cloud.

Much of the information at issue is generated outside the cloud (see Figure 6.2), and thus already has an established ownership status before it is placed in the cloud. However, information uploaded by consumer users may be more problematic evidentially. As examples, many millions of sound recording files are shared on a daily basis via consumer cloud sites, as are the more than two billion photographs that are uploaded every month on Facebook. Even if in theory the initial ownership of these files is ascertainable, in practice the complex norms of information sharing among consumers mean that identifying the owner(s) can be almost impossible in practice.[1] It seems reasonable, however, to assert that the expectation of all parties is that merely placing the information in the cloud should not alter its ownership status.

---

[1] This may be less of an issue than it seems, however, at least for collective licensing schemes that already incorporate Internet usage into their cost models. An example is the licence for YouTube content, which allows embedding into a Facebook feed or webpage. Famously, a lot of YouTube content is not available in Germany because German licensing agency GEMA failed to reach an agreement with YouTube that it felt would be satisfactory to its members. As a further example, many photographs are licensed in an open way. Flickr users are encouraged to license their work under a Creative Commons

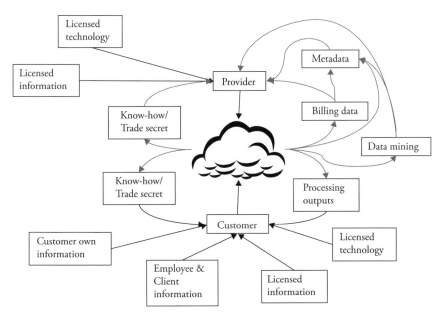

Figure 6.1 An example of information flows in a cloud relationship

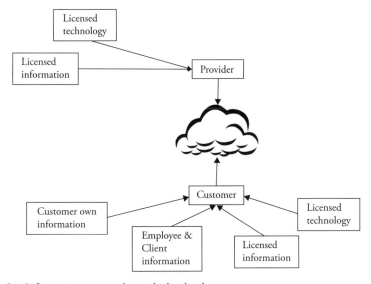

Figure 6.2 Information generated outside the cloud

For the purpose of analysing ownership, this information can be further subdivided into two categories:

1. Information generated by a party to the cloud relationship, either the customer or the provider.

licence, and such photos can see a lot of subsequent usage. Alternatively, an argument could be made that given the open, connected, and communal nature of a service such as Instagram, an implied licence for linking and sharing is granted by the initial photo post (although this would, of course, be contextualized by the ToS).

2. Information generated by a third party and placed in the cloud via the provider or customer.

As we will see below, it is comparatively easy to determine ownership rights in this class of information.

Information generated in the cloud.

The question of who owns the information generated within the cloud is more complex, as Figure 6.3 illustrates.

The main purpose of the cloud computing relationship is to enable the customer to use the cloud technology to process information and thus generate outputs. However, in doing so the customer may also generate know-how or trade secrets, which are not set out in any particular information output, but reside in the data structures or processes which the customer establishes through its use of the cloud.[2] Thus, in addition to the discrete information outputs, such as a spreadsheet or a text document, we are also interested in the information which can be derived or deduced from how the customer uses the cloud.

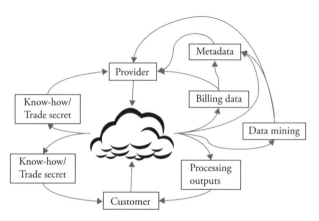

Figure 6.3 Information generated in the cloud

2.1 Ownership of information generated outside the cloud

As noted above, information generated outside the cloud will usually have an established ownership status. In most cases, this information is placed in the cloud in purely digital form, rather than via some physical carrier, and so in most jurisdictions it is unlikely that any question of personal property rights arises.[3] Instead, we must look for ownership rights in four areas of law.

---

[2] For example, the customer might devise an innovative method of doing business, implemented wholly or partly within the cloud, and this would certainly be protected as confidential information or a trade secret, and in some jurisdictions might even be patentable.

[3] Whether information can constitute personal property is still, to some extent, an open question. English law seems clear that it cannot, see *Oxford v Moss* [1979] 68 Cr App R 183, *St Albans City and District Council v International Computers Ltd* [1996] 4 All ER 481. Ken Moon, 'The Nature of Computer Programs: Tangible? Goods? Personal Property? Intellectual Property?' (2009) EIPR 396 suggests that the French Civil Code has the potential to recognize personal property rights in intangibles whereas German law does not, and also reviews the diverse US tax law decisions on this question. For the purposes of this chapter, we assume that national courts are unlikely to recognize personal property rights in digital information, though it would obviously be sensible for cloud computing terms of use to recognize the possibility that a court might do so at some future date.

The first is copyright, one of the important IP rights which might subsist in this information.[4] National copyright laws across the world recognize that copyright subsists in works in digital form, but differ in their conceptions of what constitutes a work. English law, and the law of those countries that derives from England, protects all works[5] where sufficient labour, skill, or judgement has been used in their creation.[6] There is no requirement for creativity per se, but information will not be protected if its creation required minimal effort,[7] or if what is created is too minimal to be recognized as a work.[8]

Civil law countries, which protect authors' rights rather than copyright, tend to demand a minimum level of creativity to qualify for protection. Germany provides a good example, requiring there to be a creative step (*Gestaltungshöhe*) to distinguish a work from mere information.[9] Prior to the EU Software Directive,[10] the German courts had held that some types of software (such as operating systems) were functional, rather than creative, and were thus not protected by author's right.[11] This is still likely to be the position for purely functional information such as data tables. Although a common law jurisdiction, US Federal law has rejected the 'sweat of the brow' test found in English law, and now requires a minimal level of creativity for copyright protection.[12] However, the level of creativity required is lower than, for example, in Germany.[13]

Second, if the applicable law is that of an EU Member State, then information in the form of a database receives *sui generis* protection under the Database Directive.[14] For a database[15] to qualify for this protection there must have been 'qualitatively and/or quantitatively a substantial investment in either the obtaining, verification or presentation of the contents'.[16] If so, the maker of the database has the right 'to prevent extraction and/or re-utilization of the whole or of a substantial part, evaluated qualitatively and/or quantitatively, of the contents of that database'.[17] Protection lasts for ten years from first making the database available to the public or 15 years from its creation, whichever is the shorter.[18]

---

[4] Trademark and patent rights may also subsist, but are less likely to be infringed by use of the information in a cloud computing environment. The comments below about the role of contract in relation to copyright apply equally to these rights.

[5] With the exception of databases in England: Copyright, Designs and Patents Act 1988, s. 3(1)(a) as amended by Copyright and Rights in Databases Regulations 1997 (SI 1997/3032), reg. 5.

[6] *Ladbroke (Football) Ltd v William Hill (Football) Ltd* [1964] 1 WLR 273. A similar view is taken in many other common law jurisdictions, for example see *Desktop Marketing Systems Pty Ltd v Telstra Corporation Limited* [2002] FCAFC 112 (Federal Court of Australia).

[7] *GA Cramp & Sons Ltd v Frank Smythson Ltd* [1944] AC 329.

[8] See *Exxon Corporation v Exxon Insurance Consultants International Ltd* [1982] Ch 119 (no copyright in the word 'Exxon'), *Hitachi Ltd v Zafar Auto & Filter House* [1997] FSR 50, 58 (Copyright Board, Karachi, Pakistan; no copyright in the word 'Hitachi').

[9] *Brombeer Muster*, BGH decision of 27 January 1983, 1983 GRUR 377.

[10] Directive 91/250/EEC on the legal protection of computer programs, OJ L122/42, 17 May 1991, which requires a computer program to be the author's 'own intellectual creation' to qualify for protection by copyright (Art. 1(3)).

[11] *Inkasso-Programm*, BGH decision of 9 May 1985, 1986 IIC 681; *Betriebssystem*, BGH decision of 4 October 1990, 1991 IIC 723.

[12] *Feist Publications Inc. v Rural Telephone Service Company Inc.* 499 US 340 (1990).

[13] *BellSouth Advertising & Publishing Corp v Donnelly Information Publishing Inc.* 933 F 2d 952 (11th Cir. 1991) (holding that copyright subsists in *Yellow Pages* telephone directories because of the minimal creativity in devising the business categories under which listings are set out).

[14] OJ L77, 27 March 1996, 20.

[15] ' "Database" shall mean a collection of independent works, data or other materials arranged in a systematic or methodical way and capable of being individually accessed by electronic or other means.' Directive 96/9 on the legal protection of databases OJ L77, 27 March 1996, 20 Art. 1(2).

[16] Article 7(1).   [17] Art. 7(1), subject to the lawful user's rights (Art. 8(1)).   [18] Art. 10.

From this we can conclude that much of the information placed in the cloud will be protected by copyright or database right, though not necessarily all. The owner of these IP rights will be the authors, or more likely the employers or assignees of authors. Customer and provider will continue to own the IP rights in the information they upload, subject to any contractual terms to the contrary; third-party software houses and database proprietors will similarly retain their pre-existing IP rights, and so on.

The third field of law that is relevant is that relating to the protection of confidential information or trade secrets. The international consensus on a minimum level of protection is set out in Article 39(2) of the Agreement on Trade-Related Aspects of Intellectual Property Rights (TRIPS Agreement), which provides that protection must be given to information which:

1. is secret in the sense that it is not, as a body or in the precise configuration and assembly of its components, generally known among or readily accessible to persons within the circles that normally deal with the kind of information in question;

2. has commercial value because it is secret; and

3. has been subject to reasonable steps under the circumstances, by the person lawfully in control of the information, to keep it secret.

Many jurisdictions, including England, also protect non-commercial information which is confidential in nature and has been disclosed subject to an obligation of confidence, express or implied.[19]

Much of the information in the cloud, whether protected by IP rights or not, will be of a confidential nature. So long as those involved in the cloud computing relationship accept that they owe obligations of confidence to the owner of that information, the owner will have a remedy against actual or anticipated unauthorized disclosure. Such an obligation can arise because the information is imparted in circumstances where the recipient would expect to be obliged to maintain confidence,[20] but is created most reliably by means of contractual terms. The continued maintenance of confidence in the information is important because once the information becomes known outside the confidential relationship it loses its protection[21] except, to some extent, as against a wrongful discloser in breach of confidence.[22]

As with IP rights, an owner's rights of confidentiality will not be affected by placing the information in the cloud so long as the provider, and any others who thereby have access to the information, are under an obligation to maintain its confidence. The nature of cloud computing relationships would seem to suggest that the service provider impliedly undertakes to maintain confidence in the customer's information, and this may be stated expressly in the terms of service (ToS).[23]

---

[19] *Coco v AN Clark (Engineers) Ltd* [1969] RPC 41.

[20] See, for example, *Saltman Engineering v Campbell* (1948) 65 RPC 203.

[21] See, for example, *Attorney-General v Guardian Newspapers Ltd (No 2)* [1990] 1 AC 109; *Public Systems Inc. v Towry and Adams* (Ala 1991) 587 So 2d 969 (Alabama, US).

[22] *Seager v Copydex* [1967] RPC 349.

[23] As ever, consumer use of cloud computing is likely to raise additional complexities because of the very different norms prevailing in the user community. For business use there is typically a one-to-one relationship between customer and provider, under which it is usually clear whether the provider has a duty to maintain confidentiality. However, in a service used predominately by consumers, such as Facebook, the user often maintains a one-to-many relationship with 'friends', network members, and others. Here, the nature of the provider's confidentiality obligations is less obvious, because of the more open nature of the relations between users.

Finally, contract law plays a critical role in determining ownership rights through the ToS for the cloud computing relationship. For information generated outside the cloud, this contract can clarify the copyright and confidentiality relationships in three ways:

1. Acknowledging the IP rights that the various participants own, and ensuring through appropriate drafting that no question of implied licences[24] or equitable assignments of IP rights arises.

2. Granting the licences of IP rights which are necessary for the cloud computing relationship to operate. The customer will be using software and data whose IP rights are owned by the provider or a third party, and unlicensed use of that technology will infringe. Similarly, the provider will be processing information in which the customer owns IP rights, and will also require a licence. Where third-party software or data is made available, the rights owner is likely to have licensed it to the provider on terms which place restrictions on its use. The customer needs to be made aware of those restrictions to avoid the risk of infringement, by both the customer and the provider, and the ToS are an obvious place for this to be done.

3. Defining the obligations of confidentiality which each player owes to the others, including any limitations on those obligations,[25] and agreeing the confidentiality position once the relationship terminates.

2.2 Information generated in the cloud by the customer

Ownership of the information which the customer generates through use of the cloud will depend on both the *type* of information and, to some extent, on *where* it was generated. This is most easily explained by examining three different types of output: a written report; a database of numerical information about stock prices; and an automated financial management report produced by accounting software running in the cloud.

All this information is likely to be confidential to the customer, and so the analysis of the law of confidence above applies equally here. There is likely to be little significant difference based on the location where the information was generated.

For IP rights, however, the type of information and the place of generation can have a substantial impact. Hypothetically, let us assume a customer resides in England and that the authors, who are the employees of the customer, are writing in England (a Berne Convention signatory). Thus, the report qualifies for copyright protection as a literary work in all Berne Convention countries. Since the authors are employees of the customer, the customer will normally own copyright in the report.[26]

---

[24] The difficulty with implied licences is that, although the court's analysis of the implied terms is derived from the nature of the relationship between the parties, this analysis is carried out after the event. By definition, the court would not be asked to determine the licence terms if the parties had a common understanding of the permitted uses within that relationship, and so one of them is certain to be disappointed. See, for example, the Australian decision in *Trumpet Software Pty Ltd v OzEmail Pty Ltd* [1996] 34 IPR 481 (Federal Court of Australia).

[25] As an example, a provider may receive demands for access to information under law enforcement or anti-terrorist legislation. Whether the provider intends to cooperate voluntarily or require a court order, and how far the provider will inform the customer of the demand, are matters which could be explained in the service terms.

[26] Copyright, Designs and Patents Act 1988, s. 11(2) for England. It seems universal that employers own the economic rights in works created in the course of employment, though the position for moral rights may vary.

Copyright comes into existence when the work is created, which under English law is when it is recorded.[27] However, the use of cloud computing makes it uncertain *where* the work was created. The recording may have taken place on one of the provider's servers, which might well be located outside England, or might have been produced and recorded initially on a mobile device used by one of the customer's employees outside England. It seems likely that most jurisdictions will take the position that a work is created when it is first recorded,[28] and if so the question precisely where the human author or creator was located will not affect whether copyright subsists in the report[29] though it might be relevant for other purposes.[30]

At first sight the IP rights in the database seem equally clear. The maker is an English corporation, and if the database is recorded on a server located in an EU Member State there is no question that a valid database right subsists, so long as the database meets the other requirements for protection.[31] What, though, if the server is located in the US?

The database consists of factual information, and unless there is some creativity in its structure the effect of the US Supreme Court decision in *Feist*[32] is that the database is not protected by copyright under US law. For database right to subsist,[33] the Database Directive would have to be interpreted to mean either:

1. That 'making' occurs where the maker is physically located, irrespective of the geographical location where recording of the database takes place. The wording of Article 11(3), which refers to databases 'made in third countries', suggests that 'making' has a geographical location. However, it does not help to decide whether the relevant location is the place of the maker or the place of recording (and at the date the Directive was enacted it is unlikely that the legislators envisaged that these two places might be different).

2. That the place where the 'making' occurs is not legally relevant, the question being whether the maker is a national of or is habitually resident in an EU Member State as required by Article 11(1) and (2). This approach would produce somewhat unexpected consequences, for example, a UK national who had been resident in China

---

[27] Copyright, Designs and Patents Act 1988, s. 3(2).

[28] For example, this is the position in the US under 17 USC §101 (definition of 'created').

[29] The national treatment provisions of the Berne Convention depend on a work having a 'country of origin' in a Convention Member State. If a work is unpublished, or first published outside the Berne Union (this might arise if the work is created on a server in a non-Berne country), the country of origin is that of which the author is a national and thus the place of recording is immaterial for the question whether copyright subsists: Berne Convention Art. 5(4)(c).

[30] For example, the place of creation might be in a jurisdiction which imposes formalities requirements on works created in the jurisdiction. A similar point arose recently in *Moben v 335 LLC* (unreported, D Delaware, 6 October 2009). A graphic work had been uploaded to a server in Germany, from which it immediately became accessible worldwide. The defendant was sued in the US and argued that this amounted to first publication in the US, which would prevent the action from being brought until the plaintiff had registered copyright in the work in the US. The court held that first publication had occurred on the server to which the work was uploaded, that is in Germany. If the relevant criterion had been whether the work was *created* in the US, it seems likely that the court would have adopted the same approach and held that its creation occurred in Germany.

[31] Databases, where the vast majority of investment was in creating the data, rather than in collecting or presenting it, are not protected: *British Horseracing Board Ltd et al. v William Hill Organization Ltd*, Case C-203/02 [9 November 2004].

[32] See n. 12.

[33] It is worth noting that if database right subsisted, this would give the customer a remedy in respect of any acts of unauthorized extraction or reutilization which took place in an EU Member State, but would not of course give any remedy against these acts occurring in the US where there is no database right.

for several years and created a database there would benefit from database right if unauthorized extraction or reutilization occurred in an EU country. The wording of Article 11(3) could suggest that this was not the intended interpretation, but Article 11(3) applies only to mutual recognition of equivalent rights granted by third countries, and so the geographical wording could be confined to that subsection only.

Unless and until this point comes before the courts, there must be uncertainty whether a database recorded on a non-EU server attracts any database right protection, and thus whether its maker has any IP rights at all.

The automated financial management report again raises complex geographical and jurisdictional issues because there is no international consensus whether such reports attract IP rights. English law would certainly protect the report as a literary work. Most likely it would be treated as a work of authorship, on the basis that the English customer was using the accounting software as a tool to create the report. This reasoning was adopted in *Express Newspapers plc v Liverpool Daily Post & Echo plc*,[34] where the court decided that grids of letters for use in prize draws were authored by the programmer who wrote the software to produce the grids. However, in that case the author actually wrote and operated the software, whereas in our example the customer will merely have adjusted the software settings to determine the dates on which reports should be produced, and what information they should contain; thereafter, the software will keep producing reports until the settings are changed. This input to the process is so minimal that a court might find it hard to identify the element of labour, skill, or effort which English law requires for authorship

If so, English law would still protect the report as a 'computer-generated work' under section 9(3) of the Copyright, Designs and Patents Act 1988. The author would be 'the person by whom the arrangements necessary for the creation of the work are undertaken'. Although the provider has made many of the necessary arrangements, by providing access to the cloud and making the software available, it seems to us that an English court would identify the customer's actions in configuring the software as the final, and thus *the* necessary step, though this point has not yet come before the courts.

Most jurisdictions have no concept of computer-generated work, and thus the question whether copyright subsists in the report will depend on the local courts' view as to whether the customer is the author, and merely using the software as a tool. Even if this constitutes authorship in a particular jurisdiction, the report might still not attract copyright because it is insufficiently creative to constitute a work (see the discussion in Section 2.1 above).

Contract law is, unfortunately, of little use in resolving these uncertainties. The ToS could state that certain categories of information produced by the customer are protected by copyright or database right, but this would not actually confer these IP rights if, as a matter of law, they did not subsist in the information. Such a contract term would, of course, be binding as between provider and customer, but its legal effect would be uncertain. Under the applicable law this term might be construed as a promise to treat the customer's information *as if* the stated IP rights subsisted, in which case a provider who did not do so would be in breach of contract. Alternatively, the term might merely act as an estoppel, preventing the provider from denying that the IP rights subsisted, and this might not be enough to give the customer a right of action against the provider.[35]

---

[34] [1985] FSR 306.

[35] For example, even if the contract stated that the provider acknowledged that database right subsisted in the customer's databases, this would not give the customer any claim if the provider's unauthorized extraction and reutilization took place on a non-EU server.

Contract could clarify matters, though only as between customer and provider, if the ToS were drafted so as to replicate the desired IP rights as contractual obligations.[36] Such a contract would be complex to draft and would probably need to be individually negotiated for each customer–provider relationship.

3. Information Generated in the Cloud by the Provider

3.1 Generation for the provider's internal purposes

Information generated by the provider for its own internal purposes, such as billing or management of its cloud, will belong to the provider in the same manner that information generated by the customer belongs to the customer. The analysis above thus applies equally here. If the provider's cloud spans multiple jurisdictions, the same uncertainties about subsistence of IP rights are likely to exist.

An additional complication arises because much of this provider information relates to the customer's information and activities, and as we have already seen that information is likely to be subject to an obligation of confidence. If the provider-generated information is used only for the provider's internal purposes there is no question of breach of this obligation. The primary obligation of the law of confidence is one of non-disclosure, and to the extent that the applicable law imposes restrictions on the provider using that information for its own purposes, a licence to do so would surely be implied because the use of this information is necessary for the effective operation of the cloud computing relationship with the customer.

In any event, it is likely that the service provider will use the service terms to obtain all the licences from the customer that are necessary for the operation of the service, and so the primary concern of both parties in respect of this information is likely to be preventing unauthorized disclosure.

3.2 Exploitation of derived information

As we have seen above, the service provider will generate information for its internal purposes which is derived from the customer's information and activities. The provider has the ability to use data mining and other tools to extract further information from its collection of customer data. This raises two questions: will the production of such information infringe the customer's ownership rights, and does the customer have any control over the use of this information, in particular any commercial exploitation?

3.2.1 The customer's rights

In order to produce this derived information the provider will need to process customer information, and information it has collected based on customer activities. Clearly, if there are any contractual restrictions on doing so the provider will need to comply with those obligations. If the provider is acting within the terms of its contracts with customers, the laws of confidence and copyright come into play.

---

[36] The jurisdictional problems when considering infringement of IP rights are complex and uncertain, see Paul Edward Geller, 'Rethinking the Berne-plus Framework: From Conflicts of Laws to Copyright Reform' (2009) EIPR 391.

The law of confidence imposes on the provider a duty not to disclose that information in breach of confidence. Potentially, it also goes further, requiring the provider to observe:

the broad principle of equity that he who has received information in confidence shall not take unfair advantage of it.[37]

Clearly, the provider intends to benefit from the derived information, but does this amount to unfair use of customers' confidential information? The case law on this point is unhelpful because the alleged breaches in those cases have all fallen into three classes: disclosure to a third party; use of the information to compete with the confider; or use to make a profit which could have been made by the confider.[38] The cloud computing service provider's activities in creating and exploiting derived information fall into none of these, other than by accident.[39]

It seems to us that there are two arguments which might be advanced in favour of the proposition that this conduct takes unfair advantage. The first is based on concealment; if the provider does not inform the customer that its information will be used in this way, that failure amounts to unfair conduct in the context of the confidential relationship. The weakness of this argument is that in a commercial relationship confidential information is regularly shared, but without commensurate disclosure by the parties about their business plans and how they intend to use that information. Confidentiality clauses in commercial contracts concentrate on the preservation of confidentiality against third parties, and do not normally restrain the recipient's use of that information to conduct its own business activities. The argument might perhaps be more persuasive in the case of a consumer customer, whose expectations are likely to be different from a commercial customer, and will be formed by the disclosures of the provider as to what uses will be made of the customer's confidential information.

The second argument is based on the quasi-proprietary nature of confidential information. A bailee of personal property who uses it for his own purposes, particularly to make a profit, might reasonably expect to require the bailor's consent to do so, and the argument would be that the same should be true for confidential information. This argument assumes, though, that the profits derived from exploiting derived information are somehow separate from the business of providing services to customers. It is far more likely that the price of the cloud computing service is calculated on the basis that profits will be made from derived information, and thus the customer already receives a benefit from that activity in that the provider's service charges are lower than they would otherwise have been.

All that can be concluded from this discussion is that there is real uncertainty as to whether a customer can use the law of confidence to prevent the provider creating derived information. The most obvious way to resolve this uncertainty is via transparency in the service terms: if the customer consents to this activity, there can be no suggestion that the provider is in breach of its obligations of confidentiality.

The position in respect of the customer's IP rights is much simpler. The provider will need to copy data if it engages in data mining and related activities, at least

---

[37] *Seager v Copydex Ltd* [1967] 2 All ER 415, 417 per Lord Denning.
[38] For a useful review of the cases, see Robert Flannigan, 'The (Fiduciary) Duty of Fidelity' (2008) LQR 274.
[39] Except where, for example, a disclosure of profile data about a user to a third party (perhaps for behavioural advertising purposes) results in an indirect disclosure of confidential information, which few, if any, providers would intend to occur.

temporarily in the course of that processing, and thus to the extent that the customer owns copyright in that information the provider needs a licence to copy it. The provider will certainly have an implied licence to copy for the purposes of providing the service, but reliance on such an implied licence to copy for other purposes will be dangerous as the scope of the implied licence cannot be determined until a court addresses the matter. We anticipate that a provider who wishes to create derived data will take an appropriate licence in the ToS.

If the provider has no licence, the jurisdiction in which the copying takes place becomes important. Some types of information will attract copyright in one jurisdiction but not others. The applicable law for the purposes of infringement is the law of the jurisdiction where copying occurs, and not of the jurisdiction in which the information was created, based on the national treatment provisions of the Berne Convention and World Intellectual Property Organization (WIPO) Copyright Treaty.

If derived information is created without a licence to do so for the purpose of exploitation, exploiting the derived information will be an infringement if the information contains a substantial part of the customer's copyright information. This is so even if that customer information forms only a small part of the derived information as a whole; the test is the substantiality of what is copied, not its proportion in relation to the new work which incorporates that information.[40]

So far as database right is concerned, a licence will similarly be required for extraction or reutilization of a substantial part[41] of the database if this occurs in a jurisdiction where database right subsists. However, it has been held by the European Court of Justice (ECJ) that the mere consultation of a database does not infringe database right.[42] The provider will thus only infringe if a copy of the whole or a substantial part is made for use by the data mining tools, or if a substantial part of the contents of the database is reutilized in the derived information.

3.2.2 Limits on use and exploitation

If the generation of derived data by the provider for the purpose of exploitation does not infringe the customer's ownership rights, then the only further limitation on its use and exploitation is the obligation to preserve the customer's confidentiality and trade secrets. It is assumed in this chapter that no cloud computing service provider would deliberately exploit confidential information in a way that identified the customer to which that information related, as this would be commercial suicide once the fact became known. This section therefore addresses the exploitation of anonymized derived information.

If it is not possible to discover from the derived information the identity of the customer or any other person to whom a confidentiality obligation is owed,[43] then there is little risk of a breach of confidentiality. The only danger might be that the derived information enabled a third party to discover confidential business or technical processes and

---

[40] This principle is established in a long line of cases running from *Scott v Stanford* (1866–67) LR 3 Eq 718 to *Independent Television Publications Limited & The British Broadcasting Corporation v Time Out Limited* [1984] FSR 64.

[41] The test for substantiality differs from the copyright test. If the part is not quantitatively substantial as a proportion of the whole, the qualitative test is not how important or commercially valuable the part is, but whether it represents a substantial proportion of the investment in making the database: *British Horseracing Board Ltd et al. v William Hill Organization Ltd* [9 November 2004] Case C-203/02 [71–2].

[42] *British Horseracing Board Ltd et al. v William Hill Organization Ltd* [9 November 2004] Case C-203/02 [74].

[43] This might include the customer's employees, clients, or trading partners, as examples.

reuse them. This danger is likely to be reduced if providers aggregate the data they derive from their customer information, rather than exploiting anonymized information about each individual customer.

However, anonymization of data is not a complete safeguard against confidentiality breaches. In a recent article, Paul Ohm has alerted lawyers to advances in reidentification science, which uses the recombination of separate databases to build connections between items of data, and thereby identify the person to whom they relate.[44] A service provider's obligation is probably only to take reasonable care to preserve confidentiality,[45] not an absolute duty, and so the provider will have fulfilled this obligation if the derived information cannot, in the light of the state of technology at the time, foreseeably identify the customer via the use of reidentification technology. However, a wise provider will need to keep alert to new developments in reidentification, as a failure to adapt to new technologies can also amount to a failure to take reasonable care.[46]

4. Using the Cloud to Distribute Content

In addition to storing, processing, and/or creating content within the cloud, cloud computing can also be an efficient means of distributing content. This can, of course, encompass both legal and illegal distribution.

4.1 Copyright material

The use of cloud technology to distribute copyright material can become an issue for those who believe that it is also being used for the distribution and use of copyright material owned by them, and not licensed for that subsequent use. Megaupload, while ostensibly a 'file-sharing site' and subsequently shut down and indicted by a US Federal grand jury for, *inter alia*, criminal copyright infringement and conspiracy to commit money laundering,[47] was also, in the eyes of some of its users, something akin to a cloud IaaS site. For example, the Electronic Frontier Foundation (EFF) filed suit on behalf of interested party Kyle Godwin who sought the return of high-school sports videos that are the property of his company OhioSportsNet. Goodwin maintained that the files he stored at Megaupload were the only copies of the videos. His hard drive, where he had stored other copies, crashed. The court, on the basis of such arguments, blocked the hosting company from deleting data and ordered the government, Dotcom's legal counsel, and EFF to come up with suggestions about how to return property to Megaupload users, if at all.[48]

Megaupload subsequently transformed itself into MEGA, and also transformed the service into a new cloud offering involving what they call User Controlled Encryption or UCE, so that the material uploaded is encrypted in such a way that MEGA cannot

---

[44] Paul Ohm, 'Broken Promises of Privacy: Responding to the Surprising Failure of Anonymization' (2010) 57 UCLA L Rev 1701. For a more detailed discussion of the potential impact on cloud computing, see Chapter 7.

[45] *Weld-Blundell v Stephens* [1919] 1 KB 520.

[46] *The T J Hooper* (1932) 60 F 2d 737 (ship-to-shore radio).

[47] *US v Kim Dotcom,* 12-00003, US District Court, ED Virginia.

[48] D Kravets, 'Megaupload Case Has Far-reaching Implications for Cloud-data Ownership Rights' *(Wired,* 11 July 2012), <http://www.wired.com/threatlevel/2012/11/megaupload-data-what-to-do> (accessed 1 April 2013).

decrypt it. The argument here is that if the service provider has no possibility of appreciating what information is being stored, claims of infringement (whether secondary or not) are untenable. In its previous incarnation MEGA was notorious with regard to allowing the distribution of infringing material. It now states on its website, however:

All files stored on MEGA are encrypted. All data transfers from and to MEGA are encrypted. And while most cloud storage providers can and do claim the same, MEGA is different – unlike the industry norm where the cloud storage provider holds the decryption key, with MEGA, you control the encryption, you hold the keys, and you decide who you grant or deny access to your files, without requiring any risky software installs.[49]

Cloud computing offers to those content distributors a hyperrealized version of what the Internet and digitization (allied with telecommunications) already offered: content available on any device, anywhere. Cloud computing is thus moving beyond the traditional triumvirate of SaaS, PaaS, and IaaS to include potentially 'anything', but particularly access to content, as a digital, mobile, and distributed service.

For those who already administer or manage a portfolio of content that was created outside the context of cloud computing, cloud computing offers the possibility of increased ease of access and use by a customer or other type of user base, allied with much lower costs of distribution. For those who are involved in the production and distribution of films and television (TV) programmes, cloud computing is an additional means of distributing film. Witness for example, the emergence of UltraViolet (UV),[50] a new technical rights management standard developed under the auspices of the Digital Entertainment Content Ecosystem, a consortium made up, among others, of film studios, manufacturers of electronics, and Internet service providers.[51] The UV standard ensures that UV-approved films, irrespective of the mode of purchase, which might be on DVD or as a legal online stream, involve the additional purchase of UV 'rights'. This means that a user might be able to download a digital version of a movie or TV show they purchased on a physical Blu-ray disc, or stream a show to their smartphone, tablet, or other eligible connected device, or create or obtain another physical copy such as a DVD, dependent on the 'rights' involved. All this is made possible and more attractive to the consumer (now one who expects constant access to content everywhere, on anything) by the use of cloud computing to ensure access to the content covered by the relevant UV right anywhere, on any type of device.

This example, and it is only one of many,[52] symbolizes the benefit offered by cloud computing in increasing the scope for distribution and use of existing and commercially viable (and often IP-protected) content. It also symbolizes the benefit offered to administrators of such a portfolio in relation to the previously tricky area of *control*. The cloud model offers a way to maximize the potential regarding distribution that was only

---

[49] Available at <https://mega.co.nz/#privacycompany> (accessed 1 April 2013).

[50] Available at <http://www.uvvu.com> (accessed 1 April 2013).

[51] The consortium is led by Sony Pictures; Apple and Disney are not involved, Disney being in the process of developing its own system, Keychest, and Apple working on movie storage within its iCloud system.

[52] The Tesco system blinkbox (available at <http://www.blinkbox.com> (accessed 1 April 2013)) is an interesting example, in that it allows for the purchase of, say, a TV series that is not offered as a download nor as delivery of a physical disc with the series on it but instead simply as the perpetual ability and freedom to watch the 'owned' series as many times as is liked. This would be impossible without the cloud computing model, but has huge implications in redefining the relationship between IP rights and the actual relationship a person has with a cultural artefact such as a disc or book that is legally controlled by IP (but over which artefact the IP owner has, in fact, little actual control).

hinted at during the early days of the Internet, allowing for new ways of interacting with content or data in an era of increasingly sophisticated mobile devices, and an era where expectations of access to everything everywhere is high. It also shows how access and geographical availability are developing hand in hand with increased control. Cloud computing service providers are learning from the success of iTunes, and the failures of many early digital rights management (DRM) technologies, and trying to apply them to content more generally. The overall benefit to the administrator of IP is a new level of control allied with the possibility of offering previously unachievable flexibility of access to content. Of course, not all content follows the standard IP exclusionary model, and neither do all content administrators, as we shall see; but the cloud still offers possibilities for them too.

Issues that arise with such legal use of the cloud for distribution centre around the ways in which both usage and access are regulated either by technological means or contractual means (or a mixture of both), and how such regulation can potentially conflict with the public aspects of IP law, such as statutory exceptions. This is especially complicated given how cloud computing is diminishing the effect of actual geographical/political borders whereas IP law, especially the scope and nature of exceptions, is still largely national. Copyright is in fact a number of limited exclusive rights and is also historically balanced by the existence of exceptions.[53] These exceptions limit the exclusivity offered by the copying rights, for, the argument goes, if a copyright owner were able to control absolutely the use of their work (or to charge extraordinarily high licensing fees for all use), such defining aspects of society as criticism, review, education, and satire would be nigh on impossible.[54] Exceptions operate, to an extent, as a kind of 'soft' legal measure. In other words, permission to deal fairly is not required in advance but if the copyright owner has an issue, a particular use may be challenged after the fact. The flexibility inherent in exceptions operating like this is potentially lost when content is distributed over a cloud computing model, because the possibility to exercise an exception is lessened; control and access are more centralized and less under the control of the individual. This is one potential copyright problem with the use of cloud computing for content distribution.[55]

4.2 Designs

Cloud computing may have further implications in relation to content distribution in relation to designs, not an area of the IP family most usually associated with possibilities for commercial distribution online. Visual designs are normally protected by a registered design right, though some aspects of a design may also receive copyright protection as

---

[53] For example, within UK legislation, under Chapter III of the Copyright, Designs and Patents Act (CDPA) 1988 (as amended), a list of 'acts permitted in relation to copyright works' is laid out, including: making a temporary copy (s. 28A); use for research and private study (s. 29); use for criticism, review, and news reporting (s. 30); and use as an incidental inclusion of copyright material (s. 31). These 'fair dealing' exceptions are mirrored in most, if not all, copyright regimes in the world.

[54] See, W Cornish, D Llewelyn, and T Aplin, *Intellectual Property: Patents, Copyright, Trade Marks and Allied Rights*, 7th edn (London: Sweet and Maxwell, 2010), 500–9; for further reading on copyright exceptions in the context of digitization and the Internet, see R Burrell and A Coleman, *Copyright Exceptions: The Digital Impact* (Cambridge: Cambridge University Press, 2005).

[55] See, more generally on the problem of increased digitization and subsequent control of copyright works and the difficulty of exercising copyright exceptions in such an environment, A Cunningham, 'Rights Expression on Digital Communications Networks: Some Implications for Copyright' (Spring 2005) *Int J Law Info Tech* 13(1), 1–38.

artistic works. The registered right prevents others applying the design in industrial processes. Unregistered designs for manufacturing often receive legal protection from the moment they are recorded, in the UK by means of the unregistered design right introduced by the Copyright, Designs and Patents Act 1988.

Such rights, whether registered or unregistered, will arguably have a future importance in the context of cloud computing, especially when the benefits of the cloud are allied with the technology of the so called 3-D printer.[56] Copyright, patent, and trademark will also be issues here, admittedly, but the design rights are primarily concerned with the appearance of what have, to date, more often than not been industrially produced products, and it is expected that design rights will become most contentious in this context. The 3-D printer is expected in time to undermine the dominance of the industrial factory-produced product, once cost and material issues are sufficiently streamlined. What will make or break the success of the 3-D printer, however, will be the way in which access to the designs (and indeed, any copyrights, patents, or trademarks) that allow a 3-D printer to work properly is made available, if at all.

Where does the cloud fit into this? Well, just as film studios recognize the advantages of using cloud technology to store films and provide access to those who have purchased DVDs, so holders of design rights may see cloud-stored (and accessible) designs for use with 3-D printers as a possible new way to do business. Imagine, for example, Lego.[57] It is not the manufacture of the pieces that provides value to Lego. If anything, they are an unnecessary cost in an era when the owner of the 3-D printer could be supplying the manufacturing materials him or herself. It is the look and feel that the design protects that is of most value to the company. Why not make available the 3-D printing designs for a price worldwide? Here, manufacturing costs are avoided and the inherent value of the product design is maintained. Bradshaw et al. have written how:

The exemptions for personal and private reproduction of registered designs and the exclusion of non-commercial use from UDR protection mean that the *domestic* use of a personal 3D printer to reproduce an item will infringe neither registered nor unregistered design protection.

Further, they add:

Perhaps more surprisingly the exclusive right provided by UDR appears not to cover such public but non-commercial users as schools; subject to interpretation, it may not prevent use in a commercial reproduction bureau. Even for commercial use, many items that are attractive for 3D printing, such as spare parts, may be unregistrable as registered designs and excluded from protection by UDR.[58]

If the owner of a design was making it available via a cloud site, such exceptions would need review. The technology underpinning cloud computing can be used to distribute designs that are open and not restricted by IP ownership, and such a different mode of distributing designs would have implications for developing countries. In addition, design rights themselves may well come under threat as designs for products become a much more useful currency in an era when one only needs access to 3-D printers to make a product. The best way to combat any such threat would indeed be by making designs accessible on reasonable terms, and cloud technology may well facilitate that process.

---

[56] The 3-D printer is a machine that can create physical objects from digital data by printing layer by layer; See, N V 'Difference Engine: The PC All Over Again' (*The Economist*, 9 September 2012), <http://www.economist.com/blogs/babbage/2012/09/3d-printing> (accessed 1 April 2013).

[57] While not benefiting from copyright, Lego brick will have a registered design right; see *Interlego AG v Tyco Industries Inc.* [1989] AC 217.

[58] S Bradshaw, A Bowyer, and P Haufe, 'The Intellectual Property Implications of Low-cost 3D Printing' (2010) 7:1 *SCRIPTed* 5.

5. Open Content

Most contentious cloud computing issues will relate to the question of who owns information or content stored, created, processed, or distributed in the cloud. What will be of most interest to those administrators and owners of content or creators of content who are storing, distributing, creating, and processing will be a maximization of exclusivity and revenue. Cloud computing also offers possibilities, however, to those who administer a portfolio of content or create content that they have decided, for whatever reason, should be 'copyleft', 'open', or even free, as in the sense that free software is free. In other words, data or content that is either freely accessible in terms of liberty, or freely accessible in terms of cost, or both.

In this respect, the use of cloud computing will reflect, as does the use of the Internet more generally, the political, economic, and philosophical perspective of the owner, creator, or administrator in relation to the information or property under their control. Should it be easily accessed and free (either in a liberty or financial sense)? Or should it be controlled and cost (either in a liberty or financial sense)? Cloud computing can be seen as only tweaking a distribution model that already existed and was often utilized more privately, but the choices made by service providers in relation to control, freedom of access, and cost have huge implications for the future of the market position of these providers and, most crucially, the emergence of standard technologies and cloud platforms in this field.

Most often this will occur in the case of content that would, under other circumstances, fall under copyright protection, as open and free movements are most strongly established in the area of copyright works. This is especially so for software, although the Creative Commons movement has developed the Free and Open Source model to devise copyleft licences for many other types of content.

As with copyleft and copyright, there is also the issue of cloud computing potentially making other types of restricted or closed sets of information more accessible, for example with patents (although given the more commercial nature of the patent field there is less of a subversive, open approach). Some preliminary work has been done on such projects in relation to general patent information. In 2010, Fairview Research and IFI announced the wide availability of Alexandria, which, as they stated at the time, would be 'the world's first commercial database of patents on the Amazon Elastic Cloud'. They added that:

> This marks a major milestone in patent content availability and the future of content dissemination and distribution. Alexandria is specifically designed to support the low cost, large scale extraction and manipulation of patent information content particularly to support data mining, analysis, monitoring and reporting. Clients can now have their own private patent database on which they can design their own front end for their specific end user needs.[59]

However, as of March 2013 the authors can find no presence of such an open service on the Internet, though IFI claims to be using it to service its clients.

One can also imagine that in time, once 3-D printing advances, arguments will be made in favour of open and/or free access to design rights, especially in the context of designs for products that have development implications in areas where such materials or products were previously unavailable, either for cost or other reasons. How cloud computing develops alongside these other technological and social developments will have major impacts on our future conceptions of ownership and access in relation to such content and rights.

---

[59] As reported on the Patent Information User Group (PIUG) website, <http://wiki.piug.org/display/PIUG/2010/11/11/Patents+on+the+Cloud>; see also, <http://ificlaims.com/index.php?page=start> (both accessed 1 April 2013).

6. Problems of Infringing Content

Cloud service providers will often store and transport data that may be protected by a number of rights, for example copyright or design right, and such cloud service providers may sub-contract services such as storage or processing. How sure can they be that no infringement is taking place in the sub-contracted layer? An implied licence would be the reasonable response to any copying that occurred for the purposes of making the data available to the owner or for undertaking actions necessary for the maintenance of the data,[60] but beyond such necessary copying, the issue remains that there is a lack of any more than general knowledge on the part of the user regarding when, where, why, and how their data is being copied. Given the potential cultural, commercial, and personal value of such copyright-protected works, it is reasonable to imagine potential users having concerns about this lack of certainty.

The concern of those who distribute or store copyright works on cloud services (excluding what we call administrators of commercially viable content, such as, for example, a film studio, which will have no doubt more sophisticated means of tracking and controlling) would thus appear to stem from the potential for infringement given the often opaque nature of the reality of cloud storage. Terms of service usually state no claim to ownership, although this does not mean infringement may not occur in the course of cloud use, especially given the sub-contracting that occurs in the cloud. Encryption and technological measures, either implemented by the user or put in place by the service provider, will therefore play a part in protecting users against infringement, as ToS will only ever offer soft protection to those who want to use or store the copyright material on the cloud.

As mentioned previously, it is unlikely that patent infringement will be a major issue in the context of cloud computing service use. It is also unlikely that trademark or passing-off issues will arise in the core cloud computing services, SaaS, PaaS, and IaaS, at least in relation to the particular services that are offered. Of course, a SaaS provider might engage in trademark infringement or passing off in relation to how it markets itself and its own use of trademarks, but there is nothing particular to the way cloud operates that will affect the application of the law here. In addition, a user might engage in trademark infringement or passing off in creating something within cloud services, but, arguably, the issue will remain one between the trade- or other mark owner and the cloud service user, especially given that most cloud service ToS will notify users that they must not upload anything that infringes IP rights. For example, the Apple iCloud terms (UK) state you must not:

engage in any copyright infringement or other intellectual property infringement (including uploading any content to which you do not have the right to upload), or disclose any trade secret or confidential information in violation of a confidentiality, employment, or nondisclosure agreement.[61]

In other types of cloud services, such as Content as a Service (CaaS), again, it is unlikely that anything unique to the cloud model will lead to trademark infringement or passing off. If anything, the greater degree of control inherent in CaaS would, if anything,

---

[60] And, indeed, in many of the ToS employed by cloud service providers, it is stated that use of the service grants an implied licence for the provider to undertake such copying as would be technically necessary for the use of the service.

[61] Available at <http://www.apple.com/legal/icloud/en/terms.html> (accessed 1 April 2013).

minimize trademark infringement or passing off, other than what would occur in any event, irrespective of the use of the cloud model.

7. Collaboration in the Cloud

A further category of information generated in the cloud is information produced collaboratively between users, using tools made available by the service provider. In some circumstances there will also be collaboration with the service provider or with third-party information providers.

Cloud computing facilitates access by multiple users to collaboration tools often at low cost, or even 'free' of charge. This may lead to questions regarding authorship for copyright purposes. Copyright comes into existence upon creation of a work, which in the case of an individual is usually straightforward. It may, however, be more difficult to identify the author or authors of collaborative works. Most, if not all copyright jurisdictions, recognize joint authorship of a copyright work, but assessing relevant contribution may be difficult in the context of multiple online creators and real-time creation.[62] Arguably, such changes in the way documents are authored requires a change in awareness of the responsibilities of the parties involved in relation to either claiming or managing the allocation of copyright, or, as is also possibly the case, arguing for more openness, for example copyleft.

It may even be that the new modes of creation available with cloud computing services such as SaaS will encourage new equivalent modes of ownership. For those who work for a company or organization and are encouraged to use cloud computing in the creation of documents with a potentially unknown and unfixed number of contributors on a cloud service, the contractual terms of their employment will usually regulate their claims to ownership of subsequently created content. However, for the informal consumer user or start-up enterprise, issues of ownership will need to be addressed prior to using cloud services. The central issue one can see arising here is, given the possibilities for a number of disparate actors to work on a project using cloud services and potentially resulting in copyright, how should these actors regulate their role in creation?

This will rarely be a direct concern for cloud service providers, and it is hoped that cloud users will have an awareness of potential complications regarding ownership, although for the average consumer this is probably not the case. Contracts or written policies regulating use can be employed among users to establish rights and responsibilities, but again, the average consumer will not be used to such techniques. And yet, consumers are using cloud SaaS to create collaborative works that have potential commercial and intrinsic value and, indeed, can be protected by copyright. The concurrent phenomenon of 'bring your own device' and subsequent use of cloud and mixed personal/private use will, in addition, further complicate this issue.

An analogous issue may arise in relation to other types of content or data that can become subject to rights of ownership; for example, the question of establishing patent ownership among users of cloud computing who are undertaking data processing leading, potentially, to a patentable invention. Or, rather, since a patent has to be applied for and it is therefore easier to establish one's standing in relation to the actual application, the issue is that of ensuring that those with access to the research data leading to the

---

[62] CDPA 1988 (as amended), s. 10(1) defines a work of joint authorship as meaning 'a work produced by the collaboration of two or more authors in which the contribution of each author is not distinct from that of the other author or authors'.

patent application are doing so in good faith in relation to the general administration of the research project. How can one guarantee the data remains confidential not only against outside sources, but against those partners or individuals who are involved and may see that they can access data provided by a research partner or individual? Such data may be potentially patentable in isolation from the project and that potential might not have been seen by the original controller of it.

If independent researchers are working together on a project using the benefits of cloud computing, it may well be that they need to minimize the risk cloud poses in terms of input from partner researchers by self-regulating issues of ownership and data access in advance. University or corporation-based researchers will usually have specific clauses in their contracts of employment relating to patent ownership over research they are working on as an employee. Cloud ToS all reject claims of ownership over IP, including patents, but this statement might not be enough to allay fears over breaches of confidentiality. As with copyright, encryption technologies and additional contractual agreements may be needed to allay security fears when using the cloud for data processing.

8. IP Rights of Cloud Providers

A common fear expressed among potential users of cloud computing is that information and content may become the IP of the cloud provider. However, the 2010 and 2013 contract surveys by the Queen Mary, University of London Cloud Legal Project found no evidence of cloud service providers making claims to own IP in material uploaded by users or created by them in the course of using a service.[63] Such IP clauses clearly delineate IP ownership between the user and the service provider, establishing that both parties retain ownership over IP relating to their data and service respectively. However, the majority of providers surveyed in 2010 expressly included terms in their ToS making it clear that ultimate responsibility for preserving the confidentiality and integrity of the customer's data lay with the customer. Several (eg, Amazon, GoGrid, and Microsoft) asserted that they would make 'best efforts' to preserve such data, but nonetheless included such a disclaimer. A number of providers went so far as to recommend that the customer encrypt data stored in the provider's cloud (eg, GoGrid and Microsoft), or specifically placed responsibility on the customer to make separate backup arrangements. Amazon's ToS for Amazon Web Services (AWS), for example, did this in 2010, and went on to note that 'We will have no liability to you for any unauthorized access or use, corruption, deletion, destruction or loss of any of Your Content or Applications'.[64]

Little changed in this area by 2013. All of the providers surveyed for the first time in 2013 incorporated such terms although, perhaps to assuage possible customer concerns, especially among consumers, a number of providers gave non-binding assurances about the measures they took to safeguard customer data. Linode referred, for instance, to 'industry-standard technical safeguards' and 'other storage system access control mechanisms' in its privacy policy.[65]

Similar concerns regarding confidentiality were identified in the part of our study that explored standard ToS relating to data disclosure. As explained in Chapter 3, there is a spectrum of approaches ranging from providers that have a high threshold for justifying disclosure to ones which have a much lower one. A typical example of this approach

---

[63] See Chapter 3, Section 3.2.6.
[64] AWS Customer Agreement, Section 7.2 (see Chapter 3, Section 3.2.1).
[65] See Linode Privacy Policy, <http://www.linode.com/privacy.cfm> (accessed 18 March 2013).

is IBM, which states that it has no duty of confidentiality regarding customer data stored in its cloud, and places responsibility for keeping it confidential on the customer, for example, via encryption.[66] However, as Chapter 3 also highlighted, where the data are stored under arrangements where IBM specifically has root (as in privileged) access to virtual machines (VMs), considerably tighter disclosure protection is specified. This appears to reflect the difference between customer data that IBM is not required to have access to for the provision of the service, for example straightforward data storage, and data where the nature of the service requires that IBM has unencrypted access to it, for example the hosting of VMs.

8.1 Metadata

Cloud providers too will be generating information of various different types, and some of this information will fall outside the standard categorizations of information or content previously outlined. In particular:

1. All cloud computing service providers will collect information about the operation of their systems and services for management purposes. Much of this information will amount to know-how or trade secrets belonging to the provider.

2. Customers will need to be billed for their use of the service, and thus the provider will collect billing data, which will certainly incorporate information about the customer's activities.

3. Providers will also generate and store metadata[67] about the data relationships between the customer's data and applications and any provider or third-party applications or data. The purpose of producing this information is both to enable or enhance the customer's use of the service, and also for the provider's own management purposes.

4. Finally, and most controversially, data mining[68] tools are available which may enable a provider to trawl through customer information, either individually or on a collective basis, and thereby generate new and potentially valuable information. As a hypothetical example, a service provider with a number of motor insurers as customers could mine their data to extract information on the accident rates and types for different makes and models of vehicle.

The main distinction here should be based on the *purpose* for which the provider generates information. Ownership and control issues are more pressing in relation to information which the provider collects for commercial exploitation, at least where the exploitation involves the disclosure of the information to others. Information generated for a provider's own internal purposes is less likely to be controversial, though the provider might

---

[66] IBM SmartCloud Agreement, Section 5.2 'Content Responsibilities'<http://www-935.ibm.com/services/us/en/cloud-enterprise/contracts/sc_agreement.html#5> (accessed 6 June 2013).

[67] Metadata presents known privacy risks, and in many countries telecoms service providers are limited in the metadata they can collect. See, for example, Directive 2002/58/EC of the European Parliament and of the Council of 12 July 2002 concerning the processing of personal data and the protection of privacy in the electronic communications sector, OJ L201/37 31 July 2002, Arts 6 and 9. It is not suggested in this chapter that ownership rights are in need of regulation of this kind, but there are real risks to confidentiality which might not be adequately addressed through contract, for example in the case of consumers.

[68] See, for example, Jiawei Han and Micheline Kamber, *Data Mining: Concepts and Techniques*, 2nd edn (San Francisco: Morgan Kaufmann, 2006).

subsequently decide that this information could also be exploited. Indeed, data mining tools are sufficiently sophisticated that a provider might usefully aggregate its internal data with data from one or more customers to extract even more valuable information from the mining process.

8.2 Application programming interfaces

Another area of concern for providers and regulators of cloud services is the intersection between APIs and IP. APIs are key to the success of cloud computing, especially given increased calls for data portability between cloud services (and increasing promises of data portability) and the increasing number of cloud services now available on mobile devices that use different operating systems. APIs are also key to the issue of interoperability. APIs are software packages that allow different applications, possibly coded in different programming languages and running on different platforms, to communicate with each other to enable interoperability.

To date, the question of ownership of APIs in legal and programming circles has been contentious, especially given the high odds of similarity between two APIs. Metz has written how:

As they evolve into a way of connecting modern web services and mobile applications, APIs are moving towards a common convention called REST, short for 'representational state transfer,' and the whole idea of REST is to make APIs simple. Sometimes, an API call is similar to a common English noun or verb, and it typically handles the same data formats as other REST APIs. The odds of similarity between any two RESTful APIs is quite high.[69]

The issue of copyright in APIs emerged most vividly in the recently decided US case of *Oracle v Google*.[70] In 2007, Google announced its Android software platform for mobile devices. In 2010, Oracle purchased Sun Microsystems, thus acquiring Sun's interest in the Java programming language, a language used in Android. Sun was later renamed Oracle America, Inc. Shortly after, Oracle sued Google and alleged that its Android platform infringed Oracle's Java-related copyrights and patents. Both Java and Android are complex platforms. Both include VMs, development and testing kits, and APIs. Oracle's copyright claim involved 37 packages in the Java API. The copyright issue was whether Google was and remained free to replicate the names, organization of those names, and functionality of 37 out of 166 packages in the Java API, referred to in the cases as the 'structure, sequence and organization' of the 37 packages.

In ruling on this copyright API claim, Judge Alsup stated that:

So long as the specific code used to implement a method is different, anyone is free under the Copyright Act to write his or her own code to carry out exactly the same function or specification of any methods used in the Java API. It does not matter that the declaration or method header lines are identical. Under the rules of Java, they must be identical to declare a method specifying the same functionality—even when the implementation is different. When there is only one way to express an idea or function, then everyone is free to do so and no one can monopolize that expression. And, while the Android method and class names could have been different from the names of their counterparts in Java and still have worked, copyright protection never extends to names or short phrases as a matter of law.

---

[69] C Metz, 'If You Can Copyright an API, What Else Can You Copyright?' *(Wired*, 15 May 2012), <http://www.wired.com/wiredenterprise/2012/05/api-copyright> (accessed 1 April 2013).

[70] *Oracle America, Inc. v Google, Inc.*, 810 F Supp 2d 1002 (N D Cal, 2011).

It is true that the very same functionality could have been offered in Android without duplicating the exact command structure used in Java. This could have been done by re-arranging the various methods under different groupings among the various classes and packages (even if the same names had been used). In this sense, there were many ways to group the methods yet still duplicate the same range of functionality.

But the names are more than just names—they are symbols in a command structure wherein the commands take the form

java.package.Class.method()

Each command calls into action a pre-assigned function. The overall name tree, of course, has creative elements but it is also a precise command structure—a utilitarian and functional set of symbols, each to carry out a pre-assigned function. This command structure is a system or method of operation under Section 102(b) of the Copyright Act and, therefore, cannot be copyrighted. Duplication of the command structure is necessary for interoperability.[71]

It is important to note, however, that the court did not hold that Java API packages are free for all to use without a licence. It did not hold that the structure, sequence, and organization of all computer programs may be taken freely. Rather, it simply held on the specific facts of this case that the particular elements replicated by Google were free for all to use under the US Copyright Act. Given, therefore, that many in the computing industry still believe in the copyrightablity of APIs, one can expect to see further conflicts over the potential ownership of the API glue that, in a sense, holds many cloud services together. If it were to be found that APIs could be protected by software copyright, the implications for cloud computing as an industry would be significant, with those holding the *de facto* standards for APIs in a strong position to take market leads and charge royalties for use of APIs.

In Europe, such a development seems unlikely. In the 2012 ECJ case *SAS v World Programming*, the Court ruled definitively that

neither the functionality of a computer program nor the programming language and the format of data files used in a computer program in order to exploit certain of its functions constitute a form of expression of that program and, as such, are not protected by copyright in computer programs for the purposes of that directive.[72]

This reasoning can be used to argue that APIs and other functional characteristics of computer software are, therefore, not eligible for copyright protection. It remains to be seen how US jurisprudence on this issue develops.

9. Conclusion

A user of a cloud service, whether a business, a public sector organization, or a private individual, will use information and content created both outside the cloud and within the cloud service itself. Content or information brought in will usually have an established ownership status and will normally be covered by one of the following: IP, confidential information/trade secrets, and/or contract. For information created inside the cloud service by the user, the same rights will often apply, complicated somewhat by questions of where the information is created and, indeed, as we have in seen in addressing the increasingly collaborative nature of cloud work, by how many and by whom. Cloud service providers will rarely, if at all, make claims concerning ownership

---

[71] *Oracle America, Inc. v Google, Inc.*, n. 70.
[72] *SAS Institute Inc. v World Programming Ltd* [2012] ECJ C-406/10.

of content created either outside the service or in the service by the user. However, given that providers almost universally limit their liability concerning such things as data integrity, and disclosure, the onus will more often than not be on the user to encrypt data so as to ensure with complete satisfaction that infringements, compromises of confidentiality, and ownership claims do not occur.

A cloud provider will also create information during its administration of a service. Here, the main issues of concern are transparency (so that customers are aware of the uses which will be made of their information), and the preservation of confidentiality in the light of technical advances which increase the risk of reidentification. It may be that these issues of derived information are, in fact, resolved through data protection laws and their regulation of the use and distribution of such information.[73]

Questions of information ownership and use also arise in relation to the use of cloud models for the distribution of existing information. Such distribution may be based on conventional commercial arrangements involving access charges, or the cloud may be used to facilitate a more open use of information. Issues here include how such cloud-effected distribution interacts with exceptions that exist in law regarding certain types of content, and how infringement of such distributed content is to be avoided. Again, contract and technology may play a role, along with encryption and the ToS applying to user security.

Finally, as we have seen, broader issues of ownership may arise in relation to APIs, the glue that holds much of the cloud service industry together. While courts in both the US and EU have, in recent decisions, ruled against the existence of copyright for APIs, the US decision appears to apply only to the specific facts and may be inconclusive. Given the importance of APIs in terms of connectivity and interoperability, an extension of copyright to APIs could have a deleterious effect on the development of the cloud computing sector.

---

[73] See Part III of this book for a detailed discussion of these issues.

PART III

PROTECTION OF PERSONAL DATA IN CLOUDS

As cloud computing has moved into the mainstream, questions are increasingly being asked about the protection available for information relating to identifiable individuals, or 'personal data'. Laws have already been enacted in more than 90 countries worldwide to regulate the processing of personal data. Almost all of those laws are based on specific harmonization measures, in particular the 1980 OECD Guidelines, a Convention adopted by the Council of Europe in 1981 and an EU Directive from 1995. Although the global balance is shifting, Europe still has the greatest number of jurisdictions with data protection statutes. In this part of the book, we analyse the implications for cloud computing of European data protection law with a focus on four key issues: what information is protected, who is responsible, which law(s) apply, and how international data transfers are regulated.

In Chapter 7 we consider what information in clouds is, and what should be, classified as personal data. It is crucial to tackle this question first as the rights and obligations arising under EU national data protection laws apply only to personal data and tend to do so on an 'all or nothing' basis, depending on whether a particular individual is identified or identifiable. The use in cloud computing of encryption, anonymization, data fragmentation, and other techniques has an impact on this threshold issue. Indeed, as discussed in Part I of this book, cloud computing technologies and service models are sufficiently complex that it is often the case that a provider of the whole or part of a multilayered cloud service will not even know whether its systems are being used to process personal data. With that in mind, in Chapter 8 we look at who is regulated as a 'data controller' and/or 'data processor' in various situations, and how those roles might be mapped onto typical cloud computing arrangements.

Data protection laws in the EU adopt a complicated location-based approach to regulation. Jurisdiction depends either on where a controller or processor is 'established', in which case the relevant national law has global reach to regulate activities carried on in the course of that establishment, or on the mere use of equipment located in the EU to process personal data, which may trigger regulation of activities of controllers with no EU establishment. In Chapter 9, we look at the international impact of European data protection legislation and consider which laws apply to personal data in clouds. In Chapter 10, we consider how restrictions on cross-border transfers of data work, or perhaps don't work, in cloud environments and how they might be improved.

We will focus mainly on the current European legislative framework as it is likely to remain the foundation for national laws in the EU until at least 2016. EU data protection policy has, however, been in a state of flux since the European Commission published details of a wide-ranging legislative reform package that, among other things, would replace the current Data Protection Directive with a General Data Protection Regulation.[1] Notwithstanding the frequent invocation by EU officials of 'the cloud' as a catalyst and justification for new EU data protection laws, the proposed Regulation does not look particularly 'cloud friendly',[2] nor indeed 'business friendly', 'citizen friendly', or 'future proof'.[3] The proposal will almost certainly be amended substantially before adoption, if indeed it is adopted. However, in its initial form it would broaden the already wide scope of 'personal data' and would impose even more complex and cumbersome compliance obligations on cloud providers and users of their services, including in relation to international transfers of data. Billions of cloud-enabled devices are in use already and vast amounts of personal data are transferred globally every second. In that context, it is not surprising that the EU rules have proved controversial and that there is intense international interest in the current reform proposals.

---

[1] The Regulation forms part of a package of reform proposals published by the European Commission on 25 January 2012. Full details are available at <http://ec.europa.eu/justice/newsroom/data-protection/news/120125_en.htm>.

[2] Neelie Kroes, 'Cloud Computing and Data Protection Reform', blog post, 13 January 2012, <http://blogs.ec.europa.eu/neelie-kroes/cloud-data-protection/>.

[3] Viviane Reding, 'Privacy in the Cloud: Data Protection and Security in Cloud Computing', press release, 7 December 2011, <http://europa.eu/rapid/press-release_SPEECH-11-859_en.htm>.

7

What is Regulated as Personal Data in Clouds?

W Kuan Hon, Christopher Millard, and Ian Walden

1. Introduction

Central to any consideration of cloud-based processing is the definition of 'personal data'. National laws based on the EU Data Protection Directive (DPD) only apply to 'personal data'. Information that is not, or ceases to be, 'personal data' may be processed, in the cloud, or otherwise, free of data protection law requirements. In cloud computing, the 'personal data' definitional issue is most relevant in three contexts: first, anonymized and pseudonymized data; second, encrypted data, whether encrypted in transmission or storage; and third, sharding or fragmentation of data. In each case, the question is: should such data be treated as 'personal data'? These forms of data involve the application of different processes to personal data, at different stages, and/or by different actors. We will discuss them in detail, but look first at the 'personal data' definition.

2. 'Personal Data'

Data protection law uses objective definitions for personal data and sensitive personal data, unlike privacy law's subjective 'reasonable expectations'.[1] This results in a binary, 'all or nothing', perspective and wide-ranging applicability.

The DPD defines 'personal data' as:

any information relating to an identified or identifiable natural person ('data subject'); an identifiable person is one who can be identified, directly or indirectly, in particular by reference to an identification number or to one or more factors specific to his physical, physiological, mental, economic, cultural or social identity.[2]

Stricter regulation applies to the processing of special categories of personal data deemed particularly sensitive ('sensitive data'),[3] namely personal data revealing 'racial or ethnic origin, political opinions, religious or philosophical beliefs, trade-union membership', 'data concerning health or sex life', and criminal offences or convictions.[4]

Information that is 'personal data' is subject to the DPD, whatever its nature. Similarly, sensitive data is automatically subject to stricter rules; information that person X has an embarrassing disease, or just a minor cold, must be treated the same way. Arguably, not all information merits protection as 'personal data'. Some information

---

[1] See, for example, *Campbell v MGN Ltd* [2004] UKHL 22 [21].

[2] DPD, Art. 2(a).

[3] Some other data types are also regulated more stringently, for example, 'traffic data' and 'location data' under Directive 2002/58/EC of the European Parliament and of the Council of 12 July 2002 concerning the processing of personal data and the protection of privacy in the electronic communications sector OJ L 201/37, 31.07.2002 ('ePrivacy Directive').

[4] Article 8. The DPD refers to 'special category' data. Such data are generally called 'sensitive data' or 'sensitive personal data'. Stricter requirements may include 'explicit' data subject consent to processing.

may seem intrinsically 'non-personal', for example meteorological information recorded on Mount Everest by automated equipment.[5] Leaving aside apparently 'non-personal' information, however, DPD recital 26 recognizes that information constituting 'personal data' may be rendered 'anonymous'. Unfortunately, its interpretation and application are not straightforward,[6] especially when considering how to 'anonymize' or 'pseudonymize' personal data sufficiently to take data outside the DPD.

In its Working Paper 136 (WP136),[7] the EU Article 29 Working Party (A29WP) has issued guidance on the meaning of 'personal data'. WP136 interprets the concept broadly, stating that the DPD is intended to cover all information concerning, or which may be linked to, an individual,[8] and that 'unduly restricting' the interpretation should be avoided. Seemingly over-broad application of the DPD should instead be balanced using the flexibility allowed in applying the DPD's rules.[9] A29WP opinions are persuasive but not binding. Therefore, in practice, controllers will often exercise caution when relying on such opinions.

WP136 also emphasizes that whether information is 'personal data' is a question of fact and depends on context. For example, a common family name may not single someone out within a country, but probably identifies a pupil in a classroom.[10]

Information which is not 'personal data' in the hands of one person (eg a cloud user) may, depending on the circumstances, become 'personal data' when obtained or processed by another[11] (such as a cloud provider, if it tries to process it for its own purposes). Indeed, information not originally being 'personal data' may become so if its holder processes it for other purposes, such as to identify individuals.

Similarly, when considering identifiability, account must be taken of 'all the means likely reasonably to be used by the controller or any other person to identify them'.[12] This test is dynamic. Methods 'likely reasonably to be used' may change as re-identification technology improves and costs decrease. Accordingly, the intended storage period of information is also relevant.[13]

Finally, whether information is 'personal data' may (where the processing's purpose is not identification) be affected by technical and organizational measures to prevent identification.[14] More effective measures make information more likely to be anonymous data.

---

[5] That is not strictly correct, as we see later. Even seemingly non-personal information can be 'personal data'.

[6] Particularly as many national law definitions of 'personal data' also differ from the DPD definition. See Christopher Kuner, *European Data Protection Law: Corporate Compliance and Regulation*, 2nd edn (Oxford: Oxford University Press, 2007), Ch. 2.82 (tables of comparative definitions).

[7] *Opinion 4/2007 on the Concept of Personal Data, WP 136* (2007).

[8] Even information about things can be 'personal data' if linkable to an individual—WP136, Part 2.

[9] WP136, 4–6.

[10] WP136, 13, and the contextual nature of 'personal data' has been recognized, for example, in *Common Services Agency v Scottish Information Commissioner (Scotland)* [2008] UKHL 47, (*CSA*), [27].

[11] WP136, 20, and the examples in ICO, *Determining What Is Personal Data (Data Protection Technical Guidance)* (2007), 5.2.

[12] Recital 26. WP136 considers a 'mere hypothetical possibility' to single out someone is not enough to consider the person 'identifiable'. The difficulty is, when does a 'possibility' exceed merely 'hypothetical'?

[13] WP136, 15: particular information meant to be stored for a month might not be 'personal data' as identification may be considered impossible during its 'lifetime'. If the same information is to be kept for ten years, the controller should consider that the information might become identifiable in say year nine, which would make it 'personal data' then.

[14] WP136, 17: here, implementing those measures may be 'a condition for the information precisely not to be considered to be personal data and its processing not to be subject to the Directive'.

3. Anonymization and Pseudonymization

Cloud users and/or providers may process information free of the DPD if it is not 'personal data' but 'anonymous'. Also, personal data may be 'anonymized' to facilitate future cloud processing.

As the UK Information Commissioner's Office (ICO) puts it, 'Anonymisation ensures the availability of rich data resources, whilst protecting individuals' personal data'.[15] Anonymized or pseudonymized data result from actions deliberately taken on personal data to conceal or hide data subjects' identities. Users may perform anonymization or pseudonymization procedures on data sets before processing resulting data in the cloud. Also, providers may anonymize personal data stored with them, in order to then use, sell, or share the anonymized data.[16] Some US health data storage providers anonymize and sell health data.[17]

3.1 Anonymization or pseudonymization as 'processing'

Processing anonymous or pseudonymized data involves two steps:

1. anonymizing or pseudonymizing 'personal data'; then
2. disclosing or otherwise processing the resulting data.

If step one itself constitutes 'processing' the DPD will apply; for example, requiring data subjects' consent to anonymization or pseudonymization procedures, including explicit consent for sensitive data. WP136 did not discuss whether these procedures are 'processing'. Uncertainties regarding their status may, unfortunately, discourage their use as privacy-enhancing techniques, or the production and use of anonymized or pseudonymized data for socially desirable purposes such as medical research.[18]

However, even if step one is 'processing', the ICO considers that consent is not generally needed, on the basis that the UK Data Protection Act 1998 (DPA) only entitles individuals to prevent the processing of their personal data where this would be likely to cause unwarranted damage or distress. Therefore, provided there is no 'likelihood' of anonymization causing unwarranted damage or distress, as will be the case if it is done effectively, there will be no need to obtain consent as a means of legitimizing the processing.[19] This suggests that if an anonymization procedure is not performed effectively, it

---

[15] ICO, 'Anonymisation: Managing Data Protection Risk Code of Practice Summary' (20 November 2012) and see generally ICO, 'Anonymisation Code of Practice' (2012).

[16] Such use may indeed be key to its business model: M Mowbray, 'The Fog over the Grimpen Mire: Cloud Computing and the Law' 6(1) *SCRIPT-ed* 132 at 144–5. Sometimes personal data are not even anonymized before 'processing', for example automated software scanning social networking profiles (or web-based emails) to display content-based advertisements.

[17] K Zetter, 'Medical Records: Stored in the Cloud, Sold on the Open Market' (*Wired*, 19 October 2009), <http://www.wired.com/threatlevel/2009/10/medicalrecords> (accessed 18 March 2013).

[18] I Walden, 'Anonymising Personal Data' (2002) 10(2) *International Journal of Law and Information Technology* 224. Some consider consent *should* be required for anonymization, for example where anonymized data will be used for medical research in areas where a data subject has moral objections—Walden, 'Anonymising Personal Data', at 231. In the UK, a tribunal has held that anonymization is 'processing'—*All Party Parliamentary Group on Extraordinary Rendition v The Information Commissioner & The Ministry of Defence*, [2011] UKUT 153 (AAC) (*APGER*), [127].

[19] Anonymisation Code 28, n. 15. The Code notes further difficulties with relying on consent to legitimize processing, stressing that it is 'safer' to publish anonymized data even where consent could be obtained for the disclosure of (non-anonymized) personal data.

could constitute unlawful processing. This provides an incentive to use more effective anonymization procedures.

This chapter proceeds on the basis that there are no problems with anonymization or pseudonymization procedures.[20]

3.2 Common anonymization and pseudonymization techniques

Methods to 'anonymize' personal data, particularly before publishing statistical information or research results, include (alone or in combination):[21]

- deleting or omitting 'identifying details', for example names;
- substituting code numbers for names or other direct identifiers (this is pseudonymization, effectively);
- aggregating information, for example by age group, year, or town;[22] and
- barnardization[23] or other techniques introducing statistical noise, for example differential privacy techniques with statistical databases.[24]

Many anonymization and pseudonymization techniques involve amending only part of a data set, for example disguising names or applying cryptography to other explicit identifiers. Other information in the data set, such as usage information or test results associated with names, remains available to those having access to resulting data.[25]

WP136 notes[26] that identification[27] involves singling someone out, and distinguishing them from others either directly or indirectly. Direct identification includes identification by name or other 'direct identifier'. Indirect identification includes identification by reference to identification number or other specific personal characteristics, including identification by combining different information (identifiers) held by controllers or others, which individually might not be identifying.

---

[20] A study for the EU Parliament's Committee on Internal Market and Consumer Protection, X Konarski et al., *Reforming the Data Protection Package* (European Parliament, 2012) also emphasizes the need to clarify requirements and the legal basis for anonymization itself: 26–7, 40.

[21] For details of techniques and examples, see the Anonymisation Code, n. 15.

[22] WP136, 22. Aggregation into a group may be used to make it harder to single out individuals.

[23] A statistical technique aiming to anonymize statistical counts, and ensure individuals cannot be identified from statistics, while still indicating actual numbers. 0, +1, or –1 are randomly added to all non-zero counts in table cells, recalculating row/column totals accordingly. *CSA* (n. 10) [8], [15]. After *CSA*, the Scottish Information Commissioner found that barnardization would not be adequate to anonymize data, but broader aggregation would. Statistics requested by age range 0–14, for each year from 1990 to 2003, within the Dumfries and Galloway area by census ward, were considered too identifying, even if barnardized. However, disclosure was ordered of aggregated statistics for the whole area for each year from 1990 to 2001. *Collie and the Common Services Agency for the Scottish Health Service, Childhood Leukaemia Statistics in Dumfries and Galloway*, [2010] UKSIC 021/2005 ref. 200500298.

[24] C Dwork, 'Differential Privacy: A Survey of Results, Theory and Applications of Models of Computation', in Manindra Agrawal, Dingzhu Du, Zhenhua Duan, and Angsheng Li (eds), *Theory and Applications of Models of Computation* (Berlin/Heidelberg: Springer, 2008), 1–19. This technique aims to provide accurate statistical information when querying databases containing personal information, without compromising privacy.

[25] Social networking sites share 'anonymized' data, but individuals are re-identifiable from anonymized social graphs (network of individuals they are connected to). Arvind Narayanan and Vitaly Shmatikov, 'De-anonymizing Social Networks' (Proceedings of the 2009 30th IEEE Symposium on Security and Privacy, IEEE Computer Society Washington DC, US, 17–20 May 2009), 173.

[26] 12–15.

[27] WP136 analysed all 'personal data' definitional building blocks. We consider only 'identified or identifiable'.

Omitting or deleting direct identifiers, such as names, while leaving indirect identifiers untouched, may not render information sufficiently non-personal. In particular, identification numbers or similar unique identifiers may enable linking of disparate information associated with the same indirect identifier to a given individual, and may be used to identify them. Nevertheless, deleting direct identifiers is often considered adequate to prevent identifiability.[28] Proposed guidance on minimum standards for de-identifying data sets, for instance to ensure patient privacy when sharing clinical research data, recommends deleting direct identifiers including names, email addresses, biometric data, medical device identifiers, and IP addresses. If the remaining information includes at least three indirect identifiers, such as age or sex, the authors recommend independent review before publication. Thus, they consider three or more indirect identifiers present sufficient risk of identification to require independent consideration of whether the risk is 'non-negligible'.[29]

Pseudonyms, for example nicknames substituted for names, are indirect identifiers.[30] WP136 describes[31] pseudonymization as 'the process of disguising identities', to enable collection of additional information on the same individual without having to know his or her identity, particularly in research and statistics. There are two types of pseudonymization. Retraceable, also known as reversible, pseudonymization aims to allow 'retracing' or re-identification in restricted circumstances.[32] For example, 'key-coded data' involves changing names to code numbers, with a 'key'[33] mapping numbers to names. This is common in pharmaceutical trials. Another example is the application of two-way cryptography to direct identifiers. The second type, irreversible pseudonymization, is intended to render re-identification impossible; for example, 'hashing': applying one-way cryptography (hash functions) to direct identifiers.[34] Retraceably pseudonymized data may be 'personal data', as its purpose is to enable re-identification, albeit in limited circumstances.

If each code is unique to an individual, identification is still a risk, so pseudonymized information remains 'personal data'.[35] However, if pseudonymization reduces risks for individuals then data protection rules could be applied more flexibly, and processing of pseudonymized data may be subject to less strict conditions than processing of information regarding directly identifiable individuals.[36] Austria's DPD implementation[37] illustrates this less strict approach. Information is 'indirectly personal data' if its controller, processor, or recipient cannot identify individuals using legally permissible means. Indirectly personal data are, effectively, pseudonymous data: identities can be retraced, but not legally. Key-coded pharmaceutical trials data are considered 'indirectly personal data'.

---

[28] For example, Joined Cases C-92/09 and C-93/09 *Volker und Markus Schecke (Approximation of laws)* OJ C 13/6, 15.1.2011 (not yet published in ECR) assumes deleting names and so on would adequately anonymize recipients of certain funds.

[29] I Hrynaszkiewicz et al., 'Preparing Raw Clinical Data for Publication: Guidance for Journal Editors, Authors, and Peer Reviewers' (2010) BMJ 2010, 340:c181.

[30] For example, in Germany a pseudonymous person may seek access to information that online service providers hold regarding his pseudonym. Kuner, n. 6, Ch. 2.10.

[31] WP136, 17.

[32] For example, with pseudonymized medical trials data, to identify individuals who may need follow-up treatment or to enable regulators to audit clinical trials.

[33] Accessible only to a restricted set of individuals.

[34] Ross Anderson, *Security Engineering: A Guide to Building Dependable Distributed Systems*, 2nd edn (Indianapolis: John Wiley & Sons, 2008), Ch. 5.3.1.

[35] WP136, 19 suggests risks of key hacking or leakage are factors to be taken into account when considering 'means likely reasonably to be used'.

[36] WP136, 18–19.   [37] Datenschutzgesetz 2000.

Such information, presumably because privacy risks are considered lower, has less protection than 'personal data'. It can, for example, be exported without regulatory approval.[38]

If the same code number is used, such as for all individuals in the same town, or all records for the same year, WP136 considers that the identification risk might be eliminated to render data anonymous. This effectively involves aggregating data: in WP136's examples, the aggregation is by town or year, respectively.

Key-coded medical trials data may be 'personal data'; but WP136 also recognizes:[39]

This does not mean, though, that any other data controller processing the same set of coded data would be processing personal data, if within the specific scheme in which those other controllers are operating re-identification is explicitly excluded and appropriate technical measures have been taken in this respect.[40]

Therefore, key-coded data may be non-personal data when held by another person and specifically not intended to identify individuals, and when appropriate measures are taken to exclude re-identification (eg, cryptographic irreversible hashing).[41] Furthermore, WP136 considers[42] information may not be 'personal data' in that person's hands even if identification is theoretically possible in 'unforeseeable circumstances', such as through 'accidental matching of qualities of the data subject that reveal his/her identity' to a third party,[43] whereupon the third party would have accessed 'personal data'.

The European Commission considers that transferring key-coded data to the US (without transferring or revealing the key) is not a personal data export subject to Safe Harbor principles.[44] WP136 considers itself consistent with this view as recipients never know individuals' identities; only the EU researcher has the key.[45]

We now consider 'irreversibly pseudonymized' data and aggregated data. In discussing pseudonymized data, WP136 focused on changing names or other perceived unique identifiers into code numbers, in other words key-coded data, rather than attempts to pseudonymize data irreversibly by deleting direct identifiers or one-way encrypting them. The opinion only touched on aggregation.

---

[38] Kuner, n. 6, Ch. 2.12; Peter Fleischer, 'Austrian Insights' (*Peter Fleischer: Privacy...?*, 22 February 2010), <http://peterfleischer.blogspot.com/2010/02/austrian-insights.html> (accessed 18 March 2013).

[39] Page 20.

[40] Other controllers processing that data may not be processing 'personal data' because only the lead researcher holds the key, under a confidentiality obligation, and key-coding is to enable only him/her or authorities to identify individuals if necessary, while disguising trial participants' identities from recipients of pseudonymized data. Typically, recipients include research sponsors/funders or, when publishing research containing key-coded data, readers.

[41] The UK DPA's 'personal data' definition differs from the DPD's, causing disagreement about how personal data may be anonymized and released. The Scottish Court in *Craigdale Housing Association et al. v The Scottish Information Commissioner* [2010] CSIH 43, [2010] SLT 655 [19] observed that the 'hard-line' interpretation, 'under which anonymised information could not be released unless the data controller at the same time destroyed the raw material from which the anonymisation was made (and any means of retrieving that material)', was 'hardly consistent' with recital 26. The Tribunal in *APGER* (n. 18) considered that anonymized personal data remained 'personal data' in the hands of the controller who held the key, but could be released as anonymization removed its 'personal data' character. A subsequent Court decision, *Department of Health v Information Commissioner*, [2011] EWHC 1430 (Admin) held that a controller who anonymized personal data could disclose the resulting data, which was anonymous data even if the controller had the key to identifying individuals concerned. It noted the adverse impact a contrary ruling would have on the publication of medical statistics.

[42] Page 20.   [43] How accidental matching could happen was not detailed.

[44] The Safe Harbor is one method enabling export of personal data to the US. See Chapter 10.

[45] European Commission, 'Frequently Asked Questions Relating to Transfers of Personal Data from the EU/EEA to Third Countries' (2009), <http://ec.europa.eu/justice/policies/privacy/docs/international_transfers_faq/international_transfers_faq.pdf>.

WP136 seems, initially, to equate irreversible pseudonymization with anonymization.[46] However, WP136 then states[47] that whether information is truly anonymous depends on the circumstances, looking at all means likely reasonably to be used to identify individuals. It considers this particularly pertinent to statistical information where, although information is aggregated, the original group's size is relevant. With a small group, it is more likely that identification will still be possible through combining aggregated information with other information.

Deleting or irreversibly changing direct identifiers leaves untouched other information originally associated with that identifier. For example, if information comprises name, age, gender, postcode, and pharmacological test results, and only names are deleted or changed, information about age, gender, or other details remains. Indeed, usually the deletion or change is intended to disguise identities while enabling disclosure of other information. That purpose would be defeated if age, and certainly test results, had to be deleted before disclosure.

However, age, gender, and other traits can be identifying, when combined with each other and perhaps information from other sources.[48] Information is increasingly linkable, and individuals increasingly identifiable. With automated fast data mining over large data sets, different information, perhaps from multiple sources, is linkable to the same individual for analysis. Over time, more information becomes linkable, increasingly enabling identification whether data are key-coded, irreversibly pseudonymized, aggregated, or barnardized.

To summarize, when processing data in the cloud, it is important to note that retraceably pseudonymized data, such as key-coded data, may remain personal data. However, aggregating pseudonymized data, for example through non-unique codes, may render data 'anonymous', with data set size being one relevant factor, and enabling cloud processing of anonymous data free of the DPD. Moreover, even retraceably pseudonymized data may be anonymous data in the hands of another person operating within a scheme where re-identification is explicitly excluded, and when appropriate measures are taken to prevent re-identification by them, even if, theoretically, others could 'accidentally' re-identify individuals.

Critically, whether information is 'personal data' depends on the circumstances, considering all means likely reasonably to be used to identify individuals, including, for anonymized or pseudonymized data, the strength of 'anti-identification' measures used. In addition, anonymization or pseudonymization procedures may themselves be regulated as 'processing'.

The A29WP has been criticized for 'deficient' understanding on the basis that data set size, rather than the quality and effectiveness of measures used, determines effectiveness of pseudonymization or anonymization procedures.[49] However, data set size should not be the only determinant: quality and effectiveness of measures are also major factors to consider, all in the particular circumstances. If, for example, strong encryption is applied to the whole data set, data set size may not matter.

---

[46] Page 18.   [47] Page 21.

[48] For example, a person's Internet search queries can identify them, especially when different queries by the same person are recorded against the same code number, and therefore can be combined. See the AOL search results release incident, summarized in Paul Ohm, 'Broken Promises of Privacy: Responding to the Surprising Failure of Anonymization' (2010) 57 *UCLA Law Review* 1701.

[49] Douwe Korff, 'European Commission Comparative Study on Different Approaches to New Privacy Challenges, in Particular in the Light of Technological Developments—Working Paper No. 2: Data protection laws in the EU: The difficulties in meeting the challenges posed by global social and technical developments' (20 January 2010) [48].

The DPD and WP136 certainly recognize indirect identification is possible through combining information, and WP136 mentions data set size and linkability, noting that deanonymization techniques could improve. However, the pace of technological advances seems to have been underestimated.

Re-identification methods are progressing,[50] reinforcing the reality that current techniques, such as removing identifiers and/or aggregation, may not effectively anonymize data irreversibly.[51] Indeed, any information linkable to an individual is potentially 'personal data', because it can identify them if combined with enough other information.[52] This means that anonymized or pseudonymized personal data may still be, or become, 'personal data'.

However, this does not mean that it is pointless to apply anonymization or pseudonymization techniques to personal data; far from it. Such privacy-enhancing techniques reduce *risks* of identification and therefore risks of harm to data subjects, and typify the use of Privacy by Design (PbD) and Privacy Enhancing Technologies (PETs) concepts that lawmakers wish to promote expressly.[53] Their use should be encouraged as best practice, as for example in the ICO's Anonymisation Code.

3.3 Encryption[54]

Are encrypted data in the cloud 'personal data'? Whether encrypted data are 'personal data' depends on the circumstances, particularly the 'means likely reasonably to be used' (fair or foul) to re-identify individuals, and the security of encrypted data against decryption. As with anonymization, applying cryptography to personal data may be 'processing' requiring, for example, consent or other justification. The arguments above apply equally here.

Where one-way or two-way cryptography is applied to identifiers within personal data (eg names) leaving other data readable as 'plaintext', this overlaps with pseudonymization and anonymization. Two-way cryptography may be applied to the whole data set, and data may be encrypted within the user's computer prior to transmission, using the user's own software, or the provider's. Even if users intend to process data unencrypted in the cloud, a provider may encrypt all or part of the data it receives, before using or selling anonymized or pseudonymized data (eg, applying cryptography to identifiers) or to store data more securely (applying two-way cryptography to the full data set). Transmissions may themselves be encrypted or unencrypted, usually depending on how providers set up their systems.

WP136 discusses one-way cryptography, not for password authentication or integrity checking, but to scramble irreversibly identifiers within a larger data set. WP136 states:[55] 'Disguising identities can also be done in a way that no reidentification is possible, e.g. by one-way cryptography, which creates in general anonymised data.' This suggests data containing one-way encrypted identifiers would not be 'personal data', and it does seem

---

[50] Even differential privacy is attackable. See Graham Cormode, 'Individual Privacy vs Population Privacy: Learning to Attack Anonymization' (2010) arXiv:1011.2511v1 [cs.DB].

[51] Research also continues on anonymization, for example the Purdue project on anonymizing textual data, and its impact on utility: Chris Clifton et al., 'Anonymizing Textual Data and Its Impact on Utility', <http://projects.cerias.purdue.edu/TextAnon> (accessed 18 March 2013).

[52] Even meteorological data collected automatically on Mount Everest may be linkable to researchers publishing the data.

[53] Along with 'privacy by default', see draft Data Protection Regulation Arts 23, 30.3. Also see A Cavoukian and E Khaled, *Dispelling the Myths Surrounding De-identification: Anonymization Remains a Strong Tool for Protecting Privacy* (Information and Privacy Commissioner of Ontario, 2011).

[54] Cryptography is outlined in Chapter 2.   [55] Page 18.

that 'accidental' re-identification is less likely with data anonymized through one-way cryptography. However, WP136 then discusses the effectiveness of the procedures, so in reality the crucial issue is the reversibility of the one-way process. Even one-way cryptography may be broken, and original data reconstituted.[56] The more secure the cryptography method, the less likely that information will be 'personal data'. If a cryptography technique employed to 'anonymize' data is cracked, in order to maintain 'non-personal data' status data may require re-encryption using a more secure method.[57]

Furthermore, as previously discussed, irreversibly hashing direct identifiers cannot prevent identification through indirect identifiers, other information in the data set, and/or other sources. Thus, personal data where identifiers have been deleted or one-way hashed may, after considering such 'means likely reasonably to be used', remain 'personal data', and their storage or use by providers may be subject to the DPD.

We now consider two-way encryption. WP136 focuses mainly on one-way cryptographic hashing;[58] notably, scrambling direct identifiers, supposedly irreversibly, to anonymize or pseudonymize personal data. However, often users want to store data for future use but, to ensure security and confidentiality, apply two-way encryption to the full data set (not just one component like names). The user can read encrypted data using its secret decryption key; others are not intended to decipher it.

The 'personal data/not personal data' debate concentrated on anonymizing or pseudonymizing parts of a data set. However, WP136 applies equally to two-way encryption of full data sets. Under WP136, 'anonymized' data may be considered anonymous in a provider's hands if 'within the specific scheme in which those other controllers [eg providers] are operating re-identification is explicitly excluded and appropriate technical measures have been taken in this respect'. On that basis, we suggest that if you cannot view data, you cannot identify data subjects, and therefore identification may be excluded by preventing others from being able to access or read data. By analogy with key-coded data, to the person encrypting personal data, such as a cloud user with the decryption key, the data remain 'personal data'. However, in another person's hands, such as a cloud provider storing encrypted data with no key and no means 'reasonably likely' to be used for decryption,[59] the data may be considered anonymous.

This may arguably remove cloud providers from the scope of data protection legislation, at least where data have been strongly encrypted by the controller before transmission, and the provider cannot access the key.[60] Consider a SaaS provider using a PaaS or IaaS provider's infrastructure to offer its services. The PaaS or IaaS provider may not have the keys, even if the SaaS provider does, so the information may be 'personal data' to the SaaS provider, but not to other providers. In SaaS involving mere storage, where users encrypt data before transmission, even the SaaS provider may not have the key.

---

[56] Cloud computing, in the form of Amazon's EC2 GPU cluster instances, was used to find 14 passwords of 1–6 characters long from their SHA-1 hashes in under an hour, for about US$2. Jack Clark, 'Hacker Uses Cloud Computing to Crack Passwords' (*ZDNet*, 16 November 2010), <http://zdnet.com/hacker-uses-cloud-computing-to-crack-passwords-4010021067> (accessed 18 March 2013).

[57] At least, within a reasonable period.   [58] See Chapter 2.

[59] Bearing in mind that cloud computing may itself increasingly be 'means likely reasonably' to be utilized to decrypt data! 'Cracking Passwords in the Cloud: Breaking PGP on EC2 with EDPR' (*Electric Alchemy*, 30 October 2009), <http://news.electricalchemy.net/2009/10/cracking-passwords-in-cloud.html> (accessed 18 March 2013).

[60] Storage SaaS provider Dropbox had to clarify that it held keys and could access users' encrypted data: Ryan Singel, 'Dropbox Lied to Users About Data Security, Complaint to FTC Alleges' (*Wired*, 13 May 2011), <http://www.wired.com/threatlevel/2011/05/dropbox-ftc> (accessed 18 March 2013).

When encrypting a full data set, size should not matter; unlike with key-coded data, no data remain available 'in the clear' as potentially linkable, indirectly identifying information. Encrypted data, transformed into another form, differ qualitatively from, and arguably pose fewer risks than, key-coded data or aggregated data, so there is a stronger argument that fully encrypted data are not 'personal data' (to those without the key).

The issue again is security against decryption by unauthorized persons. Stronger 'anti-identification' measures applied to data make it more likely the data will be anonymous. Again, encryption strength is important, as is the effectiveness of other measures such as key management. If personal data were not encrypted before transmission to the cloud, or only weakly encrypted, or if the key was insecurely managed, data stored might be 'personal data', and the provider a 'processor'.[61] However, if personal data were encrypted strongly before transmission, the stored data would be unlikely to be 'personal data' in the provider's hands.

However, why should whether a user decides to encrypt data,[62] or the effectiveness of their chosen encryption method or other security measures, determine whether encrypted data hosted by providers constitute 'personal data'? Generally, 'pure' cloud storage providers[63] cannot control in what form users choose to upload data to the cloud.[64] Nor would providers necessarily know the nature of the data that users intend to store. Yet the status of data stored with providers, which affects the provider's status as a 'processor' (or not) of data stored by users, will vary with each user's decisions and actions; it may differ for different users, or even for the same user storing different kinds of data, or the same data, at different times. This seems unsatisfactory.

Regarding providers' knowledge, an Italian court has considered that in order to impose criminal data protection liability on a data host for not monitoring or prescreening uploaded sensitive data, there must be knowledge and will on its part, even with a SaaS provider that is considered more than a passive storage provider.[65]

The possible encryption of data transmissions has been discussed previously.[66] If users transmit unencrypted personal data, even via secure channels, providers will still receive personal data as such, while encrypted channels may not be required for confidential transmission of already strongly encrypted data, as anyone monitoring transmissions would only obtain encrypted data.

Transmission and longer-term storage may merit different treatment. Transmission durations, and therefore possible interception windows, may be relatively short. Therefore, in many cases perhaps 'data in motion' need not be as strongly encrypted, to make transmitted

---

[61] Assuming a provider storing personal data 'processes' data for customers, and so is a 'processor', see Chapter 8.

[62] Disadvantages to storing data in encrypted form include the inability to index and therefore search encrypted data. This may lead some users not to encrypt data. However, searchable encryption is being investigated, and may some day become feasible: Seny Kamara and Kristin Lauter, 'Cryptographic Cloud Storage', in Radu Sion et al. (eds), 'FC'10 Proceedings of the 14th International Conference on Financial Cryptography and Data Security' (Springer-Verlag Berlin, Heidelberg 2010), 136.

[63] For example, providers of IaaS or PaaS for storage by users of data on the provider's infrastructure; or providers of SaaS, where the service is limited to data storage and tools to upload, download, and manage stored data.

[64] They can control it if they build it into their systems. For example, Mozy's procedures involve encrypting data on a user's local computer, using the user's key, before transfer to Mozy's servers via encrypted transmissions. Mozy Inc., 'Is Mozy Secure?', <http://support.mozy.co.uk/articles/en_US/FAQ/Is-Mozy-Secure> (*Mozy*, 15 July 2012) (accessed 25 March 2013).

[65] Liability was imposed for other reasons. Judge Oscar Magi, Milan, Sentenza, Tribunale Ordinario di Milano (Sez Pen) n. 1972/2010 (4 December 2010), *Giur Comm* 2011, 5, 1215. <http://speciali.espresso.repubblica.it/pdf/Motivazioni_sentenza_Google.pdf> (accessed 18 March 2013). The judgment was reversed on appeal—see Chapter 9.

[66] See Chapter 2.

information non-personal.[67] However, stronger encryption may be necessary for data in persistent storage to be considered non-personal.[68]

The DPD forbids exports to 'third countries' without an 'adequate level of protection'. Article 25(2) requires assessing adequacy in light of all the circumstances surrounding the export operation or set of operations, giving particular consideration to matters including the proposed processing operation(s)' duration. This implies that if an operation, and therefore presence of personal data in the country, is of a shorter duration, risks are lower, and less stringent protective measures may be considered adequate than if data were located there for longer. Similarly, information exposed unencrypted for relatively short periods for transient processing operations should arguably not lose 'anonymous' status.

However, suppose military-grade security measures are applied to data transmitted for storage, rendering the data non-'personal' in the provider's hands. For applications to process such data subsequently, such as for sorting or analysis, the data require decrypting first and currently conducting secure operations on encrypted data would take too long to be practicable.[69]

Therefore, currently, to run applications on (originally personal) data stored encrypted in cloud, the user must first decrypt the data, necessarily involving processing 'personal data'.[70] If users download data before decryption, providers would not be involved in users' local processing of decrypted personal data, but users would lose cloud processing power. If users run cloud applications on decrypted data in the provider's servers, the provider could become a 'processor'. However, as with transmissions, such operations may be transient; data may remain in encrypted form for longer than in decrypted 'personal data' form. Must all the DPD's requirements, nevertheless, be applied to those operations, or would more limited application be sensible?

An A29WP opinion on cloud computing considers that, although encryption 'may significantly contribute to the confidentiality of personal data if implemented correctly' in the cloud, 'it does not render personal data irreversibly anonymous'.[71] However, WP196 did not discuss the possibility that someone holding encrypted data, but without access to the decryption key, could be in a different position from someone who has the key. Therefore, while requiring encryption of personal data as a *security* measure (to protect confidentiality), and emphasizing the importance of key management,[72] it seems EU data protection regulators collectively take the view that encrypted personal data remain personal data, and that all data protection law requirements continue to apply to such data in anyone's hands, irrespective of key access or knowledge as to the data's nature.[73] As regards transmissions, WP196 considers that encryption of personal data must *always* be used when in transit, so that communications between cloud provider and customer and *between* data centres should be encrypted, and remote administration of the cloud platform should only occur using secure communication channels.[74] The

---

[67] Although, if transmissions between particular sources/destinations are actively monitored, brevity of individual transmissions may be irrelevant.

[68] Where, therefore, the potential attack window will be longer.

[69] For a more detailed discussion, see Chapter 2.

[70] Even if information is 'personal data' ephemerally, while operated on in decrypted form, and then encrypted and saved as such. Information which is 'personal data' ephemerally is not exempt, but, based on WP136 arguably poses lower risks to data subjects, as with data in flight.

[71] A29WP, Opinion 05/2012 on Cloud Computing, WP 196 (2012) (WP196), 3.4.3.3.

[72] WP196, 3.4.3.3: 'Encryption of personal data should be used in all cases when "in transit" and when available to data "at rest"... Encrypting data at rest requires particular attention to cryptographic key management as data security then ultimately depends on the confidentiality of the encryption keys.'

[73] This seems contrary to the position of UK courts in relation to anonymized personal data—see n. 41.

[74] WP196 (n. 71), 3.4.3.3.

ICO's cloud guidance is similar, but less emphatic and more nuanced, in relation to the realities of cloud processes. It stresses the importance of key security but states that data in transit 'should' be protected from interception, that providers 'should' be able to assure security of data in transit within the cloud service, and that cloud users 'should' consider, where it is appropriate, encrypting data at rest, depending on the nature of the data and type of cloud processing.[75]

In summary, to try to render information stored in the cloud non-'personal data' in the provider's hands, the best course seems to be to encrypt it strongly before transmission. However, the matter is unclear, and even personal data encrypted for storage as anonymous data must be decrypted for operations, with such operations constituting processing of 'personal data'. Therefore, particularly given WP196's firm stance, it seems the prudent course in practice is to treat encrypted personal data as 'personal data'.

Uncertainties regarding whether, and when, encrypted data are considered 'personal data', and to what extent users' own encryption or other decisions affect data's status in the cloud, cause practical concerns. It may also seem unfair that someone holding encrypted personal data, and who is unaware of the data's nature, should be required to comply with data protection obligations in relation to such data. However, despite exhortations to clarify the position in relation to encrypted data and encryption procedures,[76] the proposed measures to update the DPD do not show any signs of doing so. Given the widespread availability of cryptography, and the desirability of encouraging its use in order to enhance security and privacy, this omission seems particularly unfortunate.

4. Data Fragmentation

We now consider cloud data storage and its implications. In this section and the next, we do not deal with strongly encrypted data, but only data which users have not encrypted, or secured weakly. This is because we argue that strongly encrypted 'personal data' should already be considered 'anonymous' in the hands of a provider without key access.

IaaS, PaaS, and SaaS can store data as unencrypted 'plaintext'.[77] With cloud applications beyond simple storage, often data are stored unencrypted, or providers may access users' keys or their own secondary decryption keys. This enables value-added services, such as indexing and full-text searching of data, retention management, or data format conversion, which may be impossible with encrypted data.[78]

Chapters 1 and 2 of this book outlined the use of virtual machines (VMs) and how data are stored in the cloud, including the sharding or fragmentation of data across different equipment, and the replication of data to other equipment, possibly even in other data centres, for backup purposes. Where unencrypted personal data are automatically sharded[79] for distributed storage, the user uploading such data, or perhaps running cloud applications on data and receiving coalesced results, is clearly processing personal data.

---

[75] ICO, 'Guidance on the Use of Cloud Computing' (2012) [63]–[69].

[76] For example, see IaaS provider Rackspace US, Inc.'s, 'Consultation Paper on the Legal Framework for the Fundamental Right to Protection of Personal Data' (31 December 2009).

[77] This obviously includes pure storage SaaS. It may also include other SaaS like webmail where, as well as providing cloud application software, in this case email software, the provider also stores the data used in relation to that application, for example emails and contacts data.

[78] See Chapter 2.

[79] Automated sharding, as with anonymization, may itself be 'processing'. However, just as the DPD should permit or encourage anonymization, arguably sharding into non-personally identifying fragments should be allowed, at least where each shard is too small to contain personal data.

However, are individual shards, in distributed storage on providers' equipment (including any replicas or backups), 'personal data' in the provider's hands? Key-coded data may be anonymous data in another's hands, provided only the researcher has the key and adequate measures against re-identification are taken. With cloud computing, much depends on sharding or replication methods, and measures to restrict shard 'reunification' in order to allow only authorized users to access reunified data.

If a shard contains sufficient information to identify an individual, its access or replication involves 'processing' personal data. Even a small fragment may contain personal data, as the Google Street View Wi-Fi incident illustrated.[80] However, what matters is not shard size, but content and intelligibility. Even if a shard contains personal data, if the data are only intelligible to the user, when duly logged in, arguably it is 'personal data' only to that user. Providers have different sharding systems, so further analysis is difficult without exact details.[81]

Some fear data 'in the cloud' may be seized or accessed by local law enforcement authorities or others in the jurisdiction where storage equipment is located.[82] However, if a third party physically seizes hard drives or other equipment containing a shard, would it thereby retrieve 'personal data' stored by the targeted user? Not if the seized equipment holds only an incomprehensible shard and it cannot access equipment holding the remaining shards, for example because it is in another jurisdiction. Related shards are, in practice, likely to be stored in the same data centre or perhaps even in the same equipment; but it is technically possible that they may not be. Even where all shards are retrievable, the third party may not be able to reunify them intelligibly with or without the provider's cooperation, depending on the system's design and whether the data were encrypted.[83]

What about data deletion or service termination? Comprehensible 'personal data' shards may well remain temporarily on providers' equipment, pending automatic overwriting by other data, after users decide to delete data (or delete data accidentally) or terminate their accounts. How does this affect the user's compliance with its data protection law obligations? And what is the provider's status in relation to such deleted personal data?

Under data protection law, deletion of personal data is relevant in several main scenarios, bearing in mind that 'processing' expressly includes 'blocking, erasure, or destruction'

---

[80] Google's vehicles travelled streets globally, collecting data for its Street View online mapping service. It was discovered that they also captured data transmitted over open (non password-protected) Wi-Fi networks, for example, some consumers' home networks. That data included 'payload' data (content of transmitted data), as well as routing information. Various data protection authorities' investigations found 'while most of the [captured] data is fragmentary, in some instances entire emails and URLs were captured, as well as passwords'. Alan Eustace, 'Creating Stronger Privacy Controls inside Google' (*Official Google Blog*, 22 October 2010), <http://googleblog.blogspot.com/2010/10/creating-stronger-privacy-controls.html> (accessed 18 March 2013). Combining such data with geolocation to discover from whose home data originated, and correlating location with residents' identities, could allow association of usernames/passwords with individuals.

[81] For example, provider Symform offers distributed storage on users' own computers. Users' files are split into blocks, each block is encrypted, further fragmented, and distributed for storage. Even for very small files within a single data fragment:

> [T]he information about which file is associated with which data fragment and where that data fragment is located is stored separate from the data fragment itself—in Symform's cloud control. So, an attacker would have to identify a file and break into Symform to find out where its fragments are located. After this, they would have to actually have access to at least one of those fragments to be able reconstruct the encrypted contents. Last, and certainly not least, they would have to break the 256-AES encryption.

> Symform, 'Data Processing Details: How Our Backup & Storage Works'.

[82] On law enforcement issues in cloud computing, see Chapter 11.

[83] See further Section 6 of this chapter.

of personal data (so deletion is 'processing'). First, personal data must not be kept for longer than necessary. WP196 puts it thus:[84] 'Personal data that are not necessary any more must be erased or truly anonymised. If this data cannot be erased due to legal retention rules (e.g., tax regulations), access to this personal data should be blocked.' Second, data subjects are entitled to 'rectification, erasure, or blocking' of personal data whose processing is non-compliant (eg because it is incomplete or inaccurate), while similarly data protection authorities' may order rectification, erasure, or blocking of inaccurate data. Third, deleting personal data when it should *not* have been deleted may breach data protection law requirements on security (accidental or unlawful destruction or accidental loss), or accuracy (incompleteness), or indeed other laws requiring retention of certain data. So some situations require deleting personal data (which we will call 'must delete') while others require personal data to be protected against deletion (termed 'must not delete').

There are different degrees of deletion with digital data.[85] The ICO's guidance on deletion of personal data[86] acknowledged, 'There is a significant difference between deleting information irretrievably, archiving it in a structured, retrievable manner or retaining it as random data in an un-emptied electronic wastebasket'. Taking a 'realistic approach', the ICO recognized that deleting information from a digital system 'is not always a straightforward matter and that it is possible to put information "beyond use", and for data protection compliance issues to be "suspended" provided certain safeguards are in place'. Accordingly, where 'information has been deleted with no intention on the part of the data controller to use or access this again, but which may still exist in the electronic ether', for instance, where the information 'could be waiting to be over-written with other data', the ICO considers that 'this information is no longer live. As such, data protection compliance issues are no longer applicable'. The ICO uses the analogy of a bag of shredded paper waste where reconstituting information from fragments may be possible but 'extremely difficult and it is unlikely that the organisation would have any intention of doing this'. All this applies to a 'must delete' scenario.

Indeed the ICO guidance goes further, relaxing the application of data protection rules not only to deleted information 'in the electronic ether', but also to 'information that should have been deleted but is in fact still held on a live system because, for technical reasons, it is not possible to delete this information without also deleting other information held in the same batch'. The latter may also be considered 'put beyond use'.

Neither the DPD nor the DPA contains any express concept of putting information 'beyond use'. However, this concept seems akin to 'blocking' access to personal data, which is mentioned in the DPD, the DPA, and WP196. For information to be considered 'put beyond use', the ICO guidance requires that 'the data controller holding it:

- is not able, or will not attempt, to use the personal data to inform any decision in respect of any individual or in a manner that affects the individual in any way;

- does not give any other organisation access to the personal data;

- surrounds the personal data with appropriate technical and organisational security; and

- commits to permanent deletion of the information if, or when, this becomes possible'.

Unfortunately, the guidance does not address cloud computing, even though deleted data are often 'waiting to be over-written with other data'. In particular, should a cloud

---

[84] (n. 71), 3.1.4.3.   [85] See Chapter 2.
[86] ICO, 'Deleting Personal Data' (2012).

provider be considered to have been given 'access' to the deleted data? In what circumstances could deleted cloud data be considered 'surrounded' with appropriate security: would it depend on the security of the deletion procedure used? Nevertheless, users may wish to consider, at least in the UK, whether any shards of 'personal data' remaining in providers' equipment after deletion or account termination might be treated as 'put beyond use'.

Another noteworthy issue is the differential treatment of, or perhaps simply failure to focus on, methods of deletion or blocking in the separate contexts of 'must delete' and 'must not delete'. Say that an action or occurrence is treated as 'deletion' in a 'must not delete' scenario, so that the controller is liable for breach of data protection rules because it allowed personal data to be 'deleted' which should not have been. Logically, it is arguable that the same action or occurrence, in a 'must delete' context, should be treated as sufficient to comply with the obligation to delete personal data, for example deleting personal data after they are no longer needed for the controller's purpose. In particular, consider strongly encrypted personal data in the cloud. The ICO's cloud guidance states: 'It is also important to note that the loss of an encryption key could render the data useless. This could amount to the accidental destruction of personal data—this would be a breach of the DPA's security principle.'[87] That should mean that, conversely, in a 'must delete' scenario involving encrypted[88] personal data in the cloud, it should be sufficient for the controller to 'shred' the key, which could be considered putting the data beyond use, or blocking access to such data.[89] More broadly, if blocking is considered adequate under the DPD to comply with a data subject's or a data protection authority's requirement that personal data be erased, why should blocking not be considered enough to comply with any 'must delete' obligation? Effectively, the ICO has allowed this, but only it seems in a non-cloud situation, and clarification regarding the applicability of its deletion guidance to cloud computing would be helpful.

There is potential to allow cloud computing to be used while protecting personal data, by applying only certain data protection principles (or none) to personal data in the cloud that have been 'put beyond use' or blocked according to specified minimum criteria; for instance, deleted or post-account termination cloud data where the provider cannot or does not intend to reconstitute users' deleted data.[90] However, EU reform proposals have not explored or expanded upon the concept of 'blocking' or 'put beyond use', although similar issues arise with all forms of digital data storage, not just cloud. It seems the main concern here is not so much continued access by the user to 'deleted' data, but potential access by the provider (covered in the next section).

Finally, data fragments may exist in the 'live' processing context. As mentioned in Chapter 1, operations on data may be distributed, or split into smaller sub-operations running simultaneously in different nodes, and perhaps in different locations, each processing a different shard or data set subset. Sub-operation results are combined and sent to the user. When running cloud applications on data, such distributed processing may be employed automatically. While the application operates on data, shards may be stored in the provider's equipment, usually ephemerally, irrespective of whether the

---

[87] ICO, 'Guidance on the Use of Cloud Computing' (2012) [69].

[88] At least, where strongly encrypted.

[89] However, this possibility is not mentioned by the ICO in its webpage 'Deleting your data from computers, laptops and other devices' for the general public, which states, without considering encrypted data: 'Securely deleting data from the cloud or other remote storage service cannot be achieved by you running overwriting software. You should contact your cloud provider to see what service they offer to securely delete the data.'

[90] If the provider did so, it would become controller of such personal data. See Chapter 8.

user intends original or resulting data to be stored permanently in the cloud. Similar issues would arise regarding whether such shards include intelligible personal data, and whether, as with transient operations on decrypted data, such temporary operations or storage merit application in full of the DPD's requirements.

In summary, the position on storing or operating on shards, and the status of post-deletion shards, is unclear. Detailed operational aspects, which vary with services and/or users, may determine whether stored information is 'personal data'. Again, this seems unsatisfactory. More transparency by providers as to sharding and operational procedures, including data deletion as well as replication, would help inform the debate.

5. Provider's Ability to Access Data

We argued that strongly encrypted data should not be 'personal data' to those without the keys, as individuals cannot be identified without decryption. What about cloud data stored unencrypted or only weakly encrypted?

Even with personal data stored unencrypted in the cloud, re-identification of individuals through stored data is achievable only by someone who can access reunified data shards in intelligible form. What if the user is the only person who can access reunified shards of their stored data, through logging into their account with the provider, and the provider's scheme excludes anyone else from being able to access the account and access intelligible data? Arguably the data may be 'personal data' to the user, but not to anyone else.[91]

In other words, the effectiveness of measures to prevent persons other than the user from accessing a user's stored, unencrypted, personal data, may affect whether data are 'personal data' as regards those persons. A key factor will be the effectiveness of the provider's access control system, which typically only allows authenticated and authorized users to access a particular cloud account. By logging into an account, a user can access and operate on the full set of any personal data stored. That does not mean, however, that others can access the set.[92] More effective and restrictive access control measures would make it more likely that re-identification by others will be excluded, and therefore that stored data will not constitute 'personal data'.[93]

Another important factor is whether 'backdoors' exist that allow providers to sign in to users' accounts or otherwise access users' reunified data. One advantage of cloud computing is that providers usually maintain and update automatically the login software and (for SaaS) application software. While convenient for users, this also means providers can, unbeknown to users, build in and use backdoors, or even introduce backdoors at the behest of law enforcement or other authorities. While equipment containing fragmentary personal data may be seized, undesired access to cloud data may be more likely

[91] Leaving aside for now that individual shards may contain intelligible personal data. A German data protection regulator has reported the head of Google's cloud services in Central and Northern Europe as saying that if anyone broke into Google's 'top-secret computer centre', the intruder would find ' "absolutely nothing" usable, only "meaningless bits and bytes" because Google uses a proprietary file system'. The regulator, however, then expressed the view that security by transparency, with state-of-the-art security measures, is preferable to security by obscurity. Thilo Weichert, 'Cloud Computing and Data Privacy' (The Sedona Conference, Sedona, February 2011) (10–11).

[92] Subject to any 'backdoors', discussed below.

[93] Users' login password strength may also affect access control measures' effectiveness. Again, something within users' control rather than the provider's, in this case user password selection, affects whether information held by the provider is 'personal data'.

to occur through the provider's ability to access,[94] or allow third parties[95] to access, reunified shards of stored data by accessing users' accounts, wherever its data centres are located (even if in other countries).

Currently, many providers' contract terms expressly reserve rights to monitor users' data and/or data usage.[96] Where users are consumers, the provider is probably a controller of any personal data collected regarding users. This may include personal data consumers provide during sign-up, as well as, for instance, metadata[97] generated regarding their ongoing service usage. However, we do not cover monitoring of user-related personal data. We consider only any personal data, perhaps relating to others, processed by users using providers' facilities.

There is a difference between having the right and the technical ability to access data, and actually accessing data. Unless and until a provider accesses data, it may not even know that data are 'personal data'. Should not a provider who restricts access to a few employees and in tightly controlled circumstances, for example, only as necessary for maintenance and proper provision of services, and who takes other measures, such as regularly auditing access logs, be exposed to fewer liabilities than providers who, say, allow all employees access to users' data anytime for any purpose?

Providers who enable any internal or external access to users' accounts or data face difficulties, even with strictly controlled access. WP136 does not envisage limited re-identification incidental to accessing data, for example to investigate service issues, rather than to identify data subjects. The scheme must exclude re-identification before data may be considered non-'personal' for providers. Thus, it seems, if a provider can access users' unencrypted stored personal data, its scheme does not exclude identification: data stored unencrypted with it would be 'personal data'.

Many SaaS services go beyond 'pure' storage. Providers may access stored unencrypted personal data (eg, to run advertisements against content). Personal data may be exposed to widespread, even public view, such as in some social networking or photo-sharing sites.[98] Thus, excluding identification may be impossible. So too with SaaS 'passive' storage services, IaaS, or PaaS where, although stored unencrypted data are meant to be accessible only to the user, to investigate problems the provider's engineers need the ability to log in to users' accounts or view stored data, and accordingly may see any identifying information therein.[99] Similarly, where comprehensible 'personal data' shards remain temporarily on providers' equipment, pending automatic overwriting by other data after users decide to delete data or terminate accounts, at least where the provider

---

[94] Google's Site Reliability Engineers had 'unfettered access to users' accounts for the services they oversee'. In 2010, one such engineer was dismissed for accessing minors' Google accounts without consent, including call logs and contact details from its Internet phone service, instant messaging contact lists, and chat transcripts. Adrian Chen, 'GCreep: Google Engineer Stalked Teens, Spied on Chats (Updated)' (*Gawker*, 14 September 2010), <http://gawker.com/5637234> (accessed 18 March 2013). See, regarding allegedly 'universal' employee access to users' accounts on social networking site Facebook, Christopher Soghoian, 'Caught in the Cloud: Privacy, Encryption, and Government Back Doors in the Web 2.0 Era' (2010) 8(2) *Journal on Telecommunications and High Technology Law* 359 fn. 99.

[95] For example, law enforcement authorities in the country of the provider's incorporation, or who otherwise have jurisdiction over it, or private parties under court judgments made against it. These issues are discussed further in Chapter 11.

[96] See Chapter 3, Section 3.2.5.   [97] On metadata generated by providers, see Chapter 6.

[98] See Chapter 3, Section 3.2.3.

[99] Similarly with storage services offering indexing and searching facilities or other value-added services requiring the provider or its software to be able to access data. See Tim Mather, Subra Kumaraswamy, and Shahed Latif, *Cloud Security and Privacy: An Enterprise Perspective on Risks and Compliance* (Sebastopol, CA: O'Reilly, 2009).

can read shards marked for deletion.[100] Therefore, currently, it seems some data stored by these cloud services must be treated as 'personal data'.

It appears inevitable, from WP136's focus on preventing identification rather than assessing risks to privacy in context, that any remaining comprehensible 'personal data' shards must be treated as such. However, there may be policy reasons for encouraging the development of cloud infrastructure services and recognizing infrastructure providers' more neutral position. More flexible application of the DPD's requirements may be appropriate in some cloud situations, for example imposing fewer requirements on infrastructure or passive storage providers than on SaaS providers who actively encourage or conduct personal data processing.

Even with publicly accessible unencrypted personal data, one twist merits exploration. The DPD's prohibition on processing sensitive data does not apply to processing of data 'which are manifestly made public by the data subject'.[101] Such sensitive data may be processed without explicit consent: the data subject's publication justifies others' further processing. Arguably, even non-sensitive personal data publicized by the data subject should become free of the DPD's requirements, although the DPD does not so provide. Related difficulties include determining when data are 'made public',[102] especially with social networks, and the role of data subjects' intention to publicize data.

Consumers are posting unprecedented amounts of information online, including personal data, yet they are not necessarily aware of the possibly extensive consequences, both for themselves and others whose data they post. Regulators and legislators are increasingly concerned about consumer protection, and are focusing on issues such as the importance of more privacy-friendly default settings.[103] Many social networking sites' default settings make posted information available to a wider group, sometimes even publicly; yet, some consumers may believe posted data are only available to a limited group. Policymakers may, therefore, be reluctant to endorse free processing of personal data publicized by data subjects. Nevertheless, there may still be scope for relaxing the DPD requirements applicable to such data.

In summary, the effectiveness of access control restrictions and any means for a provider to access personal data stored unencrypted may affect whether data are 'personal data' in the provider's hands, even if the provider only has limited incidental access. However, arguably the DPD's rules should not be applied in full force, or at all, to infrastructure providers such as pure storage providers, who may not know the nature of the data stored in their infrastructure 'cloud of unknowing'.[104]

---

[100] Deletion is discussed further in Chapter 2, Section 2.2 and in Chapter 3, Section 3.2.2. Where providers do not promptly overwrite such 'deleted' personal data, including duplicates, would that affect the provider's status? Does the provider thereby become a controller of such data, even if it would have remained a mere processor had the user's account remained open, and even if the provider does not actually access such 'deleted' data? What if the account remains open but the user, on 'deleting' data, loses access to deleted data: can the provider (though not the user) recover deleted shards, and if so, does this technical ability mean it becomes their controller (whether or not it actually attempts to recover deleted personal data)?

[101] Article 8(2)(e).

[102] Peter Carey, *Data Protection: A Practical Guide to UK and EU Law* (Oxford: Oxford University Press, 2009), 86: a TV interview statement is public; what about a personal announcement to friends?

[103] For example A29WP and Working Party on Police and Justice, *The Future of Privacy—Joint Contribution to the Consultation of the European Commission on the Legal Framework for the Fundamental Right to Protection of Personal Data, WP 168* (2009) [48], [71]; A29WP, *Opinion 5/2009 on Online Social Networking, WP 163* (2009), 3.1.2 and 3.2.

[104] See Chapter 8.

6. The Way Forward?

We suggest a two-stage approach. First, the 'personal data' definition should be based on a realistic likelihood of identification. Second, rather than applying all the DPD's requirements to information determined to be 'personal data', it should be considered, in context, which requirements should apply and to what extent, based on a realistic risk of harm and likely severity.

The 'personal data' concept currently determines in a binary manner whether the DPD regulates information. If information is personal data, all the DPD's requirements apply to it in full force; if not, none do. However, as WP136 and courts have recognized, 'personal data' is not binary, but analogue. Identifiability falls on a continuum and the degree of identifiability can change with circumstances, who processes information, and for what purpose. Moreover, as information accumulates about someone, identification becomes easier. On this basis, almost all data is potentially 'personal data', which does not help determine applicability of the DPD to specific processing operations in practice. Similarly, whether particular information constitutes 'sensitive data' is often context-dependent. As the ICO has stated,[105] while many view health data as 'sensitive', is a management file record that an employee was absent from work due to a cold particularly sensitive in any real sense?

Advances in re-identification techniques have highlighted the inappropriateness of applying the DPD's requirements in an 'all or nothing' fashion. The ICO also considers that the 'personal data' definition needs to be clearer and more relevant to modern technologies and the practical realities of processing personal data within both automated and manual filing systems.[106] The ICO pointed out that any future framework must deal more effectively with new forms of identifiability, but suggested that different kinds of information, such as IP address logs, might have different data protection rules applied or disapplied.[107] Its overall view was that 'a simple "all or nothing" binary approach to the application of data protection requirements no longer suffices, given the breadth of information now falling within the definition of "personal data" '.[108]

In its 2010 Communication on 'A comprehensive approach on personal data protection in the European Union',[109] the European Commission did not consider changing or eliminating the 'personal data' definition. However, it noted, as regards this definition, 'numerous cases where it is not always clear, when implementing the Directive, which approach to take, whether individuals enjoy data protection rights and whether data controllers should comply with the obligations imposed by the Directive'. It felt certain situations, involving processing specific kinds of data,[110] required additional protections,

---

[105] ICO, 'The Information Commissioner's response to the Ministry of Justice's call for evidence on the current data protection legislative framework' (6 October 2010) (MoJ).

[106] Ibid.

[107] For example, for IP logs requiring security measures, but not subject access rights or consent to log recording. ICO, 'The Information Commissioner's response to the European Commission's consultation on the legal framework for the fundamental right to protection of personal data' [2]; and MoJ (n. 105) 7.

[108] MoJ (n. 105) 7; ICO, 'The Information Commissioner's (United Kingdom) response to: A comprehensive approach on personal data protection in the European Union—A Communication from the European Commission to the European Parliament, the Council, the Economic and Social Committee and the Committee of the Regions on 4 November 2010' (14 January 2011), 2–3.

[109] European Commission, 'Communication from the commission to the European Parliament, the Council, the Economic and Social Committee and the Committee of the Regions' COM (2010) 609 final.

[110] For example, location data, even key-coded data.

and that it was necessary to consider how to ensure coherent application of rules in light of new technologies.

It may be time to focus less on protecting data as such,[111] and more on properly balancing, in specific processing situations, protection of individuals' rights regarding their data, with free data movement within the EEA and, where appropriate, beyond. In particular, rather than considering solely whether information is personal data,[112] it may make more sense to consider risk of identification and risk of harm[113] to individuals from particular processing, and the likely severity of any harm. Processing should then be tailored accordingly, taking measures appropriate to those risks.[114]

Arguably the A29WP's underlying approach is already risk-based. Consider, for example, WP136's suggestion that pseudonymous data may involve fewer risks. Regarding anonymization, the ICO has pointed out different levels of identifiability and argued for a more nuanced and contextual approach to protecting 'personal data' and 'anonymized' data.[115]

Austria's treatment of 'indirectly personal data' has been mentioned.[116] Sweden's 2007 changes to its implementation of the DPD[117] also illustrate a risk-based approach, with reduced regulation of personal data contained in unstructured material such as word-processing documents, webpages, emails, audio, and images, presumably based on risks being considered lower there. Sweden relaxed compliance requirements for processing such material, provided it is not included or intended for inclusion in a document-management system, case-management system, or other database. Such unstructured data are exempt from most of the DPD's requirements, such as the restrictions on export. However, security requirements apply, and processing of such personal data must not violate data subjects' integrity (privacy).[118] Thus, the focus is on preventing harm. In a report on lacunae in the Council of Europe's Convention 108[119] arising from technological developments, the author argued it was increasingly less relevant to ask whether data constituted personal data; rather, one should identify risks relating to the use of data posed by technologies in a particular context, and respond accordingly.[120]

---

[111] The GSM Association (GSMA) has noted that EU data protection rules are based on distinguishing individuals from others, 'even though an organisation collecting and processing such information has no intention of using it to target or in any way affect a specific individual'. Martin Whitehead, 'GSMA Europe Response to the European Commission Consultation on the Framework for the Fundamental Right to the Protection of Personal Data' (*GSMA Europe*, 22 December 2009), <http://ec.europa.eu/justice/news/consulting_public/0003/contributions/organisations/gsma_europe_en.pdf> (accessed 18 March 2013).

[112] As the ICO pointed out regarding manual records (MoJ, n. 105), reliance on the 'personal data' definition has resulted in attempts to avoid regulation by trying to structure situations so that data fall outside it.

[113] As per APEC's Privacy Framework (APEC Secretariat, 2005), and see Christopher Millard, 'Opinion: The Future of Privacy (part 2)—What Might Privacy 2.0 Look Like?' (2008) 5(1) *Data Protection Law & Policy* 8–11. Technology multinational Cisco supports 'a more explicit link between harm and the necessary data protection requirements', noting that the DPD 'tends towards seeing all personal data as worthy of protection regardless of the privacy risk'. This approach's divergence from one based on privacy risk 'is exacerbated by the broad definition of personal data, which encompasses any data that can be linked to an individual'. Cisco Systems, 'Cisco Response to the Consultation on the Legal Framework for the Fundamental Right to Protection of Personal Data' (23 December 2009) [s. 3.3, 5].

[114] If you are identified as belonging to a group with 100 members, the chances (and risks) of identifying you are 1 in 100. That may entail more precautions than with data which would only identify you as belonging to a group with 1 billion members.

[115] MoJ (n. 105), 8.   [116] Text to n. 37.

[117] Personuppgiftslag (1998:204) (Swedish Personal Data Act).

[118] Swedish Ministry of Justice, *Personal Data Protection—Information on the Personal Data Act*, 4th edn (Sweden: Ministry of Justice, 2006).

[119] Convention 108 for the Protection of Individuals with regard to Automatic Processing of Personal Data, on which the DPD was largely based.

[120] Jean-Marc Dinant, 'Rapport sur les lacunes de la Convention no 108 pour la protection des personnes à l'égard du traitement automatisé des données à caractère personnel face aux développements technologiques' T-PD-BUR(2010)09 (I) FINAL (*Conseil de l'Europe*, 5 November 2010) (8).

Whether information is 'personal data' already requires consideration of specific circumstances. Assessing risks of identification and harm posed by a particular processing operation would not seem more difficult than determining whether particular information is 'personal', yet it may be more successful in making controllers consider the underlying objective: protecting privacy.

The 'personal data' definition is currently the single trigger for applying all DPD requirements. But, on this definition, given scientific advances, almost all data could qualify as such. In considering whether particular information should trigger data protection obligations, the key factor ought to be, what is the realistic risk of identification? Only where risks of identification are sufficiently realistic (eg, 'more likely than not')[121] should information be considered 'personal data'.

Where identification risk is remote or highly theoretical, for example due to technical measures taken, we suggest information should not be 'personal data'. In particular, encrypted data should be recognized as non-personal data in cloud computing, at least where strongly encrypted.[122] Clarification is also needed regarding anonymized data and anonymization and encryption procedures. The current law partly recognizes this ('means likely reasonably to be used', and WP136's reference to theoretical risks). However, in today's environment it may make sense for the threshold to be higher, based on realistic risks (such as 'more likely than not'). The boundary should be clearer.

Criteria for triggering the application of the DPD's requirements should be more nuanced, not 'all or nothing'. It may be appropriate to apply all of the DPD's requirements in some situations, but not in others. A better starting point might be to require explicit consideration of risks of harm to living individuals from intended processing, and its likely severity, balancing the interests involved, and with appropriate exemptions.

This would require an accountability-based approach, proportionate to circumstances, including those of controllers, data subjects, and any processors.[123] More sensitive situations, with greater risks of resulting harm and/or greater severity of likely harm, would require greater precautions. That would accord with the European Commission's desire to require additional protections in certain circumstances, while allowing fewer or even no DPD requirements to be applied to strongly encrypted data[124] held by someone without the key, or deleted data in systems where access by providers to comprehensible personal data is impossible or sufficiently difficult. Could such a broad, flexible approach produce uncertainty and exacerbate lack of cross-EU harmonization? Arguably, no more so than currently.[125] Indeed, it may better reflect practical realities in many Member States.

---

[121] The UK tribunal in *APGER* (n. 18) did not think that 'appreciable risk' of identification was the statutory test. However, in deciding whether, on the facts, certain information was 'personal data' it concluded that its publication would not render individuals identifiable 'on the balance of probabilities'. Thus, it seems that it applied a 'more likely than not' test in practice. *APGER* [129].

[122] The European Commission supports developing 'technical commercial fundamentals' in cloud computing, including standards (eg APIs and data formats). Neelie Kroes, 'Towards a European Cloud Computing Strategy' (World Economic Forum Davos, 27 January 2011) SPEECH/11/50. Encryption and security measures also need standardization, with a view to appropriate legal recognition of accepted standards.

[123] We use 'accountability' as per the Canadian Personal Information Protection and Electronic Documents Act 2000 ('PIPEDA'). Views differ on 'accountability'. The A29WP in *Opinion 1/2010 on the Principle of Accountability, WP 173* (2010) seems to consider 'accountability' involves taking measures to enable compliance with data protection requirements and being able to demonstrate measures have been taken. However, PIPEDA's broader approach treats accountability as end-to-end controller responsibility (eg PIPEDA Sch. 1, s. 4.1.3).

[124] At least where that is reasonable, assuming industry standards would require stronger encryption for sensitive data. If encryption under recognized standards is broken, stronger encryption might be expected to be substituted within a reasonable time.

[125] Also, given the recognized importance of harmonization and of doing more to foster a unified approach, if the EU legislature thinks fit, the data protection law reforms could provide for guidance by

It has been suggested[126] that because, in today's environment, re-identification is increasingly easy and fully anonymizing personal data near impossible, 'the basic approach should be to reduce the collecting and even initial storing of personal data to the absolute minimum'.[127] PbD and PETs will assist data minimization,[128] and we consider them significant elements in the proposed Data Protection Regulation. However, data minimization alone cannot protect personal data already 'out there'.[129] The processing of such personal data must still take account of risks to living individuals and their likely severity. Moreover, data minimization may in some circumstances limit the potential benefits of Big Data analytics, for example in epidemiology.[130]

What about sensitive data? Under current definitions, all data may potentially be sensitive, depending on context. Arguably, the distinction between 'personal data' and 'sensitive data' is no longer tenable. The European Commission is considering whether other categories should be 'sensitive data', for example genetic data, and will further clarify and harmonize conditions for processing sensitive data.[131] The ICO has pointed out[132] that a fixed list of categories can be problematic:[133] sensitivity can be subjective/cultural, set lists do not take account sufficiently of context and may even exclude data which individuals consider to be sensitive, while non-EU jurisdictions may have different lists, causing possible difficulties for multinationals. The ICO also suggested:

[A] definition based on the concept that information is sensitive if its processing could have an especially adverse or discriminatory effect on particular individuals, groups of individuals or on society more widely. This definition might state that information is sensitive if the processing of that information would have the potential to cause individuals or [sic] significant damage or distress. Such an approach would allow for flexibility in different contexts, so that real protection is given where it matters most. In practice, it could mean that the current list of special data categories remains largely valid, but it would allow for personal data not currently in the list to be better protected, for example financial data or location data. Or, more radically, the distinctions between special categories and ordinary data could be removed from the new framework, with emphasis instead on the risk that particular processing poses in particular circumstances.[134]

This indicates possible support for a risk-based approach to personal data generally, under which 'sensitive data' as a special category may not be necessary, the sensitivity of particular data in context being one factor affecting how they may, or should, be processed.

the A29WP or Commission to bind Member States and courts, and/or empower the A29WP to assess adequacy/consistency of national implementations and issue binding rulings.

[126] LRDP Kantor and Centre for Public Reform, *Comparative Study on Different Approaches to New Privacy Challenges, in Particular in the Light of Technological Developments—Final Report to European Commission* (European Commission 2010) [121].

[127] Data minimization is an existing Principle—Art. 6(1)(c). The suggestion was to focus on it primarily, or more.

[128] For example, IBM's Idemix, Microsoft's technologies incorporating Credentica's U-Prove, and the Information Card Foundation's Information Cards. Touch2ID piloted smartcards proving UK holders are of drinking age without revealing other data—Kim Cameron, 'Doing It Right: Touch2Id' (*Identity Weblog*, 3 July 2010), <http://www.identityblog.com/?p=1142> (accessed 18 March 2013).

[129] Case C-73/07 *Tietosuojavaltuutettu v Satakunnan Markkinaporssi and Satamedia Oy (Approximation of laws)* OJ C 44/6, 21.2.2009; [2008] ECR I-9831.

[130] Omer Tene et al., 'Big Data for All: Privacy and User Control in the Age of Analytics' (*Social Science Research Network*, 20 September 2012), <http://papers.ssrn.com/sol3/papers.cfm?abstract_id=2149364> (accessed 18 March 2013).

[131] See n. 109, 2.1.6.   [132] MoJ (n. 105) 10.

[133] The draft US Privacy Bill demonstrates the difficulties with defining 'sensitive personal data' using a list of categories, rather than by reference to impact, or potential impact, of processing on the individual—MoJ (n. 105).

[134] MoJ (n. 105) 11.

We suggest a two-stage, technologically neutral, accountability-based[135] approach to address privacy concerns targeted by the 'personal data' concept. First, appropriate technical and organizational measures should be taken to minimize identification risk. Only if the resulting risk is still sufficiently high should data be considered 'personal data', and trigger data protection obligations. Second, the risk of harm and its likely severity should then be assessed, and appropriate measures taken regarding the personal data, with obligations being proportionate to risks.

Accordingly, if a controller has successfully implemented appropriate measures to minimize identification risk so that information is not considered 'personal data' (such as strong encryption), risk of harm need not be addressed. However, if there is a sufficient risk of identification in specific circumstances, for example with pseudonymization or aggregation performed in certain ways, then risk of harm and its likely severity should be assessed, and appropriate measures taken.

In two situations, less restricted or even free processing of originally 'personal' data might be permissible. One is where data are so depersonalized that they are no longer 'personal', such as through strongly encrypting full data sets. The other is where data subjects intentionally make public their personal data. Account should be taken not just of what is done to data, but who does it: data subject, cloud user, or cloud provider.

7. Concluding Remarks

We have advanced proposals for data protection laws to cater for cloud computing and other technological developments in a clearer, more balanced way.

The data protection regime should be more nuanced, proportionate, and flexible, based on an end-to-end accountability approach (rather than binary distinctions). The threshold inherent in the 'personal data' definition should be raised, basing it instead on realistic risk of identification. A spectrum of parties processing personal data should be recognized, having varying data protection obligations and liabilities, with risk of identification and risk of harm (and its likely severity) being the key determinants, and with appropriate exemptions. Such an approach should result in lighter or no regulation of cloud infrastructure providers, while reinforcing the obligations of cloud providers who knowingly and actively process personal data to handle such data appropriately.

The status of encrypted and anonymized data (and encryption and anonymization procedures) should be clarified so as not to deter their use as PETs. This could be done, for example, by stating that such procedures are not within the DPD, are not 'processing' or are authorized, or that fewer obligations apply to the resulting data. This would enable more data to fall outside the regulated sphere for 'personal data' in appropriate situations. In particular, we suggest that data strongly encrypted and secured to industry standards (including on key management) should not be considered 'personal data' in the hands of non-keyholders.

As regards anonymized data, it is important to clarify when anonymization may produce non-'personal data'. Likelihood of identification should be the main determinant. For example, information should be treated as 'personal data' where it 'more likely than not' would identify individuals, but not where the realistic risk of

---

[135] For example, users remain accountable and should consider the risk of providers inadvertently deleting encrypted data, and take steps to protect data accordingly, such as by saving copies locally or with other providers.

identification is insufficient. For sensitive data, a similar risk of harm approach should be considered, with definitions as suggested by the ICO. The position in relation to personal data manifestly made public should be clarified for non-sensitive and sensitive data, such as applying fewer data protection rules to such data. More generally, consideration needs to be given to applying different rules to personal data, depending on the situation. For example, fewer rules might apply to pseudonymized data.

Providers, especially infrastructure providers, should consider developing and implementing measures to minimize the likelihood of cloud services being regulated inappropriately by EU data protection laws; for example, by implementing encryption on the user's equipment using keys generated by and available only to the user. More transparency on sharding and other operational procedures would assist regulators to treat cloud services more appropriately, as would industry standards on matters such as encrypting data for cloud storage, including PbD. Emphasizing standards, while facilitating more flexible and pragmatic regulation of cloud ecosystem actors, should also help shift the regulatory focus back to protecting individuals.

The DPD was proposed in 1990 and adopted in 1995. Technologies, in particular Internet-related technologies, have evolved significantly since. It is time to make the DPD fit for the twenty-first century. However, the proposals launched in January 2012 to update EU data protection laws may in some respects turn the clock back. The European Commission claimed that the reform measures would retain the current definition of personal data.[136] However, the drafting would mean that, effectively, all data would be 'personal data'. This is because the draft Data Protection Regulation swapped the DPD's definitions of 'data subject' and 'personal data'. Instead of defining 'personal data' by reference to information relating to an 'identified natural person or a natural person who can be identified, directly or indirectly, by means reasonably likely to be used by the controller or by any other natural or legal person', the wording quoted was used in the definition of 'data subject'. Furthermore, 'personal data' was defined to mean any information relating to a data subject. Since all information can be 'related to' some identified or identifiable person or other,[137] logically this means that *all* information would be 'personal data', which would make having any definition of personal data superfluous. As with much else in the draft legislation, the intended aims may be clear and even generally accepted, but the drafting, if unamended, may fail to achieve those aims and indeed result in far-reaching unintended consequences.

Nevertheless, there are strong policy arguments for making specific provision for pseudonymization and anonymization of personal data in order to encourage controllers to use those techniques. If even anonymized or pseudonymized personal data attract the full compliance obligations of 'personal data', why would controllers go to the trouble and expense of applying privacy-protecting anonymization or pseudonymization procedures?

The ICO has stated that 'Given the wide scope of "personal data" we consider, based on our regulatory experience, particularly in the online world, that it may be unrealistic to expect all the requirements of the Regulation to apply fully to all forms of personal data that fall within its scope . . . This is particularly important in relation to

---

[136] Impact assessment, Annex 8: 'Annexes to the Impact Assessment' available at <http://ec.europa.eu/justice/data-protection/document/review2012/sec_2012_72_annexes_en.pdf> (accessed 18 March 2013): 'it would seem counterproductive to change the definition of personal data. Specific issues such as IP addresses and geo-location data should be tackled on the basis of this proven concept, taking into account—as said in recital 26 of the Directive—of "all the means likely reasonably to be used either by the controller or by any other person to identify the said person".'

[137] See the meteorological data example given at n. 52.

pseudonymisation as there needs to be positive encouragement to data controllers to use pseudonymisation wherever possible'.[138] Subsequently, the ICO summarized its position as follows: 'The scope of the law needs to be as clear as we can make it, particularly the definition of "personal data". In particular, the status of pseudonymised data needs to be clarified and, if covered, needs to be treated realistically for the digital information society age.'[139]

Similarly a report for the European Parliament's Committee on Internal Market and Consumer Protection[140] emphasizes the need for more work to incentivize anonymization and pseudonymization and clarify the circumstances in which anonymization or pseudonymization would be considered effective. The draft Albrecht Report[141] states: 'Legitimate concerns regarding specific business models can be addressed without denying individuals their fundamental rights. In this context the rapporteur encourages the pseudonymous and anonymous use of services. For the use of pseudonymous data, there could be alleviations with regard to obligations for the data controller (Articles 4(2) (a), 10), Recital 23).' This draft proposed expanding draft recital 34 to disapply the new laws to 'anonymous data'.[142] Furthermore, anonymization or pseudonymization would be required specifically, with proposed amendments to draft Article 5.1(c) requiring that personal data can be processed only if the purpose could not be fulfilled by processing 'anonymous information'.[143] In the proposed draft Article 8.1(2a), Member States would be able to allow processing of 'health data' without consent only in certain circumstances, including that such data must be 'anonymised, or if that is not possible for the research purposes, pseudonymised under the highest technical standards, and all necessary measures shall be taken to prevent re-identification of the data subjects'. A similar approach is proposed for the use for research purposes of sensitive data or data relating to children.

This all bodes well in terms of overall legislative intentions. However, while many of the relevant issues have been raised and even spelled out explicitly,[144] it is critical for legal certainty that the drafting of the reform measures reflects these intentions properly and clearly, and provides concrete guidance regarding the relevant technical standards that would be considered adequate, particularly given the social importance of research in areas such as public health and medical research. A suggestion by the ICO[145] merits exploration, focusing on the intention of the controller rather than trying to draw fine

---

[138] ICO, 'Information Commissioner's Office: Initial Analysis of the European Commission's Proposals for a Revised Data Protection Legislative Framework' (27 February 2012).

[139] ICO, 'Data Protection Reform; Latest Views from the ICO' (22 January 2013).

[140] Reference in n. 20.

[141] European Parliament, 'Draft report on the proposal for a regulation of the European Parliament and of the Council on the protection of individual with regard to the processing of personal data and on the free movement of such data (General Data Protection Regulation)' (*Committee on Civil Liberties, Justice and Home Affairs*, 16 January 2013).

[142] Defined as 'any data that can not be related, directly or indirectly, alone or in combination with associated data, to a natural person or where establishing such a relation would require a disproportionate amount of time, expense, and effort, taking into account the state of the art in technology at the time of the processing and the possibilities for development during the period for which the data will be processed'. Specific clarification of how data may be 'related' to a natural person would be desirable for legal certainty, for example given the narrow view in the UK of 'relating to'. See C Millard and WK Hon, 'Defining 'Personal Data' in E-Social Science' (2012) 15(1) *Information, Communication and Society* 66.

[143] Again, the drafting needs consistency, for example 'anonymous information' should be changed to 'anonymous data'.

[144] For example in the report mentioned in n. 141.

[145] ICO, 'Information Commissioner's Office: Initial Analysis of the European Commission's Proposals for a Revised Data Protection Legislative Framework' (27 February 2012) [5].

distinctions regarding the status of data (emphasis added): 'A better approach might be to make it clear in the Regulation that where IP addresses or similar identifiers are *processed with the intention of targeting particular content at an individual, or otherwise treating one person differently from another*, then the identifier will be personal data and, as far as is possible, the rules of data protection will apply.'

Meanwhile, what are controllers to do in practice? Controllers need to assess the risks and take a view, which will depend on the approach of regulators in the EU Member States in which they operate. The cautious approach would be to assume that any data that might be 'personal data', particularly sensitive data, should be treated as such, and anonymization measures applied as far as possible, particularly in the UK.

8

Who is Responsible for Personal Data in Clouds?

W Kuan Hon, Christopher Millard, and Ian Walden

1. Introduction and Scope

This chapter considers which entities are regulated when 'personal data' are processed in the cloud, and what are their key obligations and liabilities. We address first how controllers can comply with current data protection laws when using cloud computing, and cloud providers' status as processors or controllers. Then we explain why current laws do not suit cloud computing, with recommendations on how they could be changed to strike a better balance between allowing potential cloud users to reap the benefits of cloud computing while protecting personal data.

2. Controllers and Processors—General Concepts

In cloud computing, the concepts of 'controller' and 'processor' under the EU Data Protection Directive (DPD) are both complex and critical. The controller has primary responsibility for complying with data protection legal obligations, including any requirement to register with the relevant national authority before processing personal data, providing data subjects' personal data to them on request, and processing personal data fairly and lawfully. The distinction affects allocation of responsibility. The controller bears most of the burden of ensuring that personal data are only processed in accordance with the DPD's data protection principles. It also faces primary liability for any data protection law breaches, including regulatory sanctions (eg fines), and/or liability to data subjects who have suffered damage as a result including possible criminal liability.

A controller is 'the natural or legal person, public authority, agency or any other body which alone or jointly with others determines the purposes and means of the processing of personal data'.[1] This definition envisages that more than one 'controller' is possible in relation to the same personal data.[2]

A controller must ensure that its processing of personal data complies with certain principles, with some exceptions. Personal data must be processed fairly and lawfully, for specified lawful purposes only, and the processing must be adequate, relevant, and not excessive for those purposes. Personal data must also be accurate and kept updated as necessary, not be kept for longer than the processing purpose requires, be processed consistently with various data subject rights, be secured against unauthorized or unlawful processing, and not be transferred outside the European Economic Area (EEA) except in

---

[1] Article 2(d).
[2] However, some Member States, for example France and Poland, may not explicitly recognize the concept of a co-controller: Christopher Kuner, *European Data Protection Law*, 2nd edn (Oxford: Oxford University Press, 2007), Ch 2.22, fn. 30.

certain circumstances. For processing to be legitimate, it must fall under one of a number of bases, of which data subject consent is one.

Furthermore, if a controller uses another entity to process personal data on its behalf, for example by outsourcing processing to a sub-contractor, Article 17 of the DPD specifies how that relationship must be governed. The controller must choose a data processor providing 'sufficient guarantees' in respect of the technical and organizational security measures governing the processing, and take reasonable steps to ensure compliance with those measures. Moreover, the controller-processor contract must be made or evidenced in writing,[3] must require the processor to act only on the data controller's instructions (instructions requirement), and must comply with obligations 'equivalent' to those imposed on a controller by Article 17(1), broadly, the security measures required by the laws of the Member State where the processor is established.[4] We shall term a contract that contains the required provisions a 'data processor agreement'.

Sub-processing arrangements may also be regulated. The controller-processor contract may restrict the use of sub-processors,[5] but if multiple processors and sub-processors are used, then they must all act on the controller's instructions; other requirements listed above also apply.[6]

The DPD defines 'processor' as 'a natural or legal person, public authority, agency or any other body which processes personal data on behalf of the controller'.[7] Processors are not normally subject directly to DPD obligations. However, as mentioned above, to enable the controller to comply with its own DPD obligations when using a processor, a processor may be required by the controller to enter into certain minimum legally binding commitments in addition to those detailed in the DPD. Also, Member States are free to impose liabilities on processors if they wish.[8]

Accordingly, it is important to consider which, if any, cloud computing actors are controllers, which are processors, and which are neither. Also, an entity may act as controller for certain processing operations, but as processor for others, so its

---

[3] According to the UK Information Commissioner's Office (ICO), the written contract may be electronic. ICO, *Personal Information Online Code of Practice* (2010), 29.

[4] For a more detailed discussion of data protection jurisdiction, see Chapter 9.

[5] For example, as in model clauses for EU controllers to export personal data for processing by non-EU entities: European Commission Decision of 5 February 2010 on standard contractual clauses for the transfer of personal data to processors established in third countries under Directive 95/46/EC of the European Parliament and of the Council (2010/87/EU) OJ L39/5, 12.2.2010. Clause 11 restricts sub-contracting by the 'data importer' without the data exporter's prior written consent.

[6] WP169 (n. 10) 27: 'one should avoid a chain of (sub-)processors that would dilute or even prevent effective control and clear responsibility for processing activities, unless the responsibilities of the various parties in the chain are clearly established'. The use of sub-processors further complicates the position, in practice. For example, the European Privacy Officers Forum, 'Comments on the Review of European Data Protection Framework' (EPOF, December 2009) pointed out the lack of harmonization in the approaches of different Member States' data protection authorities to the use of sub-processors in outsourcing: some regulators require direct contracts between the controller and every sub- or sub-sub-processor, while the 'much more pragmatic approach' of other regulators (including Spain and the UK) allows the first processor's obligations to be passed contractually to sub-processors provided the controller consents and can enforce its rights against any sub-processor.

[7] Article 2(e).

[8] Most Member States' national implementations (such as the UK's Data Protection Act 1998) do not impose direct obligations on processors, preferring to oblige the controller to bind the processor by contract to act only on the controller's instructions and implement appropriate security measures. However, a processor that processes personal data in a manner other than that instructed by the controller would thereby be rendered a controller in its own right. An example of a national implementation of the DPD where some obligations are imposed directly on processors is the Czech Republic's law Zákon č. 101/2000 Sb. o ochraně osobních údajů (Personal Data Protection Act 101/2000), such as arts 7, 9, and 10.

status as controller or processor must be assessed with regard to *specific* sets of data or operations.[9]

As data processing arrangements have become increasingly complex and multiparty, many practical difficulties have been encountered in applying the controller/processor definitions, so much so that the A29WP issued guidance (WP169) on this area.[10] Cloud computing is further 'blurring the distinction between data controllers, processors and data subjects'.[11]

3. Cloud Users

3.1 Overview

Some controllers believe that if they use cloud computing, they relinquish responsibility for data security,[12] or that security may be left to end users.[13] That is not the case in law. A controller of personal data who chooses to 'outsource' its data storage or processing to a third party still remains a controller, and is still subject to, and responsible for complying with, data protection law obligations. If problems arise from the third party's failures, the controller remains liable.[14] WP169 also discussed possible split sequential or joint processing operations within the same overall 'macro' processing, chains of processors, and joint controllership. Such arrangements would not necessarily entail joint and several liability, it would depend on the circumstances. Controllers may be responsible as such even if they cannot control all aspects, or meet all controller responsibilities, for example data subject access rights. WP169 stresses that processors with more bargaining power, for example to require controllers to accept their standard terms, are not necessarily controllers; nevertheless, controllers should not accept terms that breach data protection laws.

How can a controller process personal data in the cloud, including mere data storage, in a way that is compliant with data protection laws? Guidance to controllers, or decisions on the use of cloud services, have been issued by EU data protection regulators collectively via an A29WP opinion ('WP196'),[15] and also individually. France's CNIL

---

[9] WP169 (n. 10) 25.

[10] A29WP, *Opinion 1/2010 on the Concepts of 'Controller' and 'Processor', WP 169* (2010). For discussion and examples of practical problems, see ICC Task Force on Privacy and the Protection of Personal Data, *Summary of the Workshop on the Distinction between Data Controllers and Data Processors* (International Chamber of Commerce, Paris 25 October 2007).

[11] A29WP and Working Party on Police and Justice, *The Future of Privacy—Joint Contribution to the Consultation of the European Commission on the Legal Framework for the Fundamental Right to Protection of Personal Data, WP 168* (2009) [41].

[12] Worryingly, 88% of UK business leaders so believed, according to a survey of more than 1200 IT, finance, and legal decision-makers in mid-to-large businesses across the UK, Spain, France, Germany, the Netherlands, and Hungary, conducted at the end of 2012 by Opinion Matters for storage provider Iron Mountain: Iron Mountain, 'Business Leaders Ignore Responsibility for Data in the Cloud' (*Iron Mountain*, 27 February 2013), <http://www.ironmountain.ie/news/2013/impr02272013.asp> (accessed 18 March 2013).

[13] Robert L Scheler, 'Cloud Security: Too Important to Leave to End Users' (*CA Community*, 5 March 2013), <http://community.ca.com/blogs/perspectives/archive/2013/03/05/cloud-security-too-important-to-leave-to-end-users.aspx> (accessed 18 March 2013).

[14] And can be fined large amounts, for example when a processor engaged to destroy hard drives containing personal data, indeed health data, did not; some drives were sold online: ICO *News release: NHS Trust fined £325,000 following data breach affecting thousands of patients and staff* (1 June 2012).

[15] A29WP, 'Opinion 05/2012 on Cloud Computing' WP196 (2012). This drew on the so-called Sopot Memorandum, International Working Group on Data Protection in Telecommunications, 'Working Paper on Cloud Computing—Privacy and Data Protection Issues—"Sopot Memorandum"' (24 April 2012), <http://www.datenschutz-berlin.de/attachments/873/Sopot_Memorandum_Cloud_Computing.pdf> (accessed 18 March 2013).

has even produced suggested contractual clauses.[16] Of EU data protection authorities' decisions on specific cloud transactions issued to date, cloud use was permitted in only two instances and those were dealt with by the same authority (in Norway), which reversed its own previous contrary ruling, and left certain aspects for the controller to assess.[17] In earlier decisions, authorities in Denmark and Sweden[18] ruled that the transactions concerned were non-compliant with data protection laws.

Both conceptually and in practice, there are major issues with data protection regulators' general approach to cloud. In particular, WP196 seems problematic as a source of guidance for several reasons. Its detailed prescriptive requirements do not properly take into account cloud mechanics, operations, or key differences between cloud and traditional outsourcing.[19] It purports to use 'must' and 'should' in the same way as in technical standards although, reflecting strict legal requirements, there are relatively few 'musts'.[20] Also, WP196 does not make clear whether certain matters should be checked only as part of precontractual due diligence, or whether contract terms must also explicitly address those matters (and if so, how). Finally, there appears to be an element of 'gold-plating' and anticipation of future reforms, for instance 'isolation', 'accountability', and direct obligations on processors,

---

[16] To date, for example in Denmark, France, Germany, Ireland, Italy, Norway, Spain, Sweden, and the UK. CNIL, 'Cloud Computing: CNIL's Recommendations for Companies Using These New Services' (*CNIL*, 25 June 2012), <http://www.cnil.fr/english/news-and-events/news/article/cloud-computing-cnils-recommendations-for-companies-using-these-new-services>; ICO, *Guidance on the Use of Cloud Computing*, <http://www.ico.org.uk/for_organisations/data_protection/topic_guides/online/~/media/documents/library/Data_Protection/Practical_application/cloud_computing_guidance_for_organisations.ashx>; Data Protection Commissioner, *Data Protection 'in the Cloud'* (3 July 2012), <http://www.dataprotection.ie/viewdoc.asp?DocID=1221&m=f>; Consejo General de la Abrogacía Española, 'Utilización del *Cloud Computing* por los despachos de abogados y el derecho a la protección de datos de carácter personal' (*Agencia Española de Protección de datos*), <http://www.agpd.es/portalwebAGPD/revista_prensa/revista_prensa/2012/notas_prensa/common/junio/informe_CLOUD.pdf>; 'Cloud Computing—Protect Your Data Without Falling from a Cloud: Guidance from the Italian DPA to Businesses and Public Bodies', <http://www.garanteprivacy.it/garante/doc.jsp?ID=1906181>; Datainspektionen, 'Sidan kan inte hittas', <http://www.datainspektionen.se/press/nyheter/risker-med-otydliga-avtal-for-molntjanster>; Datainspektionen, 'Molntjänster', <http://www.datainspektionen.se/lagar-och-regler/personuppgiftslagen/molntjanster>; Der Landesbeauftragte für den Datenschutz und die Informationsfreiheit Rheinland-Pfalz, 'Entschließung der 82. Konferenz der Datenschutzbeauftragten des Bundes und der Länder' (28–9 September 2011), <http://www.datenschutz.rlp.de/de/ds.php?submenu=grem&typ=dsb&ber=082_cloud>; 'Orientierungshilfe—Cloud Computing' (26 September 2011), <http://www.datenschutz-bayern.de/technik/orient/oh_cloud.pdf> (all accessed 18 March 2013).

[17] Of Google Apps and Microsoft Office 365 SaaS—Datatilsynet, 'Use of Cloud Computing Services' (26 September 2012), <http://www.datatilsynet.no/English/Publications/cloud-computing> (accessed 18 March 2013).

[18] Datatilsynet, 'Processing of Sensitive Personal Data in a Cloud Solution' (3 February 2011), <http://www.datatilsynet.dk/english/processing-of-sensitive-personal-data-in-a-cloud-solution>; Datainspektionen, 'Tillsyn enligt personuppgiftslagen (1998:204)—Salems kommunstyrelse' (28 September 2011), <http://www.datainspektionen.se/Documents/beslut/2011-09-30-salems-kommun.pdf> on Google Apps; Datainspektionen, 'Tillsyn enligt personuppgiftslagen (1998:204)—Enköpings kommunstyrelses användning av molntjänsten Dropbox' (28 September 2011), <http://www.datainspektionen.se/Documents/beslut/2011-09-30-enkopings-kommun.pdf> on Dropbox; Datainspektionen, 'Tillsyn enligt personuppgiftslagen (1998:204)—Brevo AB' (28 September 2011), <http://www.datainspektionen.se/Documents/beslut/2011-09-30-brevo.pdf> (all accessed 18 March 2013 on a SaaS service built on Windows Azure PaaS).

[19] See Chapter 2, Section 5.2.

[20] See WP196, fn. 1 citing RFC 2119: S Bradner, 'Key Words for Use in RFCs to Indicate Requirement Levels' (March 1997), <http://www.ietf.org/rfc/rfc2119.txt> (accessed 18 March 2013). It seems 'must' ought to refer to legal requirements under the DPD, for example Art. 17, the data export restriction (Chapter 11), and fair and lawful processing. However, in some cases 'must' as used in WP196 seems to mean, 'must, in the view of the A29WP, even if not required by law'. Confusingly, WP196 occasionally applies both 'must' and 'should' to similar issues in different places, while using neither word in other places.

some of which are not currently law, but would become so under the proposed EU General Data Protection Regulation (the Regulation).[21]

Broadly, the common themes from WP196 and national regulatory guidance or decisions are as follows: a requirements and risk assessment should be conducted, including consideration of the personal data to be processed in-cloud (such as nature, sensitivity, and quantity); the type of intended processing; how to address risks of lack of control and transparency; as well as due diligence regarding potential providers. Sensitive data may require stronger protective measures.[22] As part of this assessment, contract terms should be reviewed for compliance with data protection law. Clear responsibility for compliance with data protection rules 'must' be allocated, especially if sub-providers are involved. The contract 'must' include a set of 'standardised data protection safeguards' (although none exist), *including* on security, controlling cross-border data flows, and 'additional mechanisms that can prove suitable for facilitating due diligence and accountability such as independent third-party audits and certifications of a provider's services'.[23] The key issues thus involve sub-providers, including their contracts with the direct provider, data location and data export, and security measures, including logging and auditing.

WP196 also states that a controller using cloud services must ensure the contract with its provider includes a data processor agreement with instructions requirement. Because the controller is required to choose a processor providing 'sufficient guarantees' on technical and organizational security measures, due diligence should extend to the intended provider's security measures.[24] WP196[25] considers that the *contract* 'should afford sufficient guarantees' regarding such measures, as well as other measures for data protection law compliance. The controller must 'take reasonable steps' to ensure compliance with the required security measures, by putting in place ways to check such compliance, such as contractual rights to audits, monitoring, and logs. Moreover, because the controller remains responsible for compliance with its data protection law obligations generally, it must ensure, including by conducting due diligence on possible providers and ensuring appropriate contract terms, that it can continue to comply with those obligations even after moving the relevant personal data processing to the cloud. Much of WP196 is aimed at this issue, addressing measures regarding not only security requirements,[26] but also data protection law requirements more

---

[21] The Regulation forms part of a package of reform proposals published by the European Commission on 25 January 2012. Full details are available at <http://ec.europa.eu/justice/newsroom/data-protection/news/120125_en.htm>.

[22] Regulators have often pointed to EU security agency ENISA's documents: ENISA, *Information Assurance Framework* (November 2009); ENISA's survey of SMEs' needs, requirements, and expectations for cloud: ENISA, *An SME Perspective on Cloud Computing* (Survey, November 2009); and its general risk assessment document: ENISA, *Benefits, Risks and Recommendations for Information Security* (Executive Summary, November 2009) as updated by ENISA, *Cloud Computing Benefits, Risks and Recommendations for Information Security* (Rev B, December 2012).

[23] WP196, 8.

[24] Standard checks such as the provider's financial standing should not be overlooked, as the strongest contractual commitments may be worthless if the provider goes out of business or cannot meet its liability. See Chapter 4.

[25] Page 21.

[26] DPD, Art.17: the controller must implement 'appropriate technical and organizational measures to protect personal data against accidental or unlawful destruction or accidental loss, alteration, unauthorized disclosure or access, in particular where the processing involves the transmission of data over a network, and against all other unlawful forms of processing. Having regard to the state of the art and the cost of their implementation, such measures shall ensure a level of security appropriate to the risks represented by the processing and the nature of the data to be protected.' Art. 16 on confidentiality of processing: 'Any person acting under the authority of the controller or of the processor, including the processor himself, who has access to personal data must not process them except on instructions from the controller, unless he is required to do so by law.'

generally, such as fair processing, data subject access rights, and the data export restriction. Any power imbalance as against the provider will not excuse a controller, for example an SME, who agrees to contract terms or cloud practices that are not permitted for data protection law purposes. Finally, data subjects 'should' be provided with information regarding the controller's use of cloud computing.

Detailed checklists regarding WP196's requirements have been produced.[27] We will not duplicate them here. Instead, we will highlight the problems with WP196 by discussing a few specific examples.

3.2 Data processor agreements and the instructions requirement

The instructions requirement exemplifies the difficulty of applying regulatory rules based on pre-Internet concepts to modern technologies such as cloud. Article 17.3's first sub-point simply requires the contract to stipulate that 'the processor shall act only on instructions from the controller'. However, WP196 adds that, for legal certainty, the contract 'should' cover '[d]etails on the (extent and modalities of the) client's instructions to be issued to the provider, with particular regard to the applicable SLAs (which should be objective and measurable) and the relevant penalties (financial or otherwise including the ability to sue the provider in case of non-compliance)'.

Giving 'instructions' to a provider makes sense where controllers engage providers to process data actively for the controller, as in traditional outsourcing. The controller gives the provider instructions, which the provider is obliged contractually to follow, regarding exactly how the provider must process the data. But giving processing 'instructions' is inappropriate when the controller, rather than the provider, is *itself* doing the processing via the provider's service. The problem is that, in self-service cloud, referring to 'instructions' is artificial.

What can 'instructions' mean, in cloud? WP196 states that instructions 'should' include the 'subject and time frame of the service',[28] and that the provider may even be instructed to answer data subject access requests on behalf of the client.[29] Conceptually, this, again, assumes traditional outsourcing, and seems more relevant to contract *scope* than processing 'instructions'. For example, one party does not 'instruct' the other regarding contract duration, both parties agree this. Similarly, SLAs[30] and penalties relate to service quality requirements and remedies for breach. How can you 'give instructions' regarding SLAs? 'Instructions' are not the same as contractual commitments that SLAs must not fall below certain levels, with certain remedies being stipulated if they do. It would be a stretch to class these as issues on which users give processing 'instructions'. If subject, time frame, SLAs, and penalties are treated as aspects on which users must be able to 'instruct' providers, taken to its logical extreme this would suggest that users

---

[27] For example, CSA's Privacy Level Agreement Outline for providers and Annex, CSA, *Privacy Level Agreement Working Group* (PLA Outline, 25 February 2013); and EuroCloud Austria's Cloud contracts: what providers and customers should discuss (which covers more than data protection law issues) EuroCloud.Austria et al., *Cloud Contracts: What Providers and Customers Should Discuss* (Catalogue of recommended contractual components in General Terms and Conditions of Business (AGB) and Service Level Agreements (SLAs) for Cloud Service Providers, 1 November 2012).

[28] WP196 3.4.2.1, 4.1 ('Contractual safeguards').   [29] WP196 fn. 30.

[30] So far, no standards have been agreed for 'objective and measurable' SLAs, even security SLAs, and key performance indicators may vary greatly depending on the service and intended use. See ENISA, *Procure Secure: A Guide to Monitoring of Security Service Levels in Cloud Contracts* (Security SLA Paper, 2012).

should be able to dictate unilaterally the terms (or at least key terms) of cloud contracts, even pricing![31] That cannot be right.

Could 'instructions' relate to computerized service requests? Cloud users (typically through web browsers) make computerized service requests to providers' systems. If those requests are 'instructions' which providers must follow, they would be guaranteeing service operation, including software liability. If a bug prevents users from saving changes, for example to address books in an email SaaS service, is this a failure to follow 'instructions', exposing the provider to 'penalties'? Where email applications are installed on-premise, similar failures would not expose the application provider to data protection law liability. Why should it be different with cloud? Treating service requests as 'instructions' would strain the objective and meaning of the instructions requirement too far.

Could 'instructions' relate to how users wish processing infrastructure, environment, and applications to be configured and maintained? Outsourcing the hosting or management of a private cloud[32] is the closest to classic outsourced data processing, where controllers may well impose detailed contractual requirements relating, for example, to infrastructure and environment. However, with public cloud, providers maintain standardized infrastructure and environments. Users with sufficient technical knowledge might be able to specify how infrastructure and processing environments, or providers' applications, should be set up or developed. However, that would controvert the model underlying *standardized* public cloud, and could undermine the cost-savings made possible through commoditization, shared standard infrastructure, and economies of scale. Also, should different users' instructions conflict, providers may be unable to comply. Finally, security measures are already addressed under the DPD, and we argue that it is unnecessary also to require providers to follow 'instructions' specifically regarding security measures.

Our negotiated cloud contracts research[33] found that users or providers faced an unacceptable position. Some providers refused to agree to the instructions requirement on the basis that it was impossible or made no sense in self-service commoditized cloud, perhaps compromising by agreeing to an alternative, such as to 'comply with data protection laws generally'. Some users chose to accept such compromise terms, risking regulatory action for failure to include an express instructions requirement in their cloud contracts. In other cases, providers agreed to a contractual instructions requirement to assist users with their compliance obligations, or to win the contract, taking the risk that they might be in difficulties if a user chose to issue any 'instructions' inappropriate to cloud. Neither position seems satisfactory.

The true concerns underlying regulators' interpretation of the instructions requirement in relation to the cloud seem twofold.[34] First, that providers may *access* personal data processed using their service, use such data illegitimately for their own purposes, or disclose them to unauthorized persons. Second, that cloud providers could 'unilaterally make a decision or arrange for personal data (and its processing) to be transmitted more or less automatically to unknown cloud data centres'. The latter may be addressed by a specific contractual restriction regarding data location, without any instructions requirement. As regards the former, to minimize this risk WP196 emphasizes ensuring that 'personal data are not (illegally) processed for further purposes' by providers or sub-providers, with contractual

---

[31] Many cloud *providers* currently dictate contract terms, requiring 'click-through' acceptance of their standard terms. That raises separate questions of the extent to which such terms can be negotiated by users, or are enforceable against consumers. See Chapters 4 and 13.

[32] Ignoring self-hosted, self-managed private cloud, which would not constitute outsourcing and involve no 'instructions' to others.

[33] See Chapter 4.   [34] Sopot (n. 15).

requirements and penalties 'if data protection legislation is breached'.[35] No instructions requirement is needed to hold responsible providers who process personal data illegally for their own purposes.[36] Clearly, they would then become controllers of such data in their own right, and be directly liable as such. If an explicit contractual term is considered necessary, it need only prohibit providers' use of relevant personal data for their 'own purposes', and restrict unauthorized disclosure of data,[37] without needing to refer to 'instructions'. This is similar to where sub-providers are involved, and is discussed below. Our view of the objective underlying the DPD's instructions requirement is supported by its legislative history[38] and, for example, Norway's approach,[39] whose implementation of the DPD states: 'No processor may process personal data in any way other than that which is agreed in writing with the controller. Nor may the data be turned over to another person for storage or manipulation without such agreement.' The data protection authority interprets this as requiring the processor to abide by the controller's instructions regarding the processing, and is limited to the processing purposes and methods available to the controller. If the provider processes personal data in other ways, or for other purposes, than those agreed, this would breach the data processor agreement and render it a controller. The Norwegian implementation, as well as making more sense in cloud, arguably also makes more sense than the DPD in terms of the original legislative purpose and technology neutrality.

If we liken processing personal data to cooking food,[40] current data protection laws assume that you either cook food yourself (process data in-house), or hire a chef or caterer to cook for you, who may engage sub-caterers (hire processors who use sub-processors). However, cloud involves cooking a ready meal, or renting a kitchen (which may be pre-equipped) in which you cook. Laws regulating caterers simply do not suit kitchen rentals. Rather than making kitchen rental companies and ready meal suppliers follow every customer's 'instructions' on how to configure rental kitchens or what ingredients to put into ready meals, what is most important is ensuring that customers only use kitchens and ingredients meeting certain minimum health and safety standards. In

---

[35] 3.4.1.2 and after 3.4.2.14.

[36] Certain further processing, such as indexing data to enable searching by users, would surely be considered for the purposes of users, rather than the provider.

[37] Stating, as Sopot and WP196 do, that providers should never 'use' personal data for their 'own purposes' (or risk being treated as controllers), seems over-broad and insufficiently clear. Providers mining and selling personal data may well be controllers. But, what about monitoring or logging users' processing (including of personal data) for the service's overall health, and to enable the provider to address availability or other service issues? Surely that should not be considered 'use' for the provider's 'own purposes'? Clarification that this sort of monitoring would be considered for *users'* benefit and purposes would have been helpful.

A related concern, arising from providers potentially having access to user data, is the risk of unauthorized *disclosure* of data by providers, for instance if requested by foreign law enforcement authorities, mentioned several times in both Sopot and WP196. WP196 3.4.2.13 suggests the contract 'should' (among other things) require notification of such requests (unless prohibited by criminal law), 'to ensure legal certainty'. This issue is *not* treated as part of the instructions requirement: nor should 'use' be. See also Chapter 11.

[38] The instructions requirement represented 'simplification' of earlier drafts focusing on data integrity and unauthorized disclosure: 'The provisions on confidentiality have been put into a separate Article (Article 16); the drafting of those on security affecting both the controller and the processor (Article 17) has been simplified. The consideration of the costs of the measures to be taken has been reintroduced, while maintaining the criterion of risk for assessing the suitability of the measures taken.' DPD common position explanatory statement III.B.2(ix). EurLex, 'Common position (EC) No 1/95 adopted by the Council on 20 February 1995 with a view to adopting Directive 95/.../EC of the European Parliament and of the Council of... on the protection of individuals with regard to the processing of personal data and on the free movement of such data' (Official Journal C 093, 13 April 1995).

[39] See n. 17.

[40] W Kuan Hon, 'The 12 Cs of Cloud Computing: A Culinary Confection' (*Society for Computers and Law*, 16 April 2012), <http://www.scl.org/site.aspx?i=ed26082> (accessed 18 March 2013).

other words, a requirement to follow each customer's 'instructions', for example on how to configure cloud infrastructure, seems meaningless or impossible with self-service, shared, and standardized cloud infrastructure; if required, this may negate the potential costs and flexibility benefits of commodity public cloud for SMEs and others. What should matter most is whether the infrastructure meets minimum security standards. Security of personal data in the cloud is the underlying policy objective here,[41] and that should be the main focus, rather than the instructions requirement per se.

Concerns about data protection law compliance in the cloud environment, particularly public infrastructure services, ought to be addressed not through an instructions requirement, but by updating data protection laws to recognize explicitly a status of 'resource provider',[42] to whom no instructions requirement would apply. Ensuring that controllers are better aware of the security requirements incumbent upon them, and the measures available to them, should result in their (i) using only resource providers meeting minimum security requirements, and (ii) imposing contractual restrictions on such providers' use/disclosure of any personal data processed using their resources, and/or through user encryption excluding provider access to intelligible personal data. A similar approach would be appropriate as regards restrictions on transferring personal data to countries without adequate protection, bearing in mind that confidentiality of data may be protected by user encryption, while integrity and availability may be assured by means of user backups.

However, rather than recognizing the inappropriateness of the instructions requirement in the cloud, France's CNIL would hold providers liable as controllers in cases where cloud users cannot give 'instructions' but must accept the provider's terms.[43] Similarly, the proposed Data Protection Regulation would expand requirements regarding the controller-processor contract, impose detailed direct obligations on processors, and impose controller status on processors who do not follow the controller's 'instructions'.[44] This could deter cloud providers from offering services to EU users. For example, non-EEA cloud storage services might refuse to provide services to EU residents, perhaps by filtering users' IP addresses by geography, in order to avoid exposure to liability for unknown personal data uploaded by users. This could deprive EU residents of cost-effective storage services, even if users who encrypt data first and back up elsewhere could mitigate the data protection risks.

3.3 Security requirements

WP196 would require detailed precontractual security checks, contractual security undertakings by providers, and rights for controllers to conduct post-contract monitoring and auditing. While appropriate for traditional outsourcing, and possible for

---

[41] The other chief objective being prevention of misuse of personal data by providers, which presupposes access to intelligible data.

[42] Cf the draft Albrecht Report (see Chapter 7, n. 141), which would introduce a concept of 'producer', processing system creators, and impose greater obligations on them, namely to take 'technical and operational measures to ensure…compliance [with the main data protection principles] in the design, set-up, and operation of automatic data processing or filing systems'. This could be a challenge, with uncertain scope as to what systems are covered and what measures are needed, especially as much depends on how systems are used by controllers.

[43] CNIL, 'Cloud computing: les conseils de la CNIL pour les enterprises qui utilisent ces nouveaux services' (*CNIL*, 25 June 2012), <http://www.cnil.fr/la-cnil/actualite/article/article/cloud-computing-les-conseils-de-la-cnil-pour-les-entreprises-qui-utilisent-ces-nouveaux-services> (accessed 18 March 2013), thus interpreting 'instructions' in yet another way.

[44] 'The A29WP considers that this proposal goes in the right direction to remedy the unbalance that is often a feature in the cloud computing environment, where the client (especially if it is a SME) may find it difficult to exercise the full control required by data protection legislation on how the provider delivers the requested services.' WP196, 23.

dedicated managed private cloud, these requirements are at odds with the model of shared, standardized public cloud, and do not recognize that users may have significant control over security depending on service type, for example IaaS or PaaS.[45]

Many providers are reluctant to give much information about their security measures or allow physical inspections of code or shared infrastructure, whether as precontractual information or under post-contract audits, as that could compromise security. Regulators recognize this, yet cite it as an example of lack of transparency, and under WP196 the contract 'should' impose general obligations on providers to 'give assurances' that their internal organization and data-processing arrangements, and those of any sub-processors, comply with 'the applicable national and international legal requirements and standards'.

Many users may lack expertise to assess and specify cloud or even IT security requirements. Also, as with 'instructions', providers of shared infrastructure in a standardized environment may be unable to comply with conflicting requirements of different users in relation to security policies. One practical compromise has been for providers to obtain independent expert third-party certifications or audits to check that their security measures meet certain recognized industry standards, share certifications, audit reports, or summary results with prospective or current users, and commit to maintaining such certifications.[46]

WP196 recognizes that in a multiparty, virtualized server environment, a 'relevant third-party audit' chosen by the controller 'may' be satisfactory in lieu of an individual controller's right to audit, which may be impractical technically, and can increase risks to network security. It acknowledges that independent verification 'can be a credible means for cloud providers to demonstrate their compliance with their obligations as specified in this Opinion'. However, under WP196 any such third-party audit 'would indicate that data protection controls have been subject to audit or review against a recognised standard meeting the requirements set out in this Opinion by a reputable third party organisation'. Moreover, providers 'should' provide 'documentary evidence' of measures, not just for security, but to 'deliver the outcomes of the data protection principles', such as 'Procedures to... respond to access requests, the allocation of resources including the designation of data protection officers who are responsible for the organisation of data protection compliance...'. It mentions that recognized standards might be those of the International Standards Organisation, the International Auditing and Assurance Standards Board, and the Auditing Standards Board of the American Institute of Certified Public Accountants, 'in so far as these organisations provide standards that meet the requirements set out in this opinion'. Although there are *security* standards such as ISO27001, used for example by the UK G-Cloud programme,[47] there are no standards and certifications yet that are recognized specifically for EU data protection law purposes, still less for cloud data protection. Therefore, it may be impossible for providers to offer such certifications or audits.

Under WP196, the contract 'should' ensure the controller's right to monitor the provider, audit processing operations, and oblige the provider to cooperate. The ability for the cloud platform to provide reliable monitoring and comprehensive logging mechanisms is considered paramount for investigating breaches.[48] Providers' logging and log-checking tools may vary, but increased logging may affect performance and

---

[45] See Chapter 1.   [46] See Chapter 4.   [47] See Chapter 5.
[48] The difference between 'monitoring' and 'logging' is unclear: if the former means real-time monitoring, excessive 'live' monitoring by one user may be undesirable in terms of affecting availability for other users. See Chapter 4.

raise costs. It is also questionable whether reliable tools for certain kinds of logging, for example data location audit trails, exist.[49]

WP196's recommendations on data deletion seem absolute. For example, 'it must be ensured that each instance of them is erased irretrievably (i.e., previous versions, temporary files, and even file fragments are to be deleted as well)'. No allowance is made for structural or technological protections against access to intelligible personal data, for example where the system design may prevent access to, or reconstitution of, fragments. With most public cloud services, as Google Apps' terms clearly state, only 'pointers' to data are deleted, with actual data being overwritten over time.[50] Although 'blocking' of access to data is mentioned in the DPD, it is considered an option by WP196 only if data retention is required for legal reasons. However, more secure data deletion costs more money. Requiring complete destruction of all possible fragments, and perhaps also secure destruction of hardware, could negate one of the cloud's key potential benefits.

More generally, WP196 assumes that cloud providers always have access to intelligible personal data, but users' 'self-help' use of encryption or encryption gateway services[51] can prevent this altogether, or at least mitigate the risk significantly. Regulators and lawmakers do not seem to take enough account of technological measures that *users* may implement to protect personal data that they wish to process in-cloud, quite independently of providers' own security measures. On the contrary, the draft Regulation would impose direct obligations on processors regarding security measures, irrespective of their knowledge as to whether they are even processing 'personal data'.

3.4 Sub-providers

WP196's statements regarding sub-providers again reflect traditional outsourcing where providers 'commission' sub-contractors, ignoring the fact that, with cloud, the 'direction of travel' is reversed.[52] Providers with sub-providers have *already* created services based on the sub-provider's service. While some providers might be willing to provide details of all their sub-providers to prospective users, others may not, perhaps for commercial confidentiality reasons.

Also, it is hardly realistic to oblige providers to change pre-existing commercial arrangements and rewrite contracts with sub-providers to 'mirror' the provider's obligations in their contracts with each user. Existing sub-providers may be unwilling to agree to follow the user's 'instructions', or accept increased security obligations with liability if 'data protection obligations' are breached, not least because one sub-provider's infrastructure may itself service multiple cloud providers, each with its own users.

The situation is exacerbated by uncertainties (not clarified by WP196) regarding which actors must be considered as 'sub-contractors', and down to what level. Must providers rewrite their contracts with, for example, data centre operators and equipment suppliers, and guarantee their security measures? Must providers be prohibited from making any changes, such as replacing faulty storage equipment, unless they have first notified each and every user, and each user has given its prior written consent? This would be very disruptive to operations on common standardized infrastructure. Indeed, it is likely to be completely unrealistic in most cases.

---

[49] See Chapter 10.   [50] See Chapter 7.
[51] Available, for example, for Salesforce, Google Apps, and Microsoft Office 365. See Chapter 2, Section 2.1.
[52] See Chapter 2, Section 5.2, para. 2.

Providers, especially if required to give assurances regarding all possible sub-providers' security and other compliance measures, may well suggest that prospective users should either 'consent' in advance, which makes a consent requirement somewhat artificial, or go elsewhere.

Another fundamental issue is that, as with providers, it seems too broad-brush to assume that all sub-providers can always access intelligible user data, as users may encrypt their data. A further layer of protection at provider level is also possible; for example, the provider itself could encrypt data, or its system design may otherwise prevent sub-provider access to intelligible data. Although IT security is important for data protection law compliance, data protection law should not seek to be a substitute for technical security, especially with fast-moving technologies. Some security standards may involve vetting of storage equipment, for example for possible backdoors sending data back to the manufacturer. Could not certification of services to such standards suffice, without users needing to know details of possible sub-providers, or requiring full contractual obligations all the way down the supply chain?

3.5 Other issues

The DPD restricts the transfer of personal data outside the EEA, to prevent controllers from avoiding data protection law obligations by moving data to a non-EEA country. This pre-Internet restriction can constrain the location-independent use and/or storage of personal data that is a key feature of cloud.

Under WP196, controllers' pre-contract risk assessments should include obtaining lists of not only all sub-providers, but also their locations and data centre locations. The contract itself also 'should' list all locations in which personal data may be processed or, which may be different, where 'the service may be provided'. The contract 'should' put in place safeguards if personal data could be transferred to 'non-adequate' third countries, for instance requiring the provider to sign contracts with third country sub-providers based on model clauses, and so on.[53]

However, apart from statements that relying on a provider's US Safe Harbor self-certification may be insufficient (although strictly it is for DPD purposes), little detail is provided on what exactly would be required beyond 'incorporating the expertise and resources of third parties that are capable of assessing the adequacy of cloud providers through different auditing, standardization and certification schemes'. Providers may not know their sub-providers' data centre locations, and the data export restriction does not take into account users' ability to protect data through encrypting data and taking backups internally or to other services. Therefore, providers and sub-providers may not be able to access intelligible personal data, or interfere with data availability even if their service stores personal data outside the EEA. In our view, in accordance with the DPD's objective, data location should not be an end in itself, but a means to achieve data security and compliance with substantive principles. If confidentiality, integrity, and availability, along with data subject access, can be achieved through user encryption/backup, it does not seem sensible for laws to focus on data location as such.

WP196 also emphasizes 'intervenability', which appears to mean the ability for individuals to exercise their rights—notably to access their data, and transparency. While in a traditional outsourcing arrangement a processor may have sole access to data, so that the controller needs its assistance to respond appropriately to requests from data

---

[53] Discussed in detail in Chapter 10.

subjects, this does not hold true in cloud. WP196's focus on this aspect seems misconceived. For example, the contract 'should' oblige the provider to cooperate and 'support the client in facilitating exercise of data subjects' rights to access, correct, or delete their data' and to ensure the same in relation to any subcontractor.[54] 'The provider may even be instructed to answer requests on behalf of the client.'[55] However, with self-service cloud, controllers need only ensure that the service provides indexing of personal data, or includes more sophisticated database functionality as appropriate, in order to enable the controller to search for requested personal data. Controllers may download, delete, and amend retrieved data themselves. It is unclear what cloud 'obstacles' to intervenability rights there might be, particularly from passive sub-providers. Moreover, if asked to answer data subject requests, most providers are likely to refer the matter back to the controller or charge extra for 'assisting', while many controllers would not want to ask providers to trawl through their data even if that were possible.

On transparency, 'the client should as a matter of good practice inform data subjects about the cloud provider and all subcontractors (if any) as well as about locations in which data may be stored or processed by the cloud provider and/or its subcontractors', and give data subjects 'any further information such as on the recipients or categories of recipients of the data, which can also include processors and sub-processors in so far as such further information is necessary to guarantee fair processing'. Again, data subjects are more likely to be concerned about security than data location or the exact identities of providers or sub-providers, and the relevance of encryption and backups is again overlooked.

3.6 Summary

In summary, WP196's approach may have been influenced by concerns that data protection may be reduced if controllers use cloud, coloured by the popular perception that most users cannot obtain full information about cloud services,[56] lack power to demand changes to cloud providers' (often provider-friendly) standard terms, and will lose all control over their data in the cloud.[57] It is important that any changes that are made to policy and laws in order to address such concerns are informed and are proportionate to the actual risks, and are not merely a reaction to popular perceptions.

Unfortunately, if the recommendations contained in WP196 were to be followed to the letter, it would be impossible for data controllers to use public cloud computing for processing personal data. The highly customized service that regulators demand would not be 'cloud', and would deliver neither the efficiencies nor the process improvements that make cloud computing attractive. Requirements designed for traditional outsourcing simply do not fit the public cloud model.[58] Moreover, while the European Commission in its cloud

---

[54] 3.4.3.5.   [55] WP196, fn. 30.

[56] And transparency from providers is a 'must' under WP196, although there is no legal basis in the DPD for this requirement as such.

[57] WP196 focuses on cloud users' loss of control regarding availability, integrity, confidentiality, transparency, isolation ('unlinkability'), intervenability, accountability, and portability. Lack of 'integrity' is attributed to 'sharing resources', lack of 'intervenability' is blamed on 'the complexity and dynamics of the outsourcing chain'. Lack of 'isolation' is said to arise from the ability to link different users' data. Additional safeguards are considered necessary given the perceived lack of control and insufficient provision of information regarding cloud services. However, the DPD does not specify any requirements for example on 'isolation' or 'accountability' and, as Chapter 2 explains, control in cloud is more nuanced and context-dependent.

[58] Others share this view. Dai Davis. 'Where Does the ICO's New Cloud Guidance Take You?' (*Computer Weekly*), <http://www.computerweekly.com/opinion/Where-does-the-ICOs-new-Guidance-guide-you-to> (accessed 18 March 2013), referring to similar UK ICO guidance: 'in effect, banning the

strategy asserted that the draft Data Protection Regulation would solve current problems with cloud data protection,[59] the reform measures, if adopted as proposed, could have the opposite effect.

Ignorance on the part of many cloud providers and users as to their data protection law obligations and rights may result in increased data protection risks in the cloud. However, the solution is not to impose cumbersome obligations on resource providers who provide low-priced cloud services on a standardized utility basis. The imposition of disproportionate controls may force providers to raise prices substantially or even withdraw some cloud services from EU residents altogether. In our view, the problem should be addressed through a combination of two approaches. First, raising user awareness, particularly regarding self-help measures. Second, encouraging the development, with participation by all stakeholders, of appropriate standards for cloud services, and the offering of cloud services specifically designed and certified as 'fit for personal data' according to those standards. Such services may be more expensive than standard 'no frills, no guarantees' public cloud services. This may lead to the emergence of a more sophisticated market for cloud services, with differential pricing for different levels of security and control.[60] Furthermore, while it would be possible to require controllers to use only services independently certified to such standards, it would be preferable to introduce incentives for controllers to use such services, for example by applying fewer or lighter compliance obligations to controllers who use them.

4. Cloud Providers

4.1 Introduction

We now discuss the position of cloud providers. As mentioned previously, in considering the position of an entity that handles personal data, each individual activity or set of activities should be considered separately. An entity may be a controller in relation to one processing operation, but only a processor in relation to another.

When a cloud provider has an individual user (a human being) as its customer, the provider is likely to be the 'controller' of the personal data collected relating to that customer ('user-related personal data').[61] This may include personal data provided by the customer during sign-up, as well as metadata generated regarding the customer's ongoing usage of the service.[62]

However, what is the position of a cloud provider in relation to personal data, perhaps relating to other individuals, that its users choose to store on its hardware or otherwise process via its cloud services ('cloud-processed personal data')? In this context, what *should* be its status? Those questions are the main focus of this section.

---

use of cloud services...Yes, a cloud customer could negotiate a one-off solution from a cloud provider. If the cloud customer is willing to pay enough, anything is possible. But the cloud customer would not then end up with what a normal businessman would regard as a cloud solution—it would end up with a bespoke outsourcing solution. And it would not end up with most of the benefits of the cloud—certainly not the cost benefits.'

[59] European Commission, *Unleashing the Potential of Cloud computing in Europe*, COM(2012) 529 final.

[60] See Chapter 4, Section 6.

[61] The provider may not be a controller of the user's service-related data if the user who contracts with the provider is an organization (as only data relating to living individuals are considered 'personal data'), although entities such as corporations, of course, generally act through human beings.

[62] On metadata generated by cloud providers, see Chapter 6.

If a cloud provider is a 'processor', then all requirements regarding processors discussed above apply, including contractual arrangements regarding the provider and any sub-processors.[63] If it is a 'controller' (possibly jointly with the cloud user), it will be subject to regulatory obligations and liability as such. We argue further that some cloud providers should be regarded as neither controllers nor processors.

4.2 Contractual designations of status

Only a small minority of the providers whose Terms of Service ('ToS') were included in the Queen Mary, University of London surveys in 2010 and 2013 asserted their status as controller or processor in relation to either user-related or cloud-processed personal data.[64]

A few providers, however, stated explicitly that they were processors in relation to cloud-processed personal data. For example, Google's standard terms for UK customers for Google Apps for Business state: 'for the purposes of this Agreement and in respect of Customer Personal Data, the parties agree that Customer shall be the controller and Google shall be a processor. Within the scope of this Agreement, Customer shall comply with its obligations as a controller and Google shall comply with its obligations as a processor under the Data Protection Legislation'.[65]

As regards user-related personal data, Apple states in the ToS for its iCloud service: 'you consent and agree to the collection and use of certain information about you and your use of the Service.' It goes on to assert that it is a data controller in relation to such user-related data as follows: 'personal information regarding individuals who reside in a member state of the European Economic Area (EEA) is jointly controlled by Apple Distribution International in Cork, Ireland, and Apple UK Limited in Uxbridge, United Kingdom.'[66]

In contrast, US infrastructure provider Rackspace takes a neutral position, making explicit provision both for situations where it is a controller, and situations where it is a processor; thus, it seems, acknowledging that, in different circumstances, its status could vary.[67] It will be interesting to see whether other major players adopt this approach which takes into account explicitly the different capacities in which a cloud service provider may handle personal data.

It is important to bear in mind, however, that contractual terms that purport to dictate the status of the provider, as controller or processor, are not conclusive under EU data protection laws.[68] The particular factual circumstances will determine whether a

---

[63] Which may include third-party cloud providers whose services or tools may be used or integrated with the primary cloud provider's service.

[64] The survey results are reported in Chapter 3.

[65] Google Apps for Business (Online Agreement) clause 2.2, <http://www.google.com/apps/intl/en-GB/terms/premier_terms_ie.html>.

[66] iCloud Terms and Conditions, <http://www.apple.com/legal/icloud/en/terms.html>.

[67] Rackspace, *General Terms and Conditions* (30 January 2013) Clause 23: 'Each of us agrees to comply with our respective obligations under the Data Protection Act 1998 (the "Act") as applicable to personal data that it controls or processes as part of, or in connection with, its use or provision of the Services...We agree that we will not provide access to personal data that you store through the Services to any subcontractor or affiliate outside of the EEA unless that person meets the requirements stated below during the entire time that it has access to the personal data:
23.1.1 for personal data for which we are a "controller" under the Act...
23.1.2 for personal data for which we are a "processor" under the Act...'.

[68] See text to n. 69. See also n. 99 on the SWIFT incident, where contractual terms providing that SWIFT was to act as a processor did not prevent it from being considered a controller on the facts.

provider is a controller or processor, although explicit contract terms may influence the determination.

4.3 Cloud providers' position

Under WP169 on controllers and processors, factual functional control matters most in determining controller status, not contractual provisions or labels, although contractual terms will be relevant (unless they do not affect the substance of the position).[69]

WP196 considers that cloud providers are processors, unless they become controllers because they act in a manner inconsistent with their instructions. Certain providers, such as social networking or webmail SaaS services, which run advertisements based on the content of uploaded personal data, are likely to be controllers, and we do not argue against their regulation as such. However, we consider that these kinds of providers are qualitatively different from what we term cloud 'infrastructure' providers, whether IaaS, PaaS, or SaaS, who rent out computing resources such as processing power and 'pure' infrastructure-like data storage facilities (utility storage). Our main focus is on infrastructure providers. Are they processors or controllers, or (as discussed later) should they be treated as neither?

Cloud providers often determine the 'means' of processing, such as the hardware, software, and data centres used to process users' data or sub-providers used. This may lead to them being characterized as 'controllers'. However, an alternative characterization is that the cloud *user* determines the means, at least at a high level, for example, by choosing a particular cloud provider's (pre-built) facilities and tools.

WP169 recognizes that processors have some 'margin of manoeuvre' in determining 'means' of processing, such as hardware, without that making them a 'controller'. In this context, WP169 introduces a concept of 'effective means' whereby a person who determines either the purposes of processing or the 'effective means' of processing is a 'controller'.[70] 'Effective means' under WP196 are essential elements 'traditionally and inherently reserved' to the controller, or in other words, 'substantial questions . . . essential to the core of the processing'. WP169 describes this as the 'how' of processing, such as which data to process, for how long, which third parties will have access to data, and when to delete data. However, 'effective means' do not include *non*-essential means, such as technical and organizational questions. These may be delegated to processors without turning them into controllers. Indeed, 'it is well possible that the technical and organizational means are determined exclusively by the data processor. In these cases—where there is a good definition of purposes, but little or even no guidance on technical and organizational means—the means should represent a reasonable way of achieving the purpose(s) and the data controller should be fully informed about the means used'.[71]

Accordingly, WP169 clearly envisages that providers may determine 'which hardware or software shall be used', and even *exclusively* determine technical and organizational means, while remaining 'processors'. WP196 also states: 'The cloud client may task the cloud provider with choosing the methods and the technical or organisational measures to be used to achieve the purposes of the controller.'[72]

---

[69] N. 10. Therefore, for example, a non-EEA parent company might be the 'controller' of its EEA subsidiary's operations.
[70] WP169 states that factors to consider include the level of prior instructions given by the data controller (which determines the processor's 'margin of manoeuvre'), the extent to which the controller monitors the execution of the service, the visibility of the controller to data subjects, and expectations of data subjects based on that, and the expertise of the parties.
[71] WP169, 14–15.   [72] WP169, 3.3.1.

Yet, security is considered critical by many Member States and national regulators, and WP169 acknowledged, 'In some legal systems decisions taken on security measures are particularly important, since security measures are explicitly considered as an essential characteristic to be defined by the controller. This raises the issue of which decisions on security may entail the qualification of controller for a company to which processing has been outsourced'.[73] For example, could cloud security measures such as scanning data for malware or other security risks 'determine' the purpose of the processing?

Statements such as 'the means should represent a reasonable way of achieving the purpose(s) and the data controller should be fully informed about the means used', and 'This processing activity may be limited to a very specific task or context or may accommodate a certain degree of discretion *about how to serve the controller's interests*, allowing the processor to choose the most suitable technical and organizational means',[74] clearly assume traditional outsourcing, where a controller engages a processor to perform specified processing within the scope of the controller's 'mandate',[75] with the processor being informed explicitly of the purposes of the processing. The italicized phrase indicates the assumption underlying the 'processor' concept: an agent hired to process data actively to serve the controller's interests.

Again, these are inappropriate to self-service public cloud, particularly infrastructure services. Users of such cloud services do not hire providers for stated processing purposes; providers do not then adapt their infrastructure/systems to 'process' data in furtherance of those purposes, indeed providers may not even know these purposes.[76] Trying to shoehorn infrastructure providers into the definition of 'processors' may not be the best way to achieve the understandable policy objectives underlying regulators' interpretations. This applies with even more force to sub-providers on whose infrastructure services SaaS or PaaS providers build their own services.

In WP169, the instructions requirement also seems inextricably interlinked with 'processor' status.[77] A provider is more likely to be considered a processor (rather than a controller), the clearer the instructions, the more tightly defined the processor's 'tasks', and the more limited the scope for 'discretion'.[78] There is no prohibition on 'subdividing the relevant tasks' among sub-processors as long as they all follow 'instructions'.[79] However, the difficulty with the instructions requirement in cloud has already been discussed.

While WP169 attempts to be helpful and pragmatic, and provides some useful guidance, it leaves some open issues and grey areas. The DPD itself contains no concept of 'effective means', and therefore potential controllers and processors must wait to see how regulators apply that concept in practice, with no guarantee that WP169 will be interpreted and applied consistently across EU Member States. The position regarding decisions on security measures is also uncertain. The key underlying security concerns are that cloud providers could access users' data to misuse or disclose them illegitimately, undermine the integrity of users' data by deliberately or inadvertently losing or corrupting data, or prejudice the availability of the data to the user.[80] However, as previously discussed, cloud providers (or sub-providers) may or may not be able to access *intelligible* data. Clarification is also needed, as well as harmonization across Member States,

---

[73] WP169, 15.   [74] WP169, 33.

[75] For example, 'The contract should include a detailed enough description of the mandate of the processor' WP169, 26.

[76] Unless the provider deliberately accesses the data or spies on the processing, whereupon it may become a controller (assuming it can access user data in intelligible form).

[77] WP169, 25 (III.2).   [78] WP169, 13, 28, 29.   [79] WP169, 27.

[80] WP196, 3.4.3.

regarding whether controllers may determine minimum security measures, leaving providers to meet those minimum standards as they see fit (and still remain 'processors'), or whether controllers must specify security requirements to a fine level of granularity.[81]

4.4 What should the regulatory status of cloud providers be?

Commentators tend to assume all cloud providers are processors,[82] and that the issue is whether, and to what extent, providers risk being treated as controllers. Their focus has generally been on where the line lies between processor and controller, and how that line is crossed. However, arguably, infrastructure providers should not even be regarded as 'processors'.[83] The UK ICO has, albeit briefly, acknowledged the possibility of a 'neither' status in relation to database vendors.[84] This issue was not discussed in WP169[85] or WP196.

We consider that there is a case for updating the law to clarify the status of infrastructure providers whose facilities are rented by cloud users and used to process personal data in self-service fashion. Our view is that mere providers of IT resources[86] should not be considered 'processors', unless they monitor processing with a view to accessing or using personal data,[87] or access such data for their own purposes, for example to disclose data to law enforcement authorities without the controller's authorization.

Data storage in the cloud may involve temporary caching or persistent storage.[88] Since it is the cloud user who makes use of software in-cloud to process data in a self-service fashion, and arguably controls any automatic temporary caching of data that results from such use, this should not make the hardware or software provider a processor. This argument becomes harder to sustain if data are saved to permanent storage on the provider's infrastructure, for example a server's hard drive. Where a cloud service comprises or includes permanent data storage, it would seem that, because the provider passively holds data for the customer even when the customer is not operating on the data by running application software in the cloud, the provider is storing data on

---

[81] Providers may also have more expertise on security and other technical issues than users such as SMEs or individuals. Most users are unlikely to be able to specify cloud security requirements, particularly in detail, without expert advice, with attendant costs.

[82] For example, Daniele Catteddu and Giles Hogben, *Cloud Computing—Benefits, Risks and Recommendations for Information Security* (European Network and Information Security Agency, 2009), 66; Lisa J Sotto, Bridget C Treacy, and Melinda L McLellan, 'Privacy and Data Security Risks in Cloud Computing' [2010] 15 *Electronic Commerce & Law Report* 186; Yves Poullet, Jean-Marc Van Gyseghem, Jacques Gérard and others (Research Centre on IT and Law (CRID)), Discussion paper 'Cloud Computing and Its Implications on Data Protection' (Council of Europe, 2010).

[83] IaaS provider Rackspace made this point in its contribution to the 2009 Consultation. Rackspace, *Consultation Paper on the Legal Framework for the Fundamental Right to Protection of Personal Data* (31 December 2009) (4): 'There is a need for a clear distinction of requirements for processors that have access to data and are processing such data on the instruction of the data controller and who determine the means of processing (e.g., payroll companies, accountants, call centers, market research companies); as opposed to IT hosting providers that only provide technical infrastructure and technical support to a processor who uses such equipment to perform its data processing. The IT hosting provider in this case provides processing equipment, hosting infrastructure and technical support for the use of the processor to store and transmit the data. Such processing is controlled by the data processor who is renting the hosting equipment from the IT hosting provider who has no right to access data stored on the data processor's server.'

[84] ICO, *ICO Highlights Need to Remain Compliant When Using Commercial Databases* (January 2013).

[85] The discussion of 'third party' in WP169 III.3 does not extend to the possibility of an intermediary 'non-processor'.

[86] See Chapter 2, Section 5.1. [87] The 'spyware' equivalent, text to n. 92 below.

[88] See Chapter 1, Section 2.1.2.

behalf of its customer. Under current laws, although the user initiates data uploading and downloading, during the period when the provider hosts data pending download or processing by the customer, the provider is likely to be a 'processor'. This is because 'processing' includes passive storage,[89] and knowledge of the stored data's nature may be deemed irrelevant. A provider is even more likely to be characterized as 'processor' if its services include automated data replication for business continuity.[90] Saving extra copies of personal data elsewhere would constitute 'processing'. Indeed, splitting personal data into fragments may constitute 'processing' personal data, even if the resulting fragments may not be 'personal data', just as the procedure of anonymizing data may itself be 'processing'.[91] However, arguably if personal data are fragmented into non-personal data, then subsequent storage of such fragments should not be 'processing'.

In relation to infrastructure providers or sub-providers whose services include data storage (such as data hosts), would the stored data be 'personal data', and therefore regulated under the DPD? Chapter 7's analyses regarding anonymized, pseudonymized, and encrypted data are relevant here. For example, we consider that sufficiently well-encrypted data, where the provider has no access to the key, should not be 'personal data', and similarly with sufficiently anonymized data. However, it seems unsatisfactory that the provider's status should depend on the strength of encryption or anonymization techniques used by its customer, of which it may have no knowledge or control.

We suggest that mere hosting of personal data, without knowledge as to whether it is 'personal data', should not render a provider a processor, and even more so with encrypted data. We believe that introducing an exemption or exception to data protection laws is justified here. Knowledge that 'personal data' are being processed, and control in the sense of ability to access such data in intelligible form, should be prerequisites to attributing a cloud provider with the status of 'processor'.

Generally, someone who rents out a computer or application software to you cannot access your data, unless they use secret spyware.[92] Yet, it is commonly feared that cloud providers may access stored data, and even give unauthorized third parties such access. Generally, infrastructure providers do control storage and processing hardware, and SaaS providers control the underlying code of applications run by users. However, where data are stored in securely encrypted form where the provider does not have the key, or in non-personal fragments where the provider has taken technical and organizational measures to prevent itself from reuniting the fragments (so that only the user, duly logged in, can do so), the provider has no data access and should not be considered a 'processor'. Indeed, even where unencrypted stored information is clearly personal data, there may be justification, admittedly less compelling, for arguing that a cloud provider is not (or should not be considered) a 'processor', as long as it has taken appropriate

---

[89] Perhaps even temporary storage is 'processing', as the definition is not by reference to duration.

[90] See Chapter 1, Section 2.1.2. However, providers do not necessarily make a contractual commitment to customers that they will back up data or take similar measures—see Chapter 3, Section 3.2.1.

[91] See Chapter 7, Section 4.

[92] Whereupon the spyware user would be controller of the personal data collected covertly. In the US, such spying occurred: Federal Trade Commission, 'FTC Halts Computer Spying' (*FTC*, 25 September 2012), <http://www.ftc.gov/opa/2012/09/designware.shtm>; software pre-installed by the provider on rental PCs was used, 'capturing screenshots of confidential and personal information, logging their [ie renters'] computer keystrokes, and in some cases taking webcam pictures of people in their homes, all without notice to, or consent from, the consumers'. The US Federal Trade Commission settled with the software supplier DesignerWare and several computer rental companies, for example Aaron's, but renters have commenced class action litigation. Dan Goodin, 'How Spyware on Rental PCs Captured Users' Most Intimate Moments' (*Arstechnica*, 18 December 2012), <http://arstechnica.com/security/2012/12/how-spyware-on-rental-pcs-captured-users-most-intimate-moments> (both accessed 18 March 2013).

measures to prevent access to the data by anyone other than the relevant user. What is most important is that it has put in place access control restrictions, or designed the service such that it cannot access intelligible user data.

Where infrastructure providers do have the technical ability to access a user's account and stored data, for example for maintenance, upgrades, or troubleshooting purposes, and access the user's account or stored personal data for authorized purposes,[93] the access is only incidental to the authorized access. Arguably, therefore, this is little different from where computing hardware and/or software is rented to a customer, and the provider's employee visits the customer's premises to maintain or upgrade software or hardware. The employee may incidentally have the opportunity to access personal data while performing the maintenance, but that should not render the rental provider a 'processor'.

Where a cloud provider uses a sub-provider, the sub-provider is likely to have far less control than the provider over the user's account or stored data. For example, with Dropbox SaaS storage using Amazon IaaS, Dropbox encrypts user data and has access to decryption keys.[94] However, this does not mean Amazon has such access. In the analyses below we do not always discuss sub-providers explicitly, but the point regarding sub-providers being further removed applies equally there, and should be borne in mind.

Moreover, with utility storage it is the end user who chooses what kind of data to store on the provider's equipment, and in what form. Providers normally cannot control such user actions.[95] Utility storage providers are unlikely to know whether the user is storing personal data or non-personal data, unless, and until, they inspect the data.[96] This strengthens the argument that incidental access should not render these kinds of utility providers 'processors'.[97]

However, what if an infrastructure provider, with access to intelligible personal data stored on its infrastructure, does something that exceeds its authority regarding the data, such as using personal data for its own purposes, or giving third parties access to the data without the controller's authority?[98] In these situations, it would seem reasonable to consider that the provider has thereby become not just a processor, but also a controller of the data, and accordingly should be liable as such.[99] Given the increasing integration of cloud services, a provider might also permit another provider to access stored user

---

[93] Making the fair assumption that the user has expressly or impliedly authorized provider access for such purposes. All providers surveyed in Chapter 3 that mentioned the issue stated that they would disclose stored user data on a valid court order, which presupposes they can access such data. See Chapter 3, Section 3.2.2.

[94] Dropbox, 'How Secure Is Dropbox?', available at <https://www.dropbox.com/help/27/en> (accessed 18 March 2013).

[95] A cloud provider's Acceptable Use Policy may entitle it to ban or remove certain kinds of data, but it cannot realistically control what data its users store with it, unless and until it has knowledge, or perhaps notice, that a user has stored unacceptable data. Certain material may now, upon upload to video sharing sites such as YouTube, be vetted for copyright breaches through automated checking against reference files: YouTube LLC, 'Audio ID and Video ID', available at <http://www.youtube.com/t/contentid> (accessed 18 March 2013). However, currently it is not technologically possible to conduct similar automatic checks for all possible types of 'personal data', particularly given the uncertainties with the definition and the possibility of indirect identifiers, as discussed in Chapter 7.

[96] However, with services such as social networking sites, it may be likelier if not inevitable that the provider should know that stored data were personal data.

[97] Some providers reserve monitoring rights, see Chapter 3, Section 3.2.5.

[98] See n. 93 regarding standard clauses purporting to authorize service providers to disclose user data to third parties. Leaving aside the question of whether this type of standard term will bind users, particularly consumers, it should also be considered whether, whatever the terms say, the sharing or disclosure is lawful under data protection laws in cases where the stored and disclosed 'personal data' relate, not to the user, but to others.

[99] For a well-known example of a processor that was considered to have arrogated to itself the role of controller, see A29WP, *Opinion 10/2006 on the Processing of Personal Data by the Society for Worldwide*

data. Where such access is given by the provider, rather than through the user's own actions, and the user has not authorized that access or its extent, the provider would become a controller through enabling that unauthorized access.[100] However, absent any 'line-crossing' behaviour by the provider, and assuming it has put in place appropriate measures to prevent unauthorized access, there seems no reason to impose liabilities upon it as controller or processor.

Use or further processing of stored personal data for the provider's own purposes may be more likely with certain kinds of SaaS (rather than with PaaS or IaaS), such as social networking or other consumer-focused services, which by their nature involve the storage of personal data in unencrypted, widely accessible form, and where re-identification of data subjects may be easier.[101] This is likely to increase the provider's, and third parties', ability to access intelligible stored personal data, and therefore increase risks of unauthorized or, indeed, authorized processing.[102] It may, therefore, be justifiable to treat such SaaS providers differently, even as controllers, and issues arising in that context need further consideration.[103] Nevertheless, this does not detract from arguments

Interbank Financial Telecommunication (SWIFT), WP 128 (2006). Belgian financial messaging service provider SWIFT, which facilitates transactions between financial institutions, had decided, without informing its member institutions, to comply with US subpoenas allowing the US Department of the Treasury to view or search data held in SWIFT's US data centre. SWIFT was considered to have become a 'controller' as it had exceeded its authority as 'processor': 'Even if it was assumed for a moment that SWIFT acted as "processor", SWIFT has taken on specific responsibilities which go beyond the set of instructions and duties incumbent on a processor and cannot be considered compatible with its claim to be just a "processor".' Factors included: 'SWIFT management has the power to take critical decisions with respect to the processing, such as the security standard and the location of its operating centres ... Indeed, the control mechanisms obtained and operated by SWIFT affected the purpose and scope of the transfer of data to the UST [US Department of the Treasury]. These actions exceed by far the normal capacities of a data processor in view of its supposed absence of autonomy with respect to the instructions of the data controller.'

[100] Similarly if an organization adds a third-party script to the source code of its own website, intending to use or offer visitors extra functionality promised by the script, such as ads or an icon allowing visitors to 'Like' the site on another social networking site. Some scripts may do more than the organization expected, surreptitiously collecting personal data on visitors. Should the organization be held responsible for verifying, before installation, exactly what personal data the script accesses or uses, and what the third party will do with such data? The inclusion of the Facebook 'Like' script on the UK National Health Service Direct's website enabled Facebook to track which pages on that site were viewed by Facebook users: Garlik, 'NHS.uk Allowing Google, Facebook, and Others to Track You' (*Garlik*, 23 November 2010), <http://www.garlik.com/blog/?p=405>. A study unmasked the secret collection of personal data, including the 'ushering in' of fourth- or fifth-party data collectors, by certain advertising network scripts, unbeknown to websites inserting the script—Krux, 'Krux Cross-Industry Study (2010)', updated in 2012 (*Krux*, 12 June 2012), <http://www.krux.com/pro/broadcasts/krux_research/CIS2012> (both accessed 18 March 2013).

[101] The more difficult it is to identify individuals in data, for example because of technical measures to prevent re-identification, the more likely that the data will be considered 'anonymous', and conversely easy re-identification means data are more likely to be 'personal data'. See Chapter 7. Some services even require users to register with 'real names'.

[102] Use of personal data for purposes such as running advertisements based on the text of stored emails or social networking profiles is often integral to such providers' business model and may be authorized explicitly by the ToS. However, the cloud user's consent to the provider's processing for such further purposes will not necessarily stop the provider from being a controller. There are separate, difficult, issues regarding the extent to which users are bound by providers' standard terms, and the extent to which 'pre-ticked' consent constitutes the cloud user's freely given, specific, and unambiguous consent to such use, especially where users are consumers with little awareness of security and data protection risks. See Chapter 7, n. 109; *The Future of Privacy* (n. 11) 17; A29WP, *Opinion 2/2010 on Online Behavioural Advertising, WP 171* (2010); and Edgar A Whitley and Nadja Kanellopoulou, *Privacy and Informed Consent in Online Interactions: Evidence from Expert Focus Groups* (EnCoRe, 2010).

[103] Including possibly imposing duties on such providers, and certainly educating users and raising awareness of the risks. See further the references in n. 102.

regarding what should be the status of infrastructure providers, such as utility storage providers, who are more akin to passive hosts.

Another issue arises from a provider's ability, through its physical control of storage hardware and software, to compromise data integrity. For example, it may inadvertently delete data through a systems fault. Does that apparent 'control' make it a 'processor'? Here, there seems more reason to require providers to take measures to safeguard data integrity. Many providers take such measures in practice, for example through data replication. However, at least with utility storage, it makes more sense for users to remain primarily accountable for data. Even with unencrypted data, providers cannot know whether information which their users choose to store are personal data requiring further protective measures, unless they access and check every user's data. This seems infeasible, and even if practicable, providers might not wish to access such data. If the risk of providers compromising or losing data is a concern, arguably it is the user who should be made clearly responsible for considering and addressing the risk, for example by encrypting data first, and backing up to other storage providers.[104]

Finally, we consider the theoretical ability of providers to monitor processing operations conducted on personal data by users. Again, arguably a provider who has implemented appropriate measures to prevent unauthorized monitoring should not be considered a controller. Recall the analogy with organizations that rent out computers for others to use. Under data protection laws, computer rental companies are not deemed automatically to be 'processors' merely because they supply IT resources for hire. However, like cloud providers, they may have the technical ability to monitor processing performed by users via their computers, or to interfere with stored data. Rental companies who actually spied on users[105] would become controllers, and responsible for those activities under applicable law. Nevertheless, this does not automatically make all computer rental companies 'processors'. Why should infrastructure cloud providers be treated differently? If all infrastructure providers must be considered as processors simply because personal data are processed using their equipment, so too should computer rental companies, but they are not.

Regarding all of the above, what measures would be required to avoid 'processor' status? We suggest that explicit adoption of accepted industry standards and best practices as a clear 'tipping point' would be appropriate. Cloud actors should be encouraged to develop appropriate standards and best practices on technical and other measures.[106] Alternatively, or in addition, further regulatory guidance would assist.

Discovering whether a provider has accessed or given others access to the user's stored personal data without authority, or otherwise processed the data unlawfully, is a difficulty not unique to cloud. In practice, regulators or data subjects may not know about unlawful processing or data security breaches absent technical means to detect them, and only find out if and when informed by the entity concerned.[107] This issue should, however, be addressed

---

[104] Increasingly, services are being offered to assist users to use cloud services, including encryption and key management. See for example Rob Mason, 'Data Security and the Nasuni Filer—Just the Facts' (*Nasuni Blog*, 15 March 2010), <http://www.nasuni.com/news/nasuni-blog/data-security-and-the-nasuni-filer-just-the-facts> (accessed 18 March 2013).

[105] As in n. 92.

[106] Bodies such as the Cloud Security Alliance and Cloud Industry Forum are indeed attempting to do so, and one strand of the EU cloud strategy is to facilitate technical standardization of cloud security, particularly through the European Telecommunications Standards Institute (ETSI) *Cloud Standards Coordination* (Cloud Standards Coordination meeting, 4–5 December 2012).

[107] An entity suffering a data security breach may decide to keep the breach secret, even if it is legally obliged to notify the breach under data breach notification laws (existing in most US states, and imposed on EU telecommunications providers since 2011). This may be a deliberate commercial

by legislating for greater transparency, auditing and/or monitoring, and accountability.[108] The practical difficulty of detecting unlawful processing should not detract from arguments in favour of infrastructure providers having neither processor nor controller status. Indeed, with cloud computing it may be easier to develop privacy-enhancing technologies to help detect and perhaps even notify breaches, by logging data accesses and usage against set policies and flagging up unauthorized, or possibly authorized, uses for checking.[109]

In summary, we argue that infrastructure providers, notably utility providers of processing power with no persistent data storage, and utility storage providers who provide no substantive user applications beyond storage management, merely provide resources to cloud users. Given such providers' lack of knowledge as to the nature of data stored, and/or lack of practical ability to access such data, we suggest they should not be treated even as 'processors', provided they have taken appropriate measures, unless and until they 'cross the line'. It seems to make more sense that users should be responsible and accountable end-to-end for the data they choose to store in-cloud. However, the position of certain SaaS providers who are likely to store known personal data, particularly consumer-targeted services, is different; their regulatory characterization needs careful consideration. Greater transparency by cloud providers, whether IaaS, PaaS, or SaaS, as to their internal measures, including proactive disclosure of their detailed policies and practices, would help to inform the debate.

5. Three Proposals for Reform

We have three main proposals to address the unsatisfactory allocation of responsibility for personal data in cloud computing environments, and to enable data protection laws to cater for cloud computing and other technological developments in a more clear and balanced way.

First, the binary distinction between controllers and processors is unsuitable for a cloud computing environment and should be abolished, to be replaced by a principle of end-to-end accountability. Second, we suggest that infrastructure providers should be treated as neutral intermediaries under the EU Electronic Commerce Directive ('ECD'), unless and until they have the requisite knowledge and control over data (in the form of access to data, at least for more than incidental purposes). Third, the instructions requirement should be replaced by a more technology-neutral formulation regarding purpose limitation.

Even before the current interest in cloud computing, it was clear that a simple binary controller/processor approach cannot accommodate the practical realities of modern business,[110] and may even be counterproductive.[111] The position is complicated further by the

---

decision because notification may prejudice its financial position (eg see Ponemon Institute LLC's annual studies on 'Cost of a Data Breach'). Absent such a notification, it may be difficult if not impossible for others to know that the breach occurred.

[108] The draft Regulation attempts to do this, but in a detailed and prescriptive way.

[109] See Siani Pearson and Andrew Charlesworth, 'Accountability as a Way Forward for Privacy Protection in the Cloud' in *First International Conference, CloudCom 2009, Beijing, China, December 1–4, 2009, Proceedings* (Berlin: Springer, 2009).

[110] As exemplified by the SWIFT incident (n. 99). See also ICC (n. 10).

[111] For example, the submission to the 2009 consultation by International Pharmaceutical Privacy Consortium, 'Comments in Response to the Consultation on the Legal Framework for the Fundamental Right to Protection of Personal Data' (23 December 2009) notes: 'A great deal of time and effort is spent trying to determine the appropriate categorization of the parties involved in a data processing activity, and it is reasonable to question whether this time might be better spent actually ensuring that appropriate data privacy and security safeguards are in place.'

increased potential in cloud for chains of providers and sub-providers, and possibly other actors such as physical infrastructure providers or communications providers. All this means that it is often not clear which parties determine, and to what extent, the 'means' of processing personal data in the cloud.

Arguably, WP196 was doomed to fail in its attempt to be 'cloud-friendly' while applying to cloud a traditional analysis of controller/processor obligations in conventional outsourcing arrangements. Indeed, we could perhaps go further and argue that the concepts of 'controller' and 'processor' in the DPD were already fundamentally inappropriate for many 'conventional' outsourcing deals. For some major outsourcing players, their strict stance of being 'mere processors' may not reflect the degree to which control is delegated to them in complex deals, especially in business process outsourcing, but also some IT outsourcing. The pressure to 'add value' beyond simple delegation of specific processing activities has long meant that many outsourcing customers expect providers to display a high degree of autonomy, at least in terms of processing 'means'. Providers have been keen to accommodate them, but challenging this at a regulatory level would have uncovered fundamental flaws in core concepts and rules embedded in the DPD.

For the benefit of all, including data subjects, it is desirable that legislators should clarify the respective actors' responsibilities in relation to personal data in the cloud, as well as in other complex 'controller vs processor' situations. The definitions of 'controller' and 'processor' need updating to allow a more nuanced and flexible approach. How could this be done? Eliminating the simplistic binary controller versus processor distinction would be one option.[112] However, we advocate a more flexible approach to data protection responsibilities, which may impose primary liability on one party,[113] but assign different degrees of responsibility and liability to other actors in proportion to the individual parts they play in the processing chain.[114] This would allow, perhaps even encourage, the parties involved to consider and allocate risks and responsibilities contractually. It would also promote responsibility throughout the personal data processing life cycle[115] involving a continuum or spectrum of parties, only some of whom may be

---

[112] See, for example, EPOF (n. 6), 9: 'Probably the only practical approach is to make any party processing personal data liable for compliance with the rules, but only to the extent necessary to safeguard personal information in respect to a particular processing operation, and to the extent of that person's legal right to control the data.'
   See also the submissions to the 2009 Consultation by International Chamber of Commerce: *ICC Response to the European Commission Consultation on the Legal Framework for the Fundamental Right to Protection of Personal Data* (ICC Commission on E-Business, IT and Telecoms, December 2009) (4) and Vodafone, *The Future Direction of EU Data Protection and Privacy Regulation* (Executive Summary, 30 December 2009).
   A 2010 report for the Council of Europe on lacunae in Convention 108 arising from new technologies noted that, historically, laws regarding the protection of personal data focused on the twin concepts of personal data and 'controller', but that both concepts seem to have now become both too vague and narrow to lead to effective regulation. The report also recommended that the controller/processor definitions and distinction be revisited. Jean-Marc Dinant, *Rapport sur les lacunes de la Convention n° 108 pour la protection des personnes à l'égard du traitement automatisé des données à caractère personnel face aux développements technologiques, Partie I T-PD-BUR (2010) 09 (I) FINAL* (Council of Europe). See also Jean-Marc Dinant and others, *Partie II T-PD-BUR(2010)09 (II) FINAL* (Council of Europe 2010) 17–18.

[113] For example, see Alcatel-Lucent, *The European Commission's Consultation on the Legal Framework for the Fundamental Right to Protection of Personal Data* (Alcatel-Lucent Contribution, Executive Summary, December 2009) (5): 'having a responsible party who will guarantee end-to-end protection for users, and who has sufficient financially backing (e.g., insurance) to meet its responsibilities'.

[114] Including reflecting the extent of each actor's actual ability and right to control the relevant processing operation.

[115] As observed in ICO, *The Information Commissioner's Response to the European Commission's Consultation on the Legal Framework for the Fundamental Right to Protection of Personal Data* (2010).

considered to be processing personal data from beginning to end, with varying degrees of data protection obligations and liabilities. A more nuanced approach to 'controller' and 'processor' roles would also accord with the principle of accountability,[116] whose introduction as a fundamental data protection principle is increasingly being advocated in the EU[117] and elsewhere.[118] Such an approach would help achieve a more appropriate balance between commercial and privacy considerations in light of the complexity of modern-day relationships, as typified by the potential for layers of cloud providers, and also the increasing integration of supporting services in cloud. Educating both cloud providers and potential cloud users, of whatever variety, and raising their awareness, would be important should accountability be introduced into law.

The second proposal is that, for those providers who do not process personal data in a meaningful sense, data protection law ought to recognize an intermediary role, which is neither controller nor processor, analogous to that of 'host' or 'mere conduit' under the ECD. An obvious example would be a cloud provider that merely stores data passively on behalf of its customers, or that provides infrastructure to enable its customers, including other cloud service providers, to operate on data. Such a provider may not know whether the information stored or operated on is personal data, or, regardless of knowledge as to the nature of the data, it may have no reasonable means of access to the stored information. This may be because secure encryption has been applied to the data, or because, for example, the provider's systems have been designed to prevent access to users' stored data in any circumstances. Such providers should be entitled to ECD-style 'defences' in relation to the processing of personal data, unless and until they obtain the requisite knowledge and/or access.

Although current data protection laws generally treat cloud providers as 'processors' of personal data processed using their services, we argue that these laws are inappropriate for self-service infrastructure services, where providers rent out the use of computing resources rather than actively processing data for users. In practice, the result may be either that users fail to comply with laws, taking the risk of regulatory action or liability, or that providers agree to commit to contractual obligations which they may not be able to meet if the user chooses to insist on its strict contractual rights.

Many different types of cloud providers exist. The types of service they provide and the types of customers they service[119] may not always be clear-cut, but there does seem to be a qualitative difference between 'pure' infrastructure providers, such as providers of processing power or utility storage, which serve more as neutral intermediaries, and

---

[116] At least in the sense used in the Canadian Personal Information Protection and Electronic Documents Act 2000 ('PIPEDA'). Views differ on what 'accountability' involves. A29WP, *Opinion 1/2010 on the Principle of Accountability, WP 173* (2010) seems to consider that 'accountability' involves taking measures to enable compliance with the data protection requirements and being able to demonstrate that that has been done. In contrast, the broader PIPEDA approach treats accountability as end-to-end responsibility on the part of the controller; for instance, there is no prohibition on transfer of personal data abroad, but the controller remains accountable for the data wherever it is held: PIPEDA, Sch. 1, 4.1.3. In this chapter, when we refer to accountability, we generally mean the PIPEDA approach. Accountability and the respective positions of the different actors are discussed in more detail in Chapter 14, Section 2.3.

[117] WP173 and draft DP Regulation.

[118] For example, Organization for Economic Cooperation and Development, *OECD Guidelines on the Protection of Privacy and Transborder Flows of Personal Data* (1980) [14]; Asia–Pacific Economic Cooperation, *APEC Privacy Framework* (APEC Secretariat, 2005) Pt 9; International Conference of Data Protection and Privacy Commissioners, *Joint Proposal for a Draft of International Standards on the Protection of Privacy with Regard to the Processing of Personal Data (The Madrid Resolution)* (2009); WP173 (n. 116); Alcatel-Lucent (n. 113).

[119] See further Chapter 1.

other kinds of cloud providers such as consumer-oriented Web 2.0 services. Arguably infrastructure providers are not even 'processors', particularly where they are used only for processing power. It is more difficult to argue this where the service consists of or includes persistent storage of data, in other words where the provider acts as a data host. However, often providers will not know the nature of data stored with them, so it seems problematic that their status should depend on what data their customers decide to store, and how well the customer encrypts or anonymizes the data.[120]

What requirements or exemptions should apply to such providers? The ECD was intended to foster the development within the EU of electronic commerce and 'information society services',[121] meaning[122] 'any service normally provided for remuneration, at a distance, by means of electronic equipment for the processing (including digital compression) and storage of data, and at the individual request of a recipient of a service'. It included provisions to harmonize liability defences for service providers which act as intermediaries, because it was felt that differences in intermediary liability across different Member States were impairing the development of cross-border services and distorting competition within the EU.[123]

Many cloud services are clearly 'information society services' as defined. However, the ECD expressly[124] does not apply to questions relating to information society services covered by the DPD and the E-Privacy Directive.[125] Such application was considered unnecessary as those Directives were thought to provide a complete regime for the protection of individuals with regard to processing of personal data.[126] We suggest that this assumption is no longer valid. The DPD considerably pre-dated the rise of cloud computing. Its drafters did not anticipate the current complexities and multitude of actors who could be involved in processing personal data. The ECD makes certain immunities from liability available to intermediary service providers who provide 'mere conduit', 'caching', and 'hosting' information society services, on the basis that they have no knowledge or control of the content transmitted or stored.[127]

Take the example of Internet cafes, pubs, or public libraries which permit their customers or users to use their computing and Internet connectivity resources on a shared basis. Such cafes, pubs, or libraries may be providing communications services, but they are clearly not 'processors' of any personal data processed by their customers using their services; they are more akin to 'mere conduits' under the ECD. So, too, there seems no good reason why cloud providers who are neutral intermediaries,[128] akin to hosting or caching providers under the ECD, should not benefit from similar liability defences, while also benefiting from a prohibition on having a general duty to monitor actively any data transmitted or stored by them.[129] Such an approach would dovetail well with

---

[120] The provider could set up its service such that it never has access to the data. Examples include Mozy and Firefox Sync, formerly Mozilla Weave, mentioned at n. 13 in Chapter 2, where all information is automatically encrypted on the user's computer before upload.

[121] Defined by reference to the definition in Directive 98/34/EC of the European Parliament and of the Council of 22 June 1998 laying down a procedure for the provision of information in the field of technical standards and regulations and of rules on information society services, OJ L204/37, 21.7.1998.

[122] According to recital 17 ECD.   [123] Recital 40 ECD.   [124] Art. 5(b) ECD.

[125] Directive 2002/58/EC of the European Parliament and of the Council of 12 July 2002 concerning the processing of personal data and the protection of privacy in the electronic communications sector, OJ L 201/37, 31.07.2002.

[126] See recital 14 ECD.

[127] Ian Walden, 'Mine Host Is Searching for a "Neutrality" Principle!' (2010) 26 *Computer Law and Security Report* 203.

[128] In particular, those providing processing power or acting as passive hosts for storing data.

[129] Article 15 ECD.

the previous discussion, whereby non-processor or even processor status would be lost, and controller status and associated liability would be triggered, if the provider–intermediary does, or allows a third party to do, something inappropriate to, or with, stored personal data.

What should be the conditions for immunity, and the circumstances triggering its loss in relation to personal data processing? Under the ECD,[130] the immunity, at least for 'mere conduit' and caching services,[131] is based in part on the service provider having 'neither knowledge of nor control over the information which is transmitted or stored'. In order to benefit from the liability limitation, a hosting service provider must, upon obtaining actual knowledge or awareness of illegal activities, 'act expeditiously to remove or to disable access to the information concerned' bearing in mind the balance with freedom of expression.[132] The liability exemption of hosting providers is conditioned on the provider not having 'actual knowledge of illegal activity or information' and, as regards claims for damages, not being aware of 'facts or circumstances from which the illegal activity or information is apparent', and on the provider, upon obtaining such knowledge or awareness, acting 'expeditiously to remove or to disable access to the information'.[133]

We propose that the basis for the immunity of intermediaries should similarly be knowledge and control. A cloud provider whose services are used to process data on behalf of a consumer or business customer, but who does not know that the data are 'personal data', or who knows the data's status but has no access to the data processed, should not be a 'processor' for DPD purposes because a processor, by definition, 'processes personal data'. Thus such a provider should not be subject to any data protection obligations. Any such exemptions should of course be subject to similar provisions as to the loss of immunity, and corresponding imposition of data protection obligations as a controller or processor, should the provider acquire the relevant knowledge and/or access. If it had the requisite knowledge and control, it would be treated as a processor. If, having such knowledge and control, it used or disclosed personal data for unauthorized purposes, then it would be treated as a controller.

Our third, and final, recommendation is that the instructions requirement should be abolished. Controllers should be required to restrict processors' or resource providers' unauthorized use or disclosure of personal data processed using their resources, either by contractual restrictions, with provider liability for breach, and/or through user encryption or other user measures to exclude provider access to intelligible personal data.

Cloud computing providers and users may also benefit from greater openness regarding security measures and practices, and the development of appropriate industry standards and best practices on issues such as logging, auditing, and access to cloud users' data. Such measures may help to provide a clear boundary between our proposed intermediary status and a 'processor' or 'controller' status.

---

[130] Recital 42.

[131] It is our view that it is recital 46 of the ECD which ought to apply to cloud computing storage as 'hosting', in other words expeditious action upon actual knowledge or awareness, rather than control or knowledge alone, as applied under recital 42 ECD to 'mere conduit' and 'caching'. See Opinion of Advocate General Jääskinen, 9 December 2010, Case C-324/09 *L'Oréal SA et al. v eBay International AG et al. (Reference for a preliminary ruling from the High Court of Justice of England and Wales, Chancery Division (United Kingdom))*, [138]–[142]. We argue that, in many cases, an infrastructure service provider does indeed confine 'itself to providing that service neutrally by a merely technical and automatic processing of the data provided by its customers' even if Art. 14 ECD applies to it, within [111]–[113] of Case C-324/09 *L'Oréal SA et al. v eBay International AG et al.* [2011] IP & T 819, [2011] RPC 777, [2011] ETMR 52.

[132] Recital 46 ECD.   [133] Art. 14(1) ECD, and *eBay* (n. 131).

9

Which Law(s) Apply to Personal Data in Clouds?

W Kuan Hon, Julia Hörnle, and Christopher Millard

1. Introduction

National laws based on the EU Data Protection Directive (DPD) may apply to non-European Economic Area (EEA) entities with significant consequences for providers and users of cloud computing services. An entity may, for example, be required to obtain data subjects' consent or find some other justification to transfer data 'back' outside the EEA from an EEA data centre. This may be the case even when the data were initially 'imported' to the EEA data centre from outside the EEA, and relate only to non-EEA persons. Whether EU law can be enforced against a non-EEA entity in practice is a different issue.

This chapter considers the DPD's applicability to cloud computing actors, and the jurisdiction of data protection authorities to regulate them. In particular, when do non-EEA cloud users or cloud providers become subject to EU data protection law through using EEA data centres or EEA cloud providers, or through saving cookies and so on on equipment of EEA residents, under Article 4 DPD? We argue that reform of data protection law is required to address the current uncertainties concerning the boundary between an entity falling within the jurisdiction of EU data protection law, and its not being so regulated.

2. Jurisdiction, Applicable Law, and Data Protection Law

The DPD envisaged remote data processing (eg, recital 20), where the processor is established in a 'third country' (outside the EEA). Its jurisdictional provisions were intended to ensure application of data protection obligations to personal data connected with the EEA, even if processed in third countries by non-EEA established controllers.[1]

DPD Articles 4 and 17(3) deal with applicable law and jurisdictional reach (the latter concerning mere processors). The meaning of these provisions is opaque, partly because different language versions differ, and partly because Member States could not agree on one rule of competence, such as the country of origin rule in Article 3 Electronic Commerce Directive (ECD).[2] The main obstacle is that Member States' data protection rules are not harmonized; their national law implementations of the DPD differ. This means that the provisions on applicable law and jurisdiction are subject to interpretation, and the DPD's jurisdictional scope is unclear. Review and simplification of jurisdictional grounds are, therefore, needed. This is one aim of the current proposals to update EU data protection laws, in particular the proposed General Data Protection Regulation (the draft Regulation).

[1] A29WP, *Opinion 8/2010 on Applicable Law*, WP179 (2010) (WP179).
[2] Directive 2000/31/EC of the European Parliament and of the Council of 8 June 2000 on certain legal aspects of information society services, in particular electronic commerce, in the Internal Market OJ L 178/1, 17.7.2000.

Although cloud computing involves remote data processing, the controller's and processor's respective activities are *not* removed from the DPD's scope merely because data are 'somewhere in the cloud', processed physically in one or more other jurisdictions. The location of data, or of physical operations on data, is not determinative.[3] The citizenship, residence, or domicile of persons to whom data relate is also immaterial.[4] However, the means of processing (which to an extent may overlap with processing location) are relevant in Article 4(1)(c), discussed below.

2.1 The Article 4 grounds

The central provisions are in Article 4, which contains three grounds based on which the European data protection regime becomes applicable to acts of processing personal data: establishment, public international law, and use of equipment within the jurisdiction. We will discuss each in turn.[5]

In cloud computing, these grounds determine to what extent a cloud user or provider, even if not incorporated, resident, or headquartered in an EEA Member State, may become subject to obligations under EU data protection law due to:

1. having a subsidiary, branch or agent, or even just a data centre, in the EEA (the establishment ground); or

2. making use of a data centre, or other equipment, located in the EEA (the equipment ground).

A case referred to the European Court of Justice (ECJ)[6] may provide definitive rulings on these and related issues, but a decision is unlikely before the end of 2013.

2.1.1 Establishment

Under Article 4(1)(a), each EEA Member State must apply the DPD as implemented in that Member State if 'the processing is carried out in the context of the activities of an establishment of the controller on the territory of the Member State', that is if the controller has an establishment there and processes personal data 'in the context of the activities of that establishment'.

If an EEA Member State's data protection law applies to a controller on this 'establishment' ground, the law's requirements will apply to *all* personal data processed 'in the context of the activities' of that establishment, wherever in the world the processing takes place,[7] including through using cloud computing. If it applies on the equipment ground, the controller must comply with the relevant data protection law for all processing of the personal data concerned, again even if it occurs outside the EEA.

---

[3] See also LA Bygrave 'Determining Applicable Law Pursuant to European Data Protection Legislation' in J Hörnle and I Walden *Ecommerce Law and Practice in Europe* (Cambridge: Woodhead Publishing, 2001), 1–11, 4; however, the location of equipment or means of processing is relevant (see Section 2.3 below).

[4] WP179; U Wuermeling, *Handelshemmnis Datenschutz* (Cologne: Carl Heymanns Verlag, 2000), 76.

[5] For a detailed discussion of Art. 4, see Lokke Moerel, 'Back to Basics: When Does EU Data Protection Law Apply?' (2011) 1(2) *International Data Privacy Law* 92.

[6] Case C-131/12 *Google Spain, SL, Google Inc. v Agencia Española de Protección de Datos, Mario Costeja González*, Official Journal C 165, 09/06/2012 P. 0011–0012.

[7] For example in the incident relating to Belgian entity SWIFT—A29WP, *Opinion 10/2006 on the Processing of Personal Data by the Society for Worldwide Interbank Financial Telecommunication (SWIFT)*, WP 128 (2006). However, the final decision of the Belgian authority was that Belgian law did not apply on US territory—Belgian Privacy Commission, Decision of 9 December 2008, Control and recommendation procedure initiated with respect to the company SWIFT scrl, [167].

If a controller is 'established' in more than one EEA Member State, it may have to comply with laws applicable in these different Member States: 'when the same controller is established on the territory of several Member States, he must take the necessary measures to ensure that each of these establishments complies with the obligations laid down by the national law applicable'.[8] This provision on establishments in several Member States is tautological—it attempts to determine which law is applicable by referring to the 'national law applicable'. Hence, it probably does not achieve any more than saying that, for controllers with establishments in different Member States, more than one set of national data protection laws may apply.

Article 4(1)(a) lays down a two-stage test for applicable law: does the controller have an 'establishment' on the territory of an EU Member State; and does it process personal data in the context of activities of that establishment? If the answer to both is yes, then that Member State's data protection law applies to such processing, wherever it occurs—whether outside or inside the EEA. In other words, if a controller's EEA branch or office (or other 'establishment') wishes to process personal data in the cloud 'in the context of' that branch or office's activities, when performing such processing it must satisfy the local requirements of the EEA country where the branch or office is established, wherever the processing occurs. For example, a cloud customer based in London, using a Brazilian cloud provider with servers in Portugal to process personal data, must comply with the UK Data Protection Act (not Brazilian or Portuguese laws). The UK Act would equally apply if the London office processed the data using a Belgian cloud provider with servers in France.

The A29WP's opinion on applicable law (WP179)[9] considers that the notion of 'establishment' under the DPD should be guided by the jurisprudence of the ECJ regarding freedom to provide services and freedom of establishment under Article 50, Treaty on the Functioning of the European Union (TFEU). The ECJ has clarified that 'establishment' requires at a minimum a staffed office with a degree of permanence and stability: 'both human and technical resources necessary for the provision of particular services are permanently available'.[10] Recital 19 DPD mirrors this: 'implies the effective and real exercise of activity through stable arrangements' and the 'legal form of such an establishment (. . .) is not the determining factor'.

While an EEA branch office is clearly an 'establishment', technical equipment such as a server in a Member State would seemingly not constitute a 'virtual' establishment.[11] However, *using* the server may trigger that Member State's data protection law under Article 4(1)(c), discussed below. A German court has held that German-established content delivery networks used by Facebook were not 'establishments' of Facebook.[12]

2.1.2 *In the context of activities*

More opaque than the notion of establishment is the phrase 'in the context of the activities of an establishment of a controller'. The English language version ('context') appears to be different to some of the other language versions of the DPD, for example German ('*Rahmen*'/framework) or French ('*cadre*'/framework).

---

    [8] Article 4(1)(a), second sentence.   [9] WP179 (n. 1), 11.
    [10] Case C-168/84 *Bergholz* ECR [1985] 2251 [14]; Case C-390/96 *Lease Plan Luxembourg* ECR [1998] I-2553.
    [11] WP179, text to fn. 19: 'A server or a computer is not likely to qualify as an establishment as it is simply a technical facility or instrument for the processing of information.'
    [12] See n. 16 and accompanying text.

WP179[13] states that three factors should be considered:[14] the degree of involvement of the establishment(s) in the activities in the context of which personal data are processed; the nature of the activities as a secondary consideration; and the goal of ensuring effective data protection. It states that a 'who is doing what' test should be applied, in that the test requires determining who carries out the relevant activities and whether there is data processing in the context of these activities. The involvement of the establishment in these activities is the main factor.[15]

A German court considered data protection jurisdiction in two cases involving social networking service Facebook.[16] The Schleswig-Holstein data protection authority had ordered that Facebook's 'real names' policy of blocking the accounts of users who had registered using false personal data, or pseudonyms, was against German data protection law, which provides a right to pseudonymous or anonymous use. On Facebook's appeal, the court held that the choice of law clause in contracts between Facebook Ireland and German users did not affect whether German data protection law applied, and based on German data protection law and Article 4 DPD, Irish, not German, data protection law applied, so the authority was not competent to issue its order. Interpreting German legislation, which omitted reference to context of activities, so as to be consistent with Article 4, the court emphasized that it was not sufficient that a controller had an establishment in a Member State. To apply that Member State's laws, the processing must occur within the framework of activities of that establishment:[17] exactly the point we made above. The activities of Facebook's German subsidiary were limited to advertising and marketing, and no personal data of German users were processed in Germany, so no such personal data were processed in the context of activities of the German establishment. Article 4(1)(a) applied because Facebook's Irish subsidiary, with a staffed office, was its only establishment in Europe that was a controller[18] with responsibility for personal data collected from non-US users, so Article 4(1)(c) (equipment/means) was inapplicable. The court also confirmed that the physical location of data and servers processing the data, which seemed to be the US, was irrelevant to applicable law under Article 4, and that content delivery networks used in Germany were not 'establishments'. On appeal the German Data Protection Authority had argued that Facebook Ireland also was not a relevant establishment as all decisions and policies concerning data protection are made by Facebook Inc. in the US. The Appeal Court did not accept this argument and held that all that is required is an 'establishment'.[19] In contrast the Administrative Court in Berlin found in a decision that it has jurisdiction to rule on the standard terms and privacy policy used by Apple (also headquartered in Ireland).[20] The Berlin Court referred to the Jurisdiction

---

[13] N. 9.   [14] WP179 (n. 9), 14.   [15] WP179, 30.

[16] *Facebook Ireland, Facebook Inc. v Unabhängiges Landeszentrum für Datenschutz Schleswig-Holstein,* Az 8B 60/12, Judgment of 14 February 2013 (Case against Facebook Ireland) and Az B8 61/12, Judgment of 14 February 2013 (Case against Facebook Inc.). See <https://www.datenschutzzentrum.de/facebook/Facebook-Inc-vs-ULD-Beschluss.pdf> and <https://www.datenschutzzentrum.de/facebook/Facebook-Ireland-vs-ULD-Beschluss.pdf>.

This has now been confirmed by the Administrative Appeal Court of Schleswig Holstein in a judgment on 24 April 2013 in Az 4 MB 10/13, 4 MB 11/13, see <https://www.datenschutzzentrum.de/facebook/20130422-ovg-beschluss-facebook-inc.pdf.>

[17] The court stated further that the German implementation of Art. 4 DPD, disapplying German data protection law if a controller established in another EEA State processes personal data in Germany unless this processing is carried out *by an establishment in Germany,* was incomplete.

[18] It is unclear whether Facebook Inc. could have been a joint controller—some passages suggest it considered Facebook Ireland to be the sole controller, but later the court stated that the issue did not need deciding.

[19] Fn. 16.

[20] *VZVB v Apple,* 30 April 2013, Az 15 0 92/12 available from <http://www.vzbv.de/cps/rde/xbcr/vzbv/Urteil_des_LG_Berlin_zur_Datenschutzrichtlinie_von_Apple.pdf>.

Regulation EC/44/2001, Article 5 (3) which allows a court to assume jurisdiction at the place where the harmful event occurred. This case illustrates that the contractual (and pre-contractual) relationship are governed by different rules on jurisdiction and applicable law than the question of competence of the national data protection authority.

The *Google Italy* case illustrates the wide application by an EU court of its national data protection laws.[21] Google executives were convicted of offences for infringing Italian data protection law in connection with a video uploaded by Italian youths to Google Video showing abuse of a disabled student.[22] In the first-instance court the judge decided that Italian data protection law applied to the case, since Google had an establishment in Italy. He came to this conclusion even though data in connection with the Google Video services were not processed in Italy but on servers in the US or Ireland, the defence asserted that decisions about content were not made in Italy, and AdWord links were created based on users' choices (not by Google Italy) and those links went not to the videos but to advertisers' websites.[23] The judge found:

(a) Google Italy was the 'operative and commercial hand' of Google Inc; (b) like other Google subsidiaries, it was substantially a part of the group operating as a single unit, under the direction of Google Inc; (c) Google Italy had the possibility of linking advertising to the videos using the service Google AdWords.[24]

The conviction was overturned on appeal,[25] primarily because the appeal court considered that an Internet hosting service should not be required to filter in advance data uploaded to its services. On jurisdiction, there were two different areas involved: Italian criminal law, and data protection. The appeal court agreed with the first-instance judge that Italian criminal law was applicable because the video had effects in Italy, as it was viewable by Italian users.[26] As regards the applicability of Italian data protection law, the court considered that there was a Google 'establishment' in Italy,[27] namely the Italian-incorporated company Google Italy

---

[21] The authors are grateful to Maria Frabboni and Gaetano Dimita for their kind assistance with the meaning of key paragraphs of the first instance and appeal judgments.

[22] Tribunal of Milan, Sentenza n. 1972/2010.

[23] G Sartor and MV de Azevedo Cunha 'The Italian Google Case: Privacy, Freedom of Speech and Responsibilities of Providers for User-Generated Contents' (2010) 18(4) *International Journal of Law and Information Technology* 356–78, 363.

[24] Sartor and de Azevedo Cunha 'The Italian Google Case'.

[25] Reported by for example <http://www.reuters.com/article/2013/02/27/google-italy-privacy-idUSL6N0BRCKJ20130227>.

The judgment Sentenza 8611/12 del 21-12-2012, Corte di Appello di Milano is available at <http://www.leggioggi.it/wp-content/uploads/2013/02/sentenza-google.pdf>. The Italian prosecutor has appealed this decision to Italy's highest court, the Court of Cassation, according to one of the Google executives involved, and the case is unlikely to be heard before the date of publication of this book: <http://peterfleischer.blogspot.co.uk/2013/04/the-saga-continuesnow-to-italian.html>. However, the appeal seems to relate to whether providers should pre-screen content and seek any necessary consents, so the supreme court may or may not express any views on the jurisdiction point.

[26] Articles 8–9, Codice di Procedura Penale.

[27] Under Italy's implementation of the DPD, Codice in materia di protezione dei dati personali Decreto legislativo 30 giugno 2003 n. 196 <http://www.garanteprivacy.it/web/guest/home/docweb/-/docweb-display/docweb/1311248>, there is no reference to 'context of activities', for which reason arguably the implementation might be considered defective and the Italian courts should have interpreted the Codice in the light of the DPD, reading 'context of activities' into the wording—cf the German court in the Facebook case above. Section 5 provides (English translation at <http://www.garanteprivacy.it/web/guest/home/docweb/-/docweb-display/docweb/2427932>):

'1. This Code shall apply to the processing of personal data, including data held abroad, where the processing is performed by any entity established either in the State's territory or in a place that is under the State's sovereignty.

2. This Code shall also apply to the processing of personal data that is performed by an entity established in the territory of a country outside the European Union, where said entity makes use in connection with the processing of equipment, whether electronic or otherwise, situated in the State's territory, unless such equipment is used only for purposes of transit through the territory of the European Union. If this Code applies, the data controller shall designate a representative established in the State's territory with a view to implementing the provisions concerning processing of personal data.'

srl, which the court found performed more than mere marketing or advertising functions, as, on the evidence, it had responsibility for compliance with Italian data protection laws, and was indeed processing personal data within Article 4(1)(a). Furthermore, the court held that, in any event, the Italian subsidiary itself constituted 'equipment (electronic or otherwise)', that is 'means', located in Italy,[28] irrespective of the servers being located in the US or Google's European headquarters being in Ireland. What remains unclear is whether Google Italy was an 'establishment' in its own right or an 'establishment' of Google, Inc., although the latter seems likely given the discussion about Google Italy constituting 'means' in any event (which can only be 'means' of Google, Inc.).

The A29WP's opinion on search engines takes a similar approach.[29] This considers that processing is in the context of the activities of an EEA establishment even if the establishment does not carry out or direct any processing, and its role is limited to being responsible for relations with search engine users, selling advertisements in that jurisdiction, or complying with law enforcement requests regarding user data. This wide view of 'context' arguably risks rendering 'context' as a connecting factor meaningless. In our view, although this seems implicit from Article 4(1)(a)'s reference to an establishment 'of the controller', the notion of 'context' should be linked explicitly to the processing activities of the establishment *as* a controller who determines the purposes and means of that processing. However, if, for policy reasons, lawmakers wish the net of applicability to be as wide as the A29WP in WP148 cast it, then the reference to 'context' should be deleted altogether, given the confusion it causes.

If the A29WP's wide interpretation of 'context of activities' extends to providers with one or more establishments in the EEA, two consequences arise: EU data protection laws may apply even if no processing of personal data is conducted at the establishment, and if more than one establishment in the EEA is involved in activities such as those mentioned in WP148, the controller may be subject to several different national implementations of the DPD. For example, a multinational cloud provider may have offices in the EEA, say in Rome and Dublin. It provides cloud data storage services to businesses and consumers in the EEA, but all data processing for those services is managed and performed in the US and India. Users enter into contracts for cloud services online. The provider's EEA offices are involved in software development activities and marketing. This raises the possibility, based on WP148, that the software company must comply with both Italian and Irish data protection laws. This would be a strange result, probably unintended by the original drafters of the DPD. The applicability of two sets of laws is an extremely undesirable consequence of this interpretation of Article 4(1)(a). In cloud computing (as in the search engine scenario), the provider may well have establishments in several Member States performing ancillary or indeed core functions, so that multiple, possibly conflicting, data protection laws may apply to the same processing.

The A29WP attempts to address this problem by saying that controllers may engage in several activities and that for each activity it will be necessary to decide which establishment 'owns' this activity, before deciding on applicable law: 'their practical behaviour and interaction which should be the determining factors: what is the true role of each establishment, and which activity is taking place in the context of which establishment? Attention should be paid to the degree of involvement of each establishment, in relation to the activities in the context of which personal data are processed.'[30] While initially seemingly logical, this approach may be unworkable. Activities may overlap: service improvement, advertising, local and central marketing campaigns, profiling, and so on

---

[28] See n. 27.
[29] A29WP, *Opinion 1/2008 on Data Protection Issues Related to Search Engines, WP 148* (2008) (WP148) 10.
[30] WP179, 15.

may all involve the same data-processing acts. This is acknowledged but not solved by WP148: 'situations where the same database can be subject to different applicable laws do increasingly happen in practice.'[31]

In revising the DPD, the European Commission considered intra-EEA conflicts where establishments exist in multiple EEA states. The draft Regulation would introduce a concept of 'main establishment' which, for a controller, means 'the place of its establishment in the Union where the main decisions as to the purposes, conditions and means of the processing of personal data are taken; if no decisions as to the purposes, conditions and means of the processing of personal data are taken in the Union, the main establishment is the place where the main processing activities in the context of the activities of an establishment of a controller in the Union take place'. The 'supervisory authority of the main establishment' would supervise all processing activities in all Member States, where 'the processing of personal data takes place in the context of the activities of an establishment of a controller or a processor in the Union', thus achieving a regulatory 'one stop shop' for controllers and processors.

However, the draft Regulation, which defines territorial scope by reference to processing of personal data 'in the context of the activities of an establishment...in the Union', would perpetuate the concepts of 'establishment' and 'context of activities' and the problem of determining when processing is 'in the context' of an establishment's activities, without clarifying adequately their meaning and application. For example, could an EU data centre of the controller, whether owned by the controller or a cloud provider, be a 'main establishment'? Recital 27 does state that 'the presence and use of technical means and technologies for processing personal data or processing activities do not, in themselves, constitute such main establishment and are therefore no [sic] determining criteria for a main establishment'. However, their relevance needs further explication, particularly where no 'main decisions' are taken in the EU. In particular, are EEA data centres or EEA providers 'establishments' for this purpose? Is their processing 'in the context of' their activities as 'establishments'? The European Data Protection Supervisor has also called for clarification of the criteria for identifying the 'main establishment', particularly for groups of undertakings such as multinational corporate groups.[32]

Furthermore, new uncertainties are introduced. Are decisions 'main decisions' if relating to processing of personal data worldwide, or only in the EU? If 'main decisions' are taken outside the EU, but the controller has more than one 'establishment' in the EU, which is the 'main establishment'? What does 'the main processing activities in the context of the activities of an establishment of a controller in the Union' mean?

Within the EEA, a 'consistency mechanism' would apply where a supervisory authority intends to take measures regarding processing operations related to activities such as the offering of goods or services to residents of several Member States, or to monitoring them.[33] This should help to promote consistency across the EEA, though it is

---

[31] WP179, 15.

[32] *Opinion of the European Data Protection Supervisor on the Data Protection Reform Package* <http://www.edps.europa.eu/EDPSWEB/webdav/site/mySite/shared/Documents/Consultation/Opinions/2012/12-03-07_EDPS_Reform_package_EN.pdf> paras 101, 106–7. This opinion also points out that, in areas where specific national laws may still apply, such as in employment or health, 'there is no criterion to address national applicable law issues: the "main establishment" criteria of the Proposal only allows for determination of the way in which supervisory authorities will be involved', and clarification is needed there too—paras 102–3. Similarly, the UK Information Commissioner's Office (ICO) has expressed concerns about possible 'forum shopping' due to lack of clarity 'as to whether the "main establishment" is meant to be an objective test or to allow organisations to "choose their DPA" '. ICO, 'Proposed New EU General Data Protection Regulation: Article-by-article Analysis Paper', 12 February 2013.

[33] Draft Regulation Arts 3(1), 4(13), and 51(2); see also recitals 19, 27, 63–4, 97–8; Art. 34(5).

likely to work quickly and effectively only if the relevant data protection authorities and European Commission are resourced adequately. The financial impact statement accompanying the draft Regulation estimated that the European Commission could, without any headcount increase, implement the new mechanism, conduct adequacy assessments of third countries, and prepare implementing measures and delegated acts. The assumptions underlying this estimate are that the consistency mechanism will only be invoked five to ten times per year, there will be no more than four adequacy requests per year, and the European Commission will handle up to three implementing measures per year. These assumptions all look optimistic, as the draft Regulation would establish many circumstances where the consistency mechanism may be triggered, the number of countries adopting data protection laws (and that may apply for an adequacy finding) is growing at an accelerating rate,[34] and no fewer than 30 of the 91 Articles of the draft Regulation would 'empower' the Commission to 'adopt delegated acts' or 'make decisions'.

As at 1 March 2013, the draft opinion[35] of J-P Albrecht, the rapporteur for the European Parliament Committee chiefly responsible for scrutinizing the draft Regulation (LIBE), opposes a concept of 'main establishment' and proposes a different consistency mechanism. Albrecht would introduce a 'lead authority' as a 'single contact point' for liaison only, to coordinate supervisory proceedings in cross-border situations. The final views of LIBE and the European Parliament as a whole are not yet known, nor the final views of the Council.

2.2 International law

Under Article 4(1)(b), a Member State's data protection laws may, by virtue of international law, apply to a controller not established on that Member State's territory, for example on a ship or aircraft flying a particular Member State's flag.[36] This may be relevant to cloud. For example, data centres could be established on ships moored outside the territorial waters of any Member State. While this may seem improbable, Google has obtained a US patent for such data centres, using sea water to generate power and cool equipment.[37] Such data centres may be deployed at some point in the future, using flags of convenience for data protection law purposes.[38]

2.3 Equipment

Article 4(1)(c) provides the final basis for a Member State to apply its national data protection laws to cloud services. A Member State's data protection laws may be applied to a controller 'not established on Community territory' if the controller 'makes use of equipment, automated or otherwise, situated on the territory' of that State for the

---

[34] Graham Greenleaf, 'Global Data Privacy Laws: 89 Countries and Accelerating', Queen Mary School of Law Legal Studies Research Paper No. 98/2012 (2012), <http://papers.ssrn.com/sol3/papers.cfm?abstract_id=2000034> (accessed 9 February 2012).

[35] <http://www.europarl.europa.eu/meetdocs/2009_2014/documents/libe/pr/922/922387/922387en.pdf>.

[36] Ships could be moored in, or beyond, territorial waters. If outside EU territorial waters, EU laws may not apply, but the laws of the flag state, which could be non-EU, could apply.

[37] Larry Dignan, 'Google Wins Floating Data Center Patent' (*Between the Lines*, ZDNet 2009), <http://www.zdnet.com/blog/btl/google-wins-floating-data-center-patent/17266> (accessed 9 February 2012).

[38] Although other factors may influence server location, for example tax.

purposes of processing personal data, unless the use is only 'for the purpose of transit through' Community territory. The personal data processed need not relate to EEA individuals.

If a controller uses equipment within Article 4(1)(c) so that a Member State's law applies, the controller must appoint a representative in that State.[39] This representative's role differs from Member State to Member State. In some Member States (such as Belgium, the Netherlands, and Greece) the representative may be subject to a fine for breaches; in others, representatives have no civil or criminal liability, their role being confined to communication and legal representation. The A29WP recommends harmonizing this role to allow data subjects to exercise their rights against representatives.[40]

Prima facie there seems to be a gap in the applicability of the DPD if a controller has an establishment in a Member State, but does not perform data processing *in the context of* that establishment's activities. For example, a US cloud provider providing data mining facilities, for which it is the controller, operates an office in Poland for unrelated software development. This provider also uses equipment (data centres) in several Member States for its data mining service but it has no establishment in those other countries (assuming its use of a data centre does not result in its being treated as having an 'establishment' through the data centre or data centre provider). Arguably, the processing in the context of the data mining service is not governed by Article 4(1)(a), since the only activity of the Polish establishment is software development, not data mining. In other words, the processing is not 'in the context of' the activities of the Polish establishment. Then, it is arguable that Article 4(1)(c) does not apply since the cloud provider *is* established on the territory of a Member State, Poland.

The A29WP denies there is such a gap in Article 4, by interpreting the DPD so as to discount the unrelated establishment: 'Article 4(1)(c) will apply where the controller has an "irrelevant" establishment within the EU.'[41] In the example above, according to the A29WP the Polish establishment would not count when applying Article 4(1)(c). The laws applicable would be those of the Member States where the equipment (data centres) used are situated. It seemed implicit in the German Facebook judgments[42] that, for Article 4(1)(c) purposes, 'irrelevant' establishments would not count (ie EEA establishments that did not process personal data in the framework of activities as controller). But the court did not make a clear pronouncement on this point, as it was not relevant to the case.

We now consider what is meant by 'equipment'. This need not be something solid, tangible, or materially substantive.[43] The French[44] and German[45] versions of the DPD use the even wider expression, 'means'. According to the A29WP, this 'supports a broad interpretation of the notion of equipment', more along the lines of 'means', to include even surveys or questionnaires.[46]

If a controller makes use of computers, terminals, servers, storage hardware, or data centres within a Member State's territory for the purposes of processing personal data, that Member State's data protection law would apply.[47]

What is 'making use'? WP179 states 'it is not necessary for the controller to exercise ownership or full control over the equipment'.[48] But it is generally thought the

---

[39] Article 4(2) DPD.   [40] WP179, 23.
[41] WP179, 19—it nevertheless calls for a clarification of the issue in the revision of the DPD, WP179, 30.
[42] N. 16.   [43] Bygrave (n. 3) 7.   [44] '*Moyen*'.
[45] '*Mittel*'.   [46] WP179, 20.   [47] WP148 (n. 29) 10–11.   [48] WP179, 20.

controller must have a degree of control over the equipment/means,[49] although WP179 seemingly takes a very broad view of 'making use': 'some kind of activity of the controller and the clear intention of the controller to process personal data'.[50] The question of control is relevant to whether 'lights-out' data centres amount to equipment under Article 4(1)(c), discussed further below.

A UK example arose in *Douglas v Hello (No. 2)*.[51] There, it was argued that using an ISDN line for transmitting photographs over the Internet from New York to London was 'making use of equipment' in the UK[52] not merely for purposes of transit, with the consequence that a US photographer in New York could be a 'controller' under the Data Protection Act 1998 through sending wedding photographs digitally to London which the recipient sent on to Spain, where a magazine containing the photographs was printed. The English Court of Appeal considered there was a 'good arguable claim' worth putting before a court regarding this interpretation of the legislation, 'which to some extent may be fact sensitive'.

The 'equipment' ground has frequently been criticized as being opaque and unworkable for controllers established outside the EEA.[53] The A29WP also acknowledged that the 'equipment' connecting factor may apply even where connection with the EEA is limited, and that there is obviously need for reform. It admitted the ground has 'undesirable consequences', such as possible universal application of EU laws, but recommended retaining it for certain data protection principles (such as legitimacy and security), to prevent avoidance of EU data protection laws where relevant infrastructure exists in the EU.[54]

For controllers not established in the EEA, the draft Regulation would apply based not on concepts of equipment/means, but on whether they process personal data of EEA residents in relation to offering goods or services to such data subjects (ie akin to a directing or targeting test), or 'monitoring' their behaviour (a new way whereby non-EEA controllers could be subject to data protection regulation).[55] These new tests are discussed further below.

---

[49] U Wuermeling, *Handelshemmnis Datenschutz* (Cologne: Carl Heymanns Verlag, 2000), 78.

[50] Wuermeling (ibid).

[51] (CA) [2003] EWCA Civ 139 [45]–[47].

[52] See Data Protection Act 1998, s. 5(1)(b) implementing Article 4(1)(c) of the DPD.

[53] European Commission, *First Report on the Implementation of Directive 95/46/EC COM(2003)265 final* (2003), 17; Bygrave (n. 3), 9.

[54] WP179, 21, 32.

[55] Draft Regulation Arts 3(2), 25(2)(d), 25(3); see also recitals 20–1, 63–4, 105. Recital 21 expands on what is considered 'monitoring': 'whether individuals are tracked on the internet with data processing techniques which consist of applying a "profile" to an individual, particularly in order to take decisions concerning her or him or for analysing or predicting her or his personal preferences, behaviours and attitudes'. Such a controller must also appoint an EEA representative, in only one of the Member States concerned, rather than all of them, who interacts with EEA supervisory authorities (and is liable in the EEA for penalties (Art. 78(2)), unless the controller is established in a third country ensuring an adequate level of protection, is a small or medium-sized enterprise or public authority or body, or is 'only occasionally' offering goods or services to EEA residents (Art. 25, recitals 63–4). Such a controller (and indeed, processors) must also appoint an independent data protection officer to assist it internally on compliance, if it is in the public sector, is a large enterprise, or (whatever its size) if its 'core activities' 'involve' processing operations which 'require' 'regular and systematic monitoring' (Art. 35(1), recital 75). A large enterprise is one that has at least 250 employees. As at 1 March 2013, a few points have emerged from EU institutions' consideration of the draft Regulation. The Council wants to make clear that the 'offering' test would apply whether or not the data subject was required to make any payment, and that monitoring would only relate to behaviour taking place within the EU. LIBE would also expressly include free goods or services, if 'aimed at' EU residents, and include the monitoring of data subjects (not just their behaviour). It would remain questionable whether in practice the Regulation may be enforceable against non-EU controllers who do not have any 'establishment' in the EU.

3. Cloud Computing and the Long-arm Reach of EU Data Protection Laws

We now discuss whether customers and/or providers of cloud services could become subject to EU data protection law under Article 4, even if not established in the EEA, and even if they have no connection with the EEA except for one of the following:

1. a cloud provider which is a controller saves cookies[56] or other data, or runs scripts or applications, on the computers, mobile phones, or other equipment of its EEA-based users; or

2. a data centre located in an EEA Member State is used (perhaps with non-EEA data centres and/or data centres located in other EEA Member States) to provide cloud services.

3.1 Cookies and so on

This first scenario is not uncommon with SaaS. Suppose a non-EEA established cloud provider is the controller of personal data processed in providing a particular cloud application, such as an online calendar or social networking service. Must it comply with EU data protection laws because it processes personal data by saving a cookie (or similar) or running a script on EEA-based users' computers? Several A29WP Opinions[57] state that 'installation'[58] of a cookie by a remote, non-EEA-established service provider would constitute 'making use of equipment' in a Member State, triggering application of that State's data protection laws. Indeed, in WP179, the A29WP refers expressly to a cloud computing scenario, an online diary management system, as an example of applying Article 4(1)(c): 'if the service uses calculating facilities, runs java scripts or installs cookies' to store, retrieve and aggregate personal data, then the provider must comply with data protection laws of the Member States where users are located when the facilities are installed and used.[59] Therefore, if a cloud service stores a cookie or runs a script on the computer of an EEA-based user to process personal data, in the A29WP's opinion this would suffice to trigger application of EU data protection laws.

In such situations, the 'equipment' ground may lead to the application of 28 Member States' data protection laws if the cloud service provider is the controller and provides services to users across the EU. This is obviously a practical problem for the controller, starting with the requirement to appoint representatives in all those States. It affects all online services requiring EEA users to log in with a username and password, if the login is handled by storing cookies on the user's computer (as most such services do). It

---

[56] Cookies are text files which are 'set', that is saved onto a user's computing equipment by the user's web browser, when the user visits a webpage and the browser automatically follows instructions sent by the web server to save the cookie. Cookies may be retrieved from the user's equipment and 'read' by the website on subsequent browser visits to the site. Cookies may also be set by Javascript or other scripts run by the browser, for example after automatically downloading the script from a visited webpage. Information saved in a cookie may be used for authentication, identifying a user session, saving user's preferences or shopping cart contents, or other purposes—A Barth, Internet Engineering Task Force (IETF), 'Request for Comments 6265 HTTP State Management Mechanism' (2011) ISSN: 2070-1721.

[57] WP148 (n. 29), 10–11; A29WP, *Opinion 5/2009 on Online Social Networking WP 163* (2009), 5, and WP179, 21.

[58] Presumably 'setting'.   [59] WP179, 22.

also affects some services that do not require a login but still use cookies, such as many websites.

It is important to distinguish between cloud customers and cloud providers. The cloud customer may well be a controller of personal data (eg its own clients' personal details) which it uploads to a cloud provider's service, but not all cloud providers are controllers. Often a provider may not be a controller, but merely a processor on behalf of its business customers; indeed, in some cases, such as where its services are used only for processing power and not for persistent data storage, arguably it may be neither controller nor processor.[60]

Against this, arguably the very act of storing a cookie or running a script on the user's equipment to process personal data suffices to make the provider a controller. However, much depends on the particular circumstances, which should be analysed individually. A SaaS provider may offer a cloud application to end users which stores cookies or runs scripts to process personal data, and the provider may therefore be a controller of that data. However, in a multilayered situation where the SaaS provider layers its service on another PaaS or IaaS service, it would seem only the SaaS provider should be considered 'controller' of any personal data processed using the service. Neither the PaaS nor the IaaS provider, each being a mere infrastructure provider, should be considered controller of such data, even if its service includes tools facilitating creation of and access to cookies.[61]

Furthermore, if an individual cloud customer uses a PaaS or IaaS service which stores cookies on the user's computer for their login to the service, the provider may be 'controller' of the individual user's account and login details. But if the user then processes personal data (eg of third-party clients) using the service, the provider should not necessarily be considered 'controller' of the personal data processed by the individual using this service.[62]

3.2 Data centres

The two questions to be answered in this section are whether a data centre or server farm used to provide cloud services and located in an EEA Member State (perhaps along with non-EEA data centres and/or data centres located in other EEA Member States), may constitute an 'establishment' in the EEA, and whether using an EEA data centre to provide or consume cloud services constitutes 'making use' of equipment in the EEA. We assume that providers are, at most, processors. Should a provider cross the line into the domain reserved for controllers, which would depend on the circumstances, much of the discussion below regarding cloud customers who are controllers may apply to it also.

3.2.1 Data centre or third-party data centre operator as 'establishment'?

Key to abbreviations:

'Customer' is a customer or user of cloud services, being an entity incorporated in a non-EEA country; Customer will usually be a controller of personal data.

'Provider' is a provider of cloud or related services.

'DataCentreState' is the EEA Member State where a data centre used in cloud computing is located.

If Customer, an entity incorporated in a non-EEA country, runs a data centre in EEA State DataCentreState (but has no EEA offices, branches, or subsidiaries), and uses the

---

[60] See Chapter 8.   [61] Unless and until they access the data. See Chapter 8.
[62] Although in some circumstances the PaaS or IaaS provider might become a controller. See Chapter 8.

data centre to process personal data for Customer's private cloud, is the data centre an 'establishment', and is the processing within the data centre 'carried out in the context of the activities' of that establishment so that DataCentreState's data protection laws apply to the processing?

3.2.2 'Establishment'

As discussed above, the meanings of 'establishment' and 'established' in Article 4 are not sufficiently clear, or consistent across Member States.[63] A server is unlikely to be considered an 'establishment' as 'it is simply a technical facility or instrument for the processing of information'.[64] However, a data centre comprises a building, normally with employees to maintain the servers, power, cooling, physical security, and so on. If Customer owns the building and employs those employees, it seems more likely that the data centre would be considered an 'establishment' of Customer.

Next, recall that an entity that provides cloud services using equipment within a data centre does not necessarily own the building and/or equipment.[65] If Customer rents space in a data centre in the EEA owned by a third party, Provider, would this be an 'establishment' of Customer? How much physical space or equipment would it take to constitute an 'establishment'? If a single server is not an establishment, but a data centre may be, where should the line be drawn? What if Customer rents use of servers in Provider's data centre, but does not own them? Does it matter whose employees maintain Customer's servers—Provider's, or Customer's own? What if third parties own and operate the data centre, but for the sole benefit of Customer, for example as a dedicated managed private cloud? Does that make the data centre an 'establishment' of Customer?[66] Many of these issues are relevant to data centres used in traditional outsourcing, not just cloud. Again, more clarity would be helpful.

3.2.3 'Context'

Even if a data centre can be considered an 'establishment' of Customer, is the processing within its servers and other equipment conducted 'in the context of' Customer's activities? Again, this concept is not harmonized across the EU; some Member States have not implemented this criterion.[67]

---

[63] For example, the Dutch data protection authority seems to interpret 'established' in Art. 4(1)(a) to require incorporation under Netherlands law, thus applying Dutch data protection laws on the 'establishment' ground only to Dutch corporations: Moerel (n. 5). For an outline of several different national implementations of 'establishment', see Douwe Korff, *New Challenges to Data Protection Working Paper No. 2—Data Protection Laws in the EU: The Difficulties in Meeting the Challenges Posed by Global Social and Technical Developments* (European Commission, 2010), 27–9.

[64] N. 11.   [65] See Chapter 1.

[66] In one case on freedom of establishment, Stanley (an English bookmaker) had commercial agreements with Italian operators or intermediaries regarding the creation of data transmission centres to make electronic means of communication available to Italian users, to collect and register users' intentions to bet, and to forward them to Stanley in the UK. The ECJ considered that these arrangements involved Stanley having a presence, indeed 'agencies', in Italy, and that: 'Where a company established in a Member State (such as Stanley) pursues the activity of collecting bets through the intermediary of an organisation of agencies established in another Member State (such as the defendants in the main proceedings), any restrictions on the activities of those agencies constitute obstacles to the freedom of establishment.' Case C-243/01 *Gambelli et al.* ECR [2003] I-13031 [14], [46].

[67] There is no requirement for 'context' in the laws of Finland, Greece, and Sweden, while Austria's law applies simply to 'processing of personal data in Austria'—European Commission, *Analysis and Impact Study on the Implementation of Directive EC 95/46 in Member States* (2003), 6, and Lilian Mitrou,

If a data centre is 'an establishment', in a sense *all* personal data processing conducted using its equipment could be said to be 'in the context of' its activities, because the very function of a data centre is to provide data processing facilities. On the other hand, it is arguable that a data centre has no independent activities of its own, hence it never processes data 'in the context of' *its* activities. Arguably, the processing within a data centre is a purely 'passive' technical activity, conducted in the context of *other*, 'real', activities of the controller *as such*. It could be said that the processing is carried out *as* the activity of the data centre as processor, not *in the context of* its activities as controller, and therefore the technical processing within the data centre is not a 'real' exercise of activity within recital 19.

This view seems supported by two hypothetical examples in WP179. The first involves a controller established in Austria which outsources processing to a processor in Germany: 'The processing in Germany is in the context of the activities of the controller in Austria. That is to say, the processing is carried out for the business purposes of, and on instructions from the Austrian establishment. Austrian law will be applicable to the processing carried out by the processor in Germany.' This suggests that the 'context' considered is *not* that of the mere processor in Germany.[68]

The second example involves a Japanese-headquartered entity, with an Irish office which deals with issues connected with processing the personal data of its users, and a Hungarian data centre which processes and stores that personal data but is only involved in 'technical maintenance'. WP179 states the data centre should apply Irish law to the processing in the data centre, but Hungarian law to any processing of the personal data of the data centre's employees.[69] This example is relevant where a non-EEA entity uses its own data centre located in the EEA to process personal data, that is self-hosted private cloud. It is also relevant where a non-EEA entity has an establishment, such as a sales office, in the EEA, in the context of whose activities *no* personal data are processed, and also a data centre in the EEA processing personal data in the context of its *non*-EEA activities.

The second example implies that personal data processing within a data centre should not be treated as being in the context of the data centre owner's own activities as processor, but only in the context of other, 'real', establishments' activities. Taking the example to its logical conclusion, if the data centre owner has no other 'establishment' in the EEA carrying on 'real' activities, the 'establishment' ground should not apply at all.

In other words, if the data centre is an 'establishment', it is an 'irrelevant' establishment.[70] The point here is that, for purposes of applying the equipment ground, the A29WP attempted to introduce the concept of 'relevant' establishment, to address the possible lacuna in Article 4(1)(c) previously discussed. Article 4(1)(c) only applies if the controller is not 'established on' Community territory. WP179 interpreted Article 4(1)(c) as referring only to a 'relevant' establishment.[71] Thus, even if a controller has an EEA establishment, that establishment would be discounted, and Article 4(1)(c) would apply, unless it is a 'relevant' establishment. In considering 'relevance', the A29WP effectively used the 'context of activities' test from Article 4(1)(a): if an EEA establishment

---

New Challenges to Data Protection Country Study A.5—Greece (European Commission, 2010), 6–7. Italy's law applies to 'processing of personal data, by anyone, carried out on the territory of [Italy]', Denmark's law to activities by a Denmark-based controller, but only if those activities 'are carried out within the territory of the European Community'. Korff (n. 63), 28.

[68] If Austrian and German laws conflict, however, German law would apply as regards the security requirements—see Section 4 below.

[69] 16–17.   [70] See para. containing n. 41.   [71] See para. containing n. 41.

does not process personal data 'in the context' of its activities, it is not considered a 'relevant' establishment.

We argue that if an EEA establishment is considered not to process personal data in the context of its activities, and therefore is an 'irrelevant' establishment for the purposes of Article 4(1)(c), it should equally be considered not to process personal data in the context of its activities for the purposes of Article 4(1)(a). 'Context of activities' should be approached consistently under both sub-paragraphs.

The argument, that processing in a data centre is not 'in the context of' the data centre owner/operator's activities, holds true if the non-EEA entity does not have any office or other establishment in the EEA, but only a data centre in the EEA (eg for self-hosted private cloud). In relation to a one-person office, WP179 considers[72] it should be 'actively involved in the activities in the context of which the processing of personal data takes place', in order to be an establishment. This approach supports the argument that a data centre is not an 'establishment' of the data centre owner vis-à-vis the processing within the data centre, as the owner (and even the cloud provider) is not *actively* involved in the processing, which is controlled by the cloud *user*.

Notwithstanding the implications of the Japanese/Hungarian example, WP179 generally takes a very broad view of 'context', as does WP148.[73] On that view, Customer must comply with DataCentreState's data protection law for personal data processing within the data centre in DataCentreState, even if the data were collected in Customer's own non-EEA country for its business in that country, and related only to that country's residents. This uncertainty may discourage non-EEA persons from building EEA data centres, for example for their own private clouds. It is important to resolve these inconsistencies and clarify whether 'in the context of the activities of an establishment of the controller' includes a data centre's technical processing activities (when it performs no other economic activity), or whether the processing must be considered in the context of *other* distinct 'activities' of the controller.

Assume now that Customer uses a data centre in another EEA State, where personal data can flow between data centres in DataCentreState and the other State, as may occur in cloud computing. If a data centre is an 'establishment' and processing of personal data within it is 'in the context of' the data centre's activities, Customer may have to comply with data protection laws of both DataCentreState and the other State, in relation to the same data,[74] which may be difficult or impossible as national laws differ and may even conflict. This might discourage the building or use of data centres in multiple EEA states.

Another scenario is where Customer engages the services of a third-party provider, Provider. We assume Provider is established in an EEA Member State, DataCentreState, and owns and manages a data centre in DataCentreState which is dedicated to Customer's use for Customer's private cloud.[75] In this scenario, is this third-party data centre an 'establishment' of Customer?

There is much ECJ jurisprudence on the meaning of 'establishment' in relation to freedom to provide services and freedom of establishment under Article 50 TFEU. WP179 considers that this jurisprudence provides useful guidance when interpreting

---

[72] WP179, 12. Korff (n. 63) 25 considers 'An agent used on an ad hoc basis is not an establishment of the controller but merely a "processor" (although if the arrangements between the controller and the agent become quasi-permanent, this could change)'.

[73] N. 29.   [74] See recital 19, text after n. 27.

[75] In other words a dedicated managed private cloud, but this analysis could apply equally to a traditional IT outsourcing involving dedicated managed hosting using an EEA data centre.

'establishment' under Article 4.[76] Under that jurisprudence, an entity may in certain circumstances be considered to have an 'establishment' through having a third-party agent in the territory concerned. WP179 states that even a 'simple agent' may constitute an establishment 'if his presence in the Member State presents sufficient stability'.[77]

Furthermore, some Member States explicitly include agencies as 'establishments'. For example, the Irish Data Protection Act 1988, section 1(3B)(a) has as the jurisdictional ground 'the controller is established in the State and the data are processed in the context of that establishment'. It then defines 'established in the State' in section 1(3B)(b) to include:

(d) a person who does not fall within subparagraphs (i), (ii) or (iii) of this paragraph but maintains in the State –

    (I) an office, branch or *agency* through which he or she carries on any activity, or
    (II) a regular practice.

Maintaining 'a regular practice' seems an even wider concept than agency. The UK data protection legislation is similarly broad,[78] while the French legislation seems broader still.[79]

There is, therefore, a risk for Customer that the dedicated third-party data centre could be considered an 'establishment' of Customer. Based on the Article 50 TFEU cases, the extent of Provider's independence may be a factor. The more tightly Customer tries to control the third-party data centre's activities (as seems more probable with private cloud), the more likely perhaps that it will be considered an establishment of Customer.

Now consider a scenario where Provider uses someone else's infrastructure to provide cloud services for Customer, such as renting space in someone else's building, renting someone else's servers. If Provider rents a whole data centre, or simply space or server space within another's data centre, similar questions arise regarding whether the arrangement constitutes an 'establishment' of Customer. There is, again, a need for clarity. Does the stability of the arrangement matter more than how it is provided? Is the arrangement considered more 'stable' if the whole data centre is dedicated to Customer, than if only part of it is?

Consider further the scenario where Provider is a subsidiary of Customer, incorporated under the laws of DataCentreState. Assume Provider does nothing but own and run the data centre in DataCentreState. Assume that, for Customer's business in its non-EEA country of incorporation, it is the controller of personal data processed in Provider's data centre in DataCentreState. Does this involve processing 'in the context of the activities of an establishment of the controller on the territory of the Member State', so as to subject Customer to DataCentreState's data protection laws for all personal data processing within the data centre?

Recital 19 explicitly states that a subsidiary with separate legal personality may be an 'establishment'. Again, the meaning of 'context of the activities' is critical. If the processing in the data centre in DataCentreState is 'in the context of' Customer's activities *in DataCentreState*, that is if Provider's activities in DataCentreState are attributed to Customer, then Customer,

---

[76] While acknowledging that 'it is not clear whether this and subsequent interpretations by the ECJ as regards the freedom of establishment under Article 50 TFEU could be fully applied to the situations covered by Article 4 of the Data Protection Directive'—WP179, 11. Moerel (n. 5) suggests that it would be more appropriate to consider the jurisprudence on 'establishment' under the EU legislation on e-commerce and broadcasting.
[77] WP179, 12.   [78] UK Data Protection Act 1998, s. 5 is in almost identical terms.
[79] Article 5(1) Loi du 6 janvier 1978 relative à l'informatique, aux fichiers et aux libertés: 'a controller is deemed to be established [in France] if he carries out an activity on French territory in the context of an establishment [*installation*], whatever the legal form [of that establishment]'. Translation from Douwe Korff, *New Challenges to Data Protection Country Study A.3—Greece* (European Commission, 2010).

as controller, is subject to DataCentreState's law for the processing. However, if the processing is in the context only of Customer's activities *in its non-EEA country*, then arguably DataCentreState's laws do not apply. In other words, treating a subsidiary of Customer as an 'establishment' of Customer seems to look through the corporate veil, equating the position to the one above where Customer directly owns a data centre in DataCentreState and uses it to process personal data. But should not Provider's separate legal personality be recognized?[80] Should not the position be similar to that where Provider is an independent third party?

If Provider has data centres in several Member States, the laws of multiple States may apply, as before. Also, if Provider is incorporated or headquartered in yet other Member States, the (possibly conflicting) laws of those States may apply too. This position is unsatisfactory.

Now suppose that Provider has several unrelated customers, including Customer, all of whom Provider services using Provider's data centre in DataCentreState. Public cloud services providers typically have multiple customers.

Customer may have less control over Provider here than when it is the only customer, although much will depend on the facts. With more independence for Provider, it is less likely that Provider would be considered an agency of Customer, so as to cause Customer to have an establishment in DataCentreState. In other words, with public cloud, individual users may have less control, and providers may be more independent of users, than with private cloud. Also, processing could occur in different servers at different times, not just servers dedicated to one user. Could this mean there is less stability for the user, making it less likely that the user (if non-EEA) has an EEA 'establishment'?

If Customer is, nevertheless, considered to have an 'establishment' through the 'agency' of Provider, does it matter if Provider is 'agent' solely for Customer, or if Provider is 'agent' for other customers too? Given that stability of arrangements is key, not exclusivity, it cannot be ruled out that Provider or its data centre might constitute an 'establishment' of *each* of its customers, as multi-tenancy should not affect the stability of each tenant's arrangements.

If so, the same issue arises as above regarding whether the personal data processing in Provider's data centre is in the context of 'an establishment' of a customer as controller, or whether it is only the activities of customers, *other than* the technical processing activities of the data centre, which should count when considering 'context'.

Another question is whether Customer is more likely to be considered to have an 'establishment' in the EEA if Provider offers a choice of geographical regions for hosting its customers' data or applications, and Customer deliberately selects the EEA region for its services, thus using Provider's data centres in the EEA (ie in DataCentreState) for the Customer's cloud services. Does Customer's ability to choose a region make it more likely that it is deemed to have control, and therefore deemed to have an establishment in DataCentreState? What if Customer is not offered a choice of regions by Provider, but consciously decides to use Provider's services knowing that Provider's data centres are located only in the EEA? To what extent, if at all, should that knowledge (or lack of it) affect the position?

Consider further another common public cloud scenario. What if Customer uses SaaS provided by a third party, which (through layers of other providers) is ultimately hosted on a data centre in DataCentreState? Here, Customer would have much less

---

[80] C Kuner, *European Data Protection Law: Corporate Compliance and Regulation*, 2nd edn (Oxford: Oxford University Press, 2007), para. 3.27(d)—the DPD contains no concept of piercing the corporate veil.

fine-grained control of the computing service, as it is merely using an application; Customer may have no control over which data centres the third-party provider chooses to use. Here, arguably it is least likely that Customer would be considered to have an establishment in DataCentreState. But to what extent, if at all, should the position be affected by Customer's knowledge (or lack of it) as to Provider's arrangements behind the scenes with other providers and/or their arrangements with the ultimate infrastructure provider?

Finally, consider a so-called 'lights-out' data centre. This is a data centre that has eliminated the need for direct access by personnel under normal circumstances and is operated in an automated fashion, accessed and managed by remote systems. Would such a data centre trigger application of the DPD under Article 4(1)(a)? Does it matter who employs security guards who may patrol the data centre? If the data centre is owned by the non-EEA entity Customer, and it employs the security guards and controls the processing within that data centre, the data centre might well be considered an 'establishment' of Customer. Should it matter whether that data centre is dedicated to one entity, or is multi-tenancy? It seems stability and control are the key issues, and the discussions above would apply here. Regardless of whether such a data centre is an 'establishment', it may well amount to 'equipment' or 'means', which we discuss next.

3.2.4 Data centre or data centre operator as equipment or means

Now assume that Customer has no 'establishment' in the EEA.[81] While it is unclear to what extent a non-EEA user may be said to have an EEA 'establishment' through using an EEA provider or EEA data centre, it seems much clearer that a server is 'equipment' or means, as is a data centre.[82] The key question then is, when will a non-EEA user be considered to 'make use of' an EEA server or data centre, so as to be within this ground?

As previously mentioned, WP179 considers that 'making use' involves two elements: some kind of activity of the controller, and the clear intention of the controller to process personal data. These two elements are not helpful regarding use of EEA data centres for processing personal data, as the controller clearly intends to process personal data and will be carrying out activity, technical processing, within the data centre. Unfortunately, WP179 does not discuss the intention of the controller to process personal data *using EEA equipment or means*, although WP179 implies that, elsewhere.[83] We argue that intention to process personal data using EEA equipment or means should be explicitly addressed. WP179 also states that, while not every use of equipment within the EU/EEA will lead to the DPD being applicable, the controller need not exercise ownership or full control over the equipment for the processing to fall within the DPD's scope. The equipment should simply be 'at the disposal of the controller for the processing of personal data'.[84]

If this ground applies, another uncertainty arises regarding *to what extent*, which WP179 acknowledges: 'It could be questioned whether the principles will only be applicable to the part of the processing taking place in the EU, or to the controller as such, for all the stages of the processing, even those taking place in a third country. These questions have particular significance in network environments such as cloud computing, or in the context of

---

[81] This chapter considers further below the 'transit through' exception and the condition that the 'controller is not established on Community territory'.
[82] WP148 (n. 29) 11.   [83] See text to n. 101.
[84] A29WP, *Working Document on Determining the International Application of EU Data Protection Law to Personal Data Processing on the Internet by Non-EU-based Websites*, WP 56 (2001) (WP56) 9.

multinational companies.'[85] WP179 then concludes that, if this ground applies, the full DPD should become 'applicable to the controller as such, for all the stages of the processing, even those taking place in a third country'. This includes the data export restriction, although WP179 notes the implications are problematic.[86]

If Customer owns or rents a data centre in DataCentreState for its self-hosted private cloud, clearly Customer makes use of equipment in the EEA for processing personal data, and therefore the personal data processing within that data centre is subject to DataCentreState's laws, including data export restrictions. This is the case even if the data do not relate to EEA residents, and originated outside the EEA. There is no 'context' requirement here, unlike with the 'establishment' ground. Non-EEA entities therefore risk becoming subject to EU data protection laws in relation to personal data they process using EEA data centres, even if collected outside the EEA.

If Customer has data centres in multiple EEA Member States, and personal data are transferred between them, it seems the laws of each of those States would apply to the processing of those data. In the view of the A29WP,[87] whether Customer owns or rents a data centre, rack space, or servers in a data centre is immaterial for this ground.

Next, consider the scenario where Customer has no EEA presence, but uses the services of a Provider, an EEA entity which hosts and manages Customer's private cloud on Provider's data centre located in EEA DataCentreState.[88] Assume the data centre is dedicated to Customer and its data, and does not host data of any of Provider's other customers.

Through engaging Provider, is Customer using 'equipment' or 'means' in the EEA? Of interest here is the March 2011 decision by the French data protection authority, Commission nationale de l'informatique et des libertés (CNIL), regarding use of French *processors* by non-EEA persons. In CNIL's view, non-EU entities who use the services of providers located in France to process personal data are thereby using 'means'[89] situated in France, and therefore subject to the French Data Protection Act.

However, the CNIL wanted 'to be realistic and pragmatic in applying the French law to such situations. The aim is to ensure a high level of protection of personal data while, at the same time, generating practical solutions in order not to hamper the development of service provisions propositions by French companies'.[90] Therefore, it decided to exempt from certain obligations the processing of certain types of personal data for limited purposes, when performed by French service providers on behalf of controllers established outside the EU, and to allow transborder data flows 'back' to these non-European companies.[91]

---

[85] WP179, 24.

[86] WP179, 25. Kuner (n. 80) 4.33 discusses a view that if an EEA Member State's law applies to a non-EEA person by virtue of Art. 4, the data export restriction should not apply, as the purpose of the restriction is to ensure that substantive data protection law requirements apply to the data, and that person will be bound by those substantive laws under Art. 4 so transfer of the data to it should not be restricted.

[87] WP179.   [88] Again, this applies equally to a traditional IT outsourcing.

[89] Indeed, the CNIL considers that if a controller established outside the EU sends a paper form to a data subject in France, the form constitutes a 'means' used to process data. Korff (n. 63) 30.

[90] CNIL, 'CNIL Facilitates the Use of Outsourcing Services Performed in France on Behalf of Non-European Companies' (CNIL, 2011).

[91] Délibération n° 2011-023 du 20 janvier 2011 dispensant des traitements automatisés effectués sur le territoire français par des prestataires agissant pour le compte de responsables de traitement établis hors de l'Union européenne et concernant des données personnelles collectées hors de l'Union européenne (dispense n° 15) (2011)—that is the processing of personal data relating to employees, clients and prospects, for the purposes of managing payroll, employees, clients, and prospects is exempt from obligations of: notification, authorization by the CNIL of data transfer back outside the EU, and (if it would involve disproportionate effort) informing the data subjects about that processing.

The risks to data subjects' privacy resulting from these transfers were considered to be limited as those non-European companies collected the data in their own country, that is outside the EU. However, the non-EU controller remains liable for any breaches of French data protection law, and must appoint a representative in France. Also, the contract between the non-EU controller and French processor must stipulate the processor's security and confidentiality obligations and require the processor to act only on the controller's instructions (ie the Article 17 requirements), and a policy to secure and control access to the data must be implemented.

The CNIL decision seems applicable to French data centres as well as French providers, whether for private or indeed public clouds, as it refers to 'means' situated on French territory. Therefore, if Provider is not a French entity but uses a data centre located in France, it seems these exemptions may also apply.[92] However, the decision refers explicitly to the use of a provider, so does not seem to apply to the previous scenario where a non-EEA entity directly uses a French data centre or servers in a French data centre rather than going through a provider, although logically the same policy considerations arise there. The CNIL decision is limited to French data protection law, and as stated may be understandable for pragmatic reasons, although it could be queried whether the DPD in fact permits Member States to create such exemptions.

What of other EEA Member States? WP56 considers that a controller 'makes use of' equipment 'if the controller, by determining the way how [sic] the equipment works, is making the relevant decisions concerning the substance of the data and the procedure of their processing: "In other words, the controller determines, which data are collected, stored, transferred, altered etc., in which way and for which purpose" '.[93] That last sentence does not seem to add anything because a controller, by definition, determines what data to collect and store, what analyses to perform on the data, and so on. Also, 'by determining the way how the equipment works, is making the relevant decisions' is unclear and does not assist, because the controller does not necessarily determine how the equipment works, even if using a local computer to process personal data. There are issues regarding whether Provider is a controller (rather than processor) because Provider, although engaged by Customer, determines 'means' used (ie its data centre in France).[94] But assuming only Customer is the controller, it still seems likely that Customer would be considered to be using 'equipment' in the EEA.[95]

Directly relevant is WP179's statement that 'outsourcing activities, notably by processors, carried out in the EU/EEA territory on behalf of controllers established outside EEA may be considered as "equipment" '.[96] On this basis, Customer would be using equipment in the EEA. Nevertheless, WP179 suggests that 'account should be taken of the sometimes undesirable consequences [such as a possible universal application of EU law[97]] of such an interpretation . . . if controllers established in different countries over the world have their data processed in a Member State of the EU, where the database and the processor are located, those controllers will have to comply with the data

---

[92] Whether, if Provider is incorporated in another EEA Member State, that State's laws also apply (on the 'establishment' or 'equipment' ground), is another matter, depending on that State's implementation of the DPD.

[93] WP56 (n. 84) 9.   [94] See Chapter 8.

[95] Even if Provider were considered a controller, that would not exclude the possibility of Customer (who remains a controller) still being considered to use equipment in the EEA through Provider.

[96] Assuming that Customer has no establishment in the EEA in the context of which such personal data processing is taking place. Or in the words of WP179, 20, 'provided they are not acting in the context of the activities of an establishment of the controller in the EEA—in which case Article 4(1)(a) would apply'.

[97] WP179, 31.

protection law of that Member State'. It goes on to state: 'A case-by-case assessment is needed whereby the way in which the equipment is actually used to collect and process personal data is assessed.'[98]

Given these statements and the A29WP's consistently held view that saving cookies on EEA residents' computers 'makes use' of equipment in the EEA,[99] it seems probable that use of an EEA data centre in cloud computing will bring the user within the DPD's scope. If the data centre's computers are used to analyse or data mine, rather than passively store, personal data, EU regulators might be even more inclined to consider the controller within scope, even with data collected elsewhere. More clarity on the significance of 'the way in which the equipment is actually used' would assist. Similarly, with 'lights out' data centres, it is the location of the data centre which seems determinative, rather than the location from which the controller controls the processing within the data centre.

There is also a possible issue if Provider is a subsidiary of Customer, incorporated in another Member State. It appears that, in the Netherlands, a subsidiary incorporated in the State is itself considered to be 'means' in that Member State under Article 4(1)(c), so that the Dutch data protection authority would apply Dutch law to, say, a US corporation processing data in the US, if it has a Dutch subsidiary.[100] If the State in which Provider is incorporated is a Member State taking this view, Customer could be considered to be using means in both DataCentreState *and* the other State, and thus subject to the laws of all those States regarding the same processing.

Now suppose Provider has a data centre in another EEA Member State, and personal data can flow between the data centres in DataCentreState and the other State. Here, if Customer is considered to be using equipment in the EEA (as discussed above), it seems it would be using equipment in *both* DataCentreState and the other State, so that both States' laws apply to the processing.

Another question is whether Customer can be said to be making 'relevant decisions' to use the data centres in both DataCentreState and the other State, or is that decision only Provider's, if for example Provider operates automated load balancing between its data centres? Under current law and practice, it seems likely regulators would still attribute use of data centres in both Member States to Customer.

What if more layers are involved? What if Provider is not incorporated in the EEA (or even if it is), and Customer does not know that Provider intends to use an EEA data centre to process personal data for Customer? Would Customer be considered to 'make use of' EEA equipment then? This example typifies the 'cloud of unknowing'.

WP179 considered that, 'The application of the DPD to a controller for the whole processing should be supported as long as the link with the EU is effective and not tenuous (such as by almost inadvertent, rather than intentional, use of equipment in a Member State)'.[101] Would multiple layers of providers render the link 'tenuous'? What if the controller contractually restricts its provider from using any EEA data centre or provider, but the provider does so in breach of contract—would that make the link inadvertent?

The CNIL decision provides an example of a regulator, in an 'equipment' situation, taking account of 'sometimes undesirable consequences', by applying French data protection laws to non-EEA controllers in a more limited fashion when risks are judged to be lower. It may signal the way towards a possible EEA-wide approach to cloud, whereby

---

[98] WP179, 20.   [99] WP56 (n. 84), WP148 (n. 29) 10–11, WP179.
[100] Moerel (n. 5) paragraph containing fn. 78.   [101] WP179, 24.

fewer data protection obligations are applied to non-EEA controllers who process, in EEA data centres or through EEA cloud providers, personal data collected outside the EEA and returned outside the EEA. Such an approach would, as the CNIL noted, help to foster, or at least not impede, development of services by EEA providers.[102]

More generally, WP179 suggests that a more specific connecting factor, taking relevant 'targeting' of individuals into account, could usefully complement 'equipment/means' criteria for legal certainty, and could be considered under the current revision of the data protection framework. Targeting and other possible solutions are discussed later.

Similar issues apply with public cloud. If Provider provides a cloud service using physical infrastructure in the EEA, will Customer have the necessary intention to 'make use of' EEA equipment? This seems probable if Customer can choose the EEA region for its processing, and does so. It seems less likely if Customer does not make a selection, unless it can be said that, by not selecting, it knows and accepts that its data could be processed in an EEA data centre, depending on how the service has been structured.

As with the 'establishment' ground, more control may be possible with IaaS/PaaS than most types of SaaS. With most SaaS services, Customer cannot control which data centres Provider chooses to use to provide Provider's SaaS service, and Customer may not even know which data centres are used to provide services to it or store its data. However, Customer may have more precise control with IaaS or PaaS, for example a choice of geographical regions, and generally cloud customers have more control over processing with IaaS/PaaS than with SaaS (although some SaaS services may also offer a choice of regions).

With a public cloud provider, having multiple users should not of itself affect each user's 'making use' of equipment, unless perhaps it reduces each user's control. EU data protection law may apply based on means or equipment even if the use is not exclusive. *Each* customer may be using means or equipment through Provider or its data centre. The main relevance of Provider having multiple customers is that, if Customer is Provider's only customer (or one of only a few), then perhaps Customer might be more likely to have effective control, and therefore be more likely to be considered to intend to 'make use of' Provider or Provider's equipment. The situation will depend on the facts. If infrastructure is shared, where the same physical server could be processing Customer's data one minute, and someone else's data the next (or indeed simultaneously using different virtual machines), is the server sufficiently at Customer's 'disposal'? Or is it enough that potentially it could be used for Customer's processing? A clearer test of 'make use of' is much needed, and also clarification regarding shared infrastructure and possibly transient use.

What if Provider is a non-EEA entity which uses another cloud provider Provider2 to provide its services to Customer, for example a SaaS provider using an IaaS provider Provider2, where Provider2 chooses to use an EEA data centre for the processing? To what extent should Customer be taken to know that EEA equipment is used? To what extent should such imputed knowledge require Customer to be considered as 'making use of' EEA equipment? To what extent should Customer be required to investigate sub-providers? The more layers, the further removed this may be from Customer, but the position is unclear.

Accordingly, it is uncertain what significance, if any, should be attributed to Customer's knowledge of data centre location(s), or Customer's control over the locations used, and whether it chooses to select a location. For example, should Customer be deemed to know that its data will be processed in the EEA, even with SaaS, if Provider

---

[102] WP179, 32.

only has EEA data centres? Should Customer be required to investigate all underlying layers?

3.2.5 Transit through

The 'equipment/means' ground does not apply if 'such equipment is used only for purposes of transit through the territory of the Community'.

Could processing of personal data in EEA servers or data centres be considered to be only for transit? Sometimes processing may 'move' between data centres, for example in a 'follow the sun' type of arrangement,[103] so that the personal data processed may not be permanently in EEA data centres. Can this be considered 'transit through'?

Much depends on the facts. For example, if personal data are used for local customer support in a region, this is unlikely to be considered as mere 'transit' through there. Again, this issue needs careful consideration when updating the DPD. In particular, perhaps data protection law requirements may be relaxed for data relating only to non-EEA persons where the controller has no EEA connection other than its (or its provider) using an EEA data centre for cloud computing.

Another complication is that, again, this aspect has been implemented inconsistently. Denmark, France, Italy, Luxembourg, Portugal, and Sweden, correctly, exempt transit through the European Community or EU. However, Belgium, Finland, Ireland, and the UK only exempt transit through its own national territory. The laws of Greece, the Netherlands, and Spain refer simply to 'transit'.[104] French law does not implement this exception at all.[105]

3.2.6 EEA establishment and use of equipment: the possible lacuna

As previously mentioned, there seems to be a gap in that Article 4(1)(c) on equipment use only applies if the controller 'is not established on Community territory'. This might allow a controller to avoid the application of EU data protection law.

Suppose Customer is 'established on Community territory', because it has a branch or a subsidiary incorporated in an EEA Member State. The branch or subsidiary runs a data centre in the EEA, and Customer processes personal data for its business *in its non-EEA country of incorporation* using that data centre. If the data are not processed 'in the context of' the activities of the EEA establishment, that is the branch or subsidiary (as argued earlier), then the establishment ground does not apply. But, because Customer 'is established' on Community territory, the equipment ground does not apply either. So no EU data protection laws would apply to the processing within that data centre. Similarly, if Customer directly owns a data centre in the EEA (without having any branches or subsidiaries there), and through that data centre is considered to be 'established on Community territory', but it does not process personal data 'in the context of' the establishment's activities.

This possible lacuna may be due partly to inconsistent drafting: Article 4(1)(c) refers to 'established on', Article 4(1)(a) to 'establishment of', and Article 4(1)(c) makes no reference to the context of activities of the establishment. If, instead of 'the controller is

---

[103] Moving processing to data centres which have more available energy (eg to a solar-powered facility when the sun is shining, or a wind-powered data centre when it is windy there), or to certain regions during working hours there, when employees are most likely to need to use the data.

[104] Korff (n. 63) 30.

[105] European Commission, *Analysis and Impact Study on the Implementation of Directive EC 95/46 in Member States* (2003) 7.

not established on Community territory', Article 4(1)(c) had read, 'the controller does not have any establishment on the territory of a Member State in the context of whose activities it processes personal data', there would be no gap. As mentioned above, the A29WP and, at least implicitly, a German court, has in effect interpreted that provision in that way. So, if the controller has an EEA establishment, but does not process personal data in the context of that establishment's activities, then it is an 'irrelevant establishment', ignored when considering Article 4(1)(c).[106]

3.2.7 Establishment and equipment/means: summary

In summary, when a non-EEA entity, perhaps through several 'layers' of providers, ultimately processes personal data within an EEA data centre or through an EEA-incorporated provider, it is unclear when it should be considered, through the EEA data centre or provider, to have an 'establishment' in the EEA. It may be more likely to 'make use of' 'equipment' in the EEA than to have an 'establishment'.

The likelihood that the non-EEA entity will be regulated in the EEA, whether on establishment or equipment grounds, seems greatest with private cloud where it owns the data centre, or perhaps has a dedicated private cloud managed by a third party. However, this risk still exists even with public cloud and seems greatest with IaaS, particularly if the entity chooses the EEA region, though it may decrease with PaaS and even more with SaaS, depending on the situation.

The risk perhaps becomes remoter with additional layers of providers, but the role of the entity's knowledge (or not) regarding the ultimate use of EEA data centres or EEA providers, or its ability to choose such use, is unclear, in both 'establishment' and 'equipment' contexts.

4. Cloud Service Provider as Processor—Local Obligations

The final jurisdictional provision discussed in this chapter is Article 17(3), which provides that a processor established in a Member State must also comply with technical and organizational security measures mandated by the law in that Member State. Hence a processor must comply with security measures imposed by the law of the Member State where the controller is established, and the security measures of the Member State where the processor is established. So if a cloud customer who is a controller is established in Member State A, but data are processed by cloud providers, as processors, at various points in time in data centres (whether of the same or different providers) in five other Member States, the security requirements of all six Member States would have to be complied with by the provider(s). Similarly if the customer is not an EEA entity, but uses cloud services employing data centres in multiple EEA Member States.

This is problematic since security requirements vary considerably between Member States.[107] For example, the UK requirement is simply to take 'appropriate technical and organisational measures', whereas Italy has specified the required security measures in detail, for example for reuse of storage media, and access to sensitive passwords. Denmark requires Internet transmissions of personal data to be encrypted, and Austria,

---

[106] Even so, there remains the difficult issue of what 'context' means and whether, if a data centre is an establishment, personal data processing taking place within its servers should be considered 'in the context' of its activities, as previously discussed.

[107] WP179, 25.

as well as defining detailed minimum security measures, requires documentary records of those measures.[108] Where detailed security requirements conflict, the A29WP considers that the law of the processor's Member State should prevail, and be considered sufficient even if the law of the controller's Member State imposes greater obligations. The A29WP has called for harmonization of security requirements.[109]

Article 3 of the draft Regulation would apply expressly to 'the processing of personal data in the context of the activities of an establishment of' a processor in the EEA. Therefore, cloud providers may become *directly* subject to EU data protection law obligations under the draft Regulation, unlike the current position. Although Article 1(13) would clarify that a processor's 'main establishment' is its place of central administration in the EEA, which is clearer than the position with controllers, the current problems with interpreting 'context of' activities in relation to controllers' 'establishments' would be extended to cloud providers as well as cloud users. This may deter non-EEA providers from building or using EEA data centres or using EEA sub-providers. Indeed, conceivably, cloud providers with an EEA 'administration' may be subject to the draft Regulation's requirements if the processing is 'in the context' of its EEA establishment's activities, wherever in the world the processing activities take place, even if they process personal data of only non-EEA residents. Thus, the draft Regulation may deter non-EEA cloud providers from setting up or retaining any 'establishments' in the EEA which may be considered places of 'administration', such as EEA offices. As at 1 March 2013, the Council would further stipulate that, for processors with no central administration in the EU, the 'main establishment' would be 'the place where the main processing activities take place'.[110] If non-EEA processors who process data using EEA data centres are thereby considered to have 'main establishments' in the EEA and be subject to EEA data protection laws, this would be very broad and could be a further disincentive for non-EEA providers to use EEA data centres.

The draft Regulation in Article 30 and recital 66 would also impose direct security obligations on processors, including making risk assessments. However, some cloud providers may not know whether data stored on their equipment by EEA users are 'personal data' or not. It does not seem appropriate to subject them to similar liabilities as providers who do know. Furthermore, draft Article 26(4) would explicitly make a 'processor' liable as controller if it processes personal data 'otherwise than as instructed' by the controller. While this simply reflects current laws, the requirement for processors to 'act only on instructions' from the controller does not accommodate how cloud operates.[111]

Finally, the draft Regulation still would not fully address processors' position. For example, its recital 39 acknowledges that processing 'to the extent strictly necessary for the purposes of ensuring network and information security' is a legitimate interest of controllers. However, it does not mention legitimate interests of processors, or specify (as would be desirable) that such processing for security purposes would not render a processor a 'controller'.

5. An Alternative Approach: Targeting/Directing

The complexity and ambiguity of the applicable law provisions has led to their divergent and deficient implementation in national law.[112] Accordingly, a study commissioned by the European Commission states: 'better, clearer and unambiguous rules are desperately

---

[108] Kuner (n. 80) 5.137.   [109] WP179, 25.
[110] <http://www.parlament.gv.at/PAKT/EU/XXIV/EU/08/60/EU_86013/imfname_10034284. pdf> 39.
[111] See Chapter 8, Section 3.2.   [112] European Commission Communication COM (2010) 609.

needed on applicable law'.[113] The study's main recommendation is that both EEA and non-EEA controllers should have to comply with data protection laws of one Member State *only*. This clearly would remove one layer of complexity, albeit only at the regional EEA level.

The A29WP took up this recommendation, cautiously recommending a shift to country of origin regulation, which the draft Regulation would implement.[114] This would mean all establishments of a controller within the EEA would apply the laws of the controller's main establishment, wherever the establishments are situated. However, the Opinion also stated that a prerequisite to country-of-origin regulation is comprehensive harmonization of data protection legislation, including security obligations. The draft Regulation aims to achieve this, but even a directly applicable regulation will not achieve harmonization if it lacks clarity, as there will remain scope for differing interpretations by Member States.

The A29WP also accepted that the 'equipment/means' connecting factor may be tenuous, therefore recommending its replacement with a directing/targeting test, similar to the test for jurisdiction in consumer contracts in Regulation 2001/44/EC Article 15 as interpreted by the ECJ in the *Pammer/Alpenhof* case.[115] This issue is relevant to cloud providers (typically SaaS providers) which are said to be within the scope of EU data protection law because they save cookies or run scripts and so on on EEA residents' equipment.

In *Pammer/Alpenhof*, the ECJ had to decide whether a website operator directs its activities to a particular Member State. For this to be so, the trader 'must have manifested its intention to establish commercial relations with consumers from one or more other Member States including that of the consumer's domicile'.[116] However, the ECJ also pointed out this does not mean a consumer must provide 'proof of an intention on the part of the trader to develop activity of a certain scale with those other Member States'.[117] The ECJ established a test of taking into account all circumstantial evidence surrounding the website and the trader's commercial activities in order to assess whether, objectively speaking, the trader was targeting the consumer's domicile. The ECJ listed, as non-exhaustive examples and in the context of the two cases before it, the following factors:[118]

1. the international nature of the activity;

2. mention of itineraries to reach the place of the trader's establishment or a place where the service is provided;

3. use of a language or a currency other than those used in the trader's place of establishment;

4. mention of telephone numbers with an international dialling code;

5. marketing focused on the consumer's domicile, including keyword advertising or paying for other country-specific referencing services;

6. use of a top-level domain other than that of the Member State in which the trader is established; and

7. reference to an international customer base, for example through reviews, testimony, and other circumstantial evidence.

---

[113] LRDP Kantor Ltd in association with Centre for Public Reform, *New Challenges to Data Protection—Final Report* (European Commission, 2010) [44].

[114] WP179, 31. See also LRDP Kantor Ltd (n. 113), 26.

[115] Joined Cases C-585/08 and C-144/09, *Peter Pammer v Reederei Karl Schlüter GmbH & Co. KG* (C-585/08) *and Hotel Alpenhof GesmbH v Oliver Heller* (C-144/09), ECR [2010] I-12527.

[116] *Pammer/Alpenhof* [75].   [117] *Pammer/Alpenhof* [82].   [118] *Pammer/Alpenhof* [93].

One obvious missing connecting factor is the nature of the trader's activities.

The A29WP added to these factors: delivery of goods or services in a Member State, and accessibility of the service depending on use of an EU credit card.[119] A more recent ECJ case on the Database Directive[120] also took a 'targeting' approach to jurisdiction. It considered, where data were uploaded to web servers and then accessed cross-border, that the relevant act occurred 'at least' in the recipient/downloader's Member State, 'where there is evidence from which it may be concluded that the act discloses an intention on the part of the person performing the [upload] act to target members of the public in Member State B'.[121]

A targeting/directing test to decide which Member State's data protection laws apply may indeed be preferable to the establishment/equipment grounds of Article 4. It would provide that a Member State's data protection laws apply to a particular processing of personal data if a controller directs its activities to that Member State and the processing occurs in the framework of these activities. In other words, this test would connect the processing to the activities of a controller, and connect the activities to the territory of a Member State or several Member States.

WP179 explicitly proposed the condition: 'that the activity involving the processing of personal data is targeted at individuals in the EU'.[122] It also makes the valid point that the law applicable to consumer contracts is determined by a similar targeting test, so it makes sense to apply a similar test to laws applicable to data protection, since consumer protection law and data protection law overlap to an extent,[123] for example in relation to unfair commercial practices.

To what extent would the draft Regulation improve the position for cloud computing? The proposed replacement of equipment/means with tests based on offering goods or services to EEA residents or monitoring their behaviour should result in a clearer, less artificial, approach. However, the challenge may instead be to determine when a controller 'only occasionally' offers goods or services to EEA residents, and the scope of 'monitoring' behaviour. The monitoring test, for example, seems to catch profiling, but not *collecting* personal data for profiling purposes.

The problems with any targeting/directing test are twofold. First, targeting is always a question of degree; *how much* targeting is required before the controller would be subject to a Member State's law. Second, who would have to show that a controller targeted a particular Member State and what would be the burden of proof?

Regarding the degree of targeting required, some cloud services may not appear to be 'linked' to any territory at all. Services may be provided online without reference to any particular territory, and the provider's marketing strategy may be territory-neutral. Some cloud users may not consider territory relevant when choosing to use certain online services. This raises the question whether it should be sufficient that the cloud provider, or any other online service provider, merely knows that its user base includes users domiciled in the EEA, or is likely to include such users, perhaps because of the service's nature, attractiveness to EEA users and volume of such activities. Such an argument would be similar to that developed in the 'stream of commerce' cases in the US,

---

[119] WP179, 31.

[120] Directive 96/9/EC of the European Parliament and of the Council of 11 March 1996 on the legal protection of databases, Official Journal L 077, 27/03/1996 P. 0020–0028.

[121] Case C-173/11 *Football Dataco Ltd et al. v Sportradar GmbH et al. (Legal protection of databases)* <http://curia.europa.eu/juris/document/document.jsf?text=&docid=128651&pageIndex=0&doclang=en&mode=req&dir=&occ=first&part=1&cid=522782&intEmailHistoryId=515225&intEmailListId=308&intEmailId=326334&intExternalSystemId=1>.

[122] WP179.   [123] WP179, see also Bygrave (n. 3), 10–11.

whereby a manufacturer may have constructive knowledge that its products may end up in a particular country through a chain of distributors.[124] Similarly, with online services which are ubiquitous and accessible from everywhere, it could be argued that whether a particular service provider should be subject to the laws of a particular country should depend on whether it knows that it is providing services to users in that country.[125] How much knowledge is required before a provider crosses the line of 'only occasionally' offering cloud services to EEA residents? Is it significant that the draft Regulation refers to 'offering' rather than 'supplying', in other words targeting or marketing rather than actual 'sales'?

Regarding the question of proof, the cloud provider is in the best position to know about its marketing strategy and the operation of its service and website, but it may be difficult to prove a negative (ie, that it did *not* market its services in the EEA). The draft Regulation does not address the burden of proof, and would benefit from explicit clarification on this issue.

As regards the lacuna analysed above, the draft Regulation would not 'close the loophole' for controllers. Under Article 3(1), it would apply 'to the processing of personal data in the context of the activities of an establishment of a controller or a processor in the Union'. Article 3(2) would then apply the targeting test 'to the processing of personal data of data subjects residing in the Union by a controller not established in the Union'. Therefore, if a controller is 'established in' the EEA, but is not processing personal data 'in the context' of the activities of any of its EEA establishments, the draft Regulation would not apply to it at all. It would be desirable if the draft Regulation could explicitly address this issue and clarify that 'established in' means the same as 'has an establishment in', as discussed above.

Interestingly, there is no similar loophole for processors. If a provider processes personal data 'in the context of the activities of an establishment' of the provider in the EEA, seemingly it would be subject to the draft Regulation in relation to its worldwide processing.

6. Conclusion and Recommendations

It can be seen that the DPD applies in two situations to a cloud customer who is a controller with main headquarters outside the EEA. The first is where processing is carried out in the context of activities of an establishment of the controller in the EEA. The second is where the controller has no establishment in the EEA, but it uses equipment or means in the EEA to process personal data. Hence, the territorial link is based either on an establishment, or on the use of equipment or means of processing. As regards cloud computing specifically, Article 4 would benefit from clarification, especially regarding how it applies to the use of EEA data centres or EEA providers, particularly where layers of providers are involved. The legal uncertainties need to be addressed if non-EEA entities are not to be discouraged from using EEA data centres, EEA providers, or indeed non-EEA providers which ultimately use EEA data centres.

For understandable policy reasons, EU lawmakers consider that, in some circumstances, EU data protection jurisdiction should extend extraterritorially to non-EU

---

[124] *Asahi Metal Industry Co v Superior Court* 480 US 102 (1987)—this case turned on whether there were sufficient minimum contacts, rather than knowledge as such, and it concerned goods rather than services, but the rationale can be applied by analogy.

[125] For a similar argument, see A MacDonald 'Youtubing down the Stream of Commerce' (2009) 19 *Albany Law Journal of Science and Technology* 519, 552–6.

service providers who process the personal data of EU consumers.[126] One goal of the draft Regulation is to improve harmonization across the EU, particularly regarding applicable law. The challenge is defining the boundaries with sufficient clarity for practical application, and in a way that balances interests in protecting privacy and fostering EU-wide, indeed global, development and use of cloud services by EU providers and users. The draft Regulation, while attempting to address some of the key issues, would not do so adequately.

Notably, clearer rules are needed on determining the 'main establishment' for controllers. If the concepts of 'establishment'/'context of activities' are retained, the meanings of 'establishment' and 'context' should be explained with greater precision. In particular, Article 3 of the draft Regulation should be amended to eliminate the inconsistent usages of 'establishment of' and 'established in' and clarify that both refer to the same concept. It should be spelled out that a subsidiary is not an 'establishment' of its parent, but may be a controller or processor in its own right. The implications of using EEA cloud service providers or EEA data centres need to be made very clear. As regards the targeting concept, more guidance is needed on when offering of services will exceed 'only occasionally', and the meaning and scope of 'monitoring'. It should be made explicit who bears the burden of proof on 'offering' and 'monitoring'.

Finally, the status of infrastructure providers, as well as intermediate providers should be clarified. For example, to what extent should cloud providers be subject to EU data protection laws when they are processing data for non-EEA controllers? The draft Regulation aims to eliminate national law conflicts and stipulate a 'main establishment' concept as the basis for regulating processors. This is laudable, much needed, and particularly important for security requirements. However, the draft Regulation is unclear as to the exact scope of its applicability to processors, particularly non-EEA processors who use EEA data centres, and the same issues regarding 'context of activities' arise equally here. The 'instructions' requirement, and similar requirements relating to use of processors, do not take proper account of how cloud operates. If lawmakers intend to impose EU data protection security requirements on processors having any EEA 'administration' or using any EEA data centre, regardless of the position or country of their controllers, this should be made explicit, and inappropriate provisions expressly disapplied.

---

[126] Viviane Reding, 'Your Data, Your Rights: Safeguarding Your Privacy in a Connected World' (Privacy Platform 'The Review of the EU Data Protection Framework' Brussels, 16 March 2011) SPEECH/11/183.

Appendix—Practical Application—Use of EEA Data Centres

Table 9.1 below summarizes the position of a non-EEA entity Customer, which for cloud computing services directly or indirectly uses data centres in the EEA (in Member State DataCentreState, or in some scenarios in both Member State DataCentreState and another Member State). We assume the 'transit through' exemption does not apply.

Key to abbreviations:

'Customer' means customer or user of cloud services; Customer will usually be a controller of personal data. We assume Customer is incorporated and based in a non-EEA country, and collects personal data in that country for its business there, relating only to residents of that country. We also assume Customer has no other presence in the EEA, unless otherwise stated.

'Provider' means provider of cloud or related services.

'DataCentreState' means an EEA Member State in which a data centre used in cloud computing is located.

'Multiple' means several data centres in different EEA Member States are used, between which personal data may flow.

We summarize in each alternative scenario whether EU data protection law could be applied to Customer, based on either the:

- establishment/context ground ('effective and real exercise of activity through stable arrangements'); or
- the equipment ground ('if the controller, by determining the way how the equipment works, is making the relevant decisions concerning the substance of the data and the procedure of their processing', and (i) some kind of activity of the controller, and (ii) the clear intention of the controller to process personal data).

If Provider is considered to determine 'purposes and means' of the processing so as to be considered a controller (eg through its choice of data centre(s) or any sub-provider used), then the analyses regarding Customer would apply to Provider.

Table 9.1 Practical Application—Use of EEA Data Centres

	Type	Variations	Establishment and context?	Equipment?
1	**Private cloud**—self-hosted	A. If Customer owns the data centre/servers	Uncertain. There may be enough stability for an 'establishment', especially if Customer's employees maintain the servers. However, arguably the personal data processing within the data centre is not 'in the context' of the data centre's activities. The position is unclear.	Yes
		B. If Customer rents space/servers	As in 1A. Possibly, stability increases if Customer uses more space/servers, particularly if its employees maintain the servers. Conversely, arguably the number of servers/employees dedicated to Customer should not matter—nothing turns on the 'size' of an establishment, only whether there *is* an establishment. As above, the 'context' question is unclear.	Yes
		C. If Customer has an establishment X' in the EEA, for example marketing office for hardware sales or software licensing	Arguably, same as above. However, the wide view of 'context' taken by the A29WP raises the risk that the processing in DataCentreState could be deemed to be in the context of X's activities.	This is the apparent lacuna in DPD Article 4(1)(c). WP179 would consider X to be an 'irrelevant' establishment, so that Customer is still considered to be making use of equipment in DataCentreState.
		D. Multiple	Uncertain. Either there is insufficient 'stability' in both DataCentreState and the other State, as data may not always definitively be in one centre or the other, or Customer has establishments in **both** states, subjecting the laws of both DataCentreState and the other State. Whether the second data centre is used for full replication/backup or just for 'overflow' may be relevant. NB. The context issue again arises here.	Yes, Customer would be subject to the (possibly conflicting) laws of both DataCentreState and the other State for the same processing, if distributed processing employs equipment in both those states.

2	**Private cloud**—data centre dedicated to Customer, owned and managed by Provider	E. Lights-out data centre	Uncertain. Customer may still control processing operations in the centre, albeit remotely.	Yes	Probably, although in a sense Provider also determines 'how the equipment works'. It seems a case-by-case assessment should be undertaken to avoid 'undesirable consequences'.
		A. If Provider is incorporated/established in DataCentreState	It is uncertain to what extent Customer may be considered 'established' in DataCentreState through a third party, for example Provider or Provider's data centre. Relevant factors may include the extent to which the data centre is dedicated to Customer, and the extent of Customer's control over activities therein through its contract with Provider (possibly Customer may be afforded greater control if it is Provider's only customer using that data centre). Again, the context question remains relevant.		Very probably, in DataCentreState—see 2A. The other State's laws determine whether Customer is using 'means' in the other State through its use of Provider, although the data centre is in DataCentreState.
		B. If Provider is incorporated/established in the other State	Uncertain. Customer risks being considered to have an establishment in DataCentreState, through the dedicated data centre in DataCentreState; and possibly also in the other State, through using Provider's services, as Provider is incorporated in the other State. This depends on the national laws of DataCentreState and the other State. Again, the context question is relevant.		Very probably, in DataCentreState—see 2A. 2A. The processing is still conducted on EEA territory, ie DataCentreState.
		C. If Provider (non-EEA) has no other EEA presence	Uncertain. See 2A: could the data centre be attributed to Customer nevertheless, because it is dedicated to Customer? Again, the context question arises.		See 2A. Ownership/full control is unnecessary. 'Intention' is, but activity in the EEA plus intention to process personal data suffices.
		D. If Provider rents the data centre/servers	Ownership should not matter, but it is unclear to what extent the number or proportion of servers/employees dedicated to Customer affects whether it has an 'establishment', see 1B.		

(Continued)

Type	Variations	Establishment and context?	Equipment?
	E. Multiple	If Customer is considered to have an 'establishment' through Provider or the data centre, see 1D.	Yes, in both DataCentreState and the other State—hence, both their laws would apply to the same processing.
	F. If Provider is a subsidiary of Customer	Customer may be more likely to be considered to have an establishment through Provider if Provider is its subsidiary, in some States.	Customer would be using equipment in DataCentreState. But, if Provider is incorporated in a Member State that considers a subsidiary to be 'means', Customer risks being considered to use 'means' in that Member State also.
3 **Public cloud**—Provider provides IaaS, PaaS, or SaaS to Customer; Provider has server space in a data centre (or whole data centre)	Depends on type and exact nature of service, but generally use of IaaS may be more likely to constitute an 'establishment' of Customer than PaaS or SaaS, and Customer's knowledge as to use of EEA data centres and the extent of its control may be relevant. As above, it is irrelevant whether Provider owns or rents the data centre, space, or servers. Similar questions as above arise on 'context', and, if Provider uses multiple EEA centres, on sufficient stability, and multiple laws possibly applying.	Depends on the service. Whether Provider owns or rents infrastructure is irrelevant. If Provider uses data centres in multiple EEA states and equipment use is attributed to Customer, multiple laws may apply to Customer.	

4	**Public cloud**—Provider provides cloud services to Customer using Provider2's IaaS or PaaS service; Provider2 has server space or whole data centre	The EEA data centre is even more removed from Customer than in 3. Similar questions arise as in 3 regarding the extent of Customer's control or knowledge of Provider2's use of EEA data centres, but Customer would have to investigate to find out. Should it be required to? Other issues are also similar, for example context.	The extra layer may affect whether Customer has the necessary intention, but the position is unclear (see 2D). Knowledge that Provider2's data centres are in the EEA may be relevant, but the position is further removed.
5	**Public cloud**—Provider provides cloud services to Customer using Provider2's IaaS/PaaS service, which uses Provider3's IaaS service; Provider3 provides the servers in data centre	This illustrates that even more layers are possible, including a further layer still if Provider3 does not own the data centres but rents space/servers. As with 4, a key question is whether, the further removed the data centre is from Customer, the less likely it is to be considered Customer's 'establishment'. Again, context is an issue.	As 4, but the position is even further removed.
6	**Lights-out data centre**	Depends more on type and nature of service, and layers between, than on whether the data centre is remotely controlled.	Depends on service and layers.

10

How Do Restrictions on International Data Transfers Work in Clouds?

W Kuan Hon and Christopher Millard

1. Introduction

This chapter considers how cloud computing is affected by restrictions on transferring personal data outside the European Economic Area (EEA) under Article 25 of the Data Protection Directive (DPD). We call such transfers 'data export' and in this chapter we explore the options available for complying with the data export restriction. We also make recommendations for reform of the DPD, arguing that this restriction is inappropriate in the Internet age, and should be abolished and replaced by other more suitable controls.

2. Data Export Restriction

Under Article 25(1), subject to certain derogations under Article 26, Member States must not allow a data controller to export personal data to a 'third country' outside the EEA, unless the country provides an adequate level of protection for personal data, meaning a standard in keeping with the DPD's main principles.

This applies whether the data are kept within the same entity (such as a branch), or transferred to a company in the same group or an unrelated third party in that country. One intention of this provision was to put third countries under some pressure to adopt data protection standards similar to the EEA's.[1]

This restriction is a specific additional requirement. A data export or transfer constitutes 'processing', for which a legal justification is still required in the normal way, for example data subject consent to the processing, even where export is permitted under Article 25 or 26.

The European Commission may declare that certain countries provide such adequate protection, so that personal data may be exported freely to these countries.[2] As at 1 March 2013, only a few countries, of which several are small territories in Europe, have been subject to such declarations: Andorra, Argentina, Canada (where the Canadian Personal Information Protection and Electronic Documents Act 2000 applies), Faeroe Islands, Guernsey, Isle of Man, Israel, Jersey, New Zealand, Switzerland, and Uruguay.[3]

---

[1] See Art. 25(5). For a global perspective on regulation of international data transfers, see Christopher Kuner, *Transborder Data Flows and Data Privacy Law* (Oxford: Oxford University Press, 2013).

[2] Article 25(6).

[3] For the relevant decisions, see European Commission, 'Commission decisions on the adequacy of the protection of personal data in third countries', <http://ec.europa.eu/justice/data-protection/document/international-transfers/adequacy/index_en.htm>. Although ruled adequate by the A29WP in 2012, 'Opinion 07/2012 on the level of protection of personal data in the Principality of Monaco' (adopted 19 July 2012), <http://ec.europa.eu/justice/data-protection/article-29/documentation/opinion-recommendation/files/2012/wp198_en.pdf>, as at 1 March 2013 no European Commission decision had been issued regarding Monaco. (Both accessed 2 April 2013.)

France, Portugal, and Spain allow the national data protection authority to make its own adequacy findings, and in Belgium, the Netherlands, and Sweden the Ministry of Justice or government may do so. However, such findings are rare; other Member States do not even empower national authorities to make adequacy findings, and in practice Member States simply confirm locally the European Commission's adequacy findings.[4] No Member States have issued adequacy findings for countries not already found adequate by the Commission.[5]

Therefore, effectively the DPD prohibits export of personal data from the EEA to third countries (except those listed above), unless derogations apply or special arrangements are made to assure adequacy. EU data protection regulators collectively, in the form of the Article 29 Working Party (A29WP), consider that transfer of personal data to a server outside the EEA constitutes such export.[6]

Many cloud arrangements use remote data storage and other data processing, such that the geographic location of data and/or operations on data may 'change' as data may be replicated to equipment located in other countries, including third countries. Therefore, the data export restriction creates significant challenges for cloud computing, which by its nature involves data transfers from user to cloud (and vice versa), and automated data transfers within the cloud.

This causes problems for data controllers established in the EEA, but can be even more problematic where the controller is not established in the EEA. This is because the DPD applies by virtue of Article 4(1)(c) not only to processing in the context of an EU establishment but also where a data controller based outside the EU is using 'equipment' or 'means' such as a cookie on the user's computer, or is using an EEA data centre or EEA provider.[7] Combining the jurisdictional provisions with the provisions on data export may mean that a cloud provider with no establishment in the EEA may, nevertheless, be subject to the EU data export regime when attempting to transfer data back from the EEA to its place of establishment or some other location outside the EEA, even if the data were originally collected outside the EEA and relate to non-EEA individuals.

The result may be that the DPD prevents non-EEA cloud providers offering their services remotely to users in the EEA, unless the provider complies with the requirements of the relevant national implementation(s), or an exception applies. It also raises serious issues about the enforceability of EU data protection laws in practice. For example, a US-based cloud provider offering remote storage and processing of photographs in the cloud, with data centres in various US locations, would not be allowed to offer this service to users in the EEA (unless exceptions/special arrangements apply—see below). However, it is difficult to see how EEA national data protection authorities could enforce the law against a remote US cloud provider. The A29WP has not recommended any solutions to this problem, merely stating that 'existing tools regulating the conditions for transfers should be further reflected upon'.[8]

---

[4] European Commission, 'Analysis and Impact Study on the Implementation of Directive EC 95/46 in Member States' (2003), 32.

[5] LRDP Kantor Ltd in association with Centre for Public Reform, *New Challenges to Data Protection—Final Report* (European Commission, 2010), [78].

[6] A29WP, 'Opinion 2/2010 on Online Behavioural Advertising' WP171 (2010), 21 [5.4]; and see Article 29 Data Protection Working Party, 'Opinion 10/2006 on the Processing of Personal Data by the Society for Worldwide Interbank Financial Telecommunication (SWIFT)' WP128 (2006) (SWIFT), where the A29WP considered that mirroring (automatically copying) personal data to a Belgian entity's US-located server was a 'transfer'. See further n. 99.

[7] See Chapter 9.

[8] Article 29 Data Protection Working Party, 'Opinion 8/2010 on Applicable Law' WP179 (2010), 25.

Similarly, through the establishment or equipment nexus, EU data protection laws may apply to non-EEA customers of cloud services that use data centres or providers in the EEA.[9] However, enforcement against them may again not be practicable.

It should also be noted that while some discussions centre on the jurisdiction of establishment of the cloud provider (many of whom are US corporations), in practice most cloud processing occurs using equipment housed in data centres or server farms, which may be situated in different geographical locations around the world.[10] One might say that cloud computing is 'data centre-centric'. Data may be copied or replicated to different data centres, for business continuity/backup purposes, rather than being 'moved' by being deleted from one data centre and recreated in another. Often, the provider will know where a user's data fragments (eg, for a particular application) are stored, at the data centre if not equipment level. However, whether for security or other reasons, generally providers do not disclose to *users* their data's location.[11] This is changing, as discussed later. Some providers do provide or allow users to check certain location information.[12] As technology improves, costs reduce, and customers increasingly demand greater transparency for regulatory compliance and other reasons, perhaps more providers will offer users capabilities to monitor data location and other matters, whether as a standard or additionally priced feature, in order to maintain or increase their market competitiveness.[13]

With increasing globalization, a non-EEA entity could own or rent space and/or equipment in a data centre located *within* the EEA. If it uses that data centre to provide cloud services, transfer of personal data to it might not constitute transfer of data outside the EEA, even though the entity is not established in the EEA. Conversely, if an EEA-established entity uses a non-EEA data centre for cloud computing, transferring personal data to that entity for cloud computing could constitute data export, as discussed below.[14] Also, many cloud services involve use of sub-providers and even sub-sub-providers, so the relevant location would be that of the data centre(s) used by the sub-provider in the lowest layer of the cloud 'stack' (which may not even be a cloud services provider as such, but a data centre services provider).

---

[9] See Chapter 9.   [10] See Chapter 1.

[11] Attempts are being made to identify the locations of various providers' data centres. For examples, see <http://www.datacentermap.com/cloud.html> and see Chris Gaun, 'Sniffing Out the Geographic Location of Cloud Service Data Centers' (*Ideas Insights*, 2011), <http://web.archive.org/web/20130401133847/http://ideasint.blogs.com/ideasinsights/2011/05/sniffing-out-the-geographic-location-of-cloud-service-data-centers-.html> (accessed 24 March 2013).

[12] For instance, Salesforce enables users to check the data centre location of the virtual machine (VM) 'instance' their organization is using, see <http://trust.salesforce.com/trust/status/> (accessed 22 March 2012)—which also enables monitoring of performance and maintenance data. It is not said whether a user's data, when saved to persistent storage, would be located in the same data centre, although that is probable for latency reasons (see Chapter 1).

[13] Current techniques for users to verify the geographical location of their data independently are not straightforward or reliable. Even when the provider states the data location, users must trust that the information is accurate. Even if it is accurate, location of data in one place does not exclude the possibility of copies also being located elsewhere. However, the issue of how cloud users may obtain independent, accurate verification of the location of their data is increasing in profile. Zachary NJ Peterson, Mark Gondree, and Robert Beverly, 'A Position Paper on Data Sovereignty: The Importance of Geolocating Data in the Cloud' (Proceedings of HotCloud 11, Portland, OR, US, 14–17 June 2011).

More recently, the US National Institute of Standards and Technology (NIST), working with Intel, VMWare, and RSA Archer and using their technologies, produced a proof-of-concept system that monitors and enforces geolocation restrictions by enabling users to determine and control the location of the hardware that processes and stores their data and applications in the cloud, which may serve as a blueprint for others to implement, Erin K Banks et al., 'Trusted Gelocation in the Cloud: Proof of Concept Implementation (Draft)' (*NIST*, December 2012), <http://csrc.nist.gov/publications/drafts/ir7904/draft_nistir_7904.pdf> (accessed 2 April 2013).

[14] Paragraphs containing nn. 23–5.

Given these issues and complexities, in any analysis it is important to be clear regarding what is being considered: physical location of data, physical location of the provider to whom a controller transfers data, and/or the laws of a jurisdiction where the provider is incorporated or established or where data are located? Regarding the latter, the wording of the DPD's data export restriction, and of many national implementations, focuses on the *third country* ensuring an adequate level of protection, seemingly envisaging that this be achieved through that country's data protection and privacy laws. The DPD's wording does not envisage the possibility that exported data could be adequately protected by other means, such as strong encryption or other measures taken by the controller/exporter or the recipient/importer. The DPD restriction is thus based on the assumption, exemplified by the German regulator's view mentioned below,[15] that data physically located in a particular country risk being accessed by unauthorized third parties located in that country.

However, technological developments, particularly the Internet, have undermined this assumption, and some national implementations take a different approach. For instance, the UK Information Commissioner's Office (ICO) considers that a controller is entitled to assess whether protection is adequate in the circumstances, so that, for example, it is reasonable to decide adequate protection exists where an employee takes a laptop containing personal data outside the EEA, as long as the information stays with the employee on the laptop and the employer has effective procedures to address security and other risks of using laptops (including the extra risks of international travel).[16] The German federal law, discussed below,[17] focuses on adequacy of protection offered by the data *recipient* in the third country, rather than under the laws of that country.

3. What Is a 'Transfer'? Who Makes the Transfer?

Given the importance of data transfers in cloud computing, we first consider what is a 'transfer', the exceptions for allowing international data transfers, and whether and how these exceptions might apply to cloud.

The DPD does not define 'transfer', although some national laws do. As mentioned above,[18] the A29WP considers that a transfer of personal data to a server outside the EEA would be a regulated data export for DPD purposes. Therefore, it might seem reasonable to take the view that, in considering whether a data export has occurred in a cloud operation, one should first ascertain the geographical location of the equipment used for the processing, in practice the location of the data centre(s) used to provide the cloud service.

However, in the analogous situation of web hosting, unfortunately the DPD 'does not lay down criteria for deciding whether operations carried out by hosting providers should be deemed to occur in the place of establishment of the service provider or at its business address or in the place where the computer or computers constituting the service's infrastructure are located'.[19] Pragmatically, the European Court of Justice (ECJ) noted that treating uploading of personal data to a web host as a 'transfer' to a third country would lead to impracticable and unrealistic results.[20] It concluded there was no

---

[15] Paragraph containing n. 29.

[16] ICO, 'Sending Personal Data outside the European Economic Area (Principle 8)',<http://www.ico.gov.uk/for_organisations/data_protection/the_guide/principle_8.aspx> (accessed 22 March 2013).

[17] Paragraph containing n. 28.

[18] N. 6.   [19] Case C-101/01 *Bodil Lindqvist* [2003] ECR I-12971 (*Lindqvist*) [67].

[20] 'If Article 25 of Directive 95/46 were interpreted to mean that there is "transfer [of data] to a third country" every time that personal data are loaded onto an internet page, that transfer would necessarily

data export 'where an individual in a Member State loads personal data onto an internet page which is stored with his hosting provider which is established in that State or in another Member State, thereby making those data accessible to anyone who connects to the internet, including people in a third country'.[21] The ECJ carefully confined this holding to the uploading of data to a host 'established in' a Member State, stressing that the question referred to it concerned only the uploader's activities, not hosting providers', although it recognized that the host's infrastructure might be and indeed often was located in other countries. The ECJ considered it 'unnecessary to investigate whether an individual from a third country has accessed the internet page concerned or whether the server of that hosting service is physically in a third country'. Although the ECJ did not discuss when the transfer happens, the ICO considers 'a transfer was only deemed to have occurred where the internet page was actually accessed by a person located in a third country'.[22]

How does this apply to cloud services involving data centres or server farms inside and/or outside the EEA, particularly where the cloud provider is established in the EEA? *Lindqvist*[23] seems to suggest that if a cloud customer uploads personal data to an EEA-established cloud provider, there is no data export by the customer, wherever the provider's data centres are located. However, even the ICO, generally thought one of the more pragmatic regulators, considers that if a controller uploads data to a UK-based web server intending that the information will be accessed by website visitors outside the EEA, that upload is a regulated transfer. Thus, the focus in the UK is seemingly on *intention* to allow non-EEA entities to access data, although the 'intention' aspect was not spelled out fully in the DPD or the UK implementation.[24]

On that basis, data export restrictions may be relevant to web hosting activities primarily because data are uploaded to a public website. Conversely, if a controller uploads personal data to an EEA-established cloud provider, intending to store or operate on the data using cloud computing, but not intending the data to be publicly accessible, it is arguable, based on *Lindqvist*, that the controller is not exporting data, even if the provider uses a *non*-EEA data centre (or non-EEA provider) to provide its services. Whether the *provider* exports data by doing so is another issue; it might even risk becoming a controller through taking the decision to use a non-EEA data centre or non-EEA provider.[25]

Another question is the relevance, if any, of the controller's knowledge that the provider will use a non-EEA data centre for the processing. If the controller knows that the provider uses only non-EEA data centres, does this mean that the controller 'intended'

---

be a transfer to all the third countries where there are the technical means needed to access the internet. The special regime provided for by Chapter IV of the directive would thus necessarily become a regime of general application, as regards operations on the internet. Thus, if the Commission found, pursuant to Article 25(4) of Directive 95/46, that even one third country did not ensure adequate protection, the Member States would be obliged to prevent any personal data being placed on the internet' *Lindqvist*, [69].

[21] *Lindqvist*, [69] and [71].

[22] ICO, 'The Eighth Data Protection Principle and International Data Transfers v4.0' (2010), 1.3.4. Commentators also share this view that transfer involves actual receipt of information in a third country, not potential ability to access it, for example Christopher Kuner, *European Data Protection Law: Corporate Compliance and Regulation*, 2nd edn (Oxford: Oxford University Press, 2007), 4.08.

[23] N. 19.

[24] In an ECJ case on the Database Directive, in relation to uploaded data, the Court considered that the relevant act occurred 'at least' in the downloader's Member State if there was evidence of the uploader's intention to target members of the public in the downloader's state. See Chapter 9, Section 5.

[25] SWIFT (n. 6); see also n. 99: the ability to make 'critical decisions', including on the location of SWIFT's operating centres, was considered a factor.

to export data? Must the controller ask about the location of data centre(s) used, to avoid the risk of breaching the data export restriction? Can intention to export be attributed to it from lack of inquiry? What is the controller's position if the provider declines (eg, for security reasons) to name locations of all data centres which could be used to process data for that controller? Similarly, where a controller uses a non-EEA provider that may use non-EEA data centres, or where the direct provider uses sub-providers (or even sub-sub-providers, etc.) who use non-EEA data centres—for example, where an EEA SaaS provider builds its service on an IaaS provider's platform or infrastructure, and the IaaS provider uses non-EEA data centres.

A further issue is the possible ability of the provider (and of any sub-provider, eg IaaS provider) to access cloud users' data. As discussed previously,[26] where data stored with providers are not encrypted, or only weakly encrypted, most providers have the technical ability to access the data in intelligible form. Most providers also contractually reserve the right to do so, for example for service or support reasons or if disclosure is compelled or requested by law enforcement authorities. If the controller (cloud customer) knows that the provider has the ability and legal right to access its data, and the provider is established outside the EEA, does this mean that the controller 'intended' to allow non-EEA entities to access its data? Must the controller investigate the extent of the provider's ability to access its data?[27]

Here, it is interesting to note that the German Federal Data Protection Act defines 'transfer' as 'the revealing to a third party of personal data which are stored or have been obtained by data processing in such a way that (a) the data are given to the third party or (b) the third party views or accesses data which is made available for view or access'.[28] Thus, again, the emphasis seems to be on 'transfer' involving a third party knowing or accessing data. However, where the cloud provider is outside Germany or the EEA, at least one German regulator seems to consider that cloud computing necessarily involves data export. He did not discuss the possibility that a non-EEA provider might, nevertheless, use an EEA-located data centre for certain processing, but took the view that, if data are processed in another country, persons in that country, such as law enforcement authorities, may be able to access users' data, including by demanding decryption keys for any encrypted data.[29]

Also of interest are the views of Denmark's Data Protection Agency (Datatilsynet). In connection with proposed use of Google Apps (SaaS) by the Danish municipality Odense, it ruled that, while transmission to Google Ireland Limited acting as a data processor and to data centres located in EU member countries or EEA countries would not be a third-country transmission, transmission to data centres in the US and certain countries in Europe would constitute regulated transfers subject to Danish data protection law export restrictions (the *Odense* decision).[30] The Datatilsynet did not seem to have considered the question of intention to allow access to data.

---

[26] See Chapter 7.

[27] If the provider is considered a controller (see Chapter 8) through its ability to choose sub-providers, location of data centre(s) used and/or security measures, the same issues regarding its knowledge, 'intention' to export, sub-provider's ability to access data, and so on, would be relevant equally to the provider as controller.

[28] Kuner (n. 22), 2.44.

[29] For example, the regulator for the German state of Schleswig-Holstein, Thilo Weichert, 'Cloud Computing and Data Privacy' (The Sedona Conference 2011): 'If we include entities outside the European Union, the data transfer that is inevitable with cloud computing—and which has no legitimacy under data privacy law—makes clouds inherently impermissible.'

[30] Datatilsynet, 'Processing of Sensitive Personal Data in a Cloud Solution' (2011), 3.3.

Therefore, if, for processing personal data, an EEA controller uses a cloud provider (even one established in the EEA) with data centres both inside and outside the EEA, where such data may flow to third-country data centres, the cautious view, and the one generally adopted in practice, is that export restrictions would apply to that use. This is one driver behind cloud providers increasingly offering customers the option to confine data to EEA servers only.[31]

What of the not uncommon situation where a provider uses a sub-provider's platform or infrastructure to provide cloud services to an EEA customer? If the provider is treated as a processor, its sub-provider, for example an underlying IaaS or PaaS provider, might be treated as a sub-processor, in which case the previous discussion on the customer's intention or knowledge of ultimate data centre location(s) may be relevant. If a non-EEA data centre is used, it will also be necessary to consider whether there is a data export by the customer, by the provider, or indeed by the sub-provider. If no such providers are 'controllers', then it seems the export would be effected solely by the cloud customer, assuming it has any necessary intention. The question may arise whether, by choosing to use a non-EEA data centre or a sub-provider with a non-EEA data centre, the provider thereby becomes a controller. However, equally it could be argued that it is the cloud user who controls the means, by choosing to use a cloud provider who (ultimately) uses a non-EEA data centre.

The Appendix to this chapter contains tables and notes regarding some possible permutations of countries involved, illustrating the complexities of international data transfers in cloud. Data export may occur in situations other than deliberate upload of data to a cloud provider. A German state regulator has required website owners in that state to deactivate certain features such as fan pages and the 'Like' plug-in from social networking service Facebook. These services transfer content and traffic data to Facebook in the US, with limited web analytics information (on number of visitors etc.) being provided to the website owner, enabling Facebook to track and profile visitors for two years. The regulator considered that this conflicted with German communications and data protection laws unless website users' informed consent had been given before the transfer to Facebook. Logically, this could extend to non-EEA analytics services other than Facebook's, such as Google Analytics, and indeed other web-based services such as social bookmarking. It is therefore relevant to some SaaS services as well as German and perhaps other EEA websites generally, and is 'only the beginning of a continuing privacy impact analysis of Facebook applications'.[32]

Finally, the purpose of the data export restriction merits consideration. It aims to ensure that personal data are protected, by not allowing the data to enter countries deemed to have inadequate protection. There is a view that if a non-EEA data importer is subject to the DPD through the application of Article 4,[33] and therefore must protect the imported personal data in accordance with DPD requirements, the data export restriction should not apply.[34] However, notwithstanding this view, Member States' authorities tend to treat the data export restriction as a separate stand-alone requirement.

4. Data Export Exceptions/Derogations

We now consider situations where the DPD, notwithstanding lack of adequate protection, permits export.

---

[31] See Section 6.5 below.

[32] Data Protection Commissioner's Office (Independent Centre for Privacy Protection—ULD) for Schleswig-Holstein, 'ULD to Website Owners: "Deactivate Facebook Web Analytics" ', <https://www.datenschutzzentrum.de/presse/20110819-facebook-en.htm> (2011) (accessed 22 March 2013).

[33] See Chapter 9.   [34] Kuner (n. 22) 4.33.

4.1 Consent

Under Article 26(1)(a), if the data subject has given unambiguous consent to a data transfer, the transfer may proceed notwithstanding a lack of adequate protection. However, the consent must be a freely given, specific, informed, and unambiguous indication of the data subject's wishes, which the A29WP has interpreted strictly.[35] While Article 26(1)(a) may be used to allow one-off transfers where the data subject's consent has been 'specifically given for the particular transfer or a particular category of transfers in question', in relation to repeated or structural transfers the A29WP has expressed the view that in practice consent is unlikely to provide a satisfactory long-term framework.[36]

Consent as a justification may also be difficult in practice as the A29WP considers that, for advance consent to future transfers to be valid, details of the transfer must be 'already predetermined, notably in terms of purpose and categories of recipients', as well as notified to data subjects, and that consent may be withdrawn at any time (which would require isolating the personal data concerned and preventing its export).[37] Therefore, for regular or repeated transfers made as part of a business or other commercial relationship, such as when using cloud, it may be better to try to find a justification other than consent.

Reliance on consent also raises the questions of who is the data subject from whom consent must be obtained, and who is actually transferring the personal data.

On the one hand, if a user of a SaaS service, such as a social networking site, is both a data subject and a joint controller knowing that his or her personal data will be transferred, processed, and stored in a third country without an adequate standard of protection, it could be argued that this user has given consent as data subject.

On the other hand, if the cloud user is not the data subject of the data transferred, it may be impossible to rely on the consent derogation in Article 26(1)(a). For example, if a business uses a cloud application to process customer data (such as purchase orders), it may be more difficult to rely on an argument that the data subject (the customer) has given consent.

The same may apply where an EEA user of a SaaS service such as a social networking service posts personal data of other individuals, such as friends' photographs or names. Individuals may benefit from the 'household exception' (processing personal data for a purely personal or household activity).[38] However, the A29WP considers that 'A high number of contacts could be an indication that the household exception does not apply', so the user would be a controller subject to data protection law requirements. Similarly, where access to profile information is available to all site members (or indeed the public) and/or indexable by search engines, or the user takes 'an informed decision' to extend

---

[35] Article 2(h). Not all national implementations include this wording in their definition of 'consent'; for example, the UK Data Protection Act 1998 does not. A29WP, 'Transfers of Personal Data to Third Countries: Applying Articles 25 and 26 of the EU Data Protection Directive' WP12 (1998), 24 and A29WP, 'Working Document on a Common Interpretation of Article 26(1) of Directive 95/46/EC of 24 October 1995' WP114 (2005) (WP114), 10–12 explain the A29WP's views on the prerequisites for valid 'consent' to exporting data to a country without 'adequate protection', for example properly informing the data subject of the particular risk that his or her data are to be transferred to a country lacking adequate protection. Implied consent, such as notification of transfer and failure to object, is unlikely to be considered sufficient. For a detailed discussion of the general concept of 'consent', see A29WP, 'Opinion 15/2011 on the Definition of Consent' WP187 (2011).

[36] 'In fact, particularly if the transfer forms an intrinsic part of the main processing (for example centralisation of a world database of human resources, which needs to be fed by continual and systematic data transfers to be operational), the data controllers could find themselves in insoluble situations if just one data subject subsequently decided to withdraw his consent.' WP114, 11.

[37] WP114, 12. [38] Article 3(2).

access beyond self-selected friends.[39] In that event, when posting personal data of others, including non-members of the site, users must comply with data protection laws, including data export restrictions.

The difficulties regarding data subject consent to others' processing of their personal data, let alone unambiguous consent to data export, were highlighted when Germany's Hamburg data protection authority took proceedings against social networking SaaS service Facebook. Facebook encouraged its members to use its 'Friend Finder' tool to 'import' their email address books, thereby giving Facebook access to email addresses of members' contacts and other personal data of members' contacts. Facebook used that information to send unsolicited emails to members' contacts inviting them to join Facebook, without the contacts' consent. After discussions, Facebook agreed to make changes, including allowing email recipients to block further emails from Facebook.[40]

Obtaining data subject consent when a cloud customer wishes to use cloud services involving export of third-party personal data may thus be problematic. It is possible, but the controller would have to show that the data subjects' consent to the transfer was freely given, specific, informed, and unambiguous, and it may prefer not to have to rely on this exception.

4.2 Other derogations contained in Article 26

A transfer may also be justified if necessary for the performance of a contract between the data subject and the data controller, under Article 26(1)(b). For instance, a data subject who is a cloud customer may know the service is provided from outside the EEA, and cannot be provided within the EEA, but choose to use it nonetheless. An often-used example of 'necessity' involves a travel agent sending an individual's personal data to the third-country hotels concerned when an individual books a trip abroad.

The A29WP considers that derogations, for example for 'necessity', should be construed restrictively,[41] and, as the ICO has noted, cost-efficiency is not necessity.[42] There is nothing intrinsic to cloud that necessitates transfer of data to a particular jurisdiction or a jurisdiction without an adequate standard; in fact, some cloud providers provide regional clouds to avoid the issues surrounding transfer.[43]

None of the other derogations mentioned in Article 26 seem particularly relevant to cloud. Indeed, as WP196 stresses, the A29WP's view is that the Article 26 exemptions can only apply 'where transfers are neither recurrent, nor massive or structural', so it is 'almost impossible' to rely on them in cloud.

5. Ways to Meet the Adequacy Requirement

Where no exception can apply, personal data may still be exported from the EEA if the adequacy requirement can be met. In fact, EU regulators prefer adequacy as the basis for export, considering use of a derogation to be less satisfactory, as personal data loses protection once exported through a derogation.[44]

---

[39] A29WP, 'Opinion 5/2009 on Online Social Networking' WP163 (2009), 3.1.1, 3.1.2.
[40] 'Facebook Agrees to Change "Friend Finder" Feature', Spiegel Online International, 2011, <http://www.spiegel.de/international/business/0,1518,741027,00.html> (accessed 22 March 2013).
[41] WP114 (n. 35), 13.   [42] ICO (n. 22), 25.   [43] See Section 6.5 below.
[44] WP114 (n. 35); Kuner (n. 22), 4.12.

5.1 EU–US Safe Harbor principles[45]

The US and the EU have agreed a self-regulatory regime allowing US organizations (including cloud providers) that import personal data from the EU to demonstrate an adequate standard of protection under Article 25, by participating in a 'Safe Harbor' programme. Reportedly, the popularity of this programme has increased with the advent of cloud computing.[46]

The only entities permitted to participate in the Safe Harbor are US organizations that are subject to the jurisdiction of the US Federal Trade Commission (FTC) or US air carriers and ticket agents subject to the Department of Transportation (DOT)'s jurisdiction. Many types of organizations cannot use Safe Harbor because they are not subject to relevant regulatory oversight by the FTC or DOT, including telecommunication common carriers and financial institutions.

To obtain Safe Harbor status a US organization must either join an existing self-regulatory privacy programme or develop its own privacy scheme complying with the requirements. The organization must self-certify annually that it is Safe Harbor-compliant to the US Department of Commerce, which publishes a list of all Safe Harbor participants, and state, in its publicly accessible privacy policy, its adherence to the Safe Harbor principles (of Notice, Choice, Transfers to Third Parties, Access, Security, Data Integrity, and Enforcement). Duly certified and listed organizations are often called 'Safe Harborites'.

The Safe Harbor regime is primarily supervised by the private sector, backed up by government enforcement. Participating US organizations must establish self-assessment or third-party assessment audit procedures for verifying compliance with Safe Harbor and provide dispute resolution for complainants. The dispute resolution procedures must provide for sanctions, publicity, and deletion of data, as well as suspension of Safe Harbor status. Dispute resolution may either be via a private dispute resolution provider[47] or in cooperation with a panel provided by the relevant EU data protection authority. The FTC and DOT have powers to enforce the Safe Harbor regime where an organization's failure to comply constitutes an infringement of state or federal laws prohibiting unfair or deceptive acts.[48]

It might seem that as, currently, most large cloud providers are US-based or headquartered entities, Safe Harbor would be the obvious mechanism to facilitate use by EEA controllers of US cloud providers' services. However, doubts have been raised about Safe Harbor.

There is some uncertainty regarding whether the Safe Harbor framework applies to transfers to a US processor (as opposed to controller), such as a cloud provider. The better view is that it does, and that Safe Harbor requirements such as notice and choice may be met by the controller–exporter giving notice of the processing to data subjects, or instructing the processor to do so.[49] We assume that mere processors may indeed become Safe Harborites.

---

[45] Finding of adequacy for Safe Harbor effective on 30 November 2000, under Commission Decision of 26 July 2000 pursuant to Directive 95/46/EC of the European Parliament and of the Council on the adequacy of the protection provided by the safe harbour privacy principles and related frequently asked questions issued by the US Department of Commerce, 2000/520/EC [25 August 2000] OJ L215/7.

[46] Scott Sanchez, 'Location, Location, Location—Storing EU Data with Safe Harbor' (*Cloud Computing Journal* 2010), <http://cloudcomputing.sys-con.com/node/1562070> (accessed 22 March 2013).

[47] Such as the Judicial Arbitration and Mediation Service and the American Arbitration Association. US Department of Commerce, *Safe Harbor Workbook*, <http://export.gov/safeharbor/eg_main_018238.asp> (accessed 22 March 2013).

[48] Such as s. 5 of the US Federal Trade Commission Act.   [49] Kuner (n. 22) 182.

Furthermore, a 2008 study found only about 70 per cent of organizations on the Safe Harbor list were currently certified, and only some 20 per cent of listed organizations met even basic requirements, with 13 per cent choosing non-affordable dispute resolution providers.[50] In 2009, the FTC moved against seven US businesses which falsely claimed current Safe Harbor certifications.[51] In 2011, it took its first action for breach of substantive Safe Harbor principles. This was against Google in relation to its Buzz SaaS service, for failing to give users of its SaaS webmail service Gmail any notice before, or choice about, Google's use of information collected for Gmail for a purpose other than that for which it was originally collected.[52]

The Safe Harbor adequacy decision by the European Commission should permit transfers to the US 'without additional guarantees being necessary'.[53] Indeed, some UK educational institutions use Google Apps for Education based on Safe Harbor and Google's standard terms.[54] However, the 'Düsseldorfer Kreis' group of 16 German federal and state data protection regulators[55] requires German controllers to conduct and document certain checks before transferring personal data to Safe Harborites,[56] and the A29WP in its opinion on cloud computing (WP196)[57] endorsed the view that controllers exporting personal data 'should obtain evidence that the Safe Harbor self-certifications exists and request evidence demonstrating that their principles are complied with', stressing that notwithstanding use of Safe Harbor, cloud providers' contracts must comply with national data protection law requirements (or use model clauses or binding corporate rules (BCRs), see below). Indeed, the A29WP considers that Safe Harbor principles may be insufficient to guarantee security, given cloud-specific risks, and that additional safeguards such as third-party certifications may be advisable.

Another question is, may personal data safely be exported to an US entity because it is a Safe Harborite? Or must the exporter nevertheless inquire where the Safe Harborite intends to store the exported data (US only, or outside) and/or to whom the Safe Harborite intends to or may transfer or disclose the data? The first issue, regarding location of data that is to be exported under Safe Harbor, was discussed in *Odense*. There, the Datatilsynet considered that, as Google, Inc. had subscribed to Safe Harbor, Safe Harbor permitted transfers of personal data to Google's US data centres—but *not* transfers to 'data centres located in other insecure third countries than the USA'. Without confirmation that Google's European data centres were in the EEA, the authority considered that the transfer provisions were not complied with. It considered, however, that transfer would have been permissible had model clauses (see below) been used.[58] On this basis,

---

[50] Galexia, The US Safe Harbor—Fact or Fiction? (2008).

[51] FTC, 'Court Halts U.S. Internet Seller Deceptively Posing as U.K. Home Electronics Site' (FTC File No. 092-3081) (2009) and FTC, 'FTC Settles with Six Companies Claiming to Comply with International Privacy Framework' (FTC File No. 0923137) (2009).

[52] FTC, 'FTC Charges Deceptive Privacy Practices in Google's Rollout of Its Buzz Social Network' (FTC File No. 102 3136) (2011).

[53] Recital 2, Safe Harbor decision (n. 45).

[54] For example, the University of Cambridge, which made its contract available publicly at <http://www.ucs.cam.ac.uk/googleapps/google-apps-cambridge-contract.pdf> (accessed 22 March 2013).

[55] <http://www.datenschutz-berlin.de/content/deutschland/duesseldorfer-kreis> (accessed 22 March 2013).

[56] 'Decision by the supreme supervisory authorities for data protection in the non-public sector on 28/29 April 2010 in Hannover (revised 23 August 2010)—Examination of the data importer's self-certification according to the Safe-Harbor-Agreement by the company exporting data', available at <https://www.datenschutzzentrum.de/internationaler-datenverkehr/Resolution_DuesseldorfCircle_DE%20DPAs_rev.EN.pdf> (accessed 3 April 2013).

[57] A29WP, 'Opinion 05/2012 on Cloud Computing' WP196 (2012).

[58] 'Odense Municipality and the individual data centres may enter into an agreement based on the EU Commission's standard contractual clauses, or Odense Municipality may grant Google Ireland

it is insufficient merely to check that the proposed provider is a listed Safe Harborite; the controller also needs to check that data centres to be used by the Safe Harborite to process the controller's data are located only in the US and/or EEA.

This ruling typifies the regulatory focus on location of data, rather than of the Safe Harbor-certified entity. With portable physical data storage media such as a hard drive, CD-ROM or USB stick, the fixation on data location may be understandable, but with cloud computing it is jurisdiction over the data-importing entity that is much more significant for data protection oversight purposes than data location, as discussed later.[59] Interestingly, German law generally focuses on adequacy of protection offered by the *recipient* in any third country, rather than by the country's legal system,[60] but that approach is not followed through in other respects.

We now consider so-called 'onward transfers'—Safe Harbor parlance for the increasingly common 'disclosure' of exported information by Safe Harborites to third parties.[61] Where an EEA controller exports data to a US cloud provider which is a Safe Harborite ('Safe Harborite provider'), is there an 'onward transfer' if the provider utilizes a sub-provider's infrastructure to process the data, such as where a SaaS provider uses a PaaS or IaaS provider? We argued previously[62] that many IaaS, PaaS, and some SaaS providers are not even processors, because they have a passive role and merely provide infrastructure and other resources for use by the controller. Arguably, this is the case too with sub-providers, at least with sub-providers who have no technical ability to access the data. Nevertheless, it is insufficiently clear whether use of a sub-provider involves onward transfer.

Similarly, the onward transfer rules seem to equate 'transfer' with 'disclosure'. However, this is not necessarily so. Transfer of data to a provider or sub-provider for storage or other processing does not necessarily involve disclosing data to it. For example, data will not be disclosed if they were strongly encrypted, or the system's design does not allow the provider to read data in an intelligible form, as discussed above.[63] However, for simplicity of discussion, we assume here that 'transfer' involves 'disclosure'.

Access by third parties to data exported to a Safe Harborite would also constitute 'onward transfer', including remote access. Except where a Safe Harborite provider is technically able to, and does, allow third parties access to data, for example US law enforcement authorities,[64] onward transfers via allowing third parties to access exported data would generally be controlled by the controller–exporter, not the provider. For example, a controller could enable its employees worldwide to view data stored by it with a US cloud provider. However, Safe Harbor rules seem to place onward transfer responsibilities on the Safe Harborite, although, as with arguments regarding whether processors can be Safe Harborites, arguably these responsibilities could be met through the controller–exporter's actions. These issues may be relevant not just to cloud but also to websites of EEA entities hosted using US hosting providers.

Limited a clear mandate to enter into agreements, in Odense Municipality's name and on behalf of Odense Municipality, based on the EU Commission's standard contractual clauses with the individual data centres'—but the Datatilsynet assumed that there were no such agreements as it was not informed of any: fns 30 and 114.

[59] Text to n. 113.

[60] European Commission, 'Analysis and Impact Study on the Implementation of Directive EC 95/46 in Member States' (2003), 31.

[61] US Department of Commerce, *Safe Harbor Privacy Principles* (2000). The problems with onward transfers are discussed in Christopher Kuner, 'Onward Transfers of Personal Data under the US Safe Harbor Framework', (2009) 8 *Privacy & Security Law Report* 33.

[62] See Chapter 8.   [63] See Chapter 7.   [64] See Chapter 11.

The position regarding onward transfers is problematic, not least because Safe Harbor terminology does not reflect the DPD's 'controller'/'processor' concepts. A related debate concerns whether personal data, once duly exported to a Safe Harborite, are thereafter subject only to US law Safe Harbor rules, or whether exported data and their processing (including onward transfers) remain subject to the data protection rules of the exporter's Member State, which stay 'attached' to the data wherever they go. The US government and US entities take the former view, whereas many EU regulators take the latter.

A further complication is that Safe Harbor rules regulating onward transfers differ, depending on whether the 'transfer' is to a third party 'acting as an agent' ('to perform task(s) on behalf of and under the instructions of the organization'). 'Agents' seem to map to 'processors', and other 'third parties' to 'controllers'. Requirements for non-agents involve applying the notice and choice principles, which may be difficult to fulfil in practice. For 'transfers' to 'agents', the Safe Harborite must first check that the agent 'subscribes to the [Safe Harbor] Principles or is subject to the Directive or another adequacy finding or enters into a written agreement with such third party requiring that the third party provide at least the same level of privacy protection as is required by the relevant Principles'.[65] Kuner[66] suggests that, to limit the importer/provider's risks, an 'assurance agreement' with non-EEA onward transferees would be sensible.

However, the status of sub-providers as processors or otherwise is unclear. Arguably, many sub-providers are not even 'agents', but mere infrastructure providers; some may not have access to information that is 'transferred' to them. Even assuming sub-providers are 'third parties', it is unclear whether they are 'agents' or not, and therefore it is uncertain which set of requirements must be met to enable a Safe Harborite provider to use a sub-provider. Either set may be impracticable to comply with when using cloud sub-providers. It is unclear, for instance, to what extent Safe Harborite providers in practice check that non-EEA sub-providers whose infrastructure they utilize subscribe to the Safe Harbor or process the data in an 'adequate' country, let alone enter into assurance agreements with them.

Where an EEA controller transfers data to a Safe Harborite provider intending future remote access to the data by third parties, the provider may not know or have control over who those third parties are, let alone have relationships with them. This seems to put the main burden (to give notice to data subjects, etc.) on the controller, depending on the circumstances. This raises many thorny fact-dependent practical issues. The possible lack of clarity as to the status of those third parties is exacerbated by the general difficulty, under current EU data protection laws, of distinguishing between controllers and processors.[67]

5.2 Model clauses

Article 26(4) provides that if a transfer of data to outside the EEA is made under contractual clauses the terms of which have been approved by the European Commission for this purpose, the protection is considered adequate, and the transfer must be permitted by Member States.

Standard contractual clauses have been issued by the European Commission for transfers of personal data from an EEA-established controller to a controller in a third

---

[65] Safe Harbor Principles (n. 61). It is also uncertain whether an organization may 'subscribe' to the Safe Harbor principles without being formally a Safe Harborite.
[66] N. 61.   [67] See Chapter 8.

country,[68] or from an EEA-established controller to a third-country processor.[69] The latter clauses were replaced in 2010[70] and now cover transfers by a third-country processor to a third-country sub-processor, or sub-sub-processor, and so on.

5.3 Binding corporate rules

BCRs are codes of conduct dealing with the international transfer of personal data within the same corporate group at a multinational level, subject to authorization by the relevant data protection authorities, devised by the A29WP under Article 26(2) of the DPD with industry input.[71]

Transfers to third countries under approved BCRs are permissible. However, the process for obtaining regulatory approval is currently long and expensive,[72] with different Member States having their own procedures, and some States' data protection authorities taking the view that each transfer under an approved BCR still requires individual approval.[73] Controller BCRs only allow transfers within the same corporate group, so they might be helpful for facilitating data transfers within a corporate group's private cloud, but cannot be used if a provider or sub-provider is outside the group.

Responding to calls for BCRs that would facilitate transfers to an external processor, such as a cloud provider, in 2012 the A29WP launched processor BCRs, with a similar application procedure and form as for controller BCRs.[74] Once a BCR for processors is approved it can be used by controllers and processors to ensure compliance with EU data protection rules without having to negotiate the safeguards and conditions every time a contract is entered into. Thus, processor BCRs may be used by controllers to support requests for authorization to transfer personal data to 'the different entities of their processors (for example subprocessors and data centers)'.

---

[68] There are two set of clauses for controller-controller transfers, under Commission Decision of 15 June 2001 on standard contractual clauses for the transfer of personal data to third countries, under Directive 95/46/EC (2001/497/EC), [4 July 2001] OJ L181/19, and Commission Decision of 27 December 2004 amending Decision 2001/497/EC as regards the introduction of an alternative set of standard contractual clauses for the transfer of personal data to third countries (2004/915/EC), [29 December 2004] OJ L385/74. Either set may be used, although controllers tend to prefer the latter set as it incorporates some of the changes requested by the ICC and other business groups.

[69] Under Commission Decision of 27 December 2001 on standard contractual clauses for the transfer of personal data to processors established in third countries, under Directive 95/46/EC (2002/16/EC), [10 January 2002] OJ L6/52.

[70] By Commission Decision of 5 February 2010 on standard contractual clauses for the transfer of personal data to processors established in third countries under Directive 95/46/EC of the European Parliament and of the Council (2010/87/EU), [12 February 2010] OJ L39/5, the clauses in this Decision superseded the 2001 standard controller-processor clauses, which may no longer be used.

[71] For a list of the main A29WP working papers on BCRs, see European Commission, 'Available Tools', <http://ec.europa.eu/justice/data-protection/document/international-transfers/binding-corporate-rules/tools/index_en.htm> (accessed 22 March 2013).

[72] The ICO noted, 'it currently takes 9 months to 1 year from receipt of the first draft of the BCR to it being approved by the relevant Authorities. (There are 36 approved BCRs across all DPAs and the UK has been lead authority on 15 of these applications)'. ICO, 'Proposed New EU General Data Protection Regulation' (*ICO*, 12 February 2013), <http://www.ico.gov.uk/~/media/documents/library/Data_Protection/Research_and_reports/ico_proposed_dp_regulation_analysis_paper_20130212_pdf.ashx> (accessed 3 April 2013), 59.

[73] Kuner (n. 22) 4.120–4.154.

[74] Press Release, Article 29 Data Protection Working Party, 'European data protection Authorities launch Binding Corporate Rules for processors' (21 December 2012); and see Article 29 Data Protection Working Party, 'Working Document 02/2012 setting up a table with the elements and principles to be found in Processor Binding Corporate Rules' (adopted 6 June 2012), WP 195. See also, Article 29 Data Protection Working Party, 'Explanatory Document on the Processor Binding Corporate Rules' (adopted 19 April 2013), WP204.

After a processor has secured approval by the relevant data protection authority of its processor BCR, a controller may enter into a 'service agreement' with that processor containing certain required provisions. Personal data may then be transferred from the controller to members of that processor outside the EEA who participate in the processor BCR, or to data centres of the processor or its group located outside the EEA. Processor BCRs are possible even for processors who have no group members established in the EEA. Furthermore, onward transfers to sub-processors who are not part of the processor's group are specifically permitted.

At first sight, it might seem that processor BCRs would enable EEA controllers to use cloud computing to store or otherwise process personal data outside the EEA. However, because of the A29WP's requirements for approval of processor BCRs, processor BCRs are unlikely to be used where sub-providers outside the processor's corporate group are involved, for example in a layered services situation where the non-EEA IaaS or PaaS sub-provider used by the processor is a third party, or indeed where the operator of the non-EEA data centre used by the processor is a third party. This is because, for processor BCRs to be approved, certain requirements must be satisfied in relation to any use of external sub-providers, even if the controller is willing to give its 'prior written consent' generally to the use of a long list of possible external sub-providers. For example, for a processor BCR to be approved, any external sub-provider is required, but may not wish, to agree to: third-party beneficiary rights in favour of the data subjects concerned and obligations towards the controller; compliance with security obligations to the standards of the controller's applicable law; security breach notification; a 'general duty' to 'co-operate and assist' such controllers 'to comply with data protection law' including providing information about any sub-sub-providers; obligations regarding security measures and security breach notifications; to destroy and certify destruction of personal data on service termination;[75] and more generally to change its (probably pre-existing) contract with the processor 'to respect the same obligations as are imposed on the member of the Processor's group according to the Service Agreement concluded with the data controller'. These requirements may be feasible with traditional outsourced processing, but may well not be practicable or appropriate in cloud computing, particularly with layered services, given the self-service nature of cloud and its reverse 'direction of travel',[76] the lack of knowledge on the part of many IaaS/PaaS or passive SaaS storage providers as to the nature of data processed using their services, and some SaaS providers' likely lack of bargaining power to persuade any underlying IaaS or PaaS provider to change its contract terms.[77] Providers, particularly those offering cheap utility cloud services, may also be unwilling to accept liability for failures by external sub-providers, as is required for BCR approval.

Processor BCRs may provide a workable solution in cloud computing in one situation: where the processor has effective control of the supply chain used, for instance providers who do not use sub-providers, or, more likely, providers who have vertically integrated cloud offerings or the power to dictate terms to their sub-providers, such as Amazon, Google, or Microsoft. Thus, under current laws larger providers may have an advantage over small providers, who may lack the resources or bargaining power to apply

---

[75] See Chapter 2, Section 2.2 and Chapter 8, Section 3.3.
[76] In other words, the fact that in cloud arrangements a customer will typically purchase a pre-packaged and multilayered service, which may encompass established and complex sub-provider relationships. This is in marked contrast to conventional outsourcing arrangements where a customer may be in a much stronger position to negotiate an arrangement that will ensure that the customer's instructions are passed down the chain to sub-processors. See Chapter 2, Section 5.2 para 2.
[77] These difficulties arise more generally with the use of cloud services for personal data, especially layered services (see Chapter 8).

for or implement processor BCRs, particularly EEA cloud providers who use non-EEA sub-providers.

All the same, there may still be difficulties for providers, even large providers, who may be required by law to disclose cloud data, for instance when requested by foreign law enforcement authorities, particularly where the provider is prohibited by law from revealing the request.[78] Providers may be unwilling to apply for BCR approval if they consider that the possibility of such requests may render them unable to comply with processor BCR requirements under which all members must, without any exception for other processing required by law, 'process the personal data only on behalf of the data controller and in compliance with its instructions. If it cannot provide such compliance for whatever reasons, it agrees to inform promptly the data controller of its inability to comply, in which case the data controller is entitled to suspend the transfer of data and/or terminate the contract'.

The draft Regulation would formalize the status of BCRs, which should be helpful in relation to Member States which do not currently recognize them, and would also permit processor BCRs. However, the ICO has noted that while, under the A29WP's processor BCRs, a processor can be based outside the EEA and need not have an entity established in a Member State, under the draft Regulation it seems it would not be possible to approve a processor BCR where there is no EU entity,[79] which seems retrograde.

5.4 Other options

Finally, personal data may be transferred to a third country, even if none of the above applies, under Article 26(2). This allows a Member State to authorize a transfer or a set of transfers of personal data to a third country which does not ensure an adequate level of protection within Article 25(2), where the controller adduces 'adequate safeguards' with respect to the protection of the privacy and fundamental rights and freedoms of individuals and as regards the exercise of the corresponding rights. Such safeguards may, in particular, result from 'appropriate contractual clauses'. While such authorizations should be notified to the European Commission and other Member States, very few have been notified in practice.[80] The ICO does not require transfers to be pre-authorized, but as mentioned above, allows controllers to make their own adequacy assessments.[81] Obviously, a transferor that makes its own assessment runs the risk of a data protection authority later taking the view that its assessment was wrong. The more thorough its assessment, however, the more likely that it will be able subsequently to justify it.

Most Member States are unwilling to permit data controllers' own assessments. Indeed, in Austria, Greece, Luxembourg, Portugal, and Spain, absent an European Commission adequacy finding, only national authorities can determine the adequacy of a third country, which means transfers to countries not found adequate by the European Commission or relevant national authority are not possible unless a derogation applies.[82]

---

[78] See Chapters 4 and 11.   [79] (N. 72), 61.

[80] European Commission, 'First Report on the Implementation of Directive 95/46/EC COM(2003)265 final' (2003), 4.4.5 fn. 17, and European Commission (n. 4), 13.6.

[81] ICO (n. 16) 2.3—although permitting controllers to make their own assessments seems 'out of line' with the A29WP's views: Douwe Korff, *New Challenges to Data Protection Working Paper No. 2— Data Protection Laws in the EU: The Difficulties in Meeting the Challenges Posed by Global Social and Technical Developments* (European Commission, 2010), 92.

[82] LRDP Kantor Ltd in association with Centre for Public Reform, *New Challenges to Data Protection—Final Report* (European Commission, 2010), [75].

In such cases, the authority could be requested to approve an ad hoc contract for the data export, although this has time and costs implications, and the authority might not give its approval.

6. Possible Solutions for Cloud Computing

Several possible solutions or workarounds may enable cloud computing to be used to store or otherwise process personal data, notwithstanding the data export restriction. Sometimes, a combination of these methods may be used for 'belt and braces' purposes, particularly in the not uncommon situation where the status of the provider as processor or controller is not entirely clear.

6.1 Anonymization or encryption

The data export restriction applies only to 'personal data' within the DPD's definition. If information is not, or ceases to be, 'personal data', for example because it has been adequately anonymized or strongly encrypted, it may be exported and otherwise dealt with free of the DPD's restrictions. Furthermore, data fragments stored in the cloud may not be 'personal data' in the provider's hands if the provider is unable to read the fragments, although they would remain 'personal data' as regards the cloud user storing the data, who by logging into their account with the provider may reunite the fragments. It might seem, therefore, that a cloud user need not be concerned about the data export restriction provided personal data are strongly encrypted or anonymized before being stored in the cloud, even with a provider that uses data centres located outside the EEA. However, whether the data have truly become 'anonymous' depends on the effectiveness of the anonymization, which may change over time as re-identification techniques improve, and similarly the effectiveness of the encryption (including security of key management) affects whether the data remain 'personal data'. It is also uncertain whether, even if anonymized or encrypted information is treated as anonymous data in a provider's hands, it would still be considered 'personal data' as regards the cloud user uploading the data.[83]

Until these uncertainties are resolved in all Member States, it is unclear whether encryption or anonymization of data prior to transfer to a cloud provider would be sufficient to prevent a breach of the data export restriction.

6.2 Safe Harbor

The Safe Harbor is widely used to justify data exports to US cloud providers such as Google, as mentioned above. Only US entities can apply for Safe Harbor status, though this may not be a huge barrier currently, as so many cloud providers are US entities. Even so, the Safe Harbor cannot be used by telecommunications common carriers, which are increasingly providing cloud services, and there are uncertainties as to whether the Safe Harbor applies to processors such as cloud providers. Furthermore, and perhaps more importantly, the onward transfer rules may cause difficulties when the provider uses sub-providers or when

---

[83] For detailed discussion of these issues, see Chapter 7 and Hon, '"Personal Data" in the UK, Anonymisation and Encryption' (*QMUL Cloud Legal Project*, 2011), <http://cloudlegalproject.org/Research/49700.html> (accessed 22 March 2013).

the controller wishes to allow third parties access to exported data.[84] A bigger barrier may be the doubts raised by some EU regulators about the efficacy of the Safe Harbor. Given these concerns, it is not unlikely that the EU authorities will review the Safe Harbor. The A29WP has included the Safe Harbor in its work programme for 2012–13 in any event.[85]

6.3 Model clauses

Model clauses are a possible method to enable a controller to use the services of a cloud provider who has non-EEA data centres. They may even be incorporated into the provider's online contractual terms.[86] For example, model clauses have been offered for Microsoft Office 365 SaaS since 2011,[87] while in December 2012 Google introduced Data Processing Amendments to Google Apps Enterprise Agreement[88] for Google Apps SaaS, which envisaged that EEA customers could enter into model clauses[89] with Google for transfer of data to third countries, both of which customers could opt into online.[90] Model clauses may be used for direct controller-processor transfers to a cloud provider that uses its own infrastructure.

However, there are limitations with using model clauses. They were designed for controller-to-controller or controller-to-processor transfers. They cannot be used if, as we have argued is the case in some scenarios,[91] the cloud provider is not even a processor. In such a scenario, the cloud user/controller would need to find some other exception or justification for the data export.

Also, the model clauses do not cover fully all the sub-provider scenarios that are common with cloud computing (assuming here that cloud providers are 'processors'). In particular, they 'apply only to subcontracting by a data processor established in a

---

[84] See Section 5.1.

[85] A29WP, 'Work Programme 2012–2013', <http://ec.europa.eu/justice/data-protection/article-29/documentation/opinion-recommendation/files/2012/wp190_en.pdf> (accessed 22 March 2013). In April 2013, the US Department of Commerce's International Trade Administration (ITA) published 'Clarifications Regarding the US–EU Safe Harbor Framework and Cloud Computing' in which it asserted that the Safe Harbor framework applies fully to cloud service provider agreements, <http://export.gov/static/Safe%20Harbor%20and%20Cloud%20Computing%20Clarification_April%2012%202013_Latest_eg_main_060351.pdf> (accessed 1 June 2013).

[86] In its Client-Software License Agreement for its LiveVault software, for online backup of users' data to its infrastructure, previously US provider Iron Mountain had expressly incorporated by reference the standard EU contractual clauses that address the specific restriction on the export of personal data by its EEA customers to it as processor Iron Mountain, 'Website Terms and Conditions of Use', <http://www.ironmountain.com/legal/client-software-license-agreement.html>—as at 8 September 2011, referring to the standard 2001 controller-processor clauses (n. 69). The clauses incorporated have since been superseded by a subsequent Decision (n. 70) and the version of Iron Mountain's clauses accessed on 22 March 2013 no longer incorporated any model clauses. Iron Mountain is, in fact, also on the Safe Harbor list at <http://safeharbor.export.gov/companyinfo.aspx?id=10165> (accessed 22 March 2013), so it may have decided it did not need to rely on model clauses. However, model clauses may be helpful in addition, to address other DPD requirements.

[87] Microsoft, 'Office 365 Becomes First and Only Major Cloud Productivity Service to Comply with Leading EU and US Standards for Data Protection Security', 14 December 2011, <http://www.microsoft.com/en-us/news/press/2011/dec11/12-14O365CloudPR.aspx> (accessed 3 April 2013).

[88] Google Apps, 'Data Processing Amendment to Google Apps Enterprise Agreement', <https://www.google.com/intl/en/enterprise/apps/terms/dpa_terms.html> (accessed 3 April 2013).

[89] Google Apps, 'Standard Contractual Clauses (processors) for the purposes of Article 26(2) of Directive 95/46/EC for the transfer of personal data to processors established in third countries which do not ensure an adequate level of data protection', <https://www.google.com/intl/en/enterprise/apps/terms/mcc_terms.html> (accessed 3 April 2013).

[90] Google, 'Model contract clauses for Google Apps', <http://support.google.com/a/bin/answer.py?hl=en&answer=2888485> (accessed 3 April 2013).

[91] See Chapter 8.

third country of his processing services to a sub-processor established in a third country'.[92] This means that an EEA controller may use the model clauses for cloud computing involving non-EEA sub-providers (eg a SaaS or PaaS provider that utilizes the infrastructure of a non-EEA IaaS or PaaS sub-provider), as long as its direct provider is established outside the EEA. However, if the initial cloud provider is established in the EEA, the model clauses cannot be used to enable data export to the provider's underlying non-EEA IaaS or PaaS sub-provider.

To enable data export in those situations, the EEA controller would have to enter into a direct contract with the non-EEA processor (or strictly, sub-processor), containing the model controller-processor clauses. Alternatively, the controller must authorize the EEA processor (eg in the agreement between them) to enter into a contract on its behalf with the non-EEA sub-processor incorporating those model clauses. Ad hoc contracts are another option here, but they must meet all the usual requirements, and several data protection authorities reserve the right to review any such contracts and authorize (or decline) data exports based on the contract.[93]

As the model clauses do not enable EEA cloud providers to transfer data to non-EEA sub-providers, this may incentivize EU customers to use *non*-EEA cloud providers, in order to achieve greater flexibility in terms of transfers to sub-processors. This seems to be a major limitation of the new model clauses and is a significant practical disadvantage as many EEA providers rely on the infrastructure or platforms of non-EEA IaaS and PaaS providers, such as Amazon Web Services, Google App Engine, or Microsoft Windows Azure. In order to remove the current disincentive for EEA controllers to use EEA cloud providers, it would be desirable to rectify this situation, including clarifying how processors' place of 'establishment' is determined for this purpose. It is, therefore, noteworthy that Spain's data protection authority in 2012 issued standard processor-sub-processor contractual clauses,[94] enabling Spanish processors to enter into such clauses with non-EEA sub-processors to provide adequacy, with one contract potentially covering transfers of personal data of different customers, subject to contract authorizations by the authority and the relevant controller.[95]

WP196 also states that where model clauses are used for non-EEA processors with sub-processors, 'a written agreement which imposes the same obligations on the subprocessor as are imposed on the processor in the Model clauses should be put in place'.

In order for a transfer to be recognized for adequacy purposes, the model clauses must be used 'as is' without modification, although they can be part of a larger contract whose other provisions deal with other matters. Also, the controller-processor model clauses only apply to EEA-established controllers, so they would not permit a non-EEA-established controller, to whom EU data protection laws may apply due to its use of equipment in the EEA (for example a data centre), to re-export personal data. Last but not least, many Member States

---

[92]   Recital 23 of the 2010 Decision (n. 70).

[93]   A29WP, 'FAQs in order to address some issues raised by the entry into force of the EU Commission Decision 2010/87/EU of 5 February 2010 on standard contractual clauses for the transfer of personal data to processors established in third countries under Directive 95/46/EC (WP 176)' (2010).

[94]   Relying on recital 23 of the Commission's 2010 Decision (n. 70). Gonzalo F Gállego and Belén Gámez, 'Spain Changes the Paradigm of International Transfers of Personal Data Allowing Spanish Data Processors to Be "Exporters" under the Standard Contractual Clauses for the Transfer of Data' (*HoganLovells*, 5 June 2012), <http:// www.hldataprotection.com/2012/06/articles/international-eu-privacy/spain-changes-the-paradigmof-international-transfers-of-personal-data-allowing-spanish-data-processors-to-be-exporters-under-thestandard-contractual-clauses-for-the-transfer-of-data> (accessed 3 April 2013).

[95]   Agencia Española de Protección de Datos, <https://www.agpd.es/portalwebAGPD/resoluciones/ autorizacion_transf/common/pdfs/MODELO-DEFINITIVO-AEPD_Contrato-encargado­subencargado-21-03-2012.pdf> (accessed 1 June 2013).

insist on advance authorization of contracts,[96] or the filing of contracts, sometimes in ways which effectively amount to imposing a requirement of prior approval, in some cases even though the contracts incorporate the model clauses.[97]

A final point on model clauses is that different sets must be used for controller-controller and controller-processor transfers. While cloud providers should be treated as processors (or not even that),[98] in some cases a cloud provider may risk being considered a controller. This may be the case, for example, if it uses the personal data for its own new purposes or discloses it to an unauthorized third party,[99] or perhaps even because it controls the security measures. In such a case, if the contract with the provider had utilized the processor-processor clauses, the 'wrong' clauses may have been used, and the export accordingly rendered unlawful. In practice, both sets of clauses are sometimes used, to address the not uncommon situation where it is unclear whether a provider is purely a processor or may be a controller.

6.4 BCRs

BCRs for private cloud computing within a corporate group have been mentioned above. This is the most obvious use of BCRs in cloud computing. However, in practice BCRs are cumbersome, costly, and time-consuming to obtain, so corporate groups are unlikely to go through the BCR approval procedures simply for private cloud computing purposes. The BCR approval procedures could, therefore, benefit from streamlining, harmonization, and compulsory recognition by authorities across the EEA.[100]

Processor BCRs may now be used, but it remains to be seen whether the approval procedure will be quicker or cheaper than for controller BCRs. It may also be worth considering whether BCRs could be used for transfers within a community cloud. Although community members are not necessarily part of the same corporate group, they may have enough interests in common, as for example government authorities or members of highly regulated sectors such as financial services or pharmaceutical companies, that it may be feasible for them to agree and sign up to a single legally binding self-regulatory code which will be enforceable by data subjects.

---

[96] Including Austria, Belgium, Bulgaria, Croatia, Denmark, Estonia, France, some German states, Greece, Lithuania, Luxembourg, the Netherlands, Poland, Portugal, Romania, Slovakia, Slovenia, and Spain.

[97] See Kuner (n. 22) 4.27 and appendix 12 (list of filing requirements). Chapter V of the draft Regulation would explicitly permit transfers using model clauses approved by European Commission or supervisory authorities under the specified mechanisms. This is helpful because it should mean individual authorities should no longer be able to require prior authorization of transfers incorporating such clauses.

[98] See Chapter 8.

[99] For a situation where a processor was considered to have arrogated to itself the role of controller, see the SWIFT opinion (n. 6). Here, Belgian financial messaging service provider SWIFT, which facilitates transactions between financial institutions, had decided, without informing its member institutions, to comply with US subpoenas, and allowed the US Department of the Treasury to view or search data held in SWIFT's US data centre. SWIFT was considered to have become a 'controller' as it had exceeded its authority as 'processor'; it had 'the power to take critical decisions with respect to the processing, such as the security standard and the location of its operating centres'. Contractual terms stipulating that SWIFT was to act as a processor did not prevent it from being considered a controller on the facts. This was the A29WP's opinion; the Belgian authority considered SWIFT complied with Belgian law.

[100] There are signs of some States trying to streamline procedures, for example most recently Belgium— Hunton & Williams LLP, 'Belgium Simplifies the Authorization Procedure for Binding Corporate Rules' (*Privacy and Information Security Law Blog*, 2011), <http://www.huntonprivacyblog.com/2011/08/articles/european-union-1/belgium-simplifies-the-authorization-procedure-for-binding-corporate-rules/> (accessed 22 March 2013). However, procedures need to be streamlined across all Member States if BCRs are to become more practicable. The draft Regulation arts 42(2) and 43 would explicitly recognize BCRs, which is helpful, though procedural complexity make widespread use unlikely.

It may also be possible to employ hybrid models that combine BCRs with model clauses for processors.

6.5 Regional clouds

The easiest practical solution currently is to use a regional cloud. As mentioned above,[101] some IaaS or PaaS providers offer customers the option to select broad geographical regions where their data are to be stored or their applications hosted, often on an individual basis (eg one application in one region, another application in another).[102] For example, a cloud user may choose to confine its data to the European region (rather than the US, for instance).

However, these providers don't always specify whether their European data centres are confined to the EEA.[103] This matters because 'Europe' includes some countries that are not in the EEA, such as Albania and Monaco. For example, initially Microsoft's European sub-regions for its Windows Azure PaaS service were simply designated as 'North Europe' and 'Western Europe',[104] while Google Storage for Developers (now Google Cloud Storage) on launch[105] offered a choice of 'Europe' or 'United States'. Amazon for EC2 does specify US East (Northern Virginia), US West (Northern California), EU (Ireland), Asia Pacific (Singapore), and Asia Pacific (Tokyo). Furthermore, even providers that allow customers to choose regions do not commit contractually, in their terms of service, to keep the relevant data or applications in the chosen region.[106]

This suggests that, in defining regions for users to select, the providers still primarily had in mind technological issues,[107] rather than regulatory concerns. Specifying that a 'European' region (where the provider's data centre is located) is in the EEA could make the provider more attractive to DPD-conscious users who need to keep their data within the EEA, and it is surprising that more providers do not stipulate the specific European countries in which their regional data centres are located.

In practice, many users will know that, for example, Microsoft's European data centres for cloud customers are located in Ireland and Amsterdam,[108] and those users may therefore

---

[101] Sentence containing n. 43.

[102] For example, Amazon Web Services and Microsoft Windows Azure. See Chapter 3. Google too has introduced an option for users to specify storage of their data in 'buckets' only in Europe, or only in the US—Google, 'Google Storage for Developers API Overview', <http://code.google.com/apis/storage/docs/developer-guide.html#specifyinglocations>; and Navneet Joneja, 'Google Storage for Developers Open to All, with New Features' (*Google Code Blog*, 2011), <http://googlecode.blogspot.com/2011/05/google-storage-for-developers-open-to.html> (both accessed 22 March 2013).

[103] In *Odense* (n. 30), the Datatilsynet pointed out that, 'It has not been stated whether all of Google Inc.'s data centres in Europe are located within the EU/EEA'.

[104] Now, specific countries are named such as 'Netherlands'. Windows Azure, 'Privacy', <http://www.windowsazure.com/en-us/support/trust-center/privacy> (accessed 3 April 2013).

[105] Google Developers, 'Frequently Asked Questions', <https://developers.google.com/storage/docs/faq#policy>, unrevised as at 1 March 2013 (accessed 3 April 2013), cf n. 110.

[106] Although a statement regarding regional choice may be an enforceable representation. See Chapter 3. Note that storage of personal data in EEA data centres does not preclude its export in some circumstances, for example some of the provider's support staff may be located outside the EEA, but may need access to data in the EEA data centre to investigate service problems. In such a case, access by the support staff would be restricted and would require, for example, use of model clauses or Safe Harbor, or some other solution.

[107] In particular, reducing latency so as to minimize response and data transfer times. This is improved with geographical proximity of the user to the data centre storing or operating on the data.

[108] See, for example, Microsoft, 'Microsoft's cloud data: reliable, resilient and secure' (*Telegraph*, 2 August 2011).

be willing to take a view on that basis. However, for users who rely on regional storage to avoid infringing the data export restriction, the most satisfactory position is that providers should undertake contractually that data designated for storage in the EEA will not be moved outside the EEA.

As the cloud market matures, providers have become increasingly more transparent about their data centre locations, no doubt driven partly by customers' regulatory concerns about location. In late 2012, Google finally revealed fuller details about its data centres,[109] including locations to country and even city level.[110]

It is not inconceivable that in future providers could use data centres on ships flying EEA flags in international waters.[111]

7. The Way Forward?

The DPD's data export restriction rules are neither sufficiently clear nor harmonized effectively across Member States, particularly the concepts of transfer and data location. This causes legal uncertainties in relation to the use of cloud. Also, the DPD's drafting did not take into account properly the use of the Internet in general, let alone cloud computing. The DPD's intense and narrow focus on data location made some sense when data could normally be transported between countries only by physically carrying storage media across borders. With the inception of the Internet, personal data may be emailed, instant messaged or tweeted, or copied to recipients in multiple countries across the globe in an instant, as well as being made available internationally on websites. The concept of 'location' is increasingly meaningless as well as irrelevant to data protection laws, given the ease of remote access to data.

The DPD's focus on data location should not obscure the underlying purpose of its data export restriction, namely data protection. In the data export restriction context, the specific objective was, and remains, to protect personal data against access by unauthorized persons. Unauthorized use is another risk, but data cannot be used without first being accessed, so, rather than focusing on data export, the DPD should consider protection against unauthorized access by third parties as the first line of defence, because preventing unauthorized access protects against unauthorized use.

We argue the DPD's rules should accordingly focus on restricting unauthorized access, rather than restricting data export. In other words, what matters most is not where information is stored, but who can read it: who is able to obtain access to it in intelligible form.

Where data are strongly encrypted and the decryption keys securely managed, the data's location should be irrelevant. Even if such encrypted data are stored in a third country, unauthorized persons would not be able to access data in intelligible form

---

[109] Google Official Blog, 'Google's Data Centers: An Inside Look' (17 October 2012), <http://googleblog.blogspot.com/2012/10/googles-data-centers-inside-look.html> (accessed 3 April 2013).

[110] Map at Google, 'Data Center Locations', <http://www.google.com/about/datacenters/inside/locations/index.html> (accessed 3 April 2013).

[111] Google has patented floating data centres (see Chapter 9), although currently intended to be based in territorial waters. It would be possible for a country to exempt from its national laws all data processed in data centres situated on its territory (or recognize such data centres diplomatically as territory of another country) where, for example, the data do not originate from that country and do not relate to its citizens, but are imported and re-exported. In a sense, the French CNIL ruling mentioned in that chapter is a step in that direction. It remains to be seen to what extent such 'data havens' may be promoted by countries wishing to encourage the building and use of data centres on their territory.

without the key.[112] Conversely, keeping data within the EEA does not guarantee better protection. Where data are stored unencrypted (or only weakly encrypted), even if the storage equipment is located within the EEA, unauthorized persons may be able to access intelligible data by hacking into the storage equipment, and/or the provider storing data on behalf of the cloud customer may technically be able to access the data by logging into the customer's account, and indeed may be compelled by law to do so. For example, the law of the provider's (third) country of incorporation may require it to disclose its customer's data (wherever stored) to its home law enforcement authorities.[113]

The DPD's assumption that data can be accessed by persons in a third country, simply because data are stored in that country, is undermined not only by the Internet but also by cloud computing. Depending on the set-up of the system, if authorities in the third country where a data centre is located should seize one server or even all equipment in the data centre, that may not necessarily result in their being able to read any personal data in intelligible form, due to the use in cloud computing of data fragmentation, proprietary file systems, and perhaps even distribution of parts of the relevant data across different data centres. However, if third-country authorities obtain the cooperation of the provider, they will generally be able to access unencrypted or weakly encrypted data, whether held in EEA or non-EEA data centres.[114]

In cloud computing, access to data in practice depends on two main factors. First, whether the user has encrypted the data strongly before its transfer (and manages the keys securely with the provider not having the key) and, second, whether the design of the provider's systems gives it the technical ability to access users' data (eg, the system could involve all data being encrypted strongly by default on the user's local computer such that only the user has the key), and, if so, who has authority or influence over the provider.

We suggest the DPD's legal restriction on data export be abolished.[115] Article 17 DPD already legally requires controllers (and, indirectly, processors) to take appropriate technological and organizational measures for protecting personal data, to ensure a level of security appropriate to risks represented by the processing and the nature of the data, having regard to the state of the art and implementation costs. Data protection laws should, instead of restricting data export as such, focus on requiring appropriate

---

[112] We argue that the DPD should no longer legally prohibit data export as such, because that restriction is outdated given technological developments such as the Internet and encryption. Discussion of encryption technicalities is beyond the scope of this chapter. Those who use cloud computing to process personal data, of which they are controllers, may encrypt such data before upload for cloud storage. They, therefore, have the decryption key (although the provider may not). On receiving data subject access requests they may retrieve data for decryption offline in order to meet that request. As for operating on personal data in the cloud in encrypted form, work continues on homomorphic encryption—see Chapter 7. Ensuring data subject rights may be met in other respects is not a data export concern as such, but raises general issues arising equally whether data are kept within the EEA or transferred outside it.

[113] This issue is discussed in detail in Chapter 11.

[114] See Chapter 7. Some nation states may have capability to decrypt even strongly encrypted data.

[115] For an alternative approach, see Canada's Personal Information Protection and Electronic Documents Act 2000 which does not prohibit data export or restrict data location per se, but instead makes clear that organizations are responsible for personal information under their control, even when transferred to a third party for processing, and must use contractual or other means to provide a comparable level of protection during such processing. Contrast *Odense* (n. 30), in which the Datatilsynet considered that a controller cannot ensure security measures are met unless it knows at all times the location of its data. This view seems not to take into account technological realities of encryption and cloud computing architecture and operations. However, the lack of transparency by cloud providers as to their storage and security policies and techniques has not assisted the debate.

accountability, transparency, and security measures[116] that take into account cloud computing's characteristics and many providers' status as neutral intermediaries.[117] They should do so in a technologically neutral way, rather than in an overly prescriptive way that legally requires exact technologies which may, in turn, become outdated. However, the proposals on security and accountability in the draft Regulation, which for example would impose direct security requirements on processors, are beyond the scope of this chapter.

Although we argue that the data export restriction should be replaced by requirements regarding accountability, transparency, and security, if the restriction is retained then it is important to clarify three things. First, whether it applies to the location of personal data (ie, the location of the underlying data centre(s) used) or the geographical location of the recipient (and if so, is the key test the principal place of business, or jurisdiction of residence or incorporation?), including the issue left open in *Lindqvist*.[118] Second, what is meant by 'adequate protection': the laws of the third country, the measures taken by the recipient or importer, or some other factor? Third, what is the significance, if any, of the exporter's knowledge and/or intention regarding the relevant location?

The draft Regulation would, rather than abolishing data export restrictions, create additional restrictions on transferring personal data outside the EEA. Absent an adequacy decision by the European Commission, transfers would be permissible only by adducing 'appropriate safeguards' for data protection 'in a legally binding instrument'. In particular, it is envisaged that transfers may be based on BCRs, model clauses adopted by the Commission, or clauses adopted or authorized by a supervisory authority. While the draft Regulation would allow national regulators to promulgate standard data protection clauses, they would be subject to the Commission's approval. BCRs must be approved, and contracts must either be pre-approved, by the Commission or a supervisory authority, or else a specific prior authorization must be obtained on a case-by-case basis.[119] This may eliminate the ability for authorities to allow controllers to make their own decisions on adequacy[120] and seems retrograde as it could increase bureaucracy and requests for pre-approvals, consequently increasing the workload of regulators whose resources might be better spent on investigating and enforcing breaches than approving routine transfers.

It seems unfortunate that the opportunity has not been taken to permit appropriate safeguards to be adduced by technological means, such as by the controller using encryption and taking its own backups. On the contrary, the A29WP has expressed the view that 'bindingness is one of the most important requirements for tools enabling international transfers for ensuring appropriate safeguards for data subjects. It also considers that self-assessment for transfers to third countries should remain a derogation to

---

[116] An EU official reportedly shares the view that security is more important than data location. Sophie Curtis, 'European Commission: Data Location Should Not Matter in the Cloud' (*TechWorld*, 13 June 2012), <http://news.techworld.com/data-centre/3363749/european-commission-data-location-should-not-matter-in-the-cloud> (accessed 3 April 2013).

[117] See Chapter 8.   [118] Paragraph containing n. 19.

[119] Draft Regulation, Art 42. The UK ICO (n. 72) has stated: 'The concept of prior authorisation is wholly new for some supervisory authorities, such as the ICO. We are not aware that our current approach to regulation in this area has resulted in any failure to protect personal information... [prior authorizations of transfers] could have a significant impact on us as a regulatory body if we were required to authorise these in advance. The sheer scale of this duty must not be underestimated.'

[120] Discussed at Section 5.4.

adequate safeguards with a very limited scope'.[121] Furthermore, the Committee on Civil Liberties, Justice and Home Affairs (LIBE), the lead European Parliament committee scrutinizing the draft Regulation, would require prior authorizations of transfers from national regulators even when a derogation is used.[122]

One positive aspect is that the draft Regulation Article 44(1)(h) would introduce a derogation permitting transfers necessary for 'the purposes of the legitimate interests pursued by the controller or the processor'. However, that would only apply where transfers are not 'frequent or massive' and the controller or processor has, based on assessing 'all the circumstances surrounding the data transfer operation or the set of data transfer operations', adduced appropriate safeguards to protect personal data where necessary. While a 'legitimate interests' justification could be helpful, the exclusion of transfers that are 'frequent or massive' might undermine substantially the practical utility of the justification. It is insufficiently clear what transfers would qualify as 'frequent or massive'. The focus should instead be on adducing appropriate safeguards whatever the size or frequency of transfers. Guidance as to what would be appropriate safeguards in this situation, and that safeguards may be technological not just legal, would assist here.[123]

The Commission would be able to declare particular processing sectors within a third country adequate, an innovation which the LIBE wishes to delete. The European Data Protection Supervisor has called for data protection law reforms to include a definition of 'transfer', not currently in the draft Regulation,[124] and the LIBE would introduce such a definition.

As regards third country authorities' access to cloud data, the LIBE would, as advocated by the A29WP,[125] prohibit recognition or enforcement of non-EEA courts' or authorities' requests for transfer of personal data, unless based on a mutual assistance treaty or relevant international agreement. The LIBE would require such requests to be notified to the data subject and the supervisory authority for its authorization to the transfer, which may tax the resources of data protection authorities.

Additionally, the detailed rules on data export need harmonizing across the EEA, for several reasons. Full harmonization would reduce compliance burdens for entities operating in several Member States. Furthermore, it would address any concerns of 'leakage' of personal data by a transfer of data to another EEA State, which transfer must be permitted under the DPD, and thence outside the EEA, where the transferee's restrictions on data export are less stringent than those of the originating EEA State. The draft Regulation aims to harmonize the position, being in the form of a regulation with direct effect rather than a directive but, in its current form at least, would be unlikely to achieve this objective due to lack of both clarity and certainty.

---

[121] Article 29 Data Protection Working Party, 'Statement of the Working Party on current discussions regarding the data protection reform package' (27 February 2013), <http://ec.europa.eu/justice/data-protection/article-29/documentation/other-document/files/2013/20130227_statement_dp_reform_package_en.pdf> (accessed 3 April 2013).

[122] European Parliament, 'Draft Report' (17 December 2012), <http://www.europarl.europa.eu/meetdocs/2009_2014/documents/libe/pr/922/922387/922387en.pdf> (accessed 3 April 2013).

[123] Article 44(7) of the draft Regulation would empower the Commission to adopt delegated acts 'for the purpose of further specifying . . . the criteria and requirements for appropriate safeguards'.

[124] European Data Protection Supervisor, 'Opinion of the European Data Protection Supervisor', <http://www.edps.europa.eu/EDPSWEB/webdav/site/mySite/shared/Documents/Consultation/Opinions/2012/12-03-07_EDPS_Reform_package_EN.pdf> (accessed 3 April 2013), para. 108.

[125] For example, in Article 29 Data Protection Working Party, 'Statement of the Working Party on current discussions regarding the data protection reform package' (27 February 2013), <http://ec.europa.eu/justice/data-protection/article-29/documentation/other-document/files/2013/20130227_statement_dp_reform_package_en.pdf> (accessed 3 April 2013).

In relation to the Safe Harbor, the many uncertainties discussed above need to be addressed in order for the Safe Harbor to be a truly safe framework enabling EEA controllers to use US cloud providers. In any review of the Safe Harbor it would be desirable to clarify that processors may use the Safe Harbor. Clarification is also needed regarding the mapping of EU controller and processor concepts and responsibilities to Safe Harbor principles, and indeed the distinction between controllers and processors needs attention more generally.[126] The US and EU need to agree clearly which country's rules apply to data exported under the Safe Harbor, and to what extent. In relation to onward transfers, the position and requirements need clarification, for example the meaning of 'subscribes to' Safe Harbor principles. The rules should take account of the potential use by Safe Harborite providers of non-US data centres and/or of sub-providers (US or otherwise), and the situation where providers may have possession of data but not access to intelligible data. The inconsistencies in Safe Harbor acceptance across the EU Member States also need to be eliminated. Agreeing these issues is unlikely to be a rapid process.

The position of processors and sub-processors in the context of exported data also needs specific consideration. Issues include the extent to which a cloud provider may become a controller through choosing to use a data centre located outside the EEA, or through choosing to use a sub-provider; how a processor's or sub-processor's state of 'establishment' is determined, and which Member State's security requirements, if any, apply to providers.[127] Possible solutions may involve the promulgation of processor-to-processor model clauses to enable use of layered cloud computing, in particular allowing EEA processors to transfer data to non-EEA sub-processors, more cloud-appropriate BCRs for processors, and clarification regarding the Safe Harbor uncertainties. The draft Regulation would specifically permit BCRs including for processors, but other uncertainties remain to be addressed.

In summary, restricting data export per se rather than emphasizing security, accountability, and transparency, wherever in the world data are processed, may hold back the efficient use of cloud computing, and the draft Regulation would exacerbate this.

Appendix—Practical Application of the Data Transfer Rules to Common Cloud Scenarios

The tables that follow illustrate the issues discussed in this chapter, using alternative cloud computing scenarios involving a cloud user Customer, being a controller of personal data that are to be processed in the cloud.

Key to abbreviations:

'Customer' means customer or user of cloud computing services; Customer will usually be a controller of personal data.

'Provider' means provider of cloud computing or related services.

'Multiple' means several data centres in different countries are used, between which personal data may flow automatically.

For each alternative scenario we consider whether EU data protection laws would permit a data export. For simplicity we assume, unless otherwise stated, that in scenarios where Customer is subject to EU data protection laws, any export would be from, and under the law of, the Member State which applies to Customer due to its being established or using 'equipment' or 'means' there.[128]

---

[126] See Chapter 8.   [127] See Chapter 9.
[128] See Chapter 9 for a detailed discussion of data protection jurisdictional issues.

A. Private Cloud (Self-hosted)

With a self-hosted private cloud, we assume Customer controls the location of the data centre(s) used, even though it may not be the legal owner of those data centre(s) and/or of the equipment used.

	Customer established in	Data centre location	Position
1	EEA	EEA	No data export issue.
2	EEA	Non-EEA	Data export issue—customer must find an exception, or a way to ensure adequacy of protection (see Section 6 of this chapter).
3	Non-EEA	EEA	Customer may become subject to the DPD if, through its use of an EEA data centre, it is considered to have an 'establishment' in the EEA or to make use of equipment in the EEA for processing personal data. If so, it would then have to comply with the data export restrictions and other DPD requirements, even if it initially 'imported' data to the EEA data centre for processing and re-export following the processing, and even if the data originated outside the EEA and related to non-EEA persons. See also Chapter 9.
4	Non-EEA	Non-EEA	No DPD issues if the customer has no other EEA connection.
5	EEA	Multiple	If personal data are confined to EEA data centres—see 1. If personal data could be processed in non-EEA data centre—see 2. Furthermore, differences in data export rules in different Member States could mean that personal data may legally be exported from a data centre in one State in circumstances when it could not be from a data centre in another. This might, for instance, motivate Customer to use only (or as the 'end point') data centres in States with less stringent restrictions.
6	Non-EEA	Multiple	Example: a US corporation with a private cloud using multiple data centres, including in the EEA. If personal data could never be processed in the EEA—see 4. If personal data could be processed in an EEA data centre—see 3 and, in relation to 'export' from different Member States, 5.

B. Using Provider[129]

The table that follows may apply to several possible models, where in each case Customer uses the services of a third-party Provider, involving:

- a dedicated private cloud hosted/managed by the Provider or a third party (we assume that, with a dedicated private cloud, a third party controls the location of data centre(s) used, although the location may be stipulated or restricted by Customer);

---

[129] The numbering is continued from the previous table for ease of reference.

- a community cloud (eg entities in same corporate group); or
- a public cloud service.

We do not provide a separate table for situations where Provider uses a sub-provider (eg SaaS provider utilizing IaaS/PaaS infrastructure). This is because, when a sub-provider is used, then, assuming Provider is not considered a controller through its choice of sub-provider or another reason,[130] the situation will essentially be as in the table below, but with Provider choosing the sub-provider used, and 'Data centre location' referring to the location of the sub-provider's (or *its* ultimate sub-provider's) data centre. However, the more 'layers' of providers there are, the less likely it is that Customer would be taken to know or intend any export, as discussed in the main body of this chapter.

	Customer established	Provider established	Data centre	Position
7	EEA	EEA	EEA	No data export issue for either Customer or Provider. Customer must comply with applicable EU data protection laws, including as regards its contract with Provider if Provider is its 'processor'.
8	EEA	EEA	Non-EEA	Customer—no data export issue if *Lindqvist* is followed (on the analogy of uploading data to an EEA web host), although other DPD requirements will apply. However, under *Odense* there would be an export, and in practice the cautious view would be to assume an export, and seek a solution enabling export. This suggests Customer ought to inquire as to the location of the data centre ultimately used by Provider.
				Provider—if Provider is considered to determine the 'purposes and means' of processing, for example because it chose the sub-provider or chose (or, perhaps even, did not inquire into) the location of the data centre used, it risks being considered a 'controller'—see the SWIFT scenario[131]—and thus would be subject to the data export restriction and other data protection rules.
9	EEA	Non-EEA	EEA	Customer—no data export issue, assuming the initial transfer was to the EEA data centre. This is the 'regional data centre' solution used by some non-EEA providers.
				Provider—no export issue similarly.[132]
10	EEA	Non-EEA	Non-EEA	Customer—data export issue, see 8.
				Provider—see 8; but if Provider has no EEA data centre and no other EEA connection an EEA court may be less likely to accept jurisdiction over it and there may be issues regarding whether any EEA judgment could be enforced against Provider, in practice.

[130] This possibility has already been discussed (see Chapter 8). If Provider is a controller, then the analysis regarding Customer's position applies to Provider equally, if Provider is subject to EU data protection laws through being 'established' in the EEA or using 'equipment' or 'means' in the EEA (see Chapter 9).

[131] Nn. 6, 25, 99. See also Chapter 9.

[132] However, if Provider determines the 'purposes and means' of processing the data, it risks being considered to use equipment in the EEA to process personal data and thus being caught by the DPD as 'controller'—see Chapter 8. We argue that in many cases a provider should not be treated as a processor. A separate question is whether an EEA court would accept jurisdiction over Provider, which it may be more likely to do if Provider owns (or perhaps even just uses) an EEA data centre.

	Customer established	Provider established	Data centre	Position
11	Non-EEA	EEA	EEA	Customer—re-export issue may arise as in 3, if data are to be transferred outside the EEA after cloud processing. Also, Customer risks being subject to EU data protection laws if, through its use of an EEA provider or EEA data centre, Customer is deemed to make use of equipment in the EEA, as with Provider in 8. However, the same issue arises as for Provider in 8 as to whether an EEA court would accept jurisdiction over Customer or whether any EEA judgment could be enforced against Customer in practice. If Customer is subject to EU data protection laws, there is a possible re-export issue as in 3. Provider—no data export issue even if it is a controller.[133]
12	Non-EEA	EEA	Non-EEA	Customer—no data export issue (if data are never processed in any EEA data centre, there should be no issue of a 'transfer' to outside the EEA) and (assuming use of an EEA provider is not using 'means' in the EEA), if it has no other EEA connection, should not be subject to EU data protection laws. Provider—if Provider is a controller, Provider could be subject to EU data protection laws wherever in the world processing takes place (although if data were never in the EEA, there is no data export issue).
13	Non-EEA	Non-EEA	EEA	Customer—same as for Customer in 11. Application of EU data protection laws may perhaps be less likely if its only EEA connection is through its non-EEA provider using an EEA data centre. Provider—same as for Provider in 9.
14	Non-EEA	Non-EEA	Non-EEA	No DPD issues for either Customer or Provider if it has no other EEA connection.
15	EEA	Anywhere	Multiple	Similar issues to above, depending on whether data can be restricted to EEA data centres or can move to non-EEA data centres, and (for Provider) whether EU data protection laws apply to it. Differences in different Member States' export restrictions may be relevant, as in 5.
16	Non-EEA	Anywhere	Multiple	Similar issues to above, depending on whether EU data protection laws apply to Customer through use of EEA provider or data centre, and/or to Provider through use of EEA data centre, and also depending on whether data can be kept within only non-EEA data centres or may move to non-EEA centres or be re-exported after the processing. If EU data protection laws apply and personal data may be exported, differences in national data export restrictions may be relevant, as in 5.

---

[133] Although, when acting for an EEA controller, Provider should have certain contractual obligations imposed on it by the controller, in particular implementing appropriate technical and organizational measures to protect personal data as defined by the laws of Provider's EEA State of establishment (under Art. 17(3)). Provider may apply similar measures when processing data for other customers.

PART IV

CLOUD REGULATION AND GOVERNANCE

Having looked at how cloud relationships are managed using contracts (Part II), and at rules applying to the protection of personal data in clouds (Part III), in this final part of the book we consider several specific aspects of cloud regulation and governance.

The first topic, law enforcement access to data in clouds, follows naturally from the data protection discussion. A common concern expressed by prospective customers of cloud services, in both private and public sectors, is that they may lose control over information if it is transferred to another jurisdiction or even if it is processed locally but by a service provider that is subject to the jurisdiction of foreign courts, governmental authorities, or regulators. This is a high-profile issue in Europe given that all of the leading IaaS providers, and many major PaaS and SaaS providers, are either US-based companies or members of corporate groups with ultimate control in the US. In that context, Chapter 11 examines the legal framework governing access by law enforcement authorities (LEAs) to data held in cloud environments, with particular reference to US and UK law, as well as EU and international law, especially the Council of Europe Cybercrime Convention.

Competition law issues are also emerging in relation to cloud computing, notwithstanding the relative immaturity of the sector. Chapter 12 analyses the potential application to the cloud sector of EU competition rules governing anti-competitive agreements and abuses of a dominant position. Specific issues addressed include the development of standards, the potential importance of interoperability between cloud computing services, and the impact of restrictions on data portability. The suitability of existing competition rules as a regulatory mechanism for cloud computing is also considered.

Cloud services are already widely used by individuals for their own private purposes and such arrangements are likely to be subject to consumer protection laws. Chapter 13 deals with the application of EU and UK consumer protection rules, not only to private individuals but also to small-business users. The analysis is complicated by the fact that use of cloud services by individuals is often mixed, in the sense that it can be for both personal and business purposes. Moreover, many 'free' cloud services, which appear to be targeted at consumers, may also be used by businesses. Although such demarcation issues arise in other consumer protection contexts, they appear to be extremely common in the context of cloud computing and their resolution may be difficult.

Chapter 14 reviews the overall governance arrangements for cloud computing, with reference to many of the specific issues raised earlier in the book. At the heart of the discussion is the question of how an optimal governance framework for cloud computing might be developed, or at least how its emergence and recognition by the key stake-holders might be facilitated. Both internal and external governance mechanisms are considered and the limits of state regulation are appraised. Questions of legitimacy and practical reach abound. The chapter makes it clear that cloud governance is a work in progress, and that it is likely to remain so for the foreseeable future. The global reach of cloud services, the diversity of interests of cloud participants, and the complexity of their relationships, make it very unlikely that either legislation or self-regulation alone will emerge as a credible and effective governance model. Co-regulation shows greater promise but will not be achieved without a lot of effort and goodwill on the part of the key members of the cloud community, encompassing states, legislators, and individuals, as well as the cloud industry itself.

11

Law Enforcement Access to Data in Clouds*

Ian Walden

1. Introduction

As cloud services become a mainstream Information and Communications Technology (ICT) solution for business, consumers, and governments, security and privacy issues assume increasing significance. To the extent that cloud services are used for criminal activities, or targeted by organized crime, then public law enforcement agencies (LEAs) will want and need to obtain access to data held in cloud services for forensic purposes during the course of an investigation. Such forensic data may be held on systems controlled by a suspect, victim, or an innocent third party (collectively referred to as 'cloud users'), often located in foreign jurisdictions or where the location is unknown. However, the potential for law enforcement access can generate its own commercial security and privacy concerns for cloud users, from industrial espionage to political interference. The launch of Microsoft's Office 365 in June 2011, for example, was accompanied by expressions of concern that Microsoft would not guarantee that data of European customers could not be accessed by agencies acting under US jurisdiction; while in June 2013, disclosures about the National Security Agency's (NSA) PRISM surveillance programme reignited concerns about the security and privacy of cloud-based data.[1] Similar concerns were behind the Dutch government appearing to suggest that US-based suppliers of cloud services may be 'excluded' from supplying public authorities handling government or citizen data due to the risk of access by US authorities.[2] In addition, some European providers have even tried to make a virtue out of their 'non-US' status, calling for certification schemes that would indicate where data is protected from such access.[3]

This chapter examines the legal framework governing law enforcement access to data in a cloud environment, giving particular attention to US and UK laws that govern the obtaining of data for investigative and prosecutorial purposes, as well as EU and international law, especially the Council of Europe Cybercrime Convention.[4] The Convention is the leading public international law instrument harmonizing substantive and procedural laws, with some 49 signatories, including non-European states such as

---

* This chapter is an extensively revised and updated version of a paper published as I Walden, 'Accessing Data in the Cloud: The Long Arm of the Law Enforcement Agent' in S Pearson and G Yee (eds), *Privacy and Security for Cloud Computing* (London: Springer, 2012), 45–71.

[1] Zack Whittaker, 'EU Demands Answers over Microsoft's Patriot Act Admission' (*ZDNet*, 5 July 2011), <http://www.zdnet.com/blog/igeneration/eu-demands-answers-over-microsofts-patriot-act-admission/11290> (accessed 28 March 2013). On PRISM, see *The Guardian*, 'NSA Prism program taps in to user data of Apple, Google and others', 7 June 2013, <http://www.guardian.co.uk/world/2013/jun/06/us-tech-giants-nsa-data> (accessed 8 June 2013).

[2] Zack Whittaker, 'Dutch Government to Ban U.S. Providers over Patriot Act Concerns' (*ZdNet*, 19 September 2011), <http://www.zdnet.com/blog/btl/dutch-government-to-ban-us-providers-over-patriot-act-concerns/58342?tag=search-results-rivers;item3> (accessed 28 March 2013).

[3] Cornelius Rahn, 'Deutsche Telekom Wants "German Cloud" to Shield Data from US', *Business Week* (14 September 2011).

[4] CETS No. 185, entered into force 1 July 2004 ('the Convention').

the US, Japan, and Australia.[5] Chapter III of the Convention addresses the investigation and prosecution of cybercrime within the domestic jurisdiction, as well as facilitating international cooperation against transborder cybercrimes. The Convention's provisions represent a certain consensus among the signatories about the appropriate exercise of law enforcement powers in cyberspace, including a cloud environment.

Consideration is given to how such rules interact and potentially conflict with other laws, particularly data protection and evidential rules. Recent fears voiced about US-based cloud providers[6] are partly a consequence of their current dominance in the global cloud market,[7] coupled with the potential reach of US law enforcement agents, particularly under the 'Patriot Act' and related measures.[8] It is suggested, however, that there is widespread ignorance about the existence of similar powers available to LEAs in many, if not most, major jurisdictions, including the UK.[9] Regulating LEA access to data in the cloud also illustrates the problem of operating in an environment where multiple laws are applicable concurrently; laws that differ significantly between jurisdictions at both a substantive and procedural level. Harmonization initiatives, such as the Convention, have gone some way to address these differences, but, as this chapter highlights, significant differences remain. In addition, recent proposals and calls for new LEA powers in some jurisdictions, designed to bolster cloud-related investigations, would further undermine harmonization.[10]

The exercise of LEA powers raises a number of jurisdictional questions that are examined in this chapter. The first is the question of territorial reach: when does the exercising of LEA powers in the cloud reach their territorial limit, thereby becoming potentially unlawful in the domestic jurisdiction of the LEA, as well as in the foreign territory in which they were exercised? Second, what obligations does a service provider have to assist an LEA in the course of an investigation, from delivering up data in response to a request, to the retention of data and the implementation of an intercept capability? Third, how may LEA powers differ between obtaining data which is 'at rest' within a cloud service, as opposed to data 'in transmission' to, from, or within the cloud service?[11] Finally, where

---

[5] Number of signatories is correct as of 15 March 2013, see Council of Europe, 'Convention on Cybercrime', <http://conventions.coe.int/Treaty/Commun/ChercheSig.asp?NT=185&CM=8&DF=&CL=ENG> (accessed 28 March 2013).

[6] For example, Ron Hastings, 'British internet users' personal information on major "cloud" storage services can be spied upon routinely by US authorities' (*The Independent*, 30 January 2013), <http://www.independent.co.uk/life-style/gadgets-and-tech/news/british-internet-users-personal-information-on-major-cloud-storage-services-can-be-spied-upon-routinely-by-us-authorities-8471819.html> (accessed 28 March 2013).

[7] For example, Jack McCarthy, 'The 100 Coolest Cloud Computing Vendors of 2013' (*CRN*, 13 March 2013), <http://www.crn.com/news/cloud/240150619/the-100-coolest-cloud-computing-vendors-of-2013.htm> (accessed 28 March 2013).

[8] The full title is: 'Uniting and Strengthening America by Providing Appropriate Tools Required to Intercept and Obstruct Terrorism Act of 2001' Pub L, 107-56. Related measures include the Foreign Intelligence Surveillance Act (50 USC Ch. 36, sub-Ch. VI).

[9] See Hogan Lovells, White Paper, *A Global Reality: Governmental Access to Data in the Cloud* (July 2012).

[10] For example in the UK, the Draft Communications Data Bill (Cm 8359), June 2012; while in the US, see comments made by Andrew Weismann, FBI General Counsel, speaking on 'Law enforcement & new technologies' (ABA Meeting, 20 March 2013) available at <http://www.c-spanvideo.org/program/311627-1> (accessed 28 March 2013).

[11] The distinction between data 'at rest' and 'in transmission' does not denote the technical state of the data, since data held by a cloud service provider, or 'at rest' may often be 'in transmission' between internal resources of the service provider, for example using load balancing. Rather the phrases are used to indicate a legal distinction between LEA powers of access to data.

data is obtained *ultra vires* (beyond the power of the LEA) in breach of national rules, what impact does that have on its evidential value?

Each of these issues presents a boundary issue for LEAs, service providers, and cloud users: a boundary between lawful and unlawful behaviours or regulated and unregulated activities. Such boundaries are by no means unique to cloud-based activities, but are brought into sharper focus by the anticipated shift to cloud computing by users, whether individuals, business, or public administrations. This chapter examines how and when those boundaries apply and what mechanisms and procedures have been adopted, or are proposed, to address the needs of LEAs in a cloud environment. First, however, we need to consider some of the forensic challenges for law enforcement in a cloud computing environment.

2. Forensic Challenges in the Cloud

Cloud users depend on various 'service providers' for their use of the cloud, of which three broad categories are distinguished for our purposes:[12]

- A cloud service provider, who has a direct contractual relationship with the subscriber to the service, whether offering a SaaS, PaaS, IaaS, or other variant.
- A cloud infrastructure provider, who provides the cloud service provider with some form of infrastructure,[13] such as server farms and processing capacity, including persistent storage.
- A communication service provider, who provides the transmission service enabling the cloud user to communicate with the cloud service provider.

Both cloud users and service providers may become the focus of attention in an LEA investigation, through the utilization of either covert investigative techniques, such as surveillance or interception, or the exercise of coercive powers, such as production or search and seizure orders, to obtain the forensic material. The layered nature of cloud computing services means that an LEA request could be served against a cloud infrastructure provider, such as Amazon Web Services, without necessarily either the cloud service provider, such as Dropbox, or the cloud user being aware that such a request has been made in respect of data entrusted by the user with his service provider.

Obtaining computer-derived evidence, whether 'at rest' or 'in transmission', raises formidable forensic challenges, which have been examined elsewhere.[14] While methods of forensic analysis and the tools are fairly well established, some specific forensic challenges of cloud computing can be seen in four key areas:

- *Multiplicity*—Data held by the service provider is likely to be replicated within the cloud for reasons of performance, availability, backup, and redundancy. These multiple copies are likely to be stored across different 'virtual' and physical machines, sometimes in different jurisdictions. As such, when responding to an LEA request, a cloud service provider may have to, or choose to, retrieve the data from multiple locations.

---

[12] See further Chapter 1.
[13] For the purpose of this article 'infrastructure' refers to any component of the cloud service, not an IaaS.
[14] E Casey, *Handbook of Digital Forensics and Investigations* (Burlington, MA: Academic Press, 2010) and Ian Walden, *Computer Crimes and Digital Investigations* (Oxford: Oxford University Press, 2007).

- *Distributed storage*—Techniques widely used in cloud computing, such as 'shard-ing' or 'partitioning',[15] mean that the data will likely be stored as fragments across a range of machines, logically linked and reassembled on demand, rather than as a single contiguous data set.

- *Protected data*—The cloud user may submit data in a protected form, such as by using cryptographic techniques, which render the data opaque to the cloud service provider.[16] As a consequence, when requesting data disclosure by a service provider, an LEA may not be able to obtain intelligible material. In addition, the various lay-ers of provider may each apply cryptographic tools to the submitted data, during transit or storage, which will need to be removed for LEA access.[17]

- *Identity*—Even with a stand-alone computer, it can be difficult to establish an ade-quate forensic link between the relevant evidential data, the virtual identity of the user, and a real-world person. These identity problems are more complex in a cloud environment, where there is a need to establish a link between the data held in the cloud, the user device from which data was created, submitted to, or accessed from, the cloud service,[18] and an individual user.

For the first three, the generic concern is one of access: locating the relevant data and reassembling or converting the data into intelligible form. A fundamental principle of digital forensics is that data obtained for law enforcement purposes should not be altered through the process of obtaining, especially the metadata relating to the evidential con-tent.[19] While client-side analysis will continue to offer valuable forensic material, remote data retrieval will likely become the norm in a cloud environment, which increases the risk that data changes will occur, especially where access is obtained through cloud appli-cation programming interfaces (APIs),[20] and architectures that may be unknown to the investigators. As such, the competence of investigators to testify in court about the authenticity of the process of obtaining, especially data changes attributable to their actions, may be seriously compromised.

A shift to remote data retrieval will increase LEA reliance on cooperation from cloud service providers. Otherwise, access to the material could be obtained through a user's access device, whether a suspect or not, under coercion, voluntarily or surreptitiously. In both scenarios, however, the location of the cloud-derived data at the moment it is retrieved in the course of an investigation may be unknown and unknowable, in terms of the physical machines upon which the data rests, and therefore the territory or ter-ritories in which it can be said to reside. Instead, such identification may only be pos-sible through further forensic analysis subsequent to the retrieval. As a consequence, consideration needs to be given to the impact that the inability to establish location, referred to as the 'loss of location',[21] has on the exercise of law enforcement powers and

---

[15] See Chapter 1, Section 2.1.2.   [16] See Chapter 2, Section 2.1.

[17] See generally P Swire, 'From Real-time Intercepts to Stored Records: Why Encryption Drives the Government to Seek Access to the Cloud' (2012) 2(4) *International Data Privacy Law* 200.

[18] Particularly as user applications may be configured not to record such interactions, for exam-ple Microsoft Internet Explorer's 'InPrivate' browsing setting. Referred to by JJ Schwerha IV, 'Law Enforcement Challenges in Transborder Acquisition of Electronic Evidence from "Cloud Computing Providers"' (Discussion Paper, Council of Europe, 15 January 2010).

[19] See 'The Principles of Computer-based Electronic Evidence' in the ACPO, *Good Practice Guide for Computer based Electronic Evidence*, 4th edn (October 2008).

[20] Application programming interfaces specify the manner in which software programs communi-cate with each other.

[21] See J Spoenle, 'Cloud Computing and Cybercrime Investigations: Territoriality vs. the Power of Disposal' (Council of Europe Discussion Paper, 31 August 2010).

the evidential value of cloud-derived material. Where data fragments are located in different jurisdictions, it would be possible to resolve a single location prior to disclosure to the LEA, identifying when and where the data are reassembled, which could be used as a proxy for determining the legality or enforceability of a request.

Remote data retrieval also differs in nature from the seizure of a suspect's device for forensic analysis. While the latter involves the taking of property, in the former, a copy is generally obtained of the relevant data, which raises questions about the appropriate legal characterization of the copied data. Whether such copying constitutes an interference with a person's 'possessions', engaging Article 1 of Protocol 1 of the European Convention on Human Rights (ECHR), or his privacy, under Article 8 of the Convention, may be uncertain.[22] The Cybercrime Convention refers both to the seizure and copying of data, although it does not make clear whether the distinction has legal consequence.[23] However, an earlier Council of Europe Recommendation suggested a principle of equality, whereby data that is functionally equivalent to a traditional document should be treated as the same for the purposes of procedural law governing search and seizure.[24]

Cloud forensics is an emerging discipline that will address the needs of a range of actors, including public LEAs and civil litigants engaged in e-discovery.[25] Forensic challenges from cloud-derived data impact most directly on the evidential value of such data before a tribunal. However, issues of location and how conduct is characterized also impact on the exercise of LEA powers.

3. Exercising LEA Powers

In general, the powers exercised by LEAs are expressly conferred by statute, and may be exercised either in the course of carrying out duties conferred upon the LEA, or require further and specific authorization, granted under judicial, executive, or administrative procedures. Such prior authorization is usually relevant to the exercise of covert or coercive powers, which is the primary concern of this chapter. In urgent or exigent circumstances, such as those involving an imminent danger to life, an LEA may be permitted to exercise covert or coercive powers without prior authorization[26] or subject to special procedures,[27] particularly where there is a risk that forensic material could be deleted by a suspect or the equipment on which it resides is vulnerable. Jurisdictions also often distinguish between standard LEA procedures and those applicable in cases involving 'national security' issues or agencies tasked with related duties.[28]

---

[22] See, for example, *Veolia ES Nottinghamshire Limited v Nottingham County Council et al.* [2010] EWCA Civ 1214, paras 117–22.

[23] The Convention on Cybercrime Explanatory Report ('Explanatory Report' available at <http://conventions.coe.int/Treaty/en/Reports/Html/185.htm> (accessed 28 March 2013)) explicitly leaves flexibility to states, paras 137, 187.

[24] Council of Europe Recommendation No. R(95)13, 'Concerning problems of procedural law connected with information technology', Principle 4.

[25] See K Ruan, J Carthy, T Kechadi, and M Crosbie, 'Cloud Forensics' in *Advances in Digital Forensics VII* (London: Springer, 2011), 35–46. Also A Araiza, 'Electronic Discovery in the Cloud' (2011) *Duke L & Tech Rev* 8.

[26] For example, in the US, see Department of Justice (DOJ), 'Searching and Seizing Computers and Obtaining Electronic Evidence in Criminal Investigations' (DOJ Guidance, 2009) 27 ff.

[27] For example, in the UK, Regulation of Investigatory Powers Act 2000 ('RIPA'), ss 7(2)(a), 43(1); in the US, 50 USC § 1881a(g)(1)(B).

[28] For example, Intelligence Services Act 1994. However, what comprises an issue of 'national security' is generally left to a state to determine.

The Convention expressly recognizes that the exercise of LEA powers interferes in the rights and freedoms of individuals, such as the right to privacy, and therefore any measures must be subject 'to conditions and safeguards'.[29] These can include conditions governing the obtaining and subsequent handling of data, such as a 'limitation on the scope and the duration of such power or procedure';[30] requirements to notify the subject of the investigation, which enables legal challenge;[31] and an oversight regime. The latter will usually involve some 'judicial or other independent supervision', either through the authorization procedure or an *ex post* review process, with the capability to investigate compliance with the conditions and safeguards.[32] For Member States, these criteria are found in the ECHR, which requires any interference in a person's rights to be 'in accordance with the law', to meet a 'legitimate interest', and only to be to the extent necessary and proportionate, as further expounded in European Court of Human Rights (ECtHR) jurisprudence. For non-Member States, such as the US, other 'binding international obligations and established domestic principles' should provide the source of such safeguards.[33] However, concern about the existence and adequacy of such protections under US law forms one strand of the current controversy about LEA access in the cloud.[34]

Jurisdictions can vary significantly in granting LEAs access to similar data types under different authorization procedures. In the UK, for example, stored data is generally accessed under a judicial warrant,[35] the interception of communications content under an executive warrant,[36] while access to communications data occurs under an administrative authorization.[37] By contrast, in the US, access to communications data requires a judicial warrant,[38] while interception of foreign communications can be authorized by the executive.[39] While there is a general principle under US and European human rights law that the exercise of law enforcement powers should be entrusted to the supervisory control of a judge, there is no requirement to adopt judicial authorization procedures.[40] In turn, different procedures, safeguards, and oversight mechanisms can generate uncertainty and distrust about the sufficiency of protections that foreign regimes offer against abusive deployment and infringements of individual rights.[41]

A failure to obtain appropriate authorization would generally render the LEA conduct unlawful, subject to criminal, civil, or administrative liability, unless express immunity is granted.[42] While a law enforcement officer may engage in conduct as any ordinary person without such behaviours constituting an 'exercise of power' per se, such

---

[29] Convention, Art. 15(1).
[30] Convention, Art. 15(2), for example in the UK, RIPA, s. 15 re: disclosure, copying, and retention.
[31] Either at the time of the request or subsequently, for example 18 USC § 2703(b).
[32] For example, Interception of Communications Commissioner (RIPA, Part IV). See *Kennedy v United Kingdom* (2011) 52 EHRR 4, paras 166–7.   [33] Explanatory Report, paras 145–7.
[34] See *Clapper v Amnesty International USA* 133 S Ct 1138 (2013), where respondents were denied standing to challenge 50 USC § 1881a as unconstitutional; while in *In re National Security Letter* FSupp2d, 2013 WL 1095417, NDCal, (2013), a court granted a petition declaring certain powers relating to the issuance of national security letters, permitting LEA access to telecommunication records without court approval, unconstitutional. However, in an appeal by Google, heard in June 2013, the same judge rejected a similar argument based on the constitutionality of such orders.
[35] For example, Police and Criminal Evidence Act 1984, s. 9.   [36] For example, RIPA, s. 5.
[37] RIPA, s. 22.   [38] For example, 18 USC § 3123.   [39] For example, 50 USC § 1881a.
[40] *Katz v US*, 389 US 347, 357 (1967) and *Klass et al. v Germany* (1979–80) 2 EHRR 214, § 56.
[41] See, for example, European Parliament study, 'Fighting Cyber Crime and Protecting Privacy in the Cloud' (*European Parliament*, 2012), available at <http://www.europarl.europa.eu/committees/en/studiesdownload.html?languageDocument=EN&file=79050> (accessed 28 March 2013).
[42] For example, RIPA, s. 80 ('General saving for lawful conduct').

as searching the Internet, certain 'normal' conduct may be considered unlawful on the basis that the person, as a public official, is an agent of the state.[43]

Where an LEA exercises conferred powers, the legislation granting such powers is usually expressly stated to be, or presumed to be, limited to the territorial jurisdiction of the domestic state.[44] While an LEA would be acting unlawfully if it exercised powers outside the jurisdiction, a domestic exercise of powers may have an extraterritorial effect, which would not be considered unlawful. Conversely, any domestic 'conditions and safeguards' controlling an exercise of LEA powers would also be generally limited to acts carried out within the domestic jurisdiction;[45] although whether such protections are available to 'any person' within the jurisdiction, or only nationals, can vary.[46]

When considering the legality of the 'exercise' of an LEA power, a further distinction should be made between the obtaining of the authorization, and the conduct carried out in furtherance of that authorization. In respect of the former, legality issues may arise if an LEA engages in conduct without obtaining the required authorization, or the authorization process is procedurally flawed. In respect of the latter, a validly granted authorization may be served on an entity to which it is not applicable, or on an entity residing outside the jurisdiction. While the authorization process itself may be 'in accordance with the law', the act of serving it may render it unlawful or, at least, unenforceable.

4. Convention Measures

The powers referred to in the Convention can be broadly divided into measures exercised against cloud users and those against service providers. The requirement to enable the 'expedited preservation of stored computer data' (Art. 16) while potentially applicable to any persons, is most likely to be used against an innocent third party, such as a cloud service provider, rather than a suspect. The preservation and disclosure of 'traffic data' is again primarily directed at service providers. 'Traffic data' is defined in the following terms:

any computer data relating to a communication by means of a computer system, generated by a computer system that formed a part in the chain of communication, indicating the communication's origin, destination, route, time, date, size, duration, or type of underlying service.[47]

This would include forensic material held by all three types of service provider outlined above and, indeed, the provision expressly recognizes that 'one or more service providers' may have been involved in the transmission of the communication (Art. 17(1)(b)). The Convention's data preservation obligations are potentially applicable across all types of cloud service provider, in contrast to the wholesale data retention obligations under

---

[43] For example, the incitement of crime through the actions of 'agent provocateurs' may breach an individual's right to a fair trial, under Art. 6 of the ECHR. See *Teixeira de Castro v Portugal* (1998) 28 EHRR 101.

[44] For an example of an express limitation, see the Police Act 1996, s. 30(1); while the presumption was recently restated in *R (Al-Skeini) v Secretary of State for Defence* [2008] 1 AC 153 (45).

[45] For example, *Zheng v Yahoo! Inc.*, 2009 WL 4430297 at *4, No. C-08-1068 MMC (2 December 2009), where representatives of the China Democracy Party tried unsuccessfully to bring an action for violation of the Electronic Communications Privacy Act (ECPA) of 1986.

[46] For example, *Suzlon Energy Ltd v Microsoft Corp.*, 2011 US App 9th Circuit, where the court held that the ECPA protected the domestic communications of any person, not just US citizens: <http://cdn.ca9.uscourts.gov/datastore/opinions/2011/10/03/10-35793.pdf>.

[47] Convention, Art. 1(d).

EU law, applicable only to communication service providers.[48] The contrast may be less stark, however, depending on how widely the latter category is defined, and how the preservation regime operates.[49] For example, in the US the authorities can issue 90-day blanket data preservation orders against all three types of cloud service providers, which are renewable for an additional 90-day period,[50] which equates with the minimum six-month data retention period under EU law.[51]

The expedited preservation of forensic material by the service provider is the first stage of an investigation. LEA access to such data will often comprise a separate procedure, subject to different authorization procedures. The Convention distinguishes two forms of production order: one being issued against a person who is in 'possession or control' of computer data, while the other is for a service provider to disclose 'subscriber information' (Art. 18). The former requires the person to be located 'in its territory', although the data may be held elsewhere; while a request for subscriber information can extend to any service provider 'offering its services in the territory', which could obviously mean that an order may be served where both entity and data reside in a foreign jurisdiction.

'Possession and control' reflects the terminology commonly found in the national law of signatories to the Convention.[52] 'Possession' would seem a narrower concept than 'control', even though it may extend beyond physical possession to constructive possession under certain legal systems.[53] The concept of having 'control' over data can be viewed from different perspectives:

- Managerial, for example an ability to determine the purpose and means of processing.[54]

- Technical, whether the person is capable of remotely accessing the data, for example under 'follow the sun' support services.

- Legal, as having legal rights in respect of the data, 'whether legislative, executive, administrative, judicial, contractual, or consensual'.[55]

Some cloud providers have taken the unusual step of publicly taking a position on such issues, responding to widespread concerns by offering certain assurances to users. Rackspace, for example, has recently stated that it takes the view that it has neither possession nor control over its customer stored data, since customers have the technical capability 'to lock Rackspace out, control of passwords used to access their data, and the security of data stored on those servers to the exclusion of others', as well as having contractual responsibility for the protection of any data stored with Rackspace.[56]

---

[48] See further Section 7 below.

[49] See Report for the Commission, 'Data Retention' (*European Commission*, December 2012), available at <http://ec.europa.eu/dgs/home-affairs/what-we-do/policies/police-cooperation/data-retention/index_en.htm> (accessed 28 March 2013).

[50] 18 USC § 2703(f).

[51] Council Directive (EC) 06/24 on the retention of data generated or processed in connection with the provision of publicly available electronic communications services or of public communications networks and amending Directive 2002/58/EC ('Data Retention Directive') [13 April 2006] OJ L105/54, Art. 6.

[52] Under UK law, the terminology is 'possession, custody or power' (eg in the Terrorism Act 2000, Sch. 5, para. 5); while US law refers to 'possession, custody or control' (eg in the Federal Rules of Civil Procedure, at Rules 26 and 34; Federal Rules of Criminal Procedure, Rule 16).

[53] Convention Explanatory Report, para. 173.

[54] Similar to the EU data protection law, as in Directive 95/46/EC, Art. 2(d).

[55] Convention Explanatory Report, para. 38.

[56] Statement issued by Alan Schoenbaum, General Counsel of Rackspace, available at <http://www.rackspace.com.au/company/patriot-act.php> (accessed 28 March 2013).

In deciding whether a US parent company can be compelled to require a foreign subsidiary to disclose customer data to US authorities, a court would examine the nature of the relationship between the parent company and its subsidiary.[57] This would appear to offer cloud providers the possibility of designing their corporate governance structure in a manner that could ensure that an EU-based subsidiary of a US cloud provider is legally immune from a production order issued under US law against that subsidiary. This is the converse of the current situation in Europe, where local subsidiaries of US service providers often decline to respond to domestic LEA requests on the grounds that they do not have rights of access to data held by their US parent.[58] Such Balkanization of the cloud will be unappealing for cloud providers in terms of the efficiency of the technological infrastructure, but may be a necessary response to security and privacy concerns.

In providing for a second category of production order in relation to 'subscriber information' held by a service provider, the Convention suggests the need for a distinct regime governing access to such data. 'Subscriber information' is information held by a service provider 'relating to subscribers of *its* services' (Art. 18(3)), which would exclude a cloud infrastructure provider from receiving data requests about users of a service supplied by a separate cloud provider over its infrastructure. It may also mean that LEAs have to approach a multitude of providers before locating the relevant one. In the UK, the procedure for LEA access to 'subscriber data' arises through administrative self-authorization, rather than requiring judicial sanction, which would be the norm were the same request to be made to a cloud user.[59] Such differential treatment, while clearly advantageous to LEAs, raises concerns about the quality of oversight given to disclosures by service providers. In the US, similar disclosure obligations in respect of subscriber and customer data made against providers of 'electronic communication services' and 'remote computing services' would generally be judicially authorized;[60] while requests for financial records may be made under an administrative subpoena.[61]

Although many LEA powers can be viewed as coercive in the sense that they require a person to act in a certain manner, search and seizure powers represent one of the most intrusive forms of exercise of power provided for in the Convention (Art. 19). As a consequence, such powers are generally subject to judicial authorization and are only utilized against a suspect in an investigation, for example a cloud user, rather than an innocent third party who is simply in possession of relevant forensic material, for example a cloud service provider. The latter will generally receive a production order, as described above. However, to the extent that a search and seizure order is executed against a cloud user, then it will be likely to have an impact on the cloud service provider.

In terms of cloud-located data, the Convention provides that an initial search may be extended to other computer systems connected to the user's system, for example a cloud service provider, where that other system is within the territory and such remote data access is lawful or accessible from the user's system (Art. 19(2)).[62] While accessibility is straightforward, determining legality may require that an LEA be able to determine the location of the systems being utilized by a 'domestic' cloud service provider for the

---

[57] For example, *US v Vetco, Inc.*, 691 F 2d 1281 (9th Cir 1981), where the court required the US entity to produce data held by a subsidiary outside of the US.

[58] For example, the *Yahoo! Belgium* case discussed below.

[59] Regulation of Investigatory Powers Act 2000, Part I, Chapter II. Note, however, that this was amended by the Protection of Freedoms Act 2012 to require judicial authorization in respect of requests made by 'local authorities' (RIPA, s. 23A).

[60] 18 USC § 2703(c).   [61] 31 USC § 5318(k)(3).

[62] In the UK, the Police and Criminal Evidence Act 1984, s. 20, contains a similar provision.

storage of the cloud user's data. This is likely to be extremely difficult, particularly in a timely fashion demanded by the investigators, unless the service provider has structured its service on a jurisdictional basis.[63] To address this problem, the Convention provides for Member States to enable LEAs direct access to data stored in foreign territories.

Article 32 provides that a domestic LEA may access data in another territory without authorization of the foreign state or the need to comply with mutual legal assistance procedures in one of two circumstances: where the data is 'publicly available (open source) stored computer data' or where the domestic LEA 'obtains the lawful and voluntary consent of the person who has a lawful authority to disclose the data'.[64] The former relates to the condition of the data itself, while the latter is concerned with the persons who have authority over the data.

These two circumstances do not preclude other forms of transborder access, which are 'neither authorized, nor precluded',[65] rather it represents a position acceptable to all parties to the Convention.[66] For 'publicly available' data, the implication is that it can be accessed without further authorization, although such data may obviously be subject to other rules controlling further use of any information obtained, such as copyright and data protection law. It is argued that transborder access to such data by LEAs does not invoke issues of sovereignty, because such access now comprises part of international customary law.[67]

Where implied authorization cannot be assumed, because data are placed behind some form of access control mechanism, then 'lawful and voluntary consent' is required, to prevent law enforcement personnel from the investigating state committing offences under computer integrity laws of the jurisdiction in which the cloud resource resides. Who is capable of granting 'lawful and voluntary consent'? Must it be the consent of the user who placed the data in the cloud, or can it be the cloud service provider that processes the data on behalf of the user? The provision does not use the 'possession or control' criterion used in respect of the production orders, focusing instead on the person 'who has the lawful authority to disclose the data'; although the nature of the distinction being implied between the two phrases is unclear. In a cloud environment, the cloud user will clearly have such authority, while the cloud service provider is also likely to have such 'lawful authority', generally obtained through the contractual arrangement entered into with the user.

In a survey of cloud standard terms of business undertaken by the Cloud Legal Project at Queen Mary, University of London, all cloud service providers reserve the right to disclose customer data in certain specified circumstances; both data stored by customers themselves as well as data generated by their use of the service.[68] Such circumstances range from a high threshold, such as the receipt of a valid court order, to a low threshold based on the service provider's discretion or perception of its best interests.[69] In the

---

[63] Amazon, for example, offers its customers a choice of several geographical 'regions'.

[64] Absent authorization, the party may decide to give notification to the state where the data resides. See Cybercrime Convention Committee, draft Guidance Note # 3, *Transborder access to data (Article 32)*, 19 February 2013, [3.2].

[65] Explanatory Report, para. 293.

[66] However, the provision does not represent consensus among Council of Europe Member States. In particular, Russia does not accept Art. 32(b) and wants it either amended or a supplementary agreement between the parties as to its meaning, prior to becoming party to the Convention.

[67] N Seitz, 'Transborder Search: A New Perspective in Law Enforcement?' (Fall 2004–05) Vol. 7 *Yale Journal of Law and Technology*, (38).

[68] See Chapter 3.

[69] Chapter 3, Section 3.2.3. For Apple's iCloud service, the privacy policy states that it will disclose personal information if necessary 'by law, legal process, litigation, and/or requests from public and governmental authorities within or outside your country of residence', as well as where Apple 'determine that for purposes of national security, law enforcement, or other issues of public importance, disclosure is necessary or appropriate' (available at <http://www.apple.com/privacy> (accessed 28 March 2013)).

former situation, serving a domestic court order on a foreign cloud service provider may render the order unenforceable;[70] therefore, many providers state a lower threshold, accepting requests from recognized LEAs, or in circumstances where there is a clear and immediate need to disclose in the public interest, such as a danger to life. Cloud providers may also accept an obligation to notify a user on receipt of an LEA request, to the extent compatible by law, which would empower the customer to consider legal avenues to protect the data from disclosure.[71] Lack of provider clarity and customer awareness about such contractual reservations is another source of recent concern about LEA access in a cloud environment. For example, in April 2011 Dropbox was forced to change the wording used in a 'help' article to reflect an amendment made to its terms of service. It had stated that 'Dropbox employees aren't able to access user files'; part of the security assurances made to its customers relating to its use of encryption. However, its terms incorporate a provision enabling it to hand over user data in compliance with a valid court order, which required it to clarify that its employees are 'prohibited' from accessing user files, rather than being unable to access them.[72]

'Lawful' is deployed twice in Article 32(b), first in respect of authority of the person to disclose the data, and then with regard to the consent granted by the person. In respect of the former, although a cloud provider is likely to have contractually reserved authority to disclose data, as noted above, that does not preclude the need to assess other legal rules that might prohibit any such disclosure. Such laws may be designed to protect national interests or rights-based concerns. The UK's Protection of Trading Interests Act 1980, for example, was specifically passed to restrain the extraterritorial reach of US regulatory agencies.[73] Under the Act, the government retains the power to prohibit compliance with a requirement to produce to a foreign 'court, tribunal, or authority' any commercial document or information 'which is not within the territorial jurisdiction' of the foreign country (s. 2). French law also contains provisions prohibiting certain disclosures of information of an 'economic, commercial, industrial, financial, or technical' nature for the purposes of foreign legal proceedings.[74] Data protection laws, examined further below, impose an additional layer of legal constraints over the processing of personal data, which could supersede any contractual authority the cloud provider may have obtained from the cloud user. From the requesting state's perspective, the impact that such conflicts of law may have on the 'lawful' nature of the request itself may vary between jurisdictions. In the US, for example, the leading case of *US v Bank of NovaScotia*[75] held that a breach of law in the foreign state did not invalidate the enforceability of a domestic LEA request.

---

[70] J Reidenberg, 'Technology and Internet Jurisdiction' (2005) 153 *University of Pennsylvania Law Review* 1951.

[71] For example, Microsoft Online Services, Trust Center, 'Data Use Limits' states that, in the first instance Microsoft will redirect an LEA to the customer; while if required to respond to the LEA request, it will 'use commercially reasonable efforts to notify the enterprise customer in advance of any production unless legally prohibited' (available at <http://www.microsoft.com/online/legal/v2/?docid=23> (accessed 28 March 2013)).

[72] Erik Sherman, 'At Dropbox, Even We Can't See Your Dat- er, Nevermind' (*CBS Money Watch*, 19 April 2011), <http://www.bnet.com/blog/technology-business/-8220at-dropbox-even-we-cant-see-your-dat-8211-er-nevermind-8221-update/10077> (accessed 28 March 2013).

[73] A Kapranos Huntley, 'The Protection of Trading Interests Act 1980: Some Jurisdictional Aspects of Enforcement of Antitrust Laws' (1981) *International and Comparative Law Quarterly* 30 (213, 216).

[74] Loi 80-538, at Art. 1a. See further S Mason, 'Some International Developments in Electronic Evidence' [2012] 18 *CTLR*, Issue 1, (25–8).

[75] 691 F 2d 1384 (11th Cir. 1982).

Although controversial, Article 32 is not the only example of international agreement enabling domestic LEAs to carry out an investigation in a foreign territory without the need to follow interstate mutual legal assistance procedures. Under Title III of the EU 'Convention on Mutual Assistance in Criminal Matters' (2000),[76] the issue of transborder interception is addressed. At the time of drafting, two technical scenarios were of concern: satellite and mobile communication systems. With the former, the footprint of a satellite system extends over multiple jurisdictions, but the available point of interception may be a so-called 'gateway' located in a single jurisdiction.[77] Thus, a lawful intercept of a person located in territory A may require technical assistance from territory B. This may be termed the 'remote assist scenario', which could equally be applicable to cloud-based Communications as a Service (CaaS) applications. In the second scenario, mobile network coverage in border areas may enable an interception authorized in territory A of persons located in territory B with no requirement for technical assistance from territory B. This may be termed the 'spillover scenario'.

The Convention details two different procedures by which extraterritorial intercepts may be carried out in the 'remote assist' scenario. First, the intercepting state can issue a request to the state where the intercept capability is located, based on traditional mutual legal assistance (MLA) procedures. Alternatively, however, the service provider in territory A may carry out the interception by 'remote control'[78] in territory B in accordance with Article 19, which does not require notification to an authority in territory B. The wording used seems to conceive of 'control' in a purely technical sense, although clearly such control may be organizational, when dealing with a single entity with multiple sites, or contractual, where the intercept is carried out by another service provider. A third procedure, under Article 20, is applicable to the 'spillover scenario', which requires an authority in territory A to notify the relevant authority in territory B, which may permit or refuse the extraterritorial interception.

The 'Article 19' procedure represents a surrender of territorial control over interception for the state where the 'gateway' is located, while extending the jurisdictional reach of criminal procedure for the requesting state, so it may only prove an acceptable solution within the context of the EU, with its broader political and legal remit to establish an 'area of freedom, security, and justice' (Treaty on European Union, Art. 3(2)). In addition, the loss and the gains are unlikely to be shared equally between Member States, since the location of 'gateways' is driven by business imperatives, such as favourable tax regimes or low-cost infrastructure, which results in a clustering of 'gateways' in certain states, as has occurred with cloud infrastructure.

Articles 20 and 21 of the Cybercrime Convention permit the real-time collection or recording of traffic data and the interception of communication content. Two scenarios are envisaged: the first involving conduct carried out solely by the 'competent authorities', as in the LEA; the second being where a service provider is required and compelled to engage in the conduct. As discussed further below, the concept of a service provider is broadly defined and would seem to encompass all three types of service provider we have highlighted.

The Convention attempts to distinguish between LEA access to 'stored computer data', as in data 'at rest', and data obtained 'real time', as in 'in transmission', whether

---

[76] The Convention on Mutual Assistance in Criminal Matters between the Member States of the European Union Established by Council Act of 29 May 2000 [12 July 2000] OJ C197. An Explanatory Report has been published at [29 December 2000] OJ C379 (7).

[77] The 'gateway' may be the earth station controlling the telemetry, tracking, and operation of the satellite.

[78] Explanatory Report, para. 20.

traffic data or content. The implication being, as with 'subscriber information', that separate procedures may exist for the authorization of LEAs to gather such data. While differential treatment may be justifiable in public policy terms, including on privacy grounds, the problem for LEAs and service providers is whether a distinction between data at rest and data in transmission is technically meaningful, and an appropriate boundary in a cloud environment. For example, when a user posts a message on a SaaS application for subsequent retrieval, is the message in the course of transmission until it has been 'read' or stored?[79] Alternatively, should LEA access to automated intra-cloud transmissions of data occurring in accordance with load-balancing algorithms be treated as an act of interception or a request for stored data?

The potential consequences of a blurred boundary between data at rest and in transmission in a cloud environment can be significant. An individual's rights in the content of their communications may be significantly eroded. Cloud service providers will face legal, procedural, and operational uncertainties with regard to their obligations to obtain and deliver up data that has been requested by an investigator. Finally, LEAs will be faced with legal uncertainties about the appropriate procedures to be complied with when carrying out an investigation, or risk obtained data being excluded evidentially.

5. International Cooperation

As noted already, the challenge for LEAs in a cloud environment is that there is a high likelihood that the evidence being sought is outside the territorial jurisdiction of the LEA and the suspect being investigated. Where evidence is located outside the domestic jurisdiction, with a foreign cloud provider not subject to domestic jurisdiction, an investigative LEA is generally faced with four possible courses of action:

- Initiate formal MLA procedures, established under MLA treaties,[80] to obtain assistance from a foreign LEA;
- Engage in informal cooperation with the foreign LEA;
- Liaise directly with the foreign service provider requesting voluntary assistance, or
- Engage directly with the material being sought.

Chapter III of the Cybercrime Convention is designed to facilitate the first and second of these through improved international cooperation. Broadly speaking, two forms of cooperation are addressed: the provision or exchange of information, which may be directly or indirectly evidential, and the delivery-up of the suspect, or the notion of extradition, which is not considered further in this chapter.

The provision of information under formal MLA procedures tends to occur through judicial or executive authorities, often designated as 'central authorities' or 'national points of contact' for the jurisdiction, through which requests are channelled.[81] Historically, MLA procedures have been notoriously complex, slow, and bureaucratic, which is particularly unsuitable for cloud-based investigations. In 2004, for example, a

---

[79] M O'Floinn and D Ormerod, 'Social Networking Sites, RIPA and Criminal Investigations' (2011) *Crim LR* 766. See *Edmondson & ors v R* [2013] EWCA Crim 1026.

[80] For example, 'Agreement on mutual legal assistance between the European Union and the United States of America' [19 July 2003] OJ L181/34. The Agreement entered into force on 1 February 2010, after all Member States had aligned their bilateral MLAs with the US.

[81] See further N Boister, *An Introduction to Transnational Criminal Law* (Oxford: Oxford University Press, 2012), Ch. 16.

US-based hosting and cloud company, Rackspace, received a subpoena, pursuant to an MLA Treaty, requesting delivery-up of certain log file information pertaining to a media organization, Indymedia.[82] The originating request came from a public prosecutor in Italy. To comply with the request for the information, Rackspace chose to shut down the identified host server, which was in London not the US, and deliver up drives to the FBI, on the grounds that it was unable to locate the requested files within the mandated delivery timescales. The case raises a number of interesting issues. First, execution of a legitimate bilateral MLA request required implementation in a third country, the UK, but with no involvement from domestic law enforcement, or apparent consideration of the legality of such action under English law.[83] Second, the nature of the timescales involved in complying with the order meant that Rackspace felt the need to exceed the terms of the request, an inevitable tension between the need for speed, being facilitated by Convention initiatives to reduce procedural lag, and the ability of a requested party to respond in a lawfully compliant manner. The example also illustrates that even a lawfully obtained and served order can still result in potential unlawfully obtained material. Over the years, there have been numerous calls to improve the efficiency of MLA procedures.[84]

While data preservation may be a relatively straightforward process, getting the requested data transferred to the requesting jurisdiction may be considerably more problematic. The Convention attempts to address this legacy through a number of mechanisms that, in part, effectively blur the line between the provision of formal and informal assistance. While such blurring can improve the efficiency of international cooperation, it also raises questions about the legality of such cooperation, and the impact that may have on the rights of those under investigation and those who experience collateral interference.

A first tool for improving international cooperation lies in the reforms made to substantive criminal law. The harmonization of offences and their extended jurisdictional reach means that cloud-based criminal conduct is more likely to result in an offence being committed simultaneously in multiple jurisdictions. Under traditional MLA procedures, the requesting LEA would have to evidence that the conduct being investigated constituted, theoretically, an offence of minimum seriousness in both the requesting and requested jurisdiction, the so-called 'double criminality' principle. However, in a cloud-based environment, there is a greater likelihood that a perpetrator may be held to have engaged in the types of criminal conduct addressed in the Convention in both the state in which he is located as well as the state in which the data is located; for example, offences relating to criminal content such as child sexual abuse images (Art. 9) or the storage of devices designed for criminal conduct against the confidentiality, integrity, and availability of computer systems (Art. 6). In such a situation, the foreign LEA can choose to investigate the alleged conduct without a formal request having been received, on the basis that the investigated conduct also constitutes an offence in their territory.[85]

A second mechanism for improving informal cooperation is through encouraging national LEAs to spontaneously (in other words, proactively) disclose information to foreign LEAs where it appears relevant to conduct seemingly connected to the foreign territory,

---

[82] See generally <http://w2.eff.org/Censorship/Indymedia/>.
[83] In response to parliamentary questions from MPs, Richard Allan and Jeremy Corbyn 20 October 2004, col 725W; John McDonnell MP 27 October 2004, col 1278W; and Lynne Jones 11 November 2004, col 895W; to Home Office Minister Caroline Flint, who replied: 'I can confirm that no UK law enforcement agencies were involved in the matter.'
[84] For example, International Chamber of Commerce, Policy Statement: 'Cross-border law enforcement access to company data' [7 February 2012] No. 373/507.
[85] See DOJ Guidance (n. 26) 57.

rather than waiting for the foreign LEA to commence an investigation and initiate a formal MLA request (Art. 26). Such exchanges of information are obviously largely dependent on how good relations are between the various countries involved, as well as the attitudes and opinions of the people on the ground within the LEAs. The Convention tries to encourage such good relations through requiring each party to establish a designated point of contact, available 24/7, with the appropriate technical and legal expertise and ability to facilitate communications and expedite requests for assistance (Art. 35).

The final course of action noted above, direct engagement, does not require cooperation between LEAs, and was partly addressed in the previous section in respect of legitimizing certain extraterritorial conduct by LEAs under Article 32 of the Convention. However, another mode of investigation that has been raised in a cyber-context is the possibility of an LEA actively interfering with an online resource associated with a suspect, such as a cloud service, in order to obtain evidence. Such interference could clearly constitute the commission of a criminal offence by the LEA, in the domestic and, or, foreign jurisdiction, such as an illegal access under the Convention (Art. 2). A statutory defence or immunity from prosecution would, therefore, be required for such conduct, as well as an authorization and supervision regime. Such LEA conduct, especially in a multijurisdiction context, is fraught with difficulties, on grounds of principle, legality, and practicality, and is not considered further in this chapter.

6. European Criminal Procedure

As with other areas of criminal procedure, different rules and procedures exist, or are being established, for the movement of evidence between EU Member States compared with the procedures governing the movement of such evidence between EU and non-EU states. At the moment, MLA between Member States is governed by the Council of Europe's 'European Convention on Mutual Assistance in Criminal Matters' (1959),[86] which has been amended on a couple of occasions;[87] as well as supplementary EU measures, specifically the 'Schengen Convention'[88] and the 'Convention on Mutual Assistance in Criminal Matters' (2000), discussed above.

The 1959 and 2000 Conventions, based on MLA, are progressively being supplanted by other European measures designed to facilitate the handling of evidence between Member States, based on the principle of mutual recognition, as specified in the Treaty on the Functioning of the European Union, Article 82(1). In 2003, a Decision on the execution 'of orders freezing property and evidence' was adopted by the Council.[89] This enables an LEA in one Member State to request the securing of potential evidence in another Member State against potential destruction, transfer, or disposal, through an expedited procedure. The measure builds on Article 16 of the Convention, which calls for the expedited preservation of stored computer data, by providing a cross-border mechanism. However, the mechanism does not provide for the data to be transferred to the requesting state, which is subject to a separate procedure.

---

[86] CETS No. 30, entered into force 12 June 1962. The Council of Europe includes non-EU Member States.

[87] An additional Protocol was adopted in 1978 (CETS No. 99) and a Second Additional Protocol in 2001 (CETS No. 182).

[88] Convention implementing the Schengen Agreement [22 September 2000] OJ L239/19, Arts 48–53.

[89] Council Framework Decision 2003/577/JHA of 22 July 2003 on the execution in the European Union of orders freezing property or evidence [2 August 2002] OJ L196/45.

In 2008, the European Evidence Warrant (EEW)[90] was adopted, which Member States should have transposed into national law by 19 January 2011 (Art. 23(1)). Under the EEW measure, a request for evidence issued by an 'issuing authority', which may be a judge, an investigating magistrate, or public prosecutor (Art. 2(c)), in one Member State would be recognized and directly enforced by an 'executing authority' in the recipient Member State. However, due to the political sensitivities involved in establishing such procedures, the EEW is being established in two stages. This current instrument only covers 'evidence which exists and is readily available',[91] while evidence that requires further investigative activities to be carried out in the executing state, such as real-time interception and covert surveillance, as well as access to data retained by a communications service provider under the Data Retention Directive,[92] cannot be obtained under the current EEW (Art. 4(2)).

An EEW request takes the form of a standard document, translated by the issuing authority into the official language of the executing authority. This can be treated by the executing authority in the same manner as a domestic request, with the requested information being obtained in a manner considered most appropriate by the executing authority, but 'without delay and...no later than 60 days after receipt of the EEW' (Art. 15(3)). Verification of 'double criminality' is not required for the recognition or execution of an EEW, unless it involves the use of search and seizure powers (Art. 14(1)). In the latter circumstance, verification is also not required for certain designated offences where they are punishable in the issuing state by a custodial sentence of at least three years (Art. 14(2)). The list of offences includes child pornography, fraud, computer-related crime, racism, xenophobia, counterfeiting, and piracy of products, as well as infringements of intellectual property rights and sabotage. Member States have also retained the right, in exceptional cases, to refuse to execute an EEW where the offence has been committed wholly or partly in the executing state (Art. 13(f)(1)), based on the territoriality principle, which may result in multistate jurisdictional negotiations taking place at an evidential stage, rather than when deciding where to prosecute. This can be criticized for creating new obstacles to the transfer of evidence that are not present under traditional MLA procedures.

In April 2010, a second measure of mutual recognition was proposed by certain Member State governments, 'regarding the European Investigation Order in criminal matters' ('EIO').[93] The proposal forms part of the 'Stockholm Programme',[94] adopted by the European Council in December 2009, and is designed to replace the current fragmentary regime with a 'comprehensive system for obtaining evidence in cases with a cross-border dimension'.[95] It would apply to almost all investigative measures, including those requiring the ongoing gathering of evidence, such as real-time surveillance; although it is proposed that certain forms of conduct would remain outside the regime, including the interception of satellite transmission that would remain subject to the 2000 Convention, as outlined above. Once the evidence has been obtained, it would be transferred 'without undue delay' to the issuing state.[96]

---

[90] Council Framework Decision 2008/978/JHA of 18 December 2008 on the European evidence warrant for the purpose of obtaining objects, documents and data for use in proceedings in criminal matters [30 December 2008] OJ L350/72.

[91] See Press Release from the Justice and Home Affairs Council Meeting, 9409/06 (Presse 144), 1–2 June 2006.

[92] See n. 51.

[93] Council of the European Union (COD) 2010/0817 [29 April 2010] ('EIO Proposal').

[94] 'The Stockholm Programme—An Open and Secure Europe Serving and Protecting Citizens' [4 May 2010] OJ C115/1.

[95] 'The Stockholm Programme', at 3.1.1, para. 4.   [96] EIO Proposal, at Art. 12(1).

The EIO proposal has generated much controversy and dispute concerning both the appropriateness of its legal basis as well as the scope and implications of its provisions.[97] The Justice and Home Affairs Council agreed an approach on the EIO in December 2011, the European Parliament proposed amendments in May 2012, and the trialogue discussions commenced in November 2012.[98] Were the EIO to be adopted, it would facilitate LEA access to cloud-derived data held within the EU, if its location can be determined!

7. LEA–Service Provider Relations

Where evidence is located outside the territory, another course of action available to an LEA is to liaise directly with the service provider. The success of liaising with a foreign service provider will depend on a range of factors, including the provision made in the contractual terms with the customer for the disclosure of data, as discussed above. Where the foreign service provider has a domestic presence, even though distinct from the service relevant to the investigation, that is also likely to have an impact on relations. Facebook, for example, may store evidential material on servers in the US relating to its cloud services, but its presence in the UK means that there is a domestic route through which LEA requests can be channelled to the foreign entity.[99] The manner in which such a request is treated by the recipient foreign entity will obviously vary according to internal corporate policy, but any multinational corporation is likely to be mindful of any impact that any adverse decision may have on the position of its domestic entity. In September 2010, Google launched its 'Transparency Report' to publicize the numbers of domestic and foreign LEA requests it receives for user information, as well as the extent to which such requests were fully or partially complied with.[100] The stated aim is to contribute to 'discussions about the appropriate scope and authority of government requests'.

In 2008, a conference organized by the Council of Europe adopted a set of 'Guidelines for the cooperation between law enforcement and internet service providers against cybercrime'.[101] In similar fashion to the international cooperation measures detailed in the Convention, the Guidelines are designed to structure the interactions that take place 'in an efficient manner with due consideration to their respective roles, the cost of such cooperation and the rights of citizens' (para. 7). Similar to relations between states, effective cooperation will often depend on building a 'culture of cooperation' between

---

[97] Steve Peers, 'The Proposed European Investigation Order: Assault on Human Rights and National Sovereignty' (*Statewatch Analysis*, May 2010), <http://www.statewatch.org/analyses/no-96-european-investigation-order.pdf>; and Steve Peers, 'The Proposed European Investigation Order: Update' (*Statewatch Analysis*, 24 November 2013), <http://www.statewatch.org/analyses/no-112-eu-eio-update.pdf> (both accessed 28 March 2013).

[98] Written parliamentary answer from James Brokenshire, Secretary of State at the Home Office, HC Deb 12 December 2012, col 348W.

[99] In May 2011, Twitter announced it was opening a London office at a time when it was accused of facilitating breaches of a privacy injunction against the footballer Ryan Giggs and subject to a court order requiring it to deliver up details concerning its users.

[100] Available at Google, 'Transparency Report', <http://www.google.com/transparencyreport>. In March 2013, Microsoft followed suit, publishing its '2012 Law Enforcement Requests Report', available at Microsoft, '2012 Law Enforcement Requests Report', <http://www.microsoft.com/about/corporatecitizenship/en-us/reporting/transparency> (both accessed 28 March 2013).

[101] Available at Council of Europe, 'Resources: Law Enforcement—Internet Service Provider Cooperation in the Investigation of Cybercrime', <http://www.coe.int/t/dghl/cooperation/economiccrime/cybercrime/documents/lea_isp/default_EN.asp> (accessed 28 March 2013).

service providers and LEAs (para. 11); although detailed in written procedures[102] and achieved through appropriately trained and resourced points of contact. However, whether the existence of such a culture is viewed in simply positive terms or as a potential cause for concern, in terms of facilitating non-legal disclosures of data, will depend on whether the participating entities are trusted. The decision by Amazon to terminate the provision of hosting services to WikiLeaks, purportedly under pressure from the US administration, is an example of such concerns.[103]

The Guidelines specifically refer to requests made to foreign service providers, stating that LEAs 'should be encouraged not to direct requests directly to non-domestic Internet service providers', but should make use of interstate procedures contained in international cooperation treaties.[104] This wording is obviously implicit recognition that direct liaison with foreign service providers does take place, even if the recommendation is against such practices. In addition, indirect requests made through the domestic branch of the foreign service provider would not be covered by this recommendation. It is also interesting to note that the Guidelines do not have a complementary recommendation for service providers, encouraging them not to disclose in response to a request from a foreign LEA!

From the perspective of service providers, the Guidelines recommend that they be encouraged to cooperate with LEAs, including through reporting incidents of criminality which come to their attention.[105] Similar to the provisions under the Convention encouraging spontaneous information disclosure by foreign LEAs, compliance with this recommendation would effectively circumvent the need to comply with MLA procedures. Service providers are also recommended to establish 'criminal compliance programmes', which would detail their internal procedures, including 'the extent that a service provider operates in multiple countries'.[106] From a cloud perspective, mapping a service provider's footprint of operations and data centres would be of particular value to LEAs in terms of facilitating the serving of data requests, but would not necessarily identify the jurisdiction in which the data resides at the time of the request.

Another critical factor in the relationship between LEAs and service providers is how the 'service' is characterized under national law. Under the Convention, measures may be taken against a 'service provider' defined in the broadest possible terms, encompassing all three cloud-related service providers outlined at the start of the chapter:

1. any public or private entity that provides to users of its service the ability to communicate by means of a computer system; and

2. any other entity that processes or stores computer data on behalf of such communication service or users of such service (Art. 1(c)).

Unfortunately, however, this terminology does not map neatly onto EU regulatory concepts. Under EU law, a distinction is made between the provision of 'electronic communication services' (ECS) and 'information society services' (ISS):

'electronic communications service' means a service normally provided for remuneration which consists wholly or mainly in the conveyance of signals on electronic communications networks, including telecommunications services and transmission services in networks used for broadcasting, but exclude services providing, or exercising editorial control over, content transmitted

---

[102] For example, mandatory sign-off by in-house counsel.
[103] See Ewan MacAskill, 'WikiLeaks website pulled by Amazon after US political pressure' (*The Guardian*, 2 December 2010).
[104] Guidelines, para. 36.
[105] Guidelines, para. 42. Service providers are not, however, expected to 'actively search for facts or circumstances indicating illegal activities'.
[106] Guidelines, para. 50.

using electronic communications networks and services; it does not include information society services, as defined in Article 1 of Directive 98/34/EC, which do not consist wholly or mainly in the conveyance of signals on electronic communications networks.[107]

The latter ISS are primarily regulated under the 'Electronic Commerce' Directive.[108] Taking our three types of service provider, the first two are widely seen as an ISS, while the provider of the communication service would be an ECS; although it would depend on the nature of the service being supplied in the particular circumstances. So, for example, the emergence of CaaS as a variety of cloud offering, providing enterprises with the functionality of an in-house communications system,[109] could be seen as an ECS or, alternatively, as an 'associated facility' or 'associated service',[110] which also form part of the EU communication regime distinct from the provision of ISS. The boundary is particularly blurred given the potential variety of approaches that could be adopted for interpreting the phrase 'mainly in the conveyance of signals'; from quantitative to qualitative measures, including the imputed intention of suppliers or the perception of consumers. As such, this creates legal and regulatory uncertainty for service providers, as well as LEAs.

Two key EU measures where this uncertainty becomes manifest are the Communications Privacy Directive[111] and the Data Retention Directive.[112] Both contain provisions obliging Member States to adopt measures relevant to LEA access to data processed by service providers.

Under Article 5(1) of the Communications Privacy Directive, Member States are required to prohibit the 'listening, tapping, storage or other kinds of interception or surveillance of communications and the related traffic data by persons other than users', except as authorized under Article 15(1), which includes 'the prevention, investigation, detection, and prosecution of criminal offences'. The prohibition is applicable against all persons, including the service provider and LEAs, but is only applicable to communications being transmitted by means of 'a public communications network and publicly available electronic communication services'. Communications carried over non-public networks and services would not, therefore, be subject to the EU regime, although they are covered by analogous Convention provisions (Art. 21), and national legislation may extend the scope of any such prohibition.[113] As such, for intra- or inter-cloud communications uncertainty exists as to whether such communications are subject to the additional protections granted under the Directive.

While Article 15(1) permits Member States to authorize interception or surveillance by LEAs, it does not further specify the conditions under which such authorization may take place. By contrast, the Convention states that competent LEAs should be empowered to either carry out acts of interception, or to compel a service provider 'within its existing capability' to carry out the interception, or assist LEAs (Art. 21(1)). In many

---

[107] Council Directive (EC) 2002/21 on a common regulatory framework for electronic communications networks and services [24 April 2002] OJ L108/33, (Art. 2(c)).

[108] Council Directive (EC) 2000/31 on certain legal aspects of information society services, in particular electronic commerce, in the Internal Market [17 July 2000] OJ L178/1.

[109] See, for example, Interactive Intelligence, 'Communications as a Service', <http://www.caas.com/Pages/default.aspx> (accessed 28 March 2013).

[110] Framework Directive, Arts 2(e) and (ea) respectively.

[111] Council Directive (EC) 02/58 concerning the processing of personal data and the protection of privacy in the electronic communications sector [31 July 2002] OJ L201/37, as amended by Directive 06/24/EC and 09/136/EC.

[112] See n. 51.

[113] For example, under RIPA, s. 2, it is an offence to intercept a transmission carried by means of a private telecommunication system.

states, however, the procedural regime goes beyond the Convention provision by requiring that certain entities specifically implement a lawful intercept capability to enable LEAs to carry out or compel the interception of communication content.[114] Such build obligations are generally only imposed upon providers of communication networks or services,[115] as a regulated activity, which returns us to the boundary issue of whether a cloud provider can be characterized as an ECS or ISS.

Similarly, under the Data Retention Directive, the obligations to retain data are placed upon 'providers of publicly available electronic communication services'. The regulatory boundary issue has been examined in detail by the Data Retention Experts Group,[116] in relation to webmail and web-based messaging, which is an example of a cloud-based SaaS, whether provided to corporates or consumers. Its report considers various operational scenarios, such as a person leaving a message on a website for another user, and concludes that the majority constitute an ISS, rather than an ECS, and therefore fall outside the scope of the Data Retention Directive.[117]

That this characterization issue is a real problem can be seen in an important case recently examined in Belgium involving Yahoo! Inc. (Yahoo!). In this case, a public prosecutor requested the disclosure of certain data from Yahoo! regarding certain fraudulent conduct carried out using Yahoo! webmail accounts, under article 46*bis* of the Belgium Criminal Procedure Code. Yahoo! refused to disclose on two grounds: Yahoo!, being based in the US, was not subject to Belgian jurisdiction and, therefore, the request should have been made through MLA procedures; and the service was not an 'electronic communication service' and, therefore, not subject to the relevant order.[118] The lower court held that Yahoo! had unlawfully refused to disclose and imposed a €55,000 fine, with an additional €10,000 for every day it continued to refuse to comply.[119] On appeal, the court held that Yahoo! was not a 'provider of an electronic communication service' and could not, therefore, be required to cooperate.[120] However, the Supreme Court held that the Court of Appeal had been wrong to exempt Yahoo! from the application of the criminal procedure provisions on the basis that the service was not an 'electronic communication service' under the Belgian Electronic Communications Act 2005, as the scope of the concept under criminal law was broader than that under regulatory law.[121] The decision was referred back to the Court of Appeal for reconsideration, which subsequently decided that Yahoo! was not subject to Belgian jurisdiction,[122] although this has also been appealed.

A similar regulated boundary issue exists under US federal criminal law in respect of access to stored 'communications and transactional records'; with a distinction made between providers of 'electronic communication services' and 'remote computing

---

[114] For example, Belgium, Germany, the Netherlands, Italy, Mexico, Russia, Spain, Switzerland, and the UK.

[115] Note, however, the dispute between RIM, the manufacturer of the Blackberry device, and law enforcement agencies in Saudi Arabia and India: for example, Joanne Bladd, 'BlackBerry's Response: RIM Statement in Full' (*Arabian Business*, 3 August 2010), <http://www.arabianbusiness.com/blackberry-s-response-rim-statement-in-full-339572.html> (accessed 28 March 2013).

[116] Commission Decision (EC) 2008/324 setting up the 'Platform on Electronic Data Retention for the Investigation, Detection and Prosecution of Serious Crime' group of experts [23 April 2008] OJ L111/11, 23.4.

[117] DATRET/EXPGRP (2009) 2 Final—03.12.2009.

[118] P de Hert and M Kopcheva, 'International Mutual Legal Assistance in Criminal Law Made Redundant: A Comment on the Belgian Yahoo! Case' (2011) *Computer Law and Security Review* 27, 291–7.

[119] Court of Dendermonde, Not nr DE 20.95.16/08/26, 2 March 2009.

[120] Court of Appeal of Ghent of 30 June 2010.

[121] Supreme Court, Criminal Law Section, Nr. P.10.1347.N, 18 January 2011.

[122] 12 October 2011.

services',[123] which has procedural implications.[124] While the latter, defined as 'the provision to the public of computer storage and or processing services by means of an electronic communication system', would seem to most closely match that of a cloud service provider, the US courts have struggled with the issue of characterization in a similar manner to the Belgian courts.[125] In *Crispin v Christian Audigier Inc.*,[126] the court held that Facebook and MySpace could be either an ECS or an RCS, in respect of wall postings and comments. Elsewhere, however, US law has circumvented such problems through the adoption of expansive catch-all definitions. Under the Foreign Intelligence Surveillance Act, for example, authorization can be given to specifically target the surveillance of persons 'outside the United States', with the assistance of an 'electronic communication service provider' defined in terms that encompasses all possible types of cloud and communications provider.[127]

The characterization of cloud services from a regulatory perspective has important governance implications which go beyond the scope of this chapter. In the context of law enforcement requests for assistance, however, regulatory characterization can impact directly on the legality of a law enforcement request and the obligation of the service provider to comply, potentially resulting in disputes between them.

8. Law Enforcement and Data Protection

Cloud user concerns about the long-arm reach of US law enforcement lie as much in the perceived threat to personal privacy as that of commercial secrecy.[128] To address such concerns, the EU harmonizing procedural measures discussed previously are complemented by a measure to protect personal data.[129] The measure was necessary because such matters fell outside the scope of the general data protection regime, Directive 95/46/EC.[130] This is an area for reform following the abolition of the pillars by the Lisbon Treaty and, in January 2012, the Commission published proposals for a Regulation to replace Directive 95/46/EC and a Directive to replace the 2008 Decision.[131]

The 2008 Decision is primarily directed to the exchange of personal data between law enforcement bodies, 'competent authorities', within the EU Member States. However, it also details those conditions under which it would be permissible for a competent authority to transfer such data onwards to a 'third State or international bodies', which include the need for 'consent' from the authority where the data originated, and that

[123] 18 USC § 2510(15) and § 2711(2) respectively.   [124] 18 USC § 2703(a) and (b) respectively.
[125] DA Couillard, 'Defogging the Cloud: Applying Fourth Amendment Principles to Evolving Expectations in Cloud Computing' (2009) 93 *Minnesota Law Review* 2205. Also, WJ Robinson, 'Free at What Cost?: Cloud Computing Privacy under the Stored Communication Act' (2010) 98 *Georgetown Law Journal* 1195.
[126] 717 F Supp 2d 965, (CDCal, 2010).
[127] 50 USC § 1881(a)(4). These provisions were inserted in by the FISA Amendments Act of 2008, s. 701(b)(4).
[128] For example, European Parliament resolution 'on the interception of bank transfer data from the SWIFT system by the US secret services' (P6_TA-PROV(2006)0317), which raises concerns about privacy as well as 'large-scale forms of economic and industrial espionage'.
[129] Council Framework Decision 2008/977/JHA on the protection of personal data processed in the framework of police and judicial co-operation in criminal matters [30 December 2008] OJ L350/60 ('2008 Decision').
[130] [24 October 1995] OJ L281/31 Art. 3(2).
[131] Proposal for a Regulation, COM(2012) 11 final, [25 January 2012], and Proposal for a Directive, COM(2012) 10 final, [25 January 2012] (hereinafter 'draft Regulation' and 'draft Directive' respectively).

the receiving entity 'ensures an adequate level of protection'.[132] As such, personal data obtained from an EU-based cloud user or service provider may be transferred by an EU domestic authority to a US LEA under MLA procedures in a manner designed to safeguard the rights of data subjects. The MLA agreement between the US and the EU includes provisions on the use of personal data, including detailing the range of purposes for which the data may be used.[133] Other than purpose limitation, however, no 'generic restrictions with respect to the legal standards of the requesting state' may be imposed, although additional conditions can be specified in 'a particular case'.[134]

The more concerning scenario for EU cloud users, raised at the start of this chapter, is where a US LEA directly addresses a request to a cloud service provider that it produce personal data stored by cloud users on infrastructure located within the EU. As already noted, such a request is likely to be a lawful exercise of powers, provided the recipient provider has reserved its rights to disclose under its terms of business. European data protection law, however, adds an additional compliance layer that could result in a breach of the law of the state in which the recipient provider, as data controller, is established or has 'equipment' on which the cloud user data resides: the 'requested provider's state' (Art. 4).[135]

As noted above, the general data protection regime does not encompass 'activities of the State in areas of criminal law'. This is clearly not applicable to the scenario outlined in the previous paragraph because the requested provider's state is not involved in the making or serving of the request. The current regime permits the disclosure of personal data where it is necessary either for the controller to comply with a legal obligation (Art. 7(c)) or if carried out in the public interest or 'in the exercise of official authority vested in the controller or in a third party to whom the data are disclosed' (Art. 7(e)). Both could legitimate the disclosure outlined in the scenario above, as in an EU provider to a US LEA. Under the draft Regulation, however, the Commission proposes to limit this possibility by qualifying both conditions, stating that the legal basis must be provided for in EU law, or the law of the Member State to which the controller is subject.[136] Directive 95/46/EC also exempts certain processing activities from some obligations where the processing is necessary for reasons which include the 'prevention, investigation, detection, and prosecution of criminal offences' (Art. 13).

What the regime does not disapply, however, are the provisions governing the transfer of personal data outside of the EEA, Articles 25 and 26. As such, for a cloud provider to respond to a request for personal data from a US LEA, the provider must be able to legitimize such transfer under the existing rules. Article 25 provides that transfers to a third country may take place where there is 'an adequate level of protection'; such adequacy being determined in 'the light of all the circumstances surrounding a data transfer', including sectoral laws, professional rules, and security measures.[137] US Federal law enforcement bodies, for example, are subject to the Privacy Act 1974, which broadly reflects the provisions of the EU regime, although it is only applicable to 'individuals', defined as 'a citizen of the United States or an alien lawfully admitted for permanent residence'.[138] The process by which a determination of 'adequacy' is made can vary, from the default position being that of the data controller in the first instance[139] to reliance on a Commission finding of 'adequacy'.[140] In terms of the former, therefore, a cloud provider could decide that a transfer is adequate on the basis of specific representations

---

[132] 2008 Decision, Art. 13.   [133] MLA, Art. 9.   [134] MLA, Art. 9(2).

[135] See further Chapter 9.   [136] Draft Regulation, Art. 6(3).

[137] Draft Regulation, Art. 25(1) and (2) respectively. See also Chapter 10.

[138] 5 USC § 552a(a)(2).

[139] For example, UK, Data Protection Act 1998, Sch. I, Pt I, para. 8; Germany, Federal Data Protection Act, s. 4(b)(5).

[140] See n. 130, Art. 25(6).

made by the requesting authority, such as domestic judicial oversight of the subpoena under which the data is requested. It would also seem arguable that the existence of the EU–US MLA agreement could be viewed as providing an assurance of 'adequacy' in respect of disclosures to US LEAs, which could be relied upon by cloud providers; even though the data protection provisions detailed in it fail, on the face of it, to meet the minimum criteria laid down by the Article 29 Working Party: content principles and procedural/enforcement mechanisms.[141] In respect of a Commission decision facilitating disclosures, a precedent exists in the EU agreement on 'adequacy' entered into with the US concerning the 'safe harbor privacy principles'[142] and the disclosure of passenger name records to the US Department of Homeland Security.[143]

Where the cloud provider determines that 'adequacy' is not present, then an exemption will need to be relied upon under Article 26. The most relevant exemption for this discussion is where the transfer is 'necessary or legally required on important public interest grounds'.[144] The scope of the 'public interest' exemption has been considered by the Article 29 Working Party in two situations concerning disclosures for law enforcement purposes: the operation of the whistle-blowing schemes under the US Sarbanes-Oxley Act, and the disclosure of financial data by SWIFT.[145] In these opinions, the Working Party held that the important public interests had to be related to an EU Member State to avoid circumvention of the regime, thereby preventing reliance on US public interest claims. The draft Regulation has addressed this concern, in part, by stating that the 'public interest' must be 'recognized' in EU law or the law of the Member State to which the controller is subject.[146] The wording differs slightly from that outlined above in respect of legitimate processing, as 'recognized' interests would seem to encompass requests by foreign LEAs made under MLA procedures.

What the opinions fail to address, however, is the process by which a public interest claim advanced by a requesting LEA can be held to engage concurrently a public interest of the recipient EU state. As noted earlier, the transnational nature of many serious crimes, such as terrorist acts, coupled with harmonization of substantive criminal law principles, increasingly means that criminal conduct involves the commission of offences in multiple jurisdictions. Where a requesting LEA claims a 'dual' public interest,[147] would a cloud provider be expected, or indeed be able, to look behind such a claim? Would it, for example, be expected to seek confirmation from a domestic LEA?

While the European data protection regime contains provisions that try to balance the potentially conflicting interests of privacy and law enforcement, such provisions are strictly confined to jurisdictions found to have 'adequate' protections in place. As such, despite the extended jurisdictional reach granted LEAs under the Cybercrime Convention, current data protection rules may render such disclosure by a cloud provider unlawful. Uncertainty over the treatment of personal data processed in a criminal

---

[141] WP12 'Transfers of personal data to third countries: Applying Articles 25 and 26 of the EU Data Protection Directive', July 1998.

[142] Council Decision (EC) 2000/520, [25 August 2000] L215/7, which expressly permits derogation 'to the extent necessary to meet . . . law enforcement requirements'.

[143] Council Decision 2006/729/CFSP/JHA [27 October 2006] OJ L298/27, extended by Council Decision 2007/551/CFSP/JHA.

[144] See n. 130, Art. 26(1)(d).

[145] Opinion 1/2006 on the application of EU data protection rules to internal whistle-blowing schemes in the fields of accounting, internal accounting controls, auditing matters, fight against bribery, banking and financial crime [1 February 2006] WP 117; Opinion 10/2006 on the processing of personal data by the Society for Worldwide Interbank Financial Telecommunication (SWIFT) [22 November 2006] WP 128.

[146] Draft Regulation, at Art. 44(5). See also recital 90.

[147] Analogous to the 'double criminality' requirement in international criminal law.

context, however, represents an obstacle to cloud computing, which needs to be addressed as part of the current reform process.

9. Cloud-derived Evidence

It is beyond the scope of this chapter to examine different national rules governing the admissibility of cloud-derived data as evidence in criminal proceedings; although the applicable rules will vary depending on how the cloud-derived evidence is characterized from an evidential perspective.[148] The ability of LEAs to utilize cloud-derived evidence, however, is an indirect means of regulating the investigative practices examined in this chapter. Rules of evidence and the attitude of the courts can operate so as to either deter or tolerate inappropriate conduct by LEAs. The US exclusionary doctrine based on the 'fruit of the poisonous tree' metaphor is an example of such judicial deterrence.[149]

Data obtained from a cloud-based service may be excluded from use in criminal proceedings on a number of grounds. First, statutory rules may exclude certain types of evidence. In the UK, for example, evidence obtained through an interception of communications is generally inadmissible if carried out by UK LEAs,[150] while admissible if obtained from foreign LEAs.[151] In addition, courts generally have jurisdiction, granted by statute (eg criminal procedure code) or inherent to the court (eg abuse of process) to exclude evidence in certain circumstances if that evidence is considered to undermine or cause real prejudice to the defendant's right to a fair trial, as enshrined in Article 6 of the ECHR. Article 6 does not, however, contain rules on the admissibility of evidence; therefore, the ECtHR cannot exclude evidence simply on the basis that such evidence was obtained unlawfully.[152]

If obtained in breach of law, evidence gathered by an LEA may be excluded, either as a matter of law or at the discretion of the court. Such a breach may result from the conduct of an LEA investigator exceeding the jurisdiction granted to the LEA, or the conduct itself being illegal under the relevant criminal code. In terms of the former, considerations of exclusion will often depend on whether the conduct was an intentional flaunting of the applicable rules or simply a mistake made in good faith.[153] The legality of conduct may of course differ between the foreign jurisdiction where the evidence was obtained, and the domestic jurisdiction, where the evidence is being adduced, and this may impact on the domestic court's treatment of such evidence. In the UK, for example, a breach of foreign legal procedures would only lead to the exclusion of real evidence if the nature of the breach was considered to amount to an act of bad faith on behalf of the domestic LEA.[154] On the other hand, in the US, a request for evidence obtained from a foreign computer system to be suppressed on the grounds that it breached constitutional protections was denied by the court on the grounds that the protection was not applicable to property outside the US.[155] As a consequence, for example, a breach of

---

[148] See generally, S Mason, *Electronic Evidence*, 3rd edn (London: LexisNexis, 2012). Stricter controls are generally placed over the use of testimonial and hearsay evidence, compared with real evidence generated by machines, which is what the majority of cloud-derived evidence will be.

[149] See O Kerr, 'Searches and Seizures in a Digital World' (2005) 119 *Harvard Law Review* 531.

[150] RIPA, s. 17.   [151] See *R v P et al.* (2001) 2 All ER 58.

[152] *Schenk v Switzerland* (1991) 13 EHRR 242.

[153] For example, *Herring v US* 555 US (2009).

[154] R Loof, 'Obtaining, Adducing and Contesting Evidence from Abroad: A Defence Perspective on Cross-border Evidence' (2011) *CrimLR* No. 1 (40–57).

[155] *US v Gorshkov*, 2001 WL 1024026 (WD Wash 2001).

data protection rules in the course of obtaining evidence may not constitute a bar to the admissibility of cloud-derived evidence, all other things being equal.

As a general rule, evidence gathered under formal MLA procedures, through a 'letter rogatory' or 'commission rogatoire', will be subject to the same rules of admissibility in the requesting state as evidence obtained domestically.[156] As a consequence, a defendant is generally only protected by the lowest threshold of admissibility, with evidential rules of the foreign state generally being ignored in the requesting state, even if they impose a higher admissibility threshold; while evidence obtained by unlawful means abroad, which would be inadmissible if the conduct occurred domestically, is admissible before the domestic courts.[157] In addition, although MLA procedures are available to both the prosecution and defence, mechanisms designed to streamline the efficiency of these procedures are generally put in place to assist the prosecution,[158] potentially undermining the 'equality of arms' required under the right of fair trial.[159]

The EIO proposal, outlined above, provides that an issuing state may request that its 'authorities' be able to assist the authorities of the executing state in the execution of the EIO.[160] This is not intended to constitute a grant to the LEAs of the issuing state of any extraterritorial powers in the territory of the executing state; rather, it is intended to forestall admissibility challenges to the evidence when relied upon in future proceedings in the issuing state, through the direct involvement of the domestic authorities in the evidence-gathering process.

Even if admissible in court, the evidential weight given to cloud-derived evidence will often depend on the ability of the party adducing the evidence to show that the material is authentic, has integrity, and an appropriate account can be rendered of how the material was handled, from the moment it was obtained until its presentation in court. All computer-derived evidence is vulnerable to alteration and, in a cloud environment, service providers may be required to verify the provenance of data purportedly obtained from their services.

10. Conclusion

In this chapter, a number of legal issues facing LEA investigators when gathering forensic data from a cloud environment have been examined. First, when exercising investigative powers granted to them by the state, particularly where they are covert or involve coercion, LEAs must be concerned that such powers are not exceeded, either in terms of application or territorially. As we have seen, *issues of application* may arise due to uncertainty as to the characterization of the evidence being 'at rest' or 'in transmission', or the entities against which such powers may be exercised; while *issues of territoriality* may arise from the multijurisdictional nature of cloud computing. By exceeding such powers, the LEAs may be acting illegally, which is a concern in its own right, exposing LEAs to liability and potentially infringing the rights of others, as well as impacting on the evidential use or value of the material gathered in the course of the investigation.

---

[156] For example, CPS, Legal Guidance, 'International Enquiries—Using the Evidence Obtained and Admissibility'.

[157] C Gane and M Mackarel, 'The Admissibility of Evidence Obtained from Abroad into Criminal Proceedings—The Interpretation of Mutual Legal Assistance Treaties and Use of Evidence Irregularly Obtained' (1996) 4 *Eur J Crime, Crim L & Crim Just* 98, 116.   [158] See n. 154, 46.

[159] See *Jespers v Belgium* (1981) 27 DR 61 and *X v FRG* (1984) 8 EHRR 225.

[160] EIO Proposal, Art. 8(3).

Within Europe, there is a need to address the uncertainty over the regulatory boundary between the provision of communication services and cloud-based services, as the characterization of a service has important implications in terms of the regulatory obligations of the service provider and its relationship with LEAs. Although rules in the Member States governing the investigative process, for example policing operational matters, are not substantially harmonized at an EU level, there is evidence of an overlap between EU regulatory concepts and national rules, which contributes to the uncertain legal position. A second area of uncertainty is found in the application of current data protection rules to the transfer of personal data outside Europe for the purposes of a criminal investigation. The piecemeal approach that has resulted from the restricted competence of the Community in the area of criminal law has placed cloud users and providers in an uncertain legal position, which can deter the take-up of such services.

International rules governing the transborder gathering of evidence, 'mutual legal assistance', are poorly suited to cloud-based processing activities, as with other forms of computer and networking environments. Reforms have taken place over the past 10 years to try to improve the situation, especially through resort to more informal interstate mechanisms, based on harmonized legal systems as well as building trusted networks of LEA experts. The primary concern with greater reliance upon informal procedures is that of accountability; ensuring that LEAs do not exceed their powers and inappropriately interfere with individual rights. As Boister warns: 'law enforcement effectiveness tends to predominate over values like international legality, at the expense of legitimacy'.[161]

Part of the response has also resulted in sovereignty concessions being made in limited circumstances in order to legalize certain extraterritorial conduct by LEAs. While such initiatives can be viewed as eroding traditional sovereign rights, they can also represent an extraterritorial extension of criminal procedure jurisdiction that may actually strengthen sovereignty in a transnational cloud environment.

Another component of this shift to informality is greater cooperation between LEAs and service providers. For transborder investigations, this cooperation takes the form of domestic LEAs directly or indirectly (such as through a domestic entity) contacting foreign service providers with requests for data. Such requests shift the concern over legality from the requesting LEA to the responding service provider. However, our research indicates that cloud service providers generally provide for the possibility of law enforcement disclosures of customer data in their standard terms of business, thereby facilitating informal cooperation with LEAs, while mitigating the legal risks.

The legality of gathering evidence in a cloud environment is only part of the challenge facing LEAs in an investigation. Considerable technical forensic issues will confront LEAs. Where cloud-derived material is obtained, its admissibility as evidence and evidential weight may be challenged not only on the basis of the conduct of the LEA in the course of gathering such material, but also the quality of the forensic process itself, which will depend in large part on the systems and conduct of cloud service providers.

---

[161] N Boister, 'Transnational Criminal Law?' (2003) 14 *European Journal of International Law* 953, 960.

12

Facilitating Competition in the Clouds

Ian Walden and Laíse Da Correggio Luciano

1. Introduction

Cloud computing is viewed as a key enabling development capable of boosting Europe's competitiveness. However, the development and use of cloud computing services can also raise competition concerns. While substantial competition law issues are likely to emerge only when cloud computing business models have matured, some areas of potential concern can already be discerned or have been highlighted in policy responses to cloud. This chapter identifies the potential applicability of competition law to the cloud computing sector, as well as assessing its suitability as a regulatory regime.

For the purpose of this chapter, competition law is understood as a set of rules intended to protect the process of competition and enhance consumer welfare, which are enforced primarily through specialized regulatory authorities. These rules generally involve *ex post* intervention in a market in response to the decisions and conduct of its participants that either have, or are likely to, result in market distortions.[1] As such, competition regimes are distinguished from *ex ante* regimes that proactively control the manner in which market participants behave, such as telecommunications law. However, as with any law, competition law can also be viewed as having a primary 'prophylactic'[2] purpose, designed to prevent the conduct of undertakings from resulting in competition being distorted, and to promote healthy competition in the market. Such deterrence arises, in part, from the remedies available against breaches of competition rules, which include penal remedies,[3] administrative fines of up to 10 per cent of annual total turnover,[4] and civil actions for damages.[5]

Applicable legal mechanisms under competition law are analysed, specifically prohibitions on anti-competitive agreements and abuses of market dominance. While cloud computing services often have a global reach, this chapter focuses on EU competition law. We then examine alternative legal approaches and regimes, which specifically address the demand for cloud services. In particular, we consider the use of public procurement rules, including measures taken to promote open standards and interoperability, as well as the idea of a data portability right. Despite being early days, we suggest that these latter mechanisms are likely to have a more significant impact on competition in the cloud computing sector than intervention using traditional competition law measures.

---

[1] As such, while merger regulation is *ex ante* in effect, permitting or rejecting a proposed deal, it is *ex post* by nature, since it is triggered by the decision of the parties to the transaction.

[2] On the prophylactic purpose of competition law, see DA Balto and EA Nagata, 'Proof of Competitive Effects in Monopolization Cases: A Response to Professor Muris' (2000–01) 68 *Antitrust LJ* 309.

[3] For example, Enterprise Act 2002, s. 190, a potential five-year prison term for operating a cartel.

[4] For example, Council Regulation (EC) 1/2003, on the implementation of the rules on competition laid down in Articles 81 and 82 of the Treaty [4 January 2003] OJ L1/1 (Art. 23(2)).

[5] For example, Competition Act 1998, s. 47A, enabling claims for loss or damage resulting from an infringement of the prohibitions, which include the relevant provisions of EU competition law.

2. Competition in the Cloud Computing Sector

To identify competition issues, we need first to outline the emerging markets for cloud computing services. To date, the three main categories are: Infrastructure as a Service (IaaS), Platform as a Service (PaaS), and Software as a Service (SaaS).[6] However, there may be layers of cloud providers involved in a service, often without the knowledge of customers. Therefore, a customer may purchase SaaS, but the provider uses IaaS services from another cloud computing provider, so in practice the customer is using both services.[7] It should, therefore, be noted that there may be competition issues not only in the service cloud, but also in the infrastructure layers upon which cloud services are built and depend. In particular, there may be competition issues at the network level, which impinge on end-user access to cloud services, from unbundling issues to 'network neutrality'. Access to cloud services is provided by telecommunication companies that have historically been part of concentrated markets, which have developed from previous state-owned incumbent monopolies. Connectivity, in terms of availability and affordability, is a concern not only in developing economies, but also in countries where the policy of market liberalization has not sufficiently eroded the market power of the incumbent operators. These issues fall outside the scope of this chapter, but should nonetheless be borne in mind.[8]

When cloud computing takes the form of IaaS, a computing resource such as processing power or storage is provided.[9] Most of the infrastructure offered relates to the provision of virtualized application hosting or data storage. Some providers supply software and/or hardware which enable an IaaS service to be run on a private cloud,[10] while other providers offer an IaaS service internally or to others, at times using one of those suppliers' products.[11]

At present in the IaaS market, applications as well as data can generally be stored in any infrastructure. In fact, processing capacity is increasingly becoming 'industrialized' and 'utility'-like,[12] which may eventually have regulatory implications were policymakers to consider the need to impose consumer protection rules similar to those applicable to other forms of utilities, such as electricity.[13] IaaS capacity will soon be bought and sold as a commodity available from a 'trading floor'[14] in a manner similar to other products and services, such as the online trade in voice minutes.[15] However, there may be circumstances where data and application portability is not possible or is prohibited by the service provider, which may result in distortion of competition and harm to users. Such lock-in effects in the IaaS sector could prevent, for example, a customer from using an 'Amazon Machine Image' (AMI) on another provider's IaaS services. This raises concerns, for instance in terms of application portability in the IaaS market.

---

⁶ See further Chapter 1. ⁷ See Chapter 1, at 3.2.
⁸ See generally I Walden (ed.) *Telecommunications Law and Regulation*, 4th edn (Oxford: Oxford University Press, 2012).
⁹ See Chapter 1. ¹⁰ For example, AppLogic, Smart Business Cloud, and Eucalyptus.
¹¹ For example, Amazon Web Service (AWS) and GoGrid.
¹² Commission Communication, 'Unleashing the Potential of Cloud Computing in Europe' COM (2012) 529/2 (4) (hereinafter referred to as 'Communication').
¹³ In the UK, Ofgem regulates the gas and electricity markets, see <http://www.ofgem.gov.uk> (accessed 29 March 2013).
¹⁴ See David Mayer, 'Is the Cloud Exchange Concept Ready for Primetime? Deutsche Boerse Thinks So' (Gigaom.com, 2 July 2013), <http://gigaom.com/2013/07/02/is-the-cloud-exchange-concept-ready-for-primetime-deutsche-boerse-thinks-so/> (accessed 17 July 2013).
¹⁵ See, for example, RouteTrader, available at <http://www2.routetrader.com> (accessed 29 March 2013).

When PaaS is offered, tools for the construction of bespoke applications are provided.[16] These platforms offer an environment for building, maintaining, and operating applications. There may be competition issues due to lock-in effects within the PaaS sector as well. This may primarily involve obstacles to porting an application developed on one provider's platform to another provider's, plus associated data, whether unstructured or in databases. In addition, there may be concerns in relation to abusive licensing conditions placed by the platform provider on developers of applications ('apps'). This was the subject of an investigation by the European Commission in relation to Apple's iPhone applications. In April 2010, Apple imposed restrictions pursuant to the terms and conditions of its licence agreements with independent developers of iPhone apps. Apple required the exclusive use of Apple's native programming tools and approved languages for the development of iPhone apps. Imposing such restrictions was considered by the Commission as conduct which could have resulted in harm to competition by platforms that competed with Apple's apps platform. As a result of preliminary investigations by the Commission, in September 2010, Apple voluntarily announced the removal of the restrictions, thereby allowing third-party application development environments to be used to submit apps, resulting in greater flexibility for developers.[17] This is not the only conduct of Apple that may raise competition law concerns. In fact, Apple only allows apps in the App Store which Apple has approved. This would be the equivalent of a printer manufacturer only allowing cartridges made by it, or approved by it, to be used in its printers since only apps approved by Apple may be downloaded from the App Store to non-jailbroken iPhones.[18] If considered dominant in the market, Apple's conduct could be considered abusive as it reduces the choice of consumers. Cloud computing has seen the emergence of other platforms which change distribution models for digital content.[19] These distribution models allow the controller of the distribution platform to host apps/content and/or require apps to be downloaded to user devices only from them. Such control could give the controller of the distribution platform a strong position in the market which could result in the distortion of competition.

When SaaS is offered, the service provides functionality akin to an end-user application.[20] Harm to competition and consumers may result from practices of undertakings offering SaaS, such as data and application portability obstacles to enhance network effects. Network effects are common in the Information and Communication Technology (ICT) sector and mean that the more people use a product or service, the more others will be willing to use them.[21] A simple example is the telephone, which would be of little use if there were only a couple of them in the world. The more people use telephones, the more others are incentivized to use or purchase one. An example in the cloud computing sector is Facebook, whose relevance and usefulness derives from the size of its community of members. Where network effects are present, the market

---

[16] For example, Google App Engine, Force.com, LongJump, WaveMaker, and SQL Azure.

[17] See 'EUROPA—Press Releases—Antitrust: Statement on Apple's iPhone policy changes', 25 September 2010.

[18] iOS jailbreaking is a process that unlocks all features of Apple's iOS operating system, thereby removing limitations imposed by Apple.

[19] For example, Kindle and OnePass.

[20] For example, Facebook, MySpace, Google Docs, and Office Web Apps.

[21] On network effects, see J Church and N Gandal, in 'Platform Competition in Telecommunications', *Handbook of Telecommunications Economics* (eds Majumdar, Vogelsang, and Cave) (Netherlands: Elsevier, 2005), 120–6. See also DF Spulber, 'Unlocking Technology: Antitrust and Innovation' (2008) 4(4) *Journal of Competition Law and Economics* 915.

may favour one firm's product or service and it can become the *de facto* standard in the market,[22] such as Amazon's application programming interfaces (APIs).[23]

3. Mechanisms within Competition Law

The EU competition regime comprises different elements designed to address a range of anti-competitive behaviours, including conduct between market participants or carried out against consumers. For our purposes, we are primarily concerned with two types: anti-competitive agreements and abuses of a dominant position.

3.1 Article 101

Article 101 of the Treaty on the Functioning of the European Union (TFEU)[24] prohibits agreements, decisions of undertakings, and concerted practices that have the object or effect of preventing, restricting, or distorting competition and may affect trade between Member States. Such agreements and practices may be vertical[25] or horizontal,[26] and may be exempted pursuant to Article 101(3) if they 'contribute to improving the production or distribution of goods or to promoting technical or economic progress, while allowing consumers a fair share of the resulting benefit, and (...) [do] not: (a) impose on the undertakings concerned restrictions which are not indispensable to the attainment of these objectives; [and] (b) afford such undertakings the possibility of eliminating competition in respect of a substantial part of the products in question'.[27] The exemption operates either on an individual agreement basis, or through 'block' exemptions that address particular types of agreement. A species of anti-competitive agreements relates to mergers and acquisitions, which are subject to a special regime of prior notification and approval,[28] thus appearing more akin to an *ex ante* regulatory regime.

In common with other technological sectors, cloud computing companies often engage in complex agreements and practices which are innovative and benefit consumers; therefore, the first two requirements[29] for the exemption pursuant to Article 101(3) to apply are not very difficult to satisfy. However, it may be more difficult to prove that the restrictions resulting from the agreements are indispensable to the attainment of the agreement's objectives. This also needs to be shown for the exemption to apply.

---

[22] See ML Katz and C Shapiro, 'Systems Competition and Network Effects' (1994) 8(2) *Journal of Economic Perspectives* 93, 115, and 105–6.

[23] Joe Brockmeier, 'Amazon APIs: Cloud Standard or Zombie Apocalypse?' (*Readwrite*, 12 April 2012), <http://www.readwriteweb.com/cloud/2012/04/amazon-apis-industry-standard.php> (accessed 29 March 2013).

[24] Consolidated Version of the Treaty on the Functioning of the European Union [30 March 2010] OJ C83/47.

[25] A practice is vertical when it takes place in a different level of the supply/distribution chain, for example between a manufacturer and a distributor.

[26] A practice is horizontal when it takes place in the same level of the supply/distribution chain, for example between two manufacturers.

[27] TFEU, Art. 101. For the purpose of the application of Art. 101(3), services are included in the concept of 'products'.

[28] Council Regulation (EC) No. 139/2004 of 20 January 2004 on the control of concentrations between undertakings [29 January 2004] OJ L24/1.

[29] Such as to contribute 'to improving the production or distribution of goods or to promoting technical or economic progress, while allowing consumers a fair share of the resulting benefit', Council Regulation (EC) No. 139/2004.

It must be noted that although an undertaking may be in a privileged or dominant position in a market for a certain period of time as a result of agreements or concerted practices, cloud computing is a fast-changing sector, and innovations developed by competing firms may quickly change the market structure.[30] Therefore, if all the other conditions of Article 101(3) are present, agreements and practices in an innovation sector that would be prohibited in accordance with Article 101(1) are more likely to be exempted pursuant to Article 101(3). This is due to the fact that it may be difficult to predict whether substantial competition would be eliminated, and even if that is the case, it would be difficult to predict for how long an undertaking could manage to maintain a dominant position or an anti-competitive practice. In addition, there is a block exemption under Article 101(3) for categories of technology transfer agreements,[31] which ensures that the licensing of technology is allowed when the licensor permits the licensee to exploit the licensed technology for the production of goods and services generating pro-competitive effects.

In light of the above, the Commission does not tend to be overly intrusive, in order to avoid hampering the technological development of the ICT sector in the EU, which is perceived to be a key sector of the EU economy. Joaquín Almunia, the Vice President of the Commission and responsible for competition policy, reaffirmed this view in October 2010: 'The digital economy is one of the main engines of our still uncertain recovery. Few industries have the same potential to foster Europe's potential growth and long-term competiveness.'[32] However, Almunia also highlighted that the Commission wants not only to maintain a competitive environment in this sector, but also to foster it, this being essential to preserve the opportunity for new firms to enter the market and challenge established players. Ensuring a level playing field and market access may require stronger intervention than at present, as recognized by Almunia: 'This will have implications on how [the Commission will] examine access to distribution and service platforms, access to data and intellectual property that are useful in developing new and innovative digital products and services in Europe.'[33]

The Commission may intervene, for instance, in issues relating to standard-setting agreements and the ownership of intellectual property rights within adopted standards. In relation to standard-setting agreements, guidelines on the applicability of Article 101(3) to horizontal cooperation agreements ('the Horizontal Guidelines') prescribe that the participation of all interested parties must be ensured in the standard-setting process.[34] Nevertheless, in one of the very few instances where the Commission questioned the openness of the standard-setting procedure in the ICT sector, namely the *X/Open* case,[35] the standard-setting agreement was exempted under Article 101(3)

---

[30] See, for example, JA Schumpeter, *Capitalism, Socialism and Democracy* (London/New York: Routledge, 2010), Ch. 7.

[31] Regulation No. 772/2004 on the application of Article 81(3) of the Treaty to categories of technology transfer agreements [27 April 2004] OJ L123. See also Guidelines on the application of Article 81 of the EC Treaty to technology transfer agreements [27 April 2004] OJ C101. In February 2013, the Commission has published a proposal for a revised exemption, European Commission 'Draft proposal for a revised block exemption for technology transfer agreements and for revised guidelines', <http://ec.europa.eu/competition/consultations/2013_technology_transfer/index_en.html> (accessed 29 March 2013).

[32] EUROPA—Press Releases—'Competition policy for an open and fair digital economy Second NEREC Research Conference on Electronic Communications Madrid', 29 October 2010.

[33] EUROPA—Press Releases, 29 October 2010.

[34] See Guidelines on the applicability of Article 101 of the Treaty on the Functioning of the European Union to horizontal co-operation agreements [14 January 2011] OJ C11/1 paras 280, 281.

[35] See Commission Decision of 15 December 1986 relating to a proceeding under Article 85 of the EEC Treaty [6 February 1987] OJ L035/36 (IV/31.458—X/Open Group).

because, among other reasons, it was considered that opening the process to all interested parties could create practical and logical difficulties. Therefore, the approach of the Commission suggests that a 'closed' standard-setting procedure may be permissible under certain circumstances.

Moreover, the Horizontal Guidelines recognize that the non-fulfilment of the principles regulating standard-setting agreements would not necessarily result in a breach of Article 101(1). Instead, there is a general presumption of legality, or a safe harbour, when the standard-setting procedure is open and transparent, the adoption of the standard is optional, and access to the standard is available on fair, reasonable, and non-discriminatory ('FRAND') terms.[36] However, if any of these elements is not present, an assessment would be needed to determine whether the practice is contrary to Article 101(1) and, if so, whether it could be exempted under Article 101(3).

Although, on the one hand, it is recognized by the Commission that standardization generally results in positive economic benefits,[37] on the other hand it is also recognized that, when a technology has been adopted as a standard, it may result in the creation of a barrier to entry, as other technologies and undertakings may be excluded from the market.[38] Therefore, in addition to Article 101, the standard-setting process can raise issues in relation to Article 102.

3.2 Article 102

Article 102 prohibits abuse of dominance by one or more undertakings. Products offered by undertakings in this sector may become *de facto* standards protected by intellectual property rights (IPRs), or undertakings may own IPRs which are part of standards adopted by standardization bodies, or that have been given preference by the public administration in relation to public procurements. These examples help to illustrate that the dynamics of the cloud computing sector may result in the concentration of market power and the possibility that abuses could take place.

Once a standard has been established, competitors may deny or constrain access to the IPRs that are essential for its implementation. This could take place by the licensor refusing to grant a licence of an IPR, or by requiring unreasonable terms and conditions for licensing. If an undertaking is dominant, the Commission may impose compulsory licensing of IPRs on reasonable terms[39] or negotiate other commitments, such as specified royalty rates,[40] designed to avoid anti-competitive effects.

However, if the undertaking is not dominant, there is not much that the Commission could do about the refusal, as the ownership of an IPR gives the undertaking the right to decide whether and under which conditions to license. However, the *ex ante* disclosure of potentially relevant IPRs before a standard is created can minimize cases in which standards adopted incorporate IPRs whose licence may be refused or subject to unreasonable terms, resulting in market foreclosure.[41] As a result of the disclosure exercise,

---

[36] See n. 34, para. 280   [37] See n. 34, para. 263.   [38] See n. 34, para. 266

[39] For example, Cases C-241/91 P and C-242/91 P *RTE and ITP v Commission* [1995] ECR I-743 ('*Magill*') and Case C-418/01 *IMS GmbH v NDC Health DmbH & Co KG* [2004] ECR I-5039.

[40] For example, Case COMP/38.636, *Rambus* [6 February 2010] OJ C30/17, which concerned allegedly intentional deceptive conduct by Rambus when participating in a standards-making process resulting in abusive royalty rates. See also the Commission's investigation into Qualcomm's patent licences under the WCDMA standard for 3G mobile, which was closed without a finding (Memo/09/516, 24.11.2009).

[41] See 'EUROPA—Press Releases—Being open about standards, OpenForum Europe—Breakfast seminar', 10 June 2008. Market foreclosure results when an undertaking is denied the access to a market.

participants to the standard-setting procedure should be made aware of the existence of IPRs and choose whether there is a preferred alternative (eg open source) or they could check with the IPRs owner whether the technology included in the standard would be licensed on FRAND terms.[42]

In practice, *ex ante* disclosure does not always take place when standards are created; for example, because the patent holder may not be aware or participate in the standardization activity. In addition, an undertaking may have IPRs over *de facto* standards.[43] Pursuant to Article 102 TFEU, in these circumstances a non-dominant undertaking could decide whether and under which conditions to license IPRs. However, if the undertaking is dominant, the Commission is willing to ensure that the IPRs that result in market power and are essential for the development of new products are licensed and accessible to other market players in a fair, reasonable, and non-discriminatory manner.[44]

Usually, the market share required under EU law for an undertaking to be considered dominant, if all other market conditions point in that same direction, is at least 40 per cent.[45] This threshold is lower than in the US where at least 50 per cent market share is required, although some US decisions have required much higher shares.[46] In the cloud computing sector, where, in the same way as in the ICT sector as a whole,[47] network effects are likely to be strong,[48] the non-applicability of competition law until dominance is attained could prejudice the goals of competition law. By the time that a competition authority has the legal grounds to intervene, competition may already be distorted and network effects may make it difficult for effective competition to be restored. This was recognized by the Competition Commissioner, who stated that 'a case by case ex-post intervention is not always efficient to deal with structural problems, [thus] competition and sector regulation will need to work hand in hand, pursuing the same objectives through complementary means'.[49]

US antitrust law has a potential tool available to intervene in such circumstances, namely the offence of attempting to monopolize,[50] which requires a lower market share threshold, generally between 30 and 50 per cent. The existence of such type of offence in the US is more justifiable than in the EU, as the threshold for finding a monopoly in the US is higher than in the EU for finding dominance. Moreover, under EU competition law, the definition of the relevant market is generally narrower than under US antitrust law.[51] EU competition law does not have an equivalent prohibition of attempting to monopolize to utilize when assessing the behaviour of undertakings that adopt unfair

---

[42] See n. 34, para. 268.

[43] These are standards that have been created by the market rather than by standardization bodies. It refers to a common and established practice that has no associated law or standard and yet is followed as though such enforcement existed. See Case T-201/04 *Microsoft Corp. v Commission* [2007] II ECR 03601, para. 392, where it was held that Microsoft's PC Windows Operating System is the *de facto* standard infrastructure for work group servers.

[44] See n. 32.

[45] See Guidance on the Commission's Enforcement Priorities in Applying Article 82 EC Treaty to Abusive Exclusionary Conduct by Dominant Undertakings [24 February 2009] OJ C45/7 para. 14.

[46] See Federal Trade Commission's Bureau of Competition, 'Resource Guide to Business Competition'.

[47] See C Shapiro and HR Varian, *Information Rules: A Strategic Guide to the Network Economy* (Harvard: Harvard Business School Press, 1998), 174–82.

[48] Network effects are strong in the ICT sector in general. See Shapiro and Varian, *Information Rules*.

[49] See n. 32.   [50] 15 USC § 2 ('Sherman Act').

[51] See criticisms of the narrow definition of the relevant market in the EU from the ICC Commission on Competition: ICC, 'Comments on the Reform of the Application of Article 82 of the EC Treaty' (*ICC*, 12 December 2005), <http://www.iccwbo.org/Advocacy-Codes-and-Rules/Document-centre/2004/Comments-on-the-Reform-of-the-Application-of-Article-82-of-the-EC-Treaty> (accessed 28 March 2013).

means to exclude competitors, or to raise barriers to entry, which may create difficulties for competition and innovation in the cloud computing sector. The intervention of the Commission in such circumstances would ensure that the 'prophylactic' purpose of competition law is achieved.

As there is no offence of attempting to monopolize in the EU, and the Commission appears to be aware of the need to intervene in the market before competition is distorted to the point that it would be difficult to remedy,[52] the manner in which the relevant market is defined assumes great significance. The definition of the relevant market may prove intricate and difficult for cloud computing, from defining what constitutes the product,[53] to an analysis of demand and supply substitutability given the complex characteristics of the products involved, while the relevant geographic market will often be global. To the extent that some cloud markets, such as IaaS, are becoming commoditized and less differentiated, the relevant market will consequentially be more expansive than in other areas where a single SaaS application could be held to be a distinct market.[54] When defining the relevant product market, the competition authority will have to establish whether the products and services are 'integrated' or 'complementary' to the main product or service, given that it has to determine the product used to establish whether the product is interchangeable.[55] The way in which the competition authority perceives these technological products may have an impact on how widely or narrowly the relevant market is defined and, thus, where dominance is deemed to exist, which, in its turn, confers 'special responsibilities'[56] on the undertaking in question.

Two types of abuse that may arise in the cloud computing sector are tying, or practices designed to leverage the market power of a dominant provider in aftermarkets.[57] Indeed, the ICT sector is seen as having high risks of lock-in effects. A cloud computing firm may face strong competition in the primary market but may have virtually no competition in the aftermarket. Therefore, undertakings may exploit the fact that their customers have been locked into their cloud computing service and impose the use of their own software. Customers are said to be locked into a firm's product or service when the costs or the disadvantages of switching a product or service are high, thereby discouraging customers to change. As recently stated by Joaquín Almunia:

The lessons we have learned so far from our enforcement in these ICT industries (…) is that they are highly complex sectors, characterised by the need for interoperability and by potentially strong network effects or risks of lock-in. Often, these are markets where single companies dominate and it is therefore essential to ensure competition on the merits, notably through innovation.[58]

Imposing the acquisition of a firm's own software could be done unilaterally under numerous pretexts, such as the need to ensure the safety and effectiveness of the cloud system. In addition, this practice could be done in a situation where a cloud computing

---

[52] See n. 32.

[53] For the purpose of the definition of the relevant market, services are included in the concept of 'product'.

[54] For example, Competition Commission report (4 June 2009) on the acquisition of IBS OPENSystems by Capita, which found that the revenue and benefits software system used by local authorities was the relevant market for the competition analysis.

[55] See Commission notice on the definition of the relevant market for the purposes of Community competition law [9 December 1997] OJ C372 para. 7.

[56] See n. 45, paras 1, 9.

[57] An aftermarket refers to a market where consumers are likely to buy a product or service related to the one sold in the primary market.

[58] 'EUROPA—Press Releases—New Transatlantic Trends in Competition Policy Friends of Europe', 10 June 2010.

firm that provides, for instance, data storage, enters into an exclusivity agreement with another firm that produces a certain type of software, and imposes the use of such software on its customers. In doing so, the undertaking would not be tying the product, as the customer is not obliged to purchase it. However, if the customer wants to use that service, it will have to use the software produced by the firm which has an exclusivity agreement with the cloud provider. In both these situations, the undertaking providing the cloud computing service exploits the fact that customers have been locked-in, resulting in a distortion of competition and the creation of artificial barriers to entry. Therefore, it would be possible to challenge such types of conduct under the prohibition of abuse of dominance.

However, objective justifications could apply. For instance, this could be the case if the cloud computing provider discloses existing exclusivity agreements to customers in advance, before being locked-in, or if the imposition of a specific product, such as a particular type of security application, results in a more efficient performance of the cloud computing service. Indeed, the fact that a cloud computing provider decides to choose a specific antivirus software product could be interpreted as a choice over which customers should not have a say, since it concerns the security of the cloud service, and should be a matter for the cloud service provider to decide. Moreover, what the cloud computing provider is offering is a service which uses another product, thereby offering a secondary service to customers, in this case virus protection. Instead of having one product tied to another product, or a service tied to a product, in the cloud computing sector the product may become part of the service being offered. The antivirus software could be perceived as a product that is offered as a service to the final consumer. The consumer is not paying for the licence of the software. Instead, it is paying for a service that uses a certain product. This may render it difficult to establish whether the two services relate to two different relevant 'product' markets. The final service offered would encompass a certain 'package' which customers would either agree or disagree to purchase.

If it is considered that the software chosen by the cloud computing provider constitutes a different product from the service offered to the customer, questions could be raised as to whether this situation could still harm competition. Regarding the choice of a specific antivirus product it may be easier to justify the bundling as this is a matter of security, and the cloud service provider may have good reasons for its choice which would have an impact on the security of every customer using the cloud and would ensure the safe storage of their data. However, for other components, a position based on the 'essential' nature may be more difficult to argue.[59] Therefore, it may well be that determinations about tying and bundling situations will be made on the basis of the 'essentiality' of the tied product or service to the running of the service offered.

Abusive practices can obviously arise in other layers of the cloud computing ecosystem, as well as by those offering retail cloud computing services. For example, in July 2010, the Commission launched an investigation regarding IBM's computer mainframes.[60] IBM was investigated for two practices: tying its mainframe hardware to its mainframe operating system, and discriminatory behaviour towards competing suppliers of mainframe maintenance services.[61] While tying was not found to exist, IBM did accept legally binding obligations in respect of the mainframe maintenance market, such

---

[59] For example, Case COMP/C-3.37.792—*Microsoft* [6 February 2007] OJ L32/23, in relation to Media Player.

[60] 'EUROPA—Press Releases—Antitrust: Commission initiates formal investigations against IBM in two cases of suspected abuse of dominant market position', 26 July 2010.

[61] 'EUROPA—Press Releases—Antitrust'.

as the provision of technical information swiftly and on commercially reasonable and non-discriminatory terms.[62] Mainframes can be used to build cloud platforms, particularly in private and hybrid cloud environments, so constraints on the maintenance of such equipment can have a direct impact on the costs of such solutions.

Finally, the Commission may also scrutinize interoperability limitations in clouds, such as compatibility, APIs, and the ability of clouds to 'talk' to each other. The view of the Commission as to how interoperable clouds should be was highlighted by Neelie Kroes in a speech when opening the Microsoft Centre on Cloud Computing and Interoperability: 'to offer a true utility in a truly competitive digital single market, users must be able to change their cloud provider easily... as fast and easy as changing one's internet or mobile phone provider has become in many places'.[63] Limitations to interoperability could result in the Commission finding an abuse by a dominant undertaking given that this practice could be used as a technical means to stifle competition.

It must be noted, however, that although Joaquín Almunia, the Competition Commissioner, has stated that the Commission will examine carefully such practices in the ICT sector,[64] under Article 102, the Commission will only be able to intervene in situations where the firm is dominant. ICT is a fast-changing sector[65] where innovation may quickly change the structure of the market and firms may compete *for* the market rather than *in* the market,[66] which in the words of Schumpeter could be described as 'dynamic competition' which entails a process of 'creative destruction'.[67] Under this view, competition authorities should not be concerned with the commercial strategies of dominant firms that limit interoperability, as the technology in question would likely be replaced by a new technology developed by a competitor. Although this is often true, it is also the case that network effects may allow a firm that uses such strategies not only to become dominant, but to maintain its dominance for a long period of time. During the 'temporary' period in which the undertaking is dominant, its practices can distort competition and harm consumers by depriving them of better prices, greater choice, and innovation. For this reason, competition law has the role of ensuring that competition is maintained and enforced in the market. However, in the EU some potentially anti-competitive commercial strategies, such as the limitation of interoperability, may be beyond the jurisdiction of competition authorities, at least until a firm is found to be dominant. As explained above, in such cases the definition of the relevant market may play a crucial role. Nevertheless, competition law is not the only form of regulation of practices that could harm competition and consumers. Other regulatory regimes offer mechanisms that could play a key role in maintaining and enhancing the process of competition in the cloud computing sector.

4. Demand-side Mechanisms

The previous section examined the potential application of the EU competition regime to cloud computing. However, despite its overriding prophylactic purpose, competition law continues to operate as an *ex post*, reactive regime. By controlling market participants

---

[62] Case COMP/39.692 *IBM Maintenance Services* [21 January 2011] OJ C18/6.

[63] 'EUROPA—Press Releases—European Cloud Computing Strategy needs to aim high', 22 March 2011.

[64] See n. 32.

[65] 'EUROPA—Press Releases—Competition policy for an open and fair digital economy', 29 October 2010.

[66] S Park, 'Market Power in Competition for the Market' (2009) 5(3) *Journal of Competition Law & Economics* 571, 573.

[67] See n. 30, Chs 7–8.

through behavioural and structural remedies and punitive fines, competition law can be seen as predominantly addressing supply-side competition issues. As such, its effectiveness in preventing the emergence of anti-competitive behaviours and effects within cloud computing markets must remain in doubt. The capability of cloud users to port data and applications between cloud service providers, for example, is recognized as a potential public policy concern.[68] An inability to port may have differing causes, but the consequential dependency and lock-in clearly have relevance for the competitive nature of the cloud market. Conversely, however, customer dependency does not necessarily engage competition law, since the cause may not reside within its jurisdiction. An alternative, or complementary, approach is demand-side measures, using the exercise of choice by cloud users to place pressure on market participants to offer high-quality services at competitive rates. This section examines two areas where the regulation of demand can have a beneficial influence on the competitive state of the cloud market: public procurement rules, exploiting public sector purchasing power, and portability rights, promoting consumer choice.

4.1 Public procurement rules

The EU public procurement regime[69] recognizes the potential power of the public sector as a major buyer of goods and service in markets, as well as being an effective tool for promoting the building of a single European market. The former is explicitly endorsed in the Commission's cloud strategy and forms one of the three key action areas, through the establishment of the 'European Cloud Partnership'.[70] This initiative will develop 'common procurement requirements for cloud computing', which can then be implemented through public procurement procedures. Under EU law, these procedures are only applicable to contracts over certain threshold values, although the underlying principles, such as non-discrimination and transparency (which are derived from the Treaties) are applicable to all public sector agreements whatever value.[71]

As discussed elsewhere in the book, governments and public administrations are increasingly looking to cloud solutions as part of IT procurement strategies.[72] An issue of concern in such procurements can be the specification of the services being procured. To ensure a competitive market, any specifications must be sufficiently 'open' to allow the widest possible field of potential suppliers. In a cloud context, this raises the issue of whether cloud-based solutions can in fact be specified at all in a tender, since cloud is simply one possible mode of delivering IT services that should compete with other legacy solutions in terms of value for money and other considerations. Even if a cloud solution were to be specified, a particular brand of cloud solution may not be specified unless the tender either states 'or equivalent',[73] or the closed and exclusive specification can be objectively justified by reference to technical or non-technical characteristics.[74]

---

[68] Communication (n. 12), 5.

[69] Directives 2004/18/EC, 2004/17/EC and 2007/66/EC. A set of proposals reforming the regime were published in December 2011, available at <http://ec.europa.eu/internal_market/publicprocurement/modernising_rules/reform_proposals_en.htm> (accessed 29 March 2013).

[70] Communication (n. 12), 3.5.

[71] *Bent Mousten Vestergaard v Spøttrup Boligselskab* [2001] ECR 1-09505.

[72] See further Chapter 5.

[73] For example, *European Commission v The Netherlands* [1995] ECR I-15, concerning 'UNIX'.

[74] For example, *Concordia Bus Finland Oy Ab* [2002] ECR I-7251.

An example of the latter scenario in a cloud computing context arose in the US, in *Google v US*.[75] In October 2010, Google filed a claim against the US Interior Department alleging that its public procurement practices illegally distorted competition by requiring, in relation to a US$59 million contract for ICT services, messaging technologies to be based on Microsoft Business Productivity Online Suite, therefore excluding Google from public procurements and restricting competition. On 4 January 2011, Judge Susan Braden, from the US Court of Federal Claims in Washington, granted an interim injunction in favour of Google and stated that the US Interior Department's public procurement practices violated competition rules, therefore requiring the defendant to modify the procurement criteria.[76] Although the judgment did not find bad faith or wrongdoing by Microsoft, it has in effect brought to a halt the deployment of Microsoft's Business Productivity Online Services cloud computing solution and email system at the US Interior Department. The decision was intended to avoid lock-in effects and harm to competition given that without a preliminary injunction, the award would put into motion the final migration of the US Interior's email system, achieve 'organizational lock-in' for Microsoft, and cost Google the opportunity to compete.[77] Judge Braden, therefore, considered the possible harm to a competitor and to competition resulting from the network effects that would have been created by giving preference to Microsoft in public procurement. Google eventually filed a motion to dismiss the case, having reached a settlement with the Interior Department.[78]

It is not difficult to imagine similar claims being brought in the EU for breach of public procurement rules. In addition, overreliance on, or the granting of special treatment to, a particular cloud service provider could amount to a form of 'state aid' under Article 107 TFEU, which prohibits aid 'in any form whatsoever which distorts or threatens to distort competition by favouring certain undertakings'.

When awarding contracts on the basis of the 'most economically advantageous', it is permissible to take into consideration various criteria 'linked to the subject-matter of the public contract in question'.[79] These criteria can include 'functional characteristics', such as compliance with standards and interoperability, both of which are seen as important factors in the promotion of cloud computing within Europe.[80] The following sections briefly consider EU policy concerning open standards and interoperability.

4.1.1 Mandating open standards

The EU has a policy framework for regulating standard-setting by relevant authorities in the EU and Member States. Although standardization in the EU has proven a successful tool for the achievement of the single market, the Commission has admitted the need for improvements in certain areas, including ICT.[81] In fact, the EU has not managed to deploy its standardization framework to establish an effective and competitive standardization process in the ICT sector, even following the review of standard-setting

---

[75] *Google Inc. and Onix Networking Corporation v The US and Softchoice Corporation*, 95 Fed Cl 661 (2011).

[76] *Google v US*.   [77] *Google v US*, para. 25.

[78] *Google Inc. v The US*, 'Motion to dismiss without prejudice' (22 September 2011), available at <http://www.bizjournals.com/washington/fedbiz_daily/Google-MotiontoDismiss.pdf> (accessed 29 March 2013).

[79] Directive 2004/18/EC, Art. 53(1).   [80] Communication (n. 12).

[81] Commission Communication, 'On the Role of European Standardisation in the framework of European Policies and Legislation' COM (2004) 674 final, 3.

at a European level which started in 2004. The speed and effectiveness of the standardization procedures in the EU often do not respond to market needs, especially in high-technology areas where rapid standardization may be fundamental in order to meet the requirements of rapidly changing market conditions.[82]

Conversely, the US has been at the forefront of ICT standardization. The American National Standard Institute (ANSI) has successfully promoted voluntary consensus standards for use around the globe.[83] In the US, there is no hierarchical structure similar to the one found in the EU, where national standardization bodies must drop the development of a national standard if a European Standardization Organization (ESO)[84] is already working on a standard for the same matter.[85] The US has a more informal approach to standardization with less governmental intervention than in the EU, which has meant that standards could be adopted much more quickly and in a more expedient manner than in the EU. This unregulated process has seen consortia-led ICT standards, which tend to differ from the more formal and lengthy EU process and are, therefore, better suited to responding to the needs of new technology markets.

The White Paper 'Modernising ICT Standardisation in the EU' recognizes that the ICT sector is a major driver of competitiveness that represents a key sector of the EU economy.[86] It is not surprising, therefore, that the Commission has repeatedly revised the EU standardization process in favour of greater deregulation, culminating in the publication of the 2009 White Paper.[87]

The White Paper recognized the important role played by informal standardization groups, which are credited with responding to the changing dynamics of the ICT sector. As a result, the White Paper proposes that reference to standards created by fora and consortia[88] in EU legislation and policies should be permissible, as a means of achieving public policy goals. Otherwise, most ICT standards could end up being developed outside the EU without any regard to European needs.[89]

However, the White Paper states that informal standards could be referenced in EU legislation and policies, including public procurement, only if they comply with the attributes of formal standards: openness, consensus, balance, and transparency. This reflects similar sentiments expressed in the Horizontal Guidelines; although the latter is dependent on DG Competition being willing to enforce the stringent requirements required by the EU standardization framework. Thus, it is unlikely that the attributes asserted by the White Paper would be enforced through the application of competition law. The recommendations of the White Paper seem to place public procurement as a 'second layer' of regulation which would attempt to ensure the use of informal standards that have been developed respecting the attributes of formal standards.

---

[82] See Commission, 'White Paper: Modernising ICT Standardisation in the EU—The Way Forward' (3 July 2009), 3.

[83] ANSI, 'Standards Activities Overview', <http://www.ansi.org/standards_activities/overview/overview.aspx?menuid=3> (accessed 2 April 2013).

[84] Such as the European Committee for Standardization (CEN), the European Committee for Electrotechnical Standardization (CENELEC), and the European Telecommunications Standards Institute (ETSI).

[85] Directive 98/34/EC [21 July 1998] OJ L204/37, para. 18.

[86] See n. 82, 2.   [87] See n. 82.

[88] Fora and consortia are composed by undertakings which draft technical standards and specifications outside the framework of the recognized standardization bodies. There are many fora and consortia that have been working on standards for cloud computing, for example the Open Cloud Consortium (OCC), <http://opencloudconsortium.org>; the Organization for the Advancement of Structured Information Standards (OASIS), <http://www.oasis-open.org/home/index.php>; and the Storage Networking Industry Association (SNIA), <http://www.snia.org/home> (all accessed 2 April 2013).

[89] See n. 82, 2–3.

According to Commissioner Neelie Kroes, 'The reform of the European ICT standardisation framework is a simple way to bring relevant standards from the non-traditional standard-setting organisations to an equal footing with European standards when it comes to achieving interoperability'.[90] Interoperability is, therefore, a key objective to be pursued in relation to the ICT sector and the use of any relevant standards, including those developed by fora and consortia would be accepted in public procurements. Public procurement procedures are, therefore, regarded as playing an important role in ensuring that the standards adopted comply with the rules of transparency and openness, and this would be true also when interoperability is at stake.

4.1.2 Promoting interoperability

Before considering interoperability within the context of public procurement, it is important to note that interoperability has also been addressed through the application of EU competition law, in terms of both anti-competitive agreements and as an abuse of dominant position. In the *Intel/McAfee*[91] decision, for example, the Commission approved the acquisition of McAfee by Intel subject to certain interoperability commitments. The acquisition had raised concerns that, after the acquisition, security software would suffer from technical tying between McAfee's security solutions and Intel's CPUs and chipsets or from a lack of interoperability with the latter. In addition, there were concerns about an eventual lack of compatibility between McAfee's solutions and the products of Intel's competitors. The commitments accepted by the Commission contained, among other things, an obligation by Intel to ensure that instruction, interoperability, and optimization information are documented and available, under request, to third-party vendors of Endpoint Security Software[92] pursuant to a licence or other suitable contractual agreement. The information will be provided on a royalty-free basis.[93] Another important element of the commitments regarded the obligation by Intel not to actively engineer or design its microprocessors or chips to degrade the performance of Endpoint Security Software sold by a firm other than Intel.[94] This decision is a relevant precedent for cloud computing and for the ICT sector in general, where the purposeful creation of obstacles for interoperability can be used as a strategy to create barriers to entry and exclude competitors from the market.

This decision was not the first time that the Commission has addressed such issues. In fact, it received complaints as far back as 1974 from IBM's competitors who argued that the operating principles between IBM's software and hardware should be disclosed. The Commission finally accepted an undertaking from IBM in 1984,[95] whereby IBM offered to provide timely interoperability information to its competitors, in a similar way to its own subsidiaries in the downstream market, on FRAND terms. More recently, Microsoft came under the scrutiny of the Commission and the EU courts following a complaint from Sun Microsystems. According to the complainant, Microsoft refused

---

[90] 'EUROPA—Press Releases—Neelie Kroes Address at Open Forum Europe 2010 Summit: "Openness at the heart of the EU Digital Agenda" Brussels', 10 June 2010.

[91] Case COMP M.5984, *Intel/McAfee*, 26 January 2011, available at <http://ec.europa.eu/competition/mergers/cases/decisions/m5984_20110126_20212_1685278_EN.pdf> (accessed 2 April 2013).

[92] 'Endpoint security software' encompasses products that are designed to protect endpoints [which refer to a broad array of devices, notably desktop, notebook, and handheld devices] from attack or to directly protect information residing on endpoints. See *Intel/McAfee*, para. 40.

[93] See *Intel/McAfee*, para. 3.   [94] See *Intel/McAfee*, para. 4.

[95] 'IBM's 1984 EC Undertaking' (*CPTech*, 1 August 1984), <http://www.cptech.org/at/ibm/ibm1984ec.html> (accessed 2 April 2013).

to disclose how the integration between Windows, its Office suite and its server operating system worked, and this prevented the complainant from offering some services to Windows-based users of its Solaris work group server. Microsoft was held to have abused its dominance and was required to provide the interoperability information on FRAND terms to competitors in the work group server market, and to update such information whenever it released new versions of its operating system.[96] These cases demonstrate that the Commission is aware that interoperability restrictions may distort competition in the ICT sector and is willing to intervene when necessary.

Interoperability may also be a crucial element of competition law cases that emerge in public procurements involving the ICT sector. The Digital Agenda for Europe stresses the importance of cross-border eGovernment services.[97] In order to enhance cross-border eGovernment services it will be necessary to promote interoperability among public administrations of Member States and throughout the EU, as the choice of different technical solutions that are not interoperable could create electronic barriers, and harm the single market. In December 2010, the Commission adopted a Communication 'Towards interoperability for European public services'[98] to establish a common approach for Member States' public administrations, which included the European Interoperability Strategy (EIS)[99] and the European Interoperability Framework (EIF)[100] designed to enhance interoperability among national and European public services.

The EIS and the EIF do not impose specific technical solutions on national public administrations when establishing ICT-supported solutions for public services, and they state that public administrations should not impose a specific technical solution on citizens and businesses either.[101] Public administrations should ensure interoperability when providing a European public service and ensure that they obtain the best value for money. In order to achieve this, they will have to adopt common interface standards and may even need to choose among existing standards. As discussed previously, the choice of a certain standard by a public administration may exclude competitors from the market, and is capable of distorting competition. At the same time, the adoption of standards is essential in order to achieve interoperability in the single market. Therefore, public administrations will have to make choices with regards to the standards to be adopted, but such choices must take into consideration any possible harm to competition.

One important aspect of the EIF is that it not only suggests that public administrations should adopt standards pursuant to the EU standardization framework, as in technical specifications approved by a recognized standardization organization, but also recognizes that 'formal specifications' may be adopted; such as a specification established by ICT fora and consortia.[102] This is in harmony with the recommendations of the 2009 White Paper which recognized 'informal standards' in public procurements[103] and leads to the question of how public administrations ought to decide which formal specifications to adopt.

---

[96] Case T-201/04, *Microsoft Corp. v Commission of the European Communities* [2007] II ECR 03601, para. 392.

[97] See Commission, 'A Digital Agenda for Europe' 2010, <http://ec.europa.eu/information_society/digital-agenda/index_en.htm> (accessed 2 April 2013). See also n. 63.

[98] Commission Communication, 'Towards Interoperability for European Public Services' (16 December 2010).

[99] See Commission, 'European Interoperability Strategy' (16 December 2010).

[100] See Commission, 'European Interoperability Framework' (16 December 2010).

[101] See n. 100, 12.   [102] See n. 100, 24.

[103] D Geradin, 'Pricing Abuses by Essential Patent Holders in a Standard-setting Context: A View from Europe' (2009–10) 76 *Antitrust L J* 329, 331.

According to the EIF, public administrations will decide which formal specifications and technologies will be adopted, taking into account the need to ensure functional interoperability and additional criteria, such as quality, market support, potential for reusability, and openness.[104] If public administrators abide by the openness criterion, they will choose a formal specification that allows for all stakeholders to participate equally in its development, and for a public review of the decision-making process. Moreover, the specification must be available to be examined by anyone, and IPRs must be licensed on FRAND or royalty-free terms.[105] This seems to go a step further than the 2009 White Paper which, although accepting the use of standards created by fora and consortia, stipulated that the adopted standards would have to comply with the same openness and transparency principles as formal standards.

The adoption of this public procurement policy impacting the selection process of formal specifications may result in a second layer of protection against refusals to license or abusive licensing prices and/or conditions. By promoting the adoption of open standards, as well as those which involve IPRs licensed on FRAND terms, the Commission appears to be willing to find a compromise between the need to adopt the best technology available, while having such IPRs licensed on FRAND terms, irrespective of whether the IPRs owner is dominant in the relevant market.

Nevertheless, it must be noted that the EIF also allows the public administration to choose 'less open' specifications in cases where the open specifications fail to meet requirements in terms of functional interoperability.[106] From a competition law perspective, this may result in the undesirable situation where a firm is 'given' dominance of a market due to the choice of the public administration. It is possible for the strong network effects in the cloud computing sector[107] and the prominence given to interoperability to result in public administrations conferring, at times, dominance on those undertakings who have IPRs in relation to the formal specifications chosen in public procurement processes. As a result, the choices made by a public administration can actually distort competition. Under such circumstances, undertakings which did not have their formal specifications chosen by the public administration would only be able to challenge the validity of the procurement decisions under Article 107(1) prohibitions, as already discussed. In addition, the actions of an undertaking that owns IPRs within the chosen formal specification may be challenged if it becomes dominant and refuses to license under FRAND terms.

Although the EIF allows the public administration to choose 'less open' specifications,[108] certain EU Member States may choose to follow the approach indicated by the White Paper (or an even stricter approach), according to which informal standards could be referenced in public procurements.[109] This seems to be the case in the UK, where the Cabinet Office has issued a Procurement Policy Note (PPN) on the use of open standards when specifying ICT requirements. According to the PPN, government departments should deploy open standards in their public procurement specifications in order to, among other things, enhance interoperability and avoid technological lock-in.[110] One interesting aspect of the PPN is that it not only requires standards and technical specifications chosen to have the attributes established by the White Paper, but it goes a step further. The intellectual property involved in the standards and technical specifications chosen must be made irrevocably available on a royalty-free basis, rather

---

[104] See n. 100, 26.   [105] See n. 100, 26.   [106] See n. 100, 26.
[107] See n. 48.   [108] See n. 99, 26.   [109] See n. 82, 10.
[110] Cabinet Office, 'Procurement Policy Note—Use of Open Standards when specifying ICT requirements. Action Note 3/11' (31 January 2011), 1.

than on FRAND terms. This suggests that the UK government may be willing to adopt a stricter approach to ICT standards in comparison with the Commission. This may soon be the case in other EU Member States as well, creating divergent approaches to this matter which can raise competition law issues.[111] Competition law may be invoked to ensure a level playing field throughout the EU and it is yet to be seen if such strict requirements of the UK government will be endorsed by the Commission.

It is not clear yet to what extent an obligation to license on FRAND terms is relevant in the cloud computing sector. With SaaS, an owner of IPRs does not need to license the software to the end user, as the application remains in the cloud. The customer is charged on a usage, not licence basis. Therefore, the debate about FRAND or royalty-free licensing may become increasingly inconsequential where the cloud provider is the licensor. However, where a cloud provider charges customers to use a third-party's software, then any obligations in licence terms may continue to be relevant.

4.2 Data portability

In the telecommunications market, number portability obligations are a central component of the EU regulatory regime, enabling customers to change providers rapidly, cheaply, and easily without having to change their numbers.[112] By reducing the switching costs involved in moving providers, dependency becomes less likely. Another demand-side measure in the telecommunications market is the requirement that service providers notify customers of any modification in their terms of service and offer them the right to withdraw from the agreement without penalty,[113] which again provides customers with a periodic opportunity to exercise choice. Such measures can be distinguished from traditional consumer protection laws, where the primary objective is to protect the consumer from harm, rather than help them fulfil their role in a competitive marketplace.

Migration from one cloud service to another may be restricted pursuant to the terms of an agreement with a cloud service provider or be difficult due to technical incompatibility.[114] Were a service provider to include provisions in its standard terms that constrain a customer from porting, replicating, or backing up data, this would raise concerns from a competition law as well as a consumer protection perspective. Such terms could be deemed to be in breach of competition law if they either are not necessary for providing the service, result in barriers to entry, distort competition, or harm consumers. Facilitating data and application portability would reduce lock-in effects and require competitors to compete for their existing customers as well as increasing their customer base. For the Commission, portability is seen as being both a contractual issue and one concerning standards.[115]

---

[111] See, for example, the Italian Constitutional Court decision (No. 122 of 22 March 2010), in which the Court held that a law giving greater weight to tenders involving the provision of free software and open standards was not contrary to competition law. See Carlo Piana, 'Italian Constitutional Court Gives Way to Free Software Friendly Laws' (2010) 2(1) *IFOSS L Rev*, 61–6.

[112] Such as Directive 2002/22/EC (24 April 2002) OJ L108/7, at Art. 30. Transposed into UK law through the General Conditions of Entitlement, Condition 18.

[113] Directive 2002/22/EC (24 April 2002) OJ L108/7, at Art. 20(2).

[114] Facebook is an example of a cloud computing provider that does not allow its users to move their data to competing providers. On the other hand, Google's Data Liberation Front is an initiative which intends to facilitate data portability to and from Google's products, <http://www.dataliberation.org>. See also Microsoft's 'Interoperability Elements of a Cloud Platform', at <http://www.microsoft.com/cloud/interop> (both accessed 2 April 2013).

[115] Communication (n. 12), 5.

While the Commission is aware of the potential harm that may arise from a customer's inability to port its data and applications, measures addressing these concerns are not proposed in the Communication. A right of data portability has been proposed, however, in another policy area, in the context of the reform of EU data protection law. In January 2012, the Commission published a proposal to reform the current data protection regime in the EU.[116] Among other things, it contains a proposal that a right of data portability be recognized as an individual right within a privacy context.[117] Under the provision, a data subject would have the right to obtain from the controller a copy of their personal data 'in an electronic and structured format which is commonly used', to enable further use by the data subject. Where the data have been provided by the data subject, and are processed on the basis of consent or contract, then the right to obtain and transfer encompasses not only personal data, but 'any other information provided by the data subject'.[118] As currently drafted, this provision grants data subjects a quasi-proprietary right to data supplied to the controller.

In a cloud context, the proposal has a number of implications. First, while this right is restricted to natural persons, not legal persons such as companies, it may extend to applications as well as data. While not intended as a demand-side competition measure, it could develop into something analogous to number portability. Second, the right is predicated on the data being in 'structured and commonly used formats', which relates to the standardization issues discussed previously, but does not impose any obligation to adopt such formats. As such, the provision may encourage cloud providers not to adopt such formats, which would have negative implications for competition. Third, a distinction is made between data provided by the data subject and other data, either provided by a third party (eg friends or reputational feedback[119]), or generated by the cloud service provider in the course of providing the service, so-called metadata. This implies that the data processed by a cloud provider can be distinguished into these different categories, and that the raw data submitted by the user could be easily separated from the data processed by the provider. The technical reality is likely to be much more complex, as well as generating potential conflicts over data ownership and intellectual property rights.[120]

Recognition of data portability as an individual right per se would mean it is not necessary to evidence a resulting harm to competition. The Commission has suggested that the simple fact that customers are being prevented from transferring their personal data from one application or service to another would be enough to justify action aimed at forcing providers to guarantee data portability, if it would be technically feasible.[121] Thus, regulating data portability in the cloud computing sector could prove to be more effective and straightforward via the enforcement of data portability rights under the umbrella of data protection policy than via the enforcement of competition law.

5. Contract and Consumer Protection Law

While other chapters in this book address issues of cloud, contract, and consumer protection law in detail,[122] it is important to note that both contract and consumer

---

[116] Commission proposal for a Regulation of the European Parliament and of the Council on the protection of individuals with regard to the processing of personal data and on the free movement of such data, COM(2012) 11/4 draft, 25 January 2012.

[117] COM(2012) 11/4 draft, Art. 18.   [118] COM(2012) 11/4 draft, Art. 18(2).

[119] See R Picker, 'Competition and Privacy in Web 2.0 and the Cloud' (*SSRN*, 26 June 2008), <http://ssrn.com/abstract=1151985> (accessed 2 April 2013).

[120] See further Chapter 6.

[121] Commission Communication, 'A comprehensive approach on personal data protection in the European Union' COM(2010) 609 final, 4.11.2010, at 2.1.3.

[122] See Chapters 3–5 and 13.

protection laws can be viewed as tools for facilitating competition. Where contracts are negotiated with cloud service providers, the customer may seek the inclusion of provisions that are designed to reduce dependency and the possibility of lock-in; for example, through the insertion of robust termination and exit clauses, or service level schedules that offer guarantees concerning service provider assistance for data and application portability. Procurement strategies, such as dual sourcing, can also minimize dependency risks, although with potential cost implications.[123] For standard agreements, where the customer has to accept the conditions offered by the cloud service provider, national rules may strike out certain provisions, by virtue of either regulatory or judicial intervention. Consumer protection laws may determine that certain provisions are 'unfair' and, therefore, void; while for business customers, national rules may prevent unfair commercial practices.

6. Conclusions

This chapter has considered situations in which competition can be distorted in the cloud computing sector. It has also explored existing legal mechanisms within competition law and other regulatory regimes that could be used to mitigate harm to competition in the cloud computing sector.

Competition could be distorted when a standard is developed by consortia or fora without the participation of all the interested parties. The agreements among the participating firms to the standard-setting process may create barriers to entry in respect of excluded firms. While such practices are prohibited by the Horizontal Guidelines, a lack of real and substantial openness has not, to date, been tackled by the Commission. Indeed, the Commission has openly acknowledged the difficulty of ensuring the participation of all interested parties in standard-setting processes.

As well as non-participation in standard-setting, market distortions may occur when there are IPRs within the standard created and these have not been disclosed *ex ante*. The non-disclosure may place the IPR owner in a privileged position and allow it to 'ambush' competitors. Not only may they refuse to license, but they may also impose unfair conditions to license such rights, which may be essential for the implementation of the standard. In these situations, if the firm is dominant, competition regulators may oblige licensing under FRAND terms.

Other commercial strategies, such as the creation of non-interoperable cloud computing services, may also distort competition. Where the firm is dominant this may be tackled by the Commission under Article 102. Non-intervention until the existence of dominance may be justified by the dynamic nature of cloud computing markets, where innovation is capable of rapidly changing market structures. Once dominance is achieved, strong network effects are likely to ensure ongoing dominance for some time. Market definitions, therefore, assume a greater relevance, given that, if defined narrowly, a firm may be found to be dominant more easily, allowing intervention by the Commission to prevent market abuse.

In the standard-setting scenario, the EU has pursued a continuous policy of deregulating its standard-setting procedures, culminating in the 2009 White Paper on the modernization of ICT standardization. The White Paper accepted the reference to informal standards, created by fora and consortia, in public procurements, enabling

---

[123] See T Cowen, 'Competition Law Issues in Cloud Computing' (2013) 23(6) *Computers and Law*.

public administrations to select the most suitable technology even if the standard was not brought about via a formal process. Such informal standards would need, however, to have followed the same principles of openness and transparency as if they were created by formal standardization organizations.

The Digital Agenda for Europe stresses the importance of interoperability for the provision of cross-border eGovernment services. Consequently, the EIF established that national and European public administrations must ensure the interoperability of their services. As such, firms who own IPRs in the adopted interoperable standard are potentially placed in a privileged or dominant position, although it would be necessary to ensure that the firm will license its rights on FRAND terms. This opens the possibility of competition being distorted by the choice of specifications by public administrations.

Under those circumstances, harmed competitors may challenge the choice of the public administration alleging that their specifications fit best the requirements of the EIF, or may challenge the behaviour of the firm whose specifications were chosen, but only if the firm can be considered dominant. More importantly, competitors may challenge the choice of the public administration under Article 107 if the outcome of public procurement distorts competition. The choice of formal specifications in cloud markets may soon be a source of disputes in the EU market, along the lines of the *Google* dispute in the US, although it is too early to tell how technological choices made by public administrations will be dealt with by competition authorities in the EU.

Restrictions of data portability within cloud computing services may be a barrier to entry facilitated by a firm to enhance network effects and achieve dominance; although such practices only raise competition law concerns once the firm is dominant. Thus, an individual right enshrined in the EU data protection regime may prove more effective as a pro-competitive lever, addressing the 'lock-in' problem irrespective of a firm's market power.

The issues discussed above illustrate the complexities that the Commission will likely face over the coming years when pursuing competition law and policy in the cloud computing sector. Some, such as Neelie Kroes, suggest that such public policy objectives cannot be achieved without increasing state regulation.[124] Conversely, inappropriate, pre-emptive interference in the functioning of the market for cloud services runs the risk of undermining current growth. Although most competition law issues will not emerge until cloud computing business models and technologies become better established, the issues discussed in this chapter are already apparent and of great relevance not only for competition authorities and consumers, but also for those undertakings operating in the market.

---

[124] Neelie Kroes blog post: 'The Clear Role for Public Authorities in Cloud Computing' (*European Commission*, 25 March 2011), <http://blogs.ec.europa.eu/neelie-kroes/public-authorities-and-cloud> (accessed 2 April 2013).

13

Consumer Protection in Cloud Environments

Alan Cunningham and Chris Reed

1. Introduction

The decision to use cloud computational power, storage, and/or application services has implications for all users, whether multinationals, governments, micro-, small-, or medium-sized enterprises (SMEs)[1] or private individuals. Most of these implications have a legal dimension.

Government agencies, medium and large multinational corporations, and some larger medium-sized enterprises may be able to address specific concerns during contract negotiations relating to the provision of cloud services.[2] Statutory provisions relating, for example, to data protection and copyright, may also serve to regulate other concerns. SMEs, though, will rarely have the budget to purchase a customized cloud service where terms might be negotiable, nor will they have the bargaining power to renegotiate contractual terms for an off-the-shelf service. Consumers have even less power to negotiate.

Although this chapter is concerned primarily with the relationship between consumers and cloud computing service providers, some of the issues discussed here will also be relevant for SMEs. An SME may act as a consumer in certain situations, such as is provided, for example in the UK Unfair Contract Terms Act 1977 (UCTA),[3] perhaps more especially if it is at the micro end of the SME scale.

Our primary concern though is with individual consumers, their use of cloud computing services, the Terms of Service (ToS) that apply to such use, the way in which cloud service providers communicate with consumers, and the scope of consumer protection law to regulate such interactions. A consumer who wishes to use a cloud service, irrespective of whether that service is provided without charge[4] or in return for payment, will, like the majority of SMEs, not have the opportunity to negotiate the terms under which the service is provided. In addition, the average consumer will often have neither the time, nor the technical or legal expertise to investigate the full technical and legal nature of the service being offered, and will struggle with ToS which are not presented in 'ordinary' and understandable language.

Consumers, however, share most of the same concerns as multinationals, governmental bodies, and SMEs in relation to the use of cloud computing. In order to counter

---

[1] For one definition of SME, see Commission Recommendation 2003/361/EC Art 2.

[2] See Chapter 4.

[3] Section 12 of UCTA allows for a party to a contract to 'deal as consumer' in relation to another party if that first party neither makes a contract in the course of business nor holds him or herself as doing so; the second party *does* make the contract in the course of business; and, in the case of goods, the goods are of a type ordinarily supplied for private use or consumption (although if the first party is an individual the constraint regarding goods can be ignored).

[4] It can be debated to what extent 'free' cloud services are, in fact, free, and one should bear this ambiguity in mind every time the word free is used in the text; in many instances, free cloud services involve the user becoming the product and it is their use of the service and the additional personal information relating to them and their online activity on a particular platform that is of value, subsequently adding value to the company who provides the 'free' access to their service.

(a) the lack of relative bargaining power to address them bilaterally and during individual negotiations, (b) the lack of consumer technical/legal/commercial expertise, and (c) lack of clarity concerning ToS, marketing, and advertising material, consumer protection laws act on the collective behalf of the private individual. They do so in order to ensure that the way in which companies present their goods and services to such individuals, and the ToS that apply to the provision of goods and services, are fair and reasonable. Increasingly, operating in conjunction with traditional consumer protection laws, 'soft' legal measures concerning consumer protection are also being developed, and service providers themselves are starting to realize that self-regulatory codes of practice and policies are also a good way to meet the needs and address the concerns of consumers who use and purchase their services.[5]

Generally, companies that sell to and supply to consumers apply standard, non-negotiable ToS to their customer interactions. Cloud computing service providers are no different in this regard, and the Queen Mary, University of London (QMUL) Cloud Legal Project has undertaken an extensive study of the standard ToS offered by a number of cloud service providers.[6] One focus of this chapter will be to assess the more controversial standard ToS offered on a non-negotiable basis, and to consider how far cloud service providers meet, or do not meet, their requirements under relevant consumer protection laws. Also to be explored are the various obligations imposed upon cloud service providers by consumer protection laws, and other regulations, to present information to consumers in particular ways.

There are a number of other issues of note that require exploration prior to assessing standard ToS and exploring methods of communication and advertising. First, consumer use of cloud services is often increasingly mixed in nature, in that it can often be both for personal and for professional, or business purposes.[7] Such mixed use complicates the application of consumer protection laws in many instances, for if the use is more professional than personal, the user may well not be considered a consumer for the purpose of the law. In addition, the converse is equally true: business users of cloud services may also use them in a personal way, the demarcation being often equally unclear. These two phenomena have major implications regarding the assessment of responsibilities of cloud service providers under consumer protection law. Second, cloud services, especially those that are free, may often be used in relation to activities undertaken during the foundation of a business. Again, such foundational use by a private individual makes identification of a 'consumer' difficult.

In exploring the nature of consumer protection laws and other regulatory measures in the context of cloud computing, our scope is limited to the EU and the UK, with a specific

---

[5] See, for example, the Cloud Industry Forum *Code of Practice for Cloud Service Providers* (<http://www.cloudindustryforum.org/code-of-practice/code-of-practice>), (accessed 13 July 2013). This Code does not distinguish between consumer and non-consumer customers, but it does address the first concern of consumer protection law mentioned above, that consumers should be provided with sufficient information to make a proper decision about whether to purchase the service. This concern with transparency is apparent in paragraph 1 of Part A of the Code which provides:
'Organizations complying with the Code shall conduct themselves in an open and transparent manner which facilitates rational decision-making and management by purchasers of their services. The Code, however, does not set out to and will not make decisions for purchasers, but will simply help to ensure that essential information is available to make decisions.'

[6] See Chapter 3.

[7] For example, the owner of a small business might use a cloud service to host business records and an e-commerce website, while at the same time using the service for personal emails, photographs, and other non-business purposes. Another common type of mixed use is where an individual signs up to a cloud service for personal activities, and then additionally uses that service for activities within the scope of his or her employment, such as sharing documents with colleagues.

focus on UK enforcement and interpretation of both the domestic and community rules. Admittedly, cloud computing services can easily be offered (and used) from anywhere in the world to anywhere in the world, but consumer protection laws still differ from jurisdiction to jurisdiction, even more so once the relative legislative harmony of the EU is left behind. An extensive analysis of consumer protection laws in jurisdictions beyond the UK and the EU level is, therefore, outside our scope.

2. The Consumer and the Cloud

2.1 Consumer protection

With almost minimal bargaining power, private individuals who wish to purchase either goods or services in a private capacity and for private use rely upon a complex body of consumer protection laws that act collectively on their behalf. One element of those laws aims to ensure that standard ToS set by companies are at least fair and reasonable. In addition, consumer protection law has another role: to ensure that information provided to consumers prior to the purchase or use of goods or services is clear and understandable, so that any decision made is one the consumer wants to make, and has been able to make on the basis of having access to all relevant information in a clear and understandable manner.

We can separate these consumer protection laws conceptually into *ex ante* law and *ex post* laws: those that attempt to create prior to any consumer/supplier relationship an equitable situation, and those that ensure that there is equitable redress for any imbalance that may result from a contractual relationship by, for example, imposing statutory implied terms or rendering unfair terms unenforceable.[8]

The recently enacted EU Consumer Rights Directive (CRD)[9] is a good example of *ex ante* consumer protection law; it places obligations on suppliers in different situations to provide potential consumers with certain information in certain formats. It is also worth noting the transparency provisions of the Electronic Commerce Directive,[10] which, although they apply to all online e-commerce suppliers established in the EU, are in practice mainly of relevance for consumer transactions.

In the UK, UCTA is an example of *ex post* consumer protection law. It acts to render certain unfair terms unenforceable, including terms that exclude some of the terms which would otherwise be implied into the contract. EU law also contains a more general set of *ex post* controls on unfair contract terms via the Directive on unfair terms in consumer contracts.[11] The purpose of these *ex post* controls is to prevent the seller or supplier from taking unfair advantage of the imbalance of power which enables it to impose its own terms on the consumer.

In addition to the explicit body of EU and UK consumer protection law, there also exist certain industry codes of practice, regulatory codes, and other soft law measures that act to regulate how companies deal with consumers, and advise on what information must be given out to consumers. A good example is the Cloud Industry Forum

---

[8] UK common law may also act to imply certain terms in contractual scenarios, though an analysis of the possibilities is beyond the scope of this chapter.

[9] Directive 2011/83/EU of the European Parliament and of the Council of 25 October 2011 on consumer rights, amending Council Directive 93/13/EEC; Directive 1999/44/EC of the European Parliament and of the Council and repealing Council Directive 85/577/EEC; and Directive 97/7/EC of the European Parliament and of the Council.

[10] Council Directive (EC) 2000/31 on electronic commerce, OJ L178/1, 17 July 2000.

[11] Council Directive 93/13/EEC of 5 April 1993 on unfair terms in consumer contracts, OJ L95/29, 21 April 1993.

(CIF) Code of Practice,[12] though as we shall see this concentrates on *ex ante* transparency and makes no provision for *ex post* control of contractual terms.

Before we explore which consumer protection laws have specific relevance in a cloud computing/consumer context, and what type of obligations consumer protection laws impose on cloud service providers regarding their communication with consumers, we must address a fundamental question: what is a consumer?

2.2 What is a consumer?

This question is clearly of procedural importance because we require a coherent definition before we can advance and consider what consumer protection laws will apply in the cloud computing context. It is also of substantive importance because the very technological and logistical nature of cloud computing means that there is an increased scope for a 'consumer' to use cloud services in an increasingly uncertain and mixed capacity. In fact, common uses of cloud computing services, particularly 'free' services,[13] would appear to require a reconsideration of what a consumer is understood to be for the purpose of such IT services.

The typical legal definition of a consumer under UK and EU consumer protection laws is some variation of him or her being a private individual or natural person acting for purposes outside of a professional or business-related capacity. The way in which many people increasingly use the Internet, including cloud computing services, makes drawing a distinction between what is a private use, and what is a professional or business use, increasingly difficult.

For example, it is becoming common for consumers to utilize free (and also paid-for) cloud services to facilitate what could be classed as both personal and professional activities. In such a scenario, it is often not clear whether the consumer is using the service as a consumer, or in the course of a profession or craft, or some uncertain mix of the two. Even if the cloud service is not necessarily marketed as a professional-level service it can quite easily be utilized as such. The question is crucial if the cloud service is managed or administered by the consumer him or herself, and perhaps less so if managed on his or her behalf by a firm or official department related to his or her profession.

A good example of such difficulty in classification is the use of free cloud services such as Gmail and Facebook for publicity and advertising for a small business start-up. Prior to the development of such services, advertising, marketing, and emailing cost real money. The scope of the activity was clearer, and therefore more susceptible to precise classification. Now these services are provided for free, simply in return for adding value to a social network or Internet platform. They are used for both personal and business purposes, and are particularly attractive to those founding a business because they require no investment.

A Gmail account can be set up quickly and easily to be used by a person wishing to communicate with customers, but may also be used concurrently for personal email. Conversely, a personal Gmail account already in existence might be used for such a professional purpose.

---

[12] See, further, Cloud Industry Forum, <http://www.cloudindustryforum.org> (accessed 13 July 2013).

[13] The very fact that a service is provided without charge means that more users who would typically be considered consumers will use the service for a mixture of purposes. Paid-for cloud services may also encounter mixed-purpose use by private individuals. The point is probably not so much whether the service is free, but that society increasingly uses online technology for a multitude of purposes, so that it is often not easy to separate clearly which parts are private and which professional.

Facebook is a cheap, efficient, reliable, and free way to publicize events which may have a mixed private and professional nature; and, even if the event is completely professional in nature, the Facebook profile may already exist, be predominantly private, or an uncertain mix of the two.[14] In this way, the very benefits offered by cloud computing are the same things that lead to complex, mixed use by users. Thus, the question is whether such mixed use is a consumer use, especially with regard to free cloud services.

These social, economic, and technological developments clearly challenge the standard definitions of consumer under EU and UK law, which may be inadequate to cope with those types of private individual use of cloud services which, although mixed, could not clearly be said to be definitively non-consumer uses. The problem is that the law assumes that it will always be clear whether a purchaser of goods or services is acting in a consumer capacity or not. In physical-world contracts this occasionally raised difficult questions at the margin, but for many cloud computing services this uncertainty arises at the core.

One part of the problem is whether the policy of the law is to provide such users with protection, in the form of precontractual information, and protection from unfair or unreasonable ToS. The policy is already clear in respect of the first issue, as service providers are expected under Articles 5, 6, and 10 of the Electronic Commerce Directive to provide clear information to all customers (private, SME, multinational, et al.), *ex ante*. This, though, still leaves uncertainty as to whether the additional transparency requirements of the CRD need also to be complied with, as these only apply when the customer is acting as a consumer.

Answering this policy question is much more difficult for laws which control the ToS of a contract. The UK's purely national law on this matter, UCTA, gives a clear answer. The protections of UCTA relating to consumers apply if the supplier acts in the course of a business, and the purchaser of goods or services deals as a consumer, which means according to section 12 that the purchaser does not make the contract in the course of a business (or hold himself out as doing so), and if the contract is for goods (but not services) the goods are of a kind which consumers normally buy. Thus, in relation to cloud computing services it is clear that the relevant issue is the capacity in which the user *entered into* the contract. If this was done as a consumer, it is irrelevant if the user later decides to use the cloud service for non-consumer purposes. The policy underlying the EU Directive on Unfair Terms in Consumer Contracts (UTCC Directive) is not quite so explicit, but its application is to 'unfair terms in contracts concluded between a seller or supplier and a consumer'[15] which, again, suggests that the relevant factor is the capacity as consumer at the time of making the contract.

This application of the policy makes pragmatic sense. At least theoretically, it is possible to determine this matter at the time the contract was made, whereas it is extremely difficulty to decide at a later point precisely when the purchaser ceased to act as a consumer, as this is largely controlled by the purchaser's subjective intention. An offline example will help to illustrate the difficulties. Suppose that a consumer purchases a car for private use under a contract that excludes all the seller's liability for defects (a term which would clearly be unfair, and thus unenforceable, under both UCTA and the UTCC Directive). Five days later the purchaser is asked by a friend to deliver a package

---

[14] These are very basic examples, and much more complex uses are possible. For example, it was reported that Rupert Goold, a theatre director, is using Facebook and other social media sites to premiere a mini-film trailer for a forthcoming Headlong Theatre production. See Dalya Alberge, 'Theatre turns to Facebook to bring younger audience through the doors', *The Observer* (22 April 2012). The mini-film was posted and available to watch on Mr Goold's personal Facebook profile and on the Headlong Theatre Facebook profile.

[15] Article 1(1).

for a fee. If the purchaser decides to use the car for this purpose, does he lose the benefit of the protections at the moment he forms the subjective intention to use the car (and if so what happens if he changes his mind and takes the bus)? Or do the protections cease when he starts driving? Do they resurrect on the return journey, or only when it is completed, or not at all? These are questions to which it is hard to find consistent and appropriate answers, and thus it seems more sensible to determine once and for all the question of whether the law applies, and to do so at the moment the contract is made.

If this analysis is correct, it means that the difficult problem of mixed use needs only to be considered at the time of contract formation. Outside of these more controversial types of use of cloud services, most cases will involve less complexity and will be a straightforward consumer use. How is such a straightforward consumer defined?

In the UK many of the main legislative instruments concerned with consumer protection or affiliated areas do not contain a definition of consumer, and those that do follow the general trend among EU legislative instruments.[16] The Schulte-Nölke study of EU consumer protection law isolated a number of core features among the varying statutory European definitions of a consumer stating that 'they all share a common core, as they all provide that a consumer is a natural person, who is acting for purposes which are outside some kind of business, commercial or trade activity'.[17] The study looked at a number of consumer protection Directives,[18] and even those Directives that were excluded from the terms of the study follow a similar pattern in defining a consumer.

Therefore, for the general purposes of this chapter we will utilize the conception of a straightforward consumer that emerges from the findings of the Schulte-Nölke study, that is, that a consumer is a natural person, who is acting for purposes which are outside some kind of business, commercial, or trade activity.

3. *Ex ante* Consumer Protection Law

Some consumer protection restrictions concerning how companies trade and communicate with customers obviously apply to all companies offering services to consumers, such as clarity as to price and prohibitions on misrepresentations made in the course of trade. Such basic restrictions are the foundations of any consumer/supplier legal relationship and it would be strange if any cloud service provider had an issue with complying with them. Under the Consumer Protection Act 1987 (CPA), for example, (which,

---

[16] There is no definition, for example, in the Sale of Goods Act 1979 or the Sale of Goods and Services Act 1982. The Sale and Supply of Goods to Consumers Regulations 2002 (implementing Directive 1999/44/EC) has consumer defined as 'any natural person who, in the contracts covered by these Regulations, is acting for purposes which are outside his trade, business or profession'; the Unfair Contract Terms Act 1977 s 12 contains the definition given above, and in Part II, dealing with Scottish law provisions, 'consumer' is defined as having the meaning 'assigned to that expression in the definition in this section of "consumer contract", consumer contract being defined as "a contract in which (a) one party to the contract deals, and the other party to the contract ('the consumer') does not deal or hold himself out as dealing, in the course of a business, and (b) in the case of a contract such as is mentioned in section 15(2)(a) of this Act, the goods are of a type ordinarily supplied for private use or consumption; and for the purposes of this Part of this Act the onus of proving that a contract is not to be regarded as a consumer contract shall lie on the party so contending"'.

[17] Prof. Dr Hans Schulte-Nölke, Dr Christian Twigg-Flesner, Dr Martin Ebers (eds), *EC Consumer Law Compendium, Comparative Analysis* (Universität Bielefeld, 2008), 715.

[18] Directive 85/577 (Contracts negotiated away from business premises); Directive 90/314 (Package Travel & Holiday Tours); Directive 93/13 (Unfair Terms in Consumer Contracts); Directive 94/47 (Timeshare); Directive 97/7 (Distance Contracts); Directive 98/6 (Indication of prices of products); Directive 99/44 (Consumer Goods and associated Guarantees).

despite the title, is more relevant overall to the issue of defective product liability and consumer product safety) there is a prohibition on offering misleading price indications. The Misrepresentation Act 1967 extends the legal remedies to which consumers are entitled where they have entered into a contract after a misrepresentation has been made. The purpose of this chapter is not to provide an overview of *all* aspects of consumer protection law, but rather to focus on those aspects that are of most significant interest to both the consumer of cloud computing services and to cloud service providers.

3.1 Consumer Protection from Unfair Trading Regulations 2008[19]

The Regulations prohibit unfair commercial practices as engaged in by traders.[20] A commercial practice is defined as any 'act, omission, course of conduct, representation or commercial communication (including advertising and marketing) by a trader, which is directly connected with the promotion, sale or supply of a product to or from consumers, whether occurring before, during or after a commercial transaction (if any) in relation to a product'.[21] A product means any goods or service, including immovable property, rights, and obligations.

As Naylor, Patrikos, and Blamires have pointed out, 'all of the following are potentially commercial practices: information supplied with a product; a website; all forms of advertising and marketing; oral and written communications between sales staff and the consumer; and after-sales activities, such as customer support or complaints handling'.[22] Cloud computing service providers will have an obligation to comply with the terms of the Regulation in relation to all such commercial activities.

A commercial practice as defined under the Regulations will be considered unfair in three scenarios: first, if it contravenes the requirements of professional diligence[23] and it materially distorts or is likely to materially distort[24] the economic behaviour of the average consumer with regard to the product;[25] second, if it is a misleading action under the provisions of Regulation 5, a misleading omission under the provisions of Regulation 6 or aggressive under the provisions of Regulation 7; or, third, if it is listed in Schedule 1 and, therefore, banned outright.[26] In addition, the promotion of any unfair practice by a 'code owner' in a code of practice is prohibited.[27]

---

[19] The Regulations implement Directive 2005/29/EC on Unfair Commercial Practices.

[20] A trader is defined as 'any person who in relation to a commercial practice is acting for purposes relating to his business, and anyone acting the name of or on behalf of a trader', Reg. 2(1).

[21] Regulation 2(1).

[22] Naylor, Patrikos, and Blamires 'Mass Market Contracting' in Christopher Reed (ed.), *Computer Law*, 7th edn (Oxford: Oxford University Press, 2011), 102.

[23] Defined as 'the standard of special skill and care which a trader may reasonably be expected to exercise towards consumers which is commensurate with either honest market practice in the trader's field of activity or the general principle of good faith in the trader's field of activity', Reg. 2(b).

[24] Materially distort the economic behaviour means, in relation to the average consumer, 'appreciably to impair the average consumer's ability to make an informed decision thereby causing him to take a transactional decision that he would not have taken otherwise', Reg. 2(b).

[25] Regulation 3(3). The average consumer is considered in the Regulations as being 'reasonably well informed, reasonably observant and circumspect', Reg. 2(2). For the purposes of the Regulations, a consumer is defined as 'any individual who in relation to a commercial practice is acting for purposes which are outside his business', Reg. 2(1)(b).

[26] Schedule 1 is a list of 31 commercial practices that are in all cases considered unfair such as, for example, 'claiming to be a signatory to a code of conduct when the trader is not' and 'presenting rights given to consumers in law as a distinctive feature of the traders offer'.

[27] Regulation 4. Code owner is defined as 'a trader or body responsible for—(a) the formulation and revision of a code of conduct; or (b) monitoring compliance with the code by those who have undertaken to be bound by it'. In this sense, cloud computing self-regulatory bodies, such as the CIF, are also subject to the Regulations in relation to the construction of any codes of practice.

Regulation 5 relates to misleading actions, which are those that contain false information, and are, therefore, untruthful, or those that, in overall presentation, in any way deceive or are likely to deceive the average consumer in relation to a number of matters listed in Regulation 5(4). The matters listed include such things as the nature of the product, the main characteristics of the product (including benefits, risks, fitness for purpose, geographical or commercial origin, composition of the product, results to be expected from the product) and price, among others.

This has interesting implications for cloud service providers, especially in relation to criteria such as listing the 'composition of the product' or 'fitness for purpose'. It is a common cloud industry practice to sub-contract or 'layer' facilities among and between any number of cloud companies. For example, a consumer might purchase a SaaS service through one provider, part of which might be provided by a separate (and unknown to the consumer) service provider (such as an IaaS aspect of the SaaS service).[28] Not only is it difficult to manage liabilities and risks in this type of sub-contracting arrangement, it is also difficult to communicate succinctly to a potential consumer why this might be a necessary aspect of a service, and indeed what that practically means in terms of the expected service. Similarly, with regard to fitness for purpose, it may well be that a cloud service provider advertises a service that is dependent on the adequate and timely execution of another service by a sub-contractor. In considering their initial communication with the consumer, one could easily argue that a cloud provider who sub-contracts aspects of an advertised service can only really make statements as to fitness of purpose for the service over which it has control.

Regulation 6 relates to misleading omissions. A commercial practice is a misleading omission if in its factual context, taking account of all the features and circumstances of the commercial practice, including the limitations of the medium used to communicate the commercial practice, it: (a) omits material information; (b) hides material information; (c) provides material information in a manner which is unclear, unintelligible, ambiguous, or untimely; or (d) fails to identify its commercial intent, unless this is already apparent from the context.

Material information is defined as 'the information which the average consumer needs, according to the context, to make an informed transactional decision and any information requirement which applies in relation to a commercial communication as a result of a Community obligation'. Where the commercial practice in question is an invitation to purchase, the Regulations list other specific information that will be considered material, such as the main characteristics of the product, the geographical address, the address of any other trader on whose behalf the trader is acting, and price.

The issue of misleading omissions might have some importance for cloud companies such as Facebook and products such as Gmail, where the cloud service is offered ostensibly for free, but still involves complex commercial intentions relating to the free use of the service. Could Facebook argue that its commercial intent is apparent from the mere context of the average Facebook use, and that, therefore, it has no obligation to make clear to users what its commercial operations are? Or should it be required to elaborate on the full nature of its commercial intent in connection with offering a free service?

Regulation 7 concerns aggressive commercial practices which cause a consumer to make a transactional decision he would not have taken otherwise. Although it is not impossible that potential cloud product users will be put under pressure in a way that impairs their freedom of choice, it is far more likely that there will be a misleading

---

[28] See Chapter 1 for a more detailed discussion of cloud service 'layering'.

omission or action, or that the requirements of professional diligence will be contravened so that the economic behaviour of the average consumer will be materially distorted.

3.2 Advertising standards

As its website states, the Advertising Standards Authority (ASA) exists to make sure all advertisements are 'legal, decent, honest and truthful'.[29] Its advertising codes lay down rules for advertisers, agencies, and media owners and, importantly, the rules within the codes are not written by the ASA but by the advertising industry itself through the Committee of Advertising Practice (CAP) and the Broadcasting Committee of Advertising Practice (BCAP). The ASA administers the codes and adjudicates on complaints. ASA adjudications offer important guidance regarding not only how the advertising codes will be interpreted, but also how they will be interpreted in relation to certain industries.

There has been one ASA adjudication that has particular relevance to cloud computing: *ASA adjudication on UK2 Group*.[30] UK2 Group advertised web hosting services with statements such as, 'New unlimited packages...MSQL Databases...Business Cloud...Unlimited'. Further advertising text stated: 'Web Hosting Space Unlimited...MySQL Databases Unlimited...Databases Maximum Size Unlimited'. A complainant asserted that the claim that the Business Cloud package was 'Unlimited' was misleading because he could not use the package as his database was too large.

UK2 Group argued that the resources on its unlimited packages *were* unlimited, but were dependent on the size of the server upon which the service was hosted. It stated that the way in which the customer wished to use the database on the customer's own website affected how much capacity of the server was used, thus affecting the speed at which the website would then operate. It also explained that customers whose needs exceeded the capacity of the servers for the Unlimited Business Cloud web hosting packages were advised to use one of its other web hosting packages which it believed would be better suited to their needs.

This kind of argument gets to the nub of most potential or actual consumer/cloud service provider difficulties. The very nature of cloud computing requires an outsourcing of responsibility, often even by the initial cloud service provider itself. Flexibility and mobility of access are sacrificed for knowledge of the how, what, and where, because the actual processing or storage takes place in some other part of cyberspace.

In this case the ASA upheld the complaint as 'without qualification to indicate factors, such as server capacity, which were likely to affect the optimum operation of the website', the claims that the Business Cloud web hosting package was unlimited were misleading. Such a decision is a good guide regarding the care with which cloud service providers ought to advertise their services, especially if there are a number of sub-contracted layers under the initial layer of consumer-level interaction.

3.3 The Consumer Protection (Distance Selling) Regulations 2000 (CPDSR)[31]

The CPDSR apply to distance contracts, other than those expressly excepted. A distance contract is defined as any contract concerning goods or services concluded between a

---

[29] ASA available at <http://www.asa.org.uk> (accessed 27 March 2013).
[30] *ASA Adjudication on UK2 Group*, A11-179995, 14 March 2012.
[31] These Regulations implement Directive 97/7/EC of the European Parliament and of the Council of 20 May 1997 on the protection of consumers in respect of distance contracts. It is worth noting that

supplier and a consumer under an organized distance sales or service provision scheme run by the supplier who, for the purposes of the contract, makes exclusive use of one or more means of distance communication up to and including the moment at which the contract is concluded. As most consumers contract online for cloud computing services, the CPDSR are likely to apply.

The CPDSR impose an obligation upon the supplier to provide certain information to the consumer prior to the conclusion of the contract, such as: the identity of the supplier and, where the contract requires payment in advance, the supplier's address; the description of the main characteristic of the goods or services; the price of the goods or services including all taxes; delivery costs where appropriate; the arrangement for payment, delivery, or performance; the existence of the right of cancellation; the cost of using the means of distance communication where it is calculated other than at the basic rate; the period for which the offer or the price remains valid; and, where appropriate, the minimum duration of the contract, in the case of contracts for the supply of goods or services to be performed permanently or recurrently. It also imposes an obligation to inform the consumer if, in the event of goods or services ordered by the consumer being unavailable, the supplier proposes to provide substitute goods or services of equivalent quality and price, and to inform the consumer that the cost of returning any substitute goods to the supplier in the event of cancellation by the consumer would be met by the supplier.

The Regulations stipulate that the supplier shall ensure that this information is provided in 'a clear and comprehensible manner appropriate to the means of distance communication used with due regard to the principles of good faith in commercial transactions and the principles governing the protection of those who are unable to give their consent such as minors'. The commercial purpose of the supplier must be made clear throughout in all communications.

Regulation 8 requires the supplier to provide the consumer in writing, or in 'another durable medium which is available and accessible to the consumer', certain information either prior to the conclusion of the contract; or, thereafter, in good time and in any event during the performance of the contract, in the case of services, and at the latest at the time of delivery where goods not for delivery to third parties are concerned. That information is the list previously outlined and information about the conditions and procedures for exercising the right to cancel under Regulation 10; the geographical address of the place of business of the supplier to which the consumer may address any complaints; information about any after-sales services and guarantees; and the conditions for exercising any contractual right to cancel the contract, where the contract is of an unspecified duration or a duration exceeding one year.

Crucially, Regulation 8(3) further states that 'prior to the conclusion of a contract for the supply of services, the supplier shall inform the consumer that, unless the parties agree otherwise, he will not be able to cancel the contract under Regulation 10 once the performance of the services has begun with his agreement'.[32]

There are a number of exceptions to the right to cancel, most important of which are that the consumer will not have the right to cancel the contract if the supplier has complied with Regulation 8(3) and performance of the contract has begun with

---

this Directive has been repealed by the recent CRD, although the CRD has yet to be enacted in the UK, and the statutory instrument still has full effect.

[32] Regulation 8 is subject to Reg. 9, which states that it shall not apply to a contract for the supply of services which are performed through the use of a means of distance communication, where those services are supplied on only one occasion and are invoiced by the operator of the means of distance communication. This will not apply in a normal consumer cloud contract.

the consumer's agreement before the end of the cancellation period applicable under Regulation 12.

Importantly, Regulation 25 provides that a term contained in any contract to which the CPDSR apply is void if, and to the extent that, it is inconsistent with a provision for the protection of the consumer contained in the CPDSR. In addition, where a provision of the CPDSR specifies a duty or liability of the consumer in certain circumstances, a term contained in a contract to which the CPDSR apply is inconsistent with that provision if it purports to impose, directly or indirectly, an additional duty or liability on him in those circumstances.

3.4 E-commerce Regulations (ECR)[33]

The ECR oblige any person providing an information society service[34] to make available to the recipient of the service, in a form and manner which is easily, directly, and permanently accessible, certain information, much of it similar to that required to be provided under the CPDSR: the name of the service provider; the geographic address at which the service provider is established; the details of the service provider, including his electronic mail address; details of any trade register in which the service provider is registered and his registration number of equivalent means of identification; the particulars of any relevant supervisory authority which the service provider is subject to; where the service provider 'exercises a regulated profession' the details of any relevant professional body with which the service provider is registered, the professional title of the service provider, and the Member State where that title was granted, and a reference to the professional rules applicable to the service provider and the means of access to them; and, where the service provider undertakes an activity subject to value added tax, the relevant identification number.

The ECR further provide that where there is any reference to prices, such references shall be indicated clearly and unambiguously and shall indicate whether they are inclusive of tax and delivery costs. Any commercial communication provided by the service provider and which constitutes part of an information society service shall, further, be clearly identifiable as such; clearly identify the person on whose behalf the commercial communication is made; identify as such any promotional offer, and ensure that any conditions which must be met to qualify for it are easily accessible and presented clearly and unambiguously; and clearly identify as such any promotional competition or game, and ensure that any conditions for participation are easily accessible and presented clearly and unambiguously. The service provider must also ensure that any unsolicited commercial communication sent

---

[33] The Regulations implement Directive 2000/31/EC of the European Parliament and of the Council of 8 June 2000 on certain legal aspects of information society services, in particular electronic commerce, in the internal market.

[34] Defined as having the meaning in Art. 2(a) of the Directive. The Directive states that information society services are services within the meaning of Art. 1(2) of Directive 98/34/EC as amended by Directive 98/48/EC. Directive 98/48/EC, amending Directive 98/34/EC laying down a procedure for the provision of information in the field of technical standards and regulations defines services as 'any Information Society service, that is to say, any service normally provided for remuneration, at a distance, by electronic means and at the individual request of a recipient of services. For the purposes of this definition: "at a distance" means that the service is provided without the parties being simultaneously present; "by electronic means" means that the service is sent initially and received at its destination by means of electronic equipment for the processing (including digital compression) and storage of data, and entirely transmitted, conveyed and received by wire, by radio, by optical means or by other electromagnetic means; "at the individual request of a recipient of services" means that the service is provided through the transmission of data on individual request'.

by him by electronic mail is clearly and unambiguously identifiable as such as soon as it is received.

Further information must be provided where contracts are concluded by electronic means, unless parties who are not consumers have agreed otherwise. Prior to an order being placed by the recipient of a service, the service provider must provide in a clear, comprehensible, and unambiguous manner: the different technical steps to follow to conclude the contract; whether or not the concluded contract will be filed by the service provider and whether it will be accessible; the technical means for identifying and correcting errors prior to the placing of the order; and the languages offered for the conclusion of the contract.

Again, unless parties who are not consumers have agreed otherwise, the service provider shall indicate any relevant codes of conduct it subscribes to and give information on how these codes can be consulted electronically.

Where the service provider provides ToS applicable to the contract, they must be made available in a way that allows the recipient to store and reproduce them. Contracts concluded exclusively by exchange of email or by equivalent individual communications are not subject to the requirements for contracts concluded by electronic means.

Where the recipient of a service places his order through technological means, the service provider must, unless parties who are not consumers have agreed otherwise, acknowledge receipt of the order without undue delay and by electronic means, and also make available to the recipient of the service appropriate, effective, and accessible technical means allowing him to identify and correct input errors prior to the placing of the order.

Breach of these obligations entitles the user to rescind the contract. Under the Enterprise Act 2002, the Office of Fair Trading, the Local Authority Trading Standards Services, and certain other designated enforcers have powers to take enforcement action through the courts against businesses that breach the regulations.

3.5 Consumer Rights Directive (CRD)[35]

The CRD (not yet implemented in the UK[36]) has the stated purpose of contributing to the proper functioning of the internal market, through the achievement of a high level of consumer protection, by approximating certain aspects of the laws, regulations, and administrative provisions concerning contracts concluded between consumers and traders.

Interestingly, the CRD goes beyond the usual standard definition of a consumer by including 'craft'. A consumer is defined as 'any natural person who, in contracts covered by this Directive, is acting for purposes which are outside his trade, business, craft or profession'.[37] It is also important to note that recital 17 states that: 'the definition of consumer should cover natural persons who are acting outside their trade, business, craft or profession. However, in the case of dual purpose contracts, where the contract is

---

[35] Directive 2011/83/EU.

[36] The Department of Business, Innovation and Skills consulted in 2012 on 'enhancing consumer confidence by clarifying consumer protection law' (The National Archives, 'Consultation on enhancing consumer confidence by clarifying consumer law' (13 July 2012–5 October 2012), <http://www.bis.gov.uk/Consultations/consultation-rationalising-modernising-consumer-law> (accessed 27 March 2013)). This consultation proposed placing consumer concerns into one of three distinct categories: supply of goods, supply of services, and supply of digital content. Within this new category the definition of digital content would be taken directly from the CRD, as would many of the new legal obligations. The consultation period closed in October 2012 and a Government response is expected in 2013.

[37] As previously mentioned, Commission Recommendation 2003/361/EC (concerning the definition of micro-, small-, and medium-sized enterprises) defines an enterprise as 'any entity engaged in an economic activity, irrespective of its legal form. This includes, in particular, self-employed persons and

concluded for purposes partly within and partly outside the person's trade and the trade purpose is so limited as not to be predominant in the overall context of the contract, that person should also be considered as a consumer.' In the context of cloud computing, where often a cloud user will be engaging with a service provider in a mixed capacity, this is a helpful clarification, although it will perhaps be difficult to establish when a trade purpose is so limited in the overall context of a use that such use will be a consumer use. Cloud service providers may want to clarify the main purpose of use prior to contractual engagement.

The CRD requires that certain types of information must be provided in certain contractual scenarios. Article 5 sets out the informational requirements for contracts other than distance or off-premises, but the concern of this chapter will be with the informational requirements laid down by the CRD for distance contracts, being defined in the CRD as 'any contract concluded between the trader and the consumer under an organized distance sales or service-provision scheme without the simultaneous physical presence of the trader and the consumer, with the exclusive use of one or more means of distance communication up to and including the time at which the contract is concluded'. It is possible that a consumer might sign up for a cloud computing service by signing a contract other than a distance one; but this is unlikely, and in most cases of consumer use of cloud the contract will be agreed to online.

Before being bound by such a distance contract, or any corresponding offer, Article 6 states that the trader must provide the consumer with a long list of information in a clear and comprehensible manner. Those that have some particular relevancy for cloud computing might be: if a trader is acting on behalf of another trader, the geographical address and identity of that other trader must be provided; details concerning the arrangement for payment, delivery, performance, the time by which the trader undertakes to deliver the goods or to perform the services and, where applicable, the trader's complaint handling policy must be provided; the existence of relevant codes of conduct and how copies of them can be obtained, where appropriate must be communicated; details concerning the duration of the contract, where applicable, or, if the contract is of indeterminate duration or is to be extended automatically, the conditions for terminating the contract; the conditions relating to the right of withdrawal must be provided; details concerning, where applicable, any relevant interoperability of digital content with hardware and software that the trader is aware of or can reasonably be expected to have been aware of must be provided; and, where applicable, the possibility of having recourse to an out-of-court complaint and redress mechanism, to which the trader is subject, and the methods for having access to it must be communicated to the consumer.

Importantly, it is expressly stated in Article 6(2) that these conditions shall also apply to contracts for the supply of digital content that is not supplied on a tangible medium. This is supplemented by recital 19 which states that 'similarly to contracts for the supply

---

family businesses engaged in craft or other activities, and partnerships or associations regularly engaged in an economic activity'. Beyond this, there is no assistance in defining what a craft is. The European Commission provides some assistance in interpretation, however, stating on its website that notwithstanding the lack of a formal definition, there are some characteristics craft enterprises have in common all over Europe. These relate to strong personal involvement of the owner or head of the enterprise, 'craft, technical and management competences', 'active contribution to production of products and services', including 'customisation, and proximity to the client and local activities'. This conception of craft assists in clarifying the concept. It would, for example, characterize use by an amateur photographer of a Gmail mailing list for the pursuit of his or her craft as a consumer use. 'Craft', here, is a business activity that produces craft products or services, and the craft hobbyist would, sensibly, be excluded from that definition.

of water, gas or electricity, where they are not put up for sale in a limited volume or set quantity, or of district heating, contracts for digital content which is not supplied on a tangible medium should be classified, for the purpose of this Directive, neither as sales contracts nor as service contracts'. Digital content is defined as 'data which are produced and supplied in digital form, such as computer programs, applications, games, music, videos or texts, irrespective of whether they are accessed through downloading or streaming, from a tangible medium or through other means', a definition that would cover some information provision via cloud computing.

Article 8 lays out formal requirements for distance contracts[38] and Article 9 sets out the right of withdrawal. Article 25 provides that consumers cannot, by contract, waive any of their rights conferred on them under the Directive and that any contract terms that attempt to waive their rights will not be binding. Importantly, under Article 16, it is stated that in respect of distance contracts for the supply of digital content which is not supplied on a tangible medium the right of withdrawal is not provided if the performance has begun with the consumer's prior express consent, and his acknowledgement that he thereby loses his right of withdrawal, or, in the cases of service contracts, after the service has been fully performed. This obviously could apply to a cloud computing service contract.

3.6 Soft law provisions

There are a number of soft law initiatives and instruments that act to promulgate standards regarding consumer protection in the context of electronic commerce, most notably the OECD Guidelines.[39] In the realm of cloud computing, a number of industry-led initiatives exist in various jurisdictions and sectors;[40] for the purpose of our chapter the UK CIF Code of Practice will be explored.

3.6.1 CIF Code of Practice[41]

The CIF was established as a 'direct response to the evolving supply models for the delivery of software and IT services'[42]—in other words, as a response to the development of cloud services. It is a forum for 'organizations offering to customers remotely hosted IT services of any type'.[43]

The aim of the CIF Code is to produce: 'clarity for end users when assessing and selecting Cloud Service Providers'.[44] It, therefore, concentrates on *ex ante* information requirements, rather than attempting to regulate the terms on which service providers contract with users.

There are two ways in which the CIF regulates the activity of its members in terms of the cloud. First, organizations that claim compliance with the CIF Code

---

[38] The formal requirements are an elaboration of those requirements already established in Art. 6 concerning informational requirements.

[39] OECD Guidelines for Consumer Protection in the Context of Electronic Commerce (1999).

[40] In technological industries, especially those that are 'network' industries, a lot of regulatory bodies have also a role in setting standards for the industry; in the US there is the Cloud Security Alliance, Distributed Management Task Force (DMTF), Open Cloud Standards Incubator (OCSI), US National Institute of Standards and Technology (NIST), Open Cloud Consortium, ETSI TC Cloud, and Open Grid Forum—OCCI and OASIS.

[41] See n. 5.

[42] As stated in an earlier version of the Code, CIF Code of Practice, IP10-v6.1, (1), <http://www.cloudindustryforum.org/downloads/ip10-the-code-of-practice-v6.1.pdf>.

[43] CIF Code of Practice, IP10-v6.1, (1).　　　　[44] CIF Code of Practice, IP10-v6.1, (1).

must conduct an annual self-certification process, the successful results of which are confirmed to the CIF in order to receive the authorization to use the Certification Mark (CM). The CIF spot-checks and randomly audits self-certification as well as investigates any formal complaint of non-compliance against an organization claiming compliance with the Code. Second, an organization may opt for independent certification, performed by a certification body approved by the CIF, and will then receive authorization to use the Independent Certification Mark (ICM) for the following year.

In the event of finding a 'false declaration or material non-conformity',[45] the CIF can suspend or terminate authorization to use the CM (one would presume that could happen in relation to both the CM and the ICM but the Code is not explicit about it). If authorization is suspended, such suspension will be dependent on resolution. Suspension or termination will be documented on the CIF website and 'may be reported publicly such as via press releases'.[46] According to the CIF website, 'participants must pay a nominal fee (excluding VAT and any other taxes) to assist in the administration and governance of the Code to ensure its integrity is maintained for the benefit of the industry and the market'.[47] Annual self-certification fees will be charged at the time of submitting the declaration to the CIF for approval to use the CM. As regards the costs of independent certification, no figures are currently available.

There are three pillars to the Code: transparency, capability, and accountability. Regarding transparency, the code states that 'organizations complying with the Code shall conduct themselves in an open and transparent manner which facilitates rational decision making and management by purchasers of their services'.[48] There are two categories of information that must be disclosed:

1. Information for public disclosure
    This should be 'readily available on the organization's website in the format and location specified by the CIF',[49] with a hyperlink to the CIF website. The CIF will host 'the relevant information which was provided at the time of the Certification Application'.[50] All information for public disclosure on the organization's website should be kept up to date (within four weeks of a change occurring). Some types of information for public disclosure are required and some are optional.

2. Information for contracting disclosure
    This type of information is normally disclosed in connection with proposals and contracts. Where individually negotiated and signed, the Code recognizes that this type of information may be subject to non-disclosure terms. Where non-negotiable and signed online, the Code states that the following information 'shall be made available prior to contract signing':[51] information about commercial terms; information about Personnel Profile; information about customer migration paths at contract termination; information about customer migration paths during contract execution; information about licensing and information security; information about data protection provisions; information about provisions for service continuity; information about provisions for audit; information about service dependencies; and information about complaints and escalation procedures. The CIF suggest the following means for providing the requisite

---

[45] CIF Code of Practice.   [46] CIF Code of Practice.

[47] <http://www.cloudindustryforum.org/self-certification/costs-of-self-certification> (accessed 30 March 2013).

[48] CIF Code of Practice, Section A.   [49] CIF Code of Practice, Section A.1.

[50] CIF Code of Practice, Section A.1.   [51] CIF Code of Practice, Section A.2.

information: disclosure on the organization's website and/or hyperlinked reference in the organization's contractual ToS.

Capability in the Code means 'the ability of an organization to perform essential management functions, as demonstrated by having in place auditable documented management systems'.[52] The Code states that there is no 'disclosure requirement for the details of the management systems specified by this pillar of the Code. CIF itself may audit these management systems but the organization does not need to say anything publicly about these systems, except to the extent that they are covered by the general disclosure requirement in the transparency section of the Code'.[53]

Finally, regarding accountability, the Code states that 'organizations which assert that they are complying with the Code shall be accountable for their compliance with the Code and for their behaviour with customers'.[54] Certification will be revoked by the CIF if it deems the organization to be not complying with the Code, and such revocation will be publicized on the CIF website and potentially also through the press. The potential for non-compliance may be brought to the attention of the CIF in two ways: customer or whistle-blower complaints, or as a result of a spot check or random audit conducted by either the CIF or an agent. Auditing is to be made possible by the requirement that organizations must maintain auditable records demonstrating Code compliance for a minimum of 14 months. Such records must include: copies of information for public disclosure as shown on the website and updated from time to time; and copies of information for contracting disclosure, whether shown on the website and updated from time to time, or as separately disclosed to potential customers, identifying those customers.

Regarding accountability for behaviour with customers, Code-compliant organizations are required to make two provisions in respect of this: provide formal procedures for complaint resolution within the organization, and illustrate willingness to agree to binding arbitration in local courts for the settlement of disputes. The Code further states that the above are separate from any additional requirements under legislation or regulation such as, for example, ASA requirements in the UK.

4. *Ex post* Consumer Protection Law

The Sale of Goods Act 1979 (SGA) sets out the law governing contracts for the sale of goods and governs a wide range of consumer protection matters, such as formation of contract, implied terms, the parties' rights including remedies for breach of implied terms and other breaches of contract, transfer of ownership in the goods, and performance of the contract. Given, however, that in most cases cloud computing will be considered a service for the purposes of any consumer/cloud service provider relationship, the SGA is not a matter of concern.[55] For the same reasons, the related provisions of the Supply of Goods (Implied Terms) Act 1973 are also not of concern here.

---

[52] CIF Code of Practice, Section B.   [53] CIF Code of Practice, Section B.
[54] CIF Code of Practice, Section C.
[55] For a more detailed discussion of the issues involved in categorizing cloud computing, see Alan Cunningham and Chris Reed, 'Caveat Consumer?—Consumer Protection and Cloud Computing Part 1—Issues of Definition in the Cloud' (18 January 2013). Queen Mary School of Law Legal Studies Research Paper No. 130/2013. Available at SSRN: <http://ssrn.com/abstract=2202758> or <http://dx.doi.org/10.2139/ssrn.2202758>.

4.1 Supply of Goods and Services Act 1982 (SGSA)

The SGSA has major implications for any consumer/cloud service provider relationship. The SGSA establishes standards for, among other things, the performance quality for the supply of a service, 'whatever is the nature of the consideration for the service'.[56] Although the term 'service' is not defined, it would be difficult to argue for exclusion from the remit of the SGSA of either paid-for or free cloud computing, IaaS, PaaS, or SaaS.[57]

Under section 13 of the SGSA, in a contract for the supply of a service there is an implied term that the supplier will carry out the service with 'reasonable care and skill'. The common law basis for deciding this question was established in *Bolam v Friern Hospital Management Committee*,[58] which, though addressing medical negligence, developed the standard for any professional's duty of care. McNair J said in *Bolam* that:

negligence in law means this: Some failure to do some act which a reasonable man in the circumstances would do, or doing some act which a reasonable man in the circumstances would not do; and if that failure or doing of that act results in injury, then there is a cause of action. How do you test whether this act or failure is negligent? In an ordinary case it is generally said, that you judge by the action of the man in the street . . . But where you get a situation which involves the use of some special skill or competence, then the test whether there has been negligence or not is not the test of the man on the top of a Clapham omnibus, because he has got no special skill. The test is the standard of the ordinary skilled man exercising and professing to have that special skill. A man need not possess the highest skill at the risk of being found negligent. It is well established law that it is sufficient if he exercises the ordinary skill of an ordinary competent man exercising that particular art.

Thus when addressing the question of whether a cloud service provider has provided a service with reasonable care and skill, one would have to assess the ordinary skill of an ordinary professional company/individual exercising that particular art.[59] Dependent on whether the cloud service is SaaS, PaaS, or IaaS, that particular art and level of skill may differ. For a cloud service provider offering storage, for example, one would imagine that the provision of the service should be as competent as if it were undertaken by any professional data storage company or IT employee performing that task in a professional capacity; for a provider offering email, again, one would imagine that the level of service would be as competent as if undertaken by any outsourced professional email company looking after a company's or individual's email service, or an IT employee exercising that role as a professional, and so on.

Such expectations, which may seem entirely reasonable in the context of paying for a cloud service, might become an issue in the context of a service being 'free'. Here, one might legitimately ask the question: if the service is provided at no cost, does the consumer have the same expectation as to reasonable care and skill as if he or she had paid for it? Given that, in most 'free' cases, some consideration is given, and in the context of social networks the mere use itself is an addition of value to the provider, we would argue that the consumers of such services do have a right to a similar expectation of the exercise of reasonable care and skill in the delivery of the service.

---

[56] Section 12.

[57] In the event that one could envisage cloud computing as being comprised of the delivery of both goods and services, the Act implies into contracts for services the term that they will be provided with reasonable care and skill irrespective of whether the contract is solely for services or for services and the transfer of goods.

[58] [1957] 1 WLR 582.

[59] See also, in relation to the standard for reasonable care and skill, *Kimber v William Willett Ltd* [1947] 1 All ER 361, *Nettleship v Weston* [1971] 2 QB 691, *Thake v Maurice* [1986] QB 644.

As to the scope of such a duty of care, it was stated in *South Australia Asset Management Corporation v York Montague Ltd* (a case concerning the liability of a valuer who provided a lender with a negligent overvaluation of the property offered as security for a loan) that:

> In the case of an implied contractual duty, the nature and extent of the liability is defined by the term which the law implies. As in the case of any implied term, the process is one of construction of the agreement as a whole in its commercial setting. The contractual duty to provide a valuation and the known purpose of that valuation compel the conclusion that the contract includes a duty of care. The scope of the duty, in the sense of the consequences for which the valuer is responsible, is that which the law regards as best giving effect to the express obligations assumed by the valuer: neither cutting them down so that the lender obtains less than he was reasonably entitled to expect, nor extending them so as to impose on the valuer a liability greater than he could reasonably have thought he was undertaking.[60]

In most cloud/consumer scenarios, the construction of the contract in the context of the commercial setting would lead to a reasonable expectation on the part of the consumer of a duty of care in relation to the service at issue. The scope of that duty would not be so arduous so as to make the business of the cloud provider impossible and not so ineffectual so as to make the service itself of little value to the user, even if 'free'.

In addition, under section 14 there is an implied term that the supplier will carry out the service within a reasonable time, reasonableness as to timing here being a question of fact. Finally, under section 15, there is an implied term that, unless otherwise determined by the contract in question, 'the party contracting with the supplier will pay a reasonable charge'.

Under section 16, rights, duties, or liabilities that would arise under the application of the SGSA may, crucially, be 'negatived or varied by express agreement, or by the course of dealing between the parties, or by such use as binds both parties to the contract'. However, an express term will not negate any SGSA implied term unless 'inconsistent with it'. All of this is without prejudice to any other rules of law that impose a stricter duty on a supplier than is imposed by sections 13 and 14 of the SGSA.

4.2 UCTA

UCTA limits the extent to which civil liability for breach of contract, for negligence, or other breach of duty, can be avoided by means of contract terms or otherwise. Negligence is defined as a breach of either (a) any obligation, arising from the express or implied terms of a contract, to take reasonable care or exercise reasonable skill in the performance of the contract, or (b) of any common law duty to take reasonable care or exercise reasonable skill (but not any stricter duty).[61] The main sections of the Act, sections 2 to 7, only apply in the case of business liability, that is in relation to things done or to be done by a person in the course of a business, whether their own or another's.

Under section 2, it is impossible to avoid, contractually or by reference given to persons generally or in particular, liability for death or personal injury resulting from negligence and, in the case of other loss or damage, liability for negligence insofar as the term or notice satisfies the requirement of reasonableness.[62]

Section 3 of UCTA contains important provisions regarding dealing 'as a consumer'. As against one who so deals, a supplier cannot, by reference to any contract term, exclude or

---

[60] [1996] UKHL 10, para. 15. See also, *Transfield Shipping Inc. v Mercator Shipping Inc.* [2008] UKHL 48.
[61] UCTA, s. 1(1).   [62] UCTA, s. 2.

restrict any of its liability in respect of breach, or claim to be entitled to render a contractual performance substantially different from that which was reasonably expected of him, or in respect of the whole or any part of his contractual obligation, to render no performance at all except insofar as the contract term satisfies the requirement of reasonableness. A party 'deals as consumer' in relation to another party if: that first party neither makes a contract in the course of business, nor holds him or herself as doing so, or the second party *does* make the contract in the course of business.[63]

Section 4 states further that a person dealing as a consumer cannot by reference to any contract term be made to indemnify another person (whether a party to the contract or not) in respect of liability that may be incurred by the other for negligence or breach of contract, except insofar as the contract term satisfies the requirement of reasonableness. It applies to liabilities to third parties as well as to the consumer, and to both direct and vicarious liability.

Therefore, reasonableness is an important consideration in assessing the ToS used in standard, non-negotiable cloud service contracts, those being the most commonly encountered by a consumer. Under section 11 of UCTA, reasonableness is defined, in relation to a contract term, as meaning that 'the term shall have been a fair and reasonable one to be included having regard to the circumstances which were, or ought to reasonably have been, known to or in the contemplation of the parties when the contract was made'.[64] In relation to notices, the requirement of reasonableness is that any notice should be 'fair and reasonable to allow reliance on it, having regard to all the circumstances obtaining when the liability arose or (but for the notice) would have arisen'.

In determining whether a contract term satisfies the requirement of reasonableness for the purposes of sections 6 and 7, the Act states that regard shall be had to the matters specified in Schedule 2.[65] Although it is explicitly stated that the matters outlined in Schedule 2 are only for the purposes of determining reasonableness for sections 6 and 7 of the Act, in practice these factors are often used in assessing reasonableness under the other provisions of UCTA.[66] These factors might be applied to a consumer contract with a cloud service provider as follows.

First, the parties will not be of equal bargaining power and the consumer has no real or effective power to object to standard ToS. Secondly, given the common manner in which an average consumer will engage with cloud services, it is unlikely to be reasonably practicable to obtain advice from an alternative source prior to engagement. Thirdly, the difficulty of

---

[63] UCTA, s. 12.   [64] UCTA, s. 11(1).

[65] Schedule 2 of UCTA contains guidelines for the application of the test of reasonableness in ss 6(3), 7(3)–(4), 20, and 21. It states that consideration should be given to any of the following which appear to be relevant: the bargaining strength of the parties relative to each other, taking into account (among other things) alternative means by which the customer's requirements could have been met; whether they received an inducement to agree to the term, or in accepting it had an opportunity of entering into a similar contract with other persons, but without having a similar term; whether the customer knew or ought reasonably to have known of the existence and the extent of the term (having regard, among other things, to any custom of the trade and any previous course of dealing between the parties); where the term excludes or restricts any relevant liability if some condition was not complied with, whether it was reasonable at the time of the contract to expect that compliance with that condition would be practicable; and whether the goods were manufactured, processed, or adapted to the special order of the customer.

[66] See here, *Danka Rentals Ltd v Xi Software* [1998] 7 Tr LR 74. This case involved an exemption clause that purported to exclude all express and implied warranties in the lease of a photocopier. The judge in this case applied both s. 3 and s. 7 to trigger a test of reasonableness regarding the exemption clause, and subsequently argued that there was nothing to prevent him from taking the guidelines in Sch. 2 into consideration in relation to s. 3, stating that the restriction of application of the guidelines to ss 6 and 7 *only* is of little practical difference. For specific consideration of the question of reasonableness in the context of IT, see *St Albans City and District Council v International Computers Ltd* [1996] 4 All ER 481.

the task may vary depending on whether the cloud service is SaaS, PaaS, or IaaS but it is likely to be reasonable to expect that, for example, storage of data will be done with at least reasonable care and skill. This suggests that a complete limitation of any liability would be held unreasonable. In addition there is no inherent high risk of failure when dealing with a cloud service provider. Where there is such a risk, for example there might at least be a higher *potential* for failure when cloud service providers sub-contract specific tasks which are outside their field of expertise, then this risk needs to be adequately communicated to potential users and not, as is often the case, never explicitly mentioned in advertising and sales communication. Fourthly and finally, most cloud companies could obtain insurance against at least some potential user losses, at rates which would not impinge on the service they offer.

Where a supplier seeks to restrict liability to a specified sum of money, and the question arises (under UCTA or any other Act) whether the term or notice satisfies the requirement of reasonableness, regard shall be had in particular to the resources which the supplier could expect to be available to him for the purpose of meeting the liability should it arise, and how far it was open to him to cover himself by insurance. The burden of proof regarding reasonableness lies with the one who claims the term is reasonable.

Apart from the general question of applicability of UCTA to standard ToS in cloud contracts, there are three other areas of concern when considering UCTA in the context of both consumer protection and cloud computing.

The first is that Schedule 1 states that sections 2 to 4 will not apply to a contract insofar as 'it relates to the creation or transfer of a right or interest in any patent, trademark, copyright or design right, registered right, technical or commercial information or other intellectual property, or relates to the termination of any such right or interest'. This only applies, though, to the exclusion of those contractual obligations which relate to the creation or transfer of the right,[67] for example to terms excluding the service provider's liability in the event that a third party claims to own the right. It does not exclude the application of UCTA to other liabilities, such as the obligation to provide the service using reasonable care and skill.

The second is the exemption for international goods supply contracts. A cloud service is unlikely to be a good, though it is not totally impossible to make the argument for some online content. However, a court would be likely to resist applying this exemption to cloud computing, as it would totally prevent the application of UCTA to international cloud services.

The third is section 27, which relates to choice of law clauses. Section 27(1) states that where the law applicable to a contract is the law of any part of the UK only by the choice of the parties, and that apart from such choice would be the law of some country outside the UK, sections 2 to 7 and 16 to 21 do not operate as part of the law applicable to the contract. Under Article 4(b) of Regulation 593/2008 on the law applicable to contractual obligations (Rome I) this is the law of the country where the service provider is habitually resident, and so for many cloud service contracts the relevant law would be outside the UK.

---

[67] On this point see, further, *Salvage Association v CAP Financial Services Ltd* [1995] FSR 654 concerning the installation of computer software. See also Naylor, Patrikos, and Blamires, 'Mass Market Contracting' in Christopher Reed (ed.), *Computer Law*, 7th edn (Oxford: Oxford University Press, 2011), 87: 'while there may indeed by good policy grounds for exempting certain IP transactions from the application of UCTA, 1977 allowing suppliers to exclude liability for IP-related liability in mass market transactions in the modern multi-media environment, would run entirely counter to current consumer protection policy, principles and law.'

However, section 27(2) states that UCTA has effect 'notwithstanding any contract term that applies or purports to apply the law of some country outside the UK where (either or both) the term appears to the court, or arbitrator or arbiter to have been imposed wholly or mainly for the purposes of enabling the party imposing it to evade the operation of this Act; or in the making of the contract one of the parties dealt as consumer, and he was then habitually resident in the UK and the essential steps necessary for the making of the contract were taken there, whether by him or by others on his behalf'. Thus, where the consumer is resident in the UK, a choice of some foreign law will not normally prevent UCTA applying.

4.3 The Unfair Terms in Consumer Contracts Regulations 1999 (UTCCR)[68]

The UTCCR apply specifically to unfair terms in contracts concluded between a seller or a supplier and a consumer, 'consumer' having the standard definition in European law. Under the UTCCR, contract terms that have not been individually negotiated shall be regarded as unfair if, contrary to the requirement of good faith, they cause a significant imbalance in the parties' rights and obligations arising under the contract, to the detriment of the consumer.[69] A term shall always be regarded as not having been individually negotiated where it has been drafted in advance, and the consumer has therefore not been able to influence the substance of the term, as will be the case in standard cloud computing service contracts as they relate to consumers. Even if one specific aspect of a contract has been individually negotiated, if an overall assessment indicates that the rest of the contract is a preformulated standard contract, the UTCCR still apply.

Unfairness is assessed by taking into account the nature of the goods or services for which the contract was concluded and by referring, at the time of conclusion of the contract, to all the circumstances attending the conclusion of the contract, and to all the other terms of the contract or of another contract on which it is dependent.[70] The question of the fairness of a term shall not relate to the definition of the main subject matter of the contract, or to the adequacy of the price or remuneration, as against the goods or services supplied in exchange.

Unfair terms will not be binding on the consumer and, if the contract is capable of continuing without the existence of the unfair term, its remaining terms will continue to bind the parties.[71]

Both sellers and suppliers have an obligation under the Regulations to ensure that any written term of a contract is expressed in plain, intelligible language and if there is any doubt about the meaning of a written term, the interpretation which is most favourable to the consumer shall prevail.[72]

Importantly, regarding choice of law clauses, the Regulations still apply 'notwithstanding any contract term which applies or purports to apply the law of a non-Member State, if the contract has a close connection with the territory of the Member States'.[73]

Schedule 2 of the UTCCR contains a list, indicative and non-exhaustive, of terms which may be regarded as unfair. Of particular relevance for cloud computing might be:

---

[68] The Regulations implement Council Directive 93/13/EEC of 5 April 1993 on Unfair Terms in Consumer Contracts.

[69] UTCCR, Reg. 5.   [70] UTCCR, Reg. 6.   [71] UTCCR, Reg. 8.
[72] UTCCR, Reg. 7.   [73] UTCCR, Reg. 9.

'(b) inappropriately excluding or limiting the legal rights of the consumer vis-à-vis the seller or supplier or another party in the event of total or partial non-performance or inadequate performance by the seller or supplier of any of the contractual obligations'.[74]

'(c) making an agreement binding on the consumer whereas provision of services by the seller or supplier is subject to a condition whose realisation depends on his own will alone'. It seems to us that the standard exclusion of any warranty that the service will meet particular quality standards, or indeed be provided at all,[75] is a term of this kind.

'(j) enabling the seller or supplier to alter the terms of the contract without a valid reason which is specified in the contract' and '(k) enabling the seller or supplier to alter unilaterally without a valid reason any characteristics of the product or service to be provided'. Again, we have seen in Chapter 3 that terms of this kind are extremely common, particularly those that permit the provider unilaterally to change the nature of the offering by notice, or even at will.[76]

'(q) excluding or hindering the consumer's right to take legal action or exercise any other legal remedy, particularly by requiring the consumer to take disputes exclusively to arbitration or imposing on him a burden of proof which, according to the applicable law, should lie with another party to the contract'. Compulsory arbitration clauses are clearly covered here, as are clauses which impose the exclusive jurisdiction of a court other than that of the consumer's country of residence.[77]

5. Standard Terms of Service: Issues for the Consumer

The QMUL Cloud Legal Project undertook a survey of standard, non-negotiable ToS offered by more than 30 cloud providers, as of July 2010, with a comparative analysis of changes as at January 2013.[78] The survey illustrated points of concern in standard ToS, the following being highlighted as particularly noteworthy types of standard, non-negotiable cloud computing ToS in relation to consumer protection law.

5.1 Applicable law and jurisdiction

The majority of the ToS surveyed included terms that subjected the contract to the laws of a specific jurisdiction. Typically, this jurisdiction is where the provider has its principal place of business, but sometimes the ToS specify legal systems that are dependent on user location. Thus, in 2010, 15 providers stated that the law of a US state would cover the contract and four chose English law, because it was the law of the jurisdiction where the provider was based. However, four stated English law for customers in Europe or Europe, Middle East, and Africa (EMEA); two specified the law of another EU jurisdiction for their European customers; one chose Scottish law; two the customer's local law; and three made no choice or an ambiguous one such as UK law. By 2013, certain providers

---

[74] Chapter 3, Section 3.3 has illustrated the extent to which cloud service providers attempt to exclude these liabilities. See also Section 5.11 below. [75] See also Section 5.10 below.

[76] See also Section 5.4 below.

[77] See Chapter 3, Section 3.1.4, and Sections 5.1 and 5.2 below.

[78] For a detailed discussion, see Chapter 3.

(Apple, Decho Mozy, and IBM) that had previously specified the law of another jurisdiction for customers based in the UK applied the law of the customer's usual place of residence or business address. By way of contrast, Google moved away from applying English law to customers in the EMEA region to mandating Californian law. The one provider (Flexiant) that had stipulated Scottish law in its ToS now specifies English law instead. For those providers surveyed for the first time in 2013, all had chosen to apply the jurisdiction of their corporate base.

It is important here to recall that, first, under UCTA 1977, section 27, where the law applicable to a contract is the law of any part of the UK *only* by the choice of the parties, and would otherwise be the law of some different country, sections 2 to 7 and 16 to 21 do not operate as part of the law applicable to the contract. However, this will rarely be the case for consumer cloud contracts, and section 27 states that UCTA has effect if in the making of the contract one of the parties dealt as consumer, and he was then habitually resident in the UK and the essential steps necessary for the making of the contract were taken there, whether by him or by others on his behalf.

As a result, none of the choice of law provisions will allow a cloud service provider to evade UCTA where the consumer is habitually resident in the UK. This protection would also apply to a business dealing as consumer.

In addition, clauses requiring inhabitants of one country to agree to be bound by the law of another will almost certainly be unfair, and thus unenforceable, under the UTCCR (see Section 4.3 above). Naylor, Patrikos, and Blamires assert that 'terms which prevent consumers from being able to pursue legal proceedings in their local courts (eg requiring a customer to claim via the English Courts and English law only) are likely to be considered unfair. It is not fair for the aggrieved consumer to be forced to travel long distances and use unfamiliar procedures'.[79]

Cloud providers generally specify a jurisdiction compatible with their specified legal system. Where the law of a particular US state is asserted, for example, the provider will often include a term stating that claims against it must be brought in the courts of a particular city within that state.[80] A number of providers also seek to impose relatively short limitation periods within which a customer must bring a claim in respect of service, for example Adrive state claims must be brought within six months. Again, these types of provision will probably be considered unfair under UTCCR, Schedule 2(q).

In addition it should be noted that in a recent French case[81] which concerned a provision in the Facebook ToS imposing the law and jurisdiction of Delaware, the court held that the clause was, under French law, 'unwritten' or void. The court argued, among other things, that 'provisions that directly or indirectly derogate from the rules of territorial jurisdiction are void if they are not very conspicuously specified in the commitment of the party to which she objected'. The court went on to state that 'it is therefore necessary to check if the user who deals with the company Facebook commits himself in full knowledge' arguing that 'it appears from reading the ToS, that the specific provision of the clause conferring jurisdiction on a court of the United States is embedded within numerous other provisions, none of which is numbered. It is in small print and is not distinguished from the remaining provisions'. Further, the court pointed out that 'these conditions can be even harder to read on a computer screen or mobile phone, for a French

---

[79] Naylor, Patrikos, and Blamires, 'Mass Market Contracting' in Christopher Reed (ed.), *Computer Law*, 7th edn (Oxford: Oxford University Press, 2011), 197.
[80] For example, Symantec requires that claims be brought in the courts of Santa Clara.
[81] *Mr Sebastian R v Facebook*, 23 March 2012, Court of Appeal, Pau, (authors' translation).

surfer of average skill'. We think that an English court, applying the standards set down in the UTCCR would come to a similar decision regarding the fairness of such a term.

5.2 Arbitration

Seven of the 31 ToS analysed in the study in 2010 included some form of clause seeking to impose arbitration as the sole dispute resolution mechanism. Three providers (Adrive, Nirvanix, Zoho) required customer disputes to be resolved through arbitration in all cases. 3Tera did so for claims valued at more than US$500. IBM, Iron Mountain, and LiveMesh all had terms that imposed arbitration on customers in some countries but not in others. There were no major changes noted in the 2013 survey. 3Tera's former customers now use Savvisdirect as provided by Century Link, whose ToS provide that it will pay the cost of a customer's arbitration filing fee if it exceeds the local court filing fee, and that it will pay the costs of arbitration. Again, Schedule 2(q) of UTCCR seems most applicable here and would support an argument that clauses which seek to impose arbitration on consumers based in the UK are unfair.

5.3 Acceptable use

The rules concerning acceptable use are often presented in a separate Acceptable Use Policy (AUP). Most providers surveyed in 2010 prohibited a consistent set of activities that providers consider to be improper or outright illegal uses of their service, such as spam, fraud, gambling, hacking, hosting of obscene content, and material which is defamatory or such as to promote discrimination or incite hatred. A number went further than this in setting out examples of unacceptable activity, for example ElasticHosts, which prohibits the use of its service for 'safety-critical' applications where the failure of service may result in injury or loss of life. No major changes were noted in the 2013 survey. It would be difficult to argue that such an AUP could be unreasonable or unfair, or how imposing such terms would constitute the cloud service provider not exercising their service with reasonable care and skill; if anything, such clauses could be seen as evidence of exactly the opposite.

5.4 Variation of contract terms

Eight of the providers surveyed in 2010 made no mention of any variation process, but the remainder reserved the right to do this. Among those, the procedure varied considerably. Thirteen incorporated a term that stated that they may amend their ToS simply by posting an updated version on their website and that continued use of the service by the customer is deemed acceptance of the new ToS. In the 2013 survey, only one provider (Akamai) did *not* have a term allowing ToS to be varied. Those that had introduced such a provision followed the pattern noted above, asserting the right to vary terms via unilateral notice.

A term that purports to allow the service provider to unilaterally vary the ToS will often be unfair. Schedule 2(j) and (k) of the UTCCR state, respectively, that terms which enable the seller or supplier to 'alter the terms of the contract without a valid reason which is specified in the contract' or 'to alter unilaterally without a valid reason any characteristics of the product or service to be provided' may be regarded as unfair.

Office of Fair Trading (OFT) guidance on such terms states that they will be 'under strong suspicion of unfairness' and open to 'strong objection'.[82] Also, terms that could be used to force consumers to accept new requirements or reduced benefits and perhaps even terms which are intended only to facilitate minor adjustments will be an issue if the way they are worded ensures they could be used to impose greater changes.[83]

Of course, the logistical and technical nature of cloud services requires a reconsideration of what might be considered reasonable and fair, particularly as the technology and business models for cloud are evolving rapidly. However, it seems to take flexibility too far if cloud providers can impose new terms unilaterally without giving the consumer a chance to object and walk away.

Such an approach is permissible under section 2(b) of Schedule 2 of the UTCCR, which states that 'Paragraph 1(j) is also without hindrance to terms under which a seller or supplier reserves the right to alter unilaterally the conditions of a contract of indeterminate duration, provided that he is required to inform the consumer with reasonable notice and that the consumer is free to dissolve the contract'. This would apply to almost all consumer cloud contracts, which usually continue in force until terminated by notice and are thus of indeterminate length.

5.5 Data integrity

The 2010 survey found that most providers not only avoided giving undertakings in respect of data integrity, but actually disclaimed liability for it. A majority of providers surveyed expressly included terms in their ToS making it clear that ultimate responsibility for preserving the confidentiality and integrity of the customer's data lay with the customer. A number of providers (Amazon, GoGrid, and Microsoft) asserted that they will make best efforts to preserve such data, but nonetheless included such a disclaimer. A number of providers went so far as to recommend that the customer encrypt data stored in the provider's cloud, or specifically place responsibility on the customer to make backup arrangements. In effect, a number of providers of consumer-orientated cloud services appeared to disclaim the specific fitness of their service for the purpose for which many customers would have specifically signed up to use them. The 2013 review found little change here with providers continuing to place the onus for ensuring data integrity onto customers.

One could argue that preserving the confidentiality and integrity of data held in the cloud is a question of adequate performance if it concerns carrying out the service with reasonable care and skill. As discussed in Section 4.1 above, the jurisprudence concerning what constitutes reasonable care and skill suggests that a professional service involving storage of data would be expected to preserve the confidentiality and integrity of the data. Therefore, arguably service providers who attempt to limit liability are attempting to exclude the implied terms under the SGSA that they provide the service with reasonable care and skill.

So what are the main characteristics of, for example, a cloud service provider offering cloud storage, or a cloud service provider offering cloud email accounts and storage? Arguably, such services must involve the provider being responsible for data integrity and confidentiality. If a consumer were to purchase an email software package and use it on a private personal computer, it would almost certainly be their own responsibility to preserve confidentiality and integrity of data. If, however, a company advertises a cloud-based email service or a cloud storage service, the very nature of the service may

---

[82] OFT 311, para. 10.1 and OFT 672, para. 3.46.
[83] OFT 311, para. 10.2.

imply that the service provider will exercise a level of care and skill equivalent to that of a typical professional exercising the particular art in question, that is data storage and email service administration.

It may be that the service provider selling the service is not, in fact, the only company responsible for effecting aspects of the service. In such a case, it may not be possible for the provider to take full responsibility for integrity and confidentiality. But this is not the point; consumers are entitled to expect the provider to be responsible for these matters unless informed otherwise. Thus, there should be no fudging of the issue in providers' communications with the consumer, or in the subsequent contract. Service providers have an obligation to be transparent about the nature of their services, under the *ex ante* conditions outlined above, and, indeed, under self-regulatory measures established by the industry. If they cannot ensure that part of a service will maintain the confidentiality and integrity of their users' data, they should communicate this information clearly to consumers, and they should not advertise their service in a manner that raises a reasonable expectation on the part of consumers that data will be maintained as confidential and integral.

In addition, consumers have a right to receive, in all significant respects, what they have agreed to buy, not merely something similar or equivalent. The fact that some cloud users will get a 'free' service does not excuse the provider from providing the service. These consumers contribute to the value of the provider, and consideration has been provided by mere use of the system itself.

We have already noted that the OFT considers terms that allow a supplier to unilaterally substitute something different for what it has actually agreed to supply are unlikely to be fair, and are open to 'strong objection' if they allow a supplier to do so without a valid reason.[84] A valid reason that might be reasonable in the context of cloud computing is, as the OFT states, changes to the product to be supplied that are as a 'result of reasons genuinely beyond the suppliers control' or 'other circumstances that could prevent the supply of the goods or services agreed' or 'changes which are clearly minor technical adjustments which can be of no real significance to the consumer, or changes required by law' or 'changes which are more significant, but still only limited in scope, where the consumer fully understands and agrees to the change in advance'.[85] However, terms limiting the maintenance of the integrity and confidentiality of consumer data which are included simply for the convenience of the provider are likely to be both unfair, and a contradiction of the implied term that the service will be carried out with reasonable care and skill.

5.6 Data preservation

The 2010 survey found that providers fell into three broad camps in respect of the way in which they stated they will deal with customer information following the end of their relationship: (a) they asserted that they will normally preserve customer data for a set period of time following the end of a service contract; (b) they stated that customer data will be deleted immediately the relationship ends; or (c) they engaged in a hybrid approach, stating that they are under no obligation to preserve data after the end of the relationship but not undertaking to delete data, or noting that a grace period may apply

---

[84] OFT 672, para. 3.46.
[85] Naylor, Patrikos, and Blamires, 'Mass Market Contracting' in Christopher Reed (ed.), *Computer Law*, 7th edn (2011), 164–5.

at their discretion. This separation with regard to data preservation was found to have continued in our 2013 survey. IBM, for example, in its 2013 ToS states that data will not be deleted from an account closed by a customer until the customer has confirmed that data has been exported and backed up, or six months has elapsed; Apple states it may delete data immediately the relationship ends; and Google, with regard to Google Docs, will make a reasonable effort to allow the customer the opportunity to export data.

Under the CRD, cloud service providers have an obligation to provide the consumer with, where applicable, 'the functionality, including applicable technical protection measures, of digital content' and 'where applicable, any relevant interoperability of digital content with hardware and software that the trader is aware of or can reasonably be expected to have been aware of'. One would imagine that this kind of information would be good to have after ending a relationship with a cloud provider. Such information allows for increased portability of data. There is not, as yet, any explicit provision of consumer protection law requiring portability of data, although an argument could be made that portability of data lies within the scope of the duty to take reasonable care and skill in the provision of a cloud service. There are increasing calls from the IT community regarding data portability.[86] In addition, under data protection law the question of data portability has been addressed, albeit in provisional form in the proposed data protection Regulation, Article 18.[87] Here, a right to data portability has been proposed, whereby individuals should be assisted to transfer their personal data from one service provider to another.

5.7 Data location/transfer

In 2010, some cloud providers, such as Amazon, offered in their marketing to confine customer data to regional zones. Few others undertook to store data in any particular location or zone. Fifteen of the 31 surveyed made no mention of data location whatsoever. Seven out of the remaining 16 asserted compliance with Safe Harbor procedures.

Interestingly, however, the choice of regional storage offered by Amazon was not described in the ToS, which might have constituted a contravention of the Consumer Protection from Unfair Trading Regulations 2008 as an unfair commercial practice; that is, advertising a service but not committing in contract to undertake what has been advertised.

5.8 Monitoring by provider

Three categories of ToS were found in relation to the policy on monitoring in 2010: silence; a statement that the provider monitors but only in terms of nature and pattern of use or for the purpose of quality of service provision or statistical analysis; or a statement that it monitors the data uploaded to the service in order to enforce the AUP. By 2013, a number of providers that in 2010 had not stated a policy on monitoring or

---

[86] Tim Berners-Lee has been vocal on this issue; Don Reisinger, 'Tim Berners-Lee: Tell Facebook, Google You Want Your Data Back' (*CNET*, 18 April 2012), <http://news.cnet.com/8301-1023_3-57415764-93/tim-berners-lee-tell-facebook-google-you-want-your-data-back> (accessed 28 March 2013).

[87] Proposal for a Regulation of the European Parliament and of the Council on the protection of individuals with regard to the processing of personal data and on the free movement of such data, Brussels, 25.1.2012 COM(2012) 11 final.

had stated that it was only carried out for service provision purposes had amended their ToS to state much more clearly that data was monitored for compliance with terms such as AUPs. Two major providers, in particular, did this: Apple and Google.

It would be difficult to argue under consumer protection law that such clauses were unfair, unreasonable, or not necessary for the exercise of reasonable care or skill; if anything, exactly the opposite could be argued. Any concerns regarding the act of monitoring use would arise under data protection law. This is, in a sense, a consumer protection issue, but since it does not relate to those areas of concern nominally addressed by traditional consumer protection law, it is addressed in Part III of this book.

5.9 Rights in customer content

The 2010 survey found no evidence of any provider seeking to assert intellectual property (IP) rights over content and data uploaded to the cloud. Normally, both provider and customer were stated to own the IP in their service and data respectively. A term was often included asserting that the customer grants a compulsory licence to republish some or all of the customer's data for provision of service (such a licence would in any event be implied). In 2013, little had changed with regard to such terms, and, in any event, there are no major implications for consumer protection law in relation to such clauses. However, if the ToS are drafted so as to prevent the consumer from acquiring or retaining the IP rights he or she would reasonably expect to acquire or retain, for example, in respect of content the consumer creates using the cloud service, this would be a breach of the obligation to communicate the main characteristics of the service in the CPDSR.

The 2010 survey also addressed the question whether a contract for cloud services creates some proprietary non-IP right or relationship, such as bailment or a fiduciary duty. Most contracts made no reference to such a concept. Those that did excluded the possibility that such rights could arise in relation to data in cloud. Thus, Amazon states that no right of bailment arises in respect of data sent to it for import, but the wording refers to data supplied on physical media. Again, there is no implication for consumer protection law arising from such clauses.

5.10 Warranty

Most providers surveyed in 2010 went to considerable lengths to deny any warranty about the quality of service provision. Many, including Facebook and Amazon, excluded express or implied warranties that the service provided would be fit for purpose or merchantable. However, some of those providers whose contracts are subject to the law of an EU jurisdiction either do not exclude any such warranties (UKFast), or accept statutory implied warranties where they apply (IBM and Google)—others where an EU law applied still disclaimed such Warranties (Apple and G.ho.st). Notably, in 2013, four providers provide some variation of a warranty to use reasonable skill and care (Apple, in respect of the two products reviewed in the 2013 survey, Decho, Google, in respect of Google Drive only, and IBM).

As we saw in Section 4.1 there is a statutory implied warranty that the service will be undertaken with reasonable care or skill. Those who attempt to exclude this warranty will be faced with UTCCR, Schedule 2(b), which states that 'inappropriately excluding or limiting the legal rights of the consumer vis-à-vis the seller or supplier or another party in the event of total or partial non-performance or inadequate performance by the seller or supplier of any of the contractual obligations, including the option of offsetting a debt owed to the seller or supplier against any claim which the consumer may have against him' may be unfair. Almost certainly, excluding the implied warranty under the SGSA 1982 would limit the legal rights of the consumer.

Exclusion of any warranty of merchantability or fitness for purpose is more problematic, as there is no such statutorily implied warranty for services. However, it should be noted that the courts have the power to imply such a term, and have already done so in relation to software.[88] If the court implied such a term, its reasonableness would also fall to be assessed under the UTCCR.

5.11 Exclusion and limitation of liability

In the contracts examined in the 2010 survey, direct liability was taken to mean liability for losses to the customer relating to the loss or compromise of data hosted in the cloud. All US-based providers sought to deny liability for direct damage as far as possible, either in very general terms, or phrased as relating to the consequences of inability to access data. Providers based in Europe tended to be less overt about seeking to exclude direct liability, and such exclusions as existed tended to be based on, for example, the concept of *force majeure*. Little had changed by 2013, other than some providers providing warranties relating to exercising reasonable care and skill.

The main questions here are: is excluding liability for losses relating to the loss or compromise of data hosted in the cloud a limitation of the statutory duty to exercise reasonable care and skill in providing the cloud service, and is such an exclusion of liability unfair? We do not think it is automatically improper to accept a duty to exercise reasonable care and skill in hosting data, and yet to require a user to accept a limitation of liability for loss or compromise of data hosted in the cloud. Circumstances beyond the remit of reasonable care and skill may lead to such losses, even where the cloud service provider has not sub-contracted out any aspect of the service to another provider. Limiting the provider's liability in these circumstances would be reasonable, particularly where the consumer is able to take precautions against it such as making backup arrangements. A cloud provider which assisted consumers here, for example by providing advice on backups or perhaps partnering with a backup service provider, would be in a stronger position to argue the reasonableness of the clause.

However, a clause that excludes or limits all liability arising from a breach of the reasonable care and skill requirement may well be unfair. For example, the OFT has stated that a term that excludes or limits 'the supplier's liability for damages caused by faulty goods or poor services, for example a term denying responsibility for loss of data if the consumer has not made backup copies' is likely to be unfair.[89] Again, however, the question is whether it is poor service to be subject to any loss or compromise of data; obviously, a good service would do the utmost to ensure this did not happen, but such things cannot be avoided if they are outside the provider's control.

Disclaimers of indirect liability, such as for indirect, consequential, or economic losses arising from a breach by the provider, are even more common. With the exception of Flexiant, every other provider expressly excluded them.

---

[88] *St Albans City and District Council v International Computers Ltd* [1996] 4 All ER 481.
[89] OFT 672, para. 3.124.

Because the cloud service provider is already accepting a degree of risk in managing responsibilities concerning the data of others, it may be reasonable to exclude liability for losses that were not reasonably foreseeable prior to entering into the contract, and, indeed, the OFT agrees. However, the OFT has also stated that blanket terms which aim to limit the kind of loss for which compensation is paid, including a consumer's claim to consequential losses, would be likely to be considered unfair.[90] It would, therefore, be in the interest of cloud service providers, and in the interest of fairness, since there may be losses that were not reasonably foreseeable by either party, to list expressly the categories of indirect losses for which they exclude liability, rather than trying to exclude all indirect losses per se.

Where liability is not completely excluded, it is often limited. Nineteen of the 31 companies surveyed in 2010 set a maximum liability of some multiple of the service fees with an upper limit. Where a flat liability limit was specified, the amount varied dependent on the nature of the service; for example, Adrive limited consumer claims to amounts under US$100.

Such limitations as to the amount that may be claimed would also appear to fall under Schedule 2 of the UTCCR, particularly section (b). OFCOM, in investigating the activities of Wanadoo, held that a term limiting Wanadoo's liability for any loss or damage suffered by the consumer in relation to the provision of the service to £500 in any 12-month period was unfair.[91] This does not mean that all limitations are automatically unfair, but rather that imposing too low a limitation is likely to be problematic.

5.12 Indemnification

Twenty-four of the 31 companies surveyed in 2010 required customers to indemnify the provider against any claim against the provider resulting from the customer's use of the service. This was also the case for free services such as Facebook and Dropbox. By 2013, little had changed in this regard, although 3Tera's successor CenturyLink no longer demanded such an indemnity, but Dell (newly surveyed in 2013) did. Such indemnity may be conditional; for instance, by requiring the indemnified party to allow the indemnifier to control the conduct of litigation.

A consumer cannot be made to indemnify another party to the contract or a third party to the contract except to the extent that the term meets the requirements of reasonableness under UCTA.[92] Is such an indemnity reasonable? Given the standards that would be used to assess reasonableness imposing a general indemnification as against *any* claim would most likely be unreasonable. Specific indemnifications, for example against IP infringement or defamatory statements by the customer, are more likely to be reasonable. However, the provider would be wise to communicate this to the consumer clearly, and not merely rely on the ToS of the contract.

6. Conclusion

Throughout this chapter we have emphasized that the ways in which cloud service providers communicate with their customers about the nature and characteristics of their service

---

[90] OFT 672, para. 3.124.
[91] Consumer complaint against Wanadoo about unfair contract terms CW/00779/08/04 Ofcom, 'Consumer Complaint against Wanadoo about Unfair Contract Terms' (*Ofcom*, 11 November 2004), <http://stakeholders.ofcom.org.uk/enforcement/competition-bulletins/closed-cases/all-closed-cases/cw_779> (accessed 28 March 2013).
[92] See Section 4.2 of this chapter.

are of real legal significance. There is, in any event, a legal obligation placed on providers to supply certain information and explain some matters to the customer, as discussed in Section 3 above. But even if there were no such obligation, these communications would still play a significant role in determining how fair and reasonable specific ToS are.

The extent of a provider's obligations to a consumer customer, such as the obligation to provide a service using reasonable care and skill, as well as the fairness and reasonableness of its terms, depends very much on the legitimate expectations of that consumer. Given that most consumers will not bother to read ToS before entering into the relationship, or indeed at all, the provider's informational material and advertising will be what shapes those expectations. That material may not form part of the contract, but it has legal consequences for the *ex post* assessment of the contract's validity and enforceability. If the cloud computing service is, in fact, different from what the average consumer would understand it to consist of, irrespective of whether it is free or not, then it is necessary for providers to make that difference clear before any contract is entered into.

Much of the difficulty here arises from a mismatch of starting assumptions. Many service providers conceive their consumer activities as not being a 'real' service, unlike what they provide to their commercial customers. They are merely offering the consumer a facility to use computing hardware and software in a new way, rather like the owner of a piece of land who allows drivers to park their cars on it. Neither considers that what they provide is a service, but both are wrong. This may be part of the reason why cloud providers attempt to limit all liability; why they reject an obligation to maintain data and keep it entire and secure; and why they exclude warranties that the service will be exercised with some degree of care or skill.

Consumer protection law is largely predicated on concepts of reasonableness and fairness. It does not, or at least should not, make business activities unprofitable or uninsurable. However, it does impose upon providers obligations that society considers reasonable in the exercise of their 'art'. Determining what obligations can reasonably be expected is easy for long-established commercial activities, but far more difficult for innovations like cloud computing. Service providers cannot expect society, in the form of consumers and enforcement authorities, simply to understand the new service. Rather, they have an obligation to explain its nature, addressing their explanations to these non-technical sectors of society rather than to experts in the technology. Doing so is in the interest of providers in any event, as those expectations shape the legal response to their liabilities and contractual terms.

Much of contract law is concerned with the allocation of risk between contracting parties. Consumer protection law focuses on the knowledge of consumers about those risks, and the fairness and reasonableness with which contracts allocate them. Service providers should be clear about the actual risk that a consumer is taking on, and not (for example) pretend that it is managed adequately by a sub-contractor when it is not. Where no effort has been made to communicate clearly to the consumer the essential characteristics of the service, broad limitations and exclusions of liability may not be reasonable; where an effort has been made to be clear, they might be.

A provider who uses the *ex post* and *ex ante* arms of consumer protection law in this way, ideally in conjunction with industry codes, is unlikely to face major difficulties under consumer protection law. Those cloud service providers will be able to provide the advantages of the cloud to consumers, knowing that they have conveyed an adequate understanding of the nature and risks of the service, and achieving a fair and reasonable allocation of the risks involved.

14

Cloud Governance: The Way Forward

Chris Reed

All the preceding chapters of this book have raised difficult governance questions, and in some cases have considered the potential solutions to those questions. But in each case the governance issues are, or at least might appear to be, quite different and disconnected.

This chapter will attempt to make those connections and indicate how they might be situated within a broad governance framework. It will not be possible to predict accurately the future shape of cloud governance; this is something that will follow its own evolutionary trajectory, shaped by commercial, regulatory, and individual decisions. The chapter does intend, though, to explore the issues which will need to be resolved during that evolution, and indicate some of the likely solutions.

1. What Is Governance?

The term 'governance' usually denotes a system of rule-creation and enforcement which does not depend solely on state command-and-control, but instead involves participants from a wider community.

most analytical accounts of governance rely on a definition focused on consensual arrangements, intentionally agreed upon by state and non-state actors directly involved in setting and enforcing rules.[1]

Governance of this type is most commonly referred to as co-regulation,[2] to distinguish it from governance purely by law, on the one hand, or self-regulation or contract on the other. I will argue below that state participation in cloud governance is essential, and thus this chapter will focus mainly on co-regulation.

Cloud governance encompasses two main areas: internal governance focuses on a provider's technical working of cloud services, its business operations, and the ways it manages its relationship with customers and other external stakeholders; and external governance consists of the norms, rules, and regulations which define the relationships between members of the cloud community and attempt to solve disputes between them.

Internal governance is primarily a matter for the cloud service provider to determine itself, so is not addressed in any detail here.[3] But much of the content of any internal governance system is dictated by the external governance rules, so as to enable the provider to comply with them. External governance is the primary focus of this chapter.

---

[1] Jean-Christophe Graz and Andreas Nölke, 'Introduction' in Jean-Christophe Graz and Andreas Nölke (eds), *Transnational Private Governance and its Limits* (Abingdon: Routledge, 2008), 12.

[2] See Christopher T Marsden, *Internet Co-Regulation* (Cambridge: Cambridge University Press, 2011).

[3] It will cover matters such as policies and procedures regarding how the provider evaluates and handles its own use of cloud services, internal systems and rules, risk assessments, monitoring of usage, interworking of cloud services, technical interaction with customers and others, and compliance with emerging technical standards.

2. Governance, Legitimacy, and Effectiveness

2.1 Law, self-regulation, and legitimacy

Why is law not a suitable mechanism for cloud governance? Admittedly, the existing body of national laws is ill-adapted to cloud governance, and users and providers are currently struggling to work out how to comply with it, but cannot new laws be devised to deal with at least the most pressing cloud governance issues?

The problem here is that national law lacks legitimacy. As Johnson and Post pointed out at the outset of the commercial Internet, no state has a stronger claim than any other to regulate the entirety of a cross-border computing activity:

Because events on the Net occur everywhere but nowhere in particular, are engaged in by online personae who are both 'real' (possessing reputations, able to perform services, and deploy intellectual assets) and 'intangible' (not necessarily or traceably tied to any particular person in the physical sense), and concern 'things' (messages, databases, standing relationships) that are not necessarily separated from one another by any physical boundaries, no physical jurisdiction has a more compelling claim than any other to subject these events exclusively to its laws. [4]

A state which applies its national law to online activities asserts its *de facto* power, rather than a clearly legitimate claim to exercise regulatory power. But the enforcement power of states is far lower in cyberspace than in the physical world,[5] and probably insufficient to enforce universal compliance. Thus, the legitimacy of a state's claim to regulate is fundamental to whether its laws are obeyed, and thus achieve governance.

Legitimacy derives from the acceptance by those subject to the law that they ought to accept the lawmaker as having a right to make rules to govern their conduct.[6] Residents of one state will not normally hold such a belief about the authority of a lawmaker in another state. However, where those residents are also acting via cyberspace they may temporarily become members of the other state's community, and if so are likely to accept that the other state has legitimate authority to regulate their online activity.[7] Thus, a cloud computing service provider established in, say, the US might well acknowledge the legitimate authority of the EU to make laws which apply to its activities, but only so far as those activities take place 'in' (virtually speaking) the EU.

Unfortunately, that service provider is only conducting a part of its activities as a member of the EU regulatory community. The rest of its activities are conducted elsewhere, and the EU, therefore, has no legitimate claim to regulate them. Because clouds disregards national borders, unless geography is built into their design for other reasons, legislation in any one state may effectively require cloud providers and users either to comply with it in all other states, or not to comply with it at all. If more than one state makes laws for cloud governance, it is almost certain that these laws will differ. A contradictory framework of laws can never produce a coherent governance framework.[8]

---

[4] David R Johnston and David G Post, 'Law and Borders—The Rise of Law in Cyberspace' (1996) 48 *Stanford LR* 1367, 1376. See also 1390:
'Governments cannot stop electronic communications from coming across their borders, even if they want to do so. Nor can they credibly claim a right to regulate the Net based on supposed local harms caused by activities that originate outside their borders and that travel electronically to many different nations. One nation's legal institutions should not monopolize rule-making for the entire Net.'

[5] Chris Reed, *Making Laws for Cyberspace* (Oxford: Oxford University Press, 2012), Ch. 4.

[6] See Joseph Raz, *The Authority of Law*, 2nd edn (Oxford: Oxford University Press, 2009), 29.

[7] Reed n. 5, Chs 5 and 6.

[8] Chris Reed, 'How to Make Bad Law: Lessons from Cyberspace' (2010) 73 *MLR* 903.

Indeed, I would argue that a claim to regulate part of an indivisible whole, where there is no legitimate claim to regulate the remainder, is necessarily not a legitimate claim.

These twin problems of contradiction and legitimacy could in theory be solved through law, provided the law was substantially the same everywhere. International agreement of this kind is a slow and chancy process,[9] and subordinating state lawmaking to that of a transnational body incurs substantial 'sovereignty costs'.[10] Law might one day evolve to deal with these issues, but for the immediate future some alternative form of governance is needed for cloud computing.

Self-regulatory governance is an alternative which overcomes some of the legitimacy defects explained above. Under a pure self-regulatory model those who are the primary subjects of the system's rules, in our case cloud service providers, come together to agree a governance structure and undertake to abide by the rules it produces. This voluntary subjection to the rules confers a degree of legitimacy on the rule-maker which, for a cross-border activity, no individual state could ever claim. The content of the rules tends to be well adapted to the regulated activity because those who make them are practitioners in the field, and is easy to keep up to date. All this should lead to a high level of voluntary compliance, with little need for enforcement and sanctions mechanisms.

However, self-regulation has legitimacy defects which make it even less suitable for cloud computing governance than national law. Until a mere 25 years ago the UK financial services sector, like most other countries' financial sectors, was largely governed through self-regulation. As finance became more complex, the disadvantages became apparent. The fact that the rules were created by financial services providers meant that they mainly reflected the interests of those providers, and thus gave inadequate protection to others who were affected, such as customers or the state. Frequent change in the rules made the regulation opaque to outsiders. Voluntary compliance was not always achieved, and the lack of enforcement and sanctions mechanisms allowed abuses to continue unchecked.[11] In consequence, the UK Financial Services Act 1986 substituted a co-regulatory system, which has been much modified since.[12] Self-regulation still survives in the UK Press Complaints Commission, which exhibits the same regulatory failures as the financial services system[13] but has survived because of the fundamental role that the press plays in the preservation of free speech. But the findings of the Leveson Inquiry[14] seem likely to lead to the partial abandonment of self-regulation.

The cloud computing industry has recently gone some distance towards establishing a self-regulatory governance model. The Cloud Industry Forum (CIF) has produced a Code of Practice for Cloud Service Providers[15] which deals with a number of cloud governance issues. In combination with initiatives from other bodies, such as the Cloud

---

[9] For example, discussions on many elements of the Hague Conference Preliminary Draft Convention on Jurisdiction and Foreign Judgments in Civil and Commercial Matters of 1999 were eventually abandoned because it was not possible to reconcile the differing national approaches to many issues.

[10] Kenneth W Abbott and Duncan Snidal, 'Hard and Soft Law' (2000) 54 *International Organization* 421, 436–40.

[11] The discussion about the merits and demerits of self-regulation was, of course, far more complex than this summary suggests. See Julia Black, *Rules and Regulators* (Oxford: Clarendon Press, 1997), Ch. 2 for a more detailed analysis.

[12] The current regulatory scheme is that of the Financial Services and Markets Act 2000, but further changes are under way in response to the global financial crisis.

[13] See, for example, Jonathan Coad, 'The Press Complaints Commission—Are We Safe in Its Hands?' (2005) *Ent LR* 167.

[14] <http://www.levesoninquiry.org.uk/>.

[15] <http://www.cloudindustryforum.org/downloads/Cloud%20Service%20Provider%20Code%20 of%20Practice_v6.1_(1.0).pdf>.

Security Alliance,[16] this has the potential to evolve into a pure-self-regulatory govern-ance framework. But could it actually achieve its governance functions?

At present, the CIF suffers from significant legitimacy failures. The only members of the cloud community who are certain to accept its legitimacy are those service providers who have signed up to membership. This is only a small part of the cloud community. At least under the present constitution of the CIF, the smaller cloud service providers are inadequately represented. Three of the 12 seats on the Code Governance Board are reserved for end-user, that is customer, representatives but there is no mechanism for their selection, which would give confidence that they are truly representative of the end-user community. Individuals whose data are processed in the cloud have no repre-sentation at all.

States are themselves part of the cloud community, but have no representation in the CIF. Not only are states major users of cloud computing, but also more importantly they owe duties to their citizens to provide protections for those citizens' fundamental rights. Cloud computing affects a number of those fundamental rights, most notably but not exclusively the right to privacy. States will almost certainly feel the need to step in and legislate if they perceive their own citizens to be unfairly treated by the rules.

Those who argue that online communities should regulate themselves are clear that this is because they believe such self-regulation is more legitimate than state regulation. But this is true only if the self-regulator truly represents the whole community.[17]

Even if legitimate, a self-regulatory system needs some enforcement mechanism to ensure its rules are complied with. The current CIF mechanism is that compliance with the Code is attested via self-certification by service providers, and although the Forum intends to undertake audits in the future, it is not known if the results of these audits will be made public. The sanction for failure is no more than loss of the provider's abil-ity to claim compliance. This sanction is so weak that non-provider cloud commu-nity members are unlikely to view the CIF rules as being effective, and ineffectiveness reduces legitimacy. Even if stronger sanctions were adopted, they could only be enforced through state law mechanisms such as through actions for breach of contract. And, of course, a self-regulatory structure has no means of enforcing its rules against those who are not actually members of the regulatory body, which will be true both for customers and individuals.

This analysis tells us that, by its very nature, the CIF, or any self-regulatory succes-sor, will have inadequate legitimacy to regulate. To gain legitimacy it would need wider participation in its constitutional and rule-making activities, including the participa-tion of states. It would also need the cooperation and involvement of states, both to persuade them not to legislate in its governance sphere and to assist through national law in enforcing its rules. If it were to achieve these, it would have transformed itself into a co-regulatory governance system.

2.2 Co-regulation of Internet activities

Co-regulation seems to have become the predominant governance structure for those Internet activities which extend beyond national boundaries.[18] The most obvious rea-son why this should be so is that the Internet is global in reach, and thus cuts across the

---

[16] <https://cloudsecurityalliance.org/>.
[17] See David G Post, *In Search of Jefferson's Moose* (Oxford: Oxford University Press, 2009).
[18] Marsden n. 2.

hierarchical structures of national law. There is no sovereign body which is accepted as having authority to regulate cyberspace as a whole, and as a consequence:

networked governance arrangements, in which state agencies and political offices participate along with commercial and professional groups, seem to be replacing arrangements that at least in principle were hierarchical, with the state as the sovereign power...No power holder has been sovereign or hegemonic.[19]

The decentralized structure of the online world necessitates a transnational system of governance. Each national law claims to be the centre of legal power, which leads to the kinds of conflicts that, as argued above, prevent it achieving effective governance. Self-regulation can be transnational, but lacks the necessary legitimacy. All this suggests that co-regulation is the only approach to the governance of Internet activities which has any reasonable prospect of success.

This does not tell us, though, which form of co-regulatory governance structure will be successful. Indeed, each Internet activity is likely to require a different structure, reflecting the particular regulatory settlement which is achieved through communication between the various players (including businesses, governments, and individuals) who see themselves as having a stake in that activity. These communications are continuous, not one-off, which, therefore, requires the structure to be capable of evolution rather than fixed.[20]

Inevitably, though, some players have more economic, political, or social power than others, and this will tend to shape a governance structure in a way which reflects that power balance:

the structure of power in e-commerce is formed by the mix of institutions, norms, values, and beliefs governing the electronic markets. It is the result of stakeholders' preferences, but likewise it shapes the framework of relationships where these preferences are defined and it constrains the action of governments, companies, and international organisations, both governmental and non-governmental.[21]

This creates two dangers.

The first is that the governance structure fails to take adequate account of the interests of weaker players. These will typically be individuals and small businesses, which form an inchoate and diverse community and thus find it difficult to participate in the process of determining how governance should be structured. But states, also, run the risk of being largely ignored unless they possess sufficient 'regulatory gravity'[22] to play an active part in this process. Failure to take all relevant interests into account is likely to damage the legitimacy of a governance system, which may ultimately lead to regulatory failure. It is for this reason that Mueller et al. argue that multi-stakeholder governance is always necessary.[23]

---

[19] Sven Bisley and Mikkel Flyverbom, 'Transnational Private Governance of the Internet' in Jean-Christophe Graz and Andreas Nölke (eds), *Transnational Private Governance and Its Limits* (Abingdon: Routledge, 2008), 129, 133 (emphasis in original).

[20] Andrew Murray, *The Regulation of Cyberspace* (Abingdon: Routledge-Cavendish, 2007), 24.

[21] Josep Ibáñez, 'Who Governs the Internet? The Emerging Regime of E-commerce' in Jean-Christophe Graz and Andreas Nölke, *Transnational Private Governance and Its Limits* (Abingdon: Routledge, 2008), 142, 144.

[22] See Andrew Murray, 'Nodes and Gravity in Virtual Space' (2010) 5 *Legisprudence* 195.

[23] Milton Mueller, John Mathiason, and Hans Klein, 'The Internet and Global Governance: Principles and Norms for a New Regime' (2007) 13 *Global Governance* 237, 250:
'The rhetoric of tripartite representation (government, business, and civil society) is not enough; we must pay close attention to the details of representation in governance structures and make sure that end users and individuals, who must overcome steep collective action problems, are adequately empowered.'

The second danger is that the adopted governance structure only manages to create what Marsden describes as a 'Potemkin' regulator.[24] Every appearance of regulation is present, in terms of constitution, processes, personnel, and published rules, but in practice the governance structure has little or no regulatory effect over the activity in question. To avoid this danger a governance structure needs to be effective at governance. Not only must its regulatory authority be accepted as legitimate, but also the process through which it devises substantive regulation has to be legitimate. The obligations imposed by its rules must be meaningful to those who are regulated and seen as likely to achieve the governance aims. And finally, adequate enforcement mechanisms must be in place to deal with those who are unable, or unwilling, to comply with the rules.

Thus, our analysis of cloud computing governance needs first to address in more detail these two issues. What kind(s) of structure might be perceived as having legitimate authority to regulate cloud activities; and how can the governance system be made effective?

2.3 Legitimacy and cloud governance

A governance system is legitimate if it is accepted by the relevant community as an appropriate mechanism for making rules to govern the activity, and the community also accepts that these rules are devised in an appropriate way. Both of these are important. If the community does not accept the rule-maker's authority it is irrelevant that the rules were developed through appropriate procedures and make suitable provision for the regulated activity. Conversely, a rule-maker whose authority is widely accepted will still fail to achieve governance if the rules themselves were produced in an arbitrary fashion or contain provisions which have no meaning for the regulated community.

A high level of voluntary obedience to rules, which is essential for any system to be effective in governing, derives from this acceptance of legitimacy:

All regulators, but particularly non-state regulators, need legitimacy because it is a critical element in motivating behavioural responses. They require not only that others accept them, but that they will change their behaviour because of what of the organizations or standards say. Unlike state-based regulators, whose actions are supported by law, non-state regulators cannot necessarily rely on the authority of law to motivate people to behave, or derive their legitimacy from their position in a wider legal order and constitutional settlement. They have to create the motivation for compliance or change in some other way.[25]

Black identifies four different ways in which a regulator can claim legitimacy: by asserting that it is established on a constitutionally sound footing; that the application of its rules achieves justice; that it has a democratic mandate to regulate; and that it performs its regulatory function effectively.[26]

The first three of these are all connected through the community of those who perceive themselves as having a stake in cloud computing activities. If the constitution of the governance body includes representation for all parts of that community, then the

---

[24] Marsden n. 2, 222.

[25] Julia Black, 'Constructing and Contesting Legitimacy and Accountability in Polycentric Regulatory Regimes' (2008) 2 *Regulation & Governance* 137, 148. See also 144: 'In a governance or regulatory context, a statement that a regulator is "legitimate" means that it is perceived as having a right to govern both by those it seeks to govern and those on behalf of whom it purports to govern.'

[26] Black, (2008) 2 *Regulation & Governance* 145. Black notes that this last claim, although generally not accepted by political and legal commentators, is often of real practical importance in establishing legitimacy (146).

community as a whole is more likely to accept its legitimacy. Rules produced by such a representative body are more likely to do justice as between the members of the community than rules produced by only one section of the community.[27] And proper community representation remedies the 'democratic deficit',[28] which is often suggested as the primary reason why non-state regulators lack legitimacy.

However, actually substantiating these legitimacy claims will be complex in practice because the cloud community is extremely diverse. At a minimum it consists of service providers, customers, individuals whose data is processed in the cloud, and states. Even within these sub-communities it is possible to identify further divisions; as examples, service providers who customize and re-sell cloud services have different interests from those who own and operate core cloud platforms, and major corporates who negotiate individual relationships with service providers are quite different from individuals and businesses who use standardized or off-the-shelf services. When devising a cloud governance model it will, therefore, be necessary to seek acceptance from each of these communities individually.

Different communities will inevitably require different approaches. Because national law cannot claim legitimacy to regulate the whole of a transnational activity, as explained in Section 2.1, a coherent governance system for the cloud will require the establishment of one or more non-state bodies. It seems clear that the major cloud service providers will play a large part in establishing governance organizations and their rule-setting. They will accept the system's legitimacy for this reason, and also because they have consented to it as rule-maker. This will not necessarily be true, however, for smaller service providers, and so thought will need to be given to the best method of securing their representation and consent.

So far as customers are concerned, consent (eg by agreeing in their cloud contracts to abide by the rules of the governance body) will not be sufficient on its own to secure legitimacy. In most cases there will be no opportunity for them to do anything other than consent if they wish to receive the services. Customers, therefore, need some involvement in setting the constitution and establishing the rules for governance, and this will need to be done in a way which represents the interests of potential future customers as well as existing customers.

Satisfying the legitimacy claims of individuals and states is likely to be the most challenging task for cloud governance. It is plausible to argue that states represent their citizens, and thus those individuals whose data will be processed in the cloud, so that it would be appropriate to concentrate on states and avoid the difficulties of representing individuals. But although this might address the first three of Black's legitimacy issues effectively[29] there is a risk that it might impair the governance system's functional legitimacy, which derives from the appropriateness and effectiveness of its rules. If these do not provide good solutions to the problems which they are intended to solve, there is a risk that the community will cease to respect their authority.

As an example, states may have a very different view about how data ought to be used in social networks from the view (or more likely, views) espoused by the community of Facebook users. It is not self-evident that the state's perspective is the most appropriate one on which to base rules to control that use. Online social communities develop norms which are likely to be stronger than those set out in laws or regulation, which may act as barriers to the acceptance of legitimacy by those communities.[30] Cloud governance,

---

[27] Thus, for example, the rules applied by standard form cloud computing contracts will almost inevitably favour service providers at the expense of customers—see Ch. 3.
[28] Ibáñez n. 21, 153.   [29] See text to n. 26.   [30] Reed n. 5, Ch. 7.

therefore, needs some mechanisms for identifying and taking into account these issues when rule-making.

The difficulties facing cloud governance in achieving legitimacy are not unique, and are shared by other regulators:

Regulators may thus seek to build legitimacy by conforming to the claims of all or a selective group of legitimacy communities, or by attempting to create new legitimacy beliefs and new legitimacy communities.[31]

Thus, although the democratic representation of all communities in cloud governance is a counsel of perfection, trade-offs may need to be made in the interests of workability and effectiveness. There is no perfect model for achieving regulatory or governance legitimacy; indeed, perfection may be impossible to achieve. As Black notes:

the demands of legitimacy communities may well be directly opposed—to satisfy one will necessarily lead to dissatisfaction of the other. The incompatibility of democratically rooted claims relating to representation and membership with functionally rooted legitimacy claims relating to efficiency or expertise provides a good example.[32]

And:

Actions that organizations may need to take to render them legitimate for one legitimacy community can be in direct opposition to those they need to adopt to satisfy another. Moreover, attempts to render them accountable may face an 'accountability trilemma:' they are ignored, co-opted, or destroy that which it is they seek to make accountable.[33]

Where representation of particular sub-communities in the governance system is not practicable, accountability is often suggested as way of achieving legitimacy within those groups. Accountability requires a decision-maker to explain how it arrived at its decision, which in turn permits those affected by the decision to question the justifications or challenge the outcome. The prerequisite for accountability is transparency,[34] which according to Hale:

has become the international community's standard response to accountability concerns at international institutions, appearing in the pronouncements of government and international officials, corporate executives, and activists alike.[35]

Transparency requires a governance body to disclose all the information which is necessary for its legitimacy community to determine if it is acting properly. It confers on that community, at least in theory, 'the ability to know what an actor is doing and the ability to make that actor do something else'.[36]

Hale argues that transparency, on its own, goes a substantial distance towards holding a transnational actor to account. The three mechanisms of market pressure, public criticism, and internal norms, act as powerful enforcement mechanisms in many cases. Market pressure works through the decisions of suppliers and customers; in the cloud context, customers will be more likely to choose a service provider which is subject to a legitimate and effective governance system, and suppliers will tend to choose their governance system, or improve the existing system if there is no choice, in order to attract customers. Public criticism acts intangibly, but there is evidence that it works to

---

[31] Black n. 25, 147.　　[32] Black n. 25, 153.　　[33] Black n. 25, 157.
[34] Ibáñez n. 21, 153.
[35] Thomas N Hale, 'Transparency, Accountability, and Global Governance' (2008) 14 *Global Governance* 73.
[36] Hale, 'Transparency, Accountability, and Global Governance' (2008) 14 *Global Governance* 75.

change behaviour.[37] The internal norms of a regulator require it to act in a legitimate manner, and the self-reflection which such organizations necessarily engage in leads them to adopt good practices.[38] These mechanisms are potentially backed up by external enforcement mechanisms, such as judicial review,[39] although its effectiveness for transnational governance is limited by jurisdictional difficulties.[40]

All this tells us that although accountability can be an effective way for a cloud governance body to validate at least some of its legitimacy claims, there is no single answer as to how it can be achieved. Because accountability is a dialectic relationship with the various communities who have a stake in governance, the form of accountability must vary depending on the content of that dialogue.[41] The discourse between the governance body and a state which is concerned about the privacy of its citizens will be very different from the discourse with cloud users who are concerned about their ability to migrate to a new service, and the ways in which each might hold the body to account are similarly different.

2.4 Effective governance

2.4.1 Legitimate rule-making

In any governance system there is a risk that rule-making will, in effect, be taken over by the most powerful groups. This is a criticism often levelled at governance via private bodies:

> As in other social spaces, order in cyberspace serves mainly the interests of those who establish the rules, principles, norms, and values of such order. And this represents the main limit of [transnational private governance] in electronic markets. Broader socioeconomic concerns and interests are not necessarily embedded in the order promoted by major players in cyberspace.[42]

The most powerful group in any cloud computing governance system will be the service providers. They have a level of technical knowledge which other groups cannot match, and will, therefore, understand best what can and cannot be achieved by regulation, and what the consequences of regulation are likely to be. On most issues the interests of providers are likely to be closely aligned, while the groupings of customers, individuals, and states are likely to take divergent positions. Any cloud governance system's rule-making is, thus, likely to be controlled, in practice if not in theory, by service providers.

This leads to the risk that the rules will favour the interests of service providers, even if the providers do not consciously intend them to do so. It is also likely that the rule-making calculus will be utilitarian in nature, deciding for or against a particular rule on a cost-benefit basis. Brownsword points out the dangers of a utilitarian approach, where any minority's

---

[37] Hale cites the World Bank Inspection Panel, pointing out that the mere release of information was sufficient to change behaviour in over half of the cases examined, and to produce substantial change in a quarter of them—'Transparency, Accountability, and Global Governance' (2008) 14 *Global Governance* 83–5. See also the series of reversals of privacy policy by SaaS provider Facebook, following widespread public criticism and specific interventions by regulators on both sides of the Atlantic—Chris Reed, n. 5, 213–14.

[38] Hale, 'Transparency, Accountability, and Global Governance' (2008) 14 *Global Governance* 82.

[39] Daithí Mac Síthigh, 'Datafin to Virgin Killer: Self-regulation and Public Law', Norwich Law School Working Paper 09/02, <http://ssrn.com/abstract=1374846>.

[40] Black n. 25, 143.   [41] See further Black n. 25, 149–52.   [42] Ibáñez n. 21, 147.

claims are at risk of being overridden in the interests of the greater good.[43] If this occurs, then that minority, and perhaps other groups affected by the rules, are likely to deny that those rules are a legitimate basis for regulating their use of the cloud. This results in pressure to replace it with some other system, most likely that of national law.

Brownsword proposes that the proper approach is that of a 'community of rights', where 'the substantive moral approach embedded is rights-led, being committed to the protection and promotion of individual rights'.[44] If this is achieved, regulation which has been devised in accordance with the proper procedures of the regulatory system is likely to be accepted as legitimate. However, mere proceduralism is not enough on its own:

> members will need to be satisfied that the regulators have made a conscientious and good faith attempt to set a standard that is in line with their best understanding of the community's rights commitments. Regulators do not have to claim that the standard set is right; but, before a procedural justification is accepted, regulators must be demonstrably trying to do the right thing relative to the community's particular moral commitments.[45]

This tells us that legitimate rule-making requires there to be an embedded commitment to respect the rights of all community members, most probably in the constitution of the governance body. It also requires rule-making procedures which adequately represent and take account of all members of the community, particularly the weakest and most diverse membership groups. But procedural compliance alone cannot demonstrate the legitimacy which derives from a community of rights ethos—this must be both embedded in its constitution and demonstrated in day-to-day practice. Thus the content of the rules, in terms of the fairness of the balance they strike between community members, plays as vital a role as procedural fairness.

2.4.2 Meaningful rules

Rule content, as well as constitution and procedure, is an element of the legitimacy of regulation. To be effective, the rules need to have sufficient normative force that they are obeyed by the overwhelming majority of those subject to the regulation because the costs of enforcement, in terms of policing and imposing sanctions, become insupportable if the majority do not comply with the rules voluntarily. For the rules to have normative force they must have meaning for their addressees, which requires them to be understandable, capable of being obeyed, and likely actually to achieve some purpose which the addressees perceive to be in accordance with the regulatory aims.[46] And, of course, the aims themselves need also to have meaning for the regulated community.

Cloud governance will produce two main types of regulation: rules and guidelines which relate to the technical working of cloud services; and regulations which define the relationships between members of the cloud community and attempt to solve disputes between them. The former are likely always to be meaningful, but achieving the aim of meaningfulness for the second group of rules is more challenging. Sometimes there may be overlap between the two types.

---

[43] Roger Brownsword, *Rights, Regulation and the Technological Revolution* (Oxford: Oxford University Press, 2008), 22–3.
[44] Brownsword, n. 43, 24.   [45] Brownsword, n. 43, 127.
[46] See Reed n. 5, Ch. 2—other reasons for potential meaninglessness are identified there, but these are unlikely to occur in the rules produced by a co-regulatory cloud governance system.

Technical regulation will usually consist of highly detailed rules,[47] and so at first sight it might be thought that they risk being overly complex and, thus, difficult to understand. However, the process through which they are likely to be devised avoids this pitfall, and also ensures that the rules can be obeyed and are likely to achieve their aims. Rules of this kind are usually devised and modified through continual discussion between the regulator and those to whom the regulation applies. In the cloud context, this group would be the cloud service providers and representatives of their major customers. The discussion proceeds via a series of regulatory conversations,[48] through which the regulatees negotiate the content and application of the rules with the regulator. These conversations are meaningful because the regulatory model generates an interpretive community,[49] which consists of the regulator together with those specialists within each regulated entity who work on regulatory compliance and have a deep understanding of the issues involved and the existing rules. This conversational model of regulation does not seek to establish a fixed rule-set, but rather treats the achievement of the regulatory objectives as a moving target which requires constant adjustment of the rules to take account of new technologies, behaviours, business models, and other relevant factors.

The aim of this process is to produce rules which describe as precisely as possible the conduct required from regulatees, reducing to a minimum the need for judgement or discretion on the part of both regulatee and regulator when assessing compliance. This works for technical regulation because compliance often needs to be achieved via the computing code which providers and customers use to control their cloud interactions or cloud use.[50] For example, data confidentiality can be achieved via encryption code rather than relying on normative rules.

Of course, there will necessarily be some ambiguity about how these regulatory obligations should be transposed into code, but ambiguities can be resolved through regulatory conversations. Enforcement discretion can also be used.[51] Admittedly, the meaning in practice of the rules may differ from their wording, but this is not objectionable because, through the interpretive community, regulatees know the difference between the wording of the rule and the requirements for its practical implementation and can, therefore, conduct themselves accordingly.

However, it is far from certain that this model is effective where the rules are attempting instead to describe how regulatees *ought* to behave rather than prescribe what they *must* do. Our second category of rules, which aim to define the relationships between members of the cloud community and solve disputes between them, is clearly normative rather than prescriptive, and here the conversational rule-making model fails.

Imagine that the interpretive community which devises the technical rules is also tasked with producing the normative rules. Immediately, we see that the community needs to be extended to include those others, in particular individuals and states, who have a stake in the content of the rules. Although states might be able to participate in the regulatory conversations, individuals are in no position to do so directly. Perhaps

---

[47] Though it is, of course, possible to deal with these matters by principles-based rules, leaving it to the regulatee to translate the obligation into detailed implementation via its internal governance mechanisms—see John Braithwaite, 'Rules and Principles: A Theory of Legal Certainty' (2002) 27 *Austl J Leg Phil* 47. This approach usually requires subsequent regulator approval and/or audit of the implementation.

[48] Julia Black, 'Talking About Regulation' (1998) *Public Law* 77.

[49] Julia Black, *Rules and Regulators* (Oxford: Clarendon Press, 1997), 30–7.

[50] This is a typical example of code acting as law—see Lawrence Lessig, *Code and Other Laws of Cyberspace* (New York: Basic Books, 1999).

[51] Malcolm Sparrow, *The Regulatory Craft* (Washington: The Brookings Institution, 2000).

their representatives[52] might be involved in the conversations, but they will often be less knowledgeable than the other players and, thus, at a disadvantage when deciding if the rules are appropriate.

A second difficulty is that an interpretive community whose focus is on producing technical rules is likely to approach normative rules in the same way that it approaches technical rules, that is by attempting to express them in precise and objective terms. This results in regulation which is textually complex, and which requires constant amendment and updating to account for changes in technology or the business environment. This form of rule-making is inappropriate if the rules are addressed to individuals or other players who are unlikely to be able to understand them fully. Such rules are likely to be meaningless to most of their addressees, and, thus, less likely to be effective.[53]

If the addressees of a rule are not members of the interpretive community then it is no longer possible to remedy any mismatch between the law's aims and its actual text through the use of enforcement discretion. The absence of regulatory conversation means that the enforcer is able only to guess as to how best to exercise enforcement discretion to achieve the law's aims, because the position of the rule's addressees is unknown. Because of the complexity of cloud computing, that guess is more likely to be wrong than in the physical world. Those who are attempting to frame their activities so as to comply with the law will have no easy way to discover how it is likely to be enforced, and this will inevitably produce a reduction in the law's normative effect.

A further risk of rules which are too complex to be understandable by those to whom they apply is that they may be ineffective in achieving their normative aims. Those who are attempting to comply with the rule need do no more than tick off their compliance with the various detailed obligations, even if this results in their behaving in a way which does not accord with what the rule-maker was aiming at.

Finally, it is a fundamental assumption when regulating via an interpretive community that there should be fluidity in the governance rule-sets, allowing them to evolve rapidly as circumstances change. There must be real doubt whether it is appropriate to set normative obligations in this way. How the members of the cloud community *ought* to behave towards each other is not something which is likely to change rapidly, unless some disruptive technology emerges which completely alters the fundamental basis of their relationships.[54] But if the normative obligation is embedded in detailed regulation, which requires regulatees to comply with the detailed obligations rather than the wider norm, frequent change will be inevitable if the rule-set is still to embody the norm.

This leads us to the conclusion that the second category of normative rules should at least be very different in form from those which regulate technical activities, and probably also that the rule-making process should be different. Normative regulation needs to be expressed in open-textured terms, using words like 'reasonable', 'fair', or 'necessary'. These concepts are used regularly in laws regulating human behaviour in the physical world, for example in relation to theft or negligence. There are few voices calling for these obligations to be explained in greater detail so as to reduce uncertainty.[55]

---

[52] For example, citizen advocacy groups such as EDRI (European Digital Rights), an association of privacy and digital civil rights associations, that meet EU officials and respond to consultations in an attempt to influence policy.

[53] See Reed n. 5, Ch. 8.

[54] A technology which rendered current encryption methods redundant would be such a disruptive force, requiring a complete reassessment of confidentiality and privacy relationships.

[55] Indeed, the apparent certainty of detailed regulation may be illusory—see the analysis in Reed n. 5, Ch. 8. And see also the argument that even regulation via an interpretive community can be more effective if the rules are expressed as general principles rather than detailed obligations—Braithwaite n. 47.

Cloud governance is likely to proceed primarily via the making of regulation, with compliance audited by service providers themselves or their professional advisers or independent experts.[56] Enforcement is likely to be in reaction to complaints by those affected, rather than as a result of direct monitoring by the governance body. This suggests that it is appropriate to deal with the issue of technical regulation by formulating precise rules, particularly as many elements of those rules will need to be implemented in code.[57]

However, I am strongly of the view that normative regulation should be devised by a more diversely representative group than technical regulation, and should be expressed in terms of principles. It is not appropriate to leave such regulation to the community of service providers and major users because their focus and interests will not be aligned with those of the wider community. As Ibáñez notes:

in broader social and political contexts, the limits of such private governance mechanisms are also very obvious: issues related to social concerns, economic inequalities, political legitimacy, and so on go well beyond the technical or economic functions fulfilled by those private actors at the transnational level.[58]

To be effective at regulating normative matters, a cloud governance mechanism needs to step into this wider arena and deal with those issues which concern the cloud community as a whole.

2.5 Enforcement

Enforcement is an important element of functional legitimacy, which derives from regulation which actually achieves its aims. A regulator which is otherwise accepted as having legitimate authority can easily lose that authority if it has no effective way of enforcing its rules. Conversely, a regulator which achieves a high level of compliance will enhance its legitimacy.[59] Enforcement is a particular problem with self-regulatory governance systems because they tend to lack coercive mechanisms to sanction rule-breaking.[60]

Functional legitimacy demands coercive means of enforcing regulations, even if that coercion is used only as a last resort. This might be achieved in three ways.

Some governance bodies can enforce their rules directly because they control some critical element of the regulated system. A clear example is the Internet Council for Assigned Names and Numbers (ICANN), whose Uniform Domain Name Dispute Resolution Policy[61] enforces decisions simply via modifying database registries.

---

[56] See EU Article 29 Working Party, *Opinion 05/2012 on Cloud Computing*, WP 196 01037/12/EN (1 July 2012), 4.2.

[57] Not all such regulation will necessarily be implemented through coding, however. For example, security requirements may involve not just technical implementation but also organizational measures regarding the provider's internal policies and procedures, to restrict access to users' data only to employees whose work requires them to have such access, to ensure such employees are vetted and subject to confidentiality obligations in their contracts, and so on.

[58] Ibáñez n. 21, 145.

[59] See Black n. 25, 146: 'the extent to which regulators are perceived as legitimate is not only based on cognitive and normative assessments, but on pragmatic assessments. Pragmatic legitimacy is often excluded from legal and political science accounts of legitimacy (indeed seen as an "illegitimate" form of legitimacy), but pragmatic legitimacy can be significant in practice in the creation of legitimacy for regulatory organizations, state or non-state, even though it may be normatively undesirable.'

[60] See the proposed reforms to the Press Complaints Commission, which aim to implement ' "ladders" of sanctions which will provide credible remedies'—third witness statement of Lord Black of Brentwood to the Leveson Inquiry, para. 23 (<http://www.levesoninquiry.org.uk/wp-content/uploads/2012/06/Submission-by-Lord-Black-of-Brentwood1.pdf>).

[61] <www.icann.org/udrp/udrp-policy-24oct99.htm>.

A second example is eBay, whose terms and conditions grant buyers a right to a refund in certain circumstances.[62] eBay decides these disputes itself, and implements its decisions by refunding the buyer and issuing a chargeback to the seller's PayPal account. However, the distributed nature of cloud computing means that there is no common technology which is controlled by only one organization. Thus, cloud governance will need to look elsewhere for a coercive enforcement mechanism.

The second possibility is to use contract as an enforcement mechanism. If those subject to cloud governance enter into a contract with the governance body under which they agree to comply with its regulations, any regulatory breach will also be a breach of contract. In effect this co-opts the coercive power of states, by using their national courts to seek enforcement sanctions.[63] Enforcement via an action for breach of contract has two main limitations though. The first is that it is hard to create contractual relationships with all those who are subject to the regulation. Service providers will probably sign up to the governance system in order to enhance the confidence of their customers, and governance rules can be made indirectly binding on customers if service providers include in their own terms and conditions an obligation that customers should comply with the regulation.[64] This would deal with the vast majority of regulatory breaches. The second limitation, which is more serious, is the problem of providing a remedy to individuals who suffer as a result of the regulatory breach. Even if individuals could enforce directly the contractual obligations of providers and customers,[65] in practice they are unlikely to have the economic resources to litigate, particularly if the defendant is a foreign corporation. The governance body can sue to enforce the rules, but has suffered no economic loss itself and, thus, cannot claim substantive damages. Such an action might secure an injunction ordering future compliance, but would not give an adequate remedy to the affected individual.

The final possibility is to persuade states to enforce the regulation directly through their own legal systems, or to grant the governance body the right to do this. The former might be achievable through legislation which recognizes the governance regulation directly, or more likely through indirect enforcement for breach of some more general national law. As examples, the UK Office of Fair Trading has power to act on 'super-complaints' from consumer protection organizations[66] and the US Federal Trade Commission[67] has powers to seek injunctions prohibiting traders from acting in breach of the rules with which they have publicly undertaken to comply. The concept of devolving enforcement powers to a regulator which is not an organ of the state is widely accepted, for example in legislation which sets up a regulator for financial services and gives the regulator direct enforcement powers. In all these cases, though, the regulator is purely domestic, and in most the regulator is established via primary legislation. It would be, to say the least, unusual for a state to confer enforcement powers on a foreign

---

[62] For the UK, these are set out at <http://pages.ebay.co.uk/help/policies/buyer-protection.html>, but very similar policies are applied by the other eBay sites.

[63] This is quite different from the way that ICANN and eBay use contract law. The main role of contracts there is to protect the system against claims in national courts by dissatisfied subjects of decisions, rather than to make those decisions enforceable. See, for example, *Bragg v Linden Research Inc.* 487 F Supp 2d 593 (ED Pa 2007), where the main thrust of Linden's argument was that Bragg had agreed contractually not to dispute findings under the Second Life rules.

[64] And it might even be feasible to use contractual doctrines of third-party rights to make such obligations directly enforceable by the regulator.

[65] For example, under the UK Contracts (Rights of Third Parties Act) 1990, s. 1, by virtue of expressing that they were intended to benefit the class of potentially affected individuals.

[66] Under the UK Enterprise Act 2002, s. 11.

[67] Under the US Federal Trade Commission Act, 15 USC § 45.

regulatory body, which is what a cloud governance body would be for all but the state in which it is established.[68]

At present, then, contractual enforcement seems the most likely route for cloud governance to take. The potential costs of operating such an enforcement mechanism are not trivial, but the costs of failing to secure legitimacy are likely to be greater.

3. The Route to Co-regulation

From a lawyer's perspective,[69] the most effective solution would be a single transnational governance system for all cloud activities, worldwide. This system might consist of a unitary governance body, or a group of governance bodies each regulating different aspects of the cloud and cooperating closely. The starting point has to be non-state institutions because of the difficulties of setting up state-representative bodies. However, states will need to be represented for the legitimacy reasons explained in Section 1, and so these will be co-regulatory bodies.

The journey from self- to co-regulation is a complex one, but the road has been travelled previously. In 1990, the domain name addressing system for the Internet was, essentially, managed by a single individual, Dr John Postel of the University of Southern California. Today, it is managed by ICANN, a not-for-profit corporation, under a constitution which affords representation to the global Internet community.[70]

Starting in 1993, the management of domain names transitioned to the Internet Assigned Numbers Authority (IANA) controlled by Postel, working with Network Solutions Inc. (NSI), which was contractually responsible to the US government. There was clear conflict over policy. As part of the power struggle, Postel created the International Ad Hoc Committee, which immediately faced opposition from Internet users based on its lack of legitimacy. At the same time, there was also political concern, both domestically in the US and internationally, about the role of NSI.

The ultimate resolution was the transfer of all policy matters to ICANN, established as a Californian not-for-profit corporation with by-laws and a governance structure devised by Postel as embodying the consensus of the global Internet community. ICANN soon faced further legitimacy challenges, both from non-US governments and the various non-state bodies such as the International Telecommunications Union, which had an interest in the domain name system, and from Internet users who had no representation on ICANN. Concerns arose about the choice of ICANN's directors, who had been selected as suitable persons by Postel and the US government but were now a self-perpetuating oligarchy, selecting their replacements as the directors of corporations normally do. There was further conflict over country code domains because states had a

---

[68] Although the cloud regulator would be regulating transnationally, it would need a legal personality for employing staff, making contracts to receive services, and so on. To achieve this it would need to incorporate in a state.

[69] Of course, this is not the only appropriate perspective. Political, commercial, operational, and perhaps even philosophical perspectives might produce a different ideal.

[70] The description that follows is highly simplified. For more detail, see Jonathan Weinberg, 'ICANN and the Problem of Legitimacy' (2000) 50 *Duke LJ* 187; Viktor Mayer-Schönberger and Malte Ziewitz, 'Jefferson Rebuffed: The United States and the Future of Internet Governance' (2006–07) 8 *Colum Sci & Tech L Rev* 188; Stephen M Ryan, Raymond A Plzak, and John Curran, 'Legal and Policy Aspects of Internet Number Resources' (2008) 24 *Santa Clara Computer & High Tech LJ* 335; Jay P Kesan and Andres A Gallo, 'Pondering the Politics of Private Procedures: The case of ICANN' (2008) 4 *JL & Pol'y for Info Soc'y* 345.

clear interest in setting policies for those domains but ICANN retained *de facto* control over them via the root servers.

The current regulatory settlement seems to have resolved these tensions in five ways. First, ICANN introduced public participation in its rule-making. Proposals were released for consultation, and formal processes were established for promulgating rules. Second, an internal appeal process against ICANN rulings was instituted, as was an independent external review of policy by a panel of senior lawyers. Third, stakeholder representation was introduced via representative bodies, Supporting Organizations which represent regional Internet registries, country code registries and commercial users (corporations, commercial registries, and intellectual property (IP) rights owners), and a Governmental Advisory Committee to represent states. All these have a role in selecting directors. Fourth, an Ombudsman was established to review policy and decisions on a far wider basis than the external review process. Finally, ICANN introduced transparency and accountability measures, most notably the publication of a wide range of internal documents and policy change proposals, and consultation on policy and regulation with affected sectors of the Internet community.[71]

These reforms appear to have solved ICANN's legitimacy problems, and there have been only minor changes since.

From this history we can draw a number of lessons about how a co-regulatory cloud computing body could achieve legitimacy. First, its constitution is important. Legitimacy derives from the acceptance of authority by those subject to the regulation, and, thus, requires representation of all interested parties. I suggested in Section 2.3 that there are four main groups which require representation:

1. Service providers, which comprise a comparatively small group and are easy to identify. Initially, it would seem appropriate for the largest players to be represented directly, and for an organization to be established to represent the smaller service providers, which are unlikely to have the resources available to take part in governance directly. Over time, direct representation should be abandoned, to avoid the perception that the largest service providers have a privileged position in policymaking and devising regulation.

2. Customers, which as a group are far more heterogeneous. One or more representative organizations will need to be set up, making sure that the divergent interests of different types of customer (private and public sector, large organization and SME/individual, etc.) are properly taken into account.

3. States, which have the dual function of protecting their own public interest and also the individual interests of their citizens. Individual representation would be unwieldy here, and some equivalent of the ICANN Governmental Advisory Committee would seem appropriate.

4. Individuals, whose data is processed in the cloud or whose interests are affected by cloud computing activities. It is unlikely that a properly representative organization of such a diverse group could be established immediately, but there are bodies whose remit is the protection of individual rights, such as consumer protection organizations and privacy regulators, who might be capable of cooperating to evolve an appropriate surrogate.

The main functions of these representative organizations, as is the case for ICANN, should be to appoint the directors of the co-regulatory body and to be consulted on policy and rule changes.

---

[71] ICANN accountability and transparency frameworks and principles (January 2008).

The second lesson is that legitimacy is enhanced by high levels of transparency and accountability. Transparency requires the co-regulatory body to publish rule-making proposals and policy in draft, together with minutes of its decision-making committees and other relevant information. This is to allow the regulated community to understand not only what the policy and regulation are, but also how they were arrived at. Transparency on its own achieves a degree of accountability because decision-makers are identified and know they will have to defend their decisions. Accountability is strengthened by having processes for challenging decisions on both policy and regulation. Whether a formal process for independent audit or review is necessary will only become apparent over time, but many regulators find it useful to commission regular independent reviews and publish the findings to the regulated community.

I also argued in Section 2 that there are two further elements relating to legitimacy which a co-regulatory body needs to achieve. The first is to make policy and regulation which are meaningful to the regulated community, so that members understand their aims and how they should act so as to achieve compliance. This requires the regulatory arm of the co-regulatory body to consider who is addressed by its rules. Technical standards are addressed to technicians, and so can be drafted in the kind of precise and detailed terms which enable them to be implemented via technology. Normative rules, on the other hand, attempt to modify human behaviours, and, therefore, need to be addressed to those whose behaviours are in question. This demands principles-based regulation rather than checkbox compliance lists.

The second of these elements is that the regulation emanating from the co-regulatory body should, by and large, be effective at achieving its regulatory aims. If the authority of the regulator is accepted by the community and its rules have meaning for community members, a high level of voluntary compliance can be expected. Nonetheless, there will be occasions when regulatees are in breach, either through inadvertence or deliberately, and regulation which is not enforced soon loses its normative force and, eventually, its legitimacy. Because any cloud regulator will be a transnational private organization, applying its rules globally, it is unrealistic to expect states to legislate to make those rules binding. Instead, contractual obligations will need to be imposed on those subject to the regulation, and actions brought in national courts to enforce breaches of contract. Service providers can be made to sign up to contracts with the regulator as a condition of participating in the system, and, thus, being able to advertise that they are regulated and comply. The regulator can also require providers to include clauses in their contracts which oblige their customers to comply with that regulation which imposes obligations on customers. This will capture the vast majority of regulatees against whom enforcement action might be required. The biggest challenge facing any cloud regulator will be to fund an effective enforcement campaign, as sporadic enforcement is usually perceived as largely symbolic, reducing the normative force of regulation.

4. Governance Issues

A co-regulatory system for cloud governance can only be successful if it deals with *all* the important aspects of cloud computing which require governance oversight. This is because gaps will inevitably be filled from some other source, perhaps private contracts or state legislation, either of which would necessarily lead to a lack of uniformity of governance rules. The CIF and other self-regulators currently only deal with some of the elements of governance, and if these organizations were to evolve into a transnational co-regulator they would need to expand the scope of their activities. What would they need to include?

The discussion of legitimacy in Section 2 tells us that the governance rules for cloud need to reflect the needs and interests of the wider cloud community, and can only be devised appropriately by the community itself. It is, thus, not appropriate here to lay down the precise solutions which a cloud governance system should be required, at least in my opinion, to embody in its rules.

It is, though, both appropriate and useful to pull together the governance issues which have been identified in the other chapters of this book to produce a minimum list of issues which I would suggest to a cloud governance body as requiring addressing. Rather than simply summarizing those issues, I have attempted to synthesize them under six main headings: transparency and accountability; scope and quality of service; standards; ownership and control; power imbalance; and regulatory compliance.

4.1 Transparency and accountability

We saw previously in this chapter that transparency plays a major part in holding rule-makers to account. There are similar justifications for imposing transparency obligations on members of the cloud community. As we shall see in what follows, transparency plays a fundamental role in all the other governance issues.

Providers are already subject to some explicit transparency obligations under existing law. Chapter 13 noted that, under the E-Commerce Directive,[72] a provider of information society services to EU residents is obliged to disclose to customers its identity, address, and contact information, details of trade registration and/or regulatory supervision, and its VAT number if it provides taxable services. The Consumer Rights Directive[73] imposes further transparency obligations on those who use distance means to sell goods and services to EU consumer residents. Cloud providers who sign up EU-resident customers online have a legal obligation to comply with these provisions.

Doubtless, there are similar transparency obligations, though differing in detail, in the laws of some other states. There may also be different kinds of transparency obligations which apply to the supply of cloud services into particular states.[74] It is not uncommon for the law to demand some level of transparency, but there is no global consistency in what is required.

This inconsistency suggests that there is a need for at least guidelines, and perhaps even regulation, on the minimum level of transparency which is needed to comply with the common core of obligations imposed by national laws. Guidelines for particular countries or regions, such as the EU, would also be helpful to providers. This is exactly the kind of activity that a cloud governance body is well qualified to undertake.

It should also be apparent from the other chapters of this book that transparency plays an important part in the other elements of governance which are discussed below. In many cases, the issue which needs to be resolved is that there is a mismatch between the expectations of provider and customer, and the information exchanged between them is what largely shapes those expectations. In others, one party, normally the customer, requires information about the cloud service in order to meet its obligations to regulators and third parties.

[72] Directive 2000/31/EC of the European Parliament and of the Council of 8 June 2000 on certain legal aspects of information society services, in particular electronic commerce, in the internal market.
[73] Directive 2011/83/EU on consumer rights, repealing and replacing the Distance Selling Directive, Directive 97/7/EC of the European Parliament and of the Council of 20 May 1997 on the protection of consumers in respect of distance contracts.
[74] For example, where the delivery of cloud services may involve exports of personal data to countries that are not deemed to provide an 'adequate' level of protection for such data. See Chapter 10.

This need for transparency is particularly obvious in relation to the scope and quality of service which the provider is obliged to deliver and the customer is entitled to expect. All providers tell the customer at least something about this matter, but the detail and quality of explanation is highly variable. One important function of a governance system is, therefore, to educate providers about the information which they ought to disclose to enable their customers to understand the service properly.

Some of this information is quite obvious. For commercial reasons, if for no others, providers will explain the main functionality of the service and at least something about the performance characteristics which the customer can expect. There will also be disclosure about the technical standards which the provider uses, though sometimes less than the customer needs to know.

However, other transparency issues in relation to scope and quality of service are less obvious. Chapter 13, Section 4.1 tells us that the main performance obligation of a provider is to supply the service using reasonable care and skill. That chapter also tells us that, at least as against consumer customers in the EU, the provider cannot exclude or limit liability for breach of this obligation,[75] and that the test for how much care and skill is required is based on the reasonable expectations of the customer.[76] But the level of control which the provider has over performance is very much determined by how far parts of the service are actually undertaken by other providers. Disclosing the extent of this layering helps to explain the nature and limitations of the service, and, thus, to shape the customer's expectations as to the care and skill which the provider will use. How to explain these matters, and how much information to disclose about potentially commercially sensitive relationships, is a difficult matter. Here, a cloud governance body can make recommendations and issue guidelines which reflect the best compromise between the interests of the parties involved.

A similar transparency question relates to monitoring of the customer's content by the provider. Chapter 3, Section 3.2.5 reported that providers generally undertake in the terms of service that they will not monitor content, though monitoring to check for compliance with Acceptable Use Policies is becoming more common. Chapter 11 also tells us that there are circumstances when providers may be required by law to undertake monitoring or to assist with monitoring by law enforcement authorities. Sometimes, they will be obliged to keep this monitoring secret. And Chapter 7, Section 4 explains that providers who gain sufficient knowledge of and control over content which is personal data may thereby subject themselves to regulatory obligations under data protection law by becoming data controllers. There is a delicate balance to be struck here which can only be achieved via rules or guidance produced by a governance body which legitimately represents all those whose interests are engaged.

Issues about the ownership and control of information uploaded to or generated in the cloud are immensely complex. The starting points are set by IP laws, but it is notorious that these laws are ill-adapted to cyberspace.[77] Uncertainties can be resolved through contractual terms, but only if the issues are properly understood. Because these terms are normally drafted by providers there is a clear risk that they may be held unenforceable under unfair terms legislation if they do not strike an appropriate balance between the interests engaged. Transparency in terms of what uses are to be made of customer information, and how far the provider proposes to derive and use information for its own purposes, can help to produce contractual relationships which strike the proper balance.

---

[75] See Chapter 13, Section 4.   [76] See Chapter 13, Section 4.1.
[77] See, for example, Chris Reed n. 5, Ch. 7.

It is clear that the current state of cloud contracts has not yet achieved this balance. Chapters 3 and 4 have explained that there is a consensus in cloud contracts about the ownership and control of the IP-protected information which customers and providers bring to the cloud, but little if any provision for who owns and can use derived information and metadata. Providers obviously need a licence to process customer information for the purpose of providing the service, but as Chapter 3, Section 3.2.6 shows, the current state of drafting for cloud contracts tends to grant providers use rights which potentially go far beyond what is necessary, or what their customers would expect. Transparency on these issues will assist customers in making an informed choice and also shape their expectations. The result is likely to be a fairer allocation of rights and permissions between the parties, which, in turn, will reduce the risk that terms are unenforceable and, thus, increase certainty.

In Chapter 13, we saw that much of the *ex post* consumer protection law in the EU is concerned with correcting power imbalances in B2C relationships. Transparency about the scope and quality of the service, and the uses which the provider will make of the customer's information, shapes the expectations of consumers and informs them about the risks involved in entering into the transaction and using the cloud service. The underlying assumption of the law is, to a large extent, that power imbalance derives from information asymmetry, so that if consumers are properly informed about the nature of the transaction and its risks, and enter into it freely, the law will rarely step in to upset the contractual agreement.[78]

The difficulty is, of course, that providers are not consumers, and are, thus, unlikely to find it easy to recognize what consumers need to be told in order to achieve a fair and enforceable legal relationship with them. Guidelines from a properly representative governance body would assist greatly in improving this situation.

Finally, transparency is important for customers in helping them to achieve legal and regulatory compliance. This book has investigated data protection at some length, because it is perhaps the most difficult regulatory issue currently facing a large proportion of cloud users and providers. However, customers in particular regulated sectors will face different, though closely related, compliance problems. Financial services is a clear instance.

As a general observation, it should be obvious that a high level of transparency will be of real assistance to users in persuading regulators that compliance is actually happening. To give the simplest example, if the regulator's question is 'How are you looking after data security?' then the answer 'I don't know, my cloud provider deals with that' is unlikely to be helpful.

The questions of the need for transparency to assist data protection compliance which have been raised in Part III of this book are too numerous for all to be summarized here, but it is worth examining three examples as illustrations. First, the layering business model of the cloud is fundamentally at odds with the position adopted by EU data protection regulators that the use of sub-contractors by data processors should be disclosed to and consented to by the data controller.[79] Leaving aside the commercial sensitivities, actually achieving such disclosure and consent presents real practical difficulties because of the fluid structure of many cloud relationships. The result, as explained in Chapter 4, Section 5.3.2, is that providers are very reluctant to agree to provide the help that their customers need here. Second, data controllers need to know about any unauthorized access to or processing of personal data while in the cloud,[80] but again it has proved

---

[78] See Chapter 13, Section 2.   [79] See Chapter 8, Section 3.4.
[80] See Chapter 8, Section 3.3.

difficult to negotiate appropriate contractual provisions. And finally, personal data export restrictions mean there is a need for users to know and to control the geographical locations of processing.[81] All these transparency problems require collective solutions, adopted consistently in cloud relationships. These can only be achieved through discussion between providers, users, and regulators which identify and reach a compromise between the divergent interests at stake.

Regulatory compliance is also an important consideration for cloud service providers themselves. Chapter 11 investigated the problem of access to data by law enforcement agencies, and identified that there is a mismatch between the confidentiality and security obligations which providers owe to customers (or perhaps more accurately, which customers expect from providers) and the obligations of providers under national laws to permit access to data by law enforcement agencies. Chapters 3 and 4 examined the ways in which contractual terms deal with this issue and identified divergent approaches. Some providers undertake to respond only to court orders or search warrants, and include procedural safeguards to give customers the opportunity to appeal against them, while other providers are prepared to respond to requests for access even if they are under no obligation to comply, and without notifying their customers. The issue is further complicated by the layering of services, which raises a real possibility that a restrictive policy towards access on the part of one provider may be undermined by a more permissive policy of a sub-provider. At a minimum, customers need transparency about the approach which their provider will take,[82] and ideally about the existence and policies of sub-providers (which itself raises difficult governance issues as explained above).

There is also an arguable case for imposing at least some minimal transparency obligations on users. For example, providers have an interest in knowing whether they are processing personal data on behalf of their customers because this may subject them to data protection regulation.[83] Transparency would also benefit third parties whose information is held or processed by those customers, who may have an interest in understanding how the customer's cloud use affects the relationship.

Currently, these questions of transparency are left to individual provider and customer decision-making which, as this discussion has demonstrated, produces inconsistent and far from optimal results. In all the cases considered here, the appropriate level of transparency, and how it should be achieved, can only be decided by balancing the interests of those affected by the issue. Thus transparency is clearly best determined by negotiation within the cloud community, and a properly constituted and legitimate cloud governance system will be able to provide the forum for such discussions. Transparency obligations need to reflect the needs and interests of the wider cloud community, and so can only be devised appropriately by the community itself.

4.2 Scope and quality of service

As we have seen, most of the governance issues under this heading are primarily commercial matters, and transparency will resolve the majority of them. However, there are some areas where there is little consistency of approach among providers, but perhaps ought to be, and where understanding the interests involved and defining appropriate concepts is difficult. Here, it might be appropriate for a governance body to issue guidance to help in defining scope and quality, and in interpreting what it means in practice.

---

[81] See Chapter 10, Section 2.
[82] See, for example, Google's 'Transparency Report', discussed at Chapter 11, Section 7.
[83] See Chapters 7 and 8 for discussion of this issue.

As an example, Chapter 13, Section 4.1 notes that the obligation to provide the service using reasonable care and skill is extremely open-ended, and it is usually unclear what that means in terms of important issues such as data security and integrity. What are the steps a provider should take in respect of these matters, and how much responsibility should fall on the user? The law's answer is that this depends on the user's reasonable expectations, which are clearly affected by the provider's disclosures (see Section 4.1 above). But transparency does not solve the problem entirely—it is hard to argue that a provider who takes no care at all for data security and integrity is complying with its duty of care and skill, even if this refusal is disclosed to the customer.

Interestingly, there is a recognition in negotiated cloud contracts that data integrity is a shared responsibility,[84] whereas in non-negotiated contracts the practice seems to be for the provider to disclaim all responsibility for it.[85] Given that such a disclaimer may not be enforceable against an EU consumer, it seems reasonable to assert that providers do have some responsibility for this matter. But how much, and what are the customer's responsibilities? In the fullness of time, litigation might begin to answer these questions, but that is hardly a satisfactory position. Once again, a cloud governance body is an entirely appropriate forum for developing guidelines here, and such guidelines would be very likely to influence a court's judgment about the appropriate level of care and skill.

A second issue which is difficult to negotiate, and inappropriate to leave to provider terms alone, is that of data preservation and access on exit, coupled with the question whether providers should assist the customer to migrate to different data formats and standards. Should providers offer such assistance, and at what rates, and for how long? Again, a cloud governance body is far better placed to decide these matters than a court.

4.3 Standards

Standard setting, and the adoption of standards devised by other bodies, is a role which the potential forerunners of a cloud governance body already play. The CIF has established a Special Interest Group, Industry Standards for Cloud, whose remit is to monitor standards development, review standards proposals for workability, and produce a taxonomy of standards for use by the cloud community.[86] The Cloud Security Alliance has standards creation at the heart of its work, coordinated by its International Standardization Council.[87] Others are active in this field; the US National Institute of Standards and Technology (NIST) maintains a list of standards specific or relevant to cloud computing,[88] and cloud customer groups such as the Cloud Standards Customer Council[89] and Open Data Center Alliance[90] are also attempting to influence developments.

Many of the governance issues considered in this chapter can be resolved through the adoption of standards. The implementation of these standards in computing code

---

[84] See Chapter 4, Section 5.2.   [85] See Chapter 3, Section 3.2.1.

[86] <http://www.cloudindustryforum.org/cloud-sigs/industry-standards-for-cloud>.

[87] <https://cloudsecurityalliance.org/isc/>.

[88] At   <http://collaborate.nist.gov/twiki-cloud-computing/bin/view/CloudComputing/Standards Inventory#CloudAndWebServiceStandards>. The NIST has also produced a Standards Roadmap, <http://www.nist.gov/manuscript-publication-search.cfm?pub_id=909024>. Another compilation is at <http://cloud-standards.org/wiki/index.php?title=Main_Page>. Showing how much cloud standards is a moving target, even these lists are not complete, omitting efforts by the ITU <http://www.itu.int/en/ITU-T/jca/Cloud/Pages/default.aspx> and the IEEE <http://standards.ieee.org/develop/project/2301.html> and <http://standards.ieee.org/develop/project/2302.html>.

[89] <http://www.cloud-council.org/>—whose members include providers/integrators as well as customers.

[90] <http://www.opendatacenteralliance.org/aboutus>.

entrenches the rules of behaviour for the parties involved, and indeed can achieve an unambiguous rule-set with which it is impossible to fail to comply.[91] Governance through standards can solve, wholly or in part, otherwise contentious issues without the need for complex negotiation. As examples, we saw in Section 4.2 above that customers will need assistance in migrating from one service provider to another. Such migration is greatly eased by standards for the interoperability of services across different cloud plat-forms. Similarly, many of the difficult questions about data security and data protection compliance can be answered by appropriate security standards.[92]

But the process of setting standards also raises issues of competition law. Where stand-ards entrench technology which is protected by IP rights, this offers the rights owner the opportunity to extract excessive licence fees from standards users. As Chapter 12, Section 4.1.2 explains, the normal way of resolving this issue is by requiring licences to be granted on fair, reasonable, and non-discriminatory terms. But how are such terms to be devised? Governance systems can play a role here, because determining this question (and indeed, standards setting more generally) requires the interests of all those affected to be taken into account. A governance body which meets the legitimacy criteria dis-cussed in this chapter will necessarily represent such groups adequately, and is, thus, well placed to ensure that standards are developed and implemented in a way which does not give rise to anti-competitive behaviour.

4.4 Ownership and control

We saw in Section 4.1 of this chapter that most of the difficulties in determining who has the rights of ownership in and control over information can be 'solved' through transparency and appropriate contractual provisions. It is important to note, though, that these are only solutions in that they establish a legally binding allocation of those rights. Transparency and contract do not, without more, necessarily produce a fair and just allocation of rights.

Fairness and justice are important elements of any long-term trading or service rela-tionship. If they are not achieved, that relationship is likely to break down. The party in the strongest economic position, usually the cloud service provider, might achieve a short-term advantage by securing the greatest possible extent of ownership and use rights, but this is rarely in its interest when assessed over the lifetime of the relationship.

The difficulty is to decide what is fair and just, particularly as each party to a cloud relationship views the question from the perspective of its own interests. And neither is likely to give much thought to the interests of third parties, such as those whose personal or confidential information is being processed. This is where cloud governance comes in. As discussed in Section 2.4.1 of this chapter, legitimate rule-making or issuing of guid-ance by an appropriate constituted governance body will necessarily seek to balance the rights and interests of all those involved. It is likely to produce a fair and just solution, so long as all those affected are properly represented.

In addition to this moral argument in favour of governance action here, there are also utilitarian reasons why it is desirable. First, the transaction costs of negotiating owner-ship and use rights are substantial, particularly if there is no near-consensus starting point for those negotiations. In non-negotiable contracts, providers who claim more rights than users are comfortable with will be likely to lose customers to more generous

---

[91] See Lawrence Lessig, *Code and Other Laws of Cyberspace* (New York: Basic Books, 1999).
[92] See Chapter 8, Section 3.3.

providers. Some collective consensus on fairness and justice is likely to help avoid this problem. Second, those who feel taken advantage of are likely to seek help elsewhere, probably from their national government. Governments feel an obligation to protect their citizens against abuses of power, and so legislation is not unlikely. We saw in Section 2.1 of this chapter that national legislation is generally bad for the cloud because it tends to lead to inconsistent and contradictory rules which can only be complied with by partitioning the cloud geographically. Fairness and justice in rights allocation will help to avoid this potential disaster.

4.5 Power imbalance

The analysis in Chapter 3 indicates that cloud contracts vary widely in their terms. Unsurprisingly, most of them, particularly those in standard form, are drafted very much in favour of provider interests and are often silent on, or unfavourable to, the interests of customers. This leaves those contract terms open to national law challenge on the basis of unfairness or unconscionability, which creates a high level of uncertainty for both providers and their customers.[93] It is common for terms to be changeable by the provider with minimal, sometimes no, notice; the applicable law and jurisdiction is usually that of the provider rather than the customer; compulsory arbitration by a body in the provider's country is still common, though less so than previously; promises as to performance quality are rare, and exclusion of liability for mis- or non-performance is almost universal; and providers commonly require indemnification for a wide range of third-party claims, not merely matters like defamation or IP infringement which are indisputably the customer's responsibility to control. It is clear that there is a substantial power imbalance in favour of providers, and that providers are taking advantage of it in drafting their standard terms. Chapter 12 also tells us that providers can use their power in other ways, such as by adopting proprietary data formats which impede data portability and make transfer to another provider difficult.

Chapter 13 explained how EU law tries to protect consumers from unfair or unconscionable contract terms and unfair or misleading practices on the part of businesses. The justification for this protection is the kind of power imbalance which we currently see in cloud relationships. There seems to be a global consensus that consumers and other weak parties require some protection from power imbalance, but there is no consensus about the appropriate levels of those protections which vary widely between national laws.

This diversity of approach poses real problems for cloud service providers, who will find it difficult, perhaps impossible in practice, to offer a single, global service in a way which complies with all these different national law requirements. It also poses a problem for consumers, who are rarely in a position to litigate to enforce their national law rights and are, thus, uncertain what rights will in practice be acceded to by the provider. Consumer law enforcement bodies may be unable to help because of the cost and uncertainty of cross-border law enforcement.

One way to resolve these difficulties might be for a cloud governance body to establish a normative framework which aims to prevent abuses of power. Some contractual terms and trading practices might be mandated; others proscribed. Guidelines for providers might be sufficient, or a full-blown system of regulation, dispute resolution, and enforcement might be needed. All these are matters which can only be decided by a suitably representative body.

---

[93] See Chapter 3, Section 3.3.4.

The experience of eBay's customer dispute system[94] tells us that a globally uniform set of consumer rights can be effective in resolving the vast majority of disputes, so long as it is devised to reflect community standards and not merely the interests of one part of that community. This holds true even if the system's rules fall short of the highest national levels of consumer protection. Such a system does not displace national law, but in practice makes it redundant if it provides a quicker and cheaper resolution. A cloud governance body would lack eBay's enforcement tools,[95] but as explained in Section 2.5 it is possible to devise effective ways of making rules and rulings binding and enforceable.

4.6 Regulatory compliance

There is a substantial body of external law and regulation which already applies to the cloud computing sector. The main examples reviewed in this book are data protection and privacy laws, anti-trust regulation, and laws granting access to information by law enforcement bodies. To this list must be added sector-specific regulation, such as that relating to financial services, and insolvency law. There is far more external regulation than is listed here.

Clearly, a cloud governance body has no direct role in making this regulation or enforcing it. However, there are still important functions it can perform here. First, it can coordinate the experience of the regulated cloud sector to produce advice and guidelines on how best to comply with external regulation. Second, it can work with the most important external regulators on the future shape and scope of regulation, conveying the consensus of the wider cloud community on these matters and identifying defects and improvements in proposed rule-making. And finally, the cloud regulator can introduce mechanisms to assure those who are not subject to the external regulation, but would be affected by non-compliance, that providers and users are actually complying. This links closely to the transparency issues discussed in Section 4.1 above, but alternative ways of providing assurance might also be devisable.

Four short examples might usefully illustrate the kinds of activity a cloud governance body might undertake to assist regulatory compliance. The first comes from EU data protection law, which imposes an obligation on data processors (into which category most cloud service providers are likely to fall) to process personal data only according to the instructions given by the data controller, that is the customer.[96] How this is to be complied with in practice is far from clear, and the guidance issued by the EU Article 29 Working Party[97] is, in the view of the authors of Chapter 8, so divergent from current cloud practices as to require a redesign of public cloud technology.[98] Some provider-customer contracts contain an obligation on the provider to comply with the customer's instructions, even though it is clear that the nature of the service provided makes this impossible, while others contain no such obligation, perhaps because the provider is located outside the EU and is unaware of its own compliance obligations and those which the law imposes on its customer. This is a case where a cloud governance body could attempt to negotiate acceptable means of compliance with EU data

---

[94] Text to n. 62. For further discussion, see Reed n. 5, 90–1.

[95] Ownership of PayPal, which means that sellers' accounts can be debited to satisfy customer claims which are upheld.

[96] Directive 95/46/EC on the protection of individuals with regard to the processing of personal data and on the free movement of such data, OJ L281/31, 23 November 1995, Art. 16. See the more detailed discussion of the issues in Chapter 8, Section 3.2.

[97] WP196, n. 56.   [98] See Chapter 8, Section 3.6.

protection commissioners, issue guidelines on how service providers should implement those means, mandate or recommend appropriate contractual terms, and impose transparency obligations on providers which reassure customers (on whom the primary obligation is imposed) that compliance is actually happening.

The second example is from the financial services sector, where obligations are commonly imposed on financial institutions which outsource their data processing to ensure that the service provider has the ability to undertake the processing effectively and to appropriate standards, agrees to supervision by the financial institution and the regulator, and will make disclosure of material changes which affect the service, permit audits, and so on.[99] Compliance with these obligations requires appropriate contract terms, perhaps coordination between cloud standards organizations and those who create banking technology standards, guidelines on implementation, and so on. Because these services potentially impact on the individual interests of citizens, as well as on the national interest of each state in the proper working of its financial sector, it is surely an improvement over individual contract negotiation to have these matters dealt with at the macro level, and in advance.

The need for rules and guidance on these kinds of issue is not confined to the financial sector. Chapter 4, Section 5.5 has explained how, in negotiated contracts, audit of the provider's activities (other than precontractual audit) is generally resisted. Guidance on when audit access is required by customers, and how to provide it without adversely affecting the provider's interests, would clearly help such negotiations. That chapter also noted that tools such as access logs are potentially better suited to deal with the regulatory compliance issues than audit via physical access, but regulators need to be convinced that this is the case, and guidance from a governance body would assist here as well.

---

[99] For example, the UK FSA Handbook SYSC 8.1.8 on outsourcing requires financial institutions to ensure (among other things) that:

    (1) the service provider must have the ability, capacity, and any authorisation required by law to perform the outsourced functions, services or activities reliably and professionally;

    (2) the service provider must carry out the outsourced services effectively, and to this end the firm must establish methods for assessing the standard of performance of the service provider;

    (3) the service provider must properly supervise the carrying out of the outsourced functions, and adequately manage the risks associated with the outsourcing;

    (4) appropriate action must be taken if it appears that the service provider may not be carrying out the functions effectively and in compliance with applicable laws and regulatory requirements;

    (5) the firm must retain the necessary expertise to supervise the outsourced functions effectively and to manage the risks associated with the outsourcing, and must supervise those functions and manage those risks;

    (6) the service provider must disclose to the firm any development that may have a material impact on its ability to carry out the outsourced functions effectively and in compliance with applicable laws and regulatory requirements;

    (7) the firm must be able to terminate the arrangement for the outsourcing where necessary without detriment to the continuity and quality of its provision of services to clients;

    (8) the service provider must co-operate with the FSA and any other relevant competent authority in connection with the outsourced activities;

    (9) the firm, its auditors, the FSA and any other relevant competent authority must have effective access to data related to the outsourced activities, as well as to the business premises of the service provider; and the FSA and any other relevant competent authority must be able to exercise those rights of access;

    (10) the service provider must protect any confidential information relating to the firm and its clients;

    (11) the firm and the service provider must establish, implement and maintain a contingency plan for disaster recovery and periodic testing of backup facilities where that is necessary having regard to the function, service or activity that has been outsourced.

Third, data protection compliance is a particularly difficult issue, as Part III of this book has demonstrated, primarily because the conceptual model on which the law is based is of a single processing location and unitary control of processing. It was noted in Chapter 7, Section 3 that the anonymization and encryption of personal data can be an effective means of compliance with many data protection obligations,[100] but again regulators need to be convinced. Relevant regulatory guidance, such as the Article 29 Working Party's WP136 on the concept of 'personal data', needs to be reviewed and updated to reflect technical and commercial realities. The quality of such guidance could be improved via greater transparency and by giving stakeholders the opportunity to make representations during the drafting process.

More challenging is how to deal with the cross-border application of data protection law, as Chapters 9 and 10 illustrate. This is not itself a governance issue, and the mismatch between the law's assumptions and cloud computing's reality can only be corrected by lawmakers. But even if full compliance with the law is not achievable, customers in the EU will still want their providers to do as much as is possible to achieve compliance with at least the spirit of the law, if not its letter. This would be assisted by guidance on the circumstances in which the EU regulators have an interest in the provider's and customer's compliance, and best practice in this regard. Ideally, EU and other privacy commissioners would be involved in developing these guidelines, which would provide some comfort against the risk of enforcement action.

The final example relates to advertising of cloud services. In the UK, the Advertising Standards Authority (ASA) is an independent self-regulatory authority, recognized by the government, courts, and UK regulators, which investigates and acts on complaints regarding advertisements and proactively monitors misleading, harmful, or offensive advertisements, sales promotions, and direct marketing. The ASA regulates via advertising codes[101] which are written not by the ASA but by the advertising industry itself.

Chapter 13, Section 3.2 discussed a recent ASA adjudication[102] where the complaint was that a cloud service had wrongly been advertised as being 'unlimited'. UK2 Group's position was that there was no contractual limit on database size, but in practice the size of the server upon which the service was hosted might make some uses unworkable, dependent on the way in which the customer wished to use it. This, in turn, affected how much capacity of UK2's server was used and, thus, the speed at which the customer's website would then operate. The ASA upheld the complaint, holding that making an unqualified claim of this type without indicating 'factors, such as server capacity, which were likely to affect the optimum operation of the website' was misleading and, thus, in breach of the Code.

This case illustrates the potential mismatch in knowledge between customers and service providers, and how it can affect regulatory compliance. It is probable that most cloud service providers would have agreed with the 'unlimited' description, understanding it to mean that technical limitations would inevitably exist, whereas customers lacking such knowledge would be likely to understand the term differently. Advertising guidelines from a cloud regulator in which consumer interests were represented would very likely have prevented the case from arising in the first place.

---

[100] See also Chapter 10, Section 6.1.
[101] UK Code of Non-broadcast Advertising, Sales Promotion and Direct Marketing (CAP Code) and UK Code of Broadcast Advertising (BCAP Code), available from <http://www.cap.org.uk/>.
[102] *ASA Adjudication on UK2 Group*, A11-179995, 14 March 2012.

5. Conclusion

Assiduous readers will have noticed that this chapter includes neither a detailed description of what is needed for cloud governance, nor an initial draft set of governance rules. This is deliberate. The legitimacy of any governance structure, and the rules it makes, will be derived from the consent of the regulated community and its participation in the governance process. This means that the cloud community, not a single author like myself, has to establish its preferred governance system.

What I hope to have done, though, is to explain the essential features which any cloud governance system and rule-set will need to have if it is to be accepted as legitimate, and, thus, to be effective in achieving its regulatory objectives. If the only messages I have managed to convey are that legitimacy requires community participation, and that the cloud community includes states, lawmakers, and individuals as well as the commercial players, I will have succeeded in my task.

Table of Cases

Table of UK Statutes

Table of UK Statutory Instruments

Table of International and European Legislation

Table of National Legislation

Index